D1270735

Description of Egypt

Edward William Lane

Description of Egypt

Notes and views in Egypt and Nubia,
made during the years 1825, —26, —27, and —28:
Chiefly consisting of a series of descriptions and delineations
of the monuments, scenery, &c. of those countries;
The views, with few exceptions, made with the camera-lucida

Edited and with an introduction by
Jason Thompson

The American University in Cairo Press

Copyright © 2000 by
The American University in Cairo Press
113 Sharia Kasr el Aini
Cairo, Egypt
http://aucpress.com

All rights reserved. No part of this publication may be
reproduced, stored in a retrieval system, or transmitted in any
form or by any means, electronic, mechanical, photocopying,
recording, or otherwise, without the prior written
permission of the publisher.

Dar el Kutub No. 3976/99
ISBN 977 424 525 3

Printed in Egypt

Contents

Acknowledgments

During the years that I have been engaged in the overall Edward William Lane project, of which this edition of Lane's *Description of Egypt* is a part, I have incurred scholarly debts to so many individuals that it long ago became impractical to list them all. They will, I hope, recognize their contributions, without which this work would never have come to light, and remember the shared experiences that made the project such a pleasure.

The institutions that have contributed to the project are almost as numerous as the individuals. Three require special mention. The Department of Manuscripts of the British Library, besides providing access to the final draft of *Description of Egypt*, kindly gave me permission to publish it. The Archives of the Griffith Institute of the Ashmolean Museum patiently and repeatedly allowed me to study the preliminary notebooks and the second draft of the *Description*. The Department of Western Manuscripts of the Bodleian Library permitted me to examine the first draft of the work. But I also thank the many other collections that shared their holdings and expertise with me.

Generous funding for this project came from a number of sources. The American Philosophical Society twice provided support for crucial research in Britain. The American Research Center in Egypt and the National Endowment for the Humanities funded most of the fieldwork in Egypt. Western Kentucky University supported the project in myriad ways through its Summer Research Fellowships, Faculty Research Grants, and President's Special Grant Programs. Western Kentucky also helped with several direct grants from the Division of Academic Affairs, the College of Humanities and Social Sciences, and, especially, the Department of History.

The idea for an edition of Lane's *Description of Egypt* was inspired by an invitation from the British Studies Seminar and the Center for Middle East Studies at the University of Texas at Austin to lecture about the work in 1993. Momentum was maintained by participation a year later in the Thursday evening series at the Netherlands Institute for Archaeology and Arabic Studies in Cairo. The opportunity to publish an article about the *Description* in the *International Journal of Middle East Studies* in 1996 encouraged further development, and I thank *IJMES* for permission to reproduce portions of the article in my Introduction to this edition. Now, the American University in Cairo Press must be commended for its courage and imagination in publishing the volume.

I also feel a deep sense of gratitude to Edward William Lane for the privilege of laboring among his papers and helping to realize a dream that was once very dear to him.

Jason Thompson

Editor's Introduction

Few Western students of the Arab world are as well known as the nineteenth-century British scholar Edward William Lane (1801–76).[1] During his long career, Lane produced a number of highly influential works: *An Account of the Manners and Customs of the Modern Egyptians* (1836), his translation of *The Thousand and One Nights* (1839–41), *Selections from the Ḳur-án* (1843), and the *Arabic–English Lexicon* (1863–93). The *Arabic–English Lexicon* remains a preeminent work of its kind, and *Manners and Customs of the Modern Egyptians* is still a basic text for both Arab and Western students. Yet one of Lane's most important works was never published. This was his book-length manuscript, *Description of Egypt*.[2] Apart from the *Arabic–English Lexicon*, Lane worked much longer and harder on *Description of Egypt* than on any other project, including *Modern Egyptians*, and it probably affected his life more profoundly than *Modern Egyptians*, despite the latter work's success. His failure to publish it was a serious loss to scholarship.

Description of Egypt, which would have been Lane's first book, was the culmination of youthful ambition. Lane was working as an engraver's apprentice in London in the early 1820s when his imagination was captured by Egypt. The probable cause was Giovanni Battista Belzoni's sensational exhibit at the Egyptian Hall in Piccadilly, which attracted enormous crowds. That, along with Belzoni's best-selling book, inspired one of the several waves of Egyptomania that have swept across Britain, and indeed across western Europe. Embarking on a rigorous program, Lane read everything he could find about Egypt, both ancient and modern. He resolved to travel there one day and write an illustrated book about it.

At some point during his studies, Lane's interests took a highly original turn. Most people were fascinated by Egyptian antiquities, but Lane's primary attention moved from ancient to modern Egypt, and especially to Arabic, the language of the modern Egyptians. He also

---

[1]The major biographies of Lane are: Stanley Lane-Poole, *Life of Edward William Lane* (London: Williams and Norgate, 1877); A. J. Arberry, "The Lexicographer: Edward William Lane," in *Oriental Essays: Portraits of Seven Scholars* (London: Allen and Unwin, 1960), pp. 87–121; and the definitive one by Leila Ahmed, *Edward W. Lane: A Study of His Life and Works and of British Ideas of the Middle East in the Nineteenth Century* (London: Longman, 1978).

[2]Many of the issues concerning the history of *Description of Egypt* are much too complex to be described fully here. For a more detailed account, see my "Edward William Lane's 'Description of Egypt,'" *International Journal of Middle East Studies* 2 8 (1996): 565–83. Further information will be contained in my forthcoming biography of Lane.

became intensely interested in their society, or to use the term current at the time, their manners and customs. It is unclear how he did so in spare hours in London during the 1820s, but he made substantial progress in Arabic—and not just classical Arabic but, even more remarkably, Egyptian colloquial Arabic as well. Yet Lane did not abandon his interest in ancient Egypt, leading to a duality of focus. Later, when he attempted to express his motives for going to Egypt in an early draft of *Description of Egypt* (reproduced here at the beginning of his Introduction), he had to rewrite the passage several times, finding it difficult to put the various elements into proper relationship.

Lane applied himself so assiduously to his Egyptian studies while still working as an engraver's apprentice that his health broke, rendering him susceptible to a life-threatening illness. He recovered but remained afflicted with severe chronic bronchitis for the rest of his life. Sometimes he could not walk down a London street without stopping and gasping for breath. Clearly he could not continue as an engraver, which required long hours of bending over a copper plate. It was equally clear that he needed a change of climate, both for his health and to fulfill his intellectual pursuits. On 18 July 1825, funded by a mysterious benefactor, Lane embarked for Egypt.

After a long, eventful voyage, Lane arrived at Alexandria on 17 September. Mixed emotions swept through him as he prepared to land. He remembered the moment in the first draft of *Description of Egypt*.

> As I approached the shore, I felt like an Eastern bridegroom, about to lift up the veil of his bride, and to see, for the first time, the features which were to charm, or disappoint, or disgust him. I was not visiting Egypt merely as a traveller, to examine its pyramids and temples and grottoes, and, after satisfying my curiosity, to quit it for other scenes and other pleasures: but I was about to throw myself entirely among strangers; to adopt their language, their customs and their dress; and, in associating almost exclusively with the natives, to prosecute the study of their literature. My feelings therefore, on that occasion, partook too much of anxiety to be very pleasing.[1]

When Lane reached Cairo two weeks later he made good on his vow. Immediately he forsook Western clothing for Eastern attire, dressing in none other during the rest of his time in Egypt, for his purposes required not only that he gain an intimate knowledge of the details of Eastern society, including its material culture, but also that he not be readily recognized as a European. One should bear in mind, however, that the dress and resulting public persona that he chose were not those of a native Egyptian but of a member of Egypt's ruling Turkish elite. That

---

[1]Manuscript draft of *Description of Egypt*, Bodleian Library, Department of Western Manuscripts, MS. Eng. misc. d. 234, ff. 5-5v.

facilitated his acceptance into Egyptian society and guaranteed him a degree of deference within it.

Nor was Lane's commitment merely a matter of outward appearances, for he also furnished his house in Egyptian style, learned Egyptian table manners, and became perfect in Egyptian social usages. Within a year his Arabic was fluent. He developed a wide circle of Egyptian friends who knew him as Mansur, the name—and at least to some extent the identity—that he assumed in Egypt. The result fulfilled his expectations: "I was treated with respect and affability by all the natives . . ."

Lane's circle of acquaintance in Egypt was not exclusively Eastern, for he also made a few European friends, but these were people much like himself who adopted Eastern lifestyles. Some of them, such as John Gardner Wilkinson, James Burton, Robert Hay, and Lord Prudhoe, proved very helpful to Lane in his work. Otherwise, he avoided the European residents of Cairo who mostly inhabited the Frank Quarter near the city's center. He was especially repelled by those marginal characters who went about dressed in a careless mélange of Eastern and Western clothing: "In general they look a most disreputable set of vagabonds," he wrote in one of the many pithy passages in the first draft of *Description of Egypt* that were not retained in the final one.[1] Lane lived not in the Frank Quarter but in a native area near the northwestern corner of Cairo, a short distance southeast of present-day Ramses Square.

Lane's research in Cairo took two main thrusts. One was direct experience. This might be through everyday activities such as shopping, dealing with servants, or visiting friends and receiving guests—basic interactions that can teach a careful observer much. He learned practical details about Islam so he could enter Cairo's mosques, something a Westerner could not easily do in those days, and pray in them, which he did both individually and with the congregation, as the *Description of Egypt* explicitly states. He explored the monuments and quarters of Cairo, becoming proficient in the city's urban geography, a topic left vaguely in the background in *Modern Egyptians*, where the focus is on society. He also visited the archaeological sites around Cairo. The days he spent living in a tomb at the Pyramids of Giza he remembered as the happiest of his life.

But Lane also studied Arabic literary sources for Egypt and Islam, accumulating a fine collection of books and manuscripts in the process. He greatly admired the productions of the pasha's printing press at Bulaq, becoming acquainted with its supervisor and with one of its primary distribution agents. The latter, Sheikh Ahmad al-Khutbi, later became a principal informant for the material in *Modern Egyptians*. One regrets that the list that Lane prepared of the Bulaq press's publications, along with any associated comments, is missing from the *Description of Egypt*.

---

[1] Bodleian Library, MS. Eng. misc. d. 234, f. 75.

Of course, many of the works that Lane needed existed only in manuscript. Two were of special importance for *Description of Egypt*. The *Khitat* of Taqi al-Din Ahmad al-Maqrizi, one of Lane's first acquisitions, provided historical depth to the places mentioned in *Description*, while Abd al-Rahman al-Jabarti's *'Aja'ib al-athar* became the major source for Lane's long chapter about the history of the *de facto* ruler of Egypt, Muhammad Ali. Lane was, in fact, one of the first to appreciate al-Jabarti's historiographical accomplishment. These manuscripts, along with the many others that Lane purchased, must later have constituted one of the finest personal collections of Arabic manuscripts in nineteenth-century Britain.

During this first trip to Egypt, Lane made two extended voyages up the Nile as far as the Second Cataract in Nubia. The first, in 1826, covered seven and a half months, from mid-March until the end of October. The second, which extended for six months from mid-June until mid-December 1827, he made in company with his friend Robert Hay. The latter voyage included an excursion of two weeks into the Fayyum. On both, though hampered by illness on the second, Lane repeatedly displayed his capacity to accomplish prodigious amounts of work within short spaces of time as he stopped at most of the major archaeological sites then known in Egypt and Nubia. One should, however, also note the limits to Lane's travel experience. He did not journey into Egypt's Eastern or Western Deserts, thereby missing the wonders, especially of the former, that so enchanted his colleagues Burton and Wilkinson. Lane also failed to visit the eastern Delta ("scarcely worthy of detailed description"), forcing him to rely on secondary sources when he wrote his chapter about it. These sources were not entirely trustworthy. Had Lane seen Tanis for himself, for example, his fine eye, so evident at Thebes, for the reuse of ancient building materials, probably would have saved him from his error of accepting the site as coeval with Ramses II. Nor did Lane ever travel in any Middle Eastern lands other than Egypt, forgoing the comparative perspectives he would have gained thereby.

The primary purpose of Lane's journeys into Upper Egypt and Nubia was to satisfy his persistent interest in ancient Egypt; as he wrote, "I had long entertained a wish to examine the antiquities of that most interesting country." The account of his travels on the Nile therefore expresses a little-known dimension of his intellectual life, for Lane was once among the foremost in the nascent science of Egyptology. Only a few years earlier had the secret of the hieroglyphic script been solved with Champollion's famous *Lettre à M. Dacier*. Public fascination with Egypt was at a high pitch. Yet with the exceptions of Champollion's and Lepsius' expeditions, fieldwork in Egypt during the early nineteenth century depended almost entirely on the initiative of private individuals like Wilkinson, Hay, and Lane. Had it been published when it was intended to be, Lane's *Description of Egypt* would have been a landmark in Egyptology.

Lane's Egyptological accomplishments assume even more impressive proportions when one considers their slight foundations, for the general state of Egyptological knowledge in his moment was rudimentary indeed. Lane's chronological framework for the Egyptian past extended only feebly into the Middle Kingdom (a term not yet invented) where he identified two monuments of Senwosret I. The monarchs of the Old Kingdom were but a list of unknown kings to him. His linguistic resources were scarcely more efficacious, for although the hieroglyphic script had been deciphered—and not everyone agreed even on that point—the ancient language was far from translated. At best, and only later in his studies, Lane could identify some royal names within cartouches and analyze the morphology of a few ancient Egyptian words. Even many basic Egyptological terms and conventions (such as the word 'cartouche') had yet to be standardized, compelling Lane to invent descriptive terms on his own, which he did creatively, if sometimes naively.

Hence it is not surprising that Lane made many Egyptological mistakes, so many that it would be specious to annotate them all in his text. His king "Horus" (Horemheb), for example, certainly was not the immediate successor of Amenophis III, as Lane repeatedly asserts him to have been; but Lane could not have known that, so successfully had the record of the intervening Amarna period been erased. On the other hand, we see Lane at Tuna al-Gebel and Tell al-Amarna straining against the boundaries of current knowledge as he attempted to interpret the remaining, fragmentary evidence of Akhenaten's revolutionary innovations. Much the same could be said about his encounter with Hatshepsut, likewise unknown to him, whom he identified as a regent for Tuthmosis III and placed in the correct place in his list of kings (fig. 160). In a note added at a later date, he accepted Wilkinson's identification of her as a Queen-Regent named "Amun-Neit-Gori." Of course, one of Lane's most important Egyptological contributions was to describe the condition of the monuments when he saw them; in some instances they were being destroyed before his very eyes.

Though mostly motivated by antiquities, Lane's record of his Nilotic travels reveals another dimension of his research experience that found little expression in *Modern Egyptians*: life outside of Cairo. These chapters are not just an itinerary of antiquities, but also of the towns, villages, and countryside along the way. One finds descriptions of the appearance of towns, their productions, and the state of their markets. The picture is dynamic: Fuwa flourishes because of the recent opening of the Mahmudiya Canal, but Rashid declines for the same reason, while Manfalut literally washes away, less of it remaining each time Lane sails past. Lane noted differences in the appearance and dress of the people. Since Upper Egyptian women tended to veil less, Lane could observe them more closely, but one regrets to find him occasionally hiding along the riverbank to watch them bathing. His command of Arabic enabled him to converse with the country people, or fellaheen, although the recurring topic was the oppressiveness of the pasha's government. Always in the background was Lane's developing awareness of the land of Egypt itself. He realized its close identity with the Nile and the narrow strip of fertile land along its banks. He witnessed the annual inundation spreading across the valley.

Because Lane intended to write a book from the beginning, he kept a set of diaries and notebooks. The main body of these has survived, preserved in the Griffith Institute, where they have recently been catalogued. Some of the entries are little more than hasty notes about date, place, and temperature; others are highly detailed, so much so as to contain coherent textual passages that Lane was able to incorporate into his *Description of Egypt* manuscript with little revision.

Lane also documented Egypt in pictures, thereby exhibiting his artistic dimension, one of the least appreciated of his many talents. Although he never became an engraver, his artistic training served him well by enabling him to sketch the things that he observed and, later, to transform his sketches into effective book illustrations. Lane, it should be remembered, came from a distinguished artistic environment. His great-uncle was the renowned artist Thomas Gainsborough; his brother, Richard J. Lane, was one of the leading lithographers of nineteenth-century Britain. This impeccable artistic pedigree prepared him not only to execute his own work but also to appreciate and describe the art of the Egyptians, whether ancient or Islamic.

Although Lane was capable of producing tastefully finished pictures, the best of which should rank at least as minor works of art, he primarily sought accuracy. To attain this ideal, he made extensive use of a recently invented device called the camera lucida. Easily portable, it consisted of a prism and set of lenses so arranged as to enable its operator to trace the outline of a subject onto a sheet of paper, thereby providing additional control over perspective and detail. Dozens of the camera lucida sketches that Lane made in the field are still extant, many of them providing the basis for the more developed illustrations in *Description of Egypt.*

When Lane returned to England in June 1828, he had ample material in hand to write his book. He entitled it *Description of Egypt.* This was doubtless in both admiration and defiance of the great French *Description de l'Égypte*, but it also epitomized Lane's highly descriptive literary approach. For although *Description of Egypt* was basically organized as a travelogue, it contained long passages of description that bore no relation to the itinerary of his travels, foreshadowing the topical approach that served Lane so well in *Modern Egyptians.*

Altogether, Lane wrote *Description of Egypt* through three major drafts. The first, now in the Bodleian Library,[1] was probably composed in 1829. Recognizable as the inception of the initial fifteen chapters of the final draft, it covered his journey to Egypt, impressions of Alexandria, journey to Cairo, and first trips to Giza. Topical foci were given to

---

[1]Bodleian Library, MS. Eng. misc. d. 234.

Alexandria, the physical geography of Egypt, and, most of all, to Cairo. At Giza, only the Great Pyramid was treated. The draft also contained several interesting enterprises in historiography: the political history of Egypt during Islamic times, the origin and development of Cairo, and a concise account of the career of Muhammad Ali. There were a few pages, organized into three succinct chapters, about the modern inhabitants of Egypt, covering their 1) population and revenue, 2) civil administration, and 3) religion and laws. These, of course, were the origin of *Manners and Customs of the Modern Egyptians*, although Lane as yet had no thought of writing such a book.

The first draft of *Description of Egypt* was a promising literary beginning, especially for someone not yet thirty years of age. Often it displays a strong, clear style; for example, the bridegroom passage, quoted above, is as good as anything Lane ever wrote. Other passages, as he was well aware, needed revision and development. Some of the sections with their various topics sat uneasily together, but Lane was still experimenting with placement and form. As notations in the draft show, it was intended to be the first of four projected volumes that would treat the whole of his Egyptian experience, each volume to contain approximately twenty-five illustrations. Placement points for the illustrations are indicated in the text, sometimes with a rough sketch drawn into the place, such as a preliminary sketch of the Alexandrian street scene (fig. 5). Another interesting sketch shows a man peering into a cistern among the ruins of ancient Alexandria with Pompey's Pillar in the background, but it was not included in the final draft.

As promising as the first was, Lane was soon at work on a second draft of *Description of Egypt*, the composition of which may be tentatively dated to 1830. Now among the Lane Manuscripts in the Griffith Institute,[1] this draft marked a number of improvements over its predecessor as chapters became more focused and substantial, while the manuscript grew in several areas. The chapter on the Pyramids of Giza was extended to include all of the major monuments at that site as well as those of Saqqara and Dahshur.[2] The draft closed after describing the desolate, almost obliterated ruins of Memphis with a reflective quotation from the prophet Jeremiah.

Another major area of expansion was the chapter about the history of Muhammad Ali, which grew approximately fourfold, approaching the large size it attained in the final draft. An impressive historiographical exercise, it drew primarily on al-Jabarti's manuscript history, which Lane had acquired in Egypt, and on Félix Mengin's published account of the pasha—though leaning toward the former work—in addition to Lane's own personal observations. It shows keen discernment of source material

---

[1] Griffith Institute Archives, Lane MSS 6.1.

[2] Lane may indeed have intended the Saqqara and Dahshur material to form a separate chapter as it became in the final draft, but he did not explicitly mark it as such.

as Lane weighed evidence carefully before moving to judicious conclusions. For example, although he seems to have accepted the old canard about Ibrahim not being Muhammad Ali's son, Lane observed in a footnote that the pasha always referred to Ibrahim as being so, therefore displaying unease with the unfounded yet widely accepted story. Had it been published, this chapter would have been an important contribution to the history of modern Egypt; it also would have hastened the establishment of al-Jabarti's reputation in the West.

The area that grew the most, however, was the one dealing with the modern Egyptians. The three brief chapters about population, government, and religion and law were retained, while three new, relatively short, chapters were added about Egypt's Turkish elite and Christian and Jewish minorities.[1] But the most significant addition was a new chapter of some eighty manuscript pages entitled "Manners and Customs of the Moos'lim Egyptians." The need to keep the new chapter within somewhat proportionate limits clearly frustrated Lane, but his aim was "conciseness," and the chapter's function was subordinate to that of the work as a whole.

Lane submitted this second draft, along with a set of drawings, to the publishing firm of John Murray in early 1831. Then under the direction of the founder's son, John Murray II, Murray's had published Burckhardt, Belzoni, and many other distinguished writers about Egypt and the Middle East. Lane was aiming high. Murray handled Lane's manuscript in a highly professional manner by sending it out to a qualified reader, Henry Hart Milman, an accomplished scholar who had recently published a perceptive if controversial history of the Jews in which he interpreted them in their Semitic context. Milman's report strongly recommended publication: Lane's was, he said, "the best work which has been written on the subject." He expressed two minor reservations, the first being that the chapters dealing with the modern Egyptians ought to be removed: they were good, Milman thought, but should be the basis for an entirely separate book. Milman's second reservation concerned the scope of the work, for he thought it should be extended to cover Lane's travels in Upper Egypt and Nubia, as Lane indeed intended. Murray was highly pleased with both the manuscript and the report, as well as the illustrations—"the more the work contained of them, the better," Murray said—which he considered the most accurate he had ever seen. He agreed to publish the book. But he insisted on a new title and compelled Lane to write it on the spot. So, *Description of Egypt* became:

---

[1]The chapter about the Turks is distinctly separate, but the respective texts for the Christians and the Jews are numbered one and two, as if intended for sections of one chapter. The text about the Jews was based on a passage in a loosely organized section of the first draft.

Notes and views in Egypt and Nubia,
made during the years 1825, —26, —27, and —28:
Chiefly consisting of a series of descriptions and delineations
of the monuments, scenery, &c. of those countries;
The views, with few exceptions, made with the camera-lucida:
by Edwd Wm Lane—

For the sake of consistency as well as concision, however, the title *Description of Egypt* is retained in this Introduction. It is also retained as the title of this edition, along with the revised title, which is presented as a subtitle.

But a week after Lane and Murray met, the project was delayed when the Reform Bill was introduced in Parliament on 1 March 1831. To a degree difficult to grasp now, public attention became fixed on that single political issue. Only publications about the Reform Bill were selling. Murray decided to postpone publication of *Description of Egypt* until the political crisis passed. He suggested that Lane use the delay by acting on Milman's suggestions: excising the modern Egyptians chapters and writing the new chapters about Upper Egypt and Nubia. Lane strongly opposed the changes, agreeing to them only reluctantly. It should be understood, however, that this constituted merely a delay in publication; there was no question of canceling.

Lane returned to work with characteristic assiduity. Removing the modern Egyptians chapters was the work of a moment, doing little damage to the textual fabric of the rest of the manuscript. A much more formidable task was the composition of twenty-three new Upper Egyptian and Nubian chapters, plus a long supplement about the ancient Egyptians. The chapter on Thebes alone, by far the longest, accounted for about 50,000 words. He wrote this portion of *Description of Egypt* through at least two drafts, as his footnote references to a previous draft indicate. It is unfortunate that the preliminary draft has not come to light, for it contained additional material that Lane intended to publish.

The structure of the Egyptian and Nubian chapters of *Description of Egypt* is even more emphatically the travelogue than the preceding ones. Yet it is a very contrived travel memoir, containing much more artistry than might first meet the eye. Lane compressed his two trips to Wadi Halfa and back into the narrative framework of one southward journey, ending with the preparation of his canjiah for the downstream journey: "The main-mast and yard were removed, and placed along the centre of the boat: one end resting on the roof of the cabin, and the other being lashed to the foremast. The *tarankee't* (or fore-sail) remained as usual."

Lane also revised the material that he had already composed. Most of these revisions were effective, resulting in memorable passages such as the description of his confusing initial experiences in Alexandria, his first impressions of Cairo, or the pleasure he took in his tomb-house at Giza. Yet some of the revisions are to be regretted, because he shortened then completely removed the Introduction that recounted his eventful voyage

to Egypt. Then the beautiful passage ("I felt like an Eastern bridegroom
. . . ") that so memorably expressed his conflicting emotions as he
prepared to set foot on Egypt for the first time was revised into a
detached statement that diminished the personal element almost to the
vanishing point: "I approached the beach with feelings of intense
interest, though of too anxious a nature to be entirely pleasing . . ."
Several passing comments that expressed a vibrant, personal point of
view were removed. The third draft, presented here, is naturally the most
polished of the three, but the passages within it are not invariably the
best that Lane wrote. Close study of the other two drafts, along with
their associated manuscript materials, will richly repay further attention
by researchers.

Without doubt one of Lane's largest tasks for *Description of Egypt* was
preparing the illustrations for publication. The sheer number alone was
imposing, for there were more than 150 of them, though some are
missing from the manuscript and were already missing by the 1840s,
when Lane's nephew, Reginald Stuart Poole, noted their absence in the
margins. In pre-photographic days, reproduction of illustrative material
was done by engraving, woodcutting, or the newly invented technique of
lithography. Whatever medium was used—and Lane hoped to use all
three—the artist's original work had to be copied anew, whether onto
the engraver's metal plate, the woodcutter's block, or the lithographer's
stone. Since Lane did not intend to do this himself, he needed to provide
pictures as highly finished as possible to enable the appropriate
craftsperson to realize his conception. This primarily required clarity of
line in the case of the drawings destined to become woodcuts, where
outline and contrast were paramount. But Lane hoped to have as many
of them as possible rendered by metal engraving and lithography to
achieve the delicacy of line and shading that those media, especially the
latter, could convey. Hence the high artistic quality of many of Lane's
sketches, with their delicate sepia shading and, in two instances, bright
coloration.

The maps alone were a formidable undertaking, for *Description of
Egypt* contains nine of them—thirteen if one counts each map section on
the two plates that cover the Nile Valley from Giza to Wadi Halfa. The
maps of the Delta and the Nile were based on W. M. Leake's *Map of
Egypt*, which, despite numerous shortcomings, remained a standard
through much of the nineteenth century.[1] Lane traveled along the Nile
with a copy of Leake's map, from which he made the templates for his
own. But Lane's maps were more than mere copies of Leake's,
incorporating as they did his on-site adjustments and corrections. The
same is true for the two maps of Cairo, the one of the city and its
environs and the other, more detailed one of the interior of the city,
which were both based upon maps in the French *Description de l'Égypte*.
The most original of Lane's maps is the one of Thebes, the product of his

---

[1] W. M. Leake, *Map of Egypt* (London: S. Arrowsmith, 1818).

extended stays at that site. It strikes a fine balance between detail and clarity that makes it an excellent reference tool for a book such as Lane's. In Lane's cartography for *Description of Egypt* we see yet another dimension of his talents that found no expression in his later published work.

The third draft of *Description of Egypt* constitutes a fair copy that would have delighted any Victorian typesetter. Written in Lane's beautiful hand, as the opening page of the chapter about Wadi al-Seboua shows (fig. 1), the wording was clear and the intent for note and figure placement unambiguous. His occasional, often inadvertent mistakes in spelling and grammar stood out sharply and would have been readily corrected. Only a few really rough edges remained, and he intended to smooth most of those away, such as an illustration annotation in chapter ten that was to be developed further, but never was. Temporary removal and subsequent misplacement was the likely fate of the missing appendix about the publications of the pasha's printing press at Bulaq. Inevitably, the close reader finds the occasional faulty detail, such as the omission of the letter *j* in the lettered series for the key to one of his views of Cairo (fig. 15), although a notch is there for it, and it apparently escaped his notice that he did not include the illustration for the face of the Third Pyramid at Giza. One will also observe that some of the notes to chapter twenty-six that Lane added after his second trip to Egypt are rougher than the others, but there can be no doubt that he would have worked them up to standard when the manuscript went to press, had the need arisen. One could go on; the fact remains that Lane's was an unusually clean manuscript. The finished work filled three volumes of text (removal of the modern Egyptians chapters reduced it from its initially projected four) and five volumes of illustrations. These constitute the third and final draft of *Description of Egypt,* the one presented in this edition, now housed in the British Library.[1]

Lane submitted the revised draft to Murray, who again referred it to Milman, who in turn declared it even better than the previous one. But political conditions remained unsettled, so Murray continued to postpone publication. Although Lane agreed with the wisdom of this decision, he was frustrated by the delays, which, perhaps combined with unknown personal factors, threw him into a serious mental malaise. His thoughts returned increasingly to Egypt, where he had spent so many happy, creative moments. Letters to his friends became punctuated with expressions of longing to be there again. As he sank into depression, *Description of Egypt* came to his aid.

In late spring 1833 Lane decided to write a book about the manners and customs of the modern Egyptians, something Henry Hart Milman had suggested earlier. He took the chapters that had been excluded from *Description of Egypt* and copied them into a set of new notebooks. These he submitted to the Society for the Diffusion of Useful Knowledge, an

---

[1]British Library, Department of Manuscripts, Additional MSS 34080-34088.

association that specialized in facilitating publication of meritorious works. The S.D.U.K. enthusiastically offered Lane a contract for the book. He accepted, but with the proviso that he return to Egypt to gather additional material, which a publication advance enabled him to do. In November 1833 Lane sailed for Egypt to write *Manners and Customs of the Modern Egyptians*.

When he reached Cairo in late December, Lane once again settled into his old neighborhood and resumed the Eastern lifestyle that was an essential component of his research technique. Knowing exactly what he was looking for, he worked quickly. By mid-September of the following year he had gathered almost all of his data; before the end of December he began the fair copy of *Modern Egyptians* and was preparing to return to England. At that moment a fierce outbreak of bubonic plague erupted in Alexandria and Cairo, causing him to flee to Thebes, where he spent an additional five months living in a tomb-house on the hill of Sheikh Abd al-Qurna.

Lane's time at Thebes is difficult to account for in detail. Presumably he completed the fair copy of *Modern Egyptians*, if he had not done so already, but that would not have taken the entire five months. Later, he told John Murray III that he "carefully revised all that I had written on its [Thebes'] monuments" while there, but the manuscript does not show obvious signs of such heavy revision, although he may have made another draft that is not extant. Possibly Lane was merely indulging in some justifiable exaggeration to prompt the publisher to long-overdue action. It was probably also at this time that Lane rewrote most of the Cairene chapters of *Description* into a separate manuscript, no longer extant, that was never incorporated into the original one.

Lane returned to England in autumn 1835. He made some inquiries about the progress toward publishing *Description of Egypt*, but was met with evasion or silence by John Murray III, who was becoming increasingly active in the management of the firm. Lane probably should have been alarmed; instead, he considered this just another irritating delay. Soon he was deeply engaged in making the illustrations and correcting the proofs for *Modern Egyptians*. He assumed that the success of that work would precipitate immediate publication of *Description of Egypt*.

An Account of the Manners and Customs of the Modern Egyptians was an instant success when it appeared in early December 1836.[1] The first printing sold out within two weeks; many others followed, as did several revised editions, culminating in the definitive fifth revised edition of 1860. Praised as "the most perfect picture of a people's life that has ever been written,"[2] the influence of *Modern Egyptians* can scarcely be

---

[1]Edward William Lane, *An Account of the Manners and Customs of the Modern Egyptians: Written in Egypt during the Years 1833, –34, and –35, Partly from Notes Made during a Former Visit to That Country in the Years 1825, –26, –27, and –28.* 2 vols. (London: Charles Knight, 1836).
[2]Stanley Lane-Poole, *Life of Edward William Lane*, p. 84.

overstated. As Edward Said, a strong critic of Lane's, pointed out, *Modern Egyptians* made Lane "an authority whose use was an imperative for anyone writing or thinking about the Orient, not just about Egypt."[1] This remarkable book grew directly out of *Description of Egypt*.

It should not be assumed, however, that *Modern Egyptians* is a refinement of *Description of Egypt* or that it represents a maturation and reconsideration of Lane's research approach, in which he consciously turned away from the more diffuse effort that *Description* represented. Lane was still thoroughly committed to the publication of *Description*; the possibility that it might not be published at all had not yet occurred to him. Indeed, *Description* was likely the book that he cared about the most, having spent far more time and effort on it. Students of Lane's *Modern Egyptians* should pay close attention to *Description of Egypt* and its evolution, for it is the work that not only gave birth to *Modern Egyptians* but also defined the limits that the latter work assumed. There is little textual or pictorial overlap between the two. Had Lane known that *Description* would never be published, quite likely *Modern Egyptians* would have been different in shape and content.

Buoyed by the success of *Modern Egyptians*, Lane pressed John Murray III for immediate publication of *Description of Egypt*. Murray responded by withdrawing from the project and wishing him well with another publisher. How could such a thing have happened? The possible reasons are too complicated to set forth here in detail, but the fundamental problem lay in the passing of too much time. Big, illustrated travel books—as Lane's was probably if not entirely correctly perceived to be—had passed their heyday. Also, while Lane was in Egypt, Murray's had heavily committed itself to the publication of two books by Lane's friend and colleague, John Gardner Wilkinson: *Topography of Thebes, and General View of Egypt* (1835) and *Manners and Customs of the Ancient Egyptians* (1837). Investment in the two books, especially the latter, had been heavy; *Description of Egypt*, also expensive to publish, would have competed with them. Murray's made a ruthless if unfair business decision. Lane was the loser thereby—as was the Victorian reading public.

The blow to Lane must have been devastating, even if softened by the success of *Modern Egyptians*. Efforts to place the work elsewhere came to naught. By the late 1830s a commercial publisher would have found *Description of Egypt* far too risky, while the alternative of private publication was beyond Lane's limited financial means. Lane did, however, twice try to salvage some parts of his work from the wreckage. The first attempt was a book about Thebes, based upon the Theban chapter of *Description*, which John Murray was considering, perhaps as a gesture of consolation. Lane set to work, completing a substantial portion of it. Although the manuscript has not surfaced, Lane jotted

---

[1] Edward Said, *Orientalism* (New York: Pantheon, 1978), p.23.

down a table of contents elsewhere, showing how the chapter's five sections would expand into a book of eleven chapters. Some of the later notes to the chapter, such as the references to Champollion's and Wilkinson's books, were probably added with the projected book in mind. This was also most likely the time when he added the two memoranda about inserting additional material from the supplement of *Description*. Lane's book about Thebes would have been a fine thing had it been realized, but when he was about one-third of the way through, he abandoned the project, explaining to Murray that he had no desire to compete with Wilkinson, whose two books covered much the same material, although Lane would have dealt with it much more fully than Wilkinson.

It especially pained Lane to see his illustrations lapse into oblivion; therefore he made another proposal to Murray for a volume of views of Egypt based upon the illustrations for *Description* with between 100 to 150 woodcuts and a page or two of text to accompany each. "I think that it would be acceptable to a large class of persons, as illustrating many works on Egypt; especially Wilkinson's."[1] A selection of the best of Lane's artwork from the *Description* would have made a magnificent volume, although the original works would have lost much in being translated from his delicate sepia washes into woodcuts. The preferable alternative of lithographing them all was probably too expensive to contemplate. A loose sheet inside Lane's copy of al-Jabarti's *'Aja'ib al-athar* appears to be a preliminary estimate of the size and cost of such a work.[2] On it Lane outlined a book somewhat larger than the one described in the letter to Murray, consisting of two volumes, one on the modern Egyptians and the other on "Scenery & Antiquities &c." It would contain as many as 215 woodcuts and six lithographic plates, although he also made a smaller estimate more in line with the size he had suggested to Murray. But nothing came of this idea either. By 1842, Lane had probably accepted the fact that he would never be able to publish his *Description of Egypt* or any significant portion of it.

Not that these were idle or unproductive years for Lane. His translation of the *Arabian Nights* appeared first in serialization and then in three volumes between 1838 and 1841. Though largely superseded now, Lane's reigned as the leading translation of the Arabic classic for much of the nineteenth century. Scholars still frequently consult its copious notes, much of the material for which Lane had gathered during his research for *Description of Egypt*. Lane's other major publication during this period was *Selections from the Ḳur-án* (1843). But neither project was altogether satisfactory: the publisher for the *Arabian Nights* went bankrupt before paying Lane in full, while the *Selections from the Ḳur-án* never received Lane's complete attention. Profound changes in Lane's personal life also occurred at about this time, such as the death of

---

[1] Lane to John Murray III, 4 September 1841, John Murray Archives, London.
[2] British Library, Oriental and African Collection, Or. MS. 4630.

his mother and his marriage to Nefeeseh, whom he or a friend had purchased as a child in one of the slave markets of Cairo shortly before he left Egypt in 1828. Approaching midlife, Lane must have wondered what direction his career might take.

At this juncture Lane was approached by his friend Lord Prudhoe, later the 4th Duke of Northumberland. Their friendship dated from Lane's first trip to Egypt when he had been preparing *Description of Egypt*. Lord Prudhoe had long admired Lane's proficiency in Arabic; he had also realized from personal experience in the East the need for an authoritative Arabic–English lexicon. Now he offered to support Lane in the preparation of such a work. For Lane this was the realization of one of the youthful dreams that had impelled him to Egypt in the first place. He readily accepted Lord Prudhoe's offer and soon was preparing to return to Egypt for the necessary manuscript research and collection. His one reservation was extended separation from his sister Sophia Poole and her sons, to whom he was deeply attached. But once again *Description of Egypt* came to his aid. Lane made another proposal to John Murray: he would make the *Description* manuscript available to Sophia, who would select passages from it and recast them into a book-length series of letters ostensibly recording the impressions of an Englishwoman living in Egypt. The money from this, or at least the anticipation thereof, enabled Sophia and her family to go with Lane. In July 1842 Edward, Nefeeseh, Sophia, and Stanley and Stuart set sail on Lane's third trip to Egypt. Accompanying them was the manuscript of *Description of Egypt*.

Lane's third trip to Egypt, 1842–49, was by far the longest of the three, but unlike the previous ones Lane traveled little during it and seldom went out into society. So enmeshed did he become in the lexicon project that he sometimes did not leave his house for months on end. Within the home, however, he was an affectionate family man, and he worked closely with Sophia, whose desk was within shouting distance of his, on her book. As planned, she selected passages from *Description of Egypt*, often after he had reread them and made changes in Arabic transliteration, punctuation, paragraphing, and like matters. Sometimes he updated the passages, as in the chapter about the Pyramids of Giza where Vyse and Lepsius had made important discoveries since Lane's work there. Occasionally he provided directions for turning his text into hers; for example, one of the passages about his stay at Giza received this marginal note:

> This anecdote may be introduced, commencing thus—My brother, during a long visit to the Pyr^ds, in 1825, occupied one of the tombs excavated in the eastern front of the rocky eminence on which stands the Gr^t. Pyr^d; one of those since occupied by Col. Howard Vyse; of whose quarters a Nubian has now taken possession, to afford lodgings, for a small remuneration to travellers. (Then go on: for "I," saying "my brother," &c.[)]

Lane read the resulting letters, edited them, and made the final decision whether to send them to London for publication. As she found her bearings in Cairo, Sophia later acquired a stronger voice of her own, writing about experiences that were exclusively hers, especially among the women of Cairo. In the end, roughly one-third of her book's letters, really chapters, were almost entirely based on the *Description*, while shorter passages from it were interspersed elsewhere in the letters. *Description of Egypt* was therefore the genesis of Sophia's book and provided a substantial portion of its total text. The relationship between the two works should be factored into any assessment of Sophia's *The Englishwoman in Egypt*,[1] which became a classic account of women in nineteenth-century Egypt.

Lane's nephews Stanley and Stuart were also drawn into the *Description* manuscript, the volumes of which were necessarily often readily available around the house. Their interaction with it and the resulting conversations with their Uncle Edward were surely major factors in Stanley's ultimate development into an orientalist and Stuart's into an Egyptologist. The latter's annotations, signed "R.S.P.," are to be found among the pages, especially in regard to missing illustrations. Stuart also copied, with some updating, the mysterious manuscript in which Lane had rewritten the Cairene chapters of *Description of Egypt* during the previous decade. Lane had probably intended to replace the corresponding text in *Description* with it when the work went to press. That event never occurred.

After Lane's return to England in 1849, he devoted the rest of his life to his lexicographical work. At his death on 10 August 1876 he was in the midst of preparing its sixth volume. That and the remaining two volumes were completed by his great-nephew and biographer, Stanley Lane-Poole. Lane's *Arabic–English Lexicon* remains a standard reference work to this day. Like *Modern Egyptians*, it has never gone out of print. There is no evidence that Lane gave more than passing thought to *Description of Egypt* during his later years. Its manuscript, along with some of his other papers, were sold by Lane's widow to the British Museum in 1891, a few years before her own death.

Yet Lane's *Description of Egypt* did not fade into the archival shelves without one last glimmer. This came from the posthumous *Cairo Fifty Years Ago*, published under Lane's name by his great-nephew, Stanley Lane-Poole.[2] That book was the text of the heavily revised manuscript of Lane's Cairene chapters that his nephew Stuart had copied in Cairo during the 1840s. The original manuscript later disappeared, but after

---

[1]Sophia Poole, *The Englishwoman in Egypt: Letters from Cairo, Written during a Residence There in 1842, 3, & 4.* 3 vols. (London: Charles Knight and Co., 1844–46).

[2]Edward William Lane, *Cairo Fifty Years Ago*; Stanley Lane-Poole, ed. (London: John Murray, 1896).

Lane's death Stuart gave his copy to Stanley Lane-Poole who edited and published it in 1896.[1] The publisher was John Murray.

In 1835, when Lane was preparing to leave Egypt, one of the sheikhs who was tutoring him in Arabic language and society took a piece of paper and wrote on it the *shahada*, or profession of faith: "There is no god but God and Muhammad is the messenger of God." He then tore it in two, giving one part to Lane and sticking the other into a crack in Lane's house. This was to guarantee that Lane would someday return to Egypt, for God would not allow the statement forever to remain divided. In the event, Lane did return seven years later, bringing his manuscript of *Description of Egypt*, when he began his lexicographical studies. But perhaps the sheikh's talisman was more effective than he imagined, for the *Description of Egypt* has now returned to Egypt, thereby realizing even more of the force of the sheikh's desire, for *Description of Egypt* embodies so much of Lane, his youthful experiences, and his high ideals. Essential to any full understanding of Lane's overall life and work, it is appropriate that his first book should after all these years return to Cairo for publication.

---

[1] For the history of the original manuscript and the copy, see Lane-Poole's preface to *Cairo Fifty Years Ago*, pp. v-xii.

A Note on the Text and Illustrations

Seeing one's own manuscript through press is difficult enough; doing so for someone else, especially someone who lived over a century ago, can be immensely more so. Although Lane brought his *Description of Egypt* manuscript to a high state of readiness, it nevertheless required numerous editorial decisions. Complicating these was the dual obligation of maintaining the textual integrity of Lane's manuscript while presenting it in a printed form of which he would have approved. As anyone who has undertaken such a task knows, these two goals may ultimately be irreconcilable. When they conflicted, I tended toward the former and allowed the manuscript to stand intact, yet the realities of typesetting and my sense of responsibility toward Lane often demanded textual intervention; therefore I want to make such instances as fully identifiable and reversible as possible.

The first is the title of the book, which is a new construct for this edition. As explained in the Editor's Introduction, Lane's first title was *Description of Egypt*. Later, under pressure from his intended publisher, he changed it to "Notes and Views in Egypt and Nubia [etc.]." The latter is retained here, but as a subtitle, in part to distinguish this edition clearly from any of the manuscript versions.

Lane did not prepare a table of contents. I have constructed it from his chapter titles. It ought further to be explained that Lane thought his book would be published in three volumes, not one. His first manuscript volume contained the first sixteen chapters; the second, the next ten; the third, the remaining thirteen plus the supplement. (The other six volumes in the British Library set of manuscripts are the illustrations, which Lane intended to appear in the three published volumes.) In each volume, Lane numbered the chapters anew, starting with one. Presentation in a one-volume format required renumbering all of the chapters sequentially, one through thirty-nine. His chapter three of the second volume is here chapter nineteen; likewise, his second chapter of his third volume is now chapter twenty-eight; and so on. His textual cross-references to chapters and volumes, however, are retained, with the new chapter numbers provided within square brackets.

I have retained one chapter, or rather its equivalent, that Lane cut when he prepared his final draft. This is the Introduction (his title) where he recounts his voyage to Egypt. It is certainly presumptuous of me to resuscitate an introduction that he decided to omit, but I believe the information in it is too significant to lose. The reader should be aware, however, that Lane intended his book to begin with chapter one, not the Introduction.

The preceding matters were simple compared with the myriad editorial details of preparing Lane's text for typesetting, and doing so in a manner appropriate to the time in which he intended to publish. Unfortunately, it is not possible to compare any of his published texts with their fair copies (apart from the *Arabic–English Lexicon*), for none of the latter has come to light. Fortunately, however, portions of an early draft of *Modern Egyptians* have been preserved; from them we can see numerous examples of how his manuscript conventions were translated into print. Also, during the following decade, portions of *Description of Egypt* were edited by Lane's sister and Lane himself for publication in her *Englishwoman in Egypt*. The resulting marginal annotations provide additional editorial guidance.

By far the most frequent editorial alteration in the text concerns the word 'and,' for which Lane always wrote an ampersand (&). He fully expected these to be typeset as 'and,' and so they have been here. In the case of 'etc.,' which he wrote as '&c' and used frequently, his orthography is retained, but with the addition of a terminal period (&c.), because that is how it was done in *Modern Egyptians*.

With a partial exception, Lane's system of punctuation is retained, including his use of the semicolon, which is heavy even by Victorian standards. This, in fact, was diminished somewhat—though only somewhat—by Lane's editors in the 1830s, but their criteria are too indistinct for replication here. Lane's occasional mistakes in punctuation are handled in various ways. Where the omission of punctuation is obviously inadvertent, as in the case of a complete sentence followed by spacing and a capitalized following sentence, or an unclosed set of brackets or quotation marks, the missing mark is supplied without comment. But where there is any possible doubt of Lane's intention, the passage is left uncorrected unless it causes excessive awkwardness or misreading; then the desired comma, or whatever, is inserted, but in square brackets.

The partial exception involves Lane's use of linking dashes between sentences, of which he was very fond. He tended to use them as an organizational device, to order elements within paragraphs. He also used them to give the ensuing text the force of closely appended thought, hence their frequent appearance near the end of a paragraph where related but briefly stated ideas might appear. Often, when these inter-sentence dashes occurred in the middle of overly long paragraphs— which Lane tended to write—his editors would convert them into paragraph breaks. But when they fell near the end of a paragraph with insufficient remaining text to form an independent paragraph, they were allowed to stand. Lane himself decided on reconsideration that many of his paragraphs were too long, for in some of his later notations, probably made when he was selecting text for his sister, he inserted numerous paragraph breaks, usually at points where he had written linking dashes between sentences. Where such insertion marks exist, I have taken them as license to break up despairingly long paragraphs; otherwise, Lane's paragraphing is retained intact.

Like most people, Lane had some problems with spelling, which he expected to be corrected in print. Some words he consistently misspelled, such as *ceiling* 'cieling,' *seize* 'sieze,' and *niche* 'nich.' The misspelling that occurs most frequently in this manuscript is 'pharoah' for *pharaoh.* Those words are routinely corrected in this edition without comment. In other instances the errors, even if obviously inadvertent, such as 'commitee' (in a note in chapter four), are corrected with square brackets.[1]

Occasionally Lane inadvertently used the wrong word or omitted the word that he intended to write, though not as often as one might expect. In three instances ("ten or twelves days" in chapter four, "to soon to become" in chapter six, and "was been cleaned" in chapter fifteen) I could not resist correcting the slip without comment. Otherwise, any such corrections are made within square brackets.

Lane often wrote superscripts, especially for abbreviations, but they were always brought down to the line when typeset. This is the practice here. He was, however, inconsistent about following abbreviations with periods; in this text the periods are supplied, according to editorial practice in his published works, as in the case of Mr. ('M^r'), Col. ('C^{ol}'), or Dr. ('D^r'). While Lane was fairly consistent in abbreviating and superscripting words such as the preceeding ones, others were so treated only occasionally, such as 'y^r' (year), 'morn^g' (morning), or months of the year. Here all such abbreviations are written out in full. He was also inconsistent in applying superscripts to ordinal numbers, e.g. '1st' or '4th'; here they are all brought down to the line. Another such inconsistency is 'n^o' (number), which frequently appears in the notes in reference to illustrations, and was sometimes followed by a period, but sometimes not. In some of his later, more hastily added notes, he occasionally capitalized it. Here all are standardized to 'no.' with a period.

The treatment of Lane's notes and marginal comments has required some discrimination. Lane abundantly annotated *Description of Egypt* to provide citations, additional information, and cross-references within the work. These notes are reproduced here as footnotes. Most of Lane's notes were complete, polished, and ready for the typesetters, but some that were added later, after the composition of the final draft, are rougher, obviously written in haste with the intention of further revision before going to press. This is especialy true of the additions to the Theban chapter that were probably written for the projected separate book about Thebes. These later annotations are retained in their original state, although any directions for rearrangement of text that they might contain are not followed. The marginalia and textual insertions that Lane made for *The Englishwoman in Egypt*, however, are not included here when they can be definitely identified as such, for their objective is contrary to that of *Description of Egypt*. Their textual content can be found in *The Englishwoman in Egypt*. But some of Lane's other

---

[1]Another correction is the name Quatremère, several times cited in the text, which Lane spelled once correctly with the grave e and thereafter incorrectly. All are corrected here without comment.

additions to the manuscript during the 1840s, though possibly prompted by preparation of the latter work, seem merely the product of his continuing interest in the subjects they contain. This is especially true of information derived from his friend George Gliddon. Such annotations are retained.

Some of Lane's annotations, in many instances no more than a word or a number scribbled on a facing page, are so terse as to be incomprehensible, at least without extensive annotation and explanation that far exceeds the physical limits of this volume, and therefore are not reproduced here. Other notes or memoranda, such as the momentary location of maps, are obviously ephemeral, but they also indicate placement points for references, so are retained. In some cases these memoranda bear on Lane's ultimate conception for his book: for example, a note about his intention, never fulfilled, to enlarge the description of an illustration in chapter ten.

Lane considered his illustrations to be an integral part of *Description of Egypt*. At first he planned to insert them into the text, but that intent is less clear in the final draft, where he may have been inclined to place at least some of them in separate sections. In this edition, practical considerations dictated separate presentation. The originals are to be found in six manuscript volumes;[1] their order in the first five volumes is sequential according to their main references in the text, but that of the last volume is not entirely so. Also, the contents of the last volume, which apparently were not bound during Lane's time, were to be interspersed between the others, as they are here. Lane developed a numbering system of his own, which is no longer usable, but his references are retained, with the current figure numbers following in square brackets. Lane's system, as the reader may notice, is not invariably consistent even within its own context, for it changed during the course of composition and subsequent alteration of the text. Several illustrations are missing. In one instance (fig. 41), Lane apparently forgot to include an illustration, but it (or more likely a copy of it) was located among the Lane Manuscripts in the Griffith Institute.[2]

Two classes of reproduction were envisioned for the illustrations in *Description of Egypt*. The finest were to be copper engravings or lithographs. These are the 101 contained in the first five volumes of illustrations. Most, but definitely not all, of the 56 in the last volume were to be woodcuts. As noted in the Editor's Introduction, Lane brought his illustrations to a generally high state of readiness appropriate for their anticipated medium of reproduction. Two that featured clothing were even colored (figs. 18 and 19), perhaps in contemplation of the new technique of chromolithography. In some instances, however, Lane intended further work, as he wrote on the bottom of his drawing of the

---

[1]British Library, Add MSS 34083-8.
[2]I am grateful to the Griffith Institute for permission to publish the illustration here.

Old Harbor at Alexandria: "*Note*—In a few of my drawings I have left some parts (as the water in the above) to be finished hereafter; but no part that may not be done with great correctness here [i.e., in England] as on the spot."[1] In this edition there is yet a third category of visual material, consisting of occasional rough sketches, drawings of hiero-glyphs, facsimile copies of graffiti, and staves of music that Lane inserted into his text. These are reproduced here directly from the manuscript, just as Lane drew them.

Lane prepared a list of captions for the first five volumes of illustrations. These are retained in this edition. Captions for most of the illustrations in the final manuscript volume are taken from annotations that Lane made on the drawings themselves, often on their back sides. For illustrations without such annotations, I supplied captions and identified them as mine by enclosing them in brackets. Differences in transliterations of some Arabic words in Lane's captions will be readily apparent. This results from the fact that Lane prepared the list for the first five volumes several years after completing *Description of Egypt*, after his system had changed, while his annotations on the drawings in the last volume were written much earlier when he made the drawings.

Lane's system of transliterating Arabic terms into English deserves an essay of its own, but some general points can be made about it. The first thing to note is that it was dynamic, constantly changing. The system in the first draft of *Description of Egypt* differed substantially from the one in the last; indeed, variation exists even within the final draft. Then, over the following decade and a half, Lane's ideas for transliteration changed even more radically, as his corrections for his sister's book show. No standard system had yet been developed. Though aware of the work of others, Lane ultimately had to rely on his own ear, informed by his rapidly growing knowledge of Arabic, to devise a system that suited his needs.

The result was designed to convey an approximate sense of Arabic sounds to the general reader but in such a way that someone with a knowledge of Arabic could infer the correct spelling of the original Arabic word. As much as possible, Lane proceeded phonetically, using direct correspondences (i.e., ل = l, م = m, etc.) wherever they existed, then establishing clear disctinctions between letters with subtle differences not readily apparent in English pronunciation or for letters with no English equivalent at all. While ه was simply represented as h, the harsher ح was written hh. ك was naturally written with a k, but the darker ق with ck. Lane did not, however, differentiate in transliteration between د and ض (both written as d), س and ص (both s), or ط and ت (t). The guttural خ was transliterated with kh, غ with gh, and so on. As one might expect, Lane was conditioned by Egyptian pronunciation, most evident in his transliteration of ج with a hard g rather than the soft j that would be more appropriate in other parts of the Arab world. Sun

---

[1]British Library, Add MSS 34083, ff. 4v–5.

letters he transliterated according to sound, hence "en-Neel," "es-Soo'da'n," etc.

Lane employed two diacritical marks. One, which in the manuscript resembles a rather sharply curved apostrophe, was primarily used for the letter ع, although ع was not invariably represented by it. One also finds it in place of the *fatḥa* following the ح in his "hh'sa'n" and "hh'ma'r." It is typeset here as '. The other mark resembles an apostrophe, though a straight one. Typeset here as a prime ('), its use was much more varied. In its simplest application, it served to spread stress evenly across a multi-syllabic word. Sometimes it lengthened a vowel, as in "Sa'ee'd" and "ba'b." It also indicated the doubling of a consonant by a *shadda*, as with the ق in Sack'cka'rah, م in Mohham'mad, and ل in Mel'low'ee. But it also appears in other instances where its function is less clear. As much as possible, I have left Lane's system as he wrote it. Occasionally naive, even aggravating, it helps to document the development of an especially influential scholar of the Arabic language.

One thought to retain about Lane's transliterations, and indeed about this entire edition, is that there is no absolute consistency. For example, Lane was clearly moving toward a system of capitalizing the initial article of a proper name, but not a medial one (e.g., "El-Bahhr el-Azruck"), but he did not always do so. One will also note irregularities in citation. Pliny's *Natural History* appears as "Hist. Nat." in one note and "Nat. Hist." in the next. Lane enclosed some titles of books in quotation marks, some not. Words might have macrons and breves in one appearance but not in their next. Sometimes the last item in a series of three is set off by a comma, but sometimes not. Transliterations, capitalizations, and other conventions can change, even within the same paragraph. If all were corrected within square brackets, as many are, the result would become tiresome to the reader, while application of the odious term *sic* in every pertinent situation would be intolerable. The ideal in this edition has been to be as faithful as possible to Lane's text within the parameters set forth above.

A concluding comment concerns my annotation of the text. *Description of Egypt* was a document of its time, intended for a readership in the 1830s. Since then, the readership has changed, as have the things that could be taken for granted in its understanding. My first impulse was to annotate heavily—glossing terms, supplying variant readings from earlier drafts, identifying people and places, providing contextual bibliography, and so on. Then reality intervened. The length of Lane's basic text combined with his illustrations already strained the limits of a one-volume format, even without my introductory comments. Consequently I went to the other extreme and kept my annotation to a distressingly bare minimum. But the reader is by no means left without resources. General place-names can usually be inferred from works such as Baines and Malek's *Atlas of Ancient Egypt* which also provides valuable additional information about sites as well as guides to further reading. Concise biographies of many of the individuals whom Lane mentions are available in the third revised edition of *Who Was Who in Egyptology*, the *Dictionary of National Biography*, and the many works about the history of travel and scholarship in Egypt. I did, however, feel compelled to provide some guide to the literary works to which Lane refers, often in passing and with incomplete publication data; therefore I have compiled a Bibliography. My annotations are to be found in footnotes marked with daggers, in contrast to Lane's own footnotes, which are numbered. Whenever it was necessary to insert material into one of Lane's footnotes, I did so within square brackets.

I apologize to the memory of Edward William Lane for my inevitable failure to present his work as precisely and correctly as he envisioned it. He did an exceptionally conscientious job of preparing his manuscript for press. Any mistakes or shortcomings in its presentation here are entirely my own.

Introduction.†

A zealous attachment to the study of oriental literature, and a particular desire to render myself familiar with the language of the Arabs, and with their manners and customs, induced me to visit Egypt. But these were not my only motives. I had long entertained a wish to examine the antiquities of that most interesting country: and as I felt, even before I commenced my travels, that there was a probability of my publishing the observations that I might make; I purposed to execute a series of sketches of all the most remarkable objects that I might see; well convinced that a drawing, in many cases, is worth many pages of description: and to ensure the utmost accuracy in these, I determined to make use of the Camera Lucida.

In the summer of the year 1825 I made arrangements for my passage to Egypt in a merchant brig called the Findlay bound from London to Alexandria. The passage-money was 30 guineas; the Captain engaging to supply me with provisions. I embarked on Monday the 18th of July; and on the 24th we lost sight of the English coast. On the morning of the 5th of August we saw the African mountains; and soon after sunset, on the same day, we passed Gibraltar with a delightful breeze. Throughout the remainder of that month we experienced most unfavorable weather. On the 17th we put into the port of San Antonio, in the isle of Iviça, to procure a supply of water, for our stock had become very bad. After a delay of two days we continued our voyage; but not very prosperously; for on the night of the 20th, under the south-west side of Majorca, we encountered a tremendously heavy squall, which did considerable damage to our sails and rigging. The same foul and tempestuous weather continued to attend us, interrupted only by occasional calms. On the night of the 2nd of September we were off the bay of Tunis. It was very dark and dismal; with heavy clouds and lightning from the windward quarter; and the sea ran so high that the motion of the vessel prevented the compass from traversing. A weighty storm-compass was therefore substituted; but in a few minutes it was unshipped by a heavy lurch, and was only replaced to be overturned again by the next roll of the vessel, which was several times laid on her beam-ends.

We were now drawn along in utter uncertainty between a lee-shore on the right and a dangerous reef on the left; our compass being useless. The lightning was our only guide. In this fearful state we had remained about half an hour when I retired with the master to the cabin to consult the chart. Scarcely had I entered when I heard a loud crash, occasioned by the fall of the main top-mast. The darkness still continued; but in less than an hour the moon rose above a low dark scud, and her friendly light

---

†This Introduction is primarily taken from the first draft of *Description of Egypt*, with additional details from the second.

enabled us to clear away the wreck and to steer the vessel while deprived of the aid of the compass. As daylight approached the wind somewhat abated, and we arrived at Malta without further mishap on the morning of the 4th. While we remained there to prepare a new top-mast, our two mates mutinied. They were sent on shore and put in prison. After a delay of six days we proceeded on our voyage. On the 15th we saw the high land of Candia,[†] from whence we made a direct course for Alexandria; and on Monday the 19th I beheld the shores of Egypt.

[†]Crete.

Chapter I.[1]
The Harbours and City of Alexandria.

General appearance of the coast of Egypt—Distant view of Alexandria—
The Old Harbour—Arrival in the New Harbour—First visit to the
town—Description of a crowded street—Fatal quarrel in a coffee-house—
The Quarter of the Europeans—Description of the New Harbour and the
Pharos—Short general account of the town—Climate, &c.

Egypt presents to the Mediterranean a low, sandy coast, bearing, through
out its whole extent, a most desolate aspect; and in no part more so than
in the neighbourhood of Alexandria. To the west of this town we see
nothing but a tract of yellowish calcareous rock, and sand, with, here and
there, a few stunted palm-trees, which but little diversify the dreary
prospect.

The first land-mark that we perceived was the small ruined tower of
Ab'oo Seer, situated between two inconsiderable eminences of rock, near
the shore, about seven leagues from Alexandria. A pleasant breeze bore
us rapidly along; and we soon lost sight of the "Arab Tower." My
attention was next directed to an object which appeared like a tall, distant
sail. This was the noble column named, by travellers, "Pompey's Pillar."
It seemed as if it rose from the sea; for neither the city nor the hills in its
neighbourhood could yet be discerned. Soon afterwards we saw the tops
of two lofty hills of rubbish, each crowned with a fort; and next we
distinguished the vessels in the Old Harbour, intercepting, almost
entirely, the view of the town, which lies upon a low, flat site.

The Old, or Western, Harbour (anciently called Eunostus Portus) is
deeper and more secure than the New Harbour (which was called
Magnus Portus). The former, which was once exclusively appropriated
to the vessels of the Moos'lims, is now open to ships of all nations; and
the latter, which was "the harbour of the infidels," is almost deserted.[2]
The entrance of the Old Harbour is rendered difficult by reefs of rocks,
leaving three natural passages, of which, the central has the greatest depth
of water. Frigates may enter with safety; but ships of the line cannot,
unless lightened by the removal of their guns; though there is more than
sufficient depth of water for them within the harbour. The west, and
north-west, and north winds are most prevalent; and are favourable for
vessels entering the harbour; but outward-bound vessels often remain

[1]A map [fig. 2] to accompany this volume [i.e., chapters one through sixteen] is in
the larger portfolio which I send.
[2]The permission for European vessels to anchor in the Old Harbour was
obtained by Sir John Stuart, on the occasion of the peace of Amiens.

many days or weeks before the wind will permit them to leave the port: it is well, however, that the reverse is not the case.[1]

To illustrate the descriptions which follow, I insert a small plan of the site and environs of Alexandria.[2]

As we approached the entrance of the Old Harbour, an Egyptian cruiser made towards us, and fired a gun, to bring us to. A boat was then dispatched from her, and our captain was ordered to take his papers to her commander. He soon returned, and informed us that we were to steer for the New Harbour. This was occasioned by an event which had happened shortly before our arrival. A Greek fire-ship had entered the Old Harbour, where many Egyptian men-of-war were lying among the European and other merchant-vessels. A timely discovery prevented the destruction which might otherwise have ensued; and, as it was feared that another attempt of the same kind might be made, an order was issued that no vessel should be admitted into this harbour until she had been searched.

After this short hindrance we quickly made sail again, passed before the entrance of the Old Harbour and the long, barren rock of Pharos and cast anchor in the New Harbour, not far from the fort and light-house which occupy the site of one of "the seven wonders of the world." Our vessel was almost the only one lying in this harbour, excepting some boats from Reshee'd.

The coast of Egypt had been within our view from sunrise; but three fourths of the day had passed before our vessel was safely moored, and the boat lowered to convey me to the landing-place, which was nearly three quarters of a mile distant. I approached the beach with feelings of intense interest, though of too anxious a nature to be entirely pleasing: for I was not visiting Egypt merely with the view of enjoying the

---

[1]My view of the Old Harbour (plate 1, no. 1) [fig. 3] was taken from the shore of the Necropolis, on the south-west of the site of the ancient city. It requires a few words of description.—Under the letter *a* is seen the palace of the Ba'sha, upon the long ridge of rock which was the ancient island of Pharos; at the extremity of which, under the letter *b*, is a battery. To the right of the shipping is a part of the modern town of Alexandria, and a part of the white wall which surrounds the site of the old Arab city; beyond which is seen a lofty hill of rubbish, (one of those two before-mentioned,) with a fort upon its summit, under the letter *c*.— Behind the spot whence this view was taken a battery has lately been erected. This harbour and the other are now very well defended.

[2]Explanation of the plan.*—A, gate called Ba'b el-Bahhr—B, Ba'b el-Mahhmoodee'yeh—C, Ba'b es-Sidr—D, Ba'b Reshee'd—E, the Obelisks—F, A Synagogue—G, Greek Convent—H, Roman Catholic Convent—I, Site of the Church of St. Athanasius—J,J, Two hills of rubbish; each having a fort upon its summit—K, The Pillar—L, Traces of a hippodrome—M, The great catacomb— N, The burial-ground of the Jews—O, Burial-ground of the Moos'lims—P, Palace of the Ba'sha—Q, A battery—R, The Frank Quarter—S, The New Weka'leh.

*See no. 1 of the subjects for wood-cuts [fig. 4].

examination of its pyramids and temples and subterranean wonders, and with the intention of quitting it as soon as I had satisfied my curiosity; but I was about to take up my abode there for a period of two or three years, chiefly for the purpose of studying the language and literature of its modern inhabitants, and of familiarizing myself with their manners and customs: it was requisite, therefore, that I should confine myself, almost exclusively, to the society of Moos'lims, assume their dress, and adopt their mode of life, with which I was not yet sufficiently acquainted to foresee whether it would be agreeable to me or the reverse.

It was the time of the afternoon-prayer when we reached the shore. The chant of the Moo-ed'din had just ceased, and several persons were performing the prescribed ablution with the water of the sea; while others, having finished that preparatory act were saying their prayers upon the beach. The sight of the Moos'lim engaged in his devotions never failed to impress me with some degree of veneration; but particularly when witnessed for the first time. The attitudes are peculiarly striking and expressive; and the solemn demeanour of the worshipper, who, even in the busy market-place, appears wholly abstracted from the concerns of the world, is very remarkable. The practice of praying in a public place is so general in the East, and attracts so little notice, that we cannot charge all who do so with hypocrisy or motives of ostentation.

Quitting the beach, I walked up a short lane, and immediately found myself in a narrow, crowded street. There I beheld, hemmed in between two rows of small and mean-looking shops, an assemblage of persons from almost every country bordering on the Mediterranean. Words can convey but a very imperfect idea of such a scene. The variety of costumes, and their motley appearance, owing to the contrast between the mean clothing of the barefooted poor and the gaudy or graceful habits of some of the superiors, produced an effect more remarkable and picturesque than can be imagined. While noticing the various peculiarities of dress, feature, and complexion which characterize the native of Africa and the East, I was particularly struck with the noble and hardy look of the Western Bed'awee, enveloped in his ample woollen sheet, or hooded cloak,—with the affecting spectacle of many persons nearly or totally blind,—with the sight of children in a state of perfect nudity, or clothed in rags,—and, above all, with the singular appearance of the veiled females, exhibiting, in their dull disguise, no other attraction than a degree of stateliness in their carriage, and a remarkable beauty in their large, dark eyes, which, besides being sufficiently distinguished by nature, are rendered more conspicuous by the black border of *kohhl*[1] round the lashes, and by the concealment of the rest of the features.—Most of the passengers were on foot; some, upon asses; and a few, on horses or mules. Long trains of camels, laden

---

[1]The kind of kohhl most commonly used is chiefly composed of the smoke-black produced by burning a kind of *liba'n*, or frankincense.

with water-skins, or with bales of merchandise, were winding slowly and cautiously through the midst of the crowd; their conductors bawling to the passengers to take care of themselves, and move out of the way. The cries of *O''a*! *Sa'ckin'*! and *Guarda*![1] resounded every where and every moment.

The shops of Alexandria, like those of most other Turkish and Arabian cities, resemble *cupboards*, rather than *rooms*. A raised seat of brick or stone, about three feet high, and the same, or more, in width, extends along each side of the street; and upon this the tradesman generally sits, before his shop, either smoking or at work. A shed of wood, covered with plaster, of the same width as the seat, shelters him from the sun and rain. In the evening he shuts up his shop, and goes home.

Some streets through which I passed were covered over with matting supported by rafters of wood extending across from the tops of the houses, with small, square apertures, at intervals, for the admission of light. At corners of the streets, and wherever else there was sufficient space, were groups of men and women seated on the ground, with baskets before them containing bread and vegetables for sale.

I may here introduce a sketch (made on my return from the interior) which will convey an idea of several of the streets in Alexandria.[2]

The Frank street is wide; and the houses here have an appearance somewhat European. In passing through this street I observed a number of persons collected before the open front of a Frank coffee-house. Among the mixed company within, consisting of Turks, Alexandrians, and Franks, were two Turkish soldiers, whose violent conduct had attracted the notice of the passengers in the street. The cause of their quarrel I could not learn; the result I shall not soon forget. Both were excited by intoxication; but one of them was almost mad with rage. He sprang up from his seat, drew a pistol from his girdle, and thrust it forward so that the muzzle nearly touched the face of his adversary, who sat before him on the opposite side of a table. He fired; but the intended victim, by a dexterous blow, had turned aside the pistol, and another soldier, who stood by him, received the ball, and instantly fell, a bleeding corpse. The disappointed ruffian then drew his sword, and would have shed more blood, had he not been speedily disarmed by those around him.—In the Turkish Empire a summary punishment awaits the shedder of human blood, unless protected by his rank or wealth.—In a few minutes after the commission of the crime above-related, the body of the perpetrator lay exposed to public view, with the sever'd head under the arm.[3]

---

[1]These words (which are Arabic, Turkish, and Italian) have the same meaning—"take care."

[2]Wood-cut no. 2 R.S.P. [fig. 5].

[3]After a Moos'lim is beheaded his head is placed under his arm: a Christian's is placed between his legs. A *Jew* is never *beheaded*: his blood would pollute the sword: and therefore he must be *hanged*.

The quarter occupied by the Europeans is the south-eastern part of the town; by the shore of the New Harbour. This situation appears to have been chosen for their residence because it was convenient for the landing and shipping of their merchandise: but now that the Old Harbour is open to their vessels the situation is not so advantageous for them. A large building, called the New Weka'leh[1] for the reception of merchants and others, has lately been erected on the shore of the New Harbour, quite at the extremity of the town. It surrounds a spacious square court; and the ground-floor of the building consists of magazines towards the court, and shops and the entrances of the dwellings towards the exterior. From a window of one of the apartments in this building occupied by the English Consul, Mr. Barker,[2] I made (on my return to Alexandria from the upper country) a view of the New Harbour.[3]

The modern Pharos is a poor successor of the ancient building erected by Sostratus Cnidius, from which it derives its name; but from a distance it has rather an imposing appearance.—Several Arab historians mention the telescopic mirror of metal which was placed at the summit of the ancient Pharos. In this mirror vessels might be discerned at sea at a very great distance. El-Muckree'zee[4] informs us that the Greeks, being desirous of effecting the destruction of the Pharos, of obtaining possession of the wonderful mirror, employed a deep stratagem. One of their countrymen repaired to the Khalee'feh[5] El-Welee'd Ibn 'Abd El-Mel'ik, and professed himself a convert to the faith of El-Isla'm; pretending that he had fled from his king, who would have put him to death. He informed the Khalee'feh that he had acquired, from certain books in his possession, the art of discovering where treasures were concealed in the earth, and had thus ascertained that there was a valuable treasure, consisting of money and jewels, deposited beneath the foundations of the Pharos of Alexandria. The Prince, deceived by this artful tale, sent a number of workmen with his crafty adviser to pull down the Pharos: and when more than half the building had been destroyed the Greek made his escape to his own country, and his artifice

---

[1]Generally called by Europeans *occale*.
[2]Mr. Barker succeeded Mr. Salt, who died in October, 1827.
[3][Fig. 6.] This view comprehends the whole of the western shore of the harbour. The houses in the foreground belong to European consuls and merchants. The great fort and light-house are seen in the distance (under the letter *a*), and the long causeway which connects the fort with the peninsula of Pharos.
[4]See, respecting this author, a note at the commencement of the 8th chapter of this volume.
[5]This is the title which the English generally write "Caliph."

thus became manifest.[1]—It is related by Es-Sooyoo'tee[2] that the inhabitants of Alexandria likewise made use of the mirror above-mentioned to burn the vessels of their enemies, by directing it so as to reflect the concentrated rays of sun upon them.

The causeway of stone which connects the fort and light-house with the peninsula of Pharos is built upon a ridge of rock. Granite columns and other materials of ancient buildings have been employed in its construction.

The peninsula of Pharos is now called *Ro'dat et-Teen* (or the Garden of the Fig) on account of a few fig-trees growing there. Its south-western extremity is called *Ra's et-Teen* (or the Cape of the Fig). Upon this rocky peninsula are a palace of the Ba'sha,[3] and some other building, and the burial-ground of the Moos'lims, adjacent to the town.

The New Harbour abounds with rocks and sand-banks, having little depth of water over them; and is exposed to the north and north-east winds, which are often very violent. The place of anchorage is near the causeway of the Pharos, where there is sufficient depth for corvettes and small frigates to lie.

I shall now give a brief, general account of the town: for as yet I have only described what I saw on the day of my arrival.

The modern name of Alexandria is *El-Iskenderee'yeh* الاسكندرية. It is built upon a narrow neck of land, which unites the Peninsula of Pharos to the continent and thus forms the double harbour, as did anciently the causeway which, from its length of seven stadia, was called the *Heptastadium*. The ground which is occupied by the modern town has been formed by a gradual deposit of sand on each side of the heptastadium; and the present situation is certainly more advantageous for a commercial city than the ancient site.

The houses are generally built of white calcareous stone, with a profusion of mortar and plaster. Some have the foundation-walls, only, of stone; and the superstructure, of brick. They have plain or projecting windows, of wooden lattice-work. The windows of the houses belonging

---

[1]The same author relates that part of the Pharos was thrown down by an earthquake in the year of the flight 177 (A.D. 793-4);—that Ahh'mad Ibn Too'loo'n surmounted it with a dome of wood;—and that an inscription upon a plate of lead was found upon the northern side, buried in the earth, written in the Yoo'na'nee (or ancient Greek) characters; every letter of which was a cubit in height and a span in breadth. This was perhaps the inscription placed by the original architect, and which, according to Strabo, was to this effect—"Sostratus Cnidius, the son of Dexiphanes, to the protecting gods, for the sake of the mariners."

[2]A celebrated Arab theologian and historian, so called from his birth-place, Oosyoo't, or Sooyoo't (commonly pronounced Asyoo't), in Upper Egypt. He died in the year of the flight 911 (A.D. 1515-6).

[3]This title, in Arabic, is always pronounced *Ba'sha*: in Turkish, it is *Pa'sha'*. In writing upon Egypt I think it proper to spell words as the Egyptians pronounce them: though this is a Turkish title.

to Europeans, and those of the palaces of the Ba'sha and the governor of Alexandria, and a few others, are of glass. The roofs are flat, and covered with cement. There is little to admire in the interior architecture of the houses; and the town altogether has a very mean appearance. Many ancient columns of granite and marble have been used in the construction of the mosques and private dwellings. The inhabitants are supplied with water from the cisterns under the site of the ancient city, which are filled by subterranean aqueducts from the canal, during the time of the greatest height of the Nile; but in consequence of the saline nature of the soil through which it passes from the river the water is not good. Almost every house has also its cistern, which is filled by means of skins borne by camels or asses; and there are many wells of brackish water in the town.—The number of inhabitants is about 15, or 16,000.

As the emporium and key of Egypt,[1] Alexandria is a place of considerable importance; but otherwise it is, in no respect, a desirable residence. It is a poor, wretched town; its climate is unhealthy; and nothing but sea and desert meets the eye around it. Ancient writers have extolled the *salubrity* of the air of Alexandria. This quality of the air was attributed, according to Strabo, to the almost insular situation of the city: the sea being on one side, and the Lake Mareotis on the other. The *insalubrity* of the climate in later years has been regarded as the result of the conversion of the lake into a salt marsh. The English army, in 1801, made a cut by which the water of the sea was admitted, from the Lake of Ab'oo Ckeer, into the bed of the Lake Mareotis; and the operation was repeated by 'Al'ee Ba'sha, in 1803; and again by the English in 1807: on each occasion military policy dictated the measure; and as soon as the object in view had been attained the gap was closed, as it cut off the supply of fresh water from Alexandria by interrupting the course of the canal. But while the communication between the two lakes remained open, it was not found that the climate of Alexandria was at all improved; and the evaporation of the waters of the Lake Mareotis afterwards must have had a pernicious effect. The damp and rain during the winter at Alexandria, and the heavy dew at night throughout the year have a particularly baneful influence. I may add that this town is one of the places where the plague generally makes its appearance many days earlier than in the interior of Egypt. Yet I have met with persons who consider the climate of Alexandria as more agreeable than that of the valley of the Nile; as we find those in England who prefer winter to summer.

There is a series of telegraphs, lately constructed, from Alexandria to the metropolis; a distance of more than 120 British miles. The towers composing this series are nineteen in number: the first of them is on the peninsula of Pharos: and the last, in the citadel of Musr, or Cairo.

---

[1]The northern coast of Egypt has no harbour excepting those of Alexandria.

Chapter II.
The Environs of Alexandria.

The walled site of the old Arab city—Antiquities, &c., within the wall; particularly the ancient cisterns, and the obelisks—Objects without the wall—Burial-ground of the Jews—Ancient remains along the shore of the New Harbour—Ruins of Nicopolis—The great pillar—Inquiry respecting the Serapéum, and the library which was burnt by command of 'Om'ar—The Necropolis—Dulness of a residence at Alexandria—Murder of a Frank.

The wall which surrounds the site of the old Arab city has lately been rebuilt in a plain but substantial manner. This work was commenced in 1811. Mohham'mad Ba'sha,[1] fearing another invasion of Egypt by the French, deemed it necessary to strengthen this place: for the wall above-mentioned defends the town on the land-side, and surrounds the cisterns from which the inhabitants derive their supply of fresh water. The wall has four gates: that by which the fortified enclosure is entered from the modern town is called *Ba'b el-Bahhr*, or the Sea-Gate. A scene of more complete desolation than that which is beheld on entering the enclosure can scarcely be conceived. Mounds of rubbish and drifted sand occupy nearly the whole site of the ancient city. Within the area surrounded by the present wall, besides some monuments of the ancient city, are two convents, and a synagogue, and several groups of houses, with a few walled gardens, which contain little else but palm-trees. There are also two lofty hills of rubbish, each with a fort upon its summit, which command an extensive view; but a stranger is not permitted to ascend these. The line of the principal street of the ancient city, extending in a straight direction from the shore of the Old Harbour to the *Ba'b Reshee'd* (or Gate of Reshee'd[2]), which is at the eastern extremity of the enclosure, is plainly observable: and the direction of the other great street, which crossed the former at right-angles, may also be traced; commencing near the present northern gate (*Ba'b el-Bahhr*), and terminating near the gate called *Ba'b es-Sidr*. The extent of the ancient Alexandria during its most flourishing period must have been considerably greater than that of the Arab city which succeeded it; but it is impossible to mark its precise limits. Within the area which was occupied by the latter, the most remarkable remains of antiquity are the cisterns and the obelisks.

---

[1]Mohham'mad 'Al'ee Ba'sha is commonly called only by his first name with his title.
[2]Reshee'd is the name of the town which Europeans call Rosetta.

I entered the field of ruins by the gate which is next the modern town, and having passed by the Roman Catholic convent of Terra Santa proceeded along the road which leads to the eastern gate. This road was evidently the principal street of the ancient city. On the left (or northern) side of it, a little beyond the convent above-mentioned, is the site of the church of St. Athanasius (afterwards a mosque), from which was taken, by the French, a beautiful sarcophagus, now in the British Museum.[1] Opposite this spot are two erect granite columns, of large dimensions, and a third which is prostrate. These must have belonged to some noble building which adorned the southern side of the principal street. Near them are extensive remains of very massive constructions of brick; but so much ruined and encumbered with rubbish that no idea can be formed of their plan.

Among the mounds, in many places, are seen the mouths of the ancient cisterns; each, with few exceptions, having the hollowed marble base of an ancient column placed over it. The cisterns seem to have extended under a great part of the ancient city; and there is still a sufficient number of them open and in good repair for the supply of the modern town. I have before mentioned that they are filled by subterranean aqueducts from the canal, during the season when the Nile is at its greatest height. They have arched, or vaulted roofs, which are supported by columns, or by square pillars; and some of them have two or three ranges of pillars and arches, one above another, and are very extensive.

Having deviated from the road to look into some of the cisterns in the tract on the southern side, I now retraced my steps, and, crossing the road, proceeded by the Greek convent and the synagogue towards the *obelisks*, which are situated at an angle of the enclosure, almost close to the shore of the New Harbour.

These two obelisks[2] are vulgarly called, by Europeans, *Cleopatra's Needles*; with no more reason than some tombs (which I shall have occasion to mention hereafter) are called her Baths. It is the south-western face of the erect obelisk that is seen in the view which I have given. Each obelisk is of a single block of red granite, nearly seventy feet in length, and seven feet and a half wide at the base. Three lines of hieroglyphics adorn each of the four faces of either monument. The central line bears the title and name of Thothmos 3rd, who appears, from strong evidence, to have reigned shortly before the departure of the Israelites from Egypt. The lateral lines were sculptured at a later period; for they bear the name of Rameses 2nd, or Sesostris. There is also, on the erect obelisk, a column of hieroglyphics, comparatively very small, next

---

[1]This appears to be the sarcophagus which received the body of Amyrtæus the Saite, the first native king of Egypt after the revolt of his nation from the Persian yoke to which Cambyses had subjected it. The name of Amyrtæus occurs once or more in each of the hieroglyphic legends with which the sarcophagus is so fully sculptured.

[2]See plate 2 [fig. 7].

each angle, near the base; but almost obliterated: the name of the second successor of Rameses 2nd is imperfectly legible in each of them. Upon each of the four faces of the pyramidal top, Thothmos 3rd is represented, in the form of a sphinx,[1] lying on a high pedestal (with his name inscribed both over him and on the pedestal), and presenting an offering[2] to a sitting figure of Ra, or of another deity.—Pliny relates that Rameses erected four obelisks at Heliopolis. Those at Alexandria are perhaps two of the four thus alluded to. Their antiquity, being so much greater than that of Alexandria, suggests the probability of their having been taken from Heliopolis to adorn a temple or palace in the new city. The fact of the name of Rameses 2nd being sculptured upon them may have given rise to the tradition that they were *erected* by that king.

The fort seen in the view of the obelisks occupies the site of an old tower which belonged to the former wall (that is, to the *old* wall of the *Arab* city), and which was called by European travellers "the Tower of the Romans," as it was apparently of Roman origin. The shore of the New Harbour is behind the wall on the left.

When the British army was in Alexandria in 1801, operations were commenced for transporting the fallen obelisk to England; but in consequence of the commander-in-chief refusing to sanction the undertaking, it was abandoned; and I believe is not likely to be resumed, though the present Ba'sha of Egypt offered the monument to us some years ago.[†]

After viewing the obelisks I returned to the main road, and proceeded along it to the eastern gate. On each side I observed many mouths of cisterns, such as I have before described; and in several places I saw fragments of granite and marble columns, and other materials of ancient buildings. Near the eastern gate are some modern houses, which occupy a considerable space, chiefly on the right (or southern) side of the road; and a few gardens, or plantations of date-palms, enclosed by stone walls. These gardens are irrigated with the water of the ancient cisterns, which is raised by a machine called *Sa'ckiyeh*.[3]

Having passed through the eastern gate, or Gate of Reshee'd, I turned to the left, and, proceeding along the tract lying between the wall and the small canal which empties itself into the New Harbour, came to the burial-ground of the Jews, where a broken column, or a shapeless mass of stone, is seen over each grave. If all these tomb-stones were overturned and examined, some curious inscriptions, or other sculptures,

---

[1]The sphinx was a common emblem of an Egyptian king.
[2]In this instance the sphinx has human hands and arms.
[†]Lane's belief in the unlikelihood of the removal of the obelisk was justified in the short run. Only after his death was it transported to London and erected on the Embankment in 1878. Two years later the other obelisk was transported to New York where it now stands in Central Park.
[3]A description of this machine (with an explanatory view) will be found in the fourth chapter.

might perhaps be discovered; for they all appear to be relics of ancient monuments. There was the quarter of Bruchion, bordering upon the harbour. Along the shore, from the part where the obelisks are situated to the promontory which stretches towards the Little Pharos, I looked for some remains of the Cæsarium; the Timonium of Antony, and the Posidium; but a few fragments of stone, and masses of brick and mortar, are the only existing relics of those celebrated buildings. It appears not improbable that their fall was hastened by an earthquake; and portions of their crumbling walls thus thrown into the sea; for ancient ruins are visible beneath the water near the shore. The island of Antirrhodos, which formed a little port within the Magnus Portus, near the promontory Lochias, has also disappeared. The rock which was anciently called Acrolochias is that upon which the Little Pharos is situated.

Between two and three miles beyond the eastern gate is the field of the memorable battle of the 21st of March, 1801, in which Sir Ralph Abercromby, who commanded our victorious army, received his mortal wound. At the spot where the battle raged most furiously, by the sea-shore, is a quadrangular enclosure, about 400 feet square, surrounded by substantial but now ruined walls, between 20 and 25 feet high. These are constructed of calcareous stone, and large bricks, in distinct layers, like many other Roman buildings. The ruin is called *Ckusr el-Ckaya'sireh* (or the Fortress, or Palace, of the Cæsars). It masks the site of a small town which received the name of Nicopolis, in commemoration of a famous victory obtained there by Octavius Cæsar over Antony.

Strabo speaks of a circus, or hippodrome, between this place and the city of Alexandria; but no trace of it is now seen.

On my return towards the modern eastern gate, I looked in vain for any remains by which to ascertain the site of the *Canopic Gate*, which was at the eastern extremity of the ancient city. If any vestiges of it exist, they are buried beneath mounds of sand and rubbish, which likewise probably cover the hippodrome above alluded to.

I next followed a beaten track among the mounds on the south of the wall, and arrived before the southern gate, called *Ba'b es-Sidr*. Upon an eminence about half a mile from this gate is the famous *Pillar*, vulgarly called Pompey's.[1]

The shaft of this enormous column is a single block of red granite, 68 feet in height, and 9 feet in diameter at the bottom, according to my own measurement. The capital is a block of the same kind of stone; and is 10 feet high. The base, plinth, and pedestal are likewise of red granite, and

---

[1] See the view, plate 3 [fig. 8]. In this view is seen a part of the wall which surrounds the site of the old Arab city; with the gate called Ba'b es-Sidr, to the left of the Pillar. To the right of the gate is seen the erect obelisk; to the left, the two granite columns near the site of the church of St. Athanasius; and in the extreme distance, the sea. To the right of the pillar is seen the easternmost of the two hills mentioned before, with the fort upon its summit.

each is a single block. The combined length of these three pieces is 17 feet. The total height of this superb monument is therefore 95 feet; and the substructure, which is partly modern, is 4 feet in height.—The shaft is beautifully wrought, but sadly disfigured by numerous names inscribed in very large characters, with black paint. I have not thought it necessary to disfigure my drawing of it in the same manner; as the effect would thereby be very much injured. The names have mostly been written by persons who have ascended to the summit. This they have been enabled to do by flying a large paper kite, and causing it to descend so that the cord rested upon the top of the capital; by which means they succeeded in drawing a stout rope over it; and, having accomplished this, easily rigged shrouds, by which to ascend. This exploit has been performed several times; generally by naval officers, who have caused the name of their ship to be painted on the shaft. An English lady once ascended to the summit.—The capital is of inferior workmanship; and the pedestal is not remarkable. The foundation consists of several stones cemented with mortar; but the weight of the pillar rests principally, if not wholly, on the central stone, which is a mass of breccia, five feet square. This stone is covered with hieroglyphics, which are inverted: and it is smaller at the lower, than the upper part; whence it appears that it is an inverted obelisk, or a portion of an obelisk, sunk in the ground. I have derived these particulars from the observations of preceding travellers: for the central stone was, at the time of my visit, completely surrounded with masonry.

I could not perceive any traces of the Greek inscription on the pedestal: it can only be faintly seen when the rays of the sun fall obliquely upon the surface of the stone. Every traveller who examined the pillar since the time of Pococke believed the inscription to be entirely obliterated, until Col. Squire again discovered it. That gentleman, with Mr. Hamilton and Col. Leake, deciphered the following lines, recording the dedication of the pillar, by a "prefect of Egypt" (whose name is almost wholly illegible), to the "most (revered) Emperor, the protecting divinity of Alexandria, Diocletian Augustus."

ΤΟΝΤΙΜΙ ωΤΑΤΟΝΑΥΤΟΚΡΑΤΟΡΑ
ΤΟΝΠΟΛΙΟΥΧΟΝΑΛΕΞΑΝΔΡΕΙΑC
ΔΙΟΚΛΗΤΙΑΝΟΝΤΟΝCΕΒΑCΤΟΝ
ΠΟΜΠΗΙΟCΕΠΑΡΧΟCΑΙΓΥΠΤΟΥ

The letters underlined are conjectural restorations: the rest are generally believed to be fairly deciphered: but Dr. Clarke reads διον ἀδριανον instead of διοκλητιανον.[†]

This inscription certainly proves that the column, or the building in which it stood, was *dedicated* to the Roman Emperor whose name is thus recorded; but not that the column was *erected* in honour of that

---

[†]I.e., 'divine Hadrian' instead of 'Diocletian.'

individual, any more than the lateral lines of the inscriptions on the obelisks which I have described prove that they were erected in the reign of Sesostris. The name of the "prefect of Egypt" who caused the inscription to be sculptured is plainly seen to begin with the letters ΠΟ—. It was probably ΠΟΜΠΗΙΟC; for M. Quatremère has shown that there was a prefect of that name in Egypt in the time of Diocletian. If so, the appellation of "Pompey's Pillar" is not altogether incorrect.

By the Arab historians this pillar is called *'Amoo'd es-Sawa'ree*; which may be interpreted "the Pillar of the Columns." Michaelis, in translating Ab'oo-l-Fed'a's Description of Egypt, mistook the word *sawa'ree* for a proper name; and called this monument "the Column of Severus"; but he afterwards acknowledged his error.—Abd El-Latee'f and El-Muckree'zee affirm that this pillar originally belonged to a magnificent building, containing a library, which 'Amr Ibn El-'A'see[1] burnt by command of the Khalee'feh 'Om'ar. A particular account of the destruction of this library is given by Ab'oo-l-Far'ag[2]; but the statement of that author has been disbelieved because the story is related by few other writers. Why (I would ask) should they record what they considered an event of scarcely any importance? It is evident, from the slight manner in which 'Abd El-Latee'f and El-Muckree'zee mention the fact, that they regarded it as a very unimportant occurrence. They allude to it merely as connected with the history of the great pillar. The former says—"Here was the library which 'Amr Ibn El-'A'see burnt by permission of 'Om'ar."—El-Muckree'zee says—"The pillar is of a red, speckled stone; hard and flinty. There were around it about four hundred columns, which Ckara'ga, Governor of Alexandria, in the time of the Soolta'n Sala'hh ed-Deen[3] Yoo'soof Ibn Eiyoo'b, broke, and threw into the sea, near the shore, to prevent the vessels of an enemy from approaching the walls of the city. It is said (he adds) that this pillar is one of those which stood in the portico of Aristotle, who there taught philosophy; and that this academy contained a library, which 'Amr Ibn El-'A'see burnt by direction of 'Om'ar Ibn El-Khatta'b."—The Arab general, 'Amr, having taken Alexandria, was solicited by one Johannes, surnamed "the Grammarian," to spare the library above-mentioned, and to suffer it to remain in the possession of its former owners. 'Amr, willing to oblige the philosopher, wrote to the Khalee'feh, desiring to know his pleasure respecting these books; and received the following answer—"As to the books which you have mentioned, if they contain what is agreeable with the book of God, in the book of God is sufficient without them; and if they contain what is contrary to the book of God, there is no need of them: so give orders for their destruction."—They were accordingly distributed about the city, to be used for heating the

---

[1]This name is generally, by European writers, improperly spelled "Amroo Ibn El-As."

[2]Or _____ Far'aj. I adopt the Egyptian pronunciation.

[3]Called by Europeans "Saladin."

baths; and "in the space of six months they were consumed."—"Hear what happened," says Ab'oo-l-Far'ag, "and wonder!"—The author here quoted does certainly speak of this event as one of lamentable importance; but he was a *Christian* writer. The *Moos'lims*, though they love and encourage many branches of literature, generally imagine that the books of the Christians are useless, or of an evil tendency.

It is evident, I think, that the building which contained the library above alluded to was the Serapéum.—The *first* great library of Alexandria, founded by Ptolemy Soter, was in the palace near the Great Port. This, as we learn from Plutarch and Orosius,[1] was burnt together with part of the city which took fire from the conflagration of Cæsar's fleet. The *second* library, which was that of Ptolemy Philadelphus, was in the Serapéum. This temple was erected on the same spot where a smaller edifice, dedicated to the same deity, had been built before the foundation of Alexandria; as we are informed by Tacitus. The name of the god worshipped there was Rhacotis (according to Cyrill); and hence the place where the temple was situated was called "the Hill of Rhacotis." Strabo mentions a village, or small town, of the same name, which became included within the limits of Alexandria, and was near the docks; but this was distinct from the *hill* of Rhacotis. Cyrill informs us that the Serapéum was near the Necropolis; and a general remark of Macrobius, respecting temples dedicated to Serapis, shews that it must have been without the walls of the city; while Strabo describes it as being within the canal. Ruffinus, also, says that it was situated on an eminence, to which one ascended by a hundred or more steps. It appears, therefore, that this temple was on a hill, between the canal and the city, towards the Necropolis. All these descriptions of its position agree exactly with the site of the great pillar. Therefore, as the accounts of the Greek and Arab writers coincide respecting the situation of this building, we may consider this point as clearly established; and likewise the truth of the history of the destruction of the library.

The worship of Serapis was abolished, and his temple and colossal image destroyed by order of the Emperor Theodosius; as Ruffinus relates: but that the building in which the books were contained was preserved we learn from later writers. It seems, however, that it was not the celebrated *great library* of the Serapéum which 'Amr burnt; for Orosius saw the book-cases empty in the beginning of the fifth century; but it was probably a smaller collection. Aphthonius, writing in the fourth century, after the worship of Serapis had been abolished, calls this building "the Acropolis of Alexandria." It is clear that he alludes to no other edifice; for he describes the library within it, and the great pillar.[2]

I saw no remains of any ancient building around the pillar; but this is not to be wondered at: the columns which surrounded the great pillar

---

[1] For the passages from the works of ancient authors referred to in these remarks respecting the Serapéum see White's Ægyptiaca.
[2] See De Sacy's "Relation de l'Egypte, par Abd Allatif," pp. 234 and 5.

were thrown into the sea, as before related; and the other materials were probably made use of in the construction of the walls, or private dwellings, mosques, &c., of the Arab city.—At a short distance to the south-west are traces of an ancient stadium, or hippodrome.

I completed my survey of the environs of Alexandria by visiting the ancient Necropolis, or City of the Dead. This name has been given to a tract of nearly two miles in length, on the south-west of the site of the ancient city; between the Old Harbour and the bed of the Lake Mareotis. The sepulchres are all excavated in the rock, which is calcareous and rather soft. Those which I saw were small, and rudely cut, without paintings or any other decorations.

One of the catacombs is very spacious. It is the only one that is well worthy of being examined; but I was not allowed to approach it; and had I obtained permission, I should not have been at all anxious to avail myself of it; for a battery has lately been constructed over the spot, and the Turks have converted the subterranean apartments into sinks. The principal chamber is described as being of a circular form; and the roof is excavated like the interior of a dome. Around it are three recesses, which were doubtless receptacles for mummies: one of these is opposite the entrance, and the remaining two opposite each other, on the right and left; and around each of them are three troughs, cut in the rock, each apparently, to receive a mummy. In other chambers are similar receptacles for the dead. The entrance of the principal (or circular) apartment is ornamented with pilasters and a pediment; plainly shewing the period of the formation of the catacomb to have been posterior to the founding of Alexandria.

The descriptions which several travellers have given of the catacombs of Alexandria shew that they are very inferior to those of Thebes and Memphis and many other ancient cities of Egypt. Very few traces of painting or sculpture have been discovered in them; and, I believe, no hieroglyphics: Mr. Davison mentions his having seen one or two figures of men, which, although defaced, sufficiently shewed that they were the work of no great master. Dr. Clarke, not having seen the elaborately wrought catacombs adorned with interesting and beautifully executed paintings or painted sculptures, in Upper Egypt, speaks of those of Alexandria in terms of most unqualified admiration; declaring that nothing so wonderful ever fell within his observation. His supposition that the circular chamber mentioned above was the famous Serapéum of Rhacotis is utterly inconsistent with the descriptions of that temple given by many ancient authors, as my remarks respecting it must have shewn.

The foregoing brief account of the remains of one of the most illustrious cities of ancient times may be considered somewhat uninteresting; being merely a plain description of objects which for the most part disappoint the traveller, and occasion only melancholy reflections. But history confers a deep interest on this desolate spot, once the chief seal of Egyptian learning, the theatre of many wars and bloody tragedies, the scene of the martyrdom of St. Mark, the birth-place and residence of many of the most eminent fathers of the church, and the hot-bed of schisms and heresies. Its importance as the key of Egypt, rendering it obnoxious to oft-repeated sieges and captures, may be regarded as the primary cause of the destruction of the monuments of Alexandria: but much of the work of demolition must be attributed to the fanatic zeal of the Christians during the reign of the Emperor Theodosius, and in subsequent periods. I should have found but little inducement to remain at Alexandria more than two or three days, had not my stay there been attended with other pleasures than those derived from the examination of the few monuments of antiquity. A letter of introduction procured for me much friendly attention and useful information from Mr. Salt, the British Consul-General, who received me into his country-house. Mr. Salt's house was situated within the area formerly occupied by the old Arab city, at the distance of about half a mile from the modern town, and not far from the gate called Ba'b es-Sidr. It was surrounded by a garden, which appeared like an oasis in a desert; though in another situation it would have possessed but few charms. On my arrival I had the pleasure of finding that M. Linant, with whom I had become acquainted shortly before, at Malta, was a guest at the consul's house. I also met there that enterprising antiquarian Caviglia, to whose extraordinary labours, as well as those of Belzoni, modern travellers in Egypt are so much indebted. Caviglia, who is a native of France, was master of a merchant-vessel in the Mediterranean, and has abandoned his seafaring life to prosecute researches in Egypt. He professes to be intimately acquainted with magic; and to have discovered, by means of that art, all the mysteries of the Pyramids, their secret passages and chambers, and every thing else connected with them. During my stay in Egypt, he published, at Alexandria, some portions of a periodical work on the Egyptian mythology, &c., with certain remarks upon the Christian religion which were of such a nature as to draw down a sentence of excommunication against all his readers; and the work was consequently discontinued. If an anathema had been directed against all who *understood* the work, few would have been obnoxious to the curse.

One evening, while I was sitting in the consul's garden, enjoying the mild air and a pipe, a Frank entered, in a state of great agitation, bringing information of a murder that had just been committed. A respectable European, serving as an interpreter to the Austrian consul, was returning from the town to his country-house near the Ba'b Reshee'd, when a ruffian, who appeared to be a Turkish soldier, riding up behind him, unperceived, shot him in the back, and, galloping onwards, escaped through the gate above-mentioned before the cries of a person who witnessed the murder could reach the sentinels, and cause them to stop him. The assassin was however discovered a day or two after; and it was some satisfaction to me to learn that he was a Frank, who had disguised himself as a Turk in order to avoid detection. Two murders had been committed in this place during the first week after my arrival; both, as I believed, by Turkish soldiers; and I began to think that, where such monsters abounded, the life of every European must be in constant jeopardy: but my subsequent experience proved my anticipations to be groundless.

Chapter III.
Voyage from Alexandria to the Nile.

Communication between Alexandria and the Nile by means of the New Canal—Description of the boats of the Nile—Commencement of the voyage along the canal—The Sera'b, or Mirage—Arrival at the Nile—Account of the route from Alexandria along the sea-shore to Reshee'd (or Rosetta)—Ancient sites—Canopic branch of the Nile—Similarity between an ancient and modern custom.

The traveller bound from Alexandria to the Egyptian metropolis formerly journeyed by land to Reshee'd (or Rosetta), where he embarked on the Nile; the principal part of his route to the banks of the river lying along the sea-shore, over a barren and almost desert tract: or he made a disagreeable voyage by sea to the mouth of the Nile: the *bo'gha'z* (or bar) of which was seldom passed without some risk: the surf being generally tremendous; but the sudden transition from the conflicting waves to the tranquil flood within was most delightful; and no further danger awaited the traveller, who embarked in a smaller boat at Reshee'd. A more agreeable and more expeditious course is now afforded by the canal called the *Mahh'moo'dee'yeh* المحمودیّه ; and it was this course that I pursued. M. Linant, being about to proceed to the metropolis at the same time as myself, proposed that I, with another traveller, should accompany him. As a stranger in the country, and not having at that time provided myself with a servant, I was glad to avail myself of his offer. But this obliged me to make a more rapid voyage than I should otherwise have done. I shall therefore incorporate with the few observations which I made during *this* voyage those which I was enabled to make at my leisure on my return.

The boats of the Nile are admirably constructed for the navigation of that river. Their great triangular sails are managed with extraordinary facility; which is an advantage of the utmost importance; for the sudden and frequent gusts of wind to which they are subject require that a sail should be taken in almost in a moment, or the vessel would most probably be overset. When these boats run aground (which very often happens, for the river is shallow in many parts, and abounds with moving sand-banks), they are generally pushed off without much difficulty by means of poles; or the crew descend into the water, and shove the vessel off with their backs and shoulders. In a calm the boat is towed by the crew; and it is astonishing to see how well they perform this laborious task in the very hottest weather, seldom stopping to take rest; and then, only for a very short time. In descending the river the main-sail and yard are usually taken down, and the fore-sail only left; as the wind is almost constantly from the north-west (that is, contrary to the general course of the river); and the vessel is propelled by oars, or suffered to drift down the stream. The boatmen generally sing while rowing; and while the vessel is under sail they often accompany their songs with the rude music of the *darabook'keh* and *zoomma'rah*, which are a funnel-shaped earthen drum and a double reed-pipe.[1] Though the sounds of these instruments are loud and harsh, I enjoyed their music and the songs of the boatmen as much, I believe, as the crew themselves.

The most common kind of passage-boat, or pleasure-boat, is called a *Ckan'geh* (also pronounced *Ckan'jeh*). It is long and narrow; and draws but little water. It has two masts, with two large triangular sails, and a low cabin, which is generally divided into two or more apartments, having small, square windows, which are furnished with sliding shutters, or with blinds, in the inside.[2] The traveller spreads a mat or carpet in the cabin; and he should place a narrow mattress along one, or each, of its sides, with cushions to lean against. This is the Turkish mode of furnishing the cabin; and is the most comfortable manner; for it does not admit of a person's sitting upon a high seat. The cabin of a moderate-sized boat of this kind is between six and seven feet wide, and about four feet, or four and a half, high; and the whole boat is from thirty-five to fifty feet long. The boats of the Turkish grandees are generally painted white, with a mixture of red, green, and other gay colours: bunches of flowers are commonly painted upon the pannels of the cabin, both within and without; and the blood-red flag waves at the stern. Other boats in general are not painted. The ropes are mostly made of *leef*, or the fibres of the palm-tree. The crew generally consists of six or seven men.—The *Dahabee'yeh* is larger than most boats of the former kind, and wider in proportion to its length; but it resembles them in other respects.—The *Ma'a'sh* is the largest of the boats of the Nile. It is used both as a passage-boat and for the carriage of grain, &c. In its form it differs but little from the vessels above described.[3]—The sketch here introduced represents a small dahabee'yeh; and will convey a fair notion of the other boats above described.[4]

Having hired a large and commodious boat, we embarked on the 28th of September, late in the evening; and immediately set sail.—A custom which is always observed by the Arab boatmen at the commencement of a voyage much pleased me. As soon as the wind had filled our large sails, and we began to glide along the canal, the Rei'yis (or captain of the boat)

---

[1] These instruments are seen in plate 6 [fig. 61] in the second volume of this work.
[2] In plate 6 in the second volume of this work [fig. 61] a boat of this kind is represented (that in which I made my first voyage through Upper Egypt and Nubia); and the first plate in the same volume [fig. 55] represents the interior of its cabin, which was not divided.
[3] *Mur'kab* is the *general* term for a boat, whatever be its kind, and also for a ship.
[4] See no. 3 of the subjects for wood-cuts [fig. 9].

exclaimed *El-Fe't'hhah*![1] This is the title of the opening chapter of the Ckoor-a'n,—a short and simple prayer,—which the Rei'yis and all the crew repeated together in a low tone of voice.

The great pillar, on our left, had a very noble appearance when viewed from the canal; but excepting this and a country-house of the Governor of Alexandria, nothing could we see but the high banks, which, however, only concealed from our view marshes and sandy plains.

Where the canal runs along the narrow neck of land between the salt marsh of Mareotis and that of Ab'oo Ckeer, the sides are formed by solid walls of stone, to prevent in some degree, the filtration of salt water into the Mahh'moo'dee'yeh, as it supplies the cisterns of Alexandria. In scarcely any part does this canal occupy exactly the bed of the *ancient* canal of Alexandria; which it crosses in several places. More than 300,000 men were employed to dig it; and about 12,000 of these are said to have died in the space of ten months; many of them in consequence of ill treatment, excessive labour, and the want of wholesome nourishment and good water. Their only implements in this work were the hoes which are commonly used in Egyptian agriculture; and when the soil was moist they scraped it up with their hands, and then removed it in baskets. The whole length of the canal is nearly fifty British miles; and its breadth, about 80 or 90 feet. It was commenced and completed in the year 1819. The name of Mahh'moo'dee'yeh was given to it in honour of Mahhmoo'd, the reigning Soolta'n.

During the whole of the voyage along the canal the view is intercepted by a high ridge of earth on either side, which was throw[n] up in excavating the bed. On one occasion, having landed to obtain a sight of the adjacent country, I saw, for the first time, that extraordinary phenomenon called, by the Arabs, *Sera'b*, and by Europeans, *Mirage*. In the midst of a sandy waste on the north of the canal, was the semblance of a clear and extensive lake, a mile or two distant, surrounding some hillocks, which seemed to be islands, and having its apparent shores defined with the most perfect precision. It was not without much difficulty that I was persuaded to believe it an illusion; for, though I did not find it marked in the maps, I thought it must be a real lake formed by the overflowing of the Nile. Never after did I see this phenomenon more completely deceptive.

On the 30th, just as the day began to dawn, we approached the Nile. During the latter part of the night a thick fog had prevailed; but this disappeared with the darkness, and my eyes were charmed with the delightful prospect of the Delta, doubly agreeable after the dull voyage of the preceding day. The river, then at its greatest height, had a noble appearance, and was bordered with luxuriant verdure. In the distance were seen the white ma'd'nehs (or menarets) of the town of Foo'weh, a little higher up the river, on the opposite bank.

---

[1]This word is commonly pronounced as I have written it, instead of *El-Fa'tehhah*.

The sand and mud accumulate so rapidly at the entrance of the canal, and within it, that it is found necessary, before the river becomes very low, to raise a dam of earth at the entrance, (as well as at the mouth, at Alexandria, where it empties itself into the sea), in order to retain a sufficient quantity of water, and to prevent a greater deposit within it: and goods must then be transferred from one boat to another, across the dam. If the canal had been made to branch off from the river more in the direction of the current of the latter, a greater flow of water would have been thrown into it, and the evil here spoken of perhaps avoided.

I shall now give a brief account of the land-route from Alexandria to Reshee'd (or Rosetta).

Passing through the eastern gate of Alexandria (the Gate of Reshee'd), the traveller proceeds by the ruins of Nicopolis; beyond which, nothing occurs worthy of notice for the distance of about six or seven miles; the route lying along an arid, sandy tract, interspersed in some parts with palm-trees. On the left is the sea; and on the right, the marshy lake of *Ab'oo Ckeer* ابو قير (also called the lake of *El-Ma'adee'ah*, or "the ferry"), which will, probably, soon be completely dry; the inlet which admitted the waters of the sea having been stopped up. This was done in the year 1816; before the new canal was made. A strong dike, or causeway, was raised between the lake and the sea; by which the inconvenience of the ferry was obviated. The salt water of the lake of Ab'oo Ckeer and that of Mareotis continues to filter into the new canal of Alexandria; and this cannot be wholly prevented until these lakes have entirely dried up; though the sides of the canal are lined with masonry at the narrowest part of the isthmus.

Within a league of the point of Ab'oo Ckeer are some ruins on the sea-shore which appear to mark the site of *Taposiris Parva*. At Ab'oo Ckeer is a village, and a fort with a light-house, situated on a low point (probably the "*Zephyrium promontory*" of Strabo, where the city of *Thonis* once stood). Off the point is a small rocky island, to which the name of "Nelson's Island" has been given by the English, in commemoration of "the Battle of the Nile," which was fought in the Bay of Ab'oo Ckeer.

Leaving the fort and village, the traveller proceeds along the dike which separates the marsh of Ab'oo Ckeer from the sea, and arrives at the mouth of the Lake of *At'koo* اتكو . This inlet is supposed to be the mouth of the ancient Canopic branch of the Nile; on the west of which was situated the town of *Heracléum*; so called from its containing a temple dedicated to Hercules. Hence this branch of the Nile received also the name of "Heracleotic." It was likewise called "the Naucratic branch," from the city of *Naucrătis*, which was situated at some distance inland, on the eastern bank, that is, within the *ancient* Delta. The city of *Canopus* (according to Strabo's description) was somewhat nearer to Alexandria than was the town of Heracléum; and the *canal* of Canopus must have traversed the tract which is now the bed of the lake of Ab'oo Ckeer. The remains of Canopus may be concealed by the marshes of

Ab'oo Ckeer; but its site was not so far distant as the village of that name from the Canopic mouth.

Not wholly different are the manners of the modern Egyptians from those of the ancient Alexandrians who flocked to the licentious festivals celebrated at Canopus in honour of the god Serapis. Innumerable boats covered the canal by night as well as by day, conveying pilgrims of both sexes, dancing and singing and drinking, and availing themselves in every way of the pious licence afforded them. So, in the present day, vast numbers of the male inhabitants of the metropolis of Egypt, and persons from other parts, with numerous courtesans, repair to the festivals celebrated in commemoration of the birth of the seyd Ahh'mad El-Bed'awee,[1] at Tanta, in the Delta, where swarms of dancing-girls and singers contribute to their amusement, and where almost as much *brandy* is drunk as *coffee*.

From the mouth of the lake of At'koo to Reshee'd the route lies along a narrow, sandy tract, between that lake and the sea; passing by the village of At'koo, and, towards the end, traversing a plain covered with deep, shifting sands.

---

[1] A celebrated Moos'lim saint, whom I shall have occasion to mention more particularly in the 7th chapter. *Seyd* is a title given to the descendants of the Prophet.

Chapter IV.
Physical Sketch of Egypt.

General description of Egypt and the Nile—Length and breadth of the valley of Egypt and of the plain of Lower Egypt—Of the cultivable land—Extent of the land at present cultivated—Of the annual inundation; and of the consequent, gradual rise both of the whole soil of Egypt and of the bed of the river—Further remarks upon the Nile—The climate of Egypt—Heat—Rain—Winds—Sera'b—Diseases—Egyptian agriculture—Description of the machines used for the purpose of irrigating the land; and of the manner of irrigating—Other machines, &c.—Measures of land and of grain—Vegetable productions—Animals—Physical and agricultural calendar of Egypt.

The tract described in the foregoing chapters belongs, chiefly, to the Libyan Desert. The traveller can hardly be said to have arrived in Egypt until he sets his foot upon the fertile soil which borders the Nile. Here, then, may be appropriately introduced a general, physical sketch of that singular country: for Egypt is distinguished by its natural characteristics, as well as by its monuments of antiquity, from every other region of the globe.

Egypt is called by its modern inhabitants *Musr*,[1] or *Bur'r Musr*, بَرّ مصر . It is generally divided into Upper and Lower: the former called *Es-Sa'ee'd* الصعيد. The Sa'ee'd consists of the portion which is sometimes called Middle Egypt, or the Middle Provinces[2] (*El-Ack'a'lee'm el-Woos'ta*, or *E l-Wus'ta'nee'yeh*)[,] and the Southern Provinces[3] (*El-Ack'a'lee'm el-Ckiblee'yeh*). The Northern Provinces (*El-Ack'a'lee'm el-Bahhree'yeh*), which constitute Lower Egypt, include the metropolis.

The Sa'ee'd may be described as a long, narrow, winding valley, containing a soil of amazing fertility, watered throughout its whole length by the largest river of Africa, and hemmed in on either side by mountainous and sandy wastes. Lower Egypt is an extensive plain, for the most part cultivated, and copiously supplied with moisture by the divided streams of the Nile, and by numerous canals. All the cultivable soil of Egypt owes its existence to the Nile; by which it is still annually augmented: for this river, when swollen by the summer rains which

---

[1]Only the Turks, and some other foreigners (and the Egyptians in reading the *literary* dialect of Arabic) pronounce this word *Misr*. In the Hebrew Bible, Egypt is called the land of Mizraim, and the land of Ham, or Cham. *The land of Khem*, or *Khemi*, seems to have been the true, original name.
[2]The ancient Heptanomis.
[3]The ancient Thebais.

regularly drench the countries between the northern limits of Senna'r and the Equinoctial line, is impregnated with rich earth washed down from the mountains of Abyssinia and the neighbouring regions; and in its course through Nubia and Egypt, where rain is a rare phenomenon, it deposits a copious sediment both in the channel in which it constantly flows and upon the tracts which it annually inundates: it is everywhere bordered by cultivated fields, excepting in a few places, where it is closely hemmed in by the mountains or the drifted sands of the desert.[1]

The Nile is called in Egypt simply *El-Bahhr*, or "the river": for *bahhr* signifies "a great river," as well as "a sea." It is also called *Bahhr en-Neel*,[2] or "the river Nile"; and *Neel Musr*, or "the Nile of Egypt." The Arabs generally believe the Neel Musr to be a continuation of the *Neel es-Soo'da'n*, or "Nile of the Negroes."

Of the two great branches (called *El-Bahhr el-Azruck*, or "the Blue River," and *El-Bahhr el-Ab'yud*, or "the White River,") which, uniting, form the Nile of Nubia and Egypt, the former (though less long than the other) is that to which Egypt principally owes its fertility. Its chief characteristics (its colour, the banks between which it flows, &c.) are similar to those of the Nile of Egypt. Its dark colour, arising from its being impregnated with soil during the greater part of the year, has caused it to receive the name of "the Blue River"; while the other branch, from the opposite colour of its waters, is called "the White River." The latter is considerably wider than the former: its banks are sloping lawns, richly wooded; very unlike the banks of the Nile of Egypt, which are steep and broken.

At its entrance into the valley of Egypt the Nile is obstructed by innumerable rocks of granite, which cause a succession of cataracts, or rather *rapids*. The mountains on the east of the river, as well as the islands in it, are here of granite: those on the western side are of sandstone. From this point to the distance of thirty leagues southward sandstone mountains, of small altitude, extend on each side of the river. The valley so far is very narrow; particularly throughout the upper half of the sandstone district; and there is very little cultivable land on the banks of the river in that part: in some places the mountains are close to the stream; and in others, only a narrow, sandy strip intervenes. At the distance of twelve leagues below the cataracts the river is contracted to little more than half its usual width by the mountains on each side. Here are extensive quarries, from which were taken the materials for the construction of many of the temples in the Thebais. This part is called *Geb'el es-Sil'sil'eh*, or the Mountain of the Chain.—Where the calcareous district begins are two insulated hills (*El-Gebeley'n*) on the

---

[1]The mud of the Nile, analyzed by Regnault, was found to consist of 11 parts, in a hundred, of water; 48 of alumine; 18 of carbonate of lime; 9 of carbon; 6 of oxide of iron; 4 of silex; and 4 of carbonate of magnesia.

[2]The epithet *el-mooba'rak*, or "the blessed," is often added; particularly in writing.

west of the Nile; one of them close to the river, and the other at a little distance behind the former. The valley then becomes wider, and more irregular in its direction; and the Nile winds through the middle of the cultivable land, or nearly so. Afterwards, the valley resumes a less serpentine form; and the river flows along the eastern side; in many places washing the sides of the precipitous mountains. The calcareous district continues to the end of the valley; where the mountains on both sides diverge; the Arabian chain running due east, to *Es-Soowey's* (or Suez) and the western hills extending in a north-west direction, towards the Mediterranean.—Near the termination of the valley is an opening in the low western mountains, through which a canal conveys the waters of the Nile into the fertile province of El-Fei'yoo'm. On the north-west of this province is a lake which receives the superfluous waters during the inundation.

The length of the valley of Egypt, from the cataracts to the metropolis, is about 450 geographical miles;[1] and the distance from the latter point to the sea, in a straight line, is rather more than 90 miles. The width of the valley is in few parts more than eight or ten miles; and generally *less* than that. The width of that part of Lower Egypt that constituted the ancient Delta is about 120 miles, from east to west.

The whole of the fertile country is very flat; but the lands in the vicinity of the river are rather higher than those which are more remote. This has been supposed to result from a greater deposit of mud upon the former; which, however, cannot be the case; for I have observed that the fields near the river are generally above the reach of the inundation; while those towards the mountains are abundantly overflowed: but while the latter yield but one crop, the former are cultivated throughout the whole year; and it is the constant cultivation and frequent watering (which is done by artificial means) that so considerably raise the soil; not so much by the deposit of mud left by the water as by the accumulation of stubble and manure. The cultivable soil throughout Egypt is free from pebbles, excepting in parts immediately adjacent to the desert. It almost everywhere abounds with nitre.

Between the cultivable land and the mountains there generally intervenes a desert space, too high to be inundated. This tract partly consists of sand and pebbles, covering a bed of rock, and partly of drifted sand which has encroached on the cultivable soil. In some places this desert space is two or three miles, or more, in width.

The extent of the cultivated land in Egypt I calculate to be equal to rather more than one square degree and a half; or, I might say, about 5,500 square geographical miles.[2] This is less than half the extent of the

---

[1] The distance by the river is above 500 miles from the cataracts to the metropolis; and about 400 miles from Thebes to the same point. The difference in latitude between the cataracts and the metropolis is 6 degrees, or 360 geographical miles.

[2] I make this calculation from a list of all the towns and villages in Egypt, and the extent of cultivated land belonging to each. This list is appended to De Sacy's

land which is comprised within the confines of the desert: for many parts within the limits of the cultivable land are too high to be innundated, and consequently are not cultivated; and other parts, particularly in Lower Egypt, are occupied by lakes, or marshes, or drifted sand. Allowance also must be made for the space which is occupied by towns and villages, the river, canals, &c. Lower Egypt comprises about the same extent of cultivated land as the whole of Upper Egypt.

The term *shera'ckee* is applied to those lands which are above the reach of the inundation: and the term *rei* to the rest.

The annual inundation irrigates the land sufficiently for one crop; but not without any labour of the *fella'hh* (or agriculturist): for care must be taken to detain the water by means of dams; or it would subside too soon. The highest rise of the Nile ever known would scarcely be sufficient if the waters were allowed to drain off the fields when the river itself falls.[1] A very high rise of the Nile is, moreover, an event not less calamitous than a very scanty rise; for it overflows vast tracts of land which cannot be drained; it washes down many of the mud-built villages[2] (which are generally raised on slight eminences of earth and rubbish), and occasions an awful loss of lives as well as property.[3] When the river begins to rise all the canals are cleaned out: each is closed by a dam of earth at the entrance; and opened when the Nile has nearly attained its greatest height; towards the end of September. When the river begins to fall the canals are closed again, that they may retain the water. The lands that are not innundated by the overflowing of the river are irrigated artificially, if sufficiently near to the Nile or to a canal.

As all the cultivable soil of Egypt has been deposited by the river, it might be expected that the land would at length rise so high as to be above the reach of the inundation; but the bed of the river rises at the same time and in the same degree. It appears that no greater rise of the Nile is necessary in the present day to inundate the country sufficiently than was requisite in the time of Herodotus. There is a passage in the work of that historian which confirmed the assertion that I have just made, though designed to support a contrary opinion. He says—"There is another particular of great importance to confirm what I have said respecting this country, which I received from the priests, who affirm that, in the reign of Myris, if the Nile rose to the height of *eight* cubits all the land of Egypt was sufficiently watered; and Myris had not been dead

---

"Abd Allatif." It was made in the year of the flight 777 (A.D. 1375-6); and may be rather underrated than the reverse. The estimate of M. Mengin shews that, in 1821, the extent of the cultivated land was much less; but since that period considerable tracts of waste land have been rendered fertile.

[1] "Minores aquæ non omnia rigant: ampliores detinent, tardiùs recedendo." (Pliny, Nat. Hist. lib. V, cap. 9.)

[2] The huts are built of unburnt mud bricks.

[3] The plague seldom visits Egypt excepting after a very high rise of the Nile. It is, however, far from being an *invariable* consequence of such an event.

nine hundred years when I received this information: but in our time, unless the river rises *sixteen* cubits, or at least *fifteen*, the country is not covered with water." A probable explanation of this passage has been suggested; and I find an argument in favour of that explanation in El-Muckree'zee's "Account of the Nilometers." The Arab historian relates that the first person who measured the rise of the Nile in Egypt was Yoo'soof (or Joseph, the son of Jacob) who built a nilometer at Menf (or Memphis); and that afterwards Deloo'keh (an ancient queen of Egypt, who was surnamed El-'Agoo'z, or the Old Woman) built, at An'sin'ë, a nilometer of which the cubit was *small* (that is, smaller than the former one). It seems, therefore, not unlikely that Herodotus was misled by a change which had been made in the measure; *one* cubit having been made into *two*: but as an eye-witness he must be believed when he states that the Nile in his time rose sixteen cubits; which is also the height that is affirmed to have been amply sufficient, but not too great, in the time of Pliny, 500 years later.[1] Now the common Egyptian cubit, like the Greek, was equal to about a foot and a half (English measure): therefore sixteen cubits were equivalent to twenty-four feet; and that is exactly the height of a moderately good rise of the Nile in the present day, near the modern metropolis, or near the site of Memphis.[2] It is evident, then, that the bed of the river has risen as much as the whole of the cultivable land. The rate of this rise I calculate (from data furnished by the ancient nilometer of Elephantine[3]) to be about four inches and a half in a century.—No taxes are legally levied upon the land unless the Nile rise to a certain height, which is said to be sixteen cubits; but these cubits are not measured by the scale of the modern Mickya's (or Nilometer) of the Island of Er-Ro'dah. The modern nilometric column is divided into sixteen cubits, each equal to twenty-one inches and one third. The average point of high-water is one cubit above the highest marked on this column; and the low-water mark is three cubits and a half above zero, or above the base of the column, from which the graduation begins.

At Thebes the Nile rises about thirty-six feet; at the cataracts, about forty: at Reshee'd, owing to the proximity of the mouth, it only rises to the height of about three feet and a half.

The Nile begins to rise in the end of June, or the beginning of July; that is to say, about, or soon after, the summer solstice[4]; and attains its

---

[1] "In duodecim cubitis, famem sentit; in tredecim, etiamnum esurit; quatuordecim cubita hilaritatem afferunt; quindecim, securitatem; sexdecim, delicias. Maximum incrementum ad hoc ævi fuit cubitorum decem et octo; Claudio principe: minimum, quinque; Pharsalico bello." (Pliny, Hist. Nat. lib. V, cap. 9).

[2] A commit[t]ee appointed by the French Institute ascertained this with the most scrupulous exactness.

[3] See chapter IV, vol. III [chapter 30], of this work.

[4] Some travellers have erroneously asserted that the Nile is at its *minimum* in April and May.

greatest height in the end of September, or sometimes (but rarely) in the beginning of October; that is, in other words, about, or soon after, the autumnal equinox. During the first three months of its decrease it loses about half the height it had attained; and during the remaining six months it falls more and more slowly. It generally remains not longer than three or four days at its *maximum*; and the same length of time at its *minimum*: it may therefore be said to be three months on the increase, and nine months gradually falling. It often remains without any apparent increase or diminution at other times than those of its greatest and least elevation; and is subject to other slight irregularities. The Nile becomes turbid a little before its rise is apparent; and continues so in a less degree until it has fallen nearly to its minimum, when it becomes quite clear. Its water is extremely delicious, even when it is most impregnated with earth: but *then* the Egyptians (excepting the lower orders) usually leave it to settle before they drink it; and put it in porous earthen bottles, which cool it by evaporation. At one period only, during the latter half of June, when the Nile first becomes turbid, the people of Egypt generally abstain from drinking the water fresh from the river; having recourse to a supply previously drawn and kept in cisterns.

The width of the Nile where there are no islands is in few parts more than half a mile. The branches which enclose the Delta are not so wide, generally speaking, as the undivided stream above: and the river is as wide in the upper parts of Egypt as in the lower extremity of the valley. It is scarcely less wide in Nubia.

The rapidity of the current when the waters are low is not greater than the rate of a mile and a quarter in an hour: but during the higher state of the river the current is very rapid: and while vessels with furled sails are carried down by the stream with great speed others ascend the river at almost equal rate, favoured by the strong northerly winds, which prevail most when the current is most rapid. When the river is low, the wind from the north is often more powerful than the current; and vessels cannot then descend the stream even with the help of oars.

The *climate* of Egypt is in general very salubrious. The extraordinary dryness of the atmosphere (excepting in the maritime parts) is proved by the wonderful state of preservation in which bread, meat, fruits, &c., have been found in the tombs of ancient Thebes, after having been deposited there two or three thousand years. The ancient monuments of Egypt have suffered very little from the weather: the colours with which some of them are adorned retain almost their pristine brightness. There arises from the fields a slight exhalation (though not visible) when the inundation is subsiding, from the autumnal equinox to the summer solstice; but even then it seems perfectly dry immediately within the skirts of the desert, where most of the monuments of antiquity are situated. The damp at this period, slight as it is, occasions ophthalmia, diarrhœa, and dysentery to be more prevalent than at other times.

The heat in Egypt is very great; but not so oppressive as might be imagined, on account of that extreme dryness of the atmosphere of which I have just spoken, and the prevalence of northerly breezes. The general height of the thermometer (Fahrenheit's) in Lower Egypt during the hot season, at noon and in the shade, is from 90° to 100°; in Upper Egypt, from 100° to 110°; and in Nubia, from 110° to 120°, and even 130°, though in few years. In the latter country, if placed in the sand, and exposed to the sun, the thermometer often rises to 160°, or more. The temperature in Lower Egypt in the depth of winter is from 50° to 60°.

Rain is a very rare phenomenon in the valley of Egypt. In the Sa'ee'd a heavy rain falls not oftener, on an average, than once in four or five years. I witnessed such an occurrence, a tremendous storm of thunder and lightning and rain, at Thebes, in the autumn of 1827. I had often before seen a distant, flickering lightning in Egypt; but never heard thunder there until then. It was quite terrific; and lasted throughout a whole night. The torrents which pour down the sides and ravines of the naked mountains that hem in the valley of Egypt, on these occasions, leave very conspicuous traces. At the metropolis and thereabouts there fall, on an average, four or five smart showers in the year; and those during the winter and spring. A heavy rain very seldom falls there: when it does, much damage is done to the houses. In the maritime parts of Egypt rain is not so unfrequent.

The wind that most prevails in Egypt is the north-west. The predominance of this wind is one of the most remarkable advantages of climate that the Egyptians enjoy. The north-west breeze is ever refreshing and salubrious, beneficial to vegetation, and of the greatest importance in facilitating the navigation up the Nile at almost every season of the year, and particularly at that period when the river is rising, and the current, consequently, most rapid.—During the first three months of the decrease of the river, that is, from the autumnal equinox to the winter solstice, the wind is rather variable; sometimes blowing from the west, south, or east; but still the northerly winds are most frequent. During the next three months the wind is more variable; and during the last three months of the decrease of the river, from the vernal equinox to the summer solstice, winds from the south or south-east, often hot and very oppressive, are frequent; but of short duration.

During a period called *El-Khum'a'see'n*, hot, southerly winds are very frequent and particularly noxious. This period is said to commence on the day after the Coptic festival of Easter, and to terminate on the Day of Pentecost (or Whit-Sunday): thus continuing forty-nine days. It therefore generally begins in the latter part of April, and lasts during the whole of May. This is the most unhealthy season in Egypt; and while it lasts the inhabitants of that country are apprehensive of being visited by the plague; but their fears cease on the termination of this period.

The *Semoo'm*, which is a very violent, hot, and almost suffocating wind, is of more rare occurrence than the Khum'a'see'n winds, and of shorter duration; its continuance being more brief in proportion to the intensity of its parching heat and the impetuosity of its course. Its direction is generally from the south-east, or south-south-east. It is commonly preceded by a perfect calm. As it approaches, the atmosphere assumes a yellowish hue, tinged with red. The sun appears of a deep blood-colour, and gradually becomes quite concealed, before the hot blast is felt in its full violence. The sand and dust raised by the wind add to the gloom, and increase the painful effects of the heat and rarity of the air. Respiration becomes uneasy; perspiration seems to be entirely stopped; the tongue is dry; the skin, parched; and a prickling sensation is experienced, as if caused by electric sparks. Sometimes it is impossible for a person to remain on his legs on account of the force of the wind; and the sand and dust oblige him to keep his eyes closed. I once encountered, at Ckoo's, in Upper Egypt, a semoo'm which was said to be one of the most violent ever witnessed. It lasted less than half an hour. A very violent semoo'm seldom continues longer; and, though extremely distressing, I cannot think that it ever proves mortal, unless to persons already brought to the point of death by disease, fatigue, thirst, or some other cause. The camel seems to suffer from it equally with man: he often lies down, with his back to the wind, stretches out his long neck upon the ground, and so remains till the storm has passed over.

The *Zo'ba'ah* is another very remarkable phenomenon, and very common in Egypt and in the adjacent deserts. It is a whirlwind, which raises the sand or dust in the form of a pillar, generally of immense height.[1] I have seen more than twelve of these whirling pillars of sand in one day; and often, two or three at a time; during the spring. They are carried sometimes with very great rapidity across the deserts and fields of Egypt, and over the river. My boat was twice crossed by a zo'ba'ah; but on each occasion its approach was seen, and necessary precautions were taken: both the sails were let fly a few moments before it reached us; and we thus escaped injury; but the boxes and cushions in the cabin were thrown down by the sudden heeling of the vessel: and every thing was covered with sand and dust.

The *Sera'b*, that singular mist which resembles a lake, and is so often seen in the desert, tantalizing the thirsty traveller, I have already had occasion to describe, in the preceding chapter.

To these remarks on the climate of Egypt I may add a few words respecting the two most formidable diseases to which the inhabitants of that country are liable; namely, the plague and ophthalmia.—The plague has occurred, on an average, once in three or four years; but I have only

---

[1] I measured, with a sextant, the height of one of these pillars of sand, at Thebes, under circumstances which insured a very near approximation to perfect accuracy (observing, from an elevated station, the precise moment when it passed and agitated a distant group of palm trees); and found it to be seven hundred and fifty feet. I think I have seen several of greater height. Others, measured at the same place, were between five hundred and seven hundred feet in height.

[This note is one of the few passages to be found almost word for word in both *Description of Egypt* and *Modern Egyptians*.]

heard of one undoubted case of plague in Egypt since the year 1824. The season in which it has prevailed has almost always been the spring; generally after an over-abundant inundation. It seems, therefore, to originate from the marshy state of the low lands. In accordance with this opinion of its origin, we find that it mostly makes its first appearance in the marshy neighbourhood of Alexandria or Dimya't, or within one or both of those towns; and that it is checked by the dry heat of summer: but it is sometimes introduced from Syria and other countries.— Ophthalmia is chiefly caused by impeded perspiration; and therefore is most common in the autumn. It has been supposed to result from the nitrous quality of the exhalations from the soil after the inundation: but persons are attacked by this disease even in the dryest season. In an early stage it is mitigated, if not subdued, by the desert air; and consequently cannot be attributed to the sand or dust.

As the natural characteristics of Egypt are very different from those of other countries, so also are most of the processes of Egyptian *agriculture*.

By clearing out many old canals, digging others, and raising dikes, the present Ba'sha has restored to fertility some extensive tracts which had long lain waste: but his monopoly of the produce of the land, and the extorsions to which he has had recourse in order to prosecute the wars in Arabia, Senna'r, and Greece, have so dispirited and impoverished the peasantry that absolute force is often necessary to make them work in the fields. In general, the Egyptian *fella'hh* (or agriculturist) only cares to earn a scanty maintenance for himself and his family; well knowing that if he were to accumulate any wealth beyond his neighbours it would be wrung from him. A certain sum is required by the collector of the taxes from each village; and those persons who possess most are generally made to suffer for the deficiencies of others. Mohham'mad 'Al'ee has appropriated to himself the lands which belonged to his subjects; allotting to each individual thus dispossessed a small annual pension for life. A land-tax, proportioned to the quality of the soil (on the average about ten shillings per acre), is exacted from the cultivator; and the whole, or part, of the produce is bought up by the government at a very low rate: or, in some cases, the cultivation of the land is under the sole management of agents of the government. It is no wonder then that the fella'hh will not labour with assiduity. The Sheykh (or chief) of the village is often bastinadoed by the Ka'shif (or governor of the district) because his people are remiss in their work; and the Ka'shif perhaps loses his head because his district is not in a flourishing state. Several Ka'shifs and Sheykhs were beheaded for this reason in the spring of the year 1828.

The fields in the vicinity of the river and of the great canals are irrigated by means of machines at all seasons of the year if not subject to the natural inundation. These machines are represented in plate 4,[†]

[†]Missing.

which, with the following explanation, will sufficiently shew their construction. The first (under the letter *a*) is

The *Sa'ckiyeh*. The horizontal wheel, which is turned by a cow or bull, puts in motion the two vertical wheels, which are both on the same axis. As the front wheel revolves, the pots (being attached to two ropes, the ends of which are joined together) are drawn up by it, after having dropped in the water: each pot, when it has risen to the top of the wheel, discharges its contents into a trough, and then descends, with the mouth downwards, to refil. From the trough the water flows along a narrow trench, or gutter, across the field, or garden, which is to be irrigated. The land is divided into squares, each about two yards wide, by ridges of earth about half a foot high; and the water is admitted into one of these squares after another: or parallel trenches are cut, like the furrows formed by a plow, and these are filled in the same manner, one after another. This process is generally repeated every day. The sa'ckiyeh is much used throughout the whole of Egypt (particularly for watering the gardens), and more so in Nubia.

The *Sha'doo'f* (represented under the letter *b*) is a machine of very simple construction. Two props, formed with mud, or two trucks or thick branches of trees, support a cross piece of wood, from which is suspended a lever. At one end of the lever is a weight, generally composed of mud; and from the other end hangs a long palm-branch, stripped of its leaves, to which is attached a vessel in the form of a bowl, usually made of a piece of coarse woollen stuff sewed to a small hoop. By this the water is drawn up, and poured into the trench, from which, if necessary, it is raised still higher by another sha'doo'f: and often, when the Nile is very low, three or four of these machines are seen; one above another. By each machine the water is raised to the height of seven or eight feet. When the river rises the sha'doo'fs are taken to pieces: otherwise they would be carried away by the stream. On account of the simplicity of its construction, the sha'doo'f is more used in the valley of the Nile, from the Delta nearly to the cataracts, than any other hydraulic machine; but in Nubia, the sa'ckiyeh is used in preference.[1]

The *Ta'boo't* (which is represented under the letter *c*) bears some resemblance to the sa'ckiyeh. The annular part of the great vertical wheel is hollow, and divided into small cells. In the side (at one extremity) of each cell is an aperture, through which the water enters (the wheel dipping in the river or in a reservoir); and through the same aperture each cell discharges its contents into the trough when it is brought uppermost. The ta'boo't is only used in some parts of Lower Egypt, where the banks of the river are very low. The wheel is generally about ten feet in diameter: therefore, allowing one foot for its dipping in the water, and two feet for the fall of the water into the trough, it will raise to the height of about seven feet.

---

[1] The Egyptian fella'hh is often nicknamed "Ab'oo Sha'doo'f," or the father (that is, *owner*) of the sha'doo'f.

The *Ckut'weh* (represented under the letter *d*) is generally used for the purpose of raising the water into the channel of the ta'boo't, when the river is too low for the wheel of the latter machine to dip into it. It is merely a vessel like that of the sha'doo'f, with four cords attached to it; and is raised by two men; each holding two of the cords. The water is thus thrown up into the trough with great rapidity.

By means of these machines the whole of the cultivable land might be irrigated throughout the year; for water is every where to be found by digging a little below the level of the river. In some parts of the Sa'ee'd the fields which are remote from the river are thus watered, and abundant crops are obtained from them.

The Egyptian plough is very simple, without wheels; and is drawn by a yoke of oxen. A short-handled hoe is made use of to break the clods, and to cut the gutters for irrigation, &c. To separate the grain of corn from the ear, and to cut the straw for fodder, a space of ground is rendered smooth and hard by a plaster chiefly composed of mud; the corn is then spread upon it, and a yoke of oxen draw over it, in a circle, a machine called *No'rag*, which resembles a sledge with a rustic chair fixed upon it. It runs upon a number of small, sharp, iron wheels, generally having three axles, with three or four of these wheels to each. A man sits upon it, to give it the necessary weight, and to drive the oxen.

The general measure of land is the *Fedda'n*; which is equal to about an acre and one tenth. It was formerly somewhat more. The most common corn-measure is the *Ardeb'b*, which is equivalent to about five English bushels; or rather five bushels and about four pints.

Throughout the whole of the valley of Egypt the fields in the vicinity of the river are regularly enriched by three crops of corn in the year. In March and April are the harvest of wheat and barley: in July and August is the harvest of millet: in November, another harvest of millet, and that of maize; and in Lower Egypt, at the same period, is the harvest of rice.

The amazing fertility of Egypt will appear from the following account of its principal *vegetable productions*. Those which are more extensively cultivated will be first mentioned, in the order in which they are sown, or planted.

1. In *March* or *April* are sown cotton, sesame, and indigo; and the sugar-cane is planted.

Cotton (called in Arabic *ckootn*) flourishes in Egypt remarkably well; yielding a wool of the very finest quality. A large proportion of the soil is devoted to the culture of the cotton-plant; and its produce has become one of the chief sources of the revenue. The harvest begins in August or September.

Sesame (*sim'sim*) is cultivated for the sake of the oil (called *zeyt see'reg*) which is expressed from its seed. This oil is chiefly used for lamps. Sesame is reaped in September or October.

Indigo (*nee'leh*) occupies the same soil for three successive years; but the plants degenerate so much that their seed is not employed to raise another crop. Syria supplies the seed to Egypt. The shirts of the Egyptian peasants (the exterior, and often the *only* article of dress both of the men and women) are generally died with indigo.

The *sugar-cane* (*ckus'ab es-sook'kar*) is extensively cultivated in Egypt; and arrives at maturity in about ten months. Many canes are cut in the autumn to be sucked, while green and soft. Very good sugar has been made in Egypt; but it was too expensive for the markets of the country; and therefore what is generally made there is of a coarse kind. It is formed into loaves. Its principal manufactory is at Er-Reyremoo'n, near Mel'low'ee.

2. In *April*, rice is sown.

Rice (*rooz'z*, or *arooz'z*) is cultivated only in the northernmost parts of Egypt; chiefly within twenty miles of the sea-coast, where the land is very low, and therefore easily irrigated. It is reaped in the middle of November. Not less a quantity than two thirds of the produce is exported to Turkey, Syria, Arabia, and other countries. It is too expensive to be an article of food for the peasantry.

3. In *April* or *May*, millet is sown, for the first time.

Millet (*door'ah sey'fee*) is cultivated more than any other grain throughout the valley of the Nile; being the most productive. It is that on which the peasants of Egypt chiefly subsist. The first crop is reaped in July or August: the second will be mentioned in its season. The stalks, which grow to the height of eight or ten feet, are used for forming fences, the roofs of huts, &c.; and for fuel.

4. In *July*, maize is sown.

Maize, or *Indian corn* (which is called *door'ah sha'mee*, or *Syrian door'ah*), is chiefly cultivated in Lower Egypt. The harvest is in November. When nearly ripe, some of the heads are occasionally cut, to be roasted; and are thus eaten by many. "Hot door'ah!" is one of the most common cries in the streets of the metropolis during the autumn.

5. In *August* or *September* millet is sown a second time: but it is chiefly in the southern parts of Egypt, and in Nubia, that two crops of millet are obtained in the year.

6. In the end of *October*, or the beginning of *November* (that is, as soon as the waters of the inundation have sunk into the soil), are sown wheat, barley, lentils, beans, lupins, chick-peas, kidney-beans, trefoil, fenugreek, colewort, lettuce, safflower. Most of these occupy the soil about five months.

Wheat (*ckumhh*) attains to maturity in March or April; excepting in Lower Egypt, where, being sown a little later, the harvest ends in May. The straw, cut by the no'rag, is the principal fodder for horses, camels, asses, and other cattle. About half of the wheat raised in Egypt is exported; chiefly to Europe, and a small proportion to Arabia.

Barley (*sha'ee'r*) is but little used in Egypt excepting as food for horses. The harvest is in March or April.

Lentils (*'ad'as*) are chiefly cultivated in Upper Egypt; and are reaped in March. This grain is a common article of food in Egypt; a kind of porridge, like peas-soup, but thicker, being made with it.

Beans (*foo'l*), which were abhorred, and even considered impure, by the ancient Egyptians,[1] are extremely liked by the moderns; and in their dry state they serve as food for horses and other beasts of burden. The stalks also serve for fodder.

Lupins (*tir'mis*) are another common article of food in Egypt. The seeds, which are rather bitter, are boiled in salt and water; and so eaten by the lower order of the people. A flour called *doocka'ck* is also made of the seed of the tir'mis, and is used as a substitute for soap.

Chick-peas (*hhom'moos*) and *kidney-beans* (*loo'biya*) are likewise in common use as articles of food.

Trefoil (*bursee'm*) is the usual fodder for all cattle, as long as it is in season (about three months): at other times, cut straw, beans, and barley.

Fenugreek (*hhil'beh*), which is not so much cultivated as the former, also serves for fodder; and its grain is an article of food.

Colewort (*sel'gem*) and *lettuce* (*khus's*) are cultivated for the sake of the oil obtained from their seed.

Safflower (*ckoor'toom*) is cultivated chiefly for the yellow dye which it affords. An oil is also expressed from its seed.

7. In *December* are sown tobacco and flax.

Tobacco (*dookh'kha'n*) is sown on lands close to the river. The tobacco of Egypt is of a pale green colour, very mild, and of an agreeable flavour; but not to be compared with that of Syria.

Flax (*ketta'n*) is extensively cultivated.

The other vegetable productions of Egypt are very numerous. Only the more common need here be mentioned.

Hemp (*hhashee'sh*[2]) is cultivated in Egypt only for the sake of its intoxicating qualities. The capsules, with the seeds, are bruised, and mixed with tobacco, for smoking; or with hellebore, opium, and several aromatic substances, for an intoxicating conserve. "*Hhash'sha'sh*," which means "a smoker or eater of hhashee'sh," is a term of obloquy in Egypt; and applicable to few but persons of the lower orders.[3]

The *water-melon* (*buttee'kh*) is sown upon the sloping sandy banks and islands of the Nile, soon after the retreat of the waters. There are

---

[1]Herodotus, lib.ii, cap[.] 37.

[2]Grass and any green fodder are called by this name.

[3]Herodotus (in lib. iv, cap. 75) mentions the remarkable fact of the Scythian burning the seed of hemp in religious ceremonies, and becoming intoxicated with its fumes.

very many varieties of this and other kinds of melon (*cka'-oo'n, 'abdalla'wee*, &c.), and of the *gourd* (*ckar'a*), and *cucumber* (*khiya'r*). The cucumber is often stuffed with minced meat and rice; seasoned with salt, &c.; and thus prepared it is boiled.

The *black egg-plant* (*ba'dinga'n es'wed*) affords a similar dish to that just mentioned; and its fruit resembles a short cucumber. The *love-apple* (*ba'dinga'n ckoo'tah*) is also dressed in the same manner.

Esculent hibiscus (*ba'miyeh*) is an excellent vegetable for the kitchen. The part that is eaten is a pentagonal pod, from one to two inches in length in the state in which it is fit to gather, full of seeds and nutritive mucilage. The pods are boiled, and put into stews, &c. They are also dried, as an article of provision, particularly for travellers.

The *colocasia* (*ckoolcka's*) is cultivated for its large roots, which, in taste, resemble a watery potato.

Cabbage (*kooroom'b*), *purslane* (*rig'leh*), *Jew's mallow* (*melookhee'-yeh*), and *onions* (*bus'al*), are the vegetables most used in Egyptian cookery. Many other vegetables common in most countries are also among the productions of Egypt.

The *date-palm* (*nukhl*) is the most abundant and most useful of all the trees of Egypt. It everywhere forms a chief feature of an Egyptian landscape. A palm-tree generally produces about six bunches of dates; and a moderate-sized bunch weighs about a quarter of a hundred-weight. The date-season commences in the latter part of July, and ends in December. The trees are generally between 30 and 50 feet in height. The fruit is called *bel'ahh*. Either fresh or dried it is sweet and nutritious. A paste called *'ag'weh*, is made by pressing the fresh dates together; and is enclosed in a skin, or in a basket made of palm-leaves. This retains its moisture for a considerable length of time. Many of the peasants in Egypt subsist in a great measure upon dates. There are many varieties of this fruit, differing in colour (like plums), and in size and flavour. A kind of brandy, of indifferent quality, is distilled from the date; and is in general request among the Copts. The trunk of the palm, being of a loose, fibrous nature, cannot be cut into planks; but it is cleft in two, and used for various purposes; particularly as rafters, in forming the roofs and floors of the houses of the poorer classes in Egypt: the stripped branches are laid over them transversely: the leaves are spread over these; and a plaster, chiefly composed of mud, is then added. The branches are applied to a great variety of uses; such as the manufacture of stools, coops, or cages, boxes, doors, &c. With the fibres, which are called *leef*, growing at the bases of the branches, ropes are made.[1] These fibres are also much used (in the same manner as sponge) for washing the person; particularly in the bath: but for this purpose, a superior and whiter kind is brought from Arabia. The palm-trees in Egypt are taxed. The rate of this tax varies according to the quality of the trees: it is generally one piaster and a half (or five pence of our money) on a single tree. From the

---

[1] Hempen ropes are scarce in Egypt; not being made in the country.

whole amount of the tax it appears that the number of palm-trees in Egypt is about five millions.

The *do'm palm*, or *Thebaic palm* (*do'm* is its Arabic name), requires a warmer climate than that of Lower Egypt or the lower provinces of the Sa'ee'd. The first that I saw in ascending the Nile was at the little village of Abra's, in latitude about 27°30'; a little within the limits of the Thebais. In the neighbourhood of Den'dar'a it is particularly abundant.

The most remarkable difference between this tree and the date-palm is the branching trunk of the former. A little above the ground the trunk divides into two branches; each of which divides in like manner; and so again, if the tree be of full growth. The height of the do'm palm is generally between 20 and 30 feet. The fruit is a fibrous substance, of an oval form, between two or three inches in length, and in taste not unlike gingerbread. It contains an oblong stone, of a hard, horny nature; of which beads are made, and generally dyed red, green, or black.

The *bana'na* (*moo'z*) is much cultivated in the gardens of Lower Egypt. Its large, long leaves, drooping like the branches of the palm-tree, have a very picturesque effect. The fruit is oblong; about the length of a man's finger; but much thicker; containing a soft pulp, of a delicate flavour.

The *sycamore fig-tree* (*gemmey'z*) is particularly valued for its deep, broad shade. Its figs are small; but very good: they issue from the thickest branches, and even from the trunk. Its timber is used in the construction of boats, &c. The ancient mummy-cases were made of it.

The common *fig-tree* (*teen*) is also cultivated in Egypt, and thrives there.

The *prickly-pear*, or *Indian fig* (called *teen ifren'gee*, or the *Frank fig*), is very common in the gardens of Egypt.

The *orange* (*boortoocka'n*), and several kinds of *lime* and *citron* (*leymoo'n, tooroon'g*, &c.), flourish luxuriantly in Egypt.

The *pomegranate* (*roomma'n*) also thrives in Egypt.

The *mulberry* (*too't*) is much cultivated, particularly in the Shurekee'yeh, for the purpose of rearing the silk-worms.

The *lote-tree* (*nubck*, formerly called *sidr*), the fruit of which is celebrated by Homer, as having delighted the companions of Ulysses, is still abundant in Egypt. The fruit resembles, in size, appearance, and taste, the Siberian crab. It contains a stone. The wood of the tree, being hard, is used in the construction of sa'ckiyehs, &c.

The *vine* (*kurm*) is chiefly cultivated in the Feiyoo'm; and the *grape* (*'en'eb*) is of an excellent quality. The young leaves of the vine are made use of in cookery, to envelop small balls of minced meat and rice, which are boiled, and compose a pleasant dish.

Few of the fruits which thrive in more northern climates, as the apple, pear, peach, &c., attain to perfection in Egypt.

The *Nile acacia* (*sunt*) is very common in Egypt. Its wood is used for the same purpose as that of the lote-tree; and is made into charcoal. The sunt bears an edible berry, called *ckar'ud*; which also affords a red dye.

This tree, and the *seya'l*, and *talhh*, which are likewise species of acacia, and common in Egypt, yield the gum-arabic. Two other kinds of acacia, the *fit'neh* and *lubkh*, are found in the gardens of Egypt. A tree which was called by the same Arabic name as the latter of those just mentioned was, a few centuries ago, not uncommon in Egypt. From the descriptions given of it by Arab writers it seems to have been the same which the Greeks called *Persea*. There is also, at and near Aswa'n, a small species of acacia, called *'ab'ba's* (which I regret I did not see, being ignorant of its existence when I was in Upper Egypt), possessing a remarkable sensitive property. El-Muckree'zee mentions, in his account of Den'dar'a, that there was a tree of this species at that place; adding that whenever a person approached it and said—"Ya' sheg'eret el-'ab'ba's, ga'k el-fa's"— (O thou 'ab'ba's-tree, the axe is come to thee)—its leaves contracted and shrivelled in an instant, and then became restored to their former state.[1]

The *tamarisk (tur'fa)* is not uncommon in Egypt. In the peninsula of Mount Sinai a substance like honey (called *menn*), which is supposed to be the *manna* of the Scriptures, drops from the leaves of the tur'fa, and is eaten by the Bed'awees.[2] There is another species of tamarisk, called *atl*, which is also common in Egypt.

The *Dead-Sea apple ('osh'ar)* grows wild in Egypt and Nubia. It generally rises to the height of six or eight feet; has large, broad leaves; and its fruit is a green bag, distended with air, and having in its centre a core surrounded with white, silky fibres. The stalks contain a milky, poisonous juice, the touch of which is said to be very injurious to the eyes.

The *hhen'na-tree (tem'ra hhen'na)* is cultivated for the sake of the dye afforded by its leaves, which are called *hhen'na*. These, pounded and made into a paste, are used by the women of Egypt for dying the nails of their fingers and toes, and sometimes the palms of their hands. The colour imparted is a yellowish red, or deep orange; and is very durable. A great quantity of the hhen'na of Egypt is exported to Turkey; where the same use is made of it. The plant resembles privet. The flowers are white, with a mixture of yellow: they hang in large bunches, like those of the lilac; and are extremely fragrant. The leaves are of a pale green colour.

---

[1]M. Jomard heard a person address one of these trees in the same manner, but did not quite correctly catch the sounds of the words, which he writes—"Yâ chagar el-habâs, yâ kell mangé, yâ kell fâs." He states, on the authority of M. Raige, who was misled by the word *habâs*, that the first words signify "O Abyssinian tree!" Habâs, however, only *approaches* to the sound of the Arabic name of Abyssinia, which is pronounced *Hhab'ash*. (See "Descr. de l'Egypte," tome 1, p. 131, secd. edn.)

[2]The "honey of the tamarisk-tree" is mentioned by Sir John Malcolm (in his History of Persia) as "produced by an insect, or small worm which resembles a white thread," and which "lies on the leaf of the tree, and appears inert." He adds that it is chiefly found in the province of 'Era'ck, and that he received the above account of it from an English gentleman who saw the insect on the tree when traveling through that province.

The *rose* (*wurd*) is extensively cultivated in the Feiyoo'm, where the rose-water so much esteemed in the East is made. The flower is double; and of a pale colour.

The *castor-oil-plant* (*khur'wa*) is found in the gardens of Egypt, and on the banks of the Nile in Nubia.

The *lotus*, or *water-lily of Egypt* (*beshnee'n*), grows, during the inundation, in the lakes and canals of Lower Egypt, and in the small lake called Bir'ket er-Rut'lee, on the north of Musr (or Cairo); but not in the more southern parts of Egypt. It is of two kinds: one bearing a white, and the other a blue flower. The stalk varies in length according to the depth of the water; which is generally less than four feet. The broad, round leaves rest upon the surface of the water; and the flower, in the form of a cup, rises from one to two feet higher; but when it has quite opened, its weight depresses it: for several days the flower thus expanded floats upon the water, and then sinks. The flowers are called *Ara'is en-Neel* (or the Brides of the Nile). The root, which is about the size of a walnut, is eaten, boiled: it is a mealy substance; in taste resembling a potato.—Another kind of lotus (the *nymphæa nelumbo*), described by many ancient authors, under the appellation of *faba Ægyptiaca*, and once common in Egypt, is no longer seen in that country; though found in India and China.

The *papyrus* (*bur'dee*) is still seen in the canals and marshes in the neighbourhood of Dimya't.

To complete this sketch of the natural history of Egypt, a few words must be added respecting the principal domestic and wild *animals*.

The *bull* and *cow* (*to'r* and *buck'arah*) resemble those of our own country, excepting that the withers are rather higher.

The *buffalo* (*ga'moo's*) abounds in Lower Egypt; and is chiefly valued for its milk. Its colour is nearly black. It is quite tame; but inactive and indocil; and very fond of the water; often remaining for several hours together in the shallow parts of the river, more than half immersed. Buffalo-beef is rather coarse.

The *camel* (*gem'el*) of Arabia and Africa has but one hump. The *dromedary* (*hegee'n*) differs from the *heavy* camel no more than does a saddle-horse from a cart-horse. Few camels can exist (particularly in sultry weather) more than ten or twelve days together without drinking; and it is very seldom that they are exposed to such suffering. A strong camel will carry six or seven hundred-weight, on a long journey: others, five, four, or only three hundred-weight.

The *horse* (*hh'sa'n*) is not employed in Egypt in the labours of agriculture; but only for riding; and not every person in that country who can afford to purchase and keep one is imprudent enough to give such demonstration of his wealth. The Egyptian horses are generally very inferior to those of Arabia. The mare is called *far'as*.

The *mule* (*bugh'leh*) is used for the saddle by persons of the higher classes; particularly by men of the law, and great merchants.

The *ass* (*hh'ma'r*) is one of the most useful animals in Egypt; and the breed in that country is of a very fine kind. For riding in the narrow and crowded streets of the metropolis they are very convenient; and are much used there, as well as in the country. Their paces are quick and easy.

The *sheep* (*ghan'am*) are rather lean; but their flesh is of good flavour. The price of a sheep is from one to two dollars† (4s.2d. to 8s.4d.): of a *lamb* (*kharoo'f*) half those sums.—The *goat* (*ma'az*) is reared chiefly for the sake of the milk. The female is called *'an'zeh*. The flesh of the *kid* (*ged'ee*) is generally esteemed.

The *dog* (*kelb*) and the *hyena* (*dub'ă*) are among the few kinds of wild beasts of a formidable nature that infest Egypt. The *jackal* (*ta'alab*) is very common there: the *fox* (*ab'oo-l-hhosey'n*), less so.

The *gazelle* (*ghaza'l*), a most beautiful kind of antelope, is an inhabitant of the deserts on both sides of the Nile.

The *rat* (*fa'r*) must be included among the plagues of Egypt. Rats are excessively numerous in that country; and the boats are generally infested by them.—The *weazel* (*'ers*) is also very common.—The *ichneumon* (*nims*) is often found in the Feiyoo'm, and in Lower Egypt. It is not *now* remarked for its hostility to the crocodile.

The *crocodile* (*timsa'hh*) is never seen in Lower Egypt; and seldom below the Thebais; but very frequently in the neighbourhood of Furshoo't, and in other parts of the Thebais where there are many sand-banks in the river. The animal loves to bask upon a sand-bank, sleeping, with his mouth wide open. The largest crocodiles that I have seen in Egypt were about twenty-five feet in length; and I believe few exceed that measure excepting in more southern latitudes. They seldom attack a man or woman; and generally retreat at the approach of two or more persons.—A large kind of *lizard* (*war'al*, vulgo *war'an*), frequently met with in Egypt, bears a great resemblance to the crocodile; but is solely a terrestrial animal; and seldom more than two feet and a half or three feet, in length.

The *hippopotamus* (*far'as el-bahhr*) is rarely seen in Egypt; but is not so scarce in Nubia; where it often devours, during the night, the young millet sown upon the banks of the river. I saw none in either country.

Of poultry there is great plenty, though not variety, in Egypt. The most I ever paid for a full-sized *chicken* (*fur'khah*, or, in the Sa'ee'd, *furroo'g*) was a piaster and a half (or five pence). The eggs are generally hatched in ovens.—*Pigeons* (*hhama'm*) are reared in vast numbers in most of the villages. The peasants raise pigeon-houses (often more capacious than the apartments which they themselves inhabit) upon the tops of their huts.

The *large vulture* (*nesr*) and the *aquiline vulture*, or *vultur pereno-*

---

†Lane refers to Spanish dollars, which circulated widely in the Mediterranean and served as a standard by which the value of less stable currencies such as the Egyptian piastre were measured; in this instance, however, Lane gives its value in British money.

pterus (*rukh'um*[1]), are very numerous in Egypt; and are serviceable in devouring the dead bodies of camels, asses, and other animals, which would otherwise (if dogs were not near) be left to putrefy, and taint the air. The plumage of the latter bird is white.—The *eagle* (*'ocka'b*) is less frequently met with.

The *pelican* (*gem'el el-bahhr*, or the camel of the river) and a species of white *heron* (*ab'oo ckirda'n*) and the *wild duck* (*wezz*) are principally remarked among the birds which frequent the Nile.

Several varieties of the *partridge* (*hhag'al* and *ckut'a*) are met with in Egypt and the adjacent deserts. The name of *ckut'a* applies more properly, I believe, to a kind of grouse; but in Egypt it is given to a small, grey partridge.

The *bat* (*wutwa't*) inhabits the catacombs and the dark apartments of some of the temples.

Of the *snake* (which is called *hhei'yeh*, *taaba'n*, &c.) there are many species in Egypt; and though most of them are harmless, they are much dreaded. Among them we find the horned snake; the venom of which is said to be always fatal. The tracks and cast-off skins of snakes are often observed on the surface of the drifted sand in the catacombs; but the reptile itself seldom meets the eye of the travellers in Egypt.—The *scorpion* (*'ack'rab*) is met with very frequently in that country. Its sting sometimes occasions death; but never when an antidote has been promptly applied.

The common *fly* (*dibba'n*, or *dooba'b*), the *musquito* (*na'moo's*), the *flea* (*burghoo't*), the *bug* (*buck'ck*), and the *louse* (*ckuml*) are extremely numerous in Egypt. The flies are often excessively annoying. The lice are not always to be avoided even by the most cleanly persons; but they do not attach themselves to the hair or skin; being generally found on the clothes; and are therefore easily removed as soon as their piercing bite is felt. Vermin did not trouble me so often in Egypt as to detract very much from the luxuries which the climate afforded me. From musquitoes I was effectually secured at night by curtains; and when the flies would have been troublesome, if one hand was occupied with my pipe, the other was at liberty to shake a whisk made of palm-leaves, which at meals is generally held by a servant. Bugs, indeed, once drove me from my bed-chamber to sleep upon the house-top, and finally from the house itself, which swarmed with them in consequence of its containing a great deal of old wood-work.

The Nile contains abundance of *fish*; but few kinds that are very good. The best are the *bool'tee*, or *labrus Niloticus*; the flesh of which is delicate and of a fine flavour; and the *ckish'reh*, or *perca Nilotica*, the largest of the fish of the Nile, and one of the most esteemed. The largest of the latter kind that I ever saw was about four feet long; but some are said to be more than twice that length. This fish is probably the *latus*, which was

---

[1]Burckhardt has committed a strange error in calling the rukh'um an *eagle*. By some European travellers it is called "Pharaoh's hen."

an object of religious veneration in ancient Egypt, and gave its name to Latopolis. The *bin'nee*, or *cyprimus Niloticus*, is also of a delicate flavour. The *raa'a'd*, or *torpedo*, is found in the Nile.

I conclude this chapter with a physical and agricultural *calendar* of Egypt, drawn from Arabic works, and from my own observations.

January.—The mean temperature in the afternoon during this month, at Musr (or Cairo), is about 60°.—The waters which during the season of the inundation, had been retained upon the fields by means of dams have now sunk into the soil; but water still remains in some of the large canals, their mouths having been stopped up: the river has lost about half the height it had attained: that is to say, it has sunk about twelve feet in and about the latitude of Musr. The wind at this season, and throughout the winter, is very variable; but the northerly winds are most frequent.— People should now abstain from eating fowls and all crude and cold vegetables. The poppy is sown. It is unwholesome to drink water during the night at this season, and throughout the winter. The *fifth Coptic month, Too'beh*, begins on the 8th, or 9th, of January.[1] Now is the season of extreme cold. Beef should not be eaten at this period. The fields begin to be covered with verdure. The vines are trained. Carrots plentiful. Onions sown. The date-palm sown. The ripe sugar-canes cut.

February.—The mean temperature in the afternoon during this month, at Musr, is about 66°.—End of the season of extreme cold.[2] The fields everywhere throughout Egypt are now covered with verdure. The *sixth Coptic month, Amshee'r*, begins on the 7th, or 8th, of February. Warm water should be drunk, fasting, at this season. The wind very variable. The harvest of beans. The pomegranate-tree blossoms. Vines are planted. Trees put forth their leaves. The season of the winds which bring rain (called *el-lawa'ckehh*). The cold ceases to be severe.

March.—Mean temperature in the afternoon during this month, at Musr, about 68°.—End of the season for planting trees. The *seventh Coptic month, Burmaha't*, begins on the 9th of March. Variable and tempestuous winds. *The Vernal Equinox.* During the quarter now commencing the river continues decreasing: the wind often blows from the south, or south-east; and the semoo'm winds (from the same quarters) occur most frequently during this period: the plague also generally visits Egypt at this season, if at all.—The weather becomes mild. Northerly winds become prevalent. The wheat-harvest begins. Lentils reaped. Cotton, sesame, and indigo, sown; and the sugar-cane planted. The barley-harvest begins.

April.—Mean temperature in the afternoon during this month, at

---

[1]See a note on the beginning of the *first* Coptic month, in September.—The Egyptians (Moos'lims as well as Christians) still divide the seasons by the Coptic months; but for dates, in their writings, they generally use the *lunar*, Mohhammadan months.

[2]Such is the statement of the Egyptian almanacks: but there are generally as cold days in the month of Amshee'r as in Too'beh; and sometimes colder.

Musr, about 76°.—The frogs begin to croak. Time for taking lenitive medicines. The *eighth Coptic month*, *Burmoo'deh*, begins on the 8th of April. Semoo'm winds. Time for the fecundation of the date-palm. Rice sown. The wheat-harvest in Lower Egypt. Beginning of the first season for sowing door'ah sey'fee (or millet).—The Khum'a'see'n winds[1] generally commence in this month.

May.—Mean temperature in the afternoon during this month, at Musr, about 85°.—The Khum'a'see'n winds prevail principally during this month; and the season is, consequently, unhealthy. Winter clothing disused. The *ninth Coptic month*, *Beshen's*, begins on the 8th of May. Time for taking medicine, and losing blood. Season of the yellow water-melon. Cucumbers sown. The apricot bears; and the mulberry. Turnips sown. End of the first season for sowing door'ah sey'fee. The apricot ripens. The fleas cease to be troublesome. Beginning of the season of great heat. Beginning of the season of hot winds (*el-bawa'rehh*), which prevail during forty days.

June.—Mean temperature in the afternoon during this month, at Musr, about 94°.—Strong northerly winds prevail about this time. The water of the Nile becomes turbid; but does not yet begin to rise. The *tenth Coptic month*, *B a-oo'neh*, begins on the 7th of June. The banana sown. Semoo'm winds. Strong perfumes, as musk, &c., are disused now, and throughout the summer. The yellow water-melon abundant. The plague, if any existed previously, now ceases. Honey collected. People should abstain from drinking the water of the Nile at this season, for fifteen days,[2] unless first boiled. "The Drop" (*en-noock'tah*) descends into the Nile, and, according to popular belief, causes it to increase soon after[3]: this is said to happen on the 11th of Ba-oo'neh, which corresponds with the 17th of June: it is the day before the Coptic festival of Michael the Archangel. The flesh of the kid is preferred at this season, and until the end of summer. Semoo'm winds blow occasionally during a period of seventy days, now commencing. *The Summer Solstice*; when the day is 14 hours long in Lower Egypt. During the quarter now beginning (i.e. during the period of the increase of the Nile) northerly winds prevail almost uninterruptedly, excepting at night, when it is generally calm. Though the heat is great, this quarter is the most healthy season of the year.—The Nile begins to rise now, or a few days earlier or later. The season for grapes and figs commences. Peaches plentiful.

July.—Mean temperature in the afternoon during this month, at Musr, about 98°.—The rise of the Nile is now daily proclaimed in the metropolis. Lenitive medicines should not now be taken. Locusts die, in every part of Egypt, or disappear. The *eleventh Coptic month*, *Ebee'b*, begins on the 7th of July. Violent northerly winds prevail for fifteen days. Honey abundant. Fleas disappear now. People should abstain from

---

[1] Hot, southerly winds, of which I have already spoken in this chapter.
[2] Commencing from the 10th of Ba-oo'neh (or the 16th of June).
[3] It is really a heavy dew which falls about this time.

eating plentifully at this season. The noon-day heat is now excessive. Ophthalmia prevails now; but not so much as in the autumn. The *bow'a'hhee'r*, or seven days of extreme heat, fall at the end of this month.[1] Grapes and figs abundant. Door'ah sha'mee (or maize) is now sown. Harvest of the first crop of door'ah sey'fee (or millet). The date ripens.

August.—Mean temperature in the afternoon during this month, at Musr, about 92°.—Season for pressing grapes. The *last Coptic month, Mes'ree*, begins on the 6th of August. Onions should not be eaten at this time. Radishes and carrots sown. Cold water should be drunk, fasting. Water-melons plentiful. The season for gathering cotton. The pomegranate ripens. Violent northerly winds. Sweetmeats should not be eaten at this time. "The Wedding of the Nile" (*'Ors en-Neel*) takes place on the 14th, or one of the five following days, of the month of Mes'ree (the 19th to the 24th of August): this is when the dam of earth which closes the entrance of the Canal of Musr is broken down: it having been first announced that the river has risen (in the latitude of the metropolis) sixteen cubits; which is an exaggeration.[2] Second season for sowing door'ah sey'fee (or millet). Musquitoes abound now. End of the seventy days in which semoo'm winds frequently occur.

September.—Mean temperature in the afternoon during this month, at Musr, about 88°.—White bete and turnip sown. Windy weather. The beginning of *the month Too't, the first of the Coptic year;* corresponding with the 10th or 11th of September, according as five or six intercalary days are added at the end of the Coptic year preceding.[3] Ripe dates abundant; and limes. Windy weather. *The Autumnal Equinox.* The Nile is now, or a few days later, at its greatest height; and all the canals are opened. During the quarter now commencing (i.e. during the first three months of the decrease of the river) the wind is very variable; often blowing from the west, and sometimes from the south. The exhalations from the alluvial soil, in consequence of the inundation, occasion ophthalmia, diarrhœa, and dysentery to be more prevalent in this quarter than at other seasons.—Harvest of sesame.

October.—Mean temperature in the afternoon during this month, at Musr, about 80°.—The leaves of trees become yellow. Green sugar-canes cut, to be sucked. Drinking water at night, after sleep, is pernicious at

---

[1]They are said to commence on the 20th of Ebee'b (or 26th of July).

[2]The true rise at this period is about 19 or 20 feet: the river, therefore, has yet to rise about 5 or 4 feet more, on the average.

[3]The Copts begin their reckoning of time from the era of Diocletian, A.D. 284. Their months consist each of 30 days: five intercalary days are added at the end of three successive years: and six at the end of the fourth year. Our leap-year follows next after theirs: therefore the Coptic year begins on the 11th of September only after their leap-year; or when our next ensuing year is a leap-year; and after the end of the next February the corresponding days of the Coptic months and ours will, therefore, be the same as in other years.

this season. The hhen'na leaves gathered. Winter vegetables sown. The *second Coptic month, Ba'beh*, begins on the 10th, or 11th, of October. Wheat, barley, lentils, beans, lupins, chick-peas, kidney-beans, trefoil, fenugreek, colewort, lettuce, and safflower are sown now, or a little later. Bleeding is injurious now. The dews resulting from the inundation increase.

November.—Mean temperature in the afternoon during this month, at Musr, about 72°.—The cold during the latter part of the night is now pernicious. The *third Coptic month, Ha'too'r*, begins on the 9th, or 10th, of November. Rain is now expected in Lower Egypt. The meree'see, or south wind, prevalent. The rice-harvest. The harvest of door'ah sha'mee (or maize), and second harvest of door'ah sey'fee (or millet). Winter clothing assumed. Bananas plentiful.

December.—Mean temperature in the afternoon during this month, at Musr, about 68°.—The flies die. Tempestuous and cloudy weather. Strong perfumes, as musk, ambergris, &c., are agreeable now. The *fourth Coptic month, Key'hek*, begins on the 9th, or 10th, of December. The leaves of trees fall. *The Winter Solstice*; when the day is ten hours long in Lower Egypt. The wind is variable during this quarter. Beginning of the season for planting trees. Fleas multiply. The vines are pruned. Beef is not considered wholesome food at this season.

Chapter V.
Reshee'd, or Rosetta.

Of the town of Reshee'd—Its gardens—Mosque and tomb of Ab'oo
Mundoo'r—Site of Bolbitine—The Bolbitic branch of the Nile—View
from the site of Bolbitine.

Many travellers, proceeding by the most direct route from Alexandria to
Reshee'd, have been much struck by the first view of the environs of this
place; for the sudden transition from a dreary desert to the Nile and its
fertile banks cannot fail to delight the stranger, if his expectations have
not been raised by exaggerated descriptions. To me, however, Reshee'd
did not present such pleasing novelty; as it was the last spot on the banks
of the Nile that I visited. I cannot say that I was so charmed with the
scenery as to fancy, like Savary, that I beheld in it a resemblance of the
Garden of Eden. I certainly saw little reason for such a comparison; but
still less for the very different terms in which one of our own
countrymen has spoken of the town and its inhabitants. Sir Robert
Wilson describes the street of Reshee'd as full of wretches whom the
pride of civilized man revolts at acknowledging as human; abounding
with diseased and deformed objects; and polluted by filth, intolerable
stench, and many other nuisances: he pronounces the women so ugly as
to have made him deem it fortunate that their faces were almost wholly
concealed by the black veil (the eyes alone being exposed); and he even
represents the banks of the river as rotten and putrefying with the fatness
of the slime left by the waters. Some accidental cause must have led to
the *last* of the remarks; and with regard to the *others*, I can only say that
neither at Reshee'd nor in any other part of Egypt did I see any thing to
justify them. If that country is not remarkable for varied and picturesque
scenery, it is amply compensated for the lack of such a charm by a river
of delicious water and of wonderful fertilizing properties, and a most
genial and delightful climate, which, I fully believe, is only sometimes
rendered insalubrious by the insufficient means which are adopted for
draining the fields after an over-abundant inundation. The plague has
usually been remarked to have followed an unusually high Nile: its
ravages have seldom extended far into Upper Egypt, where the land is
but scantily inundated; and the whole country has been perfectly free
from this dreadful disease of late years, since more proper measures have
been employed, by direction of its present governor, for the irrigation
and subsequent draining of the fields, by means of many new canals,
dams, and sluices. Of the inhabitants of Egypt I scruple not to say that
they are, in point of form,—at least the peasantry,—the finest race of

beings I ever beheld: a painter or sculptor could hardly find elsewhere better models from which to study.

The period of the foundation of Reshee'd رشيد I have not been able to learn. Some writers, misinterpreting a passage in El-Mekee'n's history, have asserted that it was founded in the ninth century of the Christian era.[1]

When the old canal of Alexandria ceased to be navigable, Foo'weh, which was the principal town on the western branch of the Nile, began to decline, and Reshee'd became the emporium of the trade between the metropolis and Alexandria. It was then necessary for the boats employed in that trade to unload, or to shift their cargoes, at Reshee'd; the largest vessels which could navigate the shallow Nile not being adapted to the sea. But since the formation of the new canal of Alexandria, Foo'weh has regained its commercial advantages, and is rapidly increasing in extent and population, while Reshee'd is falling to decay; a great number of the merchants and shop-keepers of the latter town having removed to Foo'weh and other places.

Reshee'd is about five miles from the sea. The Nile flows close before it, on the east: behind it is a sandy desert; and along the banks of the river, above and below the town, are extensive gardens. The only remarkable objects in a distant view of Reshee'd are its numerous, white-washed ma'd'nehs (or menarets). It is surrounded by a wall of brick, with loop-holes, and forts; but is a place of little strength: the sand-hills behind completely command it.

From the number of boats along the shore I should have imagined that Reshee'd was still a place of very considerable traffic; but on surveying the interior of the town I was surprised to see long streets of deserted shops, and many large houses empty and falling to ruin. The streets are very narrow, and rather dark; the upper part of the houses projecting two or three feet beyond the foundation-walls. In some instances each story projects beyond that below; so that at the top the opposite houses in a street nearly meet. Thus, though rather gloomy, the streets are rendered cool and shady. The houses are well built, with burnt bricks of a dull red colour, and with good mortar. The roofs are flat, and covered with a strong cement; as rain is not uncommon during the winter in the maritime parts of Egypt. Higher up the country the houses are not so substantial; and few of them have such roofs as would resist a heavy rain. The windows of the houses of Reshee'd are of wood-work, like those of Alexandria, through which it is impossible to see any object within.

---

[1]The following is the passage to which I allude.—"In his days (in the reign of the Khalee'feh El-Mootawek'kil) were built the walls of Tinnee's and Dimya't and Iskenderee'yeh (or Alexandria) and El-Boorool'loos and El-Ashmoo'm and Et-Tee'neh and Reshee'd and Nesteroo'h." (Elmacini Historia Saracenica, p. 152.)—It is probable that *all* these towns existed before that period; (we well know that several of them did;) but that the invasions of Egypt by the Franks rendered it necessary to encompass them with walls.

None of the mosques are remarkable for beauty of architecture; though containing many granite columns taken from ancient edifices. The burial-ground is in the sandy tract behind the town.

Reshee'd contains about 10,000 inhabitants; almost all of whom are Moos'lims. A few years ago the population was estimated at 13, or 14,000, or even more. It contains nothing to interest the antiquary, though its name is associated with one of the most valuable of all the relics of antiquity that have been found in Egypt,—the famous trilinguar tablet (now in the British Museum) which led to Dr. Young's important discovery of the phonetic system of hieroglyphics.[†] This was brought to light by the French, in repairing an old fort, called by them "Fort Julien," about half-way between Reshee'd and the mouth of the river.

The gardens of Reshee'd are walled or fenced enclosures along the bank of the river. Flowers and shrubs and a great variety of trees, all planted together without any order, exhibit a scene of wild luxuriance, and afford a delightful shade. Among the palm-trees, which are the most abundant, are plentifully interspersed the orange, the lime, the citron, the pomegranate, the vine, the sycamore (which affords a deep and broad shade), and the banana, which has a particularly beautiful appearance; its long leaves spreading and drooping from the summit of the stem, like the branches of the palm-tree. We also find here the hhen'na-tree, which is much esteemed for the delicious perfume which its flowers exhale, as well as for the dye afforded by its leaves. The water is raised from the river, for the purpose of irrigating the gardens, by the machines which I have described in the preceding chapter.

The Nile, opposite Reshee'd, is more than half a mile in width: a little higher up it is very much contracted; particularly at a point where, after having flowed in a westerly direction for the distance of about a mile and a half, it turns abruptly to the north, towards Reshee'd. Just below this sudden turn is the picturesque mosque, or tomb, of Ab'oo Mundoo'r, situated close to the river, at the foot of a sandy hill, on the same side as the town of Reshee'd, from which it is about a mile distant. The sketch here annexed was taken from the opposite side of the river.[1]

The memory of the Moos'lim saint, or Sheykh,[2] here buried is held in great veneration. His tomb is reputed to possess a talismanic influence, preventing the sands of the desert from pouring into the river and overwhelming the gardens which adorn its bank. It is also believed that the benign influence of the sheykh is extended to the prevention of another kind of barrenness; and many women, actuated by superstitious faith, piously visit his shrine. The boatmen of the Nile seldom neglect an opportunity to visit the tomb of a celebrated saint; in the belief that such

---

[†]The Rosetta Stone.

[1]See no. 4 of the subjects for woodcuts [fig. 10].

[2]The title of *sheykh* simply signifies "an elder," or "an aged person"; and is generally applied to the master of a family, the chief [of] a tribe, &c.; as well as to holy persons; but never to any but Moos'lims.

an act will be followed by a blessing; or that the prayers which they there offer up to the Deity will be answered for the sake of the sheykh, if not through his intercession; and they often make votive offerings at the tomb, and, if there be a guardian, give a trifling alms. These are customs which are also observed by the Egyptian fellahhee'n (or peasantry) in general. When they speak of a deceased saint they frequently testify a degree of respect for him not much inferior to that with which they regard a prophet; and quite unauthorized by any precept of their religion: they seldom even mention the name of such an individual without adding this benediction—"*Alla'hoom*[1] *ir'da 'an'hoo*"—(O God! mayest thou be well pleased with him!)—A small, square, white washed building, crowned with a cupola, is generally erected over the saint's grave; and the people of the neighbourhood honour him with an annual religious festival; on which occasion the profession of the faith, and some portions of the Ckoor-a'n, are chanted at his tomb. The tombs of sheykhs are objects that frequently meet the eye of the traveller in Egypt. They are mostly in the immediate vicinity of villages; but some are at a distance from any habitation. There are also many buildings of the same kind which are mere cenotaphs, dedicated, each, to a particular saint.

The hill behind the mosque of Ab'oo Mundoo'r is covered with drifted sand, intermixed with bricks, and broken pottery; and among the rubbish I found a great number of marine shells, and some fragments of small, ancient, Osiridean figures, of blue, glazed earthenware. It evidently marks an ancient site; supposed to be that of *Bolbitine*; which gave its name to the branch of the Nile that flows before it. Herodotus asserts that the Bolbitic branch was an artificial canal from the Canopic; which latter has now deserted a part of its ancient bed, and pours its waters into the sea through the Bolbitic branch and the canal of Alexandria.

The view from the top of the hill of Ab'oo Mundoo'r is extensive, and remarkable for its varied features. On the east, the winding river, and the fertile plains of the Delta, present a pleasing prospect; while on the opposite side lies a sandy desert, where not a spot of verdure relieves the eye. To the north is seen the town of Reshee'd; and the intermediate tract, along the bank of the river, is occupied by gardens.

---

[1]This word is commonly pronounced as I have written it: not *Al'la'hoom'ma*, as in the *literary* dialect.

Chapter VI.
Voyage up the Branch of Reshee'd.

Description of the scenery—Names of Lower Egypt and of its principal provinces—Villages—Matoo'bis—Customs of the peasants of the Bohhey'reh—Entrance of the Mahh'moo'dee'yeh—Foo'weh and its courtesans, &c.—Desoo'ck—Er-Rahh'ma'nee'yeh—Old canal of Alexandria, and ancient Canopic branch of the Nile—Remains of Sais—Canal of Sheybee'n el-Ko'm—Na'dir—Canal and town of Menoo'f—Tarra'neh, and the Valley of the Natron-Lakes—First sight of the Pyramids and the metropolis—The point of the Delta—Arrival at Boo'la'ck.

When the river is low, the traveller can see very little of the country from his boat on the Nile; and the higher he proceeds, the more elevated does he find the banks of the river, which are abrupt, and without any verdure upon their sides. The groves of palm-trees, the sycamores and acacias, the tombs of sheykhs, the water-wheels, the villages close to the Nile, and the summits of the palms which encompass those more remote, are almost the only objects within the bounds of his observation: and these soon lose the charm of novelty which at first recommended them to his notice. He will see, particularly on the sand-banks, when the river is low, flocks of pelicans and wild ducks, and numerous other birds; but the once-sacred Ibis he may in vain look for[1]; and in Lower Egypt he will meet with no crocodiles. On passing before a village he will generally see groupes of women and girls filling their pitchers, or washing their clothes, at the river; and, in many places, herds of buffaloes, lying down or standing in the shallow water near the banks, almost wholly immersed. Numerous boats oftentimes enliven the prospect; and the frequent songs of their crews are heard at a considerable distance. Occasionally, when the wind is light, the traveller may leave his boat, and walk along the shore, and amuse himself with shooting, or with botanical researches, without retarding his progress; and even in this flat and generally unpicturesque country he will find some scenes not unworthy of the exercise of his pencil. If dressed in the European style, he is seldom molested or insulted: but if habited as a Turk, he commands respect, and as he passes the peasant employed in the labours of agriculture, or driving his loaded ass or camel, or riding from one town or village to another, he gives, or returns, the salutation of peace.[2] The

---

[1] A kind of white heron, very common on the Nile, much resembles the Ibis: but its bill, instead of being curved, is straight.

[2] *Es-sela'm 'aley'koom,* or *es-sela'moo 'aley'koom* (peace be on you), is the

women mostly retreat at his approach, or make a circuit to avoid him.

In Lower Egypt, the general aspect of the country is everywhere nearly the same. Almost every village is imbosomed in a grove of palm-trees, and situated on a slight eminence, or surrounded by mounds of rubbish, to preserve it from the inundation. The sycamore generally shades a water-wheel or the tomb of a sheykh.[1] Few varieties of foliage are seen, excepting in the gardens; which are, with very few exceptions, only near towns or large villages. In the season of the inundation, extensive tracts of land in Lower Egypt are covered with water: villages are seen rising out of the flood like islands; and the inhabitants pass from one of these villages to another by dikes formed of earth, or, sometimes, by means of boats. During the next two months, the fields which have been inundated are almost impassable swamps; and in the depth of winter, they are overspread by brilliant verdure.

The principal divisions of Lower Egypt are *El-Bohhey'reh* البحيره , on the west of the branch of Reshee'd,—*El-Ghurbee'yeh* الغربيّه , between the branch of Reshee'd and that of Dimya't,—and *Esh-Shurckee'yeh* الشرقيّه , on the east of the branch of Dimya't.

The villages between Reshee'd and Foo'weh have a more respectable appearance than those higher up the country; as the climate renders a more substantial mode of building absolutely necessary; rain being of less rare occurrence; and many of them have two or three ma'd'nehs (or menarets[2]), which give them a seeming importance. The houses are generally built of burnt bricks; like those of Reshee'd: most of them are two stories high; and some, three.—One of these villages, called *Matoo'bis* مطوبس , is celebrated for the beauty of its women. Many of the dancing-girls and other courtesans in the Egyptian metropolis are said to be natives of this place.

Having left Reshee'd late in the afternoon, with a light wind, we proceeded that day no further than Matoo'bis.[†] In the evening, in

---

peculiar salutation of Moos'lims to each other: if a European traveller not qualified to pass as a Moos'lim were to give or return in the usual manner, this salutation, it would, in general, give great offence; and he would never *receive* it if known to be a Christian. The regular reply is *'aley'koom es-sela'm* (on you be peace); to which is often added *we-rahhmed Alla'h we-baraka'tooh* (and the mercy of God, and his blessings).—I once had some trouble to prevent my servant from giving a Jew a severe thrashing with a thick staff because the appearance of the latter was such as to make my man mistake him for a Moos'lim, and salute him accordingly.

[1] The sheykhs' tombs hereabouts are almost all of the same form; like that represented in my sketch of the hydraulic machines, plate 4 [missing].

[2] These are almost all similar to that represented in plate 5 (Foo'weh) [fig. 11].

[†] This is a loose end left over from Lane's combination of several journeys into a single narrative thread. In fact, Lane did not travel to Rashid until March 1828 when he was departing from Egypt. As he composed this text, he apparently failed to notice the disjuncture of writing about his departure from Rashid when he had described no journey to it.

conformity with the usual practice of the boatmen of the Nile, a stake was driven into the bank, and our boat made fast to it for the night.

Rice is chiefly cultivated in the neighbouring plains of the Delta; the land being very low in the northern parts, and artificial irrigation consequently attended with but little difficulty. On the opposite side of the river the tract of cultivable land is very narrow; and behind it is a sandy waste.

The peasants of the Bohhey'reh were described to me, perhaps with little reason, as a less civilized people than the rest of the Egyptians. They are particularly reproached for eating rats; and some of them, when questioned by me, confessed that they sometimes did so. It is also said that many of them eat the wild boar (*helloo'f*), which is not unfrequently found in their neighbourhood. As they are almost all Moos'lims, such practices are considered as deep stains upon their religious character.

The capital of the Bohhey'reh is *Demenhoo'r* دمنهور , a small town, about five miles south of the Mahh'moo'dee'yeh, in the centre of the province. It is generally supposed, by modern travellers, to occupy the site of *Hermopolis Parva*; but a passage in Strabo (p. 803),[†] stating that town to have been by the river (that is, by the Canopic branch), casts a doubt upon this supposition.

The entrance of the Mahh'moo'dee'yeh is two miles below the town of Foo'weh. It was here that I had beheld the Nile for the first time, in my voyage from Alexandria to the metropolis. My progress in that voyage I described thus far: I now continue the narrative.

The town of *Foo'weh* فوّه , viewed from a little distance, has a pleasing appearance; containing many well-built houses, and numerous mosques with white-washed ma'd'nehs, and having several gardens in its vicinity. The view which I give (plate 5[‡]) will convey an idea of the style of its buildings, which are very inferior to those of Reshee'd, though in some degree resembling them. It is likely soon to become a more respectable town, as it was three or four centuries ago: for since the formation of the new canal of Alexandria its commerce has been constantly increasing. Many boats were lying along-side of the bank at the time of our arrival; and numbers of women and girls were filling their pitchers; while others were washing clothes; which done, each proceeded to wash her hands, face, and feet, and immediately returned, with her pitcher, or bundle, on her head: a piece of rag, rolled in the form of a ring, and placed upon the head, served to secure the pitcher in its erect position, and seldom was a hand upraised to keep it steady. From my cabin-windows I could examine at my leisure the unveiled faces of these women: for in the country-towns and villages of Egypt few of the women wear the *boor'cko'*, or face-veil; and it is only in the immediate presence of men that they cover the face, by drawing the edge of the head-veil before it so as to conceal all the features excepting one eye. The fine figures and

---

[†]Lane refers to a particular edition of Strabo.
[‡]Fig. 11.

handsome countenances of most of the girls whom I saw here appeared to particular advantage from the contrast presented by the aspect of the older women, whose withered forms were generally very unsightly. Most of the boys and girls under the age of five or six years were quite naked, and of a dark, sun-burnt complexion.

In Foo'weh there is a quarter exclusively inhabited by courtesans; many of whom are constantly seen lounging upon the bank of the river, or sitting under the boo'zeh-sheds.[1] Their outer dress is generally a loose kind of shirt, of a sort of linen gauze, interwoven, in stripes, with silk. This is excessively full, of gay colours, and partly open in front, so as to expose much of the bosom. A piece of muslin covers the whole of the head excepting the face; and hangs down the back: this is the head-veil: they have no face-veil. Many of them wear the nose-ring; which is considerably larger than a finger-ring: it is passed through one of the alæ of the nose; and hangs partly before the mouth. The forehead is generally adorned with a row of small gold coins, sewed to the edge of the close-fitting, red cloth cap, called turboo'sh; round which is wound a coloured handkerchief.

Some of the public dancing-girls, who are called *ghäwa'zee* (in the singular, *gha'zee'yeh*), are also frequently seen here. Their performances are of a very indelicate kind; consisting in various amorous gestures, and particularly in a wriggling motion of the hips.—The term *'A'l'meh* (in the plural *'Awa'lim*), literally signifying "a learned female," has been improperly applied by European travellers to the common dancing-girls of Egypt. The 'Awa'lim are female singers and instrumental musicians; and most of them also dance; but they seldom perform excepting in a *hharee'm*.[2]

The most usual dress of the women of the lower order (and generally their only article of clothing except a head-veil) is a plain, blue shirt, differing little from that of the men, which is also, commonly, blue. It is a general custom of the Egyptian women of this class to tattoo some parts of their persons, particularly the front of the chin, and the lips, with blue marks; and, like the women of the higher classes, they tinge their nails with the dull red dye of the *hhen'na*, and arrange their hair in a number of small plaits, which hang down the back.

Foo'weh, like Matoo'bis, is celebrated for the beauty of its women. It is also famous for its pomegranates; which are both plentiful and excellent in flavour.

---

[1] Boo'zeh is a liquor commonly prepared in the following manner.—Some barley bread is crumbled, and mixed with water; and, after having been boiled over a slow fire, is left for two days to ferment. The liquor is then strained, and is fit for immediate use. It is also prepared from millet. Herodotus mentions the former kind as a common drink of the Egyptians in his time. (Lib. ii, c. 77.) The boatmen of the Nile are extremely fond of it: to me it is very nauseous.
[2] *Hharee'm* (called by the Turks *hhar'em'*) is a term applied by the Arabs—both to the apartments of the women and to the women themselves.

The next place worthy of notice, above Foo'weh, is *Desoo'ck* دسوق ,
where the tomb of the seyd Ibrahee'm Ed-Desoo'ckee attracts multitudes
of pious visitors. This Moos'lim saint is regarded with almost as much veneration as the seyd Ahh'mad El-Bed'awee, who lies buried at Tan'ta; and
is in like manner honoured with a festival on the anniversary of his birth.

A little higher up the river, on the opposite side, is the large village of
Er-Rahh'ma'nee'yeh الرحمانيه , by the entrance of the old canal of
Alexandria. It was often found necessary to clear out the bed of this old
canal, in consequence of the rapid and copious deposit of sand and mud
throughout the whole of its course; but it soon became choked up again,
and unnavigable at every season except in the period of the inundation.—
Nearly from the same spot may be traced the continuation of the ancient
Canopic branch of the Nile. That part of the present western branch
which is below this point was the ancient Bolbitic branch.

About four leagues above Er-Rahh'ma'nee'yeh, on the eastern side of
the river, are the remains of *Sais*, the ancient capital of the Delta, one of
the most celebrated cities of Egypt, and the reputed birth-place of
Cecrops, who, it is said, led a colony of Saites to Attica, about 1556 years
before the Christian era, founded Athens, and established there the
worship of Minerva (the Egyptian Neith), the tutelar goddess of his
native city. It seems either that there is an error in the passage of Strabo
(p. 803) which states that Sais was two schœni[1] distant from the river, or
that the Nile has here changed its course, as we know it to have done in
many parts of Egypt. The ruins above alluded to are within a mile of the
bank of the river; but their position is not otherwise irreconcileable with
the statements of ancient authors respecting Sais. That they are the
remains of that city may be concluded from two circumstances:—1st,
there are no other ruins of nearly so much importance in this part of
Egypt:—2ndly, a solitary village upon a part of the ancient site is still
called *Sa' el-Hhag'ar* صا الحجر , or "Sa' of the Stone." El-Muckree'zee
mentions the ancient city of Sa', and says that it was founded by a person
of that name, who was the son of Ckibta-ee'm[2] the son of Misra-ee'm.
The remains of Sa', viewed from the river, appear merely like lofty and
extensive mounds. They chiefly consist of a vast enclosure, about half a
mile in length, and nearly the same in breadth. This is formed by walls of
prodigious dimensions; being about fifty feet thick, and, in several parts,
considerably more than that in height; constructed of large crude bricks,
15 or 16 inches in length, 8 in breadth, and 7 in thickness. The rains,
though very rare even in this part of Egypt, have so much decayed these
walls that, from a little distance, they are hardly to be distinguished from
the rubbish in which they are partly buried. Within the enclosure are
only seen some enormous blocks of stone, and the remains of some
buildings of unburnt brick, which appear to have been tombs, and

---

[1]Six geographical miles and a half, supposing the smaller schœnus to be here
meant.
[2]Caphtorim the son of Mizraim? (Genesis, X, 14.)

several catacombs, which have been explored and ransacked. The labour of excavation in this place would probably be rewarded by interesting discoveries; but the ruins, in their present state, are scarcely worth visiting. The enclosure contained the famous temple of the Egyptian Minerva, described by Herodotus; the portico of which surpassed in its colossal dimensions all other works of a similar nature, and was adorned with gigantic figures and enormous androsphinges. Before it was a monolithic chapel; the most surprising work of Sais; being 21 cubits long, 14 wide, and 8 high. It is related by Herodotus that two thousand boatmen were employed during the space of three years in transporting this monolith down the Nile from Elephantine. There was also, before the temple, a colossus, in a reclining posture,[1] seventy-five feet in length, similar to that before the temple of Vulcan at Memphis; which latter colossus was the gift of Amasis. Behind the temple was a sepulchre, but for whom it was destined the historian declines mentioning. Lofty obelisks were likewise raised within the sacred enclosure, near a circular lake, which was lined with stone. This lake served as a kind of theatre for nocturnal exhibitions of solemn mysteries relating to the history of the unnamed person above alluded to; who was, probably, Osiris, for, from feelings of religious awe, many of the Egyptians abstained from mentioning the name of that god. Many other towns in Egypt disputed the honour of being regarded as the burial-place of Osiris. All the Pharaohs born in the Saitic district were buried within the enclosure which surrounded the sacred edifices of Sais; and one of those kings, Apries, founded here a magnificent palace. Of the grand religious festivals which were periodically celebrated in Egypt in ancient times, the third in point of magnificence was that of Sais, in honour of Neith: the most splendid being that of Bubastis; and the next, that of Busiris; both in Lower Egypt. That of Sais was called "The Festival of Burning Lamps," because on the occasion of its celebration, the houses in that city and throughout all Egypt were illuminated by lamps hung around them.[2]

A little above this place is the large village of *Ferez'duck* فرزدق , and the mouth of the canal of *Sheybee'n el-Ko'm* شيبين الكوم , which, flowing from the branch of Dimya't, traverses the Delta in an oblique direction, along a tract thirty-five miles in extent.

We continue our voyage as far as the village of *Na'dir* نادر , without meeting with anything worthy of remark, excepting the conical pigeon-houses, constructed of earthen pots, upon the roofs of the low huts of the peasants. With these cones almost every village hereabouts abounds.

At Na'dir is the mouth of the wide canal of *Menoo'f* منوف , which derives so large a supply of water from the branch of Dimya't that fears are entertained lest the former should become the principal channel, and the latter cease to be navigable when the river is low. On this account the

---

[1]More probably in a *sitting* posture, with the hands resting on the thighs.
[2]Herodotus, l. ii, cc. 59, 62, 169 et seq., 175 et seq.

entrance of the canal was partially closed, some years ago, by a dam of earth and stones; but this obstruction was almost entirely swept away by the next high Nile. The town of Menoo'f is small; the district, particularly fertile: the latter is called after the town, El-Men'oo'fee'yeh. It is generally said that a great number of the women of Menoo'f are prostitutes; and the men, infinitely worse.—At the village of Na'dir is one of the telegraphs.

Nearly two leagues above Na'dir is the large village of *Tarra'neh* طرّانه , on the western bank. It is the market for natron,[1] which, in Egypt, is called *nitroo'n*, or, more commonly, *atroo'n*. Several large piles of this salt lay upon the shore when we passed, ready for embarkation. The Lakes of Natron, which supply the salt in great abundance, are situated in a valley about ten leagues distant in the desert, west-south-west of Tarra'neh. The natron is found congealed upon the surface of the lakes; but is collected more copiously from the ground which the waters have left when the heat of summer has caused them to decrease by evaporation. It is monopolized by the government. Some Coptic monks inhabit convents in this dreary desert, near the lakes; and the Bed'awees exact contributions from them whenever they have occasion. Behind the valley of the lakes is another valley, which is called *El-Bahhr bil'a ma'*, or "the river without water." It contains various petrifactions of vegetable substances, and has every appearance of having been a channel for water.

For several miles above and below Tarra'neh, the cultivable land on that side of the river is extremely narrow; and in some places above that village the sands of the desert reach to the water's edge.

Approaching the extremity of the Delta, I descried the venerable Pyramids; but the undulations of the heated atmosphere on the surface of the intermediate plain prevented their being distinctly visible. They were five leagues distant. The ridge of Mount Moockut'tum, behind the capital, was also discernible, and the height which is crowned by the citadel. Though I had long and most ardently desired to see those stupendous monuments which are the wonder of the world, yet towards the *city* my eyes were mostly directed: for Alexandria had disappointed me, and I felt more anxious than ever to view the place in which I was about to take up my abode.

The southernmost part of the Delta is called *But'in el-Buck'arah*[2] بطن البقره, or "the low land of the cow." The river immediately above, is divided by several islands.

On the 2nd of October, at 5 o'clock in the evening, we arrived at Boo'la'ck, the principal port of Musr (or Cairo), after a voyage of four days from Alexandria. Our passage was neither a rapid nor a slow one: three days are sometimes sufficient.

---

[1] Native carbonate of soda.

[2] This name has always, as I think, been incorrectly written by European travellers, and interpreted "the cow's *belly*."

Chapter VII.

The Eastern Branch of the Nile,
and the adjacent districts, &c.

General remarks—Of the southern point of the ancient Delta—Canal of
Ckalyoo'b, part of the ancient Pelusiac branch—Other ancient branches
of the Nile—Remains of Athribis—Tan'ta, and its festivals—Ab'oo Seer,
and the ancient Busiris—Semennoo'd, and the ancient Sebennȳtus—
El-Mahhal'leh el-Kebee'reh—Bahbey't—El-Munsoo'rah—Dimya't, or
Damietta—Lake of El-Boorool'loos, and ancient Butos—The ancient
Elearchia, or Bucolia—The Shurckee'yeh—Bilbey's, and the Land of
Goshen—Remains of Bubastis—The Canal of the Pharaohs, from the
Nile to the Red Sea; and the Amnis Trajanus—Remains of Tanis—
Granite shrine of Thmuis—Lake of El-Men'zel'eh—Tinnee's—Pelusium
and El-Fur'ma—Ckut'ya, and Mount Casium—Es-Soowey's, or Suez.

This chapter will contain little more than brief notices of the more
interesting objects.[†] The subjects are, indeed, scarcely worthy of detailed
description. In Lower Egypt there are several large towns; but *one* is a
satisfactory specimen of *all*: there are also vestiges of many ancient cities;
but the ruins of the walls which surrounded the sacred edifices, and a few
prostrate obelisks, or confused heaps of sculptured blocks of stone, are
almost the only remaining antiquities. Knowing this to be the case, I did
not descend the branch of Dimya't, nor traverse the province of
Esh-Shurckee'yeh; preferring to devote my time and attention to more
interesting objects. The plan of this work, however, requires my adding
some brief notices of ancient sites and remains, and of a few modern
towns, &c., to complete the account of Lower Egypt.

I must first remark that the southern extremity of the ancient Delta
was nearly three leagues to the south-east of the point of the *present*
Delta.[1] Strabo informs us (p. 807) that it was three schœni (or nine
geographical miles and three quarters) from Memphis. It appears that the
great canal of Ckalyoo'b قليوب is a part of the Pelusiac, or easternmost,

---

[†]Lane originally wrote then crossed out: "This chapter will contain but little
more than a few illustrations derived from works of ancient and modern writers,
and from conversation with inhabitants of some of the provinces to which it
relates."
[1]To illustrate the ancient geography of some parts of Lower Egypt is very
difficult, on account of the changes which have taken place in the course of the
river.

branch. This canal is distinguished by the name of *Bahhr*[1] *Ab'ee-l-Mooneg'ga* بحر ابي المنجّا , or "The River of Ab'oo-l-Mooneg'ga"; and is so called because it was dug, or deepened, under the direction of a Jew of that name. This was done, as I learn from El-Muckree'zee, in the year of the flight 506 (A.D. 1112-13).[2] Across this canal, not far from its mouth, is a handsome stone bridge, consisting of six pointed arches. Along the top, on each side, is an Arabic inscription; and beneath that on the northern side is a frieze composed of a row of sculptured lions, about seventy in number, rudely executed, in low relief. It was built, according to El-Muckree'zee, in the year of the flight 665 (A.D. 1266-7), by order of the Soolta'n Beybur's.—The town of Ckalyoo'b is the capital of a province, called, after it, El-Ckal'yoo'bee'yeh.

The lower part of the branch of Dimya't, from the entrance of the canal of Et-Ta'aba'nee'yeh, is what was anciently called the *Phatnitic* or *Phatmetic* branch; and the rest, there is little reason to doubt, is part of the ancient *Sebennytic* branch; the continuation of which is marked by the canal above-mentioned. In the canal of El-Munsoo'rah we see the ancient *Mendesian* branch; and in that of Moowey's, the *Tanitic*; also called the *Saitic*. It is very remarkable that the two branches of the Nile which were originally the narrowest, and which were said to be artificial canals, are the only channels by which the Nile now empties itself into the sea during the whole year.

On the eastern side of the branch of Dimya't, about five leagues[3] below its commencement, are the remains of the city of *Athribis*[4]; consisting of extensive mounds of crude bricks, broken pottery, and materials of ancient temples. These mounds retain the name of *Tell*[5] *Atree'b* تلّ اتريب .—A little below this spot is the entrance of the canal of *Moowey's* مويس (the ancient Tanitic branch), which derives its name from a large village there situated.

Descending the branch of Dimya't about five leagues further, the traveller will pass two small towns, *Meet Ghumr* ميت غمر on the east, and *Zif'teh* زفته on the west, nearly opposite. About the same distance

---

[1]The term *bahhr*, which properly signifies *a sea*, is applied in Egypt to several great canals, as well as to the Nile.

[2]In consequence of a dispute arising from the expence incurred in this work its author was cast into prison. After having remained in confinement several years he contrived to procure a Ckoor-a'n, and made a copy of it, which, after having written at the end "copied by the Jew Ab'oo-l-Mooneg'ga," he sent to the market, to be sold. This caused a great commotion; and the Jew, being brought out to answer for the crime of handling and copying the sacred book, confessed that he had done this in the hope of being put to death. His case excited compassion; and he was reprimanded and liberated. (El-Muckree'zee.)

[3]This is the distance in a straight line: by the course of the river it is much more.

[4]Athribis was a considerable city in the times of the Pharaohs, and under the Greeks and Romans: in later times it was an episcopal see.

[5]*Tell* signifies *a hill*.

below these places is the town of Semennoo'd:—but I must not neglect to mention the town of *Tan'ta* طنتا , in the Delta; to arrive at which, by the shortest route, the traveller would leave the river about mid-way between Zif'teh and Semennoo'd. The town of Tan'ta is more correctly called *Tan'det'a* طندتا ; but the former is the general appellation at present. It is situated half-way between the branches of Dimya't and Reshee'd, in the midst of a very fertile tract; and is the most populous town in the Delta: the number of its inhabitants is estimated at about 10,000. Its flourishing state is chiefly owing to its containing the tomb of the seyd Ahh'mad El-Bed'awee, a highly revered Moos'lim saint.[1] As many as fifty thousand persons, from all parts of Lower Egypt, are said to assemble at this place on the occasions of the festivals celebrated here in commemoration of the birth of the seyd Ahh'mad. His tomb is in a large and handsome mosque, built through the munificence of the famous 'Al'ee Bey (the Memloo'k), who died in the year of the flight 1187 (A.D. 1773-4). The saint is honoured with three annual festivals; and as one of these takes place in the spring, which is the period of the year when, if at all, the plague generally begins, infected persons, arriving from the more northern parts (where the disorder is most frequently engendered), communicate the baneful disease to others, and by their dispersion it is spread through the country. The festival is a kind of fair; to which many resort for the sole purpose of traffic. In the ceremonies performed at the tomb, durwee'shes take a prominent part; chanting the profession of the faith, and exhibiting their strange exercises. Numerous tents are pitched, and swings erected; and the visitors are amused by jugglers and serpent-charmers, story-tellers, musicians, and female dancers and singers.[†] Swarms of courtesans also attend the festivals; and no small number of married women are attracted with the same view; as was the case on some similar occasions in ancient Egypt.

A village called *Ab'oo Seer* ابو صير , with ancient mounds, about two leagues south of Semennoo'd, is supposed to occupy the site of the ancient *Busiris*, where festivals inferior in magnificence only to those of Bubastis were celebrated in honour of Isis, who was worshipped there in a grand temple.[2] This village and several others of the same name in Egypt are called by the Arab geographers *Boo'see'r* بوصير ; but *Ab'oo Seer* is their modern appellation.

---

[1] This person died (according to Es-Sooyoo'tee) in the year of the flight 675 (A.D. 1276-7).

[†] On a small interleaved notesheet Lane noted: "Leave out what follows "musicians" to the end of the P [i.e., the rest of the paragraph]." While this may have been added when the passage was under consideration for inclusion in *The Englishwoman in Egypt*, Lane may also have worried that it echoed too closely a similar passage in chapter three. Or it may merely have been self-censorship.

[2] Herodotus, lib.ii, cap.59.—Busiris was one of the towns which claimed the honour of being regarded as the burial-place of Osiris; and Eudoxus (cited by Plutarch) asserts that this was really the place of his burial, and also of his birth.

The town of *Semennoo'd* سمنود marks an ancient site, which has been supposed to be that of *Sebenn ȳtus*; but it seems improbable that the cities of Sebennytus and Busiris, each the capital of a nome, should have been so near to each other as Semennoo'd and Ab'oo Seer. Some have regarded *Sheybee'n el-Ko'm* شبيين الكوم as the site of Sebennytus; and the canal of Melee'g مليج as part of the Sebennytic branch.

To the west of Semennoo'd, about a league distant from the river, is *El-Mahhal'leh el-Kebee'reh* المحله الكبيره, or ——— *el-Koob'ra*, a large town, the metropolis of the Ghurbee'yeh. It is famous for its manufactures of silks, &c.; particularly a kind of linen gauze, interwoven, in stripes, with silk.

About three leagues below Semennoo'd, and half a league from the river, on the western side, is a place called *Bahbey't*, or *Bahbey't el-Hhag'ar* بهبيت الحجر, where is seen a vast pile of sculptured blocks of granite, the remains of a magnificent temple. This edifice has been regarded as the temple of Venus (or Athor), mentioned by Herodotus,[1] in the city of Atarbĕchis (or Aphroditopolis), which was situated in the island of Prosopitis: but the remains belonged to a Ptolemaic structure; and it has been supposed, with more probability, that the town here situated was *Iseum*, or *Iseopolis*. The capitals of the columns have four sides, each adorned with a representation of the full face of Isis, or of Athor, like the capitals of the portico of the great temple of Den'dar'a. The hieroglyphic name of Ptolemy Philadelphus is found among the sculptures.

The town of *El-Munsoo'rah* المنصوره, at the entrance of the canal named after it,[2] was built (as El-Muckree'zee relates) by the Soolta'n El-Mel'ik El-Ka'mil, of the house of Eiyoo'b, in the year of the flight 616 (A.D. 1219-20), when the Franks besieged Dimya't. The name signifies "rendered victorious." Here the army of the French king St. Louis sustained a terrible defeat, and he himself was made prisoner, and here confined.

Between El-Munsoo'rah and Dimya't are numerous villages. The cultivable land on the eastern side of the river between these two towns is very narrow; and that on the western side is scarcely less so.

The modern town of *Dimya't* دمياط, or, as it is more commonly called, *Doomya't*, is better known to Europeans by the name of Damietta; but it does not occupy the same site as the Damietta of which we read in the history of the Crusades. The older town was believed (according to El-Muckree'zee) to have been founded by Dimya't, the fifth in descent from Noah. The Khalee'feh El-Mootawek'kil, of Bughda'd, encompassed it with a wall, and rendered it a place of great strength; notwithstanding which it was repeatedly taken by the Crusaders, who were enabled by the possession of this town to extend their conquests in Egypt. Among the various modes of defence resorted

---

[1] Lib. ii, cap. 41.
[2] Formerly called by the Arabs "the canal of Ashmoo'n."

to by the Egyptians to protect Dimya't from the Franks, it is related, by El-Muckree'zee, that two towers were built, one on each side of the river, and a chain of iron was stretched across from one to the other: but the invaders took one of the towers, and cut the chain. A bridge, or dam, was then constructed, to prevent the vessels of the Franks from approaching the town: but this the besiegers destroyed. Afterwards, a vast number of boats were sunk in the river, and more effectually obstructed the passage: the Crusaders, however, by clearing out an old canal, again succeeded in bringing their vessels into the Nile, and under the walls of Dimya't. In the course of the several sieges which it sustained, this unfortunate town was sometimes nearly depopulated. At length, in consequence of the difficulty of defending it, the Egyptians themselves destroyed it, at the command of their Soolta'n, El-Mel'ik El-Mo'ez'z 'Ezz ed-Deen Et-Toorkama'nee, in the year of the flight 648 (A.D. 1250-51). A new town, at first consisting merely of huts, was then founded, a little to the south of the site of the former; and this was the origin of the modern Dimya't. After the destruction of the old town, it was found still more necessary to defend the mouth of the Nile: the passage was therefore partially obstructed by an artificial bar, in the year of the flight 659 (A.D. 1260-61), by order of the Soolta'n Ez-Za'hir Beybur's; and since that period the merchant vessels of the Mediterranean have been obliged to anchor off the coast, and to discharge their cargoes into smaller vessels for the conveyance up the river to Dimya't. The bar is constantly increasing, from the action of the river upon one side, and of the sea upon the other; each depositing quantities of sand. Not unfrequently boats are wrecked upon it.

The modern Dimya't is a place of some importance; as it is the chief emporium of the trade between Egypt and Syria, and the principal mart for rice. This grain is cultivated very extensively in the neighbouring plains; and attains greater excellence there than in any other part of the country. Dimya't is situated at a reach of the Nile, about seven miles from the mouth; and has the form of a crescent. The principal houses, and the magazines of the merchants, are next the river. The markets are well supplied with most of the productions of Egypt and Syria; particularly with the fine tobacco of the latter country, of which there are many kinds, differing greatly in the degree of excellence, but all superior to that of Egypt. The native population of Dimya't has been estimated at 13,600; but, as the town abounds with Syrians, Turks, and other foreigners, the whole population probably amounts to at least 20,000.

The northern part of the Delta is a sandy waste, containing nothing worthy of remark, excepting the vestiges of many ancient towns, and the large lake of *El-Boorool'loos* البرلس , which is bordered on the south by extensive marshes. El-Boorool'loos was the Arabic name of a neighbouring town, the ancient *Paralos*, which no longer exists. The lake now known by that name was anciently called the Butic Lake,[1] from the city of *Butos*, which was situated on its southern side, near the Sebennytic branch. This city contained a temple dedicated to Apollo and Diana (the Elder Horus and the Bubastis of the Egyptian mythology), and the oracular chapel of Latona, which was formed, with the exception of its roof, of a single mass of stone; each side forty cubits wide: the roof, also, was one piece of stone, four cubits thick.[2] Among the numerous islands now existing in the lake above mentioned, that of *Chemmis*, which was said to be a floating island, and bore a temple of Apollo,[3] is not recognized with any degree of certainty. Upon a narrow, sandy strip, which separates the lake from the sea, water-melons are raised in great abundance.

The marshy districts bordering on the lake of El-Boorool'loos and the lower part of the Sebennytic branch have been supposed to be the *Elearchia*, or *Bucolia*, of ancient writers, called by the Egyptians *Bashmûr*, or *Beshmoo'r*. Aboo-l-Fed'a, however, states that the island formed by the canal of El-Munsoo'rah and the branch of Dimya't constituted the province of Beshmoo'r; and its having retained that name in his days is decisive, I think, that this was at least a *part* of the tract which was anciently called so; more particularly as the lower part of the branch of Dimya't bore the appellation of the *Bucolic* branch.[4] The name of Beshmoo'r was perhaps given to *all* the marshy districts of Lower Egypt. These were inhabited by an uncivilized race; some of whom lived in huts, and others in boats; free from the control of the Pharaohs. They afforded refuge to deposed Egyptian kings, and, probably, to many proscribed individuals.

It remains for me to speak of some parts of the extensive and populous province of *Esh-Shurckee'yeh*, and of the relics of ancient cities, &c., which it contains. The modern capital of this province is *Bilbey's* بلبيس . El-Muckree'zee states that the district of Bilbey's is the same that is called in the Pentateuch *"the land of Goshen"*; and other reasons would lead us to bel[ei]ve it so.

The site of *Bubastis*,[5] now called *Tell Bus'tah* تل بسطه , is on the west of the Pelusiac branch, and very nearly approached by the Tanitic branch. Of its celebrated temple nothing remains but a pile of sculptured blocks of granite and other materials, within a spacious enclosure of crude brick. The temple of the goddess Bubastis was situated on a small peninsula formed by two wide canals; the banks of which were planted with trees. Within the wall which surrounded it was a grove; and in the midst of the grove, a statue of the goddess. The site of the temple was considerably lower than that of the town; the latter having been raised artificially, long

---

[1]Strabo, p. 802.
[2]Herodotus, lib. ii, cap. 155.
[3]Ibid, ii, 156.
[4]Ibid. ii, 17.
[5]The Pi-beseth of Ezekiel (xxx, 17): in Coptic Φουβασθι, or Πουβαϛε.

after the foundation of the temple. Sabacon, the Ethiopian conqueror and king of Egypt, ordained that no criminal should be punished with death, but should be compelled to transport a quantity of earth, proportioned to his crime, for the purpose of raising the site of the town to which he belonged; and Bubastis was one of the cities which derived the most benefit from this law.[1] The most magnificent of all the religious festivals of ancient Egypt was said to attract to Bubastis no fewer than 700,000 persons of both sexes.

A little above Bubastis was the entrance of the canal which communicated with the Red Sea. This was commenced, according to Herodotus, under the direction of Necos, or Pharaoh Necho.[2] It is related that 120,000 of his subjects perished in the execution of this laborious undertaking; and that the voice of an oracle, intimating that his project was for the benefit of barbarians (or foreigners), caused Necos to put a stop to the work.[3] It was continued by Darius, king of Persia; but not finished; and again carried on by order of Ptolemy Philadelphus, who also failed to complete it.[4] The canal which was made by command of Adrian, and named, after his predecessor, *Amnis Trajanus,* is that which is now called *Khalee'g Musr,* or the Canal of Musr. This extended as far as the Canal of the Pharaohs; or united with it by means of a part of the Pelusiac branch. In the middle of the seventh century of the Christian era, 'Amr Ibn El-'A'see, the Arab conqueror and governor of Egypt, cleared out both the Amnis Trajanus and the Canal of the Pharaohs; and the two, being united, and rendered navigable throughout their whole extent, received the name of *Khalee'g Emee'r El-Moo-minee'n,* or the Canal of the Prince of the Faithful. Vessels continued to pass by this canal from the Nile to the Red Sea until the year of the flight 145 (A.D. 762-3), when the Khalee'feh El-Munsoo'r caused it to be stopped up; and so it has remained.[5]—Traces of the canal of the Pharaohs still exist. The present Ba'sha of Egypt has caused a part of it to be cleared out, to convey the water of the Nile from the canal of Moowey's and that of Ab'oo-l-Mooneg'ga to *Ra's el-Wa'dee* راس الوادي , where there is now a plantation of mulberry-trees, and a large establishment of silk-worms.

The site of *Tanis,* the *Zoan* of the Scriptures, is now called *Sa'n* صان . Several prostrate obelisks, bearing, among their hieroglyphics, the name

---

[1]Sesostris is said to have been the first king who raised the sites of Egyptian towns, or defended them by embankments; causing the earth which was thrown up in the digging of canals to be applied to these purposes.

[2]According to some, it was Sesostris who commenced this work. (See Strabo, p. 804).

[3]Herodotus, lib. ii, cap. 158.

[4]Pliny, Nat. Hist.[,] lib. vi, cap. 29.—Diod. Sic. lib. i, cap. 1.

[5]El-Muckree'zee.—'Amr cleared out this canal for the purpose of transporting provisions to Arabia; and it was closed on account of a rebellion in that country, that the insurgents might not so easily derive supplies from Egypt.

of Rameses 2nd, or Sesostris, attest the grandeur of the sacred edifices of this city, and shew their high antiquity.[†] These monuments lie within a vast, oblong enclosure, similar to that of Sais, bounded by ruined walls of crude brick.

At a place called *Tama'yeh* طمايه, the ancient *Thmuis*, which, according to Ptolemy, was the capital of the Mendesian nome, is a monolithic granite shrine, resembling an enormous sarcophagus placed on one end upon a cubic pedestal. Its height is above twenty-three feet; and the substructure, or pedestal, is nearly half the height of the shrine itself.

The large *Lake of El-Men'zel'eh* بحيرة المنزله , which is very shallow, and bordered by extensive marshes, extends along the northern part of the province of Esh-Shurckee'yeh. *Tinnee's* تنيس, the ancient *Thennesus*, was a large and opulent town, situated on an island in this lake. It was celebrated for the manufacture of embroidered stuffs. El-Muckree'zee relates that, in the earlier ages of the Isla'm, the covering of the Ka'abeh was woven there. "There was not in all Egypt" says this historian "a finer city than Tinnee's, until El-Mel'ik sacked it, in the year 624 (A.D. 1226-7); but now there remain only its ruins, in the midst of the lake."— This lake abounds with fish; particularly with a kind of mullet, called *boo'ree*; and vast numbers of pelicans frequent it. It occupies a part of the tract which was traversed by the Mendesian and Tanitic branches of the Nile. A very narrow isthmus separates it from the sea.

Pelusium has long since ceased to exist; and *El-Fur'ma* الفرما, which succeeded it, and was a considerable city for some centuries after the Arabian conquest, has also fallen to utter ruin.[1]

Ckut'ya قطيا , a halting-place on the road to Syria, was once a large town; but neither inhabitants nor ruins are now seen there. *Mount Casium* (where, it is said, the ashes of Pompey were buried[2]) is supposed to be recognized in a sandy ridge on the sea-shore, to the north of Ckut'ya.

Es-Soowey's السويس (or Suez), though a place of considerable traffic, is a small and miserable town; unhealthy, in consequence of the salt marshes in its vicinity, and without any good water in or near it. The journey from Musr (or Cairo) to this place (a distance of about eighty British miles by the shortest route) usually occupies three days. The intervening tract is entirely desert.

[†]Had Lane visited the site, he might have noticed that these materials had been reused in later construction.

[1]El-Fur'ma was plundered and burnt by the Franks (under Baldwin II, King of Jerusalem) in the year of the flight 545 (A.D. 1150-1); and finally destroyed, a few years after, by Sha'wir, the Wezee'r of the last of the Egyptian Khalee'fehs.— (El-Muckree'zee).—The Arabs pretend that it was the birth-place of Hagar the mother of Ishmael; and that Galen was buried there.

[2]Strabo, p. 760.

Chapter VIII.

Historical Illustrations
of the Topography of Musr (or Cairo)
and its Environs.[1]

Sources of information respecting these subjects—Of the successive seats of government since the Arabian conquest—El-Foosta't—El-'As'kar— El-Ckata'-e', or El-Ckata'ye'—Of the town of El-Mucks— El-Cka'hireh—Of the changes which have taken place in the river in the neighbourhood of El-Foosta't and El-Cka'hireh.

Little is to be found in the works of European travellers respecting the history and topography of the Egyptian metropolis and its environs; and that little is, in many cases, incorrect. It is hoped, therefore, that some authentic illustrations of these subjects, chiefly derived from El-Muckree'zee's historical and topographical account of Egypt and its metropolis (of which work I had the good fortune to obtain a copy during my residence in Musr), will not be unacceptable to the English reader. This work of El-Muckree'zee is chiefly a compilation from the writings of other Arab historians and geographers; and those parts of it

---

[1]Explanation of the Plan (plate 6 [fig. 12]).—A, The Citadel—B, Place called the Roomey'leh—C, The Ckar'a Meyda'n—D, Ckal''at el-Kebsh—E, Bir'ket el-Feel—F, El-Ezbekee'yeh—G, El-Hhasanee'yeh—H, Space between the Ba'b en-Nasr of the *first* wall of El-Cka'hireh (marked by the dotted line) and that of the *second* wall—I, Space between the Ba'b el-Footoo'hh of the first wall and that of the second—K, Space between the Ba'b Zoowey'leh of the first wall and that of the second—L, Ba'b el-Bahhr; now more commonly called Ba'b el-Hhadee'd—M, Tract formerly called Ard et-Tabba'leh—N, Site of the garden of El-Ba'al—O, El-Loo'ck, and Ba'b el-Loo'ck—P, Tract which was occupied by the gardens of Ez-Zah'ree—Q, Ckusr esh-Shem'ä—R, Mosque of 'Amr—S, Convent of Durwee'shes—T, Ckusr El-'Ey'nee; now a college—U, V, Palace and Hharee'm of Ibrahee'm Ba'sha—W, Kufr 'Abd El-'Azee'z (a village)—X, Kufr Cka'id Bey (a village)—Y, Ckusr er-Ro'dah—Z, The Mickya's, or Nilometer— a,b, Mosque and Fort on Mount Moockut'tum—c, Ruin called Ckoob'bet el-How'a—d,d,d,d,d,d,d,d, Forts erected by the French on the mounds of rubbish—e, Cemetery of Ba'b en-Nusr—f, Bir'ket er-Rut'lee—g, Telegraph—h, Ga'me' Ez-Za'hir (a ruined mosque)—i,i,i,i,i, Western canal, formerly called El-Khalee'g en-Na'siree—k,k, New canal.—(A plan in the great French work on Egypt was of some assistance to me in drawing the first lines of that above described [*Description de l'Égypte*, "État moderne," vol. 1, pl. 15]).

of which I here avail myself contain observations of many authors of different ages.[1]

The first city founded by the Arabs in Egypt was El-Foosta't. It was the residence of the governors of that country for more than a century: but after the overthrow of the dynasty of the Oomawee'yeh (or race of Oomei'yeh) a new city, called El-'As'kar, adjoining El-Foosta't, became the seat of government. Afterwards, another city, which received the name of El-Ckata'-e', or El-Ckata'ye', was built in the neighbourhood of El-'As'kar; and the independent princes of the family of Too'loo'n resided there. After the extinction of this dynasty, El-'As'kar became again the seat of government, and continued so until the general of El-Mo'ez'z obtained possession of Egypt, and founded El-Cka'hireh, which is now called Musr, or (by Europeans) Cairo.

El-Foosta't الفسطاط was built upon the spot where the army of the Arabs encamped for a short time after their conquest of Egypt in the 20th year of the flight (or A.D. 641). It received this name, which signifies "the Tent," from its having been founded around the tent of the Arab general 'Amr Ibn El-'A'see; or (according to some authors) merely because *foosta't* is a term applicable to any city. It was, however, more commonly known by the name of *Musr* مصر ; which name has been latterly transferred to El-Cka'hireh. The appellation of *Musr 'Atee'ckah*[2] (or *Old Musr*) is now given to the small town which at present occupies a part of the site of El-Foosta't. This town has been improperly called, by European travellers, *Old Cairo*: as well might Egyptian Babylon be called *Old Foosta't*.—The site of El-Foosta't, at the period of the Arabian conquest, was unoccupied by any buildings, excepting a Roman Fortress, still existing, called Ckusr esh-Shem'ă, on the north of the hill of Babylon: but in the neighbourhood were many churches and convents. The Nile, at that period, flowed close by the fortress above mentioned. El-Foosta't is described as a very fine city, containing houses five or six stories high, constructed of brick. The primary cause of its decline was the great famine which happened in the reign of the Khalee'feh El-Moostun'sir, in the middle of the fifth century after the flight, and which lasted seven years. About a century after this awful calamity the greater part of the city was purposely destroyed by fire, to prevent its falling a prey to an invading Christian army.[3] It was partly rebuilt; but never regained its former opulence.

El-'As'kar العسكر was founded in the year of the flight 133 (A.D. 750-1), long before the decline of El-Foosta't, which continued to be the

---

[1]Tuck'ee ed-Deen Ahh'mad, commonly called El-Muckree'zee (because his family was of El-Muckree'z, a quarter of Baalbek'k), was born at El-Cka'hireh (now called Musr, or Cairo) in the year of the flight 769 (A.D. 1367-8), and died in 845.

[2]More properly (though not commonly) written *Musr el-'Atee'ckah*, and *Musr el-Ckadee'meh*, which has the same meaning.

[3]Under Amaury, King of Jerusalem, called by the Arabs *Mer'ee*.

metropolis of Egypt, though the Governors no longer resided there. El-'As'kar was rather a suburb of El-Foosta't than a distinct city.

El-Ckata'-e', or *El-Ckata'ye'*, القطايع was founded in the year of the flight 256 (A.D. 869-70). It lay immediately on the west of the hill which is now occupied by the citadel of the modern Musr; and was about a mile in extent, from north to south and from east to west. In the year 292, when the dynasty of the race of Too'loo'n was subverted, this town was plundered, and partly destroyed by fire; and the great famine in the reign of El-Moostun'sir destroyed all its inhabitants, leaving it to fall to ruin. The site has become included within the suburbs of the modern Musr; and its great mosque, founded by Ibn Too'loo'n, yet remains.

The site of another town, which was called *El-Mucks* المقس , and which existed before the period of the conquest of Egypt by the Arabs, is also now included within the suburban districts of the modern Musr.

Medee'net El-Cka'hireh مدينة القاهره (or the City of El-Cka'hireh) originally occupied a space about three quarters of a mile square. It was founded in the year of the flight 358 (A.D. 968-9). Its first wall was pulled down in the year 480 (A.D. 1087-8), and a new one built, which included a small additional space on the north and south. This was pulled down in the year 572 (A.D. 1176-7), and the Citadel and a third wall were built, by Sala'hh ed-Deen (the Saladin of European historians). The third wall extended from the Citadel along the eastern and northern sides of the metropolis; being left unfinished. It was the intention of its builder to have made it to surround El-Cka'hireh and the Citadel and El-Foosta't.—The suburbs of El-Cka'hireh have become much more extensive than the city itself.

I must now give a brief account of the remarkable changes which have taken place in the bed of the river in the neighbourhood of El-Foosta't and El-Cka'hireh, chiefly since the foundation of the latter of those cities.

We are informed by El-Muckree'zee that, at the period of the conquest of Egypt by the Arabs, Er-Ro'dah was the only island existing in the neighbourhood of the sites of the two cities above-mentioned. It was believed that the colossal figure called Ab'oo-l-Ho'l (the great Sphinx near the Pyramids of El-Gee'zeh) and a similar colossus on the opposite side of the Nile were talismans contrived by the ancient Egyptians to prevent the sands of the adjacent deserts from encroaching upon the banks of the river: but in spite of the popular opinion respecting their magic influence, the latter of these colossi was demolished, in the year of the flight 711 (A.D. 1311-12); and about the year 780 (A.D. 1378-9) the face of Ab'oo-l-Ho'l was mutilated by the fanatic sheykh Mohham'mad, surnamed Sa'im ed-Dahr, or "the Faster of the Age." Immediately after these periods, it is affirmed, the sands of the eastern and western deserts began to overspread the cultivable land intervening between them and the Nile, and to cause a considerable contraction of the bed of the river: in truth, however, the eastern limits of the river in the neighbourhood of El-Cka'hireh had become very much contracted in the sixth and seventh centuries after the flight; and have experienced but little change since the commencement of the eighth century.

Before this contraction of its bed, the river flowed by the walls of the Ckusr esh-Shem'ă and the Mosque of 'Amr: to the northward of El-Foosta't, its eastern limits were bounded by the town of El-'As'kar, the gardens of Ez-Zah'ree, the eastern part of the quarter called El-Loo'ck, the town of El-Mucks, the tract called Ard et-Tabba'leh, the garden of El-Ba'al, and the village of Min'yet es-See'reg. Thus we see that the Nile formerly flowed close by the western suburbs and gardens of El-Cka'hireh.—Towards the close of the period of the dynasty of the Fawa'tim (the Khalee'fehs of Egypt) a large vessel, called El-Feel (or the Elephant), was wrecked in the Nile, near El-Mucks, and, remaining where it sank, occasioned an accumulation of sand and mud which soon became an extensive and fertile island. This new island, from the circumstance which gave rise to it, received the name of Gezee'ret el-Feel (or the Island of the Elephant). It is laid down in the plan prefixed to this chapter, according to the description of its situation and extent given by El-Muckree'zee. In the year of the flight 570 (A.D. 1174-5) this island became united with the main land on the east; and from that period, the river gradually retired from the neighbourhood of El-Mucks, forming, by the deposit of soil during the successive seasons of the inundation, the wide plain upon which the town of *Boo'la'ck* is situated. Boo'la'ck was founded in the year of the flight 713 (A.D. 1313-14); and the island which is named after it (Gezee'ret Boo'la'ck) was formed about the same time.

Chapter IX.
Boo'la'ck.

Distant view of Musr (or Cairo), &c.—General appearance of Boo'la'ck—
Its extent and population, mosques, manufactories, and printing-office.

The distant view of the Egyptian metropolis and its environs I enjoyed
to great advantage on my first approach: the Nile being at its highest
point, many objects which at other seasons would have been concealed
by its banks were visible from our boat; and the charm of novelty, with
the effect of a brilliant evening sunshine, contributed as much to the
interest of the scene as those romantic fascinations with which history
and fiction have invested it. I was most pleased with the prospect when
about a league distant from the metropolis. The river (here about half a
mile in width) was agitated by a fresh breeze, blowing in direct
opposition to the current. Numerous boats were seen around us: some,
like our own, ploughing their way up the rapid stream: others drifting
down, with furled sails. On our left was the plain of Heliopolis. The
Capital lay directly before us; and seemed to merit the pompous
appellation by which Europeans have long dignified it: I believe,
however, that it was originally called by them "Grand Cairo" merely to
distinguish it from the town improperly named "Old Cairo." It certainly
had a grand appearance; though partly concealed by nearer objects; being
situated on an almost perfect flat, and about a mile distant from the river.
I might have counted nearly a hundred ma'd'nehs (or menarets),
towering above the crowded houses. These, while they shewed the extent
of the town, seemed, from their vast number, and from their noble
proportions, to promise a degree of magnificence far beyond what I had
previously expected; and I began to think that I might find in the
Egyptian capital some of the very finest existing specimens of Arabian
architecture: nor was I disappointed by the subsequent examination of
the monuments of this city. At the further extremity of the metropolis
was seen the Citadel, upon a rocky elevation, about two hundred and
fifty feet above the level of the plain. The yellow ridge of Mount
Moockut'tum, behind the city, terminated the prospect in that direction.
The scene on the opposite side of the river possessed, with less varied
features, a more impressive interest. Beyond a spacious, cultivated plain,
interspersed with villages and palm-groves, we beheld the famous
Pyramids of El-Gee'zeh. Viewing them under the effect of the evening
sun (the sides presented towards us being cast into shade), their
appearance was peculiarly striking; their distance not being diminished
to the eye, as it is, through the extraordinary clearness of the air, when
they reflect the rays of the sun towards the spectator. As we approached

71

Boo'la'ck, the second and third pyramids became gradually concealed from our view by the greatest. Arriving within a mile or two of this town, our boatmen began to testify their joy by songs adapted to the occasion, according to their general custom[1]; and to these songs succeeded the ruder music of the zoomma'rah and darabook'keh (the double reed-pipe, and earthen drum), which was prolonged until we reached the port.

Boo'la'ck بولاق , the principal port of the metropolis,[2] has now a more respectable appearance, towards the river, than it is described to have had when Egypt was occupied by the French. The principal objects seen in approaching it by the Nile, from the north, are the warehouses and manufactories belonging to the government; which are extensive, white-washed buildings, situated near the river. In the same part of the town are seen large mounds of corn and beans, piled up in spacious enclosures, in the open air: such being the general mode of storing the grain throughout Egypt; for there is little fear of its being injured by rain. The great mosque, surrounded by sycamores and other trees, has a very picturesque appearance.[3] The landing-place presents a lively scene; the bank being lined by numerous boats, and thronged by noisy boatmen, porters, sack'ckas (or water-carriers), and idle Turkish soldiers, besides camels, asses, &c. The costume of the lower orders here is the same as throughout Lower Egypt; generally the blue shirt, and the white or red turban. The dresses of the middling classes, and of the Turks, being gay and varied, contribute much to the picturesque character of the scene. Above the general landing-place is a palace which was built for the late Isma'ee'l Ba'sha, son of Mohham'mad 'Al'ee.[4] It is a large building, white-washed, and painted with festoons of flowers, like many of the palaces of Constantinople; and having glass windows. Of late, it has occasionally been made use of as barracks for some of the Niza'm Gedee'd, or regular troops.

Boo'la'ck is about a mile in length; and half a mile is the measure of its greatest breadth. It contains about 20,000 inhabitants; or nearly so. Its houses, streets, shops, &c. are like those of the metropolis, of which I shall give a description in the next chapter. Of the mosques of Boo'la'ck, the large one called Es-Sin'a'nee'yeh, and that of Ab'oo-l-'El'ë, are the most remarkable; the former, for its size; the latter, for the beauty of its ma'd'neh. The principal manufactories are those of cotton and linen cloths, and of striped silks of the same kind as the Syrian and Indian. Many Franks find employment in them. A printing-office has also been established at Boo'la'ck, by the present viceroy. Many works on military

---

[1]Two specimens of these songs will be found in the first chapter of the second volume [chapter 17] of this work.

[2]Some of the vessels from the Sa'ee'd (or Upper Egypt) unload at Musr 'Atee'ckah.

[3]See plate 7[,] no. 1 [fig. 13, upper].

[4]See plate 7, no. 2 [fig. 13, lower].

and naval tactics, and others on Arabic grammar, poetry, letter-writing, geometry, astronomy, surgery, &c. have issued from this press. The printing-office contains several *lithographic* presses, which are used for printing proclamations, tables illustrative of military and naval tactics, &c.[1]

---

[1]A list of the works printed at Boo'la'ck will be given in a appendix to this volume. The appendix will also contain an account of the Egyptian Measures, Weights, Money, &c.

[This appendix is missing from the manuscript. In *Modern Egyptians*, first published in 1836, after a general description of the products of the Pasha's press at Boulaq, Lane adds, "I have transmitted a list of these works to the Royal Asiatic Society (p. 558, n. 1, 1860 edition)." He may therefore have contemplated a separate publication by the Royal Asiatic Society in addition to the appendix, which he may not yet have written as such or may have removed to send to the R.A.S. This communication, however, never appeared in the Society's publications, nor is its receipt recorded in the Society's archives, which are indeed incomplete for the early years of its existence. The "account of the Egyptian Measures, Weights, Money, &c." appeared as Appendix B of *Modern Egyptians*.]

Chapter X.

Description of Musr (or Cairo).[†]

Names of Musr—The approach to Musr from Boo'la'ck—Its extent and population—The walls and gates—The streets and quarters, &c.—The mosques, and other buildings.

The city which is known to Europeans by the name of *Cairo*, or *Grand Cairo*, is called by the Egyptians *Musr*[1] مصر ; and in letters, and other writings, the epithet *El-Mahhroo'seh*[2] (or the Guarded) is generally added. *El-Cka'hir* (or the planet Mars), an unpropitious star, being the ascendant at the period of its foundation, it was originally called *El-Cka'hireh*[3]; whence the Italianized name *Cairo*. It was founded at night. Astrologers had been consulted, and had fixed upon a propitious moment for laying the foundations of the city-wall. They were to have given a signal at that precise moment by ringing a number of bells, which were suspended to cords supported by poles along the whole circumference of the intended wall; but a raven happening to alight upon one of the cords, the bells were put in motion before the chosen time; and the builders, who were waiting for the signal, immediately commenced their work. Thus the city was founded at an inauspicious, instead of a fortunate, moment.[4]

From the landing-place at Boo'la'ck to the nearest gates of the metropolis the distance is a little more than one mile. There are two great roads. The southern road leads to the Ezbekee'yeh, and the Frank quarters. It is straight and wide; and is raised a few feet above the level of the plain, so as to be above the reach of the inundation. On either side, at the time of my arrival (in October), were marshes, and inundated fields. These, as soon as the waters have subsided, are sown with corn, &c. The plain is bounded on the east by extensive mounds of rubbish; behind which lies the capital, nearly concealed by them; little of it being visible but its numerous and lofty ma'd'nehs, and its Citadel, backed by the ridge of Mount Moockut'tum. The road crosses two canals; over each of

---

[†]Lane's map of Cairo is fig. 14.

[1]The Turks, and many other oriental foreigners, pronounce it *Misr*; and thus it is pronounced in the *literary* dialect of Arabic.

[2]In government-documents this epithet is often used alone to designate the Egyptian metropolis.

[3]*El-Cka'hir* and *El-Cka'hireh* (masc. and fem.) signify *Victorious*.

[4]El-Muckree'zee's Account of the First Wall.—The year in which El-Cka'hireh was founded, and the periods at which its second and third walls were built, I have already mentioned, in chap. viii.

which is a stone bridge.[1]—The northern road leads (but not in a straight course) to the gate called Ba'b el-Hadee'd, at the north-west angle of the metropolis. At a short distance from this gate it passes by a high mound of rubbish; upon which is a round tower, with a telegraph. This tower commands a magnificent view of the metropolis, the citadel, and Mount Moockut'tum. I made a very elaborate drawing of this scene.[2]

The area which the metropolis occupies is about three square miles. Its extreme length is three miles; and the extreme breadth, one and a half. The population is about two hundred thousand.—Some travellers (judging from the narrowness of its streets, and from the crowds that are met in the great thoroughfares) have represented Musr as a close, overpeopled city; and have attributed to this supposed closeness the origin and rapid spread of those epidemic diseases with which it has been visited: but the case is far otherwise: it is a less close or crowded city than London or Paris, or, perhaps, any European metropolis. For a population of 200,000 persons the space of three square miles is certainly

---

[1]See the plan (plate 6 [fig. 12]).
[2]See plate 8 [fig. 15], of which the following is an explanation.—a, The gate called Ba'b el-Footoo'hh—b and e, Two ma'd'nehs of the great mosque of El-Hha'kim—c, Tomb of the Soolta'n Burckoo'ck (behind the city)—d, Ba'b en-Nusr—e, see b.—f, Fort Menou, built by the French—g, Tomb of Cka'id Bey (behind the city)—h, Fort Dupuis—i, The Bur'ckoo'ckee'yeh—k, Mosque of the Soolta'n Ckala-oo'n, adjoining the Ma'rista'n, or hospital—l, The Hhasaney'n (a dome and two ma'd'nehs)—m, Fort Reboul—n, The great mosque El-Az'har—o, The Ashrafee'yeh—p, Mosque of Mohham'mad Bey—q, The Ba'b el-Hhadee'd (the gate at the north-west angle of the city, near the foreground)—r, Mosque of El-Ghoo'ree—s, Ckoob'bet el-How'a (a small ruin on the side of the mountain)—t,u, Dome and two ma'd'nehs of the great mosque of El-Moo-ei'yed, adjoining the Ba'b Zoowey'leh—v, Fort on the mountain—w, New mosque in the Citadel—x, Old mosque on the mountain—y, New palace in the Citadel—z, Telegraph in the Citadel—aa, Old mosque in the Citadel—bb, Old Palace—cc, Deewa'n—dd, Great mosque of the Soolta'n Hhas'an—ee, Palace in the Ezbekee'yeh—ff, House of Mahhmoo'd Bey, by the Bir'ket el-Feel—gg, Tomb of the Ima'm Esh-Sha'fe'ee, in the cemetery on the south of the metropolis—hh, House of the Defturda'r, on the west side of the Ezbekee'yeh—ii, Ma'd'neh of the great mosque of Ibn Too'loo'n, or Tey'loo'n.

[Apparently because of a copying lapse, Lane did not include letter j either in the foregoing description of the view or on the index line, although he made a notch for it. But in another description of the view written some time later he identified the missing letter as marking the "Mosque of Sultán Saláh ed-Deen," i.e., al-Salih Nagm al-Din Ayyub, the last ruler of the Ayyubid dynasty in Egypt. To his overall description of the view, Lane added, "The bridge across the canal in the foreground is called Kantarat el-Leymoon. The canal is the western one; not that which runs through the city. Two branches are seen: that nearer the eye brings the water from the Nile: the other branch supplies the Ezbekeeyeh, &c. (BL Add 34083, f. 1v.)" Strangely, Lane did not mention the other detailed, two-card view of the city that he made from a vantage point further south, although it is among the illustrations for *Description of Egypt*. See figure 16.]

very ample. The streets are made narrow for the sake of shade: but most of the houses are large enough for twice as many inmates as they contain; and they are very airy; the windows being merely of lattice work.

The *walls* by which nearly the whole of Musr is surrounded are of the calcareous stone of the neighbouring mountains, and partly of the materials of some pyramidal tombs which were near the principal pyramids of El-Gee'zeh: but they are not of uniform strength, nor the work of one period. The metropolis is bounded on the eastern side partly by a portion of the third wall (which was built by Sala'hh ed-Deen), uniting with the walls of the Citadel, and partly by modern walls, of rude construction. The northern wall is well built, and lofty. The walls on the western and southern sides are irregular in their direction, low, and for the most part very ill constructed; more like the walls of a garden than those of a great city. High mounds of rubbish rise on every side of the metropolis. The French erected many forts upon these mounds, which completely commanded the town; but they are now in a state of ruin. The Citadel overawes the town; but is itself commanded by the neighbouring mountain.

Three of the *gates* of Musr are very fine structures. They were built with the second wall of the city, in the year of the flight 480 (A.D. 1097-8), during the reign of the Khalee'feh El-Moostun'sir; and are almost the only monuments of the times of the Khalee'fehs now remaining in Egypt. Two of these, called *Ba'b en-Nusr* (or the Gate of Victory) and *Ba'b el-Footoo'hh* (or the Gate of Conquests) are in the north wall, and between six and seven hundred feet apart. They are each about seventy feet high; and eighty feet, or more, in width. The former has two square towers: the latter, two round-fronted towers; and this gate is particularly handsome; but it cannot be viewed to advantage, as there are houses almost close before it. The third of the gates above alluded to is that called *Ba'b Zoowey'leh*.[1] Though in the very heart of the metropolis, it marks the southern limit of the part particularly called "the city." It has two massive, round-fronted towers; from each of which rises a lofty and elegant ma'd'neh; presenting a grand and picturesque effect. The ma'd'nehs belong to the great mosque of El-Moo-ei'yed, which is immediately within the gate, on the left of a person entering. They were built, with the mosque, in the year of the flight 819 (A.D. 1416-17). Before this gate, criminals are generally executed.—Among the other gates, that called *Ba'b el-'Ad'awee*, in the centre of the north wall, may be mentioned, as one of solid construction, but not otherwise remarkable: also, the Ba'b el-Hhadee'd, which was built with the third wall (Sala'hh ed-Deen's wall), and which is seen in my general view of Musr.—I now proceed to describe the *interior* of the metropolis.

Musr is dignified with the name of *Oomm ed-Doon'ya* (the Mother of the World), and other sounding appellations. Though it has much declined since the discovery of the passage to India by the Cape of Good

---

[1]Originally called *Zawee'leh*. This was the name of an Arab tribe.

Hope, it is still one of the most considerable cities in the East. It is altogether an Arabian city; and the very finest specimens of Arabian architecture are found within its walls. The private houses are in general well built; the lower part of stone, and the superstructure of brick; but some are little better than huts. I shall describe them more particularly in the course of this chapter.

The *streets* are unpaved; and very narrow: generally from five to ten feet wide. Some are even less than *four* feet in width; but there are others as much as *forty* or *fifty* feet wide; though not for any great length. The general term for a street is *sik'keh*; which also signifies a *road*, or *path*. I must describe the streets under their different appellations.

A *sha'rë*', or *great thoroughfare street*, is generally somewhat irregular both in its direction and width. In most parts the width is scarcely more than is sufficient for two loaded camels to pass each other; while in some parts only one camel can proceed at a time; and hence much inconvenience is often occasioned to the passengers; though there are no carriages to be encountered but those of the Ba'sha and of another grandee, which are seldom seen in the streets. All burdens are borne by camels if too heavy for asses; and vast numbers of the former, as well as many of the latter, are employed in supplying the inhabitants of Musr with the water of the Nile; which is conveyed in skins: the camel carrying a pair of skin bags; and the ass, a goat-skin, tied round at the neck.[1] The great thoroughfare streets, being often half obstructed by these animals, and generally crowded with passengers, some on foot, and others riding, present striking scenes of bustle and confusion; particularly when two long trains of camels happen to pass; which is often the case. Asses are in very general use, and most convenient, for riding through these narrow and crowded streets; and are always to be procured for hire. I purchased a very good one for fifteen dollars (or 3*l*.2*s*.6*d*.). Their paces are quick and easy; and the kind of saddle with which they are furnished is a very comfortable seat: it is a broad, parti-coloured pack-saddle. A servant generally runs beside or before the donkey; and exerts himself by almost incessant bawling to clear the way for his master: but the rider himself must be vigilant and alert; otherwise he may be swept off the back of his donkey by the wide load of a camel; or his legs may be cut by the shovel-shaped stirrup of a horse. A horseman proceeds with less comfort and less speed; seldom beyond the rate of a slow walk; though preceded by a servant with a long staff in his hand, and sometimes by two servants, to clear his way; and he is often obliged to turn back: it is therefore not often that a numerous cavalcade is seen in the more frequented streets; and there are some streets so contracted that a person on horseback cannot pass through them. It is not uncommon for individuals of the higher and middle classes in Musr

---

[1]See plate 9 [fig. 17] which shews, also, the front and interior of a coffee shop; and will convey an idea of the other shops and houses of the more frequented streets.

to exchange salutations in the streets; though unacquainted with each other. Thus the Moos'lim salutation was often given to *me*: a fact which I mention merely to shew the fallacy of the opinion that the natives of the East can easily detect, even by a glance, a European in Oriental disguise.

A stranger, with lofty ideas of Eastern magnificence, must be surprised at the number of meanly dressed persons whom he meets in the streets of Musr. Blue is the prevailing colour; as the principal article of dress, both of the men and women of the lower orders, is a full shirt, of cotton or linen, died with indigo. The blue shirt of the men, particularly of the servants, often conceals vests of silk and cloth. Some persons are so poor as not even to possess a ragged turban; their only head-dress being a close-fitting cap of white or brown felt, or an old turboo'sh[1]: and many are without shoes. Christians and Jews are distinguished by a black or blue or light brown turban.[2] The costumes of the women, and especially of the ladies, are the most remarkable in the eyes of the European stranger. The elegant dress which the ladies wear at home is concealed whenever they appear in public by a very full silk gown (called *to'b*), and a large black silk covering (called *hhab'arah*), enveloping almost the whole person; or, instead of the latter, in the case of unmarried ladies, a *white* silk covering, or a shawl: the face-veil (*boor'cko'*) is of white muslin; and reaches, from the eyes, nearly to the feet.[3] Thus encumbered, it is with some difficulty that the ladies shuffle along in their slippers; but they are seldom seen in the crowded streets on foot: well-trained donkeys are hired for their conveyance; and are furnished, for this purpose, with a very high and broad saddle, covered with a carpet, upon which the lady sits astride, attended by a servant on each side.[4] A long train of ladies, and female slaves attired in the same manner, one behind another,—a whole *hharee'm*,—is often seen thus mounted; and passengers of all ranks make way for them with the utmost respect. The women of the inferior classes wear a *black* face-veil, which is sometimes adorned with gold coins and beads; or they draw a part of the head-veil before the face, leaving only one eye visible.[5] The eyes of the women in general are exquisitely beautiful: they are black, very large, and of the fine almond-form; and always set off with the black border of *kohhl*: their charming expression seems to be heightened by the concealment of

---

[1]The red cloth scull-cap, round which the turban is wound.

[2]See plate 10 [fig. 18]—The figure over the letter *a* shews the costume of a Moos'lim tradesman. b, A Christian. c, A tradesman in his shop. (The green turban distinguishes a sheree'f, or descendant of the Prophet). d, A Moos'lim of the lower orders. e, A private of the Niza'm Gedee'd, or regular troops. f and g, Two women of the lower orders.

(Mem. A more full description to be given of this and the next plate). [The fuller description is not found in the manuscript; it was probably never written.]

[3]See the two foremost figures in plate 11 [fig. 19].

[4]See plate 11 [fig. 19].

[5]See plate 10 [fig. 18].

the other features. The dress of the women of the lower orders often leaves the bosom partly exposed.—Numbers of blind persons are seen in the streets of Musr; and many more with a bandage over one eye, but I seldom saw a *woman* with diseased eyes.

Shops generally occupy the front part of the ground-floor of each house in a great street.

The *dookka'n*, or *shop*, is a square cell, generally about four feet in width, and six or seven feet in height.[1] Its floor is even with the top of the *mus'tub'ah*, which is a raised seat of stone or brick, built against the front, about two feet and a half in height, and the same in breadth. The shutters commonly consist of three leaves, or divisions, one above another: the uppermost of these is turned up in front: the other two leaves, folded together, are turned down on the mus'tub'ah. The shop-keeper generally sits on the mus'tub'ah, which is covered with a piece of carpet or matting, and sometimes furnished with cushions. Here he transacts his business, smokes, eats, occasionally says his prayers, and chats with his customers; some of whom take off their shoes, and seat themselves with him, and remain, some time, smoking, and sipping coffee, which is brought from a neighbouring coffee-shop, and served (I need hardly say without sugar or milk) in small china cups, each placed within a cup of brass, similar in form to our egg-cups. The coffee is paid for by the shop-keeper; who also often presents his own pipe to his customer, when the latter has not brought one. Bargains are seldom conducted without some degree of haggling: there is frequently ample time to smoke a pipe before a purchase is concluded.—The shops do not communicate with the apartments above; which are in few cases tenanted by those who occupy the former. The walls of the ground-floor are of stone. The superstructure is of brick; and its front projects a foot or two beyond the lower part. It has either *projecting* windows of unpainted wood or of boards, or *flat* windows, which are generally partly formed of lattice-work, and partly closed by hanging shutters.[2] The houses are mostly two or three stories high.—On either side of the great streets are by-streets and quarters.

A *durb*, or *by-street*, differs from a sha'rë' in being narrower, and not so long. In most cases, the durb is about six or eight feet wide; is a thoroughfare; and has, at each end, a gateway, with a large wooden door, which is closed at night.[3] Some durbs consist only of private houses: others contain shops. The private houses much resemble, in their exterior appearance, those houses which I have already described: the walls of the ground-floor being of stone; and the superstructure, which is of brick, projecting about two feet.[4] The upper windows are also similar to those before described; but the windows of the lower apartments, towards the

---

[1] See plate 10, and plate 9 [fig. 18 and fig. 17].
[2] See plate 9 [fig. 17].
[3] In plate 10 [fig. 18], the entrance of a durb is seen.
[4] See again plate 10, and plate 11 [fig. 18 and fig. 19].

street, are small, square, wooden gratings, placed very high. The houses being thus constructed, and the streets so narrow, many of the projecting windows would quite meet, face to face, were it not that few of them are placed so as to be exactly opposite, one to another. These streets have, of course, a dull appearance; and the more so as the principal windows of the larger houses look into an inner court; but they afford a delightful shade; and, to heighten the luxury obtained by the exclusion of the sun, the people, in sultry weather, frequently sprinkle water before their houses. Some of the by-streets present a singular contrast, by their comparative solitude, to the bustle witnessed in the greater thoroughfares.

A *hha'rah*, or *quarter*, is a particular district consisting of one or more streets or lanes. In general, a small quarter contains only private houses, and has but one entrance, with a wooden gate, which, like that of a durb, is closed at night.

The *soo'cks*, or *ba'za'rs*, or *markets*, are short streets, or short portions of streets, having shops on either side. In some of them, all the shops are occupied by persons of the same trade. Many soo'cks are covered over-head by matting, extended upon rafters, or by a roof of wood. Most of the great thoroughfare streets, and many by-streets, consist wholly, or for the most part, of successions of soo'cks.

Some of the *kha'ns* of Musr are similar to the soo'cks just described; but in general, a kha'n consists of shops or magazines surrounding a square or oblong court.

Kha'n El-Khalee'lee—which is situated in the central part of the *city*, a little to the east of the principal street, and occupies the site of the cemetery of the Fawa'tim (the Khalee'fehs of Egypt)—particularly deserves to be mentioned; being one of the chief soo'cks of Musr. It consists of a series of short lanes, with several turnings, and has four entrances, from different quarters. The shops in this kha'n are mostly occupied by Turks, who deal in ready-made clothes, and other articles of dress; together with arms of various kinds, the small prayer-carpets used by the Moos'lims, and other commodities. Public auctions are held there (as in many other soo'cks in Musr) twice in the week; on which occasions the kha'n is so crowded that, in some parts, it is difficult for a passenger to push his way through. The sale begins early in the morning, and lasts till the noon-prayers. It is conducted by numerous *della'ls* (or brokers), who carry up and down the market the goods that they are commissioned, by the shop-keepers or others, to dispose of; holding up the articles, and calling out the sum last bidden. Clothes (old as well as new), shawls, arms, pipes, and a variety of other goods, are offered for sale in this manner. Several *sack'ckas* (or water-carriers), each with a goat-skin of water on his back, and a brass cup for the use of any one who would drink, attend on these occasions. Sherbet of raisins, and bread (in round, flat cakes), with other eatables, are also cried up and down the market; and on every auction-day, two or three durwee'shes, and several real or pretended idiots, with a distressing number of other beggars, frequent the kha'n. The answer these mendicants generally receive is *Al'lah yoosa''edak!* (God help thee!), or some similar phrase: for an alms conferred upon *one* would immediately attract swarms of others.

Another of the principal kha'ns of Musr is that called the *Hhamza'wee*; which is the principal market of the drapers and silk-mercers.

There are few other kha'ns in Musr; or rather, few buildings so designated; but there are numerous buildings, called *weka'lehs*, which are of the same description as the generality of kha'ns.

A *weka'leh* surrounds a square or oblong court. The ground-floor consists of vaulted magazines (often used as shops), facing the court; and above these are lodgings, or other magazines, which are entered from a gallery extending round the court. Most of the buildings of this kind have only one common entrance; which renders them very secure in cases of riot. Musr contains about two hundred weka'lehs; and about a hundred and fifty of these are within the precincts of the *city*. Some of them are more than a hundred feet in length, and scarcely less in breadth; and have a small oratory in the centre of the court. They are the places where merchants and others keep their main stock of goods; and where strangers often take up their quarters.

The *Weka'let el-Gella'beh* (or Weka'leh of the Slave-merchants), which is near the Kha'n El-Khalee'lee, is the market for black slaves. It surrounds a spacious square court; in which are generally seen several groups of male and female slaves, besmeared with grease (of which they are very fond), and nearly naked, excepting in winter, when they are better clad, and kept within doors. As there is a thoroughfare through this weka'leh, the slaves are much exposed to public view; and they amuse themselves by observing and quizzing the passengers. They appear careless and happy; for their greatest troubles are passed; and they know that the slave of the Moos'lim fares even better than the free servant. Some of the more valuable of the female slaves (like the *white* female slaves, to whom another weka'leh is appropriated) are only shewn to those persons who express a desire to become purchasers.

Having now described the streets and markets of Musr, I may mention some *particular quarters*, &c.—There are some parts which are inhabited exclusively by persons of the same religion or nation. Many quarters are inhabited only by Moos'lims.[1]

The *Quarter of the Jews* (*Hha'rat el-Yahoo'd*) is situated in the western part of the *city*.[2] It is very extensive; but close and dirty. Some of its streets, or rather lanes, are so narrow that two persons can barely pass each other in them; and in some parts, the soil has risen, by the

---

[1] About three fourths of the population of Musr are native Moos'lims.
[2] That part of the metropolis which was included within the second wall (being about a fourth of the present extent of Musr, lying north of the Ba'b Zoowey'leh, and east of the Canal) is still called *el-medee'neh*, or *the city*.

accumulation of rubbish, a foot, or more, above the thresholds of the doors.—The *Greeks* have two quarters; and the *Ckoobt* (or *Copts*) have several, of which some are very extensive.—The *Franks* inhabit not only what is called the *Quarter of the Franks* (*Hha'rat el-Ifren'g*) but are interspersed throughout a considerable district, situated between the *city* and the Ezbekee'yeh. The motley population of this part of the metropolis gives it the appearance of a quarter in a sea-port town, like Alexandria: some of the Franks retain their national costume: others adopt partly or wholly the Turkish dress. The chief thoroughfare-street in this part of the town is the soo'ck called the *Moo'skee*, where are a few shops filled up in the European style, with glass fronts, and occupied by Franks, who deal in various European commodities. The Hha'rat el-Ifren'g is a short street leading out of the Moo'skee, on the southern side. At the end of it is a Frank inn; the only one in Musr.

There are several vacant spaces, of considerable extent, in the interior of the metropolis; some of which, during the season of the inundation (the autumn), become lakes. The principal of these are the Bir'ket el-Ezbekee'yeh and Bir'ket el-Feel.

The *Ezbekee'yeh*[1] is an irregular place; the greatest length of which is nearly half a mile: and the greatest breadth, about a third of a mile. On the south are two modern Turkish palaces, with gardens. On the west is a plain wall (part of the wall of the metropolis), and another Turkish palace, occupying the site of the mansion of the famous Memloo'k Bey *El-El'fee*, which became the residence of Napoleon, and of Kleber, who was assassinated in the adjacent garden. On the north-east side of the Ezbekee'yeh is a Christian quarter, presenting a long row of lofty, but neglected, houses. During the season of the inundation, the water of the Nile enters the Ezbekee'yeh by a canal; and the whole place is inundated, with the exception of a narrow space along the whole, or part, of each side. The water remains three or four months; after which the ground is sown with wheat, &c. The place has a more pleasing appearance when covered with green corn than when it is a lake; for the water is very turbid.

The *Bir'ket el-Feel* (or Lake of the Elephant)[2] also receives the water of the Nile during the season of the inundation. Only a small part of it is open to the public.

There are two small lakes in the western part of the metropolis, and several others in its vicinity.—There are also several cemeteries in the western part of the town,[3] and many large gardens. These gardens are chiefly stocked with palm-trees, acacias, sycamores, oranges, limes, pomegranates, &c. Little arrangement is displayed in them. They have generally one or more sa'ckiyehs, which raise the water for their irrigation from wells. The foliage is very much sullied by dust (which is

---

[1]See F, in the plan, plate 6 [fig. 12].
[2]See E, in the plan, plate 6 [fig. 12].
[3]The principal cemeteries are *without* the town.

one of the few evils of the delightful, dry climate of Egypt), and does not possess that brilliant verdure that is seen in other countries which are subject to frequent rains, fogs, and heavy dews.

The Canal (*El-Khalee'g*) which traverses the metropolis, is no ornament to it.[1] In most parts of its course through the town it is closely hemmed in on each side by the backs of houses: therefore it cannot be seen, excepting in a few places, by the passengers in the streets. Most of the bridges over it are moreover lined with shops on both sides: so that a person passing over them cannot see that he is crossing over the canal. The water of the Nile is admitted into the canal in August; and the entrance is closed by a dam of earth when the river begins to subside: consequently, after two or three months only stagnant puddles remain in it. While it continues open, boats enter it from the Nile; pass through the whole length of the metropolis; then along the western canal, and into the Ezbekee'yeh.

Of the *public buildings* of Musr, the most interesting are the *Mosques*.

A mosque in which a congregation assembles every Friday, to recite the noon-prayers appointed for that day, is called a ga'më'. Its doors are also open every day in the week from day-break till night, or, at least, at the stated times of prayer. During the intervals between the times of prayer, particularly in the afternoon, persons may be seen sleeping upon the matting which covers the floor; their shoes placed one upon the other, sole to sole, beside them: others, talking, or reading, or reciting portions of the Ckoor-a'n: and in some mosques I have even seen shoemakers and other mechanics at work. I visited the mosques both with the congregation[2] and on other occasions; sometimes joining a lecturer's auditory, sitting in the form of a ring upon the floor.—A *collegiate* mosque is called *Med'res'eh*.—The general plan of the more extensive mosques may be described as a square court surrounded by porticoes, and having, in the centre, a tank or fountain for ablution. The porticoes are open towards the court; and that on the side towards Mek'keh is more spacious that those on the other three sides; as it is the principal place of prayer: it generally has several rows of columns, supporting arches and a flat roof; and its pavement is covered with mats. In the centre of the wall on this side is a niche (*mehhra'b*), which is designed to shew the direction of Mek'keh; and to the right of this is the pulpit (*mim'bar*), placed against the wall. The mosques, in general, are built of stone; the alternate courses of which are coloured red.[3] Both without and within they are ornamented with inscriptions of passages from the Ckoor-an, forming long friezes, which, to my taste, are far more pleasing than any unmeaning decoration. Most of the domes and

---

[1]This canal is the ancient Amnis Trajanus; as I have had occasion to mention in chapter VII.

[2]The congregation pray *silently*; keeping time with the Ima'm in their performance of the various attitudes.

[3]See my view of the mosque of Cka'id Bey, plate 14 [fig. 22].

ma'd'nehs are very elegant. The columns and rich marbles used in the construction of many of the mosques are mostly the spoils of ancient temples.

El-Ga'më' el-Az'har (or the Splendid Mosque[1]), which is situated midway between the principal street of the city and the eastern gate called Ba'b el-Ghoorei'yib, is the principal mosque of Musr, and *the University of the East*: it is also the first with regard to the period of its foundation of all the mosques of the *city*; but it has been so often repaired, and so much enlarged, that it is difficult to ascertain exactly how much of the *original* structure we see in the *present* state of the mosque. It was founded about nine months after the first wall of the city, in the year of the flight 359 (A.D. 969-70). Though occupying a space about three hundred feet square it makes but little show externally; for it is so surrounded by houses that only its entrances and ma'd'nehs can be seen from the streets. It has two grand gates, and four minor entrances. Each of the two former (which were built about 60 years ago) has two doors, and a school-room above, open at the front and back. Every one takes off his shoes before he passes the threshold of the gate; although, if he enters this mosque by the principal gate, he has to cross a spacious court before he arrives at the place of prayer. He carries his shoes, placed sole to sole, in his left hand: this custom is observed in every mosque. The principal gate is in the centre of the front of the mosque: it is the nearest to the principal street of the city. Immediately within this gate are two small mosques: one on either hand. Passing between these, we enter the great court of the Az'har; which is paved with stone, and surrounded by porticoes. The principal portico is that which is opposite this entrance: those on the other three sides of the court are divided into a number of *riwa'cks*, or apartments for the accommodation of the numerous students who resort to this celebrated university from various and remote countries of Africa, Asia, and Europe, as well as from different parts of Egypt. These persons, being mostly in indigent circumstances, are supported by the funds of the mosque; each receiving a certain quantity of bread and soup at noon and in the evening. Many blind paupers are also supported here. The riwa'cks are separated from the court and from each other by partitions of wood which unite with the columns or pillars. Those on the side in which is the principal entrance are very small; there being only one row of columns on this side; but those on the right and left are spacious halls, containing several rows of columns. There are also some riwa'cks above the ground-floor. Each riwa'ck is for the natives of a particular country, or of a particular province of Egypt: the Egyptian students being, of course, more numerous than those of any other nation. In going the round of these apartments, after passing successively among natives of different divisions of Egypt, we find ourselves in the company of people of

---

[1]European travellers have strangely misinterpreted the name of this building, calling it "the Mosque of Flowers."

Mek'keh and El-Medee'neh; then, in the midst of Syrians; in another minute, among Moos'lims of central Africa; next, amidst Magha'r'beh (or natives of western and northern Africa); then, with European and Asiatic Turks; and, quitting these, we are introduced to Persians, and Moos'lims of India: we may almost fancy ourselves transported through their respective countries. No sight in Musr interested me more than that of the interior of the Az'har.—To the left of the great court is a smaller one, containing the tank at which the ablution preparatory to prayer is performed by all those who have not done it before entering the mosque.—The great portico is closed by partitions of wood between a row of square pillars, or piers, behind the front row of columns. The partition of the central arch-way has a wide door; and some of the other partitions have smaller doors. The great portico is very spacious; containing eight rows of small marble columns, arranged parallel with the front. That part beyond the fifth row of columns was added by the builder of the two grand gates. The walls are white-washed: the niche and pulpit are very plain: and simplicity is the prevailing character of the whole of the interior of the portico. The pavement is covered with mats; and sometimes a few small carpets are seen here and there. A person of rank or wealth is generally accompanied to the mosque by a servant bearing a *segga'deh* (or small prayer-carpet, about the size of a hearth-rug) upon which he prays. During the noon-prayers of the congregation on Friday, the worshippers are very numerous: ranged in parallel rows, they sit upon the matting during the two *khoot'behs* (an exhortation and a prayer); and when the Ima'm descends from the pulpit to recite the prayers in which they are silently to join, they all rise: when he bows and prostrates himself, they do the same. The devout manner of the whole assembly, and the exactly simultaneous changes in their attitudes of prayer, are, to an unaccustomed observer, singularly striking. Different scenes are presented at other times in the great portico of the Az'har: lecturers are seen addressing their circles of attentive listeners, or reading to them commentaries on the Ckoor-an; persons conversing together; others eating and drinking, or asleep; and sometimes, men carrying about bread and other eatables for sale: many houseless paupers, too, pass the night there. Such customs are not altogether in accordance with the sanctity of the place; but peculiarly illustrative of the simplicity of Oriental manners.

I shall add little more than the names and respective ages of such of the other mosques of Musr as I found particularly worthy of examination; chiefly for the guidance of any travellers who may make this book their companion during a visit to the Egyptian capital.[1]

Adjacent to the Az'har is the fine mosque of *Mohham'mad Bey*, founded in the year of the flight 1187 (A.D. 1773-4).

---

[1] It is not safe (or at least was not at the period of my visit to Musr) for an undisguised Christian to *enter* the mosques: he would be in danger of being mobbed and ill-treated.

The mosque of the *Hhasaney'n*,[1] which is situated to the north of the Az'har, and not far distant, is generally esteemed the most sacred mosque in Musr. It was founded in the year of the flight 549 (A.D. 1154-5); but has been more than once rebuilt. The present building was erected about 60 years ago. The fore-part consists of a handsome hall, or portico; the roof of which is supported by numerous marble columns, and the pavement covered with carpets. Passing through this hall, I found myself in that holy place under which the head of the martyr Hhosey'n is buried deep below the pavement. It is a lofty, square saloon, surmounted by a dome. Over the spot where the sacred relic is buried is an oblong monument, covered with green silk, with a worked inscription around it. This is enclosed within a high screen of bronze, of open work; around the upper part of which are suspended several specimens of curious and elegant writing. Every visiter walks round this enclosure, from left to right; reciting, but inaudibly, the Fe't'hhah (or opening chapter of the Ckoor-a'n)—a ceremony also observed on visiting *other* tombs.—My first visit to the shrine of Hhosey'n was rather a hurried one; for I was fearful of exciting suspicion by gazing too long: but I was afterwards enabled to gratify my curiosity more fully, when the visiting [of] other mosques had given me confidence in my presence of mind.

The great mosque of that impious impostor the Khalee'feh *El-Hha'kim* (who professed to be a prophet, and afterwards to be God incarnate) derives an interest from the name it bears, and from its antiquity. It is situated immediately within that part of the northern wall of the city which connects the Ba'b en-Nusr and Ba'b el-Footoo'hh. This mosque was completed in the reign of El-Hha'kim, the year of the flight 403 (A.D. 1012-13); but was founded by his predecessor. It is now in a state of ruin; and no longer used as a place of worship. It occupies a space about 400 feet square; and consists of arcades surrounding a square court.

Several of the finest mosques of Musr front the principal street of the *city*. In proceeding along this street from north to south, the first mosque that particularly attracts our notice is the *Bur'ckoo'ckee'yeh*, on the right side. This was founded in the year of the flight 786 (A.D. 1384-5). It has a fine dome, and a lofty and elegant ma'd'neh; and the interior is particularly handsome.

Just beyond this, on the same side of the street, are the Tomb and Mosque and Hospital of the *Soolta'n Ckala-oo'n*, composing one united building. The tomb and mosque form the front part: the former is to the right of the latter; and a passage, which is the general entrance, leads between them to the hospital (*Ma'rista'n*[2]). These three united buildings were founded in the year of the flight 683 (A.D. 1284-5). The tomb has a very large ma'd'neh; and is a noble edifice: its front is coloured red and

---

[1]By "the Hhasaney'n" are meant Hhas'an and Hhosey'n, the grandsons of the Prophet.

[2]Vulgarly pronounced *Moorista'n*.

white, in squares: the interior is very magnificent. The mosque is not remarkable. The hospital contains two small oblong courts, surrounded by small cells, in which mad persons are confined, and chained; men, in one court; and women, in the other. Though these wretched beings are provided for by the funds of the establishment, it is the custom of visiters to take bread to distribute to them. Male visiters are not admitted into the women's court.

Proceeding still southwards along the principal street, we arrive at a fine mosque called the *Ashrafee'yeh*, on our right. It was built by the Soolta'n El-Ash'raf Bursaba'y: consequently between the years 825-41 (A.D. 1421 et seqq.). Frequently criminals are hanged against one of the grated windows of this mosque; as the street before it is generally very much crowded with passengers.

Still proceeding along the principal street, through that part of it called the Ghoo'ree'yeh (which is a large soo'ck, or market), we arrive at the two fine mosques of the Soolta'n *El-Ghoo'ree*, facing each other, one on each side of the street, and having a roof of wood extending from one to the other. They were both completed in the year of the flight 909 (A.D. 1503-4). That on the left, El-Ghoo'ree designed as his tomb; but he was not buried in it.

Arriving at the southernmost part of the great street, we have on our right the great mosque of the Soolta'n *El-Moo-ei'yed*, which was founded in the year of the flight 819 (A.D. 1416-17). It surrounds a spacious square court; and contains the remains of its royal founder and some of his family. It has a noble dome, and a fine, lofty entrance-porch, at the right extremity of the front. Its two great ma'd'nehs, which rise from the towers of the gate called Ba'b Zoowey'leh (the southern gate of the *city*), I have already mentioned.

Of the mosques in the *suburban* districts of the metropolis, the most remarkable are those of the Soolta'n Hhas'an and of Ibn Too'loo'n.

The great mosque of the *Soolta'n Hhas'an*,[1] which is situated near the Citadel, and is the most lofty of the edifices of Musr, was founded in the year of the flight 757 (A.D. 1356). It is a very noble pile; but it has some irregularities which are unpleasing to the eye; as, for instance, the disparity of its two ma'd'nehs. The great ma'd'neh is nearly three hundred feet in height, measured from the ground. At the right extremity of the north-east side of the mosque is a very fine, lofty entrance-porch. From this, a zig-zag passage conducts us to a square hypæthral hall, or court; in the centre of which is a tank, and by this, a reservoir with spouts, for the performance of ablution; each crowned with a cupola. In each of the four sides of the court is a hall with an arched roof, and open front. That opposite the entrance is the largest; and is the principal place of worship. Its arched roof is about seventy feet in width. It is constructed of brick, and plastered (as are also the other three arches); and numerous small glass lamps, and two large lanterns of bronze, are

---

[1]See plate 13 [fig. 21].

suspended from it. The lower part of the end-wall is lined with coloured marbles. Beyond it is a square saloon; over which is the great dome; and in the centre of this saloon is the tomb of the royal founder. Most of the decorations of this mosque are very elaborate and elegant; but the building, in many parts, needs repair.

The great mosque of *Ibn Too'loo'n* (or, as it is more commonly called, *Ga'më' Teyloo'n*), situated in the southern part of the metropolis, is a very interesting building. It was founded in the year of the flight 263 (A.D. 876-7); and was the principal mosque of the city of El-Ckata'-ë', or El-Ckata'yë' (which I have mentioned in chapter VIII),—a city nearly a century older than El-Cka'hireh. The space which it occupies is about 400 feet square. It is constructed of brick, covered with plaster; and consists of arcades surrounding a square court; in the centre of which is a tank for ablution, under a square stone building, surmounted by a dome. The arches in this mosque are slightly *pointed*: this is very remarkable; for it proves—as the mosque was constructed A.D. 876-7, and has never been rebuilt—that the Eastern pointed arch is more ancient than the Gothic.—A great ma'd'neh, with winding stairs round its exterior, stands on the north-west side of the mosque; with which it is only connected by an arched gate-way. The whole of this great mosque is in a sad state of decay; and not even kept decently clean, excepting where the mats are spread. It is the most ancient Arabian building, excepting the Nilometer of Er-Ro'dah (which is about twelve years older), now existing in Egypt: for the mosque of 'Amr, though founded more than two centuries before, has often been rebuilt.

In the neighbourhood of the mosque above described is a large ruined castle, or palace, called *Ckal''at el-Kebsh* (or the Castle of the Ram[1]), occupying, and partly surrounding, an extensive rocky eminence. It was built in the middle of the seventh century after the flight (or of the thirteenth of our era). Its interior is occupied by modern buildings.

The mosques of the *sey'deh Zey'neb* (or *sit't Zey'neb*), the *sey'deh Sekee'neh*, and the *sey'deh Nefee'seh* (the first and second situated in the southern part of the metropolis, and the third in a small southern suburb without the gates) are highly venerated, but not very remarkable as buildings.[2]—There are many other mosques in Musr well worthy of examination; but those which I have mentioned are the most distinguished. I shall hereafter have to point out some in the *vicinity* of the town.

There are, in Musr, many *Tekee'yehs*, or convents for durwee'shes, and others, mostly built by Turkish Ba'shas, for the benefit of their country-men. Some of these are very handsome structures.

---

[1]*Kebsh* not only signifies a *ram*, but is also the name of the *mountain sheep* (both male and female) which is found in the deserts adjacent to Egypt.

[2]The sey'deh Zey'neb was the daughter of the Ima'm 'Al'ee, the cousin and son-in-law of the Prophet; Sekee'neh was the daughter of Hhosey'n, the son of 'Al'ee; and Nefee'seh was the great-grand-daughter of Hhas'an, the son of 'Al'ee.

Many of the *Sebee'ls* (or public Fountains) are remarkable buildings. The general style of a large sebee'l may be thus described.—The principal part of the front is of a semicircular form, with three windows of brass grating. Within each window is a trough of water; and when any one would drink, he puts his hand through one of the lowest apertures of the grating, and dips in the trough a brass mug, which is chained to one of the bars. Above the windows is a wide coping of wood. Over this part of the building is a public school-room, with an open front, formed of pillars and arches; and at the top is another wide coping of wood. Some of these buildings are partly constructed of alternate courses of black and white marble.

Hho'ds, or Watering-places for beasts of burden, are also very numerous in Musr. The trough is of stone, and, generally, in an arched recess; over which is a public school-room.

There are about sixty or seventy *Hhamma'ms*, or Public Baths, in Musr. Some are exclusively for men: some, only for women: others, for men in the morning, and for women in the afternoon. When the bath is appropriated to women, a napkin, or any piece of linen, is hung over the door. The apartments are paved with marble; have fountains and tanks and are surmounted by cupolas, pierced with small, round holes, for the admission of light.

Musr contains above a thousand *Ckah'wehs*[1], or Coffee-shops.[2] Only coffee is supplied at these; the persons who frequent them taking their own pipes and tobacco.

Of the *Private Houses* I have already described the exterior appearance, in speaking of the streets. I shall add little more respecting them than a brief description of one of the principal apartments in a house of moderate size. In general, such a house encloses a small, uncovered, and unpaved court; and has, on the ground-floor, an apartment called a *mun'dar'ah*, in which male visiters are usually received. This has a wide, wooden, grated window, next the court. The floor is paved with common stone, or with marble; and a small part of this pavement (extending from the door to the opposite side) is about half a foot lower than the rest. Every person who enters the room slips his feet out of his shoes or slippers before he steps upon the raised part of the floor; which is covered with matting or a carpet, and has a mattress and cushions placed against the wall on each side (on the right and left, and at the end), composing what is called a *deewa'n*. In most large houses, the mun'dar'ah has, in the middle of the depressed part of the floor, a fountain, which plays in a small, shallow pool, lined with coloured marbles, &c. The walls are plastered: the ceiling is of wood.— The other apartments are nearly similar. A room is completely furnished when it has a mat or carpet spread upon the raised part of the floor, and a

---

[1] *Ckah'weh* is also the name of the *beverage* which we call coffee: the *berries*, either whole or pounded, are called *boon'n*.

[2] See plate 9 [fig. 17].

deewa'n. For meals, a round tray of tinned copper is placed upon a low stool; and the company sit round it on the ground. The bed is spread upon the floor, and rolled up and removed in the morning.

I resided at Musr, at different times, a little more than a year and a quarter. As my pursuits required that I should not be remarked in public as a European, I separated myself as much as possible from the Franks, and lived in a part of the town (near the Ba'b el-Hhadee'd) somewhat remote from the Frank quarters. Speaking the language of the country, and conforming with the manners of my Moos'lim neighbours, renouncing knives and forks (which, till I saw the really delicate mode of eating with the fingers, as practised in the East, I was rather averse from doing), and abstaining from wine and swine's flesh (both, indeed, loathsome to me), I was treated with respect and affability by all the natives with whom I had any intercourse.

Chapter XI.
The Citadel of Musr, or Cairo.

Situation, &c., of the Citadel—Old Palace and Mosque—View from the western brow of the hill—Well of Yoo'soof—Modern Palaces, &c.

The Citadel (*El-Ckal''ah*) is situated at the south-eastern extremity of the metropolis, upon an extensive, flat-topped, rocky eminence, about 250 feet above the level of the plain, and near the point of Mount Moockut'tum, which completely commands it. It was founded by Sala'hh ed-Deen (the Saladin of our historians), in the year of the flight 572 (A.D. 1176-7); but not finished till 604; since which latter period it has been the usual residence of the Soolta'ns and Governors of Egypt.— Before it is a spacious square, called the *Roomey'leh*[1]; where a market is held; and where conjurors, musicians, and story-tellers, are often seen each surrounded by a ring of idlers.

The *Ba'b el-'Az'ab*[2] is the principal gate of the Citadel. Within this is a steep and narrow road, partly cut through the rock; so steep that, in some parts, steps are cut, to render the ascent and descent less difficult than it would otherwise be for the horses and camels, &c. This confined road was the chief scene of the massacre of the Memloo'ks, in the year 1811.

A great part of the interior of the Citadel is obstructed by ruins and rubbish; and there are many dwelling-houses, and some shops, within it. The most remarkable monuments that it contains are an old palace and a great mosque, both of the same age.

The Old Palace[3] is commonly called *Ckusr Yoo'soof*, or *Deewa'n Yoo'soof*; and believed to have been the palace of Yoo'soof Sala'hh ed-Deen; but erroneously. European travellers have adopted the same opinion; and call it Joseph's Hall. It was built by the Soolta'n Mohham'mad Ibn Ckala-oo'n, in the early part of the eighth century after the flight (or of the fourteenth of our era). Huge, ancient columns of granite are employed in its construction: their capitals, of various kinds, and ill wrought; but the shafts, very fine. It had a large dome; which has fallen. On entering it we observe, in the centre of the south-eastern side, a niche, marking the direction of Mek'keh, like that of a mosque, which, in other respects, this building does not much resemble.

---

[1]See plate 12 [fig. 20].
[2]Seen in plate 12 [fig. 20], under the letter *a*.
[3]Seen in plate 12 [fig. 20], under the letter *b*.

Both within and without are remains of Arabic inscriptions, in large letters of wood; most of which have fallen.[1]

The Great Mosque, built by the same Soolta'n, lies to the south-east of the former building. It is in a ruinous state; and no longer used as a place of worship. It consists of porticoes surrounding a square court.

A little to the west of the Old Palace are the remains of a very massive building,[2] called "the House of Yoo'soof Sala'hh ed-Deen"; partly on the brow, and partly on the declivity, of the hill.

Here, from the edge of the hill, we have a most striking view of the metropolis and its environs. A small portion of this extensive view I made the subject of a drawing,[3] which includes the most prominent object in the whole; namely, the mosque of the Soolta'n Hhas'an; before which is seen the great square called the Roomey'leh. The principal part of the town lies to our right. Its numerous ma'd'nehs and domes, its flat-topped houses with the sloping sheds which serve as ventilators, and a few palms and other trees among the houses, give it an appearance quite unlike that of any European city. Beyond the metropolis we see the Nile, intersecting a verdant plain; with the towns of Boo'la'ck, Musr 'Atee'ckah and El-Gee'zeh: on the south, the aqueduct, and the mounds of rubbish which occupy the site of El-Foosta't; and in the distance, all the pyramids of Memphis, and the palm groves on the site of that city. On the north of the metropolis are seen the plains of Heliopolis and Goshen. The world can hardly boast a more interesting view.

The famous Well of Yoo'soof (Sala'hh ed-Deen), so called because it was excavated in the reign of that Soolta'n, is near the southern angle of the Great Mosque. It is entirely cut in the calcareous rock; and consists of two rectangular shafts; one below the other; with a winding stair-way round each to the bottom. The upper shaft is about 155 feet deep; and the lower, about 125: therefore the whole depth of the well is about 280 feet. The water, which is rather brackish, though doubtless derived from the Nile, is raised by a sa'ckiyeh at the top of each shaft.

The Mint, and a palace,[4] are in the southern quarter of the Citadel.—In the Quarter of the Inkisha'ree'yeh (or Janisaries), which did not form a part of the *Old* Citadel, and lies to the east, is another palace, just erected, and very handsome. Some of the walls near this, together with many houses, on the northern slope of the hill, were overthrown by the explosion of a magazine of powder, in the year 1824.—On the western slope of the hill is an arsenal, with a cannon-foundry, &c.

---

[1]This noble ruin has been pulled down since I left Musr.
[2]Seen in plate 12 [fig. 20], under the letter *c*.
[3]See plate 13 [fig. 21].
[4]The palace is seen in plate 12 [fig. 20], under the letter *d*.

Chapter XII.

The Environs of Mu'sr, or Cairo.[1]

The Mountain—Gardens, &c.—Cemeteries—Aqueduct—Island of Er-Ro'dah—Musr 'Atee'ckah and its Environs—El-Gee'zeh—Shoob'ra—Heliopolis.

Mount Moockut'tum, which overlooks both the town and citadel of Musr, is composed of a yellowish calcareous rock, abounding with testacious fossils: and is entirely destitute of verdure. Upon its flat summit, a strong fort has been erected; with a steep causeway, upon high, narrow arches, ascending to it. On each side of this causeway the rock has been extensively quarried. In the western side of the mountain are many ancient sepulchral grottoes; rather difficult of access: I could find no traces of hieroglyphics or other decorations in any of them.

On the north of the metropolis are many gardens, and, in the season of the inundation, several lakes, in one of which (called Bir'ket er-Rut'lee) abundance of lotus-plants are seen, in the month of September, in blossom. In the same tract is a large, ruined mosque, which was founded by Ez-Za'hir Beybur's, in the year of the flight 665 (A.D. 1266-7). The French converted it into a fort.—Opposite the Ba'b en-Nusr is a large cemetery, occupying a desert tract.[2]

The great Eastern Cemetery, in the sandy waste between the metropolis and the mountain, contains the tombs of many of the Memloo'k Soolta'ns.[3] Some of these mausolea (which have been erroneously regarded by European travellers as the tombs of the Khalee'fehs[4]) are very noble buildings; particularly those of the Soolta'ns *Burckoo'ck*[5] and *Cka'id Bey*.[6] Of the latter I have given a view[7]; as conveying a good idea of many of the mosques of Musr. The central part of this cemetery contains several alms-houses, and is commonly called "Cka'id Bey," or "Cka'itbe'y." Here, and for some distance towards the

---

[1] For the position of the buildings, &c., mentioned in this chapter, see the plan, plate 6 [fig. 12].
[2] The tomb of Burckhardt is here.
[3] Several of these buildings are seen in the distance in my general view of Musr, plate 8 [fig. 15, lower].
[4] None of the tombs of the Khalee'fehs of Egypt now exist: Kha'n El-Khalee'lee (as I have mentioned in chapter X) occupies their site.
[5] Built by his son and successor Far'ag, in the beginning of the ninth century after the flight (or of the fifteenth of our era).
[6] Built about a century after the former.
[7] See plate 14 [fig. 22].

Citadel, the tombs are closely crowded together; and the whole cemetery, being intersected by roads like streets in a town, may justly be called a Necropolis, or City of the Dead. All the tract is desert; and few persons are to be met here, excepting on the Friday morning, when it is the custom of the Moos'lims to visit the tombs of their relations and friends. Numerous groups of women are then seen repairing to the cemetery; each bearing a palm-branch, to decorate the tomb she is about to visit.

On the south of the metropolis is another great cemetery, called *El-Ckara'feh*, still more extensive, but not containing such grand mausolea. This, also, is in a desert plain. Many of its tombs are very beautiful: one kind struck me as particularly elegant; consisting of an oblong monument, generally of marble, canopied by a cupola, or by a pyramidal roof, supported by marble columns. In the southern part of this cemetery is the tomb of the celebrated *Ima'm Esh-Sha'fe'ee*, the founder of one of the four orthodox sects of the Isla'm,[1] who died in the year of the flight 204 (A.D. 819-20). The present mosque which covers his tomb is a plain, white-washed building, with a dome cased with lead. The mosque of the Ima'm has been twice rebuilt: the present being the third building; and about two centuries and a half old. A little to the north of it is a low building, which is the burial-place of the present Ba'sha's family.—Between this cemetery and the mountain are many ancient mummy-pits, choked with rubbish. They evidently shew that this tract was the Necropolis of Egyptian Babylon.

Along the *western* side of the metropolis are several lakes and gardens and extensive mounds of rubbish; which last, though not so large or lofty as those on the east and south, conceal much of the town from the view of persons approaching it in this direction. All the camels, asses, &c., that die in the metropolis are cast upon the surrounding hills of rubbish, where hungry dogs and vultures feed upon them.—On the bank of the river, between Boo'la'ck and Musr 'Atee'ckah, are a palace of Ibrahee'm Ba'sha, another appropriated to his women, a large, square building called Ckusr El-'Ey'nee (which is an establishment for the education of youths destined for the army, &c.), and a small convent of Durwee'shes. A little to the south of these buildings is the entrance of the Khalee'g, or Canal of Musr; and just above this commences the Aqueduct by which the water of the Nile is conveyed to the Citadel. A large, hexagonal building, about sixty or seventy feet high, contains the sa'ckiyehs which raise the water to the channel of the aqueduct. The whole length of the aqueduct is about two miles. It is built of stone; and consists of a series of narrow arches, very gradually decreasing in height, as the ground has a slight ascent, imperceptible to the eye. The water, towards the end of its course, enters a subterranean channel, and is raised from a well in the Citadel. This aqueduct was built (in the place of a former one, of wood) in the early part of the tenth century after the flight (or of the sixteenth

---

[1]That sect to which the people of Musr mostly belong.

of our era).—To the south of the aqueduct lies the town of Musr
'Atee'ckah: the principal houses of which face the river and the Island of
Er-Ro'dah.

Gezee'ret er-Ro'dah (or the Island of the Garden) is about a mile and
three quarters in length, and a third of a mile in breadth. The branch of
the river on its eastern side is very narrow; and when the Nile is at its
lowest point, the bed of this narrow branch becomes quite dry. The
island contains several pleasure-houses and gardens; but the greater part
is sown with corn, &c. Along part of its western side is a row of majestic
sycamores; and here we find remains of a massive Roman wall (which is
said to have surrounded the whole island): it supports the bank; and is
constructed of brick, with several courses of stone. At the southern
extremity of the island is the *Mickya's*, or Nilometer; which was built, or
completed, in the year of the flight 247 (A.D. 861-2), on the site of one
more ancient. The Nilometric column is of marble, and of an octagonal
form: each face is divided into sixteen cubits, of $21^{1/3}$ inches each. It
stands in the midst of a square apartment; which may be called a *well*; for
its walls rise but little above the level of the island. On the western side
of the Mickya's is a mosque, and adjacent to it is a powder-magazine: on
the east are some small remains of a palace of Negm ed-Deen, built
nearly six centuries ago.

Musr 'Atee'ckah,[1] though more than a mile in length, is a small,
straggling town, lying along the bank of the Nile, and occupying a part
of the site of El-Foosta't. It contains about 4,000 inhabitants. Many of
the vessels from Upper Egypt unload here; and a constant intercourse is
kept up, by means of numerous ferry-boats, between this town and
El-Gee'zeh. Behind the town are extensive, low mounds of rubbish,
covering the rest of the site of El-Foosta't. In this desolate tract are
situated the Mosque of 'Amr, the Ckusr esh-Shem'ă, and several
Christian convents.—The *Ga'më' 'Amr*, or Mosque of 'Amr, has been so
often repaired and rebuilt, that almost every part of it may now be
regarded as modern: yet I could not help being impressed with
sentiments of veneration when I entered it, and stood upon the spot
where the conqueror of Egypt, surrounded by "Companions of the
Prophet," so often prayed. The building occupies a space about 350 feet
square. Its plan is a square court surrounded by porticoes; and its whole
appearance, very simple and plain. The exterior is formed by high, bare
walls of brick. The portico at the end of the court (towards Mek'keh) has
six rows of columns; that on the left side, four rows; that on the right,
three; and on the entrance-side, only one row. The columns are of veined
marble: some being too small, have an additional plinth, or an inverted
capital, at the base. The capitals are of many different kinds; having been
taken, as also the columns, from various ancient buildings.—The *Ckusr
esh-Shem'ă* is an old Roman Fortress, which was the strong-hold of

---

[1]Respecting the name of this town, and the impropriety of calling it "Old Cairo,"
I have remarked in chapter VIII.

Egyptian Babylon, and the head-quarters of the Greek army which the Arabs, under 'Amr, contended with and vanquished. It is said that this building was, in ancient times, illuminated with candles on the first night of every month; and hence it derived the name it now bears, which signifies "the fortress, or palace, of the candles." The area which it occupies extends about a thousand feet from north to south, and six or seven hundred feet from east to west. Its walls are very lofty; constructed of brick, with several courses of stone; and strengthened by round towers. The interior is crowded with houses and shops, occupied by Christians; and it contains several churches; among which is that of St. Sergius, where a small grotto, like an oven, is shewn as the retreat of the Holy Family.—The Egyptian *Babylon* was situated on a rocky eminence on the south-east of the Ckusr esh-Shem'ă. El-Muckree'zee and other Arab historians prove that this was the "Musr" which 'Amr besieged and took. There was another fortress here (besides the Ckusr esh-Shem'ă), called "Ckusr Ba'belyoo'n" (or the Fortress, or Palace, of Babylon). This, I believe, was the spacious square building since called *Istub'l 'An'tar* (or the Stable of 'An'tar), which in later times became a convent, and is now converted into a powder-magazine.—To the west of the Hill of Babylon, and close to the Nile, is the small village of *At'ar en-Neb'ee*; so called from a stone, bearing the impression of the Prophet's foot, preserved in a small mosque, which rises, with a picturesque effect, from the verge of the river.

El-Gee'zeh الجيزه , which is opposite to Musr 'Atee'ckah, is a small, poor town, surrounded, excepting on the side towards the river, by a mean wall, which would scarcely avail to defend it from a party of Bed'awees. It has been supposed to occupy a part of the site of Memphis; but this conjecture is now known to be erroneous.

A few places northward of the metropolis remain to be mentioned.

A fine, straight road, bordered by mulberry-trees, sycamores, and acacias, leads to Shoob'ra, the favourite country-residence of the Ba'sha, rather more than three miles from Musr. The palace of Shoob'ra is situated by the Nile. It has an extensive garden, laid out with some taste.

About six miles distant from the northern gates of the metropolis, towards the north-north-east, is the site of *Heliopolis*, the City of the Sun; called by the ancient Egyptians *On*; and by the Arabs, *'Eyn Shems*, or the Fountain of the Sun; though, to bear this signification, the name should be written *'Eyn esh-Shems*, which may also be interpreted "the rays, or light, of the sun." The route from Musr to the site of Heliopolis lies along the desert; but near the limits of the cultivable soil. This part of the desert is a sandy flat, strewed with pebbles, and with petrified wood, pudding-stone, red sand-stone, &c. A small mountain of red sand-stone, called *El-Geb'el el-Ahh'mar* (or the Red Mountain), lies at a short distance to the right, or east. On the left of the route is a large settlement of courtesans, composing a complete village. Passengers generally attract several of these girls from their huts; and are often much annoyed by their importunity. On approaching within a mile of the site of

Heliopolis, the traveller passes by the village of *El-Mut'aree'yeh*; where are pointed out an old sycamore, under the shade of which (according to tradition) the Holy Family reposed, and a well which afforded them drink. The balsam-tree was formerly cultivated in the neighbouring fields: it thrived nowhere else in Egypt; and it was believed that it flourished in this part because it was watered from the above-mentioned well. The name given by the Arabs to Heliopolis was perhaps derived from this well.—In a space above half a mile square, surrounded by walls of crude brick, which now appear like ridges of earth, were situated the sacred edifices of Heliopolis. The only remaining monument appearing above the soil, is a fine obelisk, standing in the midst of the enclosure. The Arabs call it *Misel'let Far'oo'n* (or the Obelisk of Pharaoh).[1] It is formed of a single block of red granite, about sixty-two feet in height, and six feet square at the lower part. The soil has risen four or five feet above its base: for, in the season of the inundation, the water of the Nile enters the enclosure by a branch of the Canal of Musr. Upon each of its sides is sculptured the same hieroglyphic inscription; bearing the name of Osirtesen the First,[†] the most ancient known Pharaoh of whom any sculptured monument remains. There are a few other monuments of his reign: the obelisk of the Feiyoo'm is one of these. 'Abd El-Latee'f, in speaking of 'Eyn Shems, says that he saw there (about the end of the twelfth century of the Christian era) the remains of several colossal statues, and *two* great obelisks, one of which had fallen, and was broken into two pieces. These statues and the broken obelisk, probably, now lie beneath the accumulated soil.—Such are the poor remains of Heliopolis, that celebrated seat of learning where Eudoxus and Plato studied thirteen years, and where Herodotus derived much of his information respecting Egypt. In the time of Strabo, the *city* was altogether deserted; but the famous temple of the sun still remained, though much injured by Cambyses. The bull Mnevis was worshipped at Heliopolis, as Apis was at Memphis.—It is probable that the "land of Goshen" was immediately adjacent to the province of Heliopolis, on the north-north-east.

Thirteen miles from Musr, in the same direction as Heliopolis, are the village of *El-Kha'n'keh* (once a large town) and the Camp of the Niza'm Gedee'd, or Regular Troops, of which an account will be found in a subsequent chapter of this volume.[‡] El-Kha'n'keh is two miles to the north of the *Bir'ket el-Hha'gg*, or *Bir'ket el-Hhog'ga'g* (the Lake of the Pilgrims) which is so called because the pilgrims collect and encamp by it before they proceed in a body to Mek'keh. This lake is more than two miles in length, from west to east; and a mile in breadth. It is filled by the Canal of Musr during the season of the inundation.

---

[1]See no. 5 of the subjects for wood-cuts [fig. 23] (to be introduced here).
[†]Senwosret I.
[‡]Chapter fourteen, section six.

Chapter XIII.
The Moos'lim Dynasties in Egypt.

The conquest of Egypt by the Arabs; and the subsequent changes in its government—The Viceroys appointed by the Khalee'fehs—The Dynasty of the Ben'ee Too'loo'n—The Ikhsheedee'yeh—The Fawa'tim, or Khalee'fehs of the race of Fa't'meh—The Eiyoobee'yeh—The Bahh'ree Memloo'k Soolta'ns—The Boor'gee Memloo'k Soolta'ns—The conquest of Egypt by the Turkish Soolta'n Selee'm; and its government by Turkish Ba'shas and Memloo'k Beys—Its conquest by the French; and restoration to the Turks.

In the 20th year of the flight (A.D. 640-41) Egypt was conquered by the Arabs; and since that period it has continued to be subject to Moos'lim rulers. It has been governed by Arab Viceroys, and by Turkish independent Princes; by Arab Khalee'fehs; by a dynasty of Koords; by Turkish and by Cherkassian Soolta'ns, who, in their youth, were Memloo'ks (or slaves): it has been annexed to the great Turkish Empire, and governed by Turkish Ba'shas, in conjunction with Memloo'ks; has become a prey to the Memloo'ks alone; been conquered by the French; wrested from them by the English, and restored to the Turks: it has been a scene of sanguinary contention between the Turks and Memloo'ks; and is now, again, solely under a Turkish ruler. Of these various revolutions I shall give a short account.

During the space of nearly two centuries and a half, the authority of the Khalee'fehs was maintained in Egypt by Viceroys whom they appointed, and who were frequently changed. The first of these Viceroys was 'Amr Ibn El-'A'see, the conqueror of the country. The history of their times, transmitted to us by Arab writers, contain, as far as they relate to Egypt, little that is worthy of mention. On the occasion of the overthrow of the dynasty of the Oommawee'yeh (or Khalee'fehs of the race of Oomei'yeh) the seat of whose empire was Damascus, there ensued no change in the form of government to which Egypt had been subject; but the town of El-'As'kar was then founded, and became the residence of the successive Viceroys appointed by the new dynasty of the 'Ab'ba'see'yeh (or Khalee'fehs descended from El-'Ab'ba's, an uncle of the Prophet) who changed the seat of the Arabian Empire to Bughda'd.

At the close of the period above-mentioned, the empire of the Khalee'fehs of Bughda'd had begun to decline: those princes had no longer sufficient power to overawe their lieutenants in distant provinces. The Viceroy of the greater part of Northern Africa had already set the example of rebellion against the successor of the Prophet, and had secured his independence; and now, at the close of the year of the flight

269 (A.D. 883), the Governor of Egypt, actuated by motives of self-defence, rather than ambition, threw off his allegiance to his sovereign, the Khalee'feh El-Mo'atum'id, and rendered himself absolute master not only of Egypt but also of Syria, after having governed the former country as Viceroy during the space of fifteen years. This prince was *Ahh'mad Ibn Too'loo'n* (commonly called Ibn Teyloo'n), the founder of the noble city of El-Ckata'-e' (which he made the seat of his government), and of the grand mosque which is called by his name, and which remains a proud monument of his reign. He was the son of a Turkish slave, who had been promoted to a high office in the court of Bughda'd. Though he became the independent sovereign of Egypt, the Khalee'feh continued to be acknowledged, in that country, as the head of the religion; and, as such, was still named in the public Friday-prayers in the mosques. Four independent princes of the same family succeeded Ibn Too'loo'n; and thus, during rather more than twenty-two years, the Khalee'fehs of Bughda'd remained deprived of one of the finest provinces of their wide empire. The dynasty of the *Ben'ee Too'loo'n* was overthrown in the year of the flight 292 (A.D. 905) by Mohham'mad Ibn Sooleyma'n, who, at the head of a numerous army, set fire to El-Ckata'e', plundered El-Foosta't, and reestablished the supreme authority of the Khalee'fehs in Egypt.

At the expiration of about thirty years after that period, the great Arabian Empire began to be dismembered on every side. In the year 323 (A.D. 935) a Ta'ta'r, or Turk, named *Mohham'mad El-Ikhshee'd* (or El-Akhshee'd), acceded, for the second time, to the government of Egypt, and soon after acquired the sole dominion of that country and of Syria. The latter was wrested from him; but it again became subject to his authority. This prince was the founder of the dynasty of the *Ikhsheedee'yeh* (or Akhsheedee'yeh); the second and third of whom were his sons: the fourth was a black eunuch, surnamed Ka'foo'r, whom he had purchased and emancipated. On the death of this eunuch, a dispute arose respecting the succession; and though a grandson of the founder of the dynasty was proclaimed, and acknowledged by many, still the general voice seemed to be against him. This was in the year of the flight 358 (A.D. 968-9).

Of this crisis, advantage was taken by El-Mo'ez'z, the fourth of the *Fawa'tim* (or Khalee'fehs of the race of Fa't'meh), who ruled over the greater part of Northern Africa. The Fawa'tim had succeeded the dynasty of the Ben'ee-l-Agh'lab, founded by Ibrahee'm Ibn El-Agh'lab, who, having been appointed Governor of Africa Proper by the Khalee'feh Ha'roo'n Er-Reshee'd, rendered himself an absolute prince. Immediately upon hearing of the distracted state of affairs in Egypt, El-Mo'ez'z sent thither a numerous army, and secured to himself, without the least opposition, the possession of that country. The city of El-Cka'hireh (the modern Musr), which his general Go'har founded, became the residence of El-Mo'ez'z and his successors. The title of "Khalee'feh," as applied to a Moos'lim sovereign, signifies the legitimate successor of the Prophet, and, consequently, the head of the Mohhammadan religion: the Fawa'tim, therefore, by assuming that title, excluded the princes of the race of El-'Ab'ba's from the honour of being prayed for in the mosques of Egypt; considering that as their own pre-rogative. The period of their sway was most eventful. To the horrid impi-ety and tyranny of El-Hha'kim,—the seven years' famine in the reign of El-Moostun'sir,[1]—and the burning of El-Foosta't, under El-'A'did, the last of the Fawa'tim, I have before had occasion to allude. This dynasty, which consisted of eleven Khalee'fehs (besides the three predecessors of El-Mo'ez'z), lasted until the year of the flight 567 (A.D. 1171).

The Fawa'tim were succeeded by the *Eiyoo'bee'yeh*, or Soolta'ns of the race of Eiyoo'b; who were a Koord family. The first of these was the renowned Sala'hh ed-Deen (the Saladin of European historians). He had been sent by Noo'r-ed-Deen, Soolta'n of Syria, with an army commanded by his uncle Sheerkoo'h, to assist El-'A'did, the last of the Fawa'tim, against the Crusaders, who had taken the town of Bilbey's, and laid siege to El-Cka'hireh; El-Foosta't having been burned (as before mentioned) to prevent its falling into their hands: the invaders, however, accepted a sum of money to raise the siege, and evacuated the country before the arrival of the troops which Sheerkoo'h and Sala'hh ed-Deen accompanied. These two chiefs were most honourably received by El-'A'did, who, soon after their arrival, appointed the former of them his Wezee'r: but Sheerkoo'h died only two months and five days after his promotion; and the office which he had enjoyed during that short period was conferred upon Sala'hh ed-Deen, who requited his benefactor with ingratitude. In the year above-mentioned (567), while El-'A'did was suffering from a fatal illness, Sala'hh ed-Deen, urged by his former sovereign (the Soolta'n of Syria), ordered that the Khalee'feh of Bughda'd should be prayed for in the mosques of El-Cka'hireh, to the exclusion of El-'A'did, who died that year, ignorant of this act of his Wezee'r. Immediately after his death, Sala'hh ed-Deen caused himself to be proclaimed Soolta'n of Egypt. The title of Khalee'feh he did not presume to take; not being descended from any branch of the family of the Prophet: he therefore continued to acknowledge the Khalee'feh of Bughda'd as the head of the religion. To secure his independence, he had to contend with many difficulties; but his energetic mind, and personal bravery, aided by the possession of vast treasures amassed by the Fawa'tim, enabled him to overcome every obstacle. Soon after his assumption of royalty, he had to quell an insurrection raised by the adherents of the family of Fa't'meh. The Soolta'n of Syria, while meditating the invasion of Egypt, died in that same year; and Sala'hh ed-Deen subsequently added Syria to his former dominions; whence resulted his frequent conflicts with the Crusaders, which spread his fame over Europe. The apprehension of insurrections or invasions induced him to build the Citadel and third wall of El-Cka'hireh; but the wars in

---

[1]A wise and prudent prince, who reigned sixty years.

which he afterwards engaged were those of conquest rather than defence. There were eight princes of his dynasty, which lasted 81 years and a few days: several of them rendered themselves memorable by their exploits against the Crusaders. Syria was under princes of the same family, descendants of Sala'hh ed-Deen.

To the dynasty of the Eiyoobee'yeh, succeeded that of the *Turkish* or *Toorkama'n Memloo'k Soolta'ns*, also called *El-Memalee'k El-Bahhree'yeh*, or the *Bahh'ree Memloo'ks*.[1] Nearly a thousand of this class of memloo[']ks had been purchased by El-Melik Es-Sa'lehh Negm-ed-Deen, the last but one of the Soolta'ns of the race of Eiyoo'b: they resided in his palace on the island of Er-Ro'dah; and hence they received the appellation of "the Bahh'ree Memloo'ks"[2]; the word "Bahh'ree," in this case, signifying "of the river." After having been instructed in military exercises, these slaves constituted a formidable body, whose power soon became uncontrollable. A very beautiful female slave, called Sheg'er ed-Doorr (or the tree of pearls), of the same race as these Memloo'ks, was the favourite wife of Negm-ed-Deen. This prince died at El-Munsoo'rah; whither he had gone to protect his kingdom from the Crusaders, who, under Louis IX, had taken Dimya't. Too'ra'n Sha'h succeeded his father Negm-ed-Deen on the throne of Egypt[3]; but reigned only seventy days: he was put to death by the Memloo'ks; to whom he had rendered himself obnoxious; as he had also to Sheg'er ed-Doorr, who was an instigator of his death. Under this Soolta'n, the French invaders of Egypt suffered a signal defeat, and Louis himself was taken prisoner. Sheg'er ed-Doorr caused herself to be proclaimed queen of Egypt, with the concurrence, and through the influence, of the Memloo'ks; and thus commenced, with a female, the dynasty of the Bahhree'yeh, in the year of the flight 648 (A.D. 1250): but this queen was soon obliged to abdicate; and one of the Bahh'ree Memloo'ks, 'Ezz-ed-Deen Ey'bek Et-Toorkama'nee, was raised to the throne, with the surname of El-Mel'ik el-Mo'ez'z. Sheg'er ed-Doorr became his wife; but being slighted by him on account of her age, she caused him to be put to death after he had reigned nearly seven years. His successor, who was his son by another wife, delivered this infamous woman, Sheg'er ed-Doorr, into the hands of his mother, who, together with her female slaves, beat her to death with their wooden clogs, or pattens: her body was stripped naked, and thrown outside the walls of the Citadel, whence, after some days, it was taken, and buried in a tomb which had been constructed for her by her own order.—Syria, as well as Egypt, was under the government of the Soolta'ns of this dynasty: it was several times wrested

---

[1] The term "memloo'k" is generally restricted to a white slave; particularly a military slave.

[2] El-Muckree'zee.

[3] D'Herbelot and some other European writers have fallen into an error in saying that Sheg'er ed-Doorr was the mother of Too'ra'n Sha'h. She bore, to Negm-ed-Deen one son, who died in infancy.

from them; but promptly regained. The dynasty of the Bahhree'yeh consisted of the queen above-mentioned and twenty-four Soolta'ns; and lasted, according to El-Muckree'zee, 136 years, 7 months, and 9 days. Several of these Memloo'k Soolta'ns (as El-Mel'ik Ez-Za'hir Beybur's, Ckala-oo'n, Mohham'mad Ibn Ckala-oo'n, and some others) are celebrated for their conquests, and for the noble mosques and other public edifices which they founded. Few of them died a natural death: many of them were deposed, and banished, or imprisoned; and a still greater number were victims of assassination. It is remarkable that the first of their dynasty was a woman, and the last, a boy, only six years of age.

The Bahh'ree Soolta'ns increased the number of Memloo'ks in Egypt by the purchase of Cherkassian slaves, who, in process of time, acquired the ascendancy. During the short reign of the child El-Mel'ik Es-Sa'lehh Hha'ggee, the last of the Bahhree'yeh, a chief of the Cherkassian Memloo'ks, named Burckoo'ck, was regent. In the year of the flight 784 (A.D. 1382), the latter usurped the throne; and with him commenced the dynasty of *Cherkassian Memloo'ks*, also called *El-Memalee'k El-Boorgee'yeh*, or the *Boor'gee Memloo'ks*; which name was given to them because the Soolta'n Ckala-oo'n had purchased a considerable number of this tribe of slaves (three thousand, seven hundred) and placed them, as garrisons, in the towers of the Citadel[1]: the word "boorg" signifying "a tower."—Syria continued subject to the Boor'gee Soolta'ns. This dynasty consisted of twenty-three Soolta'ns; and continued 138 years and a half. Ez-Za'hir Burckoo'ck, El-Moo-ei'yed, Cha'id Bey, and El-Ghoo'ree may be mentioned as the most renowned of these princes: their splendid mosques and mausolea, as well as their military exploits, or private virtues, have kept up the remembrance of their names. Many of the Soolta'ns of this dynasty were deposed; and several voluntarily abdicated; but nearly all of them died a natural death.

The conquest of Egypt by the Turks, under the Soolta'n Selee'm, in the year of the flight 923 (A.D. 1517), put an end to the dynasty of the Boorgee Memloo'k Soolta'ns. El-Ghoo'ree, the last but one of those princes, was defeated in a dreadful engagement with the army of Selee'm, near Aleppo, and was rode over by his own troops. His successor, Too'ma'n Bey, offered an ineffectual opposition to the invading army of Turks, in the neighbourhood of his capital: he was hanged (or, according to some authors, crucified) at the Ba'b Zoowey'leh, one of the gates of Musr (or Cairo).—A different form of government, in which the Memloo'ks were allowed to share, was now established. Egypt was divided into four and twenty provinces; each of which was placed under the military jurisdiction of a Memloo'k Bey; and the twenty-four Beys were subject to the authority of a Turkish Ba'sha, or Pa'sha', a general governor, appointed by the Soolta'n. Other members of the new administration were seven Turkish chiefs, the generals of seven military corps, called, in Turkish, O'ja'cklees, and by the Egyptians, O'ga'cklees,

---

[1] El-Muckree'zee.

or Wooga'cklees: these composed the Ba'sha's council. One of the Beys was styled Sheykh el-Bel'ed, or Governor of the Metropolis; and this chief enjoyed a higher rank than any of the other Beys; among whom, consequently, there were seldom wanting some whose ambition rendered them his secret or avowed enemies. By means of intrigue, or by the sword, or the poisoned cup, the office of Sheykh el-Bel'ed was generally obtained. The Memloo'ks who thus shared, with the Turkish Ba'shas, the government of Egypt were commonly called, collectively, El-Ghooz'z, الغز; that being the proper name of the tribe to which most of them belonged.[1] They disdained marrying Egyptian women; preferring females of their own or other more northern countries: but few of them had children; for most of the foreign females in Egypt are sterile; or have weak, sickly children, who die in early age. Such being the case, the Memloo'ks were obliged continually to recruit their members with newly purchased slaves from the same countries. Most of them, when first brought to Egypt, were mere boys, unable to wield the sabre: purchased by a Bey or other great officer, they served, for a while, as pages: those who were handsome were sure to be great favourites of their master; and every favourite who (after having been instructed in military exercises) displayed remarkable courage, fidelity and other good qualities, was emancipated, and promoted to some high office: perhaps he became a Ka'shif, and soon after, a Bey. Thus it often happened that several Beys owed their advancement to one and the same patron; to whose interests they generally remained devotedly attached. Each Bey was constantly intent upon multiplying his Memloo'ks; and frequent arbitrary exactions from the peasants of the province under his command were the base means which enabled him to accomplish this object.— During nearly two centuries after the conquest of Egypt by the Soolta'n Selee'm, the authority of each successive Ba'sha was, with few exceptions, respected by the Beys; but the latter, by degrees, obtained the ascendancy; and after the period above-mentioned, few of the Ba'shas possessed any influence over the Sheykh el-Bel'ed and the other Beys. Egypt thus became subject to a military oligarchy; and the condition of its inhabitants was rendered yet more miserable by frequent sanguinary conflicts between different parties by the Ghooz'z. Such was the state of that country when it was invaded by the French; of whose government, in general, the people of Musr speak in terms of commendation; though they execrate them for particular acts of oppression. After the expulsion of the French, Egypt remained in a very disturbed state, in consequence of the contentions between the Beys and the Turkish Ba'shas, until the power of the former was completely annihilated by Mohham'mad 'Al'ee, the present ruler.

---

[1]The Egyptians, in speaking of the times of the Memloo'ks who governed Egypt after its conquest by the Turks, say "in the days of the Ghooz'z such an event happened":—"in the days of the Ghooz'z we were less oppressed than at present."

Chapter XIV.

History of Mohham'mad 'Al'ee, and of the remarkable events which have taken place in Egypt since its evacuation by the French, in the year 1801.[1]

Introduction. Birth and early life of Mohham'mad 'Al'ee, and commencement of his military career in Egypt.

Mohham'mad 'Al'ee was born in the year of the flight 1182 (A.D. 1768-9), at Cavalla, a small sea-port town, situated in that part of European Turkey which was the ancient province of Macedonia. In early life, he lost his father, Ibrahee'm A'gha, who was a chief of patrol, after which event, he was brought up in the house of the governor of his native town. He first distinguished himself by undertaking, with a few armed men, to quell an insurrection in a neighbouring village; in which

---

[1]The greater part of this history I have composed from the valuable work of the sheykh 'Abd Er-Rahhma'n El-Gebur'tee, already mentioned in the first chapter of this volume.[†] Very few copies of that work are in existence. From one of these belonging to John G. Wilkinson Esqre., a copy was transcribed for James Burton Esqre., who, with the consent of Mr. Wilkinson, very obligingly caused another to be written at Musr for myself. I am proud to express my gratitude to these my highly respected friends.—El-Gebur'tee's narrative of the events which took place in Egypt from the period of the departure of the French army until the accession of Mohham'mad 'Al'ee agrees most remarkably with that of M. Mengin, in his excellent work entitled "Histoire de l'Egypte sous le gouvernement de Mohammed-Aly." Each of these writers seems to have kept a very faithful journal; but El-Gebur'tee has more particular claims upon our credit, as he was intimate with the Sheykhs of Musr, was often present at the councils of the 'Ool'ama, and had every opportunity of acquiring authentic information.—The notices contained in the introductory paragraph of this chapter, respecting the early life of Mohham'mad 'Al'ee, his joining the Turkish army in Egypt, and his elevation to the rank of beem-ba'shee are derived from Mengin's work. The reader is to understand that, for every thing related in this chapter, El-Gebur'tee is my authority, excepting when it is otherwise stated.

[†Lane refers to a volume organization and an earlier reference that were not retained. He was even tentative about the inclusion of this chapter in the final draft. In a pencilled note at the end of the previous chapter he wrote that next would come a "sketch" of the history of Muhammad Ali followed by the "Description of the Pyramids." He added, "the History of Mohham'mad 'Al'ee to be abridged if inserted as above proposed, or to be added in full as a Supplement to the 1st Vol." The chapter is, however, reproduced in full here.]

enterprise, he was successful; and for this service, his patron, the governor, conferred upon him the rank of *booloo'k-ba'shee*, or chief of forty soldiers, and gave him, in marriage, a widow of his own family, by whom, it is said, Mohham'mad 'Al'ee had three sons, Ibrahee'm, Too'soo'n and I'sma-ee'l: but it is generally asserted that Ibrahee'm was that lady's son by a former husband.[1] He then, without resigning his military rank, became a trader in tobacco; continuing to reside in his native place, until the 33rd year of his age. The Porte was at that time preparing to dispatch an expedition against the French in Egypt; and the governor of Cavalla was required to furnish his contingent, consisting of 300 men, who were placed under the command of his son 'Al'ee A'gha. Mohham'mad 'Al'ee was ordered to accompany them, and soon after their arrival in Egypt, he was raised to the command of the troop of 'Al'ee A'gha, who returned to his father. This appointment gave him the nominal rank of *beem-ba'shee*, or chief of a thousand men; and placed him in a situation to display his intrepidity and military skill, which soon attracted the notice of his superiors.

The personal appearance of this extraordinary man but little corresponds with his character. He is rather short, somewhat corpulent, and has an animated countenance, expressive of benignity rather than severity. His beard is now grey. The Turkish and Albanian languages he naturally speaks with fluency; but of Arabic, the language of Egypt, he knows very little. In his later years, he has learned to read and write.

Section 1. Hostile intentions of the Turkish government towards the Ghoozz, or Memloo'ks, manifested by an attempt of the Turkish Admiral to ensnare the principal Beys—*Mohham'mad Ba'sha Khoos'roof*—His operations against the Beys; and the defeat of his forces—Departure of the British army from Egypt, accompanied by El-El'fee—Rebellion of the Arnaoo't troops against Mohham'mad Khoos'roof, who saves himself by flight—*Ta'hir Ba'sha* succeeds him, and is assassinated—*Ahh'mad Ba'sha* is proclaimed Governor; but on the following day, deposed by the Arnaoo'ts.

Soon after the evacuation of Egypt by the French, that ill-fated country became a scene of more severe troubles, in consequence of the attempts of the Turks to subvert the power of the Ghooz'z, or Memloo'ks. The Porte had professed an intention to reinstate the Beys in the authority and dignities which had been accorded to them by former Turkish Soolta'ns; and England, confiding in her ally, had guaranteed the fulfilment of the promise: but Hhosey'n Bey, the Turkish Grand Admiral, who was then in Egypt, received orders from his government

---

[1]Mohham'mad 'Al'ee always calls Ibrahee'm his *son*.

to ensnare the principal Beys, and to send them to Constantinople. To accomplish this, he invited several of those chiefs to an entertainment on board his ship, in the Bay of Ab'oo Ckeer. They accepted the invitation, repaired to the vessel, and all of them, having gone on board, waited upon the deck, expecting their host to come up and receive them; but, to their surprise, they were informed by an officer, that the Admiral was on shore; that he had received orders to convey them to Constantinople, and that they must instantly give up their arms. On hearing this message, Mohham'mad Bey El-Menfoo'kh immediately drew his sword, and killed the captain of the ship. The other betrayed chiefs and their attendants followed his example; and the conflict which ensued was desperate and sanguinary. 'Osma'n Bey Et-Tamboor'gee, 'Osma'n Bey El-Ash'ckar, Mohham'mad Bey El-Hhas'anee, Moora'd Bey the Younger, and Ibrahee'm Kikh'ya Es-Senna'ree (a black) were among the chiefs who were killed. Of the rest, some were made prisoners, and others[1] escaped in a boat, and sought refuge at Alexandria; that city being still occupied by the English, who, on being informed of the perfidious conduct of Hhosey'n Ba'sha, immediately expelled all the Turkish troops who were quartered there, and shut the gates: but the Turkish Admiral, fearing their resentment, begged for a conference, gave up to them the killed, wounded, and captive Memloo'ks, and thus pacified our countrymen, who buried the slain chiefs with the honours due to their respective ranks.[2]

Mohham'mad Ba'sha Khoos'roof was the first of the Ba'shas of Egypt after the expulsion of the French. He entered the metropolis, as governor, on the 17th of Rumada'n, 1216 (January, 1802). But Egypt was not to be subjected to the same form of government as before the French invasion. The Ghoozz were not reinstated. Four of the most influential of their chiefs were summoned to Constantinople, in order that the Soolta'n might confer with them and "bestow his favours upon them"; but they were not unwise enough to obey the summons. They were then in Upper Egypt, subsisting by pillage. The Ba'sha sought to disunite their forces; inviting all but the four chiefs above alluded to (whose followers would of course remain with them) to repair to the metropolis, and there await the further orders of the Soolta'n. He next proposed to cede to them the province of Is'na, and the county southwards. Both of these proposals being rejected, he resolved on endeavouring to subdue them by force of arms. In the month of Reg'eb, 1217 (November 1802) the Ghoozz had descended to Lower Egypt, and were encamped in the neighbourhood of Demenhoo'r. Thither a considerable Turkish force was dispatched against them. Some English troops, then at Demenhoo'r, endeavoured to dissuade El-El'fee (one of the most powerful of the Beys)

---

[1] Among these was 'Osma'n Bey El-Burdee'see, who afterwards became the most powerful chief of the Ghoozz.
[2] Such is El-Gebur'tee's account of this tragical affair. It is related by Sir R. Wilson and M. Mengin somewhat differently.

from engaging the enemy advancing against him and his allies.—"What is this that you are doing?" said they, on seeing the Memloo'ks preparing for battle.—"We will charge them and combat them," replied the Bey.— "But," rejoined the English, "the enemy approaching you is 14,000 strong; and you are but few."—"Victory is in the hand of God!" exclaimed the courageous Memloo'ks; and immediately they galloped on, charged impetuously upon the enemy, threw them into the utmost disorder, and, in a few minutes, were masters of the field.[1] How many they killed is not recorded: but they took, besides the ammunition and artillery of the Turks, about 700 prisoners, whom they drove before them like a flock of sheep.[2]

In the month of Zoo-l-Cka'adeh (March, 1803) the British troops evacuated Alexandria. Mohham'mad Bey El-El'fee, the chief above-mentioned, accompanied them to England, with fifteen of his Memloo'ks, to consult with the British cabinet respecting the means to be adopted for reinstating himself and the other Beys[3] in their former authority.

About six weeks after (in the beginning of the year 1218) the Arnaoo't soldiers in the service of the Ba'sha importunately demanded of him their pay. He referred them to the Defturda'r, and the Defturda'r sent them to Mohham'mad 'Al'ee, who informed them that he had received nothing, and therefore could not satisfy their demands. This answer appeased them in some measure; but on the seventh succeeding day, their rebellious disposition was manifested in a more alarming manner. A considerable number of the discontented troops surrounded the house of the Defturda'r, and again urged their claims. This officer, after vainly endeavouring to persuade them to accept a portion of the sum that was due to them and to wait a few days for the remainder, despatched a letter to the Ba'sha, earnestly begging him to comply with the demands of the troops. The Ba'sha returned for answer that he would neither pay them, nor authorize others to do so; and that, if they did not quit Egypt immediately, they should all be put to death.—"Go again," said the Defturda'r to his messenger; "and tell him that the house is filled with soldiers, both the upper and lower apartments, and I am beset in the midst of them."—This information served only to increase the anger and obstinacy of the Ba'sha: thinking to terrify the riotous soldiers by a few discharges of the artillery of his palace, he gave orders instantly to cannonade the house of the Defturda'r, who received no intimation of

---

[1]Mengin says (in vol. 1, p. 23) that El-El'fee withdrew his force; leaving El-Bardee'see, with 800 men, to meet the enemy.

[2]Mengin relates that Yoo'soof Bey, the commander of the Turks, on this occasion, attributed his defeat to his not having been joined by Mohham'mad 'Al'ee and the forces under his command; and that the latter chief thereby incurred the displeasure of the Ba'sha.

[3]By the term "Beys," I mean the chiefs of the Memloo'ks; who, when their number was complete, amounted to twenty-four.

this, until a cannon-ball entered the apartment in which he was sitting, and fell close before him.[1] Musr has often been the theatre of similar disturbances; and the citizens did on this, as on previous occasions of the same kind: they shut their shops, as well as the doors of the by-streets and quarters; and every one who had a sword or other weapon, armed himself; some for their own defence, and others to assist their Ba'sha. The tumult, which commenced on Friday, the 7th of Mohhar'ram, about the time of the general assembling to prayer (that is, at noon), continued with unabated rage during the remainder of that day; but throughout the ensuing night, the firing was discontinued. On the following morning, the Ba'sha sent forth a body of his regular troops (white and black slaves and free negroes, whom he had caused to be disciplined by French instructors) to attempt to reduce the mutinous Arnaoo'ts, who, notwithstanding, succeeded in carrying off the Defturda'r, together with his books and papers (after having pillaged his house, which was then in flames) and conveying him to their chief, Ta'hir Ba'sha. The hharee'm of Mohham'mad Khoos'roof, who were residing in a house adjoining that of the Defturda'r, were rescued, and brought to the palace of their lord. Ta'hir Ba'sha next repaired, with a company of his Arnaoo'ts, to the Citadel; but on arriving at the great gate, he found it shut. Some of his soldiers, however, entered by an embrasure near the ground, and having ascended to the summit, demanded of the treasurer, who had been left in command, the keys of the gate. Having obtained them, they opened to their commander and the rest of his troops. As soon as he had thus gained possession of the Citadel, Ta'hir employed its artillery to cannonade the palace of the Ba'sha. He then descended to the Ezbekee'yeh; taking with him several guns and mortars and ammunition, with which to besiege the palace more closely. The Ba'sha, during the next night, had nothing but biscuit for his supper; and his horses were fed with rice. On the following day (which was Sunday) his palace was set on fire by a shell; and in the afternoon, he fled, with his hharee'm (consisting of seventeen women), his slaves and servants, certain of his principal officers, and his regular troops, who remained faithful to him. With these he embarked at Boo'la'ck, and descended the Nile to El-Munsoo'rah, and thence to Dimya't. The duration of his government was one year, three months and twenty-one days.

Ta'hir Ba'sha now caused himself to be proclaimed Governor of Egypt; but being unwise enough to follow the same line of conduct which had been the ruin of his predecessor, he experienced a more severe fate, after a tyrannical sway of only twenty-three days.—About 250 of the 'Osma'nlee (or Turkish) troops, with their two A'ghas, Isma'ee'l and Moo'sa, repaired to the palace of Ta'hir on the 4th of Suf'ar, to demand

---

[1]The house of the Defturda'r was situated on the *south*, and the palace of the Ba'sha on the *west* of the Ezbekee'yeh; only a quarter of a mile apart, and no building intervening. The house of the *present* Defturda'r occupies the site of the latter.

their pay; but meeting with a positive refusal, one of them rushed upon the Ba'sha, cut off his head, and threw it out of the window by which he was sitting, into the court. A desperate conflict immediately ensued between the Arnaoo'ts there present and the 'Osma'nlees; and after the shedding of much blood, the palace was set on fire and plundered. The most fierce animosity continued to prevail between those two parties. Of the former, Mohham'mad 'Al'ee now became the leading person. His faction, however, was weak: he therefore entered into an alliance with Ibrahee'm Bey and 'Osma'n Bey El-Bardee'see, the famous Memloo'k chiefs.

A certain *Ahh'mad Ba'sha*, who was then in Musr, and about to proceed to a province, of which he had been appointed governor, in Arabia, was raised to the more important post of Governor of Egypt, through the influence of the 'Osma'nlees and the favour of the Sheykhs; the latter of whom wrote to Mohham'mad 'Al'ee, begging him to sanction their choice: but this chief replied that Ahh'mad Ba'sha was unfit for the high office to which he had been raised, and that he must immediately depart from the city, with his troops. Mohham'mad 'Al'ee and his Arnaoo'ts were in possession of the Citadel: Ahh'mad Ba'sha residing in a palace in the quarter called Ed-Daoodee'yeh. On the following day (the day after the assassination of Ta'hir) the main force of the Ghoozz crossed over from El-Gee'zeh, where they were encamped, and came to the metropolis. Ahh'mad Ba'sha already saw his cause to be hopeless: in the afternoon, he abandoned his palace to be plundered by the Arnaoo'ts, and proceeding with his partisans through the city, went out by the Ba'b el-Footoo'hh, and sought refuge in the great ruined mosque of Ez-Za'hir, which the French, during their occupation of Egypt, had converted into a fortress. There he remained with his adherents, besieged by the Arnaoo'ts, during the whole of the night and half the following day; and being without provisions, was then obliged to surrender. He was taken to the Ckusr El-'Ey'nee; and the two A'ghas Isma'ee'l and Moo'sa, who were with him, were conveyed to Ibrahee'm Bey, and confined in the palace of El-Gee'zeh, two days; after which they were brought back to the metropolis, and there beheaded, to avenge the murder of Ta'hir Ba'sha; to whose widow, their heads were first taken, in pompous procession, and next, to his nephew,[1] in the Citadel.

Section 2. The Ghoozz again become masters of Egypt, in conjunction with the Arnaoots under Mohham'mad 'Al'ee—Their successful expedition against Mohham'mad Khoos'roof, who is taken prisoner, after the defeat of his forces at Dimya't—*'Al'ee Ba'sha* appointed Governor of Egypt by the Porte; but opposed by the Beys—Calamitous state of Egypt; particularly of the metropolis—'Al'ee Ba'sha proceeds towards the metropolis, with his troops, whom the Ghoozz and Arnaoo'ts

---

[1]Hasan Pasha, to whom reference is made further on.

compel to retire to Syria—'Al'ee Ba'sha, also, is conducted, under an escort, towards the Syrian frontier, and killed on the way—El-El'fee returns from England—Proceeding to join his partisans, he is opposed by the majority of the Ghoozz and by the Arnaoo'ts, and flies for refuge to a tribe of Arabs—The Arnaoo'ts rise against the Ghoozz, and expel them from the metropolis—Mohham'mad Khoos'roof again proclaimed Governor of Egypt, and again deposed—El-El'fee comes forth from his concealment and joins his partisans.

On the 15th of the same month in which happened the events related in the close of the last letter, the Arnaoo'ts descended from the Citadel, and put the Ghoozz in possession of it. Thus the latter became once more, virtually, masters of Egypt, in conjunction with the Arnaoo'ts under Mohham'mad 'Al'ee.—On the following day, information was received in Musr of the Wah'ha'bees' having entered Mek'keh (on the 10th of the preceding month); and on the 22nd, the Sheree'f of the holy city arrived, with about sixty persons, his family and officers.

An expedition was soon after sent, under the command of Mohham'mad 'Al'ee and El-Bardee'see, to Dimya't, against Mohham'mad Khoos'roof, the deposed governor, who, having been joined by considerable numbers of the 'Osma'nlee troops, and favoured by the strength of his position, was enabled to make a vigorous defence; but, after much bloodshed on both sides, he was taken prisoner, and brought to the capital, where he remained in confinement, but was treated with much respect. The victorious soldiery plundered the shops, weka'lehs and kha'ns of Dimya't, and even entered the private houses of the inhabitants, and carried off a vast number of young women, married and unmarried; as was their usual practise on such occasions. The messenger who brought the news of the victory and of the capture of Mohham'mad Khoos'roof to Ibrahee'm Bey was rewarded, by that chief, with a handsome dress, and with the lands, house and *wife* of a great officer whom he had killed. I mention this merely as illustrative of Turkish and Memloo'k manners.

A few days after this, the Ghoozz received information that *'Al'ee Ba'sha Et-Tar'a'bool'oosee*[1] had landed at Alexandria, bearing a furma'n which constituted him Governor of Egypt. This 'Al'ee Ba'sha was, originally, a memloo'k of a Governor of El-Jeza'ir (which the Egyptians call El-Geza'ir, and we, Algiers), and afterwards Ba'sha of Tara'booloos el-Ghurb, or Western Tripoli. He besieged, took, and plundered the latter city, of which he had been appointed governor through the influence of the Turkish Grand Admiral, Hhosey'n Ba'sha: but the former governor soon after retook the city; and 'Al'ee fled to Egypt, where he was received by Moora'd Bey. He next performed the

---

[1]Whom Mengin calls "Gezaïrly."

pilgrimage. At Mek'keh, he was recognised with two handsome Tripolitan boys, who were his constant companions, by some pilgrims from Tripoli, who cut off his beard, which was particularly handsome, and would have put him to death, had not the Emee'r el-Hha'gg (or Chief of the Pilgrims) interfered in his favour. They did, in fact, draw their swords, and wounded him. Returning to Egypt, he remained above six years in the service of Moora'd Bey, until the invasion of Egypt by the French: he then deserted, and retired to Syria: but he again visited Egypt, and was sent by the Vezee'r with despatches to Constantinople. There he obtained his nomination to the government of Egypt.

The Beys, being anxious to maintain the ascendancy which they had acquired,—for Upper Egypt, as well as the capital, and nearly the whole of Lower Egypt had become subject to them—determined to offer the utmost opposition to the approach of the newly appointed governor. The combined forces of Mohham'mad 'Al'ee and El-Bardee'see marched, therefore, against Reshee'd, which had been taken by the seyd 'Al'ee, the brother of 'Al'ee Ba'sha. They besieged and recovered that town; and the seyd 'Al'ee retired to the fort (named by the French "Fort Julien") between Reshee'd and the sea; but he was compelled to surrender, and was taken prisoner to the capital, where he was received with much honour. El-Bardee'see purposed next to besiege Alexandria; but various circumstances deterred him: the troops under his command had manifested much discontent at not having received their regular pay; and he had not then the means to satisfy their demands: besides which, 'Al'ee Ba'sha had cut the dyke that separated the lakes of Ab'oo Ckeer and Mareotis, in order to render the approach to Alexandria more difficult. El Bardee'see, therefore, and Mohham'mad 'Al'ee, returned with their troops to the metropolis.

The troubles of Egypt were aggravated that year by an insufficient inundation; provisions, consequently, becoming very dear. The granaries at Boo'la'ck were thrown open to supply the markets; and a small quantity of corn (nearly a bushel) was granted to each poor person. In order to satisfy the troops, the chiefs and subordinate officers contributed each a certain sum, according to their respective ranks; and then, to requite themselves, they exacted heavy contributions from the citizens.

At the same time, the troops of 'Al'ee Ba'sha, at Alexandria, conducted themselves in a most outrageous manner towards the Europeans; the principal of whom, with their consuls, consulted their personal safety by taking refuge on board the Turkish vessels then in the harbour: but through the mediation of Khoo'rshee'd Ba'sha, the Turkish Admiral, tranquillity was restored, and the consuls, with the other Europeans, returned to their houses.

Dreadful were the troubles which now prevailed in the metropolis: the inhabitants were not only afflicted with a scarcity of provisions, and oppressed by exorbitant taxation, to which the Beys were obliged to have recourse in order to satisfy the frequent demands of their troops;

but many persons were even robbed in the public streets, at all hours of the day, by the riotous soldiers, who seized the turbans, and stripped off the clothes, of the unarmed citizens, and carried off by force many women: so that the utmost alarm pervaded all classes of the people; obliging the tradesmen to keep their shops shut, and to remain in their houses.

The Sheykhs had written to 'Al'ee Ba'sha, inviting him to repair to the capital without delay, to assume the reins of government, and to put an end to these disorders. While preparing to comply with their request, the Ba'sha received a Khut'ti Sheree'f (or letter with the sign-manual) of the Soolta'n); and on the 1st of Shaaba'n (in the middle of December, 1803) his secretary brought it to the capital. It announced that it was the Soolta'n's pleasure that the Beys should remain peaceably in Egypt, with an annuity of fifteen purses,[1] and certain other privileges, to each; but that the government should be in the hands of the Ba'sha. The Beys, in reply to 'Al'ee Ba'sha, expressed their gratitude to the Soolta'n, and their eagerness to welcome the former at the capital. A grand council of the Ghoozz was forthwith held to elect, from among their most distinguished Ka'shifs and A'ghas, fifteen new Beys, in the places of those who had died or been killed during the late troublesome years; and these having been chosen and invested, the number of twenty-four was complete.

But the approach of 'Al'ee Ba'sha to the capital excited considerable anxiety in the minds of the Beys; for he had been detected in endeavouring, in a correspondence with the Arnaoo'ts, to bring them over to his side against the Ghoozz. His letters were shown to the Beys, and answers calculated to mislead him were returned by their directions. Ensnared by the advice of his supposed friends, he proceeded towards the capital, and encamped at Shalacka'n, accompanied by 2,500 troops. The forces of the Beys, with the Arnaoo'ts, went forth to meet him, and pitched their camp near the same place; which induced him to retreat to Zoofey'teh. The seizure of the boats which conveyed some of 'Al'ee Ba'sha's soldiers and other persons and ammunition and baggage was the first act of hostility. The Ghoozz and the Arnaoo'ts then proceeded towards Zoofey'teh, and sent a messenger to demand of the Ba'sha for what reason he had brought with him so numerous a body of troops; for that, in so doing, he had acted in opposition to long established usage, and had, moreover, been warned against such a proceeding before he left Alexandria. He replied that the soldiers who accompanied him intended to perform the pilgrimage, as soon as he should have arrived at the Citadel and given them their pay. Finding, however, that his opponents were determined not to allow his troops to proceed with him, he would have returned to Alexandria; but this, also, was forbidden: notwithstanding which, he persisted in refusing to advance without

---

[1]Equivalent to 234*l.*7s.6*d.* The piaster was then equal to 7¹/₂ pence, English: therefore the purse, being 500 piasters, was equal to 15*l.*12s.6*d.*

them. The Beys, after having expressed their resolution not to allow his troops to approach nearer to the capital, waited till the next morning, in order to afford the Ba'sha time to deliberate; but he still adhered to his former declaration, and on finding his army surrounded, on the following morning, by the Ghoozz and the Arnaoo'ts, would have hazarded a battle; but his troops being of a different mind, he was at length obliged to repair to the camp of the Beys, and consent to accompany them alone to the capital. His troops were compelled to retire to Syria; and, of their seven chiefs, six, who were found to be persons who had shortly before been banished from Musr, were put to death.

While almost a prisoner in the camp of the Beys, 'Al'ee Ba'sha had recourse again to intrigue and perfidy. During the very first night that he passed there, a horseman suddenly galloped forth from the Ba'sha's tents, and, though pursued as soon as possible, made his escape. The Ba'sha, being interrogated respecting this occurrence, observed that the person whom they had seen flying with such speed was probably a thief who had been disturbed while in the attempt to steal something. On the following night, a number of armed memloo'ks surrounded his tents, and told him that they should remain there, to take care that no more thieves came or went. He had, however, contrived to despatch a messenger on a dromedary, with a seductive letter to 'Osma'n Bey Hhas'an, governor of Ckin'ë, in Upper Egypt. The courier was stopped near El-Bes'a'tee'n, a little to the south of the metropolis, and the letter was taken back to the camp, and delivered to the Beys. This incident afforded the Ghoozz a fair pretext for ridding themselves altogether of 'Al'ee Ba'sha: the letter was therefore shown to him, and after a few words of reproach, he was ordered, without a moment's preparation, to mount a horse that was in readiness by the tent to convey him to the frontiers of Syria. He departed, under a guard of forty-five men; among whom were two Beys; and about a week afterwards, letters were received in Musr, from his attendants, announcing his death. It was said that, having overtaken some of the soldiers who were dismissed before him in the same direction, a skirmish ensued, in which the Ba'sha, by accident, received a mortal wound. Thus Egypt was saved from the yoke of a perfidious tyrant. He had promised to allow his troops, on his arrival at the seat of his government to plunder the city and do as they would with the inhabitants during the space of three days.

The country was now in a state of tranquillity; but only for a few days. On the eve of the 5th of Zoo-l-Cka'adeh (in the middle of February, 1804) the Beys at Musr received the news of the return of Mohham'mad Bey El-El'fee from England, and his arrival at Reshee'd. This event caused an extraordinary commotion among the grandees of Musr; yet the guns of the Citadel and of El-Gee'zeh and Musr 'Atee'ckah and even those of the palace of El-Bardee'see (to whom the news was particularly unwelcome) were fired twice that evening and once on the following morning, in honour of El-El'fee. A degree of jealousy had before subsisted between El-El'fee and El-Bardee'see; and this was greatly heightened now that the latter had raised himself above all the other Beys. El-El'fee the Younger was at El-Gee'zeh, where Sha'hee'n Bey joined him on the following day, for the purpose of proceeding with him to meet and escort El-El'fee the Great. Hhosey'n Bey El-El'fee also crossed over to the western bank, with the same intention; and encamped a little to the north of El-Gee'zeh; but at midnight, he was assassinated by some emissaries of El-Bardee'see; who, in concert with Mohham'mad 'Al'ee and the Arnaoo'ts, had determined to oppose the progress of El-El'fee the Great, and, if possible, to take his life. Mohham'mad 'Al'ee had crossed over that same night to the south of El-Gee'zeh; and towards morning he advanced against that place. El-El'fee the Younger at first resolved to defend his position; but found that the guns had been spiked during the night; and therefore fled. The Arnaoo'ts plundered the palace and the houses of the townspeople, and behaved in the same brutal manner towards the women as they had done at Dimya't.

Meanwhile, El-El'fee the Great had embarked at Reshee'd, and was proceeding towards the capital by the river and the Canal of Menoo'f. After having passed the town of Menoo'f, his crew were obliged to have recourse to the tow-rope, for the wind was contrary; and while El-El'fee and his officers were walking, they met a party of Arnaoo't soldiers, descending the canal, and saluted them; inquiring whither they were bound. They replied that they were seeking El-El'fee.—"He is here," said the Bey's attendants. Upon receiving this intelligence, the Arnaoo'ts made towards the boats of El-El'fee, and took possession of those which contained the baggage, costly goods, presents and merchandise which the Bey had brought from England. El-El'fee immediately sent to demand the reason of this aggression: guessing it, however, too well, he waited not for the return of the messenger, but descended into his own boat, which was at a short distance in advance of the others, with only his Memloo'ks (who were sixteen in number) and another person who had been sent to him, with two boats, containing provisions, by the younger El'fee; and thus he made his escape; his memloo'ks plying the oars with all their energy. They gained the Eastern branch of the Nile, and soon after, saw two boats conveying down the river a number of El-Bardee'see's soldiers; but these, fortunately, passed them at a considerable distance; the river being wide. Arriving before the village of Shoob'ra esh-Shih'a'bee'yeh, they observed a courier on the shore, and hailed him. They found that he was jouneying to Sooleyma'n Ka'shif El-Baouwa'b, who had hospitably received El-El'fee at Menoo'f; and they learned from him some important news.

To proceed higher in the boat was now dangerous: they therefore landed on the eastern bank. They now discovered that numerous detachments were in search of them in the neighbourhood; and one party passed so near to them that they were obliged to lie down in the high grass to avoid being seen. Proceeding thus on foot, they sought refuge among some Arabs, at the village of Ckurn'fee'l, and were received with hospitality by a woman of the tribe. Some troops arrived soon after at the same place, and inquired respecting the fugitives: the Arabs answered that they had passed by them and had continued their flight. El-El'fee and his companions were concealed in a hut, and heard this conversation. The woman, as soon as these soldiers had gone, brought, for the Bey, a swift horse, and two attendants on dromedaries, as guides; and so he departed; his Memloo'ks walking: but they had not proceeded far when they were attacked and surrounded by another party of Arabs. The Bey alone effected his escape, and galloped on towards the mountains; while his Memloo'ks were engaged with the Arabs. El-Bardee'see himself, happening to be near, and hearing the reports of fire-arms, hastened to the spot; and, finding that El-El'fee had escaped, despatched emissaries in various directions, with orders to kill him. Saad Ibrahee'm, the chief of the hostile Arabs, discovered the Bey's track, and nearly overtook him. At this critical moment, El-El'fee, with admirable presence of mind, threw down all the gold and jewels which he carried about him, and his rich pelisse; and the Arab, to secure this valuable booty, was obliged to discontinue the pursuit, while El-El'fee got far ahead, and out of sight. As it was known that the Bey had taken refuge among some tribe of Arabs, a diligent search was maintained for several days; but unattended with success.

The attention of El-Bardee'see was now drawn to events of a different kind, which threatened his speedy overthrow.—The Arnaoo't troops, having returned to the capital, demanded their pay; and in order to satisfy their claims, El-Bardee'see gave orders for the levying of heavy contributions from the citizens. This oppressive measure roused the people to rebellion. So great was the commotion which it excited, that even the Arnaoo't soldiers became alarmed for their own safety, and found it necessary to assure the people that they would not allow this order to be put into execution: their pay, they said, should be derived from the regular taxes, and not from such unjust exactions. Mohham'mad 'Al'ee caused a proclamation to this effect to be made throughout the metropolis; and thus the tumult was appeased: the Arnaoo'ts became the favorites of the people; and the Beys, the objects of their hatred and execrations. Three days afterwards, the Arnaoo'ts assembled in the Ezbekee'yeh, and thence proceeded, in the afternoon, and beset the mansion of Ibrahee'm Bey, in the quarter of Ed-Da-oodee'yeh, and that of El-Bardee'see, in the quarter of En-Na'siree'yeh. In the evening, about sunset, the latter chief sallied forth, with his Memloo'ks, and with several dromedaries loaded with his most valuable property, under a heavy discharge of musketry, and fled towards Musr 'Atee'ckah. Early on the following morning, the Memloo'ks in the Citadel directed a fire of shot and shells towards the Ezbekee'yeh, where the houses of the Arnaoo't chiefs were situated; but on hearing of the flight of El-Bardee'see, they discontinued, and descended from the Citadel by the Ba'b el-Geb'el, the gate leading to the desert and the mountain. They would have taken with them Mohham'mad Khoos'roof and other prisoners (who had been brought thither a day or two before, that they might be in more safe custody); but they were prevented by the Magha'r'beh[1] soldiers. On the south of the town, they joined the aged Ibra'hee'm Bey, who had effected his escape, though with the loss of several of his Memloo'ks, that same morning.

Mohham'mad 'Al'ee, after having garrisoned the Citadel with his Arnaoo'ts, brought down Mohham'mad Khoos'roof, who had been a prisoner just eight months, and caused him to be proclaimed Governor of Egypt. The Arnaoo'ts were now revelling in the plunder of the houses of the Beys and other Memloo'k chiefs, whose wives and female slaves they treated in their usual shameless and brutal manner. Mohham'mad Khoos'roof enjoyed the title of Governor of Egypt this second time only for the space of one day and a half. On the second night after his restoration, he was sent away under a guard towards the sea coast, together with his old friend Ibrahee'm Ba'sha, formerly governor of Dimya't, and since the fellow-prisoner of Khoos'roof. The enmity of the relations of the late Ta'hir Ba'sha and other chiefs of the Arnaoo'ts towards this unfortunate prince was the cause of his second degradation.

El-El'fee, having heard of the misfortunes of El-Bardee'see and the other Beys, deemed it unnecessary to remain any longer in concealment. He had been protected by a tribe of Arabs at Ra's el-Wa'dee. He now left that place, and following a route among the mountains, arrived at Shurek Atfee'hh, about two days' journey south of the capital; on the east of the Nile.

Section 3. Ahh'mad Ba'sha Khoo'rshee'd elected governor of Egypt by the chiefs in Musr—His oppresive exactions—The Beys collect their forces on the south of the metropolis—El-El'fee makes proposals of alliance to the Ba'sha—The majority of the Beys, with their Memloo'ks, pass to the north of the metropolis, and plunder the towns and villages—Distress occasioned by the scarcity and exactions in the metropolis—The Memloo'ks on the north continue their depradations; but are repulsed—El-El'fee retracts his proposal to the Ba'sha, and, with his partisans, approaches the capital on the south—Fresh contributions raised by the Ba'sha—The Beys on the south take the fortresses of Toor'a, which Mohham'mad 'Al'ee recovers from them—The forces of the Beys on the north are defeated—They return to the south of the metropolis; and send to request the Sheykhs to mediate between them and the Ba'sha—They retire to Upper Egypt—The troops in the metropolis manifest a disposition to desert—The Ba'sha sends an expedition against the Ghoozz in Upper Egypt—Arrival of a corps of Del'ees from Syria; and return of Mohham'mad 'Al'ee, with the Arnaoo'ts, from Upper Egypt—

---

[1]Western Arabs.

Depredations committed by a party of Memloo'ks and Arabs—Infamous
conduct of the Del'ees—Tumults in the metropolis—Moham'mad 'Al'ee
appointed Ba'sha of Jid'deh—The Del'ees continue their depredations.

After the dismissal of Mohham'mad Khoos'roof, the chiefs in Musr
invited *Ahh'mad Ba'sha Khoo'rshee'd*, who resided at Alexandria, to
repair to the capital and to assume the reins of government. He willingly,
and without delay, acceded; and on the 14th of Zoo-l-Hheg'geh (the
latter part of March, 1804) he made his entry into Musr. After having
resided a few days in the mansion which belonged to Ibrahee'm Bey, in
the Da-oodee'yeh, he took up his abode in a palace on the south of the
Ezbekee'yeh.

To raise a sum of money sufficent to satisfy the troops which had
exalted him to this dignity,[1] and to prosecute the war with the Beys, was
the first difficulty that Khoo'rshee'd had to encounter. To accomplish
this object, he gave orders for the levying of the taxes of the whole year
which was about to commence,—namely, the year 1219: but this measure
excited so much discontent among the people, that he was constrained to
reduce his demand one half.

El-Bardee'see had first encamped at El-Bes'a'tee'n, a few miles to the
south of the metropolis: afterwards, he had proceeded to Hhelwa'n;
several miles further. Many of the Beys to whom he had written before
his expulsion from the capital—for he foresaw the fate that awaited
him—had now joined him, with their forces, from various parts of
Egypt. Some were on the western side of the river; plundering the
villages in the province of El-Gee'zeh, and intercepting the boats bound
to the metropolis with corn and other provisions.

El-El'fee had joined his partisans, and was eager to revenge himself
upon his rival El-Bardee'see. With this view, he resolved upon joining
the party of the Ba'sha. A messenger whom he sent to the capital, to
make known his wishes, was very favourably received, and was
presented with a horse by Mohham'mad 'Al'ee.

Towards the middle of Mohhar'ram (the first month of the year
1219—or the end of April, 1804) El-Bardee'see and most of the other
Beys had brought together their troops to the provinces north of the
metropolis, where they were plundering the villages, carrying off the
threshed corn, and burning the rest upon the threshing-grounds,
destroying the crops, and slaughtering the oxen and sheep. They
besieged Bilbey's, the capital of the great province of Esh-Shurckee'yeh,
and after two days, compelled the governor to surrender, took him
prisoner, with two other chiefs, put his troops to the sword, and
plundered the town. Ckalyoo'b was afterwards besieged by them, and
the governor and garrison, after bravely defending themselves for three

---

[1]His election was soon afterwards confirmed by the Porte.

days and nights in a mosque, were obliged to fly, and escaped by the river to the metropolis.

The wheat-harvest had begun in Upper Egypt two months before, and was not yet finished in Lower Egypt: consequently great distress now prevailed in the metropolis from the scarcity of corn; the supplies which were expected there having been intercepted by the Ghoozz. Some engagements had already taken place between the forces of the Ba'sha and those of the Beys; but without any important advantage to either party. The Turkish troops which were in Upper Egypt at the period of the rupture with the Ghoozz were not opposed in their march to the capital by the latter; for the Beys feared that the troops of the Ba'sha might retaliate by seizing their women whom they had left in Musr. The governor of the Shurckee'yeh, and the two other chiefs who were taken prisoners at Bilbeys were also liberated, and suffered to join their comrades in the capital. The Ba'sha had been put in possession of the Citadel, and seemed to be in favour with the Turkish and Arnaoo't troops; but he could only partially satisfy their demands for pay; though he exacted heavy contributions from the Ckoobt (or Copts) and the inhabitants of the principal towns in Lower Egypt, and even from the Turkish chiefs. He attempted to obtain a considerable sum of money from the sitt' Nefee'seh, the widow of Moora'd Bey, a lady held in very great respect by all classes; but the 'Ool'ama boldly and severly remonstrated with him on the injustice of such a proceeding, and he was obliged to withdraw his first demand. His plea was that one of that lady's female slaves had endeavoured to persuade one of the chiefs of his forces to join the Ghoozz, by promising to pay the troops under his command. He, however, succeeded in exacting from her and the other wives of the Beys not less than 800 purses.[1] Not being able to raise a sufficient sum by the various means which he had already adopted, he gave orders for the levying of a tax from the trades people and artisans of the metropolis. No sooner was this order made known than all the shops were shut, and crowds of the poor people repaired to the great mosque El-Az'har, where they humbly supplicated the interposition of providence in their favour; crying *"Ya' Latee'f! Ya' Latee'f!"*—"O Gracious God!"—The Ba'sha, hearing of the commotion thus excited, sent for the Nackee'b (the chief of the Sheree'fs, or descendants of the Prophet, and one of the principal 'Ool'ama) and informed him that he should not require the *poor* to pay the tax. The Nackee'b replied that the trades people and artisans were *all* of them poor, and were suffering enough from the scarcity then existing and from the stagnation of trade, without being compelled to pay his troops. The Ba'sha, notwithstanding, persisted in requiring that all but the very poorest of the citizens should pay this tax.

The Memloo'ks, taking advantage of the discontent and insubordination of the Turkish and Arnaoo't troops, approached,

---

[1] The purse was then equivalent to the sum before stated, viz. 15*l*.12*s*.6*d*.

sometimes, to the very gates of the metropolis. They also gained a victory over the Ba'sha's forces at Belucks, in the province of Ckalyoo'b; and obtained possession of Shalacka'n, by which they were enabled to cut off the communication by the river between the northern provinces and the capital. They were then in considerable force in the province of Ckalyoo'b; but were soon after compelled to retreat, by the troops of Mohham'mad 'Al'ee and Hhas'an Bey. They retired to the Men'oo'fee'yeh and the Gharbee'yeh; plundering and levying contributions at every village in their way.

El-El'fee and 'Osma'n Bey Hhas'an were approaching the capital on the south. They had both made professions of allegiance to the Ba'sha, who had appointed the former of them governor of Gir'ga, and the latter governor of Ckin'ë; but they soon after declared against him. El-El'fee, in a letter to the Sheykhs of Musr, affirmed that the Ba'sha had made him his enemy by his oppressive conduct to the wives of the Beys.

On the 20th of Rebee'ă el Aou'wal (towards the end of June) the Ba'sha held a court, and a furma'n from the Porte was read to the assembly. It contained an exhortation to the Arnaoo'ts and 'Osma'nlees to remain faithful to their governor Khoo'rshee'd, and zealous in their opposition to the Ghoozz. After the reading of the furma'n, several Sheykhs and others received pelisses; and among those who were so honoured were the principal Ckoobt scribes, twenty-two in number: but in the afternoon of that very day, the Ba'sha sent for these same Ckoobt, threw them into prison, and exacted from them a thousand purses. Contributions were also extorted from various wealthy persons, Moos'lims, Christians, and Jews: yet with all that was thus collected, there was not sufficient to satisfy the troops; many of whom deserted.

The forces of the Beys on the south of the metropolis—that is to say, those of the two El'fees and of 'Osma'n Bey Hhas'an—approached as near as Toor'a, where are two fortresses, one by the river, and the other on the side of the mountain, connected together by a stone wall; a formidable barrier to an enemy descending towards the capital.[1] One of these fortresses, the Memloo'ks attacked and took. They then proceeded to El-Bes'a'tee'n, and came to an engagement with a small body of troops; but the Ba'sha, who had observed their approach from the Citadel, sent a fresh force against them, and obliged them to retreat. On the same day, these Beys sent to the Ba'sha to propose a negociation, which was rejected. Three days after, a considerable force, under the command of Mohham'mad 'Al'ee, was sent against them; but a troop of Memloo'ks, who were lying in wait behind a ridge of the mountain, made a sudden descent upon them, and compelled them to retreat, with great loss. Mohham'mad 'Al'ee endeavoured in vain to rally them: they

---

[1]These fortresses and the wall were built by Isma'ee'l Bey, in the year of the flight 1204 (A.D. 1789-90) to prevent Moora'd Bey and his party, who had retired to Upper Egypt, from descending upon the capital by the eastern bank. (El-Gebur'tee).

returned, with their wounded, to the capital. They also lost, on that day, the other fortress of Toor'a.

On the second evening after the above-mentioned occurrences, Mohham'mad 'Al'ee received a sum of money from the Ba'sha, to pay his troops: having distributed this, he informed them that it was his intention to surprise the enemy that night at Toor'a. He had previously written to the chiefs of those Memloo'ks, in order to put them off their guard, affirming that he wished to become their ally. At the fifth hour of the night, he departed, with about 4,000 men[1]; cavalry and infantry; whom, when he drew near to the enemy, he divided into three parties; one of which proceeded to the fortress by the river; another, to that of the mountain; and the third, to the intermediate fortifications. But this expedition was not attended with complete success: the Memloo'ks were roused from their sleep by the too hasty discharges of musketry, and, with their chief, Salehh A'gha, of the house of El-El'fee, betook themselves to flight; losing but a small number of men, and two pieces of cannon, a quantity of baggage, eight dromedaries, and thirteen horses. The two fortresses were recovered by Mohham'mad 'Al'ee's troops. The victorious chief returned, with his forces, before day-break; taking with him five heads of the slain.

On the morning of the preceding day, a party of Memloo'ks of the other faction entered the northern suburb, El-Hhasanee'yeh. The Turkish troops fired upon them from the walls; but did not go forth from the gates; and in the afternoon, the Memloo'ks retreated; after having sent one of the principal inhabitants of the suburb to mediate between them and the Ba'sha, who detained the messenger, and would return no answer. A few days after, a battle took place at Shoob'ra, between the forces of the Ba'sha and those of El-Bardee'see and his confederates. Both parties suffered severely, the former losing four (or, as some said, five) of their great officers. After the first watch of the night, the battle was renewed, and the 'Osma'nlees and Arnaoo'ts obtained possession of the retrenchments which the enemy had raised at Shoob'ra, and also those at Beysoo's and Shalacka'n. The Ghoozz sustained a heavy loss in this defeat, and were forced to retreat to El-Kha'n'keh. The Ba'sha's army returned to the metropolis, with seven heads, which were hung up at the gate called Ba'b Zoowey'leh. Three of these were the heads of chiefs; for they had beards; and one so much resembled that of the aged Ibrahee'm Bey, that most of the people who saw it supposed it to be his, until it was ascertained that he was still alive.

On the same night in which this victory was gained the Ba'sha received orders from the Porte to send 500 soldiers to Yem'bo' el-Bahhr, with a year's pay, and provisions for the same period, to protect that town from the Wah'ha'bees. In rather less than a month, 'Al'ee A'gha, the Wa'lee, a man much detested by the people of Musr for his cruelty, was sent

---

[1]Mengin says *one* thousand.

thither, with the title of Ba'sha, and with him above one hundred soldiers.

The Memloo'ks who had retreated to El-Kha'n'keh remained at that place two days. On the third day, they abandoned the northern provinces, and passing behind the mountains, proceeded towards the province of Atfee'hh, *south* of the metropolis. The forces of El-Bardee'see and his confederates and those of El-El'fee now became, in a measure, united; though the two rival chiefs were not reconciled. El-El'fee and Ibrahee'm Bey, with their Memloo'ks, crossed over to the opposite side of the Nile; and 'Osma'n Bey Hhas'an remained with El Bardee'see and the other Beys on the eastern side. They then commenced raising retrenchments and forts on each side of the river. Immediately after their retreat to this place, they sent a letter to the Sheykhs of Musr, requesting their intercession with the Ba'sha. They demanded that he should dismiss the troops who were oppressing the inhabitants of Musr, and ruining the country, and declared that they would themselves serve the Soolta'n without any pay: or else, that he would grant to them the southern provinces of Egypt: or, if neither of these propositions pleased him, that he should send forth his army into the plain, to meet them, and see to whom it would please God to give the victory. The Sheykhs consulted the Ba'sha, and were desired to write, in reply to this letter, that he was willing to grant to the Ghoozz the province of Is'na; but they declared that they could not take upon themselves to do so.

The Beys remained but a short time in the province of Atfee'hh. El-El'fee proceeded to El-La'hoo'n; 'Osma'n Bey Hhas'an, to Geb'el et-Teyr; and El-Bardee'see and the rest, to El-Min'yeh and Asyoo't.

The troops in the metropolis took advantage, as usual, of their exemption from service, to indulge in the utmost licentiousness and in overbearing tyranny towards the inhabitants. Several of their chiefs, who had amassed considerable wealth by plunder and other means, were desirous of leaving the country; but were detained by their troops, who required of them their pay. Shortly after, Mohham'mad 'Al'ee and some other great officers professed a desire to return to their own countries, and sold such of their property as they could not take with them; but the people expressed great uneasiness at this: the soldiers, also, became more insolent and riotous, thus proving that the fears of the citizens were not groundless; for Mohham'mad 'Al'ee had often overawed these undisciplined hordes, and interposing in favour of the townspeople, had checked their depredations. It is probable that this subtle chief wished to ascertain what degree of influence he possessed over the people of Musr and over the troops; therefore, having satisfied himself as to this point, he renounced his intention of quitting Egypt.

Until the expiration of two months after the Beys had retired to Upper Egypt, the Ba'sha was unable to send an expedition against them, in consequence of the discontent and insubordination of the 'Osma'nlee and Arnaoo't troops; many of whom deserted, and returned to their own countries. In the beginning of Reg'eb (or the beginning of October) an army, under the command of the Sila'hhda'r, was despatched to Upper Egypt: six weeks afterwards, a second force, under the command of Mohham'mad 'Al'ee, departed for the same destination; and a third force, under Hhas'an Ba'sha,[1] nephew of the late Ta'hir Ba'sha, followed. Several severe battles were fought before the town of El-Min'yeh, which was occupied by El-Bardee'see and the main force of the Ghoozz; but no great advantage resulted to either party. The siege of that place was protracted until the middle of Zoo'l'Hheg'geh, when the Ghoozz abandoned the town.

On the 27th of the same month, about 3,000 Del'ees[2] arrived in Musr, from Syria. Mohham'mad 'Al'ee and Hhas'an Ba'sha, hearing of this event, and learning that Khoo'rshee'd had sent for these troops in order to counterbalance or to destroy the power of the Arnaoo'ts, determined to leave the 'Osma'nlee troops at El-Min'yeh, and to return immediately to the capital. With the view of preventing this, the Del'ees and other troops were stationed at Toor'a; but these dared not oppose the Arnaoo'ts; upon the arrival of whom, they retired. Mohham'mad 'Al'ee and his troops entered the metropolis on the 19th of Mohhar'ram, 1220 (16th of April, 1805). Having made the Arnaoo'ts, and particularly their chiefs, his enemies, the Ba'sha was thrown into the utmost alarm by their presence in the capital.

Sooleyma'n Ka'shif El-Baouwa'b availed himself of this opportunity to overrun, with his Memloo'ks and a large troop of Arabs, the province of El-Gee'zeh and part of the Bohhey'reh and the Menoo'fee'yeh, levying contributions at every village. El-El'fee, also, descended to the province of El-Gee'zeh.

The metropolis was crowded with riotous soldiers; and in the town and neighbourhood of Musr 'Atee'ckah, the Del'ees conducted themselves in a most atrocious manner; expelling the people from their habitations, and seizing their property and their women. (Non solum mulieres, sed etiam pueros senesque constuprabant). The Sheykhs, informed of these execrable proceedings, complained to the Ba'sha, who sent a furma'n to the Del'ees, commanding them to quit the houses of which they had taken possession: but this order was utterly disregarded: the Sheykhs, therefore, repeated their complaints; and the Ba'sha informed them that after three days those troops would take their departure. They, however, did not.

To hasten the crisis of which they plainly saw the approach, the Sheykhs called together a number of boys, and sent them about the town to order the tradespeople to shut their shops, lest they should be plundered. As soon as the Ba'sha heard of this, he sent his Kikh'ya to the

---

[1]He had been promoted from the rank of Bey to that of Ba'sha rather more than a fortnight before.

[2]Called in Arabic "Da'lihs." They are cavalry soldiers; mostly Koords. They wear a high cylindrical felt cap, with a scanty turban wound round the bottom of it.

great mosque El-Az'har, to confer with the Sheykhs. This minister, not finding them there, repaired to the house of one of them, the Sheykh Esh-Shurcka'wee. On leaving that house, he was insulted and pelted with stones by a crowd of boys.

The Ba'sha received, that same day, a furma'n from Constantinople, conferring upon Mohham'mad 'Al'ee the appointment of Ba'sha of Jid'deh, the port of Mek'keh; and sent to demand the attendance of that chief at the Citadel, that he might invest him: but Mohham'mad 'Al'ee, suspecting treachery, refused to go thither: the Ba'sha therefore descended to the house of Sa'ee'd A'gha, to perform that ceremony; after the completion of which, Mohham'mad 'Al'ee took his leave; but at the door of the house, he was stopped by his soldiers, demanding of him their pay.—"The Ba'sha is here," he replied; and passed on unmolested to his house in the Ezbekee'yeh, scattering gold and silver to the people on the way. The troops at the door of Sa'ee'd A'gha's house opposed the return of the Ba'sha to the Citadel; but in the evening, Hhas'an Ba'sha persuaded them to disperse: he then took Khoo'rshee'd to his own house, whence he was escorted to the Citadel, a little before day-break, by 'A'b'dee Bey, the brother of Hhas'an.

The Del'ees, like a swarm of locusts, after having plundered Musr 'Atee'ckah of every thing that they could carry off, repaired to Ckalyoo'b and Ab'oo-l-Gheyt, to commit the same excesses.

Section 4. Mohham'mad 'Al'ee Ba'sha constituted governor of Egypt by the 'Ool'ama—Khoo'rshee'd prepares to defend himself in the Citadel—The Citadel is besieged—Tumults in the metropolis—The Sila'hhda'r of Khoo'rshee'd returns, with his army, from Upper Egypt, to aid the besieged—The metropolis is cannonaded and bombarded by the Citadel, and the Citadel is cannonaded by batteries on the mountain—Arrival of an Envoy from Constantinople—Rejoicings and conflicts in the metropolis—The Envoy above-mentioned arrives in Musr, with a furma'n, confirming Mohham'mad 'Al'ee, and commanding Khoo'rshee'd to repair to Alexandria; but the latter refuses to obey this order—Tumults in the metropolis—The Ghoozz return from Upper Egypt, at the invitation of Khoo'rshee'd, and destroy the fortifications of Toor'a—The Turkish Grand Admiral arrives in Egypt, bringing fresh orders to Khoo'rshee'd to surrender—The schemes of the partisans of the latter defeated—Khoo'rshee'd evacuates the Citadel, and departs from Musr.

This state of anarchy could be endured no longer. On the 12th of Saf'ar (May, 1805) the Sheykhs repaired to the Cka'dee's house, and were followed by such a concourse of people that both the hall of judgement and the great court[1] before it were crowded with persons of all classes; some calling aloud upon God, and others upon the 'Ool'ama, to protect them from the tyranny of their governor. Several high officers of the Ba'sha were summoned to this assembly; and the 'Ool'ama wrote a full statement of the various heavy wrongs which the people had endured under the administration of Khoo'rshee'd; particularly of late. This was laid before the Ba'sha; who, in the following evening, sent a letter to the Cka'dee, desiring him and the rest of the 'Ool'ama to come to him at the Citadel; but they refused; fearing some treachery; for they had been informed that the Ba'sha had sent some soldiers to lie in wait, to murder them on the way. On the next day, another assembly was held in the house of the Cka'dee. From thence the 'Ool'ama proceeded to the mansion of Mohham'mad 'Al'ee, and informed him that the people would no longer have Khoo'rshee'd to govern them.—"Then whom will ye have?" said Mohham'mad 'Al'ee.—"We will have *thee*," they replied, "to govern us according to the laws; for we see in thy countenance that thou art possessed of justice and goodness."—Mohham'mad 'Al'ee seemed, for a little while, to hesitate; and then complied: he was forthwith invested, by the seyd 'Om'ar[2] and the sheykh Esh-Shurcka'wee, with a pelisse and an inner robe (a ben'ish and ckufta'n), and his elevation to this high dignity was proclaimed throughout the metropolis.

A messenger was despatched to inform Khoo'rshee'd; who replied that he was appointed Governor of Egypt by the Soolta'n, and would not resign at the desire of *peasants*; nor would he descend from the Citadel, unless he were commanded to do so by the Soolta'n.—He immediately laid in a store of biscuits, corn, and other provisions, and ammunition, in the Citadel; and prepared, in every possible way, to make an obstinate resistance. Two powerful chiefs of the Arnaoo'ts, 'Om'ar Bey and Sa'lehh Ckoo'sh, joined his party. Mohham'mad 'Al'ee and the Sheykhs endeavoured, in vain, to dissuade them. On the other hand, many of Khoo'rshee'd's troops deserted. Vast numbers of the inhabitants of the metropolis armed themselves with swords and staves and whatever else they could procure, and, with the seyd 'Om'ar and the Sheykhs at their head, repaired frequently to the Ezbekee'yeh, to receive the commands of Mohham'mad 'Al'ee; not feeling sufficient confidence either in the numbers or fidelity of his troops. A strict watch was also kept each night by the armed populace in every quarter of the town.

On the 19th of the same month, Mohham'mad 'Al'ee laid siege to the Citadel. Retrenchments were raised in the Roomey'leh and neighbouring places; and some of the troops of Mohham'mad 'Al'ee ascended the great ma'd'neh of the mosque of the Soolta'n Hhas'an, and thence fired into the Citadel. On the evening before the 24th, the troops of Khoo'rshee'd sallied forth from the great gate of the Citadel, and attempted to drive

---

[1]This is about 150 feet square, or rather more.
[2]The Nackee'b el-Ashra'f, or Chief of the Sheree'fs.

their besiegers from the retrenchments; but were repulsed. On the following day, Hhas'an Ba'sha, who was unwilling to take an active part in the operations against Khoo'rshee'd while so many of his fellow countrymen (the Arnaoo'ts) were among the besieged, sent his brother, 'A'b'dee Bey, to the Citadel, to invite 'Om'ar Bey to a conference, and to remain as a hostage to insure the latter's safe return. This chief came to the house of Hhas'an Ba'sha, where the seyd 'Om'ar endeavoured, but without success, to induce him to pay allegiance to Mohham'mad 'Al'ee. He returned to the Citadel, and 'A'b'dee Bey rejoined his brother. Khoo'rshee'd availed himself of this short cessation of hostilities to procure supplies of provisions and water night and day; for 'Om'ar Bey remained three days with Hhas'an Ba'sha. The siege recommenced; and several guns were drawn up to the top of the mountain, to fire down upon the Citadel.

In the following month (Rebee'ã el-Aou'wal) the troops of Mohham'mad 'Al'ee demanded of him their pay; and the answer which he returned them, that they could receive nothing until Khoo'rshee'd should have evacuated the Citadel, incited them to acts of violence and mutiny, and several frays took place between them and the armed populace. Nevertheless, the siege was prosecuted, partly by the soldiers and partly by the townspeople; and Khoo'rshee'd was prevented from deriving any supplies of provisions, of which he stood in great need. He sent a furma'n to the Del'ees, at Ckalyoo'b, desiring them to come to his assistance; but as soon as this document reached them, they sent it to Mohham'mad 'Al'ee. These troops took no part in the affairs of the capital: they continued to ravage the villages; committing the same horrible excesses as at Musr 'Atee'ckah.

About the middle of this month, the Sila'hhdar returned from El-Min'yeh, with the main part of his army, for the purpose of relieving Khoo'rshee'd; and took up his quarters at Musr 'Atee'ckah; whence he contrived to send secretly, to the Citadel, supplies of bread, meat, and other provisions, which were received, unobserved by the besiegers, at a small gate towards the quarter of 'Ar'ab el-Yesa'r. But he was unable to render much assistance: the plan of an assault which he concerted with Khoo'rshee'd was divulged and frustrated; and some soldiers and servants whom he sent, with sixty camels laden with provisions for the Citadel, were attacked, on the south of the town, by a party of the armed inhabitants of the Roomey'leh, who dispossessed them of their charge, killed two men, and took three others prisoners: these were brought to Mohham'mad 'Al'ee, and by his order put to death.

Khoo'rshee'd, exasperated at this occurrence, gave orders to cannonade and bombard the town, and particularly the houses of Mohham'mad 'Al'ee and Hhas'an Ba'sha and the neighbourhood of the Az'har. A heavy fire of shot and shells was kept up from morning till noon; and again from dusk until the sixth hour of the night. The firing recommenced early the next morning, and continued all that day and the following night and day. On the latter day, the Citadel was cannonaded by the batteries on the mountain. The firing was kept up, both from the mountain upon the Citadel and from the Citadel upon the town, three days longer, after which it was discontinued, because it was the eve of Friday, which is the Sabbath of the Moos'lims. Several houses were destroyed by the shells and shot. On the eve of the Friday above mentioned, a party of the armed townspeople attempted to set fire to one of the gates of the Citadel; that which is towards the mountain and the desert, called Ba'b el-Geb'el. The guards stationed upon the mountain, observing a light, and thinking that the troops of the Citadel were sallying forth to surprise the besiegers, fired several guns towards the spot. This gave the alarm to the besieged, who also fired upon the assailants and compelled them to retire without having effected their purpose. On the Friday afternoon, the cannonading and bombarding recommenced, and was kept up until the eve of the next Friday. Many houses in the quarters towards which the firing was principally directed were destroyed; and numbers of the citizens fled to the suburbs and to Boo'la'ck.

On the day following (which was the first of Rebee' ǎ et-Ta'nee) a messenger from Alexandria brought, to the capital, information of the arrival, at the former place, of Sa'lehh A'gha, an envoy from Constantinople. This news inspired the people of Musr with the hope of a speedy restoration of tranquillity; and in the ensuing night, they testified their joy by frequent discharges of artillery and musketry.

Their enemies imagined this firing to the be result of a fray between the soldiers in the metropolis and the citizens: the Sila'hhda'r, with his troops at Musr 'Atee'ckah, marched, therefore, in all haste towards the Citadel; while, at the same time, a party of the besieged descended to the quarter of 'Ar'ab el-Yesa'r, and there raised retrenchments, favoured by the darkness, and protected by the guns of the Citadel: but a considerable force, composed of the armed inhabitants of the neighbourhood of the Roomey'leh and of the soldiers stationed there, soon collected against them, and compelled them to retreat. The events of this night were such as the natives of Musr, perhaps, never before witnessed: while some of them were thus engaged in fighting and bloodshed, others were going about with drums and hautboys and other musical instruments, rejoicing and shouting and discharging their fire-arms into the air; and all this time the town was cannonaded and bombarded by the Citadel, and the Citadel by the batteries on the mountain behind.

On the 11th of this month, the Envoy, Sa'lehh A'gha, accompanied by the Sila'hhda'r of the Vezee'r, entered the metropolis, amid the rejoicings of the inhabitants (though the firing from the Citadel still continued), and proceeded to the house of Mohham'mad 'Al'ee, in the Ezbekee'yeh, where the furma'n which he brought was read, in the presence of the Sheykhs of Musr and the other 'Ool'ama. By this document, Mohham'mad 'Al'ee was confirmed in the government of Egypt, and Khoo'rshee'd was commanded to repair to Alexandria; there to await the further orders of the Porte. On the following day, the firing from the Citadel ceased; but Khoo'rshee'd still refused to surrender, declaring that he was appointed Governor of Egypt by a *khut'ti sheree'f*, and would not yield to a mere furma'n.

Thus the hopes of the people were diappointed. Their troubles, indeed, were rather aggravated than assuaged. Robberies and murders were committed every day by the soldiers; and the trades people were obliged to shut their shops, and even to barricade the entrances of some of the streets. Notwithstanding these disturbances, two of the Sheykhs of Musr demanded and obtained, of Mohham'mad 'Al'ee, permission to issue an order that all the inhabitants of the metropolis (the soldiers excepted) should lay aside their arms during the day, and only resume them to keep watch at night; and that they should open their shops again. The doors of the great mosque El-Az'har, which had been shut many days, were now thrown open, and the professors and students were called together to resume their usual employments. Most of the people declared that they would not lay down their arms; but many were forced to do so.

El-El'fee, meanwhile, was besieging Demenhoo'r, the capital of the Bohhey'reh; and the other Beys, with their troops, were returning towards the metropolis; Khoo'rshee'd having called them to his assistance. They arrived at the province of El-Gee'zeh; and then, crossing over to the eastern side of the Nile, rased to the ground the fortifications of Toor'a. Mohham'mad 'Al'ee went forth against them, with a considerable force, and compelled them to retreat. They then returned, and the army of the Sila'hhda'r with them, to the western bank, and occupied the town of El-Gee'zeh; while the forces of Mohham'mad 'Al'ee took up their quarters at Musr 'Atee'ckah; and each party cannonaded and bombarded the opposite town during the space of one day and a night.

On the day following, the Del'ees returned, after having plundered the towns and villages of Lower Egypt, and established themselves at Boo'la'ck, in whatsoever houses they chose, driving out the lawful possessors.

On the same day, Mohham'mad 'Al'ee gave orders for the levying of contributions from the Christians and merchants and the inhabitants of the towns and villages. These were the first contributions that he exacted. He also sent five hundred workmen to rebuild the fortifications of Toor'a.

A squadron under the command of the Turkish Grand Admiral had, a few days before, arrived and cast anchor in the Bay of Ab'oo Ckeer; and on the 26th of this month, the Admiral's Sila'hhda'r arrived at the capital, with his despatches, which were nearly to the same purport as those which Sa'lehh A'gha had brought; again ordering Khoo'rshee'd to evacuate the Citadel; authorising Mohham'mad 'Al'ee to continue to discharge the functions of Governor; and commanding him to send troops to Arabia, with provisions and ammunition and all things necessary, and to confer the rank of Ba'sha upon their commander.

Khoo'rshee'd, however, still refused to surrender; urging that he owed about five hundred purses to his troops, and had not any property whatever but the clothes which he wore.

On the following day, some soldiers of Mohham'mad 'Al'ee intercepted a packet of letters addressed to Khoo'rshee'd by his Sila'hhda'r and Ya'see'n Bey, one of his officers, (who were at El-Gee'zeh), detailing the plan of an intended attack upon the capital. They were to discharge seven rockets at El-Gee'zeh, early on the following Friday (which was two days afterwards); and upon this signal, Khoo'rshee'd was to cannonade and bombard the town in the direction of the house of Mohham'mad 'Al'ee: the forces of the Sila'hhda'r were then to cross the river: El-Bardee'see was to pass behind the mountains, and so bring round his troops to the north of the metropolis: and the other Beys were to attack the town on the south. The bearer of these letters was put to death.

After many messages and conferences, Khoo'rshee'd at length agreed to evacuate the Citadel; stipulating that his troops should be paid. On the 9th of the next month (Gooma'da-l-Oo'la) a considerable number of his troops marched out, and a guard, appointed by Moham'mad 'Al'ee, took possession. Khoo'rshee'd himself descended, with the rest, on the following morning, and passing on the east and north of the town, outside the walls, repaired to Boo'la'ck, and was received there in a house belonging to the seyd 'Om'ar. He embarked, a few days after, for Reshee'd.[1]

Section 5. Critical situation of Mohham'mad 'Al'ee—His exactions—He causes a party of the Memloo'ks to be inveigled into the metropolis; and many of them are massacred—A force despatched against another party of Memloo'ks is defeated—The Del'ees who had been ravaging Lower Egypt retire to Syria—Two of Mohham'mad 'Al'ee's sons arrive from their native country—El-El'fee gains a victory over the Ba'sha's troops; and most of the Beys retire to Upper Egypt—The Ba'sha sends officers to negociate with those Beys; but his proposals are rejected—He receives the three-tailed standard—He despatches an army against the Beys—The Porte consents to reinstate the Beys, and to make El-El'fee their chief; which project gives offence both to the Ba'sha and to most of the Beys—A Turkish squadron, under the command of the Grand Admiral, arrives at Alexandria, with troops to aid in the restoration of the Beys, and an officer to succeed Mohham'mad 'Al'ee, who evades the orders of the Porte—El-El'fee gains a signal victory over the forces of Mohham'mad

---

[1]Khoo'rshee'd subsequently served in the war with Russia; was afterwards Ba'sha of Hhal'ab (or Aleppo); and lastly, was employed to reduce the rebel 'Al'ee Pa'sha, of Yan'ina: after having accomplished this arduous undertaking, he was beheaded; being suspected of having possessed himself of the rebels' wealth. (Mengin).

'Al'ee—The Grand Admiral abandons the cause of the Beys, confirms Mohham'mad 'Al'ee in the government of Egypt, and departs—Death of El-Burdee'see—Death of El-El'fee—The party of Sha'hee'n Bey, the successor of El-El'fee, is surprised and routed by Mohham'mad 'Al'ee—A British army is despatched to Egypt, in aid of the Beys—The British forces land, and take possession of Alexandria—Disastrous fate of a detachment which they send against Reshee'd—Mohham'mad 'Al'ee gains a victory over the Beys in Upper Egypt—The Beys combine with him to expel the British—The British made a second attempt upon Reshee'd, and are again defeated—Rebellion of Ya'see'n Bey—Disunion among the Memloo'k Beys—The British army departs from Egypt—Rebellion among the Ba'sha's troops—Sha'hee'n Bey and his partisans conclude a pacific arrangement with Mohham'mad 'Al'ee, and take up their abode at El-Gee'zeh—The other Beys occupy part of Upper Egypt, and make an arrangement with the Ba'sha; but do not perform their engagements—The Ba'sha conducts an army against them; and they conclude a treaty with him, by which they bind themselves to return to the metropolis—The Ba'sha prepares an expedition to Arabia—The Beys from Upper Egypt arrive at El-Gee'zeh, and suddenly retire, together with Sha'hee'n Bey and his party—The Ba'sha again marches against them; and many are induced to return—*Massacre of the Memloo'ks* in the Citadel and in Upper Egypt—A few Memloo'ks escape to Nubia.

Mohham'mad 'Al'ee was now in undisputed possession of the title of Governor of Egypt; but his authority scarcely extended beyond the walls of the capital: he was menaced by formidable enemies within a few miles of the metropolis. The main force of the Ghoozz was on the south of Musr: others of the Memloo'ks were with the army of the Sila'hhda'r of Khoo'rshee'd, who had joined the cause of the Beys, and still occupied El-Gee'zeh: El-El'fee had raised the siege of Demenhoo'r, and was near Tarra'neh. The Del'ees were committing their usual excesses: they had plundered the houses and shops of Semennoo'd, and carried off many of the young women and boys; and were doing the like at El-Mahhal'leh-el-Kebee'reh. El-El'fee the Great and the younger El'fee shortly after joined the forces at El-Gee'zeh. Many of the Arnaoo'ts in the service of the Ba'sha also attempted to join the same forces; but a body of troops was sent against them; and twenty of these deserters were killed: the rest fled in various directions.

To raise sufficient funds to enable him to prosecute the warfare against the Beys, Mohham'mad 'Al'ee arrested and threw into prison the intendant of the Ckoobt, Gir'gis El-Go'haree, and other wealthy persons of the same tribe; and shortly after, compelled them to pay him 4,800 purses. The m'al'lim Gha'lee became the successor of Gir'gis.

On the 20th of this month (or the 16th of August,)—the Nile having attained a sufficient height,—it was announced that the dam wich closed the entrance of the Canal of Musr would be cut, with the usual ceremonies, on the following morning. On the same day on which this proclamation was made, several of the Memloo'k Beys, with their troops, passed behind the mountains, and encamped on the north of the metropolis. A plan was laid to ensnare them. Some of the chiefs of Mohham'mad 'Al'ee's troops sent letters to these Beys, inviting them to enter and take possession of the city, and stipulating (in order to deceive them more effectually) for a sum of money, as their reward for proposing this scheme and cooperating to accomplish it. The Beys were informed by these letters, that, on the following morning, before day-break, Mohham'mad 'Al'ee would go forth, with almost all his troops, to be present at the ceremony of opening the Canal; and that they might then enter the city without finding any to oppose them: that only some chiefs (whom they named) would be in certain quarters, ready to assist them, if necessary. These insidious professions were believed.—The dam of the Canal was cut early in the night, without any ceremony. On the following morning, the Beys above alluded to, with their Memloo'ks, composing a very numerous body, approached the city. They broke open the gate of the suburb El-Hhasanee'yeh, and proceeded to the Ba'b el-Footoo'hh, which they found just opened to some peasants with camels laden with straw: so they entered after these. Seeing no troops, their hopes were strengthened. They proceeded along the principal street, with kettle-drums behind each company, and as they passed along, the people greeted them with apparent joy. After having passed the Ashrafee'yeh, they divided into two parties; one of which turned to the left, to the great mosque El-Az'har, and some of them to the house of the seyd 'Om'ar; but his door being shut against them, they went to the house of the sheykh Esh-Shurcka'wee, whither the seyd 'Om'ar repaired to confer with them: the other party still proceeded along the principal street, passed through the Ba'b Zoowey'leh, and thence a little way up the street called Ed-Durb el-Ahh'mar; when some soldiers fired upon them from the houses, and compelled them to return by the way that they came. Their enemies now quickly multiplied against them, and pursued them along the street. The gates at the entrances of the by-streets leading towards he Az'har were shut; so that they could not join the other party of Memloo'ks. Arriving at the part called Beyn el-Ckusrey'n, they met another body of troops. Thus opposed before and behind, and confined in a narrow street, they remained not long exposed to the fire of their assailants: some dismounted, and entered the mosque El-Burckoo'ckee'yeh, and shut themselves in: the remainder forced their way through the midst of their opponents and arrived at the Ba'b en Nusr; but found it closed: they therefore passed up a narrow street on the right, and leaving their horses, escaped over the city wall.— While they were retreating along the principal street, as above described, two Memloo'ks forced their way into a by-street leading towards the Az'har, just before the gate at its entrance was closed. They found this street so crowded with passengers, that they were obliged to dismount and creep between the legs of the camels and horses. Passing trough the

Az'har, they proceeded to the house of the sheykh Esh-Shurcka'wee, where they found their comrades who had parted from them. These all, immediately on learning what had happened, betook themselves to flight; and escaped by the Ba'b el-Ghoorei'yib.—Those who had taken refuge in the Burckoo'ckee'yeh begged for quarter, and surrendered. They were despoiled of their costly arms and all the money which was about their persons, and stripped nearly naked. About fifty of them were slaughtered on the spot, and about the same number dragged away to the house of Mohham'mad 'Al'ee, in the Ezbekee'yeh. These wretched prisoners were naked, barefooted and bareheaded: their hands were tied together; and their unmanly conductors reviled them and beat them on the backs of their heads and on their faces as they pulled them along. The Ba'sha, in a state of great anxiety and alarm, had descended from his saloon, when the prisoners, among whom were four Beys, were brought before him. He was overjoyed at seeing them; and exclaimed to Ahh'mad Bey, who was one of them,—"So thou hast fallen into the snare, Ahh'mad Bey!"—The captive chief made no reply; but asked for some water to drink. This was given him; and his arms were unbound that he might take the bottle; but instead of doing this, he snatched a yatagha'n[1] from the gridle of one of the soldiers, and rushing forward, aimed a blow at the Ba'sha. The soldiers fell upon him and despatched him; but not until he had killed several of their comrades, and wounded others. The other prisoners were fettered and chained, and left in the court of the house, in the state in which they had been brought thither, without clothes or shoes. On the following day, the heads of the Memloo'ks who had been slain were skinned, and these stuffed with straw before the eyes of the captives; all of whom, excepting one Bey and two others who paid a certain sum for their ransom, were, during the following night, tortured[2] and put to death. Their heads were cut off and stuffed, and sent, with those before mentioned and many others (in all eighty-three) to Constantinople; with a letter, stating that the Memloo'ks were utterly destroyed, and that the said heads were those of their chiefs: but many of these horrible trophies were the heads of Frenchmen (who had joined the Memloo'ks) and of Arnaoo'ts.

During the same night, 'A'b'dee Bey went forth, with his Arnaoo'ts, some by land and others by water, to Toor'a, and attacked the Memloo'ks under Ibrahee'm Bey and his son Murzoo'ck Bey; but he suffered a complete defeat and very heavy loss, and returned to Musr.

A few days after, some troops were sent by Mohham'mad 'Al'ee against the Del'ees, who (after traversing nearly every part of Lower Egypt, and committing, in every town and village in their route, the same horrid excesses and cruelties as at Musr 'Atee'ckah, &c.) had encamped at El-Kha'n'keh. These barbarous wretches, fearing to hazard a battle,

---

[1] A weapon resembling a very long knife.
[2] The word which I have translated "tortured" bears also a less harsh meaning: I should, perhaps, have written "beaten."

lest they should lose the vast spoils which they had amassed, determined to quit the country: they therefore seized five hundred camels from a tribe of Arabs, and retired by the way of Ra's el-Wa'dee. They took with them, altogether, above four thousand camels, a great number of sheep, and many women and boys (whom they had carried off by force), besides money, and other spoils. They had been ever since their arrival in Egypt, a most dreadful scourge to the country, and of no avail to Khoo'rshee'd, who had called them to his assistance.

In the beginning of the next month (Gooma'da-t-Ta'niyeh) two of Mohham'mad 'Al'ee's sons, Ibrahee'm[1] and Too'soo'n, arrived at Musr from their native country.

The Beys now seemed to have abandoned every hope of reestablishing themselves in all their former power. El-El'fee demanded, as the reward of his submission, the government of the Feiyoo'm, the provinces of Ben'ee Soowey'f and El-Gee'zeh, and the Bohhey'reh. This being refused, he attempted to make himself master of the Feiyoo'm by force of arms; and gained a victory over the troops sent thither by the Ba'sha.—The other Beys and their troops retired to Upper Egypt; and took the town of Asyoo't.—In the middle of the next month (Reg'eb) Mohham'mad 'Al'ee made preparations for an expedition to Arabia, against the Wah'ha'bees, who had taken El-Medee'neh. He gave the command of the army destined for this service to his nephew Ta'hir Ba'sha; but he afterwards counterordered the expedition, and employed Ta'hir Ba'sha and his troops to suppress the incursions of the Arabs in the province of El-Gee'zeh.

In Rum'ada'n, Mohham'mad 'Al'ee sent two envoys to the Beys who were in Upper Egypt, to make certain propositions as to the territory to be allotted to them, which were rejected. They were sent a second time; and held a conference with 'Osma'n Bey Hhas'an and El-Bardee'see, at Asyoo't; Ibrahee'm Bey being higher up the country, at Tahh'ta. The Ba'sha offered them the whole of the country south of Gir'ga; but with this they were not satisfied: they demanded a much more extensive territory; from El-Min'yeh upwards; and required that the Ba'sha should only retain about two thousand soldiers, and dismiss the remainder of his troops from Egypt.[2]

On the 17th of Mohhar'ram, 1221 (1st of April, 1806) seventy Ta'ta'rs arrived from Constantinople, bringing to Mohham'mad 'Al'ee the three-tailed standard; for every Governor of Egypt should be a Ba'sha (or Pa'sha) of three tails. They were followed by a cka'pijee-ba'shee, the bearer of a furma'n which confirmed that prince in the government of

---

[1] I have before mentioned that Ibrahee'm is generally believed to be the son of Mohham'mad 'Al'ee's wife by a former husband.

[2] El-Gebur'tee's annals—from which the materials of this history have thus far been derived—terminate at this period. For the remainder of this *fifth* section and the account which will follow of the campaigns in Arabia, Mengin is my principal authority.

Egypt and commanded him to abstain from levying any extraordinary contributions.

Mohham'mad 'Al'ee found it impossible to conclude any pacific arrangement with the Beys, unless by granting to them the whole of Upper Egypt: he therefore made every possible preparation to subdue them in the field: but the first and chief force that he employed against them, which consisted of 3,000 men (2,000 infantry, and 1,000 cavalry) under Hhas'an Ba'sha, was defeated near Rick'ckah, about forty miles above the metropolis, by the Memloo'ks of El-El'fee, who afterwards descended to the province of El-Gee'zeh; while Hhas'an Ba'sha, with his army, proceeded to Ben'ee Soowey'f.—This was not the only adverse fortune that now befell Mohham'mad 'Al'ee; for many of his troops revolted, and joined the party of the Beys.—El-Bardee'see and his partisans were at Asyoo't. They sent a detachment to blockade the town of El-Min'yeh; but this force was repulsed, and the garrison of the town was reinforced.

At length the Porte was induced, by the remonstrances of the English, and a promise, made by El-El'fee, of a large sum of money (1,500 purses) from himself and the other Beys, to consent to restore to the twenty-four Beys their former privileges, and to place El-El'fee in the highest rank among them. This intention of the Porte gave the utmost uneasiness not only to Mohham'mad 'Al'ee, but also to El-Bardee'see, whose enmity towards El-El'fee had not subsided, and whose influence over most of the other Beys was so great, that he could, in almost every case, command their concurrence. The main party of the Ghoozz determined, therefore, to oppose this measure of the Porte, merely because El-El'fee was to be at their head. They renewed negociations with Mohham'mad 'Al'ee; demanding that he should cede to them nearly the whole of Upper Egypt; from El-Min'yeh, southwards. The Ba'sha returned an evasive answer; but sent back the envoys with rich presents for the principal Beys.

A squadron consisting of four vessels, having on board 3,000 regular troops, under the command of Sa'lehh Pa'sha, lately appointed Grand Admiral, arrived at Alexandria on the 1st of July. The Admiral was accompanied by Moo'sa Pa'sha, who was sent to succeed Mohham'mad 'Al'ee; and the latter was to receive the Pa'shalick of Salonica, which Moo'sa had vacated. To the orders which were transmitted to him, Mohham'mad 'Al'ee replied, that he was desirous of obeying the commands of his sovereign; but that his troops, to whom he owed a vast sum of money, opposed his departure from the capital. In fact, he was supported by the Sheykhs, and by his Arnaoo't troops, whose chiefs he persuaded to swear allegiance to him by the most sacred oaths. The sum of 2,000 purses was contributed by the Arnaoo't chiefs, and sent by land to Constantinople, to purchase the favour of the Porte for Mohham'mad 'Al'ee; and the Sheykhs and other 'Ool'ama were induced to sign a letter to the Soolta'n, praying him to revoke the commands which he had given for the reinstating of the Beys.

El-El'fee was at that time besieging Demenhoo'r, the capital of the Bohhey'reh; but finding that the Ba'sha's troops in that province had received reinforcements, he raised the siege and marched against them. He gained a signal victory over them before the village of En-Negee'leh; after which, he renewed the siege of Demenhoo'r, but met with no better success.

The jealousy which subsisted between El-El'fee and El-Bardee'see, dividing the Ghoozz into two hostile factions, was not the only circumstance that now favoured the cause of Mohham'mad 'Al'ee: El-El'fee and his partisans were unable, or unwilling, to pay the promised bribe; and the other Beys refused to contribute any portion. The Grand Admiral, therefore, totally changed his plans. In consequence of the letter of the 'Ool'ama of Musr to the Soolta'n, Sa'lehh Pa'sha had been authorised to adopt whatever course he deemed most conducive to the interests of his sovereign. He accordingly entered into a negociation with Mohham'mad 'Al'ee, and decided that he should retain the office of Governor of Egypt on the condition of his paying to the Porte a fee of 4,000 purses. He was also required to endeavour to make some pacific arrangement with the Beys. The Admiral took back with him Mohham'mad 'Al'ee's eldest son, Ibrahee'm Bey, as a hostage. He set sail in October.

Fortune continued to favour Mohham'mad 'Al'ee.—In the following month, the famous 'Osma'n Bey El-Bardee'see died; aged forty-eight years. He was by birth a Cherkassian. Moora'd Bey purchased him; and when he promoted him to the rank of a Bey, he gave him the town and lands of Bardee's,[1] as an appanage; whence he derived his surname, El-Bardee'see, by which he was commonly called.

Another of Mohham'mad 'Al'ee's most formidable enemies died soon after.—The want of provisions excited the troops of El-El'fee to revolt, and obliged that Bey to raise the siege of Demenhoo'r, and to bend his course southwards; which he was very reluctant to do; being in daily expectation of the arrival of a British army in Egypt, to second his views. At the village of Shoob'ra-ment, in the province of El-Gee'zeh, he was attacked by sudden illness, and died on the 30th of January, 1807; aged fifty-five years. He was a memloo'k of Moora'd Bey, who purchased him for a thousand ardeb'bs of wheat[2]; for which reason, he received the name of El-El'fee; *elf* signifying *a thousand*. He was succeeded by Sha'hee'n Bey, who marched, with the troops which thus fell to his command, to Bah'nes'ë.—El-Bardee'see and El-El'fee were the most distinguished warriors among the Memloo'ks of their time.

Mohham'mad 'Al'ee thought this a fit opportunity to make pacific overtures to Sha'hee'n Bey; but met with a stern denial: he therefore marched against him, surprised his army by night, killed or made prisoners about three hundred men, put the rest to flight, and took all their artillery and baggage.

---

[1] Near Gir'ga, in Upper Egypt.
[2] Five thousand bushels.

The Porte having failed to reinstate the Beys, the British government deemed it requisite to accomplish by force of arms the object which it could not effect by negociation; and accordingly despatched an army to Egypt. The enterprise which it contemplated was considered as one which presented little difficulty: the cooperation of the Memloo'ks was regarded as certain: and therefore a very small force was employed.[1]

On the 17th of March, 1807, a British fleet appeared off Alexandria, having on board nearly 5,000 troops, under the command of General Fraser. On the 21st, they took possession of the town, without firing a gun; the garrison of the place being disaffected towards Mohham'mad 'Al'ee.—Here they were informed of the recent death of El-El'fee, upon whose powerful aid they had mainly founded their hopes of triumph. To the successor of that chief, and to the other Beys, all of whom were then in Upper Egypt, they immediately despatched messengers, inviting them to repair, without delay, to Alexandria.

In consequence of the representations of Major Misset, the British resident at Alexandria, that the inhabitants of that city ran the risk of being starved, unless Reshee'd and Er-Rahhma'nee'yeh were soon taken by our forces, General Fraser, with the concurrence of the Admiral, Sir John Duckworth, detached the 31st regiment and the Chasseurs Britanniques, under Major General Wauchope and Brigadier General Meade, to obtain possession of those places. These troops entered Reshee'd without encountering any opposition; but as soon as they had dispersed among the narrow streets, the garrison poured forth upon them; and other troops, with many of the inhabitants of the town, fired upon them from the latticed windows and from the roofs of the houses. A hundred and eighty-five of our troops, including General Wauchope and three officers, were killed; and two hundred and sixty-two wounded; among whom were General Meade and seventeen officers: the remainder retired to Ab'oo Ckeer and Alexandria. A considerable number of the heads of the slain[2] were conveyed, with the prisoners, to the metropolis, and fixed upon stakes in the Ezbekee'yeh, on each side of the road which crosses that place.

Mohham'mad 'Al'ee, meanwhile, was advancing against the main force of the Ghoozz. His army arrived at the village of Munckaba'd, about five miles below Asyoo't; and there, while a burning semoo'm darkened the air with dust, he engaged his enemies; but it was only a portion of the Memloo'k force which took part in this battle. Three Beys, four Ka'shifs, and fifteen others of the Memloo'k army were killed; and a few became prisoners: the remainder fled towards the desert, with their baggage, which was borne by two thousand camels. They descended to Mel'laou'ee; while Mohham'mad 'Al'ee proceeded to Asyoo't.

---

[1] The account of the operations of the British army in Egypt, here given, is chiefly taken from official papers which were printed and published by order of our government.

[2] According to Mengin, ninety.

Here the Ba'sha received information of the landing of the British
army at Alexandria. In great alarm, he immediately sent messengers to
the Beys (who, being far to the north of him, might then easily have
joined the British forces), promising that he would comply with all their
demands if they would unite with him in repelling the Christian
invaders. The proposal was accepted; and both parties marched towards
the metropolis; the Ba'sha's army on the eastern side of the Nile, and that
of the Beys on the western.

Major Misset having again urged the necessity of taking Reshee'd,
Brigadier General Stewart and Colonel Oswald, with a force of about
2,500 men, were despatched thither. On the 7th of April, they arrived
before the town. Having in vain summoned the garrison the surrender,
they besieged and battered the town until the 12th; and again summoned
the garrison in vain. Expecting the Memloo'ks to arrive and join him,
General Stewart still prosecuted the siege: he continued the cannonading
until the night of the 20th; and determined to retire on the following day,
if the Memloo'ks did not arrive. Early next morning he received
intelligence that sixty or seventy large vessels were coming down the
Nile; doubtless with great reinforcements for the enemy. This
information was sent by Major Macleod, who commanded the advanced
guard, stationed near the village of El-Hhama'd, about four miles and a
half south-south-east of Reshee'd. This force consisted of a detachment
of 71st, two companies of the 78th, one of the 35th, and De Rolle's
regiment; with a picquet of dragoons. General Stewart, as soon as he
received the message above-mentioned, sent a dragoon with orders to
Major Macleod to fall back upon the main army; but the messenger was
unable to penetrate to the spot. The advanced guard, surrounded by an
overwhelming force (despatched against them by the Ba'sha), could not
rejoin the main army; and all who survived became prisoners of war;
after having expended the whole of their ammunition. General Stewart
regained Alexandria, with the remainder of his army; having lost (killed,
wounded and missing) nearly nine hundred men. Seven hundred and
thirty-three were missing: these composed the advanced guard at
El-Hhama'd. The prisoners were conducted to the metropolis and were
made to pass along the road which was lined with the heads of their
countrymen who had fallen at Reshee'd on the former occasion. Some
hundreds of British heads[1] were now exposed upon the stakes along the
sides of the same road.

Though thus successful, Mohham'mad 'Al'ee found himself somewhat
critically circumstanced. Ya'see'n Bey, a chief who had served under
Khoo'rshee'd, and on the deposition of that prince had submitted to
Mohham'mad 'Al'ee, but soon after revolted, now took up his quarters
at Boo'la'ck. Having been joined by vast numbers of the Ba'sha's troops,
his party had become very formidable. He conceived the design of

---

[1]Mengin says four hundred and fifty.

supplanting Mohham'mad 'Al'ee; but his resolution failed him at the last; and he retired.

Disunion still subsisted among the Beys: one party was desirous of joining the British army: the other wished to conclude a pacific arrangement with the Ba'sha.

Mohham'mad 'Al'ee had set forth, at the head of 4,000 men, against the British, when he received proposals on the part of the latter to evacuate Alexandria. Not having met with the expected cooperation of the Beys, the British army had abandoned all hope of the success of their enterprise. They obtained the restoration of the prisoners (with the exception of a few who had embraced the Mohham'madan religion), and set sail on the 14th of September.

Mohham'mad 'Al'ee proceeded to Alexandria, and remained there three weeks. Immediately after his return to the metropolis, an alarming rebellion broke forth among his troops, who imperiously demanded their pay. Through the mediation of the Sheykhs, and some concessions on the part of the Ba'sha, the tumult was appeased.

The Ba'sha now renewed his negociations with the Beys. Sha'hee'n Bey yielded to his invitation, and took up his abode in the town of El-Gee'zeh. His Memloo'ks encamped in the neighbourhood. The Ba'sha ceded to him the province of El-Feiyoo'm, thirty villages in the province of Bah'nes'ë, and ten in that of El-Gee'zeh; and loaded him with honours. Several of the other Beys also accepted the proposals of Mohham'mad 'Al'ee. These events happened at the close of the year 1807—or in the last quarter of the year of the flight 1222.—The rebel Ya'see'n Bey was reduced soon after, and banished from Egypt.

With the Beys in Upper Egypt, no treaty had been definitively arranged; but they remained in undisturbed possession of the Sa'ee'd, with the understanding that they were to remit to the Ba'sha the amount of the land-tax to which the districts which they occupied were subject. More than a year and a half elapsed without their fulfilling this promise; but they sent frequently during that period to beg for a delay in their remittance of the tribute. While they thus evaded the Ba'sha's orders, and withheld a considerable portion of the revenue of Egypt, Mohham'mad 'Al'ee was burdened with an enormous army, to support which, he was obliged to have recourse to the most tyrannical exactions. Thus he reduced his subjects to a state of great misery. The 'Ool'ama in vain remonstrated with him: one of them, the seyd 'Om'ar, who had ever been foremost in advocating the cause of the oppressed people of Musr, and who had been one of the main instruments of the elevation of Mohham'mad 'Al'ee to the government of Egypt, was banished, for boldly protesting against these exactions.

In consequence of the backwardness of the Beys in Upper Egypt to fulfil their engagements, the Ba'sha at length marched against them, at the head of an army, of which Sha'hee'n Bey and his Memloo'ks formed a part. The refractory Beys, as soon as these forces approached them, perceived that opposition on their part would be vain. They entered into a treaty with Mohham'mad 'Al'ee, pledged themselves to pay the tribute which they had withheld, and consented to return to the metropolis. This was in October, 1809,—or in the year of the flight 1224. The Ba'sha returned, without delay, by the Nile. Landing at the village of Deyr et-Teen, he and his suite mounted donkeys which they hired of some peasants, and so proceeded, incognito, to the Citadel.

Mohham'mad 'Al'ee was now obliged, in compliance with the reiterated commands of the Porte, to commence very active preparations for an expedition against the Wah'ha'bees, whose sect was making alarming progress in Arabia.

In the beginning of the following summer (A.D. 1810—or in the year of the flight 1225) the Beys with whom the Ba'sha had concluded a treaty in Upper Egypt, as above related, had descended, distrustfully, by short journeys, interrupted by long stoppages, and encamped near the town of El-Gee'zeh. Here, directly opposite the metropolis, separated from it only by the river and a narrow plain, they suddenly took alarm and retired. They were joined in this movement by Sha'hee'n Bey and his party. Their enemies pursued them; and in the first engagement, a body of the Memloo'ks suffered a defeat, and lost two officers and many others, being surprised by night; but their party soon after gained a signal victory. They then again encamped before El-Gee'zeh; and four of the Beys passed over to the Ba'sha: the remainder, with their forces, marched southwards, to El-La'hoo'n.

The Ba'sha again conducted an army against them, and pursued them into Upper Egypt. Three more Beys demanded safe conduct to the metropolis; which the Ba'sha gladly granted.—Meanwhile, the Chief of the Soolta'n's Eunuchs, an officer held in very great respect, had arrived in Musr, with very important despatches; and Moham'mad 'Al'ee was in consequence obliged to return prematurely. The furma'n which this personage brought conveyed an injunction to Mohham'mad 'Al'ee to conduct, in person, an expedition against the Wah'ha'bees; but he was too wise to comply with such an order.—One of the Beys who had submitted to the Ba'sha was now employed to persuade those who had continued refractory to follow his example; and the result of his mission was, that Sha'hee'n Bey was induced a second time to return, with his partisans, and to take up his abode in the metropolis.

Early in the following year, the preparations for the expedition to Arabia, against the Wah'ha'bees, were completed; and the Ba'sha invited all his great officers, and particularly those Memloo'k Beys and their followers who were then in Musr, to repair to the Citadel, to witness the ceremony of his investing his son Too'soo'n Ba'sha with a pelisse, and conferring upon him the command of the army which was about to depart; after which they were to join in a grand procession through the metropolis, to escort the young general to the camp. Sha'hee'n Bey and the other chiefs of the Memloo'ks (one only excepted) proceeded with their retinues, in grand costume, to the Citadel, on the day appointed, the 1st of March, 1811. The Ba'sha greeted them with politeness and affability; and coffee was served to them. As soon as all the persons who were to compose the procession had arrived, the whole assembly took leave of the Ba'sha. The Beys and their Memloo'ks, preceded and followed by the Ba'sha's troops, slowly descended the steep and narrow road, or rather passage, leading to the great gate of the Citadel, which opens into the square called the Roomey'leh. As soon as the Memloo'ks arrived at this gate, it was suddenly closed before them. The last of those who made their exit before the gate was shut were Sa'lehh Ckoo'sh and his Arnaoo'ts. To these troops, their chief now made known the Ba'sha's orders to massacre all the Memloo'ks within the Citadel. Many have since confessed with shame the part which they acted in this horrible tragedy: they were taken by surprise: a few promptly obeyed their chief; and the remainder were led on by the example of their more savage comrades. Having returned by another way, they gained the summits of the walls and houses which hem in the road in which the Memloo'ks were incarcerated; and some stationed themselves upon the eminences of the rock, through which that road is partly cut. Thus securely placed, they commenced a heavy fire upon their defenceless victims; and immediately, the troops who closed the procession, and who therefore had the advantage of higher ground, followed their example. Of the betrayed chiefs and their attandants, many were laid low in a few moments: some, dismounting, and throwing off their outer robes, vainly sought, sword in hand, to return, and escape by some other gate. The few who regained the summit of the Citadel experienced the same cruel fate as the rest (for those whom the Arnaoo't soldiers made prisoners met with no mercy from the chiefs, or from the Ba'sha); but it soon became impossible for any to retrace their steps even so far: the road was obstructed by the bleeding bodies of the slain Memloo'ks, and their richly caparisoned horses, and grooms.[1] Four hundred and seventy Memloo'ks entered the Citadel; and of these, very few, if any, escaped.[2] The Ba'sha, in the saloon in which he had received them, awaited the result of the plot, listening to the discharges of musketry, in a state of anxiety and agitation that may easily be conceived. Only one Bey, of all those who were in the metropolis at that period, escaped this massacre.[3] This chief, Emee'n Bey, had been detained by important business when his colleagues repaired to the Citadel: he, however, followed them, and arrived at the great gate when the Ba'sha's troops were coming out: not being able to enter, he waited outside, to take his place in the procession; but seeing the gate closed before his friends, he perceived that they were betrayed, and therefore instantly betook himself to flight.[4] He had the

---

[1]The *sa'ïs* (or groom) runs before his master, bearing a long staff. (See plate 5, in this volume [missing]).

[2]Mengin says that *none* of them escaped.

[3]Too'soo'n Ba'sha, who was a young man of very noble character, took no part in this transaction, and probably was not privy to the plot.

[4]Thus the escape of Emee'n Bey is related by Mengin. Others say that he was

good fortune to escape to Syria, under the protection of a Sheykh of Arabs, upon whose generosity he cast himself.—After having despoiled the dead of their costly arms, clothes and money, the Ba'sha's soldiers proceeded to plunder the houses of the Memloo'ks: they broke into the hharee'ms, and robbed, abused, and even carried off by force, many of the women: the female slaves being looked upon as articles of property, in the same light as furniture and other possessions. Booty of almost incalculable value fell into their hands. Many of the houses of the private citizens (particularly those in the neighbourhood of the residences of Memloo'ks) were also pillaged: scarcely anybody, but the riotous soldiers, was seen in the streets: the shops were all shut on the first rumour of the massacre.—On the following day, the Ba'sha descended from the Citadel, with a large body of armed men, marching on foot, to put an end to these horrible proceedings; and on the second day after the massacre, Too'soo'n Ba'sha rode about the town, with a numerous guard, and caused every one whom he found engaged in pillage to be put to death. More than five hundred houses had been entirely plundered.—The massacre in the Citadel was followed by the murder of most of the Memloo'ks in Upper Egypt. Orders were transmitted to the Turkish governors of the various provinces to destroy every Memloo'k upon whom they could lay their hands. The heads of all these victims were brought to the metropolis; and those of the Beys were sent to Constantinople, whence the order for their destruction had been transmitted to Mohham'mad 'Al'ee. To him, therefore, the odium of these horrible massacres does not solely attach.

A small remnant of the Memloo'ks escaped into Nubia; leaving Egypt in a state of tranquillity to which it had long been unaccustomed, and which has, on very few occasions since been interrupted.

The Ba'sha, in the following year, sent an expedition, under his son (or his wife's son) Ibrahee'm Bey (now Ibrahee'm Ba'sha), against the surviving Memloo'ks, who established themselves in the fortified town of Ibree'm; a place which was strong from its position (being perched upon a rocky hill), but then in a ruinous state. The unfortunate refugees were unable to sustain a siege, in consequence of their want of provisions: they were (with the exception of a few who surrendered themselves and were beheaded) driven into the desert, and compelled to seek a retreat in the more southern parts of Nubia. They chose for their residence a village in the province of Dun'ckal'ah (or Dun'gal'ah); built for themselves a number of new houses, or rather huts, and having thus made the place of their abode a considerable town, gave it the name of "New Dun'ckal'ah." The venerable Ibrahee'm Bey (the Memloo'k Chief) died at this place, in 1816, at the advanced age of 80 years. While death gradually thinned their party, the Memloo'ks endeavoured to maintain

---

with his insnared colleagues in the Citadel, and that he urged his horse to leap from the walls, a fearful height. The horse, it is said, was killed by the fall; but the Bey escaped unhurt.

their little power by training some hundreds of blacks for their service. They retained possession of Dun'ckal'ah and the country of the Sha'ckee'yeh (or Sha'gee'yeh) until the approach of Isma'ee'l Ba'sha (the son of Mohham'mad 'Al'ee) at the head of an army destined for the subjugation of Nubia and Senna'r induced some of them to return to the capital of Egypt, where they settled in security; being no longer objects of the Viceroy's jealousy: the rest, amounting, I believe, to about a hundred persons, fled before Isma'ee'l's army, and sought refuge in the countries adjacent to Senna'r, dispersed in small parties.

Section 6. Expedition under Too'soo'n Ba'sha against the Wah'ha'bees in Arabia—Mohham'mad 'Al'ee repairs to Arabia, to direct the operations of his army—Too'soo'n concludes a treaty with the Wah'ha'bee Prince— Mohham'mad 'Al'ee returns to Egypt—His attempt to introduce the European military tactics excites a revolt—Return of Too'soo'n to Egypt—Second expedition, under the command of Ibrahee'm Ba'sha, against the Wah'ha'bees—Death of Too'soo'n Ba'sha—The capital of the Wah'ha'bees is taken by Ibrahee'm Ba'sha: their Prince is sent to Constantinople, and beheaded; and Ibrahee'm returns to Egypt— Mohham'mad 'Al'ee monopolizes the principal manufactures of Egypt; founds several large fabrics, &c.; and puts in execution some useful public works—An army, under the command of Isma'ee'l Ba'sha, is despatched to Nubia and Senna'r; and these countries, with Koordoofa'n are subjugated—Insurrection in Greece—Fate of Isma'ee'l Ba'sha— Mohham'mad 'Al'ee forms an army of regular troops, who are disciplined by European officers—Rebellion in Upper Egypt—A regiment of regular troops despatched to the southern countries; another, to Arabia; and four regiments, under the command of Ibrahee'm Ba'sha, to Greece—Six new regiments formed—The Camp of El-Kha'n'keh, the institutions connected with it; &c.—The Navy—Concluding remarks.

Being now in undisputed possession of the government of all Egypt, Mohham'mad 'Al'ee was at liberty to turn his whole attention to the state of Arabia; and, accordingly, lost no time in preparing an expedition, the grand object of which was the subjugation of the Wah'ha'bees, who had taken the two holy cities of Mek'keh and El-Medee'neh, and latterly put a stop to the annual pilgrimage from Egypt, as well as that from Syria. The army destined for this entreprise was composed of 8,000 men; one fourth of which number consisted of cavalry; and the whole force was placed under the command or Too'soo'n Ba'sha, who, young as he was (only 16 years of age), proved himself not less fit for so important a charge than many an experienced general.

The army departed from Es-Soowey's (or Suez) in the autumn of the year 1811 (corresponding with the year of the flight 1226). The campaign commenced successfully: the sea-port town of Yem'bo' being taken by assault, the invading army proceeded inland, towards El-Medee'neh, and made themselves masters of Yem'bo' en-Nakhl, in their route; but on their arrival at the entrance of the valley of Suf'ra and Joodei'yideh, where a large force of Wah'ha'bees had taken up a strong position, they were completely routed, and one half of their number perished; most of them, of hunger and thirst, during their retreat by night. After this defeat, Too'soo'n, with the remnant of his army, returned to Yem'bo'.— In the following year, he received reinforcements from Egypt, and again advanced against El-Medee'neh. The Wah'ha'bees had committed the defence of the pass of Suf'ra and Joodei'yideh to the inhabitants of the two villages from which it takes its name, who betrayed their trust. Too'soo'n's army marched through unopposed, and arrived before El-Medee'neh which they took after a siege of more than two months.

The young general, after having detached some troops to take possession of the town of Hhana'kiyeh, next conducted a division of his army to Jid'deh; where he was received by Gha'lib, the Sheree'f of Mek'keh, with much honour. He thence proceeded to Mek'keh and Et-Ta'if; the Wah'ha'bee forces which were at those places retiring at his approach. He pursued, and defeated them at a place called Besl; and their chief, 'Osma'n El-Mada'ifee, was taken prisoner in his flight, and sent to Constantinople, where he was put to death.

Thus far were the Turks successful in this quarter; but shortly after, a detachment under the command of Moos'tuf'a Bey, the brother of Mohham'mad 'Al'ee's wife, was defeated before the town of Tar'abah (or,—as the Bed'awees call it—Toor'abah) by a large Wah'ha'bee force, commanded by a *woman* named Gha'liyeh, the wife, or widow, of a chief. About the same time, So'oo'd, the Sovereign of the Wah'ha'bee sect, at the head of a numerous army, retook Hhana'kiyeh, and advanced against El-Medee'neh.

Not long after the departure of Too'soo'n from Egypt, Mohham'mad 'Al'ee had determined to place himself, as soon as possible, at the head of the army in Arabia. He had banished from Egypt several chiefs who had returned from Arabia immediately after the first defeat of Too'soo'n's army, and had removed, by the sword, or by other means, some persons besides upon whose allegiance he could not rely during his proposed absence from his proper dominions. Notwithstanding these precautions, soon after the departure of Mohham'mad 'Al'ee, an emancipated memloo'k of his court, who had been sent on an important mission to Constantinople and there raised to the rank of a Ba'sha, manifested a degree of ambition which gave umbrage to the Kikh'ya Bey and other great officers to whom Mohham'mad 'Al'ee had confided the government of Egypt: he was therefore arrested and put to death.

Mohham'mad 'Al'ee embarked at Es-Soowey's in the summer of the year 1813, and sailed for Jid'deh. After having stayed a few weeks at the latter place, he repaired to Mek'keh, and performed the pilgrimage. One of his first acts of importance after his arrival in the holy city was to cause Gha'lib, the Sheree'f, whom he had as yet treated with the greatest respect, to be arrested, while paying a visit of ceremony to Too'soo'n Ba'sha. Yahh'ya, a nephew of Gha'lib, was proclaimed his successor. His sons also were inveigled, and sent with him to Egypt. His property was confiscated; but Mohham'mad 'Al'ee received orders from the Porte to restore it. At Musr, he was treated with all the respect due to an illustrious prisoner. He was finally conveyed to Salonica, where he died.

Mohham'mad 'Al'ee remained several months in Arabia without making any considerable advance towards the accomplishment of the object which had brought him thither. It was impossible for him to unite his forces and strike one grand and decisive blow: for his enemies were scattered, in numerous tribes, throughout a vast extent of country, the desert nature of which, as well as the mode of warfare of its inhabitants, or occupants, presented difficulties of formidable magnitude to an invading army. Garrisons had been left at every conquered town or village of any strength: the remaining disposable force was divided, and despatched to different points occupied by the enemy; but Mohham'mad 'Al'ee did not as yet himself conduct any enterprise. A division, under Too'soo'n Ba'sha, was sent against the town of Tar'abah; but the want of provisions caused this attempt to fail: the Turks had hardly commenced the siege when they were obliged to retreat; and the enemy pursued them to Koola'kh. The sea-port town of Ckoon'food'ah was taken by another detachment of the Turkish army; but soon after abandoned; being besieged and deprived of water. Other conquests were obtained, and, in like manner, relinquished. About the same period, So'oo'd, the Prince of the Wah'ha'bees, died, at his capital, Ed-Dir'ee'yeh. He was a man of very noble character; brave and generous. His son 'Abd Al'lah succeeded him.

After the reverses above mentioned, Too'soo'n Ba'sha was despatched northwards, to Yem'bo', to receive reinforcements which had arrived there from Egypt, and to march into the province of Nejd. Mohham'mad 'Al'ee remained in the Hheja'z; and after having a second time performed the pilgrimage, made a very successful campaign against the Wah'ha'bees in that province. Having taken several fortified towns, among which were Tar'abah and Ckoon'food'ah, he embarked at the latter place for Jid'deh, and thence proceeded to Mek'keh.

The expedition commanded by Too'soo'n Ba'sha was not altogether unsuccessful. After having penetrated, with the aid of a large force of Arabs, as far as the town of Er-Rass, and taken that and several other fortified places in his route, he received, from the Wah'ha'bee Prince, proposals of peace, which the wretched state of his own army induced him to accept. A treaty was accordingly concluded; by which 'Abd Al'lah bound himself to renounce those tenets which were peculiar to the Wah'ha'bees, to pay allegiance to the Turkish Soolta'n, to acknowledge him as the head of the religion, to obey all his commands, and to restore the plunder which the Wah'ha'bees had taken from the tomb of the Prophet.

While Too'soo'n was engaged in this campaign, Mohham'mad 'Al'ee visited El-Medee'neh, and returned to Jid'deh. Having, at the former place, received information of Napoleon's escape from Elba, and fearing that he meditated a second expedition to Egypt, he determined to return with all possible speed to his government. He embarked at Jid'deh for El-Ckoosey'r, and arrived at his capital in the middle of the year 1815 (which corresponded with the year of the flight 1230). The tranquillity of Egypt had been but little interrupted during his absence in Arabia; though the people suffered greatly during that period from the exactions necessary for the prosecution of the war. It was soon after his departure that the tyrannical measure of confiscating the lands which belonged to private individuals, and merely allotting to these persons a pension for life, as a partial compensation, was put in execution.

A few weeks after his return from Arabia, the Ba'sha avowed his intention of training his troops according to the European system; or of instituting what is called in Egypt, "*the Niza'm Gedee'd*": but the attempted innovation excited an alarming mutiny. Having received private information of the danger which awaited him, Mohham'mad 'Al'ee had retired, by night, to the Citadel; and the riotous troops, disappointed at not finding him in his palace in the Ezbekee'yeh, dispersed themselves throughout the city and plundered the shops, the warehouses, and even some of the private dwellings. The conduct of the Ba'sha on this occasion, was highly praiseworthy: he ordered his treasurer to make a full compensation to all those who had been pillaged; and, by means of presents, reduced the discontented soldiery to their allegiance. The project which had caused them to revolt was for a time abandoned.

Too'soo'n Ba'sha, having left garrisons in some of the conquered towns in Arabia, returned to Egypt, with the remainder of the troops under his command, soon after the conclusion of the treaty with 'Abd Al'lah Ibn So'oo'd. But this treaty was not altogether approved of by Mohham'mad 'Al'ee; and some of its conditions 'Abd Al'lah failed to fulfil: he asserted that the spoils of the Prophet's Tomb were no longer in his possession; and prayed also to be excused going to Constantinople, as the Soolta'n had commanded.

Under these circumstances, Mohham'mad 'Al'ee determined to send another army to Arabia; and availed himself of the opportunity to get rid of the disaffected troops who had lately frustrated his plans of military reform. Ibrahee'm Ba'sha was placed at the head of this army, which took its departure in the autumn of the year 1816 (or in the latter part of the year of the flight 1231).

Shortly after this period, Too'soo'n Ba'sha died, very suddenly, at his camp in the Gharbee'yeh, between the lake of Boorool'loos and the western branch of the Nile. It is believed that his malady was the plague, communicated by a beautiful slave-girl, sent to him, as a present, from Constantinople.

Ibrahee'm sailed up the Nile, with his troops; and, at Asyoo't, seized a vast number of peasants, for the service of the army. He then proceeded to Ckin'ë, and crossed the desert to El-Ckoosey'r: he embarked at the latter place, and landed at Yem'bo'. El-Medee'neh lay in the route which the army had to pursue: they paid their adoration at the tomb of the Prophet, and remained in that town several weeks. Proceeding towards their destination, they were joined by large bodies of Arabs. With these allies they pursued their course, through sandy and rocky deserts, towards the Wah'ha'bee capital; and after having achieved several victories (though none of great importance), they arrived before Er-Russ, one of the largest towns in their route. A Wah'ha'bee garrison, aided by the native inhabitants, very bravely defended this place. Ibrahee'm Ba'sha, after having battered the town, and repeatedly attempted to take it by assault, during the space of more than three months, and lost nearly the half of his army, was obliged to raise the siege. The Wah'ha'bee Prince might, at this time, have brought an overwhelming army against the invaders, and utterly have destroyed them: but he kept back from an unreasonable dread of the Turks; with whose mode of warfare he was but ill acquainted.

Ibrahee'm advanced by slow steps; but with more success; making himself master of every town and village in the line of his march; and frequently waiting for a considerable period for reinforcements from Egypt, or for ammunition, or provisions. Vast numbers of his troops perished from fatigue and privations during their progress through the deserts of Nejd. At the town of Door'amah, the last place of strength that lay in his route to Ed-Dir'ee'yeh, Ibrahee'm met with a brave resistance; in revenge for which, he caused all the inhabitants to be put to death, as soon as they had surrendered; with the exception of a number of women and children; the former of whom were spared not from motives of pity.

As Ibraheem's army advanced, that of 'Abd Al'lah Ibn So'oo'd, the Wah'ha'bee Prince, retired to Ed-Dir'ee'yeh, his capital, which consisted of a cluster of five small walled towns. The Turkish army arrived before that place in the spring of the year 1818 (or in the middle of the year of the flight 1233); and month after month they prosecuted a vigorous, but unsuccessful siege. During this period, a terrible misfortune befel them. All the powder in the Turkish camp, excepting a small quantity which had been distributed among the troops, was stored up in the same spot; and an accident occasioned its explosion. Ibrahee'm was therefore obliged to send for all the ammunition that could be spared from the various towns in Arabia where Turkish troops were stationed. Had the besieged been fully acquainted with his situation at that time, the mishap above mentioned would doubtless have proved fatal to his enterprise. Ed-Dir'ee'yeh fell, after a siege of more than five months. 'Abd Al'lah was received with much respect by Ibrahee'm Ba'sha. He was under the necessity of submitting to be conducted to Egypt, and thence to Constantinople, together with his treasurer and secretary; and took with him all that remained in his possession of the spoils of the Tomb of the Prophet;—namely, three richly adorned copies of the Ckoor-a'n, three hundred pearls, and an emerald. After having been paraded through the streets of Constantinople, he and his two faithful companions were beheaded; notwithstanding the intercession of Mohham'mad 'Al'ee in his favour.

After the fall of the capital of the Wah'ha'bees, Ibrahee'm Ba'sha remained in the province of Nejd nearly a year; occasionally making excursions, either to subdue tribes which still maintained their independence (whether in villages or in the open desert), or to procure provisions, which, in that barren country, were very scarce. By order of Mohham'mad 'Al'ee, Ed-Dir'ee'yeh was entirely destroyed, and its inhabitants dispersed. The fortifications of the principal towns and villages which Ibrahee'm had taken were also demolished. Several members of 'Abd Al'lah's family were sent to Egypt; where they remained in exile: but pensions were allowed them by Mohham'mad 'Al'ee.

During the course of this war in Arabia, rebellion broke forth, on several occasions, among the Turkish troops, and the life of their commander was more than once in imminent danger, but his courage and firmness never failed him.—Ibrahee'm returned, with his army, to El-Medee'neh, and thence proceeded to Mek'keh. Having performed the pilgrimage, and sacrifised three thousand sheep, he again bent his course northwards, embarked at Yem'bo', for El-Ckoosey'r, and in the end of the year 1819 (or the beginning of the year of the flight 1235), arrived at the capital of Egypt.

Mohham'mad 'Al'ee had begun, since his return from Arabia, to engage very largely in commerce. He had founded an extensive sugar manufactory, with a distillery of rum, at Er-Reyremoo'n, near Mel'laou'ee, in Upper Egypt, under the direction of an Englishman of the name of Brine, since dead. At a later period, he devoted large sums of money to the establishment of fabrics for the weaving of woollen, cotton, and linen cloths, and of silks; but the nation has suffered very severely from his monopoly of these manufactures; while European and other foreign goods of the same kinds, but of better qualities, may be procured at less expence; with the exception, perhaps, of the striped silks; some of which are not inferior to those of India. The cotton and linen cloths manufactured in the new fabrics are not of so good a quality as those which were made in Egypt before the monopoly. Natives of Egypt are mostly employed in these establishments, and, besides them, a few slaves; but the superintendents are Europeans. Shortly after the foundation of these fabrics, Mohham'mad 'Al'ee formed, at Ra's el-Wa'dee, in the Sharckee'yeh, a large plantation of mulberries, and a complete establishment for the rearing of silk-worms. He also founded, in the Citadel of Musr, an arsenal, containing a cannon-foundry, and a manufactory of small arms. His mercantile speculations, though in themselves prejudicial to the interests of his people, gave rise to some works of general utility; one of the first and most important of which was the new Canal of Alexandria, called the Mahh'moo'dee'yeh, which was dug during the year 1819. The *old* canal of Alexandria had long before become unnavigable; and a safe channel for the conveyance of merchandise by water between the Nile and the principal harbour of Alexandria was much wanted: the passage of the *bo'gha'z* (or bar) at the mouth of the western branch of the Nile being generally attended with considerable danger.

Since Mohham'mad 'Al'ee had found his Turkish and Arnaoo't troops so violently opposed to the adoption of the European military tactics, he had formed the project of raising a regular army of slaves. In order to procure a sufficient number of captives for this purpose, and, at the same time, to extend his dominions, and to get rid of a considerable proportion of his refractory troops, he despatched, in the summer of the following year (1820), an expedition to subdue the countries of Nubia and Senna'r. The army destined for this service consisted of between 4 and 5,000 men—Turkish and Arab cavalry and infantry, and a corps of 'Aba'b'deh Arabs—with ten pieces of cannon, and one mortar. The commander was Isma'ee'l Ba'sha, the youngest son of Mohham'mad 'Al'ee; then about sixteen years of age. The progress of the troops was slow; for they were obliged to keep near the boats in which their stores were conveyed; and, at each of the numerous cataracts, or rapids, which obstruct the navigation of the river, the army waited while these vessels were drawn up by means of a rope. The Nubians offered no resistance; but immediately beyond the province of Dun'ckal'ah (or Dun'gal'ah, as the name is commonly pronounced), which is the southernmost district of Nubia, the advanced guard, with Isma'ee'l at their head, encountered and defeated a force of Sha'ckee'yeh[1] Arabs, equal in number to the whole of the invading army; and a few days after, they again engaged the same enemies, and again defeated them, and received their submission. These Arabs were a tribe who subsisted chiefly by plunder. The arms, both of their cavalry and infantry, were, like those of the Nubians, a spear, a straight, double-edged sword, and a shield of the skin of the hippopotamus, or of the crocodile. A few of them had matchlocks. No further opposition of a formidable nature was encountered by Isma'ee'l's army in their march to Senna'r; and that country was subdued without a battle.—Ibrahee'm Ba'sha, soon after, joined this expedition; but ill health obliged him to return to Egypt after a short campaign.

Not content with the conquest of Nubia and Senna'r and the intermediate petty kingdoms, Mohham'mad 'Al'ee despatched a second army southwards, consisting of about the same number of troops as the former, under the command of his son-in-law, Mohham'mad Bey, Defturda'r. The object of this expedition was the subjugation of the country of Koordoofa'n, which lies between Senna'r and Da'r Foo'r; to the latter of which it was then tributary. A single battle decided the fate of Koordoofa'n. The Turks achieved the victory; but not without a hard contest; their enemies being a brave and warlike people: many of them

---

[1]Commonly pronounced *Sha'gee'yeh*.

well mounted, and clad in armour, such as was worn by the ancient Arabs;—a coat of iron mail, and a head-piece of iron, with a point at the crown and a piece of mail-work hanging behind, to defend the neck. Their other arms were the spear, javelin, sword, and shield; similar to those of the Nubians: but they were unused to contend with fire-arms; and the artillery of the Turks quite affrighted them.

In the years 1821 and 22, the insurrection in Greece obliged Mohham'mad 'Al'ee to send large subsidies to the Porte. Many armed vessels, and several numerous bodies of Arnaoo't and Turkish troops (amounting altogether to 7 or 8,000 men) were despatched at different periods; some to the Morea, some to Cyprus, and some to Candia, to aid in reducing the insurgents. Perhaps Mohham'mad 'Al'ee was not sorry to send away so considerable a proportion of his army of irregular troops, at a period when he was about to raise a new force, to be organized according to the European system, which the Turks and Arnaoo'ts so much disliked.—It was during this period, that the Ba'sha established the series of telegraphs between Alexandria and the metropolis.

In the latter part of the year 1822, Isma'ee'l Ba'sha fell a victim to the revenge of an Arab chief, whom he had insulted. Having parted from his army, with a very small retinue, he had proceeded to a neighbouring village, to levy contributions. The Mel'ik, or chief, of the province, whose name was Nimr,[1] demurred complying with the demand of the Ba'sha, who struck him on the face with his pipe. Nimr, suppressing the rage which this indignity excited in his breast, promised that he would endeavour to raise the required tax, and bring it on the morrow: but during the ensuing night, he repaired, with a party of his people, to the hut in which Isma'ee'l and almost all his retinue were sleeping, and having piled around it a quantity of straw and reeds, set fire to these combustibles. All who were within perished in the flames; and some troops who had accompanied the young Ba'sha part of the way from his head quarters were massacred by another party of Nimr's people. Isma'ee'l's remains were afterwards discovered, and conveyed to Musr, where they were buried, in the great cemetery called El-Ckara'feh.—The Defturda'r now took the supreme command of the army. Eager for vengeance, he made a diligent search for Nimr and his principal associates: these having escaped, he tortured and slaughtered in their stead a prodigious number of the innocent inhabitants.

During the year above-mentioned (1822), an army of regular troops was at length organized. Eight thousand men (chiefly slaves, from Senna'r and Koordoofa'n) were trained in the European manner, by French officers, at Aswa'n. I have mentioned before that one of the chief objects of the invasion of the countries on the south of Egypt was to procure captives for this purpose. Vast numbers of the inhabitants of the two countries above named were seized and despatched to Egypt; but many died of privations and fatigue during the journey. Not a few were

---

[1]"Nimr" signifies "a leopard."

accompanied by their wives and children: on their arrival in Egypt, the women, as well as all of the males who were not eligible for the army, were parted from their families and friends, and sent to Musr, to be sold. Spacious barracks, enclosing a square court, had been built at Aswa'n. Thither were despatched several memloo'ks (or white slaves), who were to be instructed as officers for the new troops. Many Egyptian fel'la'hhee'n (or peasants) were incorporated with the new troops. All who had not had the small-pox were vaccinated. The organization of this force was superintended by Col. Sève, a Frenchman, who afterwards became a Moos'lim, and received the name of Sooleyma'n, and the rank of a Bey.—A great mortality ensued among the Ethiopian troops, most of them being affected with hypochondria.[†] This was attributed, in a great measure, to the climate of Aswa'n; and they therefore changed their position to Is'na; whence by degrees, they descended lower and lower. In 1823, their camp was fixed at Ben'ee 'Al'ee, in Middle Egypt. The fel'la'hhee'n not only preserved their health, but proved very good troops: accordingly vast numbers of this class were pressed for the service; and of such the Egyptian army is now mainly composed. In 1823, the new conscripts amounted to about 24,000 men. These composed six regiments of infantry (*'asa'kir moosha'h*), of five battalions each (or 4,000 men): the battalion consisting of 8 companies; and each company of 100 men. The constitution of each regiment of the Egyptian army is still the same as was then adopted. Every regiment (*a'la'y*) is commanded by a colonel (*meer-a'la'y*, or *emee'r-a'la'y*) and a lieutenant colonel (*cka'im-macka'm*). Each battalion (*o'rtah*) has its chief (called *beem-ba'shee*, which literally signifies "chief of a thousand"); and each company (*booloo'k*) has its captain (called *yoo'z-ba'shee*, or chief of a hundred"). Every regiment has also a surgeon (who is called *hhakee'm-ba'shee*); and each battalion has an assistant surgeon (who is simply called *hhakee'm*). There is, besides, an *ima'm* (or religious minister), who presides at the prayers. A Ckoob'tee secretary (called *ka'tib*, or vulgarly *m'al'lim*) is also attached to each regiment. Besides the officers above mentioned, are adjutants, lieutenants, sergeants, corporals, drummers, and fifers. The common soldier is usually called *'as'ker'ee*, or *toofen'kjee*, which is pronounced by the Egyptians, *toofek'shee*: but in official papers, &c., the troops in general are dignified with the name of *El-Gih'a'dee'yeh*, which properly signifies "warriors who fight against infidels": they are commonly called, collectively, the Niza'm troops, or *en-Niza'm el-Gedee'd*, which literally means "the new system," and is understood to signify "the troops trained according to the new system." Their uniform is of red, coarse, woollen stuff, in winter; and of white cotton in summer. The jacket fits closely: the trousers are tight from the knee downwards; the upper part very full; tied round the body by a running band; and confined also by a leathern girdle. On the head is worn the common, close-fitting, red cloth cap, called *turboo'sh*; without

---

[†]Morbid depression.

a turban: on the feet, red shoes. The arms are the musket and bayonet.
The dress of the officers is similar in form; but richly embroidered with
gold; and they have an outer jacket, with hanging sleeves. They do not
wear the turban; but only the turboo'sh; like the common soldiers.—
Mohham'mad Bey, formerly Kikh'ya Bey, was, for several years,
Minister of War.¹ Ibrahee'm Ba'sha was named Commander in chief of
the forces. The latter set a useful example to the Turkish officers who
were under him, by submitting to be instructed by Col. Sève.—While
Mohham'mad 'Al'ee was employing French officers to organize his new
army, he was preparing to supply the places of these foreigners with his
own memloo'ks. A school for the instruction of young memloo'ks and
others intended for various military and civil posts had been established
in the palace of the late Isma'ee'l Ba'sha, at Boo'la'ck. This school was
under the direction of 'Osma'n Efen'dee Noo'r ed-Deen (now 'Osma'n
Bey), a young man who, with several others, had been sent by
Mohham'mad 'Al'ee to Europe, to prepare himself for this situation. He
made himself acquainted with the French and Italian languages, and
translated into Turkish several European works on military tactics, for
the use of his pupils. The school was afterwards removed to the building
called Ckusr El-'Ey'nee. I shall speak of it again hereafter.

   In the beginning of the year 1824, the 1st regiment of regular troops
received orders to march to Senna'r and the neighbouring countries to
take the place of the irregular troops under the Defturda'r. They arrived
at Aswa'n, and a small detachment of them had proceeded considerably
further, escorting some boats which conveyed their stores, when an
alarming rebellion broke forth among the fel'la'hhee'n of Upper Egypt.
A sheykh named Ahh'mad, an inhabitant of the village of
Es-Sa'limee'yeh, a few miles above Thebes, had proclaimed himself a
prophet, and denounced Mohham'mad 'Al'ee as a tyrant, who should be
put to death. Many thousands of the peasants of the villages between
Thebes and Is'na were roused by him to rebellion; and their party daily
increased. The troops above-mentioned, with the exception of one
battalion, marched back, to quell this insurrection; but, on approaching
the disturbed district, many of them deserted, and joined the rebels. The
detachment which had proceeded into Nubia also revolted, and returned
with the intention of uniting with the insurgents: they were, however,
met and opposed by the battallion which had been left at Aswa'n: a
desperate conflict ensued between these two parties, and the greater
number of the former were killed; the loss on the other side being very
trifling. The rebels in Upper Egypt amounted to between twenty and
thirty thousand; but few of these peasants had any other weapon than
the nebboo't, or long staff. Assaulted at the same time by the troops
from Aswa'n (about 2,000 men) and another force of regular troops on

---

¹He died in August, 1827; and Mahhmoo'd Bey was appointed to fill his place.
The latter had succeeded Mohham'mad Bey as Kikh'ya; and was himself
succeeded, in that quality, by Sheree'f Bey.

the north, they offered an obstinate resistance; but were overcome; and about one fourth of their number perished. Hundreds of swollen and putrefying bodies were seen floating down the Nile during several ensuing days.—The sheykh Ahh'mad, the false prophet, escaped, and has never since been heard of in Egypt.

In the ensuing summer, the 1st regiment of regular troops commenced their march, through Nubia, to Senna'r and Koordoofa'n. The irregular troops who occupied those countries, under the command of the Defturda'r, returned to Egypt immediately after the arrival of the former, in the autumn. The most intractable of these undisciplined soldiers (the Arnaoo'ts) were sent to Candia. These were the troops who had defeated Mohham'mad 'Al'ee's first attempt to introduce the European military tactics.

In the beginning of the same year, the 2nd regiment of regular troops was despatched to Arabia, to repel the Wah'ha'bees: for, notwithstanding the loss of their sovereign, this sect had but little decreased in number; and at this period they had collected considerable forces on the east and south of that part of the Hheja'z which Mohham'mad 'Al'ee had overrun. The new troops employed in this expedition acquitted themselves in a very creditable manner, and with complete success: they returned to Egypt in the latter part of the year 1826. As soon as Mohham'mad 'Al'ee thought it prudent to dismiss his Turkish garrison from the metropolis, he chose the above-mentioned regiment of regular troops to supply their place. The guards in the Citadel, at the town-gates, &c., are now composed of these Niza'm troops.

In 1824, as soon as the 1st and 2nd regiments had left the camp for their respective destinations, as above stated, Mohham'mad 'Al'ee prepared to despatch the remainder of his new troops (namely, the 3d, 4th, and 6th regiments, to Greece; the Soolta'n having imposed upon him the chief burden of prosecuting a war which had proved too difficult for the Turkish forces. Ibrahee'm Ba'sha was appointed to the command of this expedition; which Sooleyma'n Bey (formerly Col. Sève) also accompanied; being colonel of one of the regiments. The army embarked in the summer, and after a cruise of seven months, in search of the Greek fleet, landed at Modón, in the Morea.—An account of Ibrahee'm's campaigns in that country need not here be given; as it would be foreign to the main subject of this work.

The whole of Mohham'mad 'Al'ee's then-existing force of regular troops being thus employed abroad, recruits were forthwith raised for three new regiments,—the 7th, 8th, and 9th. The camp was soon after removed from Ben'ee 'Al'ee to the immediate neighbourhood of the metropolis; and finally, it was fixed near the village of El-Kha'n'keh, 13 miles, in a north-north-east direction, from the capital. Thousands of fel'la['] hhee'n were now pressed in every province of Egypt, dragged away from their homes, bound with ropes, like criminals, and conducted to this place; many of them followed by their wives and children. From these were selected a sufficient number to form three more regiments.

The 7th and 8th regiments, as soon as they were fit for service (in the latter part of the year 1825), were sent to join Ibrahee'm's army in the Morea. In the following year, the 9th regiment was despatched to Arabia, to relieve the 2nd, which (as I have already mentioned) returned to Egypt; and shortly after, the 12th was also sent thither; the 9th having been defeated by the Wah'ha'bees, and forced to retreat to Jid'deh. The 10th embarked, in August, 1827, for the Morea. There remained, therefore, in Egypt, only one complete regiment of regular troops, namely the 11th.

A few words may here be added respecting the camp of El-Kha'n'keh, the various institutions connected with it, and the improvements which have been made in the system of discipline pursued there.—The camp is salubriously situated, just within the confines of the desert, immediately on the right of the route to Syria; the village of El-Kha'n'keh lying at a short distance behind it, close to the cultivated land. The metropolis being thirteen miles (or between four and five hours' march) distant, the troops are beyond the sphere of its attractions; for they cannot repair thither without leave of absence for a whole day, which is not easily obtained. A number of French officers have been constantly employed in training the troops at El-Kha'n'keh; but none of them have ever held any rank or command in the army, excepting a few who have embraced the Mohham'madan faith. For the space of about a year and a half, General Boyer superintended the course of military discipline, and received, for his services, a handsome salary. Mohham'mad 'Al'ee was very anxious that some of his own subjects should be qualified to perform the office of these Frank instructors: but few of his memloo'ks or Turkish officers, would apply, with any degree of spirit or diligence, to the necessary studies. One of the few friends to European innovations was 'Osma'n Noo'r ed-Deen, whom I have before mentioned. Not many months after the establishment of the camp at El-Kha'n'keh, this young man, who had been until that period, director of the school of the Ckusr El-'Ey'nee without having ever held any military rank, received the title of Bey, and was placed next in command to Mohham'mad Bey, the Minister of War, who, finding him well qualified for that high post, confided to him nearly the entire management of the affairs of the camp.—*The School of the Ckusr El-'Ey'nee*[1] is an establishment for the instruction of youths destined for the army, the navy, or civil employments under the government. Originally, a number of young memloo'ks and Turks received, in this institution, a very superficial kind of education, and were then appointed captains in the army of regular troops; the inferior officers being mostly native Egyptians, selected from among the conscripts: but latterly, the system pursued in this school has been much improved. The number of scholars is generally about a thousand. Most of them are memloo'ks and Turks, between the ages of twelve and

[1] For the situation of this building, see letter T in the plan of the environs of Musr.

sixteen; but there are also a few adult pupils. Of those intended for the army, each, on leaving the school, receives the appointment of second lieutenant (*moola'zim ta'nee*); there being two lieutenants to each company of regular troops. At the same time he enters an upper school, at the camp; where he is instructed in higher branches of knowledge. At the Ckusr El-'Ey'nee, the scholars above alluded to, and those destined for the navy, or for civil posts, are instructed in the Arabic and Turkish languages (and some of them, also, in French and Italian), as well as in writing and arithmetic, and the principles of geometry. The elements of military and naval tactics are also taught at this establishment. Most of the professors are Europeans. Besides the scholars above mentioned, there are also, at the Ckusr El-'Ay'nee, about three hundred military conscripts, under a course of instruction.—The *upper school*, for officers of the army, is in the vicinity of the camp; at a little distance from the village of El-Kha'n'keh. This school, and the residences of the principal officers attached to the camp, compose an assemblage of buildings which have quite a European aspect; being white-washed, and having glass windows. The name of *Giha'd-A'ba'd* is given to this groupe of houses. Adjacent to them are extensive gardens, laid out with somewhat of European taste. The officers who enter as pupils in the school of Giha'd-A'ba'd pursue the study of the Arabic, Persian, and French languages, arithmetic, geometry (practical as well as theoretical), and various other branches of science more or less connected with military affairs. The art of drawing is also taught there; but, as their religion forbids the application of that art to the representation of any thing that has life, none of the officers at the camp are *obliged* (nor were any, at first, easily *persuaded*) to study it: however, by degrees, the scruples of many of them, on this point, have been overcome. Most of the professors in this institution are Europeans.—Another very important establishment connected with the camp is *the Hospital of Ab'oo Za'abal*; so called from a neighbouring village of that name; and situated about two miles from El-Kha'n'keh, in a north-north-west direction. It is a low, but very spacious building, surrounding a square court. The apartments are all on the ground-floor. They afford accommodation for above a thousand patients. In the centre of the court is a building which contains the dispensary, a school of medicine and anatomy, baths, kitchens, and other offices. Dr. Clot, a clever French physician, the founder and director of this useful institution, has about a hundred young men, natives of Egypt, under his tuition; and he has so far overcome their religious prejudices as to induce them to dissect human bodies. Some of them have already attained considerable skill in most of the ordinary surgical operations; but they are regarded, by the vulgar, as utter infidels. After about three years' study, they are appointed surgeons in the army. A teacher of the French language, and several other European professors, besides Dr. Clot, are attached to this institution.—Of the Printing-Office at Boo'la'ck, I have given an account in the former volume of this work.— If the officers of the Egyptian regular troops be not well instructed, it will be for no want of zeal on the part of Mohham'mad 'Al'ee. He has sent thirty or forty young men (Turks, Memloo'ks, and Egyptians) to France; and several others to England; to study various sciences and arts. The very high pay which he awards to his military officers must excite among them much emulation. The pay of a colonel of a regiment is 16 purses per month (or $111l.2s.2^{2/3}d$); that of a chief of a battalion, 4 purses (or $27l.15s.6^{2/3}$); that of a captain of a company, one purse (or $6l.18s.10^{2/3}d$)[1]; besides rations, horse, arms and uniforms. The common soldier receives half a piaster per day (or a penny and two thirds), besides his rations. The new Egyptian troops are certainly inferior to those of most European nations; but greatly superior to the *Turkish* Niza'm troops. Besides the twelve regiments already mentioned, a corps of artillery has also been organized according to the European system; but no cavalry. At the period of my departure from Egypt (in the spring of the year 1828), the Egyptian regular troops were calculated to amount to about 40,000 men. Only one complete regiment was then in Egypt. The irregular troops, consisting of Turkish cavalry and Arnaoo't infantry, then remaining in Egypt, probably did not amount to more than 10,000.

It was only about two years before that period that Mohham'mad 'Al'ee began to introduce the European tactics in his navy. During the last two years of the war in Greece, he considerably augmented his naval force by the purchase of European and American vessels; and several ships (chiefly corvettes, with one or more frigates) were built for him at Marseilles, Genoa, and Leghorn. At the same time, French officers were employed in instructing a vast number of Egyptian boatmen of the Nile, who had been pressed to man the fleet, and several young Turks, and memloo'ks, intended for naval officers. Until the year 1827, a degree of jealousy had prevented the due cooperation of the fleet of Constantinople with that of Egypt: to obviate this evil, and to transfer a heavy expence to one who was considered better able than his sovereign to support it, Mohham'mad 'Al'ee was appointed commander in chief of the whole naval force of the Turkish Empire; but he was not required to take the personal command. The fleets of Constantinople and Egypt sailed together for the Morea in the month of August, that same year, with the 10th Egyptian regiment.[2] Their almost total destruction at Navarino, by the combined squadrons of England, France, and Russia, is well known. The news of this event spread consternation among the Europeans resident in Egypt; but Mohham'mad 'Al'ee had assured them, when the intervention of the three powers above mentioned first became known in the East, that they need entertain no apprehensions as to their

---

[1]The purse is 500 piasters. I reckon the piaster at 3 pence and one third of a penny, or 72 piasters to the pound stirling [sic]; which was the general rate of exchange during my stay in Egypt.
[2]The departure of this regiment I have before mentioned.

own safety or liberty; and on this occasion, no popular movement against the Franks was allowed to take place in Egypt.[1]

The eventful career of Mohham'mad 'Al'ee is not yet ended. In the spring of the year 1828 (when I quitted Egypt) he was in expectation of the speedy return of his army from Greece. It remains to be seen whether his sway will be less oppressive when he is no longer burdened with the heavy expenses attending the prosecution of difficult and tedious wars. Perhaps, under other circumstances, he might not have exercised that system of monopoly which has rendered him so unpopular. In his character, as displayed by the foregoing history, we see much to admire and much to censure. He has achieved surprising conquests over powerful, turbulent factions, and over religious and national prejudices. But has he ameliorated the condition of the nation which he governs?—He has exterminated the Memloo'ks who had so long usurped almost the entire dominion of Egypt; a body of tyrants, under whom that ill-fated country could never be in a state of tranquillity. Shocking as were the means employed for their destruction, the result has been most beneficial. The security which the European traveller enjoys in every part of Egypt is an evidence of this. Had there been no such object to be attained, the Ba'sha would, probably, have refused to obey the commands of his sovereign, from whom the order for the extirpation of the Ghooz'z doubtless proceeded. It is well known that, soon after the commencement of the insurrection in Greece, Mohham'mad 'Al'ee received orders to massacre all the Greeks who had taken refuge in Egypt: but while the blood of that unfortunate people streamed in the streets of Constantinople and in other parts of the Turkish Empire, Egypt still afforded an asylum to all who fled thither. Mohham'mad 'Al'ee has, moreover, relieved Egypt, and particularly its metropolis, from the presence of an undisciplined army of Turks and Arnaoo'ts, who availed themselves of every opportunity to revel in plunder and rapine and murder, and has substituted a force of well organized native troops. Thus he has restored peace and order to the whole country; and this is almost the sum total of the good which he had wrought for the present inhabitants; while the evils which he has imposed upon them are vastly preponderant. He has, in some parts, carried cultivation to a much greater extent, by digging new canals, repairing others, and forming dams and sluices; thus fertilizing large tracts of land which had long lain waste[2]: but he has impoverished the

---

[1]Mr. Salt, our consul-general in Egypt (as well known by his literary productions and by the honourable mention which has been made of him by many travellers), died, at Desoo'ck, in the Delta, on the 29th of October, in this year; nine days after the battle of Navarino, and shortly before the news of that event reached the place of his death. In him I lost a most kind and valued friend. [Other sources give Salt's date of death as 30 October 1827.]

[2]In one of the Egyptian newspapers, I find it stated that the number of trees planted in Lower Egypt, by order of the government, during the year of the

inhabitants—I might almost say that he has ruined and famished them—by monopolizing the produce of the fields, and all the principal manufactures. By confiscating the lands which belonged to private individuals, and giving these persons nothing in the way of compensation but a pension for life, he has reduced the whole of the Egyptian peasantry almost to the condition of slaves. The agriculturist rents the land of the government, and the whole of its produce he must take to the agents of the Ba'sha, who receive it at a very low price: or the latter give out the seed, receive the produce, and pay the cultivator for his labours: the corn which he may require for the support of himself and his family he is obliged to purchase of the government for about double the original price, or prime cost. So is it also with the produce of the loom, and with many other manufactured commodities. Though the Egyptian peasant has no other bed than a piece of coarse matting, even *that* he is not allowed to make for his own use. Under these regulations with regard to agriculture and manufactures, the misery of the labourer in Egypt sadly contrasts with the amazing fertility of the soil. There is, perhaps, no country in the world where the peasant is so cruelly oppressed: but the genial nature of the climate renders his privations light in comparison with what they would otherwise be; and we find him generally cheerful; though often murmuring.—Mohham'mad 'Al'ee may justly be compared with Ahh'mad Ibn' Too'loo'n, who governed Egypt with the same despotic sway, carried his victorious arms into neighbouring countries, executed many important public works, and enormously increased the revenue of his dominions. Mohham'mad 'Al'ee pays the same kind of allegiance to the Turkish Soolta'n that Ibn' Too'loo'n did to the Khalee'feh of Bughda'd; and if the jealousy of the Porte should cause him to be declared a rebel, he will, probably, in the same manner defy his sovereign, and become the founder of an independent dynasty; such as the Ben'ee Too'loo'n, and such as the Eiyoo'bee'yeh, who, though absolute monarchs, acknowledged the Khalee'feh of Bughda'd as the head of the religion: in that light might Mohham'mad 'Al'ee, to favour the prejudices of his people, still regard the Turkish Soolta'n; and, though he should pay him no tribute, still cause him to be prayed for in the mosques. Many persons have supposed that Mohham'mad 'Al'ee has long been desirous of throwing off his allegiance to his sovereign: that he would rather do so than be deposed, I have little doubt. It has also been frequently reported that attempts have been made to poison him. This would be difficult to accomplish: for he never eats in the houses of his grandees, or of any other persons; and whenever he pays a visit, no strange hand prepares or presents his coffee: this, and his pipes, are brought by his own confidential, well-paid officers. Among the qualities for which Mohham'mad 'Al'ee deserves most commendation may be

---

flight 1245 (commencing on the 1st of July, 1829 of our era) was 2,105,520. Of these, 820,999 were mulberry-trees, for the silk-worms—281,103, sunts (or Nile acacias) for charcoal—404,646, tamarisks—219,588, vines—145,778, peach-trees.

mentioned his disposition (unusual among Turks) to receive the advice and instruction of intelligent foreigners. It is from them that he has acquired those notions which have gained him so much renown throughout Europe. He receives European visiters with courtesy, and converses with them, by means of his interpreter, in a free and lively manner. Coffee is usually presented to them; but not pipes, unless to persons of high rank. Those who wear the Frank habit, during such visits, conform with the etiquette of their own countries, opposed as it is, in many points, to Oriental notions of propriety.

"Turn we to yonder rocky desert, now,
Where, to th'admiring gaze, majestic rise
Those monuments to which all others bow
In conscious littleness, unto the skies
Lifting their heads in glory; vast, sublime,
That have alone, for untold ages past,
Proudly defied the ravages of time,
And o'er so many generations cast
Their mystic shadows."
"Come! and let us scan
Their form, position, structure, now descending
Through lonely passages, with dubious light,
And, now, our steps in strange emotion bending
To lofty galleries, whose fearful height
Mocks the dim taper's radiance, till we come
Unto a desolate chamber, and a tomb
Of polished granite fashion'd, vain display!
For ev'n the very bones are swept away,
Nor, through the gloom obscure, is ought descried
Save, here and there, a solitary bat,
Sole tenant of this mansion of high state,
That flaps his dusky wings in scorn of human pride."

The above lines are from a little work entitled "Egypt, a Descriptive Poem, with notes, by a Traveller,[1]" printed at Alexandria, in 1824.

---

[1] Mr. Salt.

Chapter XV.
The Pyramids of El-Gee'zeh.[1]

Journey to the Pyramids—Description of their general aspect—The author's abode in an ancient sepulchral grotto near the Pyramids—Name of the Pyramids—Description of the Great Pyramid, and of three small pyramids in its vicinity, &c.—The Second Pyramid, and remains around it—The Third Pyramid; its temple and causeway; and 3 small pyramids adjacent to it—Tombs in the vicinity of the Great Pyramid—The Great Sphinx—Sepulchral grottoes and catacombs—History and destination of the Pyramids.

---

[1]Though I spent (during three different visits) not less than thirty-two days[†] at the Pyramids of El-Gee'zeh, employed in making drawings, notes, &c., and a week at the more southern Pyramids, I did not accomplish all that I had proposed to do in that time. It yet remained for me to make some notes of the sculptures in a few of the sepulchral grottoes (which I had not sufficiently examined) in the neighbourhood of the Pyramids of El-Gee'zeh, to take measurements of the interior of one of the Pyramids of Dah'shoo'r, and to finish one of my drawings. I therefore intended to pay one more visit to these monuments; but illness and other circumstances prevented my doing so. The drawing above alluded to is that from which the 6th plate [fig. 24] (here annexed) is engraved: in no. 1 of this plate, the tombs marked *g,g* were merely sketched in from the top of the Great Pyramid; and I may, perhaps, have omitted a few less conspicuous than the rest: in no. 2, the topography of the plain between the Pyramids and the Nile is laid down from too few observations to be as accurate as the other parts of the plan; though it is sufficiently correct to illustrate my remarks respecting the site of Memphis, &c.—In no. 1, the letters *a,b,c* indicate three deep trenches, cut in the rock—*d,e,f*, three small pyramids—*g,g*, oblong tombs, in the form of truncated pyramids—*h*, one of the most remarkable of these tombs—*i*, a tomb containing beautiful painted bas-reliefs—*k,k*, a row of oblong tombs, in a state of ruin—*l*, a ruined structure, called "the Temple of the Second Pyramid"—*m*, a sepulchral grotto—*n,o*, the "Temple" and Causeway of the Third Pyramid—*p*, a square pit, lined with masonry—*q,r,s*, three small pyramids—*t*, a sepulchral grotto, containing interesting sculptures—*u*, a sepulchral grotto called "the Sheykh's Grotto"—*w*, a ruined structure which appears to have been a pyramid—*x*, a groupe of sycamores and palms—*y,y,y*, sepulchral grottoes—*z*, grotto called "the Tomb of Numbers"—*aa*, an excavated tomb—*bb*, a ruined causeway—*cc*, a ruined wall of massive stones, nearly buried in the sand.—In no. 3, of the same plate, *a* indicates the principal Pyramid of Sack'cka'rah, called "the Pyramid of Steps"—*b*, a large mummy-pit—*c*, a large sepulchral grotto—*d*, a grotto with arched chambers—*e*, catacombs of birds, or ibis-mummies—*f*, an unfinished pyramid called "Mus'tab'at Far'oo'n"—*g*, Great Northern Pyramid of Dah'shoo'r—*h*, Great Southern Pyramid of Dah'shoo'r—*i*, brick pyramid—*k*, brick pyramid.

[†]Lane does not count his first, brief trip to Giza.

During the first five days after my arrival in the metropolis of Egypt, I found so much amusement in strolling through the narrow, intricate streets, and gazing at the public buildings, the shops, and the thronging populace of that picturesque and interesting city, besides the business of making sundry purchases of clothing, arms, &c., seeking for a house in which to take up my abode, then procuring the necessary furniture, and hiring servants, that I delayed, thus long, visiting the Pyramids; though they had been many times within my view, and, in a direct line, less than three leagues distant.[1] On the sixth day (the 8th of October, 1825), while the house which I had hired was being cleaned and prepared for my reception, I set out, in company with a small party of Europeans, with the intention of gratifying my curiosity by only a slight inspection of the principal pyramids; intending, on another occasion, to spend several days in the examination of these monuments. The journey thither occupied about six hours; for, in consequence of the inundation, we were obliged, after having crossed the river, to follow a very circuitous route. At other seasons of the year, when the water has disappeared from the fields, and when the canals are dry, or fordable, the journey may be easily performed in about *half* that time.

Mounted on asses, we left the city at noon, and proceeded to Musr 'Atee'ckah, where we embarked, with our donkeys, on board a ferry-boat, and passed over to El-Gee'zeh.[2] At that season, the Nile was at the highest. The view of the Pyramids, of which an engraving is here annexed (plate 7[†]), taken from an island just above the town of El-Gee'zeh, was made at a period when the river was very low, in the spring of the year 1827. To the right is seen a small part of the town of El-Gee'zeh. The Pyramids are about five miles and a half distant. The first to the right is the Great Pyramid. Before it are three small monuments of the same kind. The Second Pyramid, standing on rather higher ground, *appears* as lofty as the first. Before it is discerned a ruined building called "the Temple of the Second Pyramid." Before the Third Pyramid is a similar building; and on the *southern* side are three small pyramids, of which only two are seen in this view. The clearness of the atmosphere renders all these objects distinctly visible even from a greater distance.

At El-Gee'zeh, we again mounted our donkeys, and, instead of crossing the fields in a direct line towards the Pyramids, bent our course to the southward, and proceeded, for more than an hour, towards the site

---

[1]The distance of the Pyramids of El-Gee'zeh (or rather, of the Great Pyramid), in a direct line, from the nearest part of Musr, is about 7 British miles and a quarter: from Musr 'Atee'ckah 5 and three quarters; and from the Nile, or from the town of El-Gee'zeh, 5 and one quarter.

[2]Thus the natives of Egypt, in general, pronounce this name—the g hard, as in the word *give*:—The Arabs of other countries would pronounce it El-Jee'zeh; and travellers often write it so.

[†]Fig. 25.

of ancient Memphis; winding through extensive groves of lofty and luxuriant palm-trees, loaded with ripening dates, and encompassing several villages and small lakes. This part of our route was not far from the bank of the river. The pyramids were almost constantly in sight; sometimes to our right; at other times nearly behind us; and they appeared as if only separated from us by a few narrow fields. Our journey afterwards became less agreeable. Leaving the palm-groves and the vicinity of the river, we passed along a winding, narrow dike, formed of earth, and elevated several feet above the reach of the inundation, which now overspread extensive tracts on either side of us: for the cultivable land is lower towards the desert than it is near the banks of the river. We thus approached the sandy Libyan waste; and looking beyond the swamps and floods and distant villages, beheld no fewer than twenty pyramids, of various dimensions and in different states of preservation, rising from the low calcareous range: the three ruined pyramids of Ab'oo Seer lying at a short distance before us: those of El-Gee'zeh to the right of the former, and more distant; and those of Sack'cka'rah and Dah'shoo'r to the left. But the nearer we had as yet approached towards the objects of our destination, the less grand and imposing did they appear. From their aspect, as I first drew near to them, I should have formed a very inadequate opinion of their dimensions. The extraordinary clearness of the atmosphere caused them to appear much nearer than they really were. I could scarcely believe my conductor when he informed me that they were a league distant from us. When we had arrived within a mile of the Great Pyramid, the illusion became greater: the courses of stone were then plainly discernible; and I could easily calculate that they were not more in number than the courses of brick in a house about 50 or 60 feet high. These presented a scale by which the eye was much deceived in estimating the altitude of the structure; being unaccustomed to the sight of stones of such enormous magnitude employed in building. But neither of these causes would be sufficient to produce such an illusion if there were any neighbouring object with which the pyramids might be contrasted. I was fully convinced of this when I arrived at the base of the Great Pyramid. It was then curious to observe how distant appeared those places where I had thought myself nearly at my journey's end. The clearness of the air would have deceived me then, as before; but I was looking at objects which were less strange to me; such as palm-trees, and villages, and the tents of Arabs.

    I approached the Pyramids at sunset, and was much struck with the solemn effect of the scene, which I have endeavoured to represent. (See plate 8[†]). The principal object in this view is the Great Pyramid. Of the three small pyramids which are before it, one (being lower than the others) is not here visible. In the abrupt front of the rock are seen the entrances of several sepulchral grottoes; in one of which we passed the night. Near the centre of the view is the Second Pyramid, with a portion

---

[†]Fig. 26.

of its casing remaining upon the upper part. Before it is seen its "temple," and, nearer to the foreground, the head of the Great Sphinx. To the left of the Second Pyramid is the Third, with its "temple" on the east, and three small pyramids on the south. Before this, and considerably nearer, is seen a ruined building, on a base of rock, which also appears to have been a pyramid. To the left, and still nearer, is a small groupe of sycamores and palms, which thrive luxuriantly in the midst of the sandy waste. The natural strata observable in the point of the mountain at the left extremity of the view cause it to appear as if partly cased with masonry.[1] Before this mountain is a ruined wall of massive stones, nearly buried by the sand.

Another engraving, here annexed, (plate 9[†]) shews the aspect of the Pyramids from a somewhat nearer position, on the east of the Great Pyramid. To the left of the Great Pyramid are seen the Second and Third; and at the left extremity of the view is seen a part of the head of the Great Sphinx; beyond which is the ruined building mentioned in the description of the 8th plate.[‡] At the other extremity of the view is seen an old, ruined causeway, doubtless a part of that which was built by Ckar'a'ckoo'sh, for the convenience of transporting stones from the pyramids to El-Cka'hireh, when he constructed the Citadel and the Third Wall of that city; and this portion may have been raised upon the ruins of that which Herodotus describes. The more ancient causeway was raised for the purpose of facilitating the conveyance of stones from the quarries on the eastern side of the Nile to the site of the Great Pyramid, to line the passages of that structure, and perhaps to case its exterior.—In the same view are also seen the ancient sepulchral grottoes before mentioned; in one of which I passed the night, the first time that I visited the Pyramids. This visit was a very short one; for I left at sunrise on the following morning; having entered the Great Pyramid in the evening, and ascended to its summit before day-break.

On the 17th of December, in the same year, I again visited the Pyramids, to examine them at my leisure. Taking with me my two servants (an Egyptian and a Nubian), and necessary stores and utensils, I followed the same circuitous route as on the former occasion, and arrived, as before, at about the hour of sunset. I chose for my abode one of the above-mentioned grottoes, more capacious and convenient than that in which I slept during my first visit. Upon the steep before these ancient depositories of the dead were strewed many bones and rags of mummies; and opposite the entrances of some of the grottoes lay heaps of limbs and whole bodies, stripped of their bandages, and the skin quite black. Some of the sculls, I remarked, were of an extraordinary thickness. The grotto of which I made choice may be distinguished from the rest by

---

[1] It has been thus erroneously represented by Denon, in the back ground of his view of the Sphinx.

[†] Fig. 27.

[‡] I.e., in the footnote at the beginning of this chapter describing fig. 24.

its having three small apertures, which served as windows, to the left of the entrance. The interior was about 8 feet in width, and twice as much in length; and was divided into two apartments by a modern wall. The sculptures with which it had been adorned were almost wholly effaced. Its appearance, when I first arrived, was rather gloomy; but when the floor was swept, and a mat, rug, and mattress spread in the inner apartment, a candle lighted, as well as my pipe, and my arms hung about upon wooden pegs driven into crevices in the walls, I looked around me with complacency, and felt perfectly satisfied. However, as my abode was in the desert, I thought it prudent to hire two Arabs from the nearest village, to sleep at the door of the grotto; for many Bed'awees daily passed near the place, and could not fail of observing inhabitants there. Before the door of my dwelling was an agreeable terrace, where, *in the shade of the rock*, I sat every evening (at Christmas), with my pipe and coffee, enjoying the mild air, and the delightful view over the plain, towards the capital. The thermometer, at that season, generally rose to 75°, in the shade, in the middle of the day. In this tomb I took up my abode for a fortnight; and never did I spend a more happy time; though provided with fewer articles of luxury than I might easily and reasonably have procured; but I had fancied, though perhaps unjustly, that the more comforts I had, the less intent should I be upon my work. My appearance, at that time, corresponded with my mode of living; for, on account of my being exposed to considerable changes of atmospheric temperature in passing in and out of the Great Pyramid, I assumed the *hhera'm* (or woollen sheet) of the Bed'awee, which is a most convenient dress under such circumstances; a part, or the whole, being thrown about the person, according to the different degrees of warmth which he may require. I also began to accustom myself to lay aside my shoes, on many occasions; for the sake of greater facility in climbing and descending the steep and smooth passages in the Pyramid; and would advise others, in similar cases, to do the same. Once or twice my feet were slightly lacerated; but after two or three days, they were proof against the sharpest stones. From the neighbouring villages I procured all that I wanted in the way of food; as eggs, milk, butter, fowls, and camels' flesh; but bread was not to be obtained any where nearer than the town of El-Gee'zeh, without employing a person to make it.—One family, consisting of a little old man (named 'Al'ee), his wife—who was not half his equal in years—and a little daughter, occupied a neighbouring grotto; guarding some antiquities deposited there by Caviglia. Besides these, I had no nearer neighbours than the inhabitants of a village about a mile distant. The sheykh 'Al'ee made himself useful in bringing water from a well which Caviglia had dug in the sandy plain, just at the foot of the slope before the grottoes. He was a poor, half-witted creature; but possessing strong feelings; as was exemplified by an occurrence which happened during my stay at the Pyramids.—One afternoon, my cook had sent old 'Al'ee's little girl to the neighbouring village, to purchase some tobacco. The child not having returned at sunset, I became uneasy, and despatched the servant to search for her, and bring her back. 'Al'ee had also become anxious, and had sent his wife for the same purpose: but when the night had closed in, and he had received no tidings of the little girl, he seemed almost frantic: he beat his breast, stamped upon the ground, and continued, for some time, incessantly screaming "Ya' Mebroo'keh! Ya' Mebroo'keh!" After I had in vain endeavoured, for a little while, to pacify him, he set off running towards the village. About five minutes more elapsed, and I was sitting before the grotto, wondering that no one had returned, and that not even my two Bed'awee guards had come as usual, when I was alarmed by loud and piteous cries in the desert plain before me. Leaving my other servant at the grotto—for a strange youth was there—I ran towards the spot whence the voice seemed to issue. As it was dark, I could see nothing; but after I had proceeded some little distance, I heard these words repeated very rapidly over and over again,—"I testify that there is no deity but God! and I testify that Mohham'mad is God's Apostle!"—I soon after found poor old 'Al'ee, lying on the ground. He told me that an 'Efree't (or demon) had seized him by the throat, and thrown sand into his mouth, and that he was almost suffocated.[1] My two Bed'awees, whom my cook and 'Al'ee's wife had engaged to assist them in their search, had found the child, and were, like myself, drawn to this spot by the old man's cries. They helped him to walk back; but the poor creature had been so much terrified and distressed, that, for several days after, he was quite idiotic.— On the second day after I had taken up my quarters at the Pyramids, a young Bed'awee—the stranger before-mentioned—claimed the rights of hospitality from me. He remained with me until I quitted my sepulchral abode, and, being a very clever and witty youth, amused me exceedingly, every evening, while I was smoking my pipe, by reciting stories and verses from the popular romance of Ab'oo Zeyd: but at the same time, he gave much offence to my Egyptian servant, by his contempt of the Fella'hhee'n (or Peasants). He had deserted from the Ba'sha's army of regular troops, as the frankly told me; and was afraid to enter the villages, lest he should be recognized and sent to the camp of El-Kha'n'keh.—I now proceed with the description of the Pyramids.

The Pyramids of El-Gee'zeh are called, in Arabic, هرام الجيزه *Hira'm El-Gee'zeh*; or simply *El-Hira'm* (the Pyramids), as being superior to all other monuments of the same kind. The word هرم *har'am* (of which هرام *hira'm* and اهرام *ahra'm* are the plural forms) is the common designation of a pyramid, in the Arabic language; and also signifies the state of extreme old age, and decrepitude. *Har'am* is, probably, an ancient Egyptian word; and the latter signification may have been derived by the Arabs from that word; decrepitude being considered rather as the natural concomitant of extreme old age, than as having any reference to the state of the Pyramids. It has been suggested to me by a

---

[1] It seems that the Arabs are subject to a spasm in the throat, which they attribute to the above cause. These people are dreadfully afraid of 'Efree'ts.

friend that the word *pyramid* is derived (through the Greek πυραμίς) from *pi har'am*; *pi* being the ancient Egyptian article. The word حرم *har'am* has no relation to حرم *hhar'am*, which signifies "sacred," or "forbidden"; and which is forcibly distinguished from the former in pronunciation.

The bed of rock on which the Great Pyramid is situated is about 150 feet above the sandy plain which intervenes between it and the cultivated land. It is a soft, testaceous lime-stone; abounding, particularly, with those little petrifactions described, by Strabo, as found in great quantities around the Pyramids, and supposed to be *petrified lentils*, the leavings of the workmen who built the Pyramids! These abound in many parts of the chain of mountains by which the valley of the Nile is confined on this side. The stone, when newly cut, is of a whitish colour; but, by exposure to the air, it becomes darker, and assumes a yellowish tint. The level parts and slopes of the rock are covered with sand and pebbles and fragments of stone, among which are found pieces of granite and porphyry, rock crystal, agates, and abundance of petrified shells, &c. The relative situations of the Pyramids are shewn by the plan which I have given. The four sides of each of these monuments face the four cardinal points.

The Great Pyramid is that which is described, by Herodotus, as the work of a Pharaoh named Cheops, whom Diodorus Siculus calls Chem'nis.[1] The height of the Great Pyramid is not much greater than that of the Second: the former having lost several ranges at the top; while the upper part of the latter is nearly entire: but the base of the former is considerably larger; though the difference is not very remarkable to the eye; and in the solidity and regularity of its construction, it is vastly superior. The pleasure which is felt by the modern traveller in surveying the Pyramids is not a little increased by the consideration of their mysterious antiquity, and the reflection that many philosophers and heroes of antient times have in like manner stood before them, wrapt in admiration and amazement. The stupendous magnitude of the Great Pyramid is most clearly apparent when the observer places himself near one of its angles. From such a station, therefore, I made a most careful and accurate view, with the camera-lucida. (See plate 10[†]). As travellers generally approach the Pyramids from the east, or north-east, and ascend to the summit up the north-eastern angle, I chose the point from which to make my view opposite that angle, rather than any of the others; and because the entrance of the Pyramid is also seen from that position. In order to shew the magnitude of the stones, I have represented a person standing at the angle. The view of the Pyramid from this point, though it is the best that we can obtain, conveys a very inadequate idea of its size,

---

[1]Diodorus adds that some attributed this pyramid to a king named Armæus. According to Manetho (a better authority in that case) it was founded by Suphis, the second king of the 4th Dynasty, which was the second Dynasty of Memphite Kings. Some remarks on this subject will be added at the end of this chapter.
[†]Fig. 28.

for the gap in the angle, which appears to be near the summit, is not much more than half-way up; and the entrance is rather nearer to the angle which is next the observer, than to the other; though the reverse would be imagined from the view. Thus greatly is the eye deceived by this extraordinary object.

The base of the Great Pyramid is 733 feet square, and the perpendicular height is 460 feet, according to my measurement.[1] It consists of 204 courses, or layers, of stone; therefore the average height of a single course is about two feet and a quarter: but the courses vary in height from about *four* feet to *one* foot. The lower courses are higher than the rest; and the lowest is hewn out of the solid rock; as is also part of the second. Opposite the angle from which my view was taken, about 12 feet distant, is a square space, 12 feet in width, and between 2 and 3 inches in depth; apparently marking the place of the original corner-stone of the Pyramid. About the middle of each side of the Pyramid, the exterior stones have been much broken by the masses which have been rolled down from above; but at the angles, they are more entire; and *there*, consequently, the ascent is not difficult. The upper and lower surfaces of the stones are smoothly cut; but the sides have been left very rough, and, in many cases, not square: the interstices being filled up with a coarse cement, of a pinkish colour; of which I brought away some specimens. This cement is, in some parts, almost as hard as the stone itself; and I found it, sometimes, very difficult to detach. Among the dust and small fragments of stone which have crumbled away from the sides and yet rest upon the upper surfaces of the steps, or exterior stones, we find a great number of the small petrifactions in the form of lentils, which I have before mentioned.

It is not to be doubted that the sides of the Great Pyramid were originally plain. The upper part of the Second Pyramid still remains nearly perfect; its sides being quite plain; and the lower part of the Third Pyramid is yet entire; the exterior stones of this structure being of granite, and so cut as to form an uniform, smooth surface. The Great Southern Pyramid of Dah'shoo'r is very nearly in a perfect state; its sides being quite smooth. The word "casing" does not convey a proper notion of the manner in which the sides of the Great Pyramid and of the other

---

[1] A hundred and sixteen feet higher than St. Paul's Church, in London.—I made, with the most scrupulous care, a trigonometrical measurement of the height of the Great Pyramid; which I thus found to be 460 feet. Two members of the French Institute measured it step by step; and their computation of the whole height was 39 metres and 117 millimetres, or 456 feet 5 inches English measure: thus very nearly agreeing with my own calculation. Mr. Davison also measured the height of the Pyramid in 1764, in the same manner, and thus computed it to be 460 feet 11 inches; but at that period there were 206 courses; whereas there are now but 203: the height of the three upper courses then existing was 6 feet 7 inches and one third; and therefore, that of the 203 courses, 454 feet 3 inches and two thirds, by his admeasurement; which, still, very nearly agrees with my own.

monuments of the same kind were finished: for the structure was raised, as Herodotus says, in the form of steps; and the sides were then cut plain; the workmen beginning at the top. This has been disbelieved by some travellers, because no stones which could have belonged to such an exterior now remain upon the Pyramid or around its base: but it must be remembered that the materials of several small pyramids which were situated in the vicinity were used in the construction of the Citadel and the Third Wall of El-Cka'hireh, and in the building of the Bridges of El-Gee'zeh, across the Bahhr Yoo'soof; and the exterior stones of the Great Pyramid were probably used for the same, or similar, purposes. The hinder part of the Great Sphinx was cased with masonry, in the same manner; and I saw many of the stones torn down and carried away to be employed in modern buildings. Most of the casing of the Second Pyramid has also been thrown down, and the stones of which it was composed employed in the construction of other buildings. If any suppose that only the upper part of the Second Pyramid was ever cased, I must tell him that upon the Great Northern Pyramid of Dah'shoo'r only small portions of the plain casing now remain, here and there, like patches—clearly shewing that the whole was once so cased—, and that the stones which have been thrown down have likewise been carried away. The stones which formed the casing of the Great Pyramid were, doubtless, like those upon the Second Pyramid, of a more compact kind than the materials of which the main body of the structure consists, and also superior to those of the surrounding tombs now remaining; for which reason, it would seem, they were taken in preference.

On each side of the Great Pyramid is an accumulation of fragments of stone and mortar which have fallen down from the summit and sides of the building and have composed a very compact mass, which rises, in the centre, to about 50 feet above the base. The sand of the desert has contributed but little to augment these slopes of rubbish, which are nearly of the same height on each side of the Pyramid. That on the northern side forms a convenient acclivity to the entrance.

The ascent to the summit of the Great Pyramid is not dangerous; though rather tedious; as my view and description of its exterior must have shewn. At, or near, any of the angles, we find, on almost every course, or range of stone, a secure and wide footing. Some of the steps are breast-high; and these, of course, are awkward masses to climb. Rather more than half-way up the north-eastern angle is a gap, formed by the displacing of several stones; from which I often saw vultures fly out. I very frequently observed several of these birds soaring above and around the two principal pyramids. Many stones have been thrown down from the top of the Great Pyramid; which, consequently, wants about 25 feet (or, perhaps, rather more) of its original height; for, without doubt, it terminated in a point.[1] It is worthy of remark that Diodorus Siculus describes the top of the Pyramid as being 6 cubits (or 9

---

[1]It appears, therefore, that its original height was, at the least, 480 feet.

feet) square: Pliny states it to have been, in his time, 25 feet; or, according to some copies of his work, 15 feet; the latter of which readings must be considered the more correct. Several courses of stone have been thrown down in later ages; so that now, on arriving at the summit, we find a platform 33 feet square, upon which, near the eastern edge, are a few stones yet remaining of two upper courses.—see plate 11.[†] Upon these the names of many travellers are cut. The platform is quite flat: the stones being well joined and cemented. The ascent to the summit generally occupied me between fifteen and twenty minutes.

The view from the summit of the Great Pyramid is of a most extraordinary nature. On the eastern side, the eye ranges over an extensive, verdant plain, watered by numerous canals, and interspersed with villages erected upon mounds of rubbish and surrounded by palm trees. In the distance is the Nile; beyond which are seen the lofty ma'd'nehs and Citadel of Musr, backed by the low, yellow ridge of Mount Moockut'tum. Towards the hour of sunset, it is curious to observe the enormous shadows of the two principal pyramids stretching across the cultivated plain.—Turning towards the opposite side, we behold a scene exactly the reverse of that which we have just been contemplating. Instead of the palm-groves and corn-fields, we have before us the undulating, sandy hills of the great Libyan desert.—The view of the Second Pyramid, from this commanding situation, is extremely grand. This Pyramid, with the area bounded by the hewn, perpendicular face of the rock on its northern and western sides, and its "temple," on the east, are seen in plate 11.[‡] A small portion of the Third Pyramid is also seen; with one of the small pyramids on its southern side. The space which lies on the west of the Great Pyramid, and north of the Second, is covered with oblong tombs, having the form of truncated pyramids; which, from this height, appear like patches of gravel.—The head of the Great Sphinx, and the distant pyramids of Ab'oo Seer, Sack'cka'rah, and Dah'shoo'r, are seen towards the south-south-east; but not included in the view above referred to.

I sometimes loitered about the Pyramids until half an hour or more after sunset, when the gloom contributed much to the grandeur and solemnity of the scene: and on one occasion I ascended the Great Pyramid about two hours before day-break, and waited upon the summit until sun-rise. It was extremely cold; and the wind, sweeping up the northern side of the Pyramid, sounded like a distant cataract. The Second Pyramid was at first faintly discernible; appearing of vastly more than even real magnitude. Soon afterwards, its eastern side was lighted up by the rising moon; and the effect was truly sublime. By the side of the pile of stones on the top of the Great Pyramid, I found shelter from the wind; and there I sat, muffled up, by my snoring servant, till I, also, was overcome by sleep. I awoke a little before sunrise; but was so chilly and

[†]Fig. 29.
[‡]Fig. 29.

hungry that I could not remain much longer to enjoy the prospect, which, at that hour, is particularly beautiful.

On the second day after I had taken up my quarters at the Pyramids, I went out without my pistols; and in the evening, one of my guards reproved me for having done so. "How easy," he observed, "would it be for one of our people (the Bed'awees) to rob you, and, if you resisted, to murder you, and throw you down one of the mummy-pits; and who, then, would ever know what was become of you?"—On the following day, I ascended the Great Pyramid; but not unarmed. While on the summit, I perceived a solitary Arab, making towards the Pyramid, from the west. He began to ascend at the southwestern angle, and when he arrived about half-way up, little thinking that my telescope was directed towards him, he stopped, and took out a pistol from the case which was slung by his side, looked at it, and then continued the ascent. As it was evident that the fellow had no good intentions, I called out, and desired him to descend; but he either did not hear me, or would not obey. I therefore discharged a pistol, to shew him that I was not without the means of defence. Upon this, he immediately began to return, and, having reached the base, walked slowly away into the desert.

The entrance of the Great Pyramid[1] is over the sixteenth course, or layer of stone, about fifty feet above the base; a slope of rubbish, as I said before, leading up to it.[2] It is nearly in the centre, or equidistant from either angle of the northern side of the Pyramid: the eye would hardly discover that it is not *exactly* so; though really 20 feet, or rather more, to the eastward of the centre. The opening of the Pyramid seems to have been attended with considerable difficulty; a vast number of stones having been torn down above and before the aperture. The inclined plane before the entrance forms an angle of twenty-six degrees and a half with the horizon: being in the same plane with the floor of the first passage. The size of the stones above the entrance, and the manner in which they are disposed, are worthy of remark. There is no *granite* at the entrance of the Pyramid: all the blocks are of lime-stone.—Before the traveller enters the Pyramid, he should divest himself of some of his clothes: for the heat in the interior is rather oppressive; and he will require to cover himself warmly on coming out, to prevent any check of perspiration.

The passage by which we enter the Great Pyramid is only 4 feet high, and 3 feet 6 inches in width; and we are consequently obliged to descend in a crouching position. It is lined above and below and on each side with blocks of lime-stone,[3] of a more compact kind than that of which the Pyramid is mainly constructed. This superior kind of stone appears to have been brought from the quarries on the eastern side of the Nile, directly opposite the site of Memphis; for stone of the same quality is not

---

[1]See plate 12 [fig. 30]; and *b* in the section, plate 13 [fig. 31].
[2]See *a* in the section [fig. 31].
[3]Some travellers, their memory deceiving them, have described this passage as lined with *granite*: others have asserted that it is of *white marble*.

found nearer; and Herodotus and several other ancient writers inform us that the quarries of the Arabian mountains[1] supplied materials for the construction of the Pyramid. Indeed they assert that the Pyramid was entirely built of stones from those quarries; but this, evidently, was not the case: the stone of which the structure is mainly composed was quarried from the rock in its neighbourhood.—The nicety with which the stones are united in the sides of the first passage is very remarkable. In some parts, the joint cannot be discovered without a close and minute examination. In the flooring of this passage, and of all the sloping passages in the Pyramid, notches have been roughly cut, like steps, to prevent the feet from slipping. This has been the work of modern explorers. At the distance of nearly seventy feet (measuring from the outer surface of the huge block above the entrance), we find that one of the stones which form the roofing of the passage has been hewn away precisely at the point where the second passage branches off, in an ascending direction: (see the letter *c* in the section). Here we discover the square end of a granite block, which closes the entrance of the second passage; being exactly fitted to fill up the aperture. The persons who opened the Pyramid, being unable to remove this obstacle, have made a forced communication with the ascending passage. At the distance of 80 feet (from the entrance of the Pyramid) is the forced aperture, on the right side of the passage: (see *d* in the section). It has been made by hollowing out the roofing, and cutting away the upper part of the side of the lower passage. Here the explorer lights his candle (if he have not done so before), and, having ascended through this opening, finds himself in a large place, which appears like a natural cavern in a rock. Here I made the sketch from which the annexed engraving was taken; looking back towards the aperture by which I had entered.[2]

We now see the upper end of the granite block before mentioned, or of a second block. Above it is another, of which a part has been broken off. Above this, the passage (*e*, *f*) is seen, clear of other incumbrances, running upwards, but in the same southern course as the first, or descending passage. It is of the same dimensions as the first, and has the same inclination; but its sides and roofing are very rough; and, consequently, it has the appearance of a passage cut through solid rock; which is not really the case. It is 109 feet long (measuring from the southernmost of the granite blocks above mentioned); and the flooring projects a foot and a half further, in the same direction. The ascent of this passage is rather fatiguing.

On emerging from it, the explorer finds himself at the foot of the Grand Passage; the singular appearance of which the reader will best conceive from an inspection of the view here annexed: (see plate 14[†]: see

---

[1]The mountains on the east of the Nile are thus called by ancient Greek and Roman writers; and those on the west, "the Libyan mountains."
[2]See no. 6 of the subjects for wood-cuts [fig. 32].
[†]Fig. 33.

also *f, m*, in the section). On the right, he will observe the entrance, or mouth, of what has been called "the well": (*g*). Under the grand, ascending passage, runs another, which is horizontal, low, and narrow. The entrance of the latter (*h*) is 15 feet 3 inches from the projection of a foot and a half before mentioned. This passage is 3 feet 11 inches high, and 3 feet 5 inches wide: it continues of the same dimensions to the distance of 93 feet. Here there is a descent of 1 foot 8 inches in the floor; so that the remainder of the passage is nearly high enough for a person of middling stature to walk along it without bending down his head. At the distance of 110 feet 9 inches (from its entrance), it terminates (see *i* in the section) at the eastern corner of the north side of a chamber which is 19 feet long and 17 feet broad: (see *k*). This has been called, by some travellers, "the Queen's Chamber"; from the supposition that the Queen of the founder of the Pyramid was buried in it. The roof is formed of long blocks of stone, leaning against each other. The height of the chamber, to the commencement of the roof, is 13 feet and a half, and to the summit, about 7 feet more. The floor, sides, and roof are constructed of the same kind of lime-stone as the passages. In the eastern end (not in the middle, but rather to the right), is a high and narrow recess, five feet wide at the bottom, but becoming narrower towards the top; like the sides of the grand passage; as the annexed sketch will shew. It is 3 feet 5 inches deep. Within it, 4 feet from the floor, is the entrance of a forced passage, 4 feet wide.[1] At the commencement it is square, and smoothly cut; but further in, it becomes irregular; and at the distance of 50 feet, it terminates at a hollow space, wider and more irregular than the rest. In this chamber and forced passage there is little to detain us. We return to the grand passage.

Above the entrance of the horizontal passage which leads to the chamber above described (see plate 14,[†] before referred to) is a perpendicular; (marked *h* in the section, plate 13[‡]). This perpendicular, together with the height of the said passage is 7 feet 3 inches. The flooring then ascends in the same direction as the other ascending passage; at an angle of twenty-six degrees and a half. At the distance of 3 feet 5 inches, is another perpendicular, or step, of only 8 inches; above which, the floor has the same inclination again; and notches have been cut in it, to facilitate the ascent, which is not easily performed, unless with naked feet. There is a bench of stone on each side, all along the passage; and in the tops of these benches, are oblong holes, at short intervals: their use unknown. The width of the passage (including the benches, which are 1 foot 8 inches and a half square) is 6 feet 10 inches, about four ancient Egyptian cubits. The sides of the passage are composed of nine courses of stone, from the benches upwards. The stone is of the same kind as that of which the lower passages are constructed.

---

[1]See no. 7 of the subjects for wood-cuts [fig. 34].
[†]Fig. 33.
[‡]Fig. 31.

Some travellers have asserted that it is *white marble*: but no white marble is found in any part of the Pyramid. The two lower courses are even with each other: but each course above projects 3 inches beyond that below it; and so does each corresponding course at the upper and lower ends of the passage. The length of the whole passage is 158 feet. At the distance of 5 feet and one inch before we reach the upper end, we ascend another perpendicular of 2 feet 11 inches. The floor beyond is horizontal; forming a small platform: (see *l* in the section). From this commences a horizontal passage, 3 feet 7 inches and a half in height, and 3 feet 5 inches and a half in width: (see *m*). Within it, on the right, is the entrance of a *forced* passage, made in search for other chambers than those already known. At the distance of 4 feet 5 inches (from the entrance of the *true* passage) commences an open space above, (see *n*); the upper part of which is nearly twice as wide as the passage, and 9 feet 8 inches in length: but the passage below is contracted again to its former height by a kind of portcullis, formed of two blocks of granite, one above another, each one foot three inches thick: these have been let down from the space above, between two small projections on each side which form a pair of grooves. Beyond this, the passage (which is here of *granite*) is open, as before, to the space above; and there are grooves for the reception of three other portcullises of granite, by which the architect thought that he should for ever prevent access to the mysterious chamber which contains the sarcophagus: but these have been broken, and their fragments carried away. The passage, beyond, (see *o*), is of its former dimensions, and continues so to the distance of 8 feet 5 inches; its whole length, from the top of the grand passage, being 22 feet and a half. It terminates at the eastern extremity of the north side of the Grand Chamber. (See plate 15.[†] See, also, *p*, in the section).

The Grand Chamber is 34 feet 4 inches in length, and exactly half that measure (17 feet 2 inches) in width. The height is about two feet more than the width. It is entirely constructed of red granite.[1] Near the western end is the sarcophagus; which is also of red granite. It is 7 feet and a half in length, 3 and a half in breadth, and the sides are half a foot thick.[2] No hieroglyphics, nor sculptures of any kind, adorn it either within or without: its sides are perfectly plain and polished; and its form is simply that of an oblong chest, in every way rectangular. Its lid has been carried away; as well as its original contents; and we find in it

---

[†]Fig. 35.

[1]All the granite employed in the construction of the Pyramid is of the same kind, large-grained, and of a dull red colour. It appears to have been brought from the quarries of Syene, the modern Aswa'n.

[2]As the sarcophagus is exactly of the same width as the first passage of the Pyramid, and about half an inch wider than the passage by which the grand chamber is entered, it is evident that it must have been placed there before the chamber was finished: not introduced by the passages.

nothing but dust and small fragments of stone.[1] It has been much injured at one of its corners by a number of travellers, who have broken off pieces to carry away as memorials. When struck with any thing hard, or even with the hand, it sounds like a bell. It rests upon a block of granite considerably larger than any of the other blocks of which the floor is composed. A stone which was next to this large mass, at the north-west corner of the chamber, has been removed; and, in clearing out the rubbish from the hole, I observed the block above mentioned to be of an extraordinary thickness. The hole was not deep enough for me to discover the bottom of the great stone; therefore I can only say that it is at least between 4 and 5 feet thick; perhaps, considerably more. Why was such an enormous mass placed there? The alabaster sarcophagus in the great tomb opened by Belzoni in the Valley of Beeba'n el-Mooloo'k, at Thebes, closed the entrance of a deep descent of steps, which has never been explored to its termination: the soft and crumbling nature of the rock through which it is cut rendering any attempt to clear it out extremely dangerous. The enormous mass of granite under the sarcophagus in the Great Pyramid may have been placed there for a similar purpose; or to cover the mouth of a vault, or pit: so that, if any violater of the sacred edifice should succeed—notwithstanding the portcullises of granite—in effecting an entrance into the great chamber, he might, on discovering the sarcophagus, believe the object of his search to be accomplished. It would require great labour to ascertain whether this be the case; as the stone in question is surrounded by other blocks of the same hard granite, which, though of smaller dimensions, are yet very formidable masses to break, or to remove.—The sides of the chamber are formed of six regular courses of granite blocks, which are united with the greatest exactness, and their surfaces perfectly even and polished; without hieroglyphics or any other inscriptions or ornaments. In the northern side, near the corner of the entrance, is a small aperture, and opposite to it, in the southern side, is another. Their termination and use are unknown: palm-sticks, tied together, have been thrust into them to a great distance. The roof of the chamber consists of nine long granite blocks, which extend from side to side. The half, only, of the stone at each end is seen; the other half resting on the wall.

Returning from this chamber, we stop at the platform at the upper end of the grand passage[2]: (see *l* in the section). Here we observe, at the top of the eastern wall (that is, on the left of a person facing the end of the passage), at the height of 24 feet, a square aperture, which is the entrance of another passage; (*q*). Small notches have been cut at the corner, all the

---

[1] Diodorus Siculus says that the founders of the First and Second Pyramids were not buried in those monuments; though they had designed them for their tombs: they feared that the populace who had groaned under their tyranny would tear in pieces their remains, if they could discover the place of the interment.

[2] There is a remarkable echo in this passage; on account of which, it is a custom of travellers to fire a pistol here.

way up, for the reception of the ends of short pieces of wood, which were thus placed one above another, so as to form a kind of ladder. These have been taken away; and the ascent without them is difficult and dangerous. Two Arabs, however, contrived to climb up, by means of the little notches, and took with them a strong rope, the end of which I tied round me, and they drew me up to the top. As soon as I was freed from the rope, they demanded of me a present; threatning, that, if I refused, they would descend, and leave me there. Though I laughed, they would not, for some minutes, confess that they were joking. The passage in which I now found myself is only 2 feet 4 inches square. It turns immediately to the right; and, to the distance of a few feet, it continues square, and of the same dimensions as before; but much clogged with bats' dung and other dirt: afterwards, it becomes irregular both in direction and in the construction of its sides; and it is difficult for a man to drag himself along it. A great many bats endeavoured to make their escape from within, and flew against my face. They would have put out our candles; but these were held by the Arabs behind me: I had been careful, also, to leave another lighted candle in the grand passage; fearing such an accident; and was, besides, provided with a flint, steel, &c. At the distance of 24 feet, the passage terminates at the north-east corner of a large, but low place, (*r*),[1] directly above the grand chamber. It is of the same width as the chamber below; but 4 feet longer. The long granite blocks which compose the roof of the lower chamber form the floor of this; and the first and last of these blocks are here seen entire. The upper surfaces of all of them are very rough; and they are not all of the same thickness. The roof also of this place is formed of long blocks of granite, 8 in number. The height is scarcely more than 3 feet. In the south-east corner is a small forced passage, which extends a few feet.[2]—Being let down again by the rope, I next descended to the bottom of the grand passage, to examine "the Well"; as it is usually called.[3]

The entrance, or mouth, of the well is seen in my view of the grand passage; it is marked *g* in the section. The the right of that passage, two feet below the floor, are three low steps, occupying a space of 4 feet and a half in length. Beyond them is the mouth of the first shaft, which is 2 feet 2 inches square. There are little notches, roughly cut, in the sides, in

---

[1] This chamber (if such it may be called) was discovered by Mr. Davison, who was British Consul at Algiers, and who visited Egypt, with Mr. Wortley Montagu, in 1763 and 4.

[2] The second roof above the grand chamber was made to secure the lower roof, which might otherwise have been broken down by the superincumbent masses. I think I noticed that one or two of the blocks which compose the upper roof had yielded to the pressure, and cracked.

[3] The well was explored by Mr. Davison, and afterwards, (in 1801), by Col. Coutelle; but its termination and use remained involved in uncertainty and mystery, until it was cleared out, in 1817, by Caviglia, whom I mentioned in the second chapter of the former volume [chapter two] of this work.

which to place the fingers and toes; and, as the space is narrow, a person may descend without the aid of a rope; as I did myself; but I found it difficult and dangerous to do so. The ascent is attended with less danger: it is precisely like climbing a chimney. At the depth of a few feet, it becomes very rugged and irregular; and continues so for nearly 50 feet. After descending rather more that [sic] 60 feet, an aperture is seen on the southern side, which is the entrance to a kind of grotto (*s*), between 5 and 6 feet high, and about three times as long, turning to the right. It is hollowed out in a vein of coarse, but compact gravel; and the well, in consequence of this vein, is lined with masonry for the space of a few feet above and below the grotto. Where the masonry ceases (*t*), the well takes a sloping direction, and continues so to the bottom; but towards the bottom (see *u* in the section), the slope becomes more steep. All of the sloping part is cut through the solid rock, below the foundation of the Pyramid, and is of a square form. At the bottom of the well (*v*) is a horizontal passage, 6 feet long, communicating with the first passage of the Pyramid, 212 feet below the aperture by which one ascends to the second passage. The first passage of the Pyramid, from the aperture last mentioned, continues in the same direction, and is of the same dimensions, but is cut through the solid rock, and is not lined with masonry. The aperture which communicates with the bottom of the well is 2 feet 10 inches broad. It is on the right of a person descending the first passage. This passage continues in the same direction to the distance of 23 feet further, (see *w* in the section); beyond which it is horizontal, and so low and encumbered with rubbish that the explorer is obliged to drag himself along in a prostrate position. At the distance of 16 feet 9 inches, there is a recess (*x*), on the right side, 3 feet 4 inches deep and 6 feet 5 inches wide. Four feet and a half beyond this, the passage terminates at the eastern extremity of the north side of a large excavated chamber, (*y*).—See plate 16.[†]

The Great Excavated Chamber is nearly under the centre of the Pyramid. It is 27 feet broad, and 66 feet long. The roof is flat; but the floor is very uneven. At the entrance, the chamber is 15 feet high: towards the western end, the rock rises perpendicularly half-way towards the ceiling; and there are masses of strange forms, but not altogether irregular, rising still higher, and nearly touching the top of the chamber. In the floor, at the lower end, is a wide, hollow space, nearly filled with bats' dung. Immediately opposite the entrance is a level passage, (*z*), low and narrow, running towards the south: it terminates abruptly at the distance of 55 feet. The floor of the chamber is just a hundred feet below the level of the external base of the Pyramid.—It appeared evident to me that this great chamber was an unfinished excavation. Mr. Salt thought otherwise. "He had flattered himself that this chamber would turn out to be that described by Herodotus as containing the tomb of Cheops, which was insulated by a canal from the

---

[†]Fig. 36.

Nile; but the want of an inlet, and its elevation of 30 feet[1] above the level of the Nile at its highest point, put an end to this delusive idea."—An account of Caviglia's operations in the Great Pyramid and in the neighbouring tombs has already been published.[2] After having explored "the well," and endeavoured, in vain, to draw up the rubbish with which the lower part was filled, he turned his attention to the clearing of the first passage of the Pyramid, which, until that time, had been supposed to terminate just below the aperture which communicates with the second passage. In the prosecution of this work (which was one of much difficulty, as the passage was choked with large fragments of stone), he discovered the communication with the bottom of the well, and, continuing his operations, soon after entered the great excavated chamber.

Such is the description of all that is now known of the interior of the Great Pyramid. Other passages and chambers may yet remain concealed. It has been calculated that there *might* be, within this stupendous fabric, 3,700 chambers, each equal in size to the sarcophagus chamber, allowing the contents of an equal number of such chambers to be solid, by way of separation.[3] Yet this enormous pile seems to have been raised merely as a sepulchral monument, to contain, perhaps, one single mummy, not a particle of which now remains in the place in which it was deposited with so much precaution[4]; unless there be, yet undiscovered, any other receptacle for the royal corpse than the sarcophagus in the granite chamber. Herodotus and Diodorus Siculus assert that the building of the Great Pyramid occupied about 20 years; and, according to the former, 100,000 men—according to the latter, 360,000—were employed in its construction. Herodotus also says that Cheops, having exhausted his treasures in this work, had the baseness to prostitute his own daughter, to obtain an additional sum of money, sufficient to complete his pyramid; and that the daughter obliged each of her lovers to bring a stone, for the purpose of raising another pyramid, for herself; by which means she obtained the necessary materials, and, with them, built the pyramid which is "the middlemost of the three in front of the Great Pyramid."

---

[1]According to my measurement, it is 60 feet, or more, above the level of the inundation.

[2]In the 38th number (or second part of the 19th volume) of the Quarterly Review. It is there stated that there is a passage at the eastern end of the excavated chamber, which "commences with a kind of arch, and runs about 40 feet into the solid body of the Pyramid." This is a mistake. There is a passage of this peculiar description (but a little longer) at the eastern end of the chamber with the pointed roof, which I have already described, and of which I have given a sketch. This accounts for the above mis-statement.

[3]Quarterly Review, vol. 19, p. 401.

[4]Most ancient authors who have described this monument assert, in opposition to Diodorus, that its founder was buried in it.

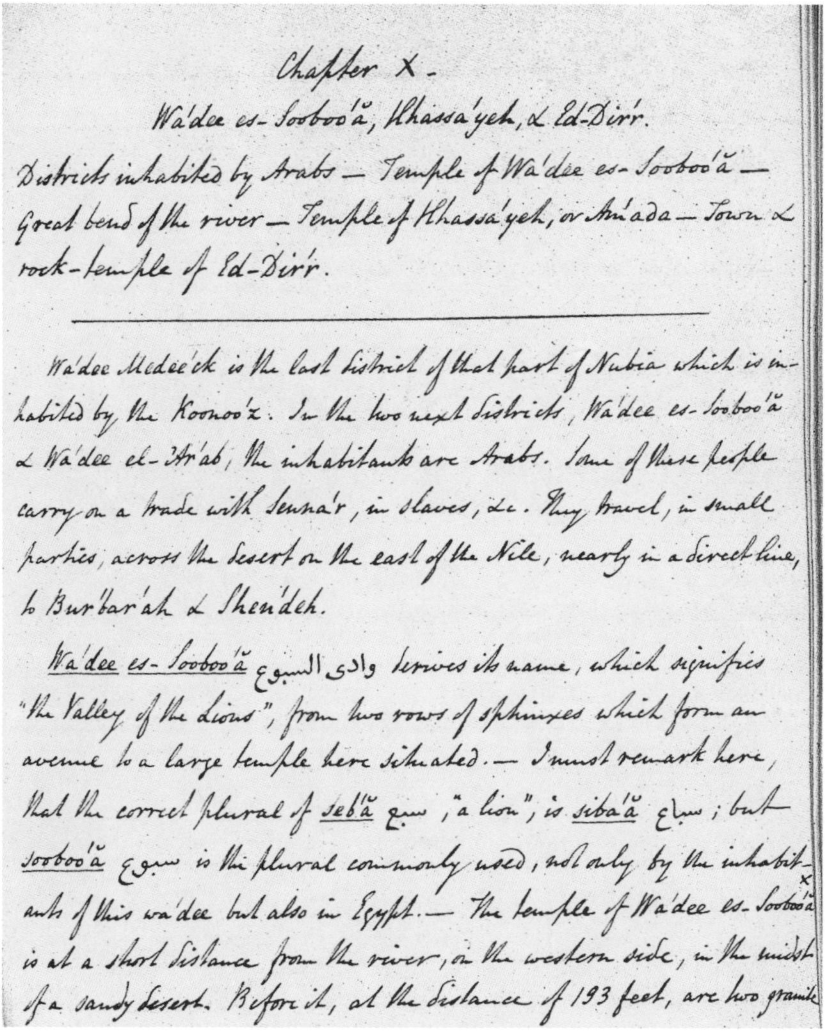

Chapter X.

Wa'dee es-Sooboo'ä, Khassa'yeh, & Ed-Dirr.

Districts inhabited by Arabs — Temple of Wa'dee es-Sooboo'ä — Great bend of the river — Temple of Khassa'yeh, or Amäda — Town & rock-temple of Ed-Dirr.

Wa'dee Medee'ck is the last district of that part of Nubia which is inhabited by the Koonoo'z. In the two next districts, Wa'dee es-Sooboo'ä & Wa'dee el-Ä'ráb, the inhabitants are Arabs. Some of these people carry on a trade with Senna'r, in slaves, &c. They travel, in small parties, across the desert on the east of the Nile, nearly in a direct line, to Bur'bar'ah & Shen'deh.

Wa'dee es-Sooboo'ä وادى السبوع derives its name, which signifies "the Valley of the Lions", from two rows of sphinxes which form an avenue to a large temple here situated. — I must remark here, that the correct plural of sebä' سبع, "a lion", is sibä'ä سباع; but Sooboo'ä سبوع is the plural commonly used, not only by the inhabitants of this wa'dee but also in Egypt. — The temple of Wa'dee es-Sooboo'ä is at a short distance from the river, on the western side, in the midst of a sandy desert. Before it, at the distance of 193 feet, are two granite

Figure 1: [A page from the manuscript of E. W. Lane's *Description of Egypt*—the opening of the chapter (36 in this edition) about Wadi al-Seboua to al-Derr.]†

---

†Captions enclosed by brackets are supplied by the editor.

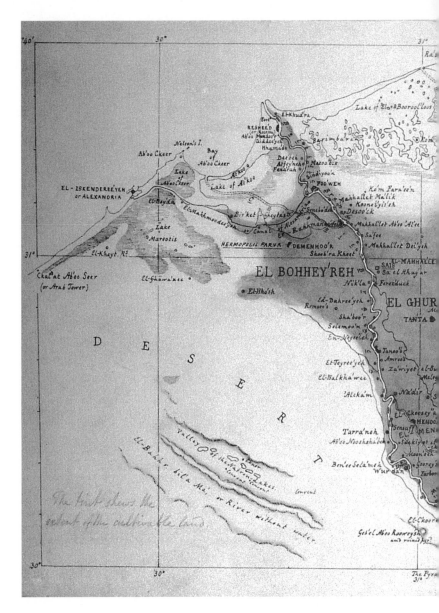

Figure 2: [Map of Lower Egypt.]

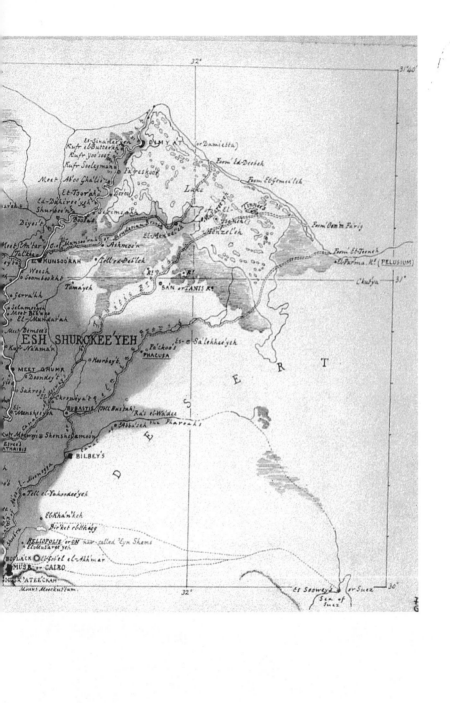

32°   31°40'

Es-Sinanee'yeh
Kufr el-Butterah
Kufr Yoo'soof   DIMYAT (or Damietta)
Kufr Sooleyman   Fa'reskoor   Foom Ed-Deebeh
Meet Ab'oo Gha'lib   Foom El-Gemee'leh
Et-Toorah   Serou   Lake
Ed-Dahiree'yeh
Shurbee'n   Sekimea'h
Diyee't   Tinnees
                              Ashmoo'n   El   Foom Oom'm Fariy
Meet Am'bar   El-Mansoo'rah or Ashmoo'n   El-Menzeh   Menzel'eh
Tal'kha   Foom Et-Treeeh
          EL-MUNSOO'RAH   Tell-el-Deb'leh   El-Purma K.¹ (PELUSIUM)
Weesh
Soombookht   C'kul'ya   31°
Serra'kh   Tamayeh   R?   R?
Selamooni   SAN or TANIS K?
Meet Bil'эно
El-Mundarah
Meet Demsee's
ESH SHURCKEE'YEH   Es-o Sa'lehkee'yeh
Kufr Na'aman   Fa'koo's   D   E   S   E   R   T
MEET GHUMR   Hoorbey't   PHACUSA
Boondey't
Sakregt
          Ckropkiya't
El-Mensheyeh   BUBASTIS (Tell Busjah)   Ra's el-Wadee
Kufr Megwys Shenshe Damoon   Abba'seh the Pharaoh's
Elree's
ATHRIBIS
          BILBEY'S   D   E   S   E   R   T

          Tell el-Yahoodee'yeh

          El-Kha'n'keh
          Bir'ket el-Haggg
HELIOPOLIS or ON now-called 'Eyn Shems
El-Matare't'yeh
BOOLA'CK Kubbel el-Akhmar
MUSR or CAIRO
BOOR 'ATEE'RAH
Mount Mookuttum.   32°   Es-Soowey's or Suez   30°
                                                  Sea of
                                                  Suez

                                                                    7
                                                                    G

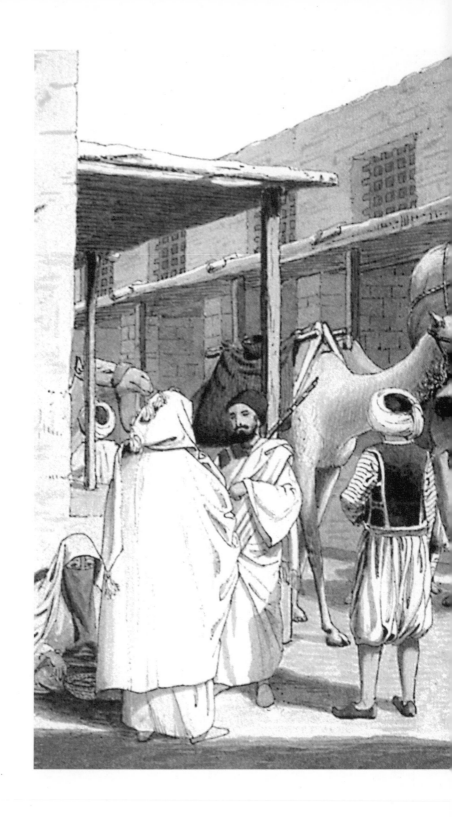

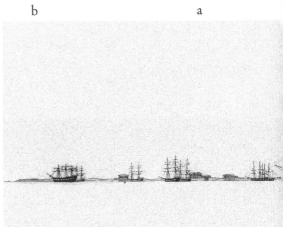

b   a

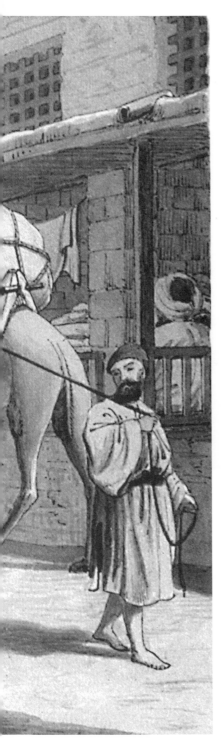

Figure 5: Sketch of a street
of Alexandria.

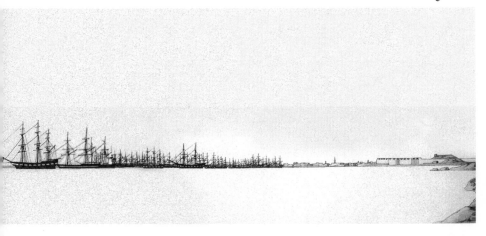

Figure 3: Old Harbour of Alexandria.

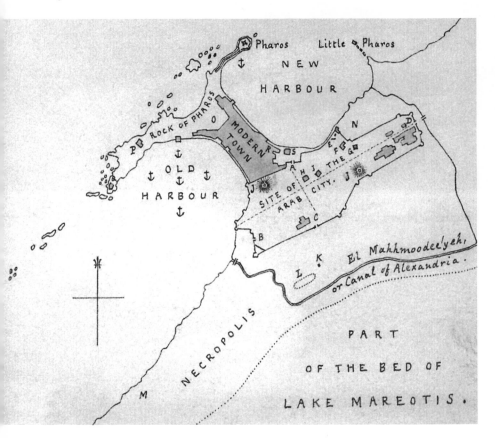

Figure 4: Topography of the site and environs of Alexandria.

Figure 7: The Obelisks of Alexandria, from the S.W.

Figure 8: The Pillar of Alexandria.—a, Two granite columns: a third is prostrate. b, Obelisk. c, Fort. d, Báb es-Sidr.

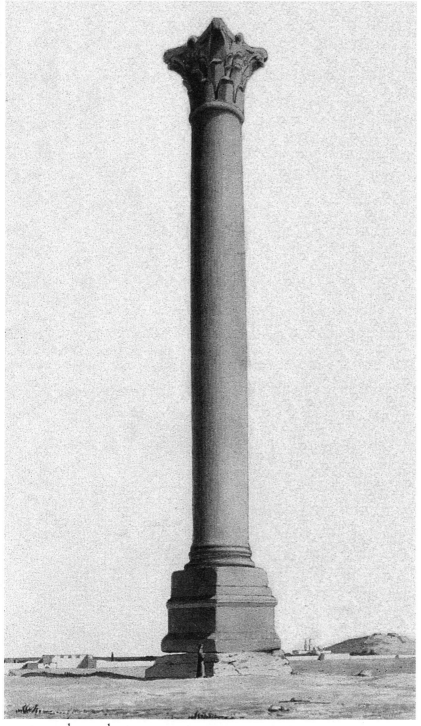

a   d   b   c

A boat of the Nile

Figure 10: Mosque and Tomb of Ab'oo Mandoo'r near Reshee'd.

Figure 11: Fooweh.

Figure 9: A boat of the Nile.

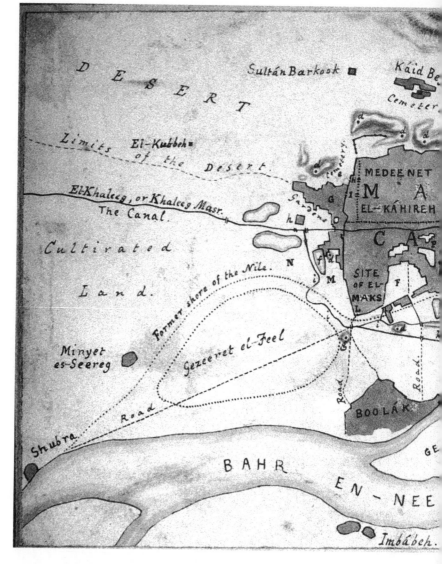

Figure 12: Musr (or Cairo) and its Environs.

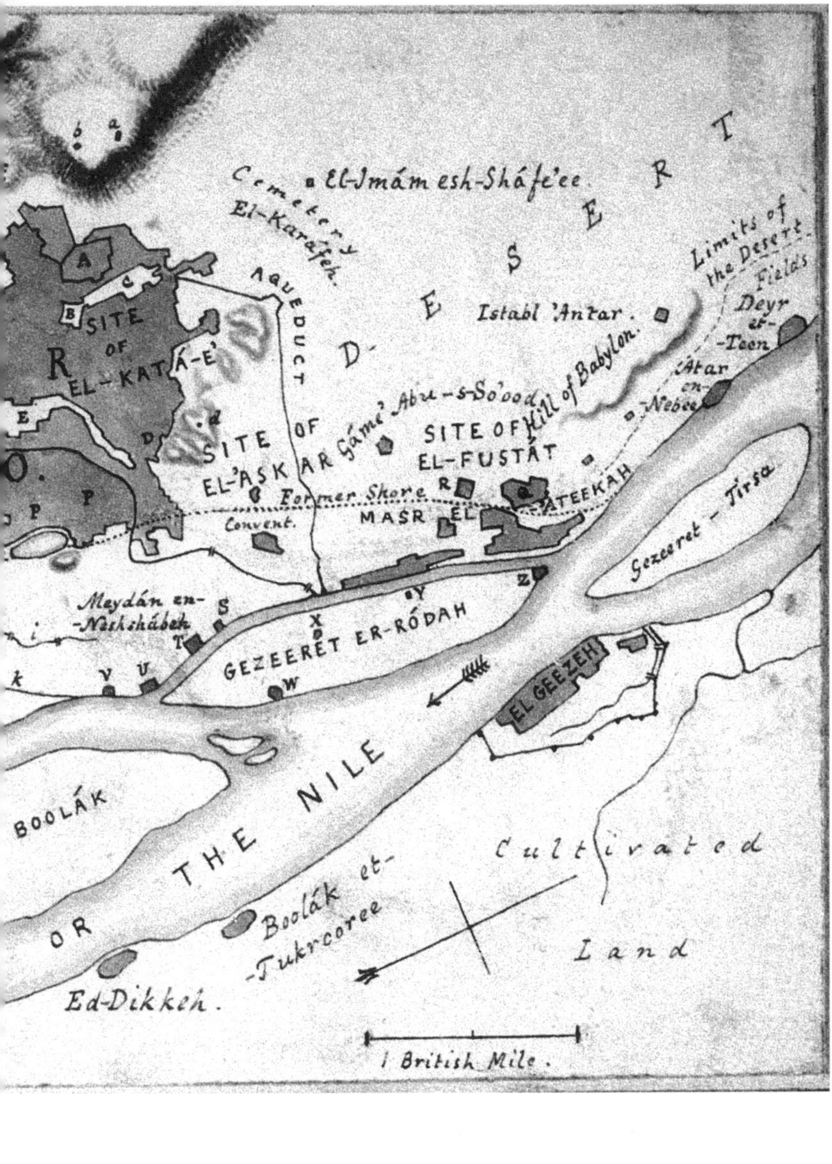
El-Imám esh-Sháfe'ee
Cemetery
El-Karáfeh
DESERT
Limits of the Desert
Fields
Istabl 'Antar
Deyr et-Teen
AQUEDUCT
SITE OF EL-KATÁ-E'
Hill of Babylon
'Atar en-Nebee
Gáme' Abu-s-So'ood
SITE OF EL-'ASKAR
SITE OF EL-FUSTÁT
Former Shore
Convent
MASR EL-'ATEEKAH
Gezeeret - Tirsa
Meydán en-Neshshábeh
GEZEERET ER-RÓDAH
EL GEEZEH
BOOLÁK
THE NILE
OR
Cultivated Land
Boolák et-Tukrooree
Ed-Dikkeh
1 British Mile

Figure 13: The General landing-Place at Boolák.—Palace of Isma'eel
Básha, at Boolák.

Figure 14: [Cairo.]
[Lane may have decided not to
retain this map: he removed a reference to it, leaving none in the
manuscript, and did not include a
key to it in the final draft. The key
reproduced here is from an incomplete preliminary draft on a loose
sheet in the second draft of
Description of Egypt in the Griffith
Institute. His reliance on the map
of Cairo in the French *Description
de l'Égypte* ("État Moderne,
Plates" vol. 1, pl. 26) is clear both
from the general appearance of his
map and from the original numbering on his manuscript, which he
changed to his own system as he
simplified the map. The signifi-
cance of his abbreviations are A =
'Atfa; B = Bab (except in two
instances, both indicated in the text
below, where it signifies "Birka");
Ck = Qantara; D = Darb; G =
Gama'; H = Hara; M = Mosque;
P = Palace; and W = Wikala. Lane's
transliterations of course differed
somewhat from these. As in other
instances in Lane's *Description of
Egypt*, there are occasional incon-
sistences in spelling ("Sik'ket" and
"Sikket") as well as unusual
spellings ("Moo's'kee").]

A 1, Sik'ket el Hhas'anee'yeh.
2, Durb es Semma'kee'n.
3, B[irkat]. Goona'ck.
4, D. el Bagha'leh.
5. Ck. el Kharoo'bee.
6, G. el Hha'kim.
7, H. el 'Otoo'f.
8, H. el Ckalyoo'bee'yeh.
9, Soo'ck el 'Asr.
10, W. es Sa'boo'n.
11, A. ed Doobabee'yeh.
12, El Hhadda'dee'n. 13, Beyn es
Seya'rig. 14, El Murgoo'sh.
15, Sikket el Ghumree.
16, D. el Goo'wa'nee'yeh.
17, D. er Reshee'dee.
18, D. el Us'far.
19, W. es Sila'hhda'r.
20, M. of Beybur's [sic] (2nd), and
site of the Da'r el Wiza'rat, or P. of
the Wezee'rs of the Fawa'tim.
21, El Gum'a'lee'yeh.
22, Khutt er Rookn.
23, Es Saba'tee'yeh.
24, El Burgawa'n.
25, El Khooroon'fesh, (or
Kharenshef). 26, Sikket esh
Shaara'wee.
27, A. esh Shoor'beeg'ee.
28, Rs [Remains] of the Ckusr
el Kebee'r, or Grt. [Great] P. of the
Fawa'tim: the street before it is
called Beyn el Ckusrey'n.
29, The Burckoo'ckee'yeh,
(Mosque). 30, Tomb and Mosque
of S. Ckala-oo'n, and Hospital
(Marista'n). 31, Sikket el Marista'n.
32, En Nahh'hha'see'n.
33, Es Sa'ghah.
34, Es Surema'tee'yeh.

35, El Gohargee'yeh. 36, Kha'n Khalee'lee. 37, Kha'n en Nahha's. 38, Kha'n el Khen'na. 39, W. el Gella'beh. 40, El Khoordagee'yeh. 41, El Khar'ra'tee'n. 42, G. Mohham'mad bey. 43, G. el Az'har, (Principal M. of Musr). 44, H. el Az'har. 45, G. El Hhasaney'n. 46, Beyt el Cka'dee. 47, D. esh sheykh Moo'sa. 48, Ckusr esh Sho'k. 49, El Goo'wa'nee'yeh. 50, H. el Ga'eedee'yeh. 51, El Mesh'hed'ee. 52, Sikket esh sheykh Moos'tuf'a. 53, Sikket esh sheykh Hhamoo'deh. 54, El Ashrafee'yeh, (Mosque). 55, El War'ra'ckee'n. 56, El Hhamza'wee. 57, Sikket el Hhamza'wee. 58, H. el Yahoo'd. 59, Sikket Beybur's [sic]. 60, El Loob'oo'dee'yeh. 61, El Ghoo'ree'yeh. 62, Et Turbee''ah. 63, Sikket et Tubley'tah. 64, Tomb and Mosque of El Ghoo'ree. 65, El 'At'ta'ree'n. 66, Sikket el Kahhkee'n. 67, El Ba't'lee'yeh. 68, Hho'sh Ckud'am. 69, El Fahh'hha'mee'n. 70, El Goo'daree'yeh. 71, D. Sa'a'deh. 72, Sebee'l Too'soon ba'sha, and El Mena'khilee'yeh. 73, H. er Roo'm. 74, Es Sookkara'yeh. 75, G. el Moo-ei'yed. 76, D. el Ahhmar. 77, D. el Mahhroo'ck. 78, Tahht er Rub'ă. 79, Sikket esh sheykh Far'ag. 80, Sikket Fa't'meh en Neb'awee'yeh. 81, El Hhad'da'dee'n. 82, Ba'b el Khurck. 83, G. Isken'der. 84, Sikket B. el Khurck. 85, Ck. el emee'r Hhosey'n. 86, Sikket el Moo's'kee. 87, Sikket el Loob'oo'dee'yeh. 88, El Moo's'kee. 89, H. el Ifren'g, (Q[uarter]. of the Franks; but which is only part of the district inhabited by them). 90, Ck. el Moo's'kee. 91, Beyn es Soo'rey'n. 92, D. el G'ney'neh. 93, Ck. el Gedee'deh. 94, Sikket esh Shaara'wee. 95, B. esh Shaaree'yeh. 96, Sikket B. esh Shaaree'yeh.

B 1, D. el Fegga'leh. 2, D. et Tam'bel'ee. 3, Ck. B. esh Shaaree'yeh. 4, Sikket el 'Arya'n. 5, Soo'ck ez Zal'at. 6, B. el Bahhr. 7, D. el Wa'se'. 8, D. el Ibrahee'mee. 9, Ck. ed Dikkeh. 10, H. en Nasa'ra. 11, Sikket G. el Ahhmar. 12, D. Moos'tuf'a. 13, D. el 'El'weh. 14, D. el Bara'b'rah. 15, House of the British Consul. 16, D. el Hheen. 17, El Moo's'kee. 18, P. of Abba's ba'sha. 19, P. of Ahhmad ba'sha. 20, Soo'ck el Bekree. 21, D. el Beydah. 22, Sikket Ck. el emee'r Hhosey'n. 23, Gheyt Ab'oo Shawa'rib.

C 1, Soo'ck B. el Khurck.
2, Sikket B. el Loo'ck.
3, El Kafa'r'weh. 4, Sikket
esh sheykh Ruhha'n. 5, Sikket
'Abdee'n. 6, Sikket er Rahh'abah.
7, H. 'Abdee'n. 8, D. el Hhag'ar.
9, H. en Nasa'ra.
10, H. es Sack'ka-ee'n. 11, Soo'ck
Mis'keh. 12, H. el Hhan'afee.
13, G. el Hhan'afee.
14, D. el Gem'a'mee'z.
15, Sikket el Isma'ee'nee.
16, G. Emee'r A'khoo'r.
17, House of the French Institute.
18, Ck. es Siba'ă. 19, G. es sitt
Zey'neb. 20, Sikket es sitt Zey'neb.
21, Sikket el Moosal'la. 22, Sikket
es Sy'r'geh. 23, Ck. 'Amr shah.

D 1, El Loob'oo'dee'yeh. 2, Soo'ck
es Sooghei'yir. 3, 'Atfet es Sa'da't.
4, Sikket B[irkat]. el Feel.
5, Ck. el Gem'a'mee'z.
6, D. el Gem'a'mee'z.
7, El Hhab'ba'nee'yeh.
8, Ck. Soon'ckoor. 9, Tekee'yeh
and Sebee'l of the Hhab'a'nee'yeh.
10, Sikket el Hhab'a'nee'yeh.
11, Dal'ă es Sem'ek.
12, Ck. el Gedee'deh. 13, Sikket
D. el Faou'a'khee'r. 14, Sikket
el Hheen. 15, Ck. B. el Khurck.
16, Soo'ck el 'Asr.
17, Ed Da'-oo'dee'yeh.
18. Sikket Beyt esh Shurcka'wee.
19, Ckus'abat Ridwa'n.
20, Sikket El Ma'r'da'nee.
21, El Mooghurbeelee'n.
22, Es Soor'oo'gee'yeh.
23, D. Ckeysoo'n.

24, P. of Mahhmoo'd bey, kikh'ya.
25, D. esh sheykh Dala'm.
26, Sikket el Hhad'arah. 27, Sikket
er Roomey'leh. 28, Sikket
es Salee'beh. 29, Es Salee'beh.
30, El Khoodaree'yeh.
31, G. Sheykhoo'n. 32, Soo'ck
es Sem'ek. 33, El Moora'hhelee'yeh.
34, D. es Salee'beh.
35, D. er Rookbee'yeh.
36, H. Teyloo'n. 37, G. Teyloo'n.
38, Ckal'at el Kebsh. 39, Soo'ck
el Magha'r'beh. 40, D. el Hosr.
41, D. el Khalee'feh. 42, G. es sitt
Sekee'neh. 43, G. es sey'deh
Nefee'seh. 44, D. el Buck'lee.
45, G. es Soolta'n Hhas'an.
46, Soo'ck es Sila'hh. 47, Soo'ck
el 'Ez'zee. 48, Et Tebba'neh.
49, G. El Ma'r'da'nee.
50, D. El Ma'r'da'nee.
51, El Bara'de'ee'yeh. 52, Sikket
G. Asla'n. 53, Sikket
el Khurbakee'yeh. 54, Sikket
B. el Wezee'r.

E [For letter E, the pentagonal sec-
tion containing the Citadel in the
southeastern corner of the map,
Lane made several entries on his
draft key but did not number them
either on the draft key or on the
map. His entries:] Ba'b el 'Az'ab,
(principal gate of the Citadel).
Quarter of the 'Az'abs. Old Palace.
Beyt Yoo'soof Sala'hh ed Dee'n.
Greek Mosque. Well of Yoo'soof.
Deewa'n. Quarter of the
Inkisha'ree'yeh. New Palace.
Mosque. 'Arab el Yesa'r. Telegraph.

Figure 16: View of Cairo from the mounds on the right of the upper road from Boolák.

a, House of the Deftardár.
b, Machine for raising water for the House of the Deftardár.
c, The gate called Báb El-Elfee, beyond which is the place called the Ezbekekeeyeh [sic].
d,d, Two mád'nehs of the great mosque of El-Hákim. e, Street on the other side of the Ezbekeeyeh leading towards the Frank Quarter: above it is seen Fort Menou, built by the French.
f, Mád'neh of the Barkookeeyeh.
g, Mád'neh of the mosque of the Sultán Kala-oon, adjoining the Máristán, or Hospital. h,j, Palace of the Páshá. i, Fort Dupuis.
j, see h. k, Great Mosque El-Azhar, and mosque of Mohammad Bey. l, Mosque of El-Ghóree. m,n, Dome and two mád'nehs of the great mosque of

dd   ee   ff   gg   hh

El-Mu-eiyad, at Báb Zuweyleh.
These are in the distance, beyond
a smaller mosque. o, New mosque
in the Citadel. p, Fort on the
mountain, behind the Citadel; and
new palace in the Citadel.
q, Old mosque on the mountain.
r, Telegraph in the Citadel.
s, Old mosque in the Citadel.
t, Old Palace. u, Deewán, and, a
little nearer, the great mosque of the
Sultán Hasan.

Figure 17: Street-view in Cairo (Sakkas, or water-carriers; a coffee-shop; and other shops).

Figure 18: Costumes of Cairo.

Figure 19: Costumes of the ladies of Cairo.

a   b   c

Figure 20: View of the Citadel of Cairo, from the opposite side of the
place called the Rumeyleh. a, The gate of the Citadel. b. The Kasr
Yoosuf. c, An old ruin. d, The Deewán.

cc

bb

aa

Figure 21: View from the Citadel of Cairo, looking upon the Rumeyleh and the mosque of the Sultán Hasan. aa, The gate of the Citadel. bb, A Tamarind-tree in the Birket el-Feel. cc, The Nile.

Figure 22: Mosque and tomb of Káïd Bey, in the eastern cemetery of Cairo.

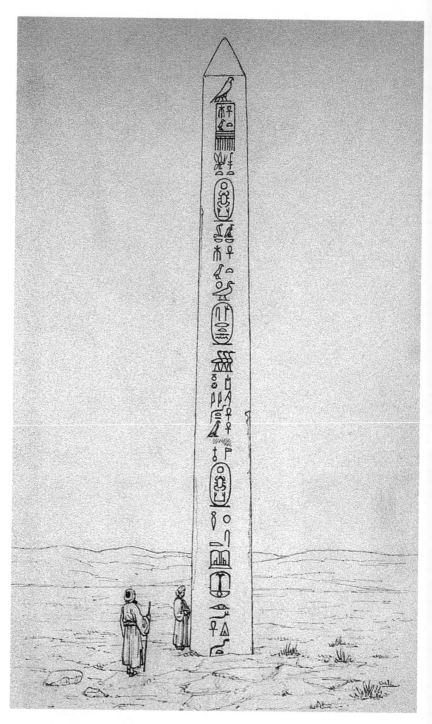

Figure 23: The Obelisk of Heliopolis.

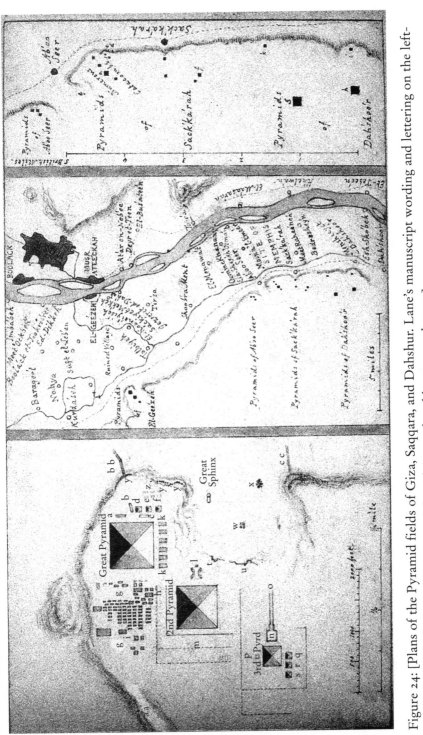

Figure 24: [Plans of the Pyramid fields of Giza, Saqqara, and Dahshur. Lane's manuscript wording and lettering on the left-hand panel, which are difficult to read, have been replaced by typeset letters.]

Figure 25: The Pyramids of El-Geezeh, from an island in the river, about five miles distant.

c

Figure 27: Third view
of the Pyramids of
El-Geezeh, from the east.
a, The Great Pyramid.
b, The Second Pyramid.
c, The Sphinx.
d, The Causeway.

Figure 26: Second view of
the Pyramids of El-Geezeh.

a   d

Figure 28: The Great Pyramid, from before the north-eastern angle.

Figure 29: The Top of the Great Pyramid, with a view of the
Second Pyramid.

Figure 30: Entrance
of the Great Pyramid.

Figure 31: [Cross-
Section of the Great
Pyramid. Lane's
manuscript letters
have been replaced
by typeset letters.]

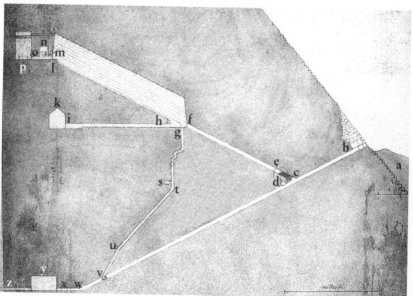

Figure 32: Ascent from the first to the second passage in the Great Pyramid.

Figure 33: The Grand Passage in the
Great Pyramid.

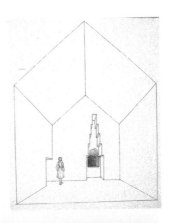

Figure 34: Middle Chamber in the Great
Pyramid.

Figure 35: The Grand Chamber in the
Great Pyramid.

Figure 36: Great excavated chamber in the Great Pyramid.

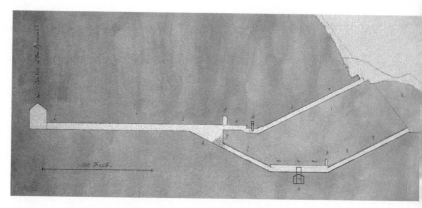

Figure 37: [Cross-Section of the Second Pyramid.]

Figure 38: [Entrances to the Second Pyramid.]

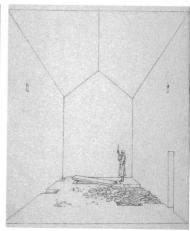

Figure 40: Inscription on the perpendicular rock on the north side of the
Second Pyramid.

Figure 39: [Burial Chamber of the
Second Pyramid.]

Figure 41: [Face of the
Third Pyramid above
Its Covered Entrance.]

Figure 42: [Mastaba in
the Western Cemetery at
Giza, Second Pyramid in
the Background.]

Figure 43: Sculptures in
the Sheykh[']s tomb, at
the Pyramids.

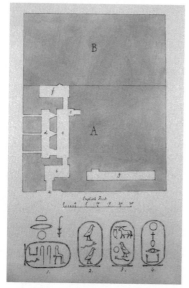

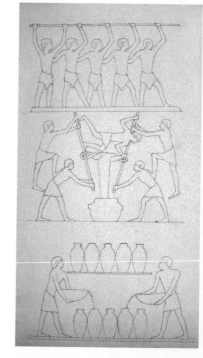

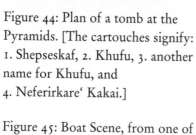

Figure 44: Plan of a tomb at the Pyramids. [The cartouches signify: 1. Shepseskaf, 2. Khufu, 3. another name for Khufu, and 4. Neferirkareʿ Kakai.]

Figure 45: Boat Scene, from one of the Tombs at the Pyramids.

Figure 46: Ploughing, from the tomb of the boats, at the Pyramids.

Figure 47: The making of wine, from the tomb of the boats, at the Pyramids.

Figure 48: The Great Sphinx.

The Great Sphinx (restored)

Name on the   Large Tablet.

Thothmos 4th.

Figure 49: The
Great Sphinx
(restored).

a

Figure 50: Pyramids of Sakkárah.

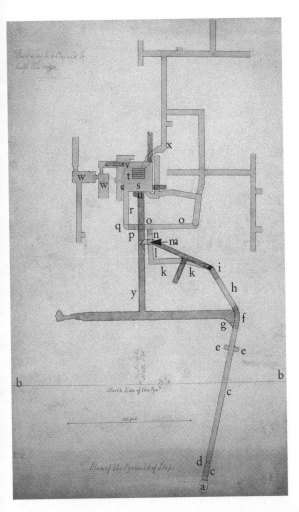

Figure 51: Plan of
the Pyramid of Steps.
Lane's manuscript
letters have been
replaced by typeset
letters.

Figure 52: [Inscription] Round a door-way under the principal Pyramid
of Sack'cka'rah. [The serekhs are those of Nedjeriket (Djoser).] The royal
title marked <u>a a</u> is sculptured four times down each side of the door.

Figure 53: Tomb at Sakkárah. [The cartouches are those of either Psammetichus I or II.]

Figure 54: 1st view, Pyramids of Dahshoor, &c. 2nd view, Two Great Pyramids of Dahshoor.

Figure 55: [The author in the cabin of his canjiah.]

Figure 56: Map of the Valley of the Nile from the Pyramids to
Thebes— corrected from former maps. The extend of the cultivable

C

Figure 57: [The Pyramid of Meidum.]

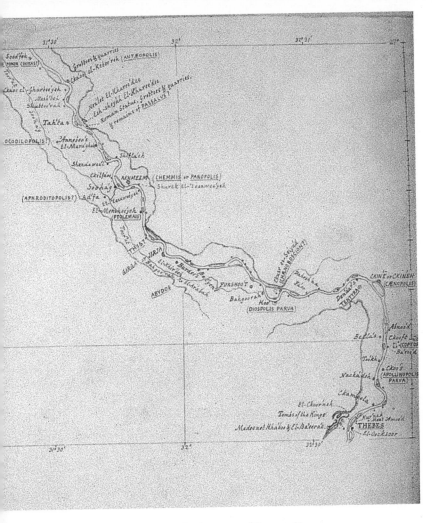

land is to be shewn by a tint, as in the map of Lower Egypt.
[The tint was never added.]

Figure 58:
The Obelisk of Begeeg.
a, Village of Begeeg.
b, Medeenet el-Feiyoom.
c, Mounds of Arsinoë.
d, Pyramid of Hawárah.

Figure 59: The Lake of El-Karn, and Island El-Karn.

Figure 60: The Kasr Károon, from the east.

Figure 61: Gebel et-Teyr, with the author's boat and crew.

Figure 62: 1st view, El-Minyeh. 2nd view, Mountain of Benee Hasan.

Figure 63: Grotto at Benee Hasan.

Figure 64: Grotto at Ben'ee Hhas'an.

Figure 65: Wrestlers—from the paintings of a grotto at Ben'ee Hhas'an.

Figure 66: Ancient Boat—from the paintings of a grotto at Ben'ee Hhas'an.

Figure 67: Sculptures near Too'na el-Geb'el.

Figure 68: [Interior of the Tomb of Ahmes (no. 3) at Tell el-Amarna.]
[The cartouches are those of the god Aten and the king Akhenaten.]

Figure 69: 1st view, Asyoot. 2nd view, Mountain of Asyoot.

Figure 70: Part of the great edifice of Abydos.

Figure 71: Small temple at Dendara, and distant view of part of the great temple, &c.

Figure 72: Front of the great temple of Dendara.

Figure 73: Portal at Koos.

Figure 75: Two views of
El-Uksur.

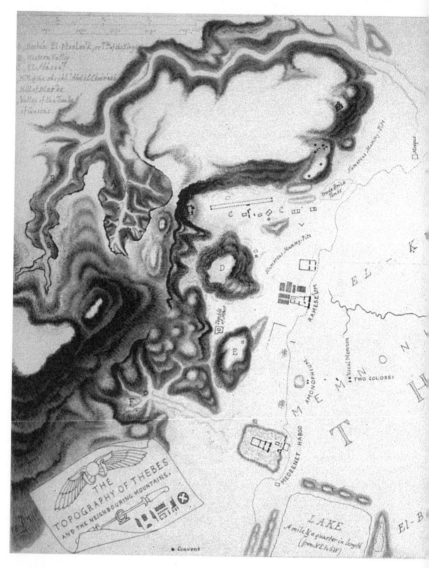

Figure 74: The Topography of Thebes and the Neighbouring Mountains.
AA, Beeba'n El-Mooloo'k, or Tbs. of the Kings.
BB, Western Valley.
CC, El As'a'see'f.
D, Hill of the Sheykh 'Abd el-Ckoo'r'neh.
E, Hill of Mar''ee.
F, Valley of the Tombs of Queens

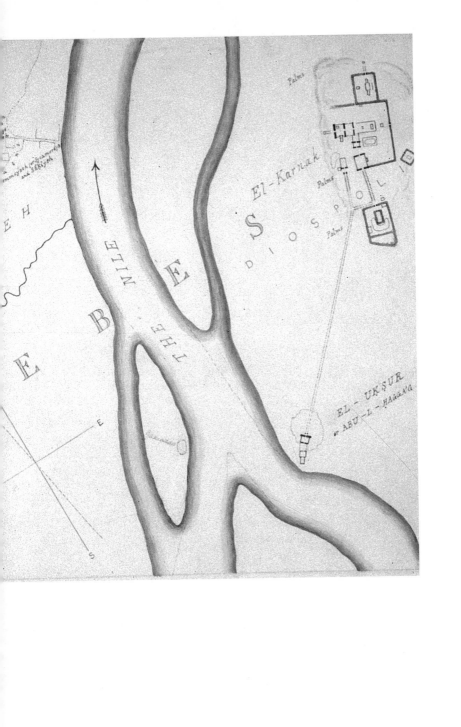

Figure 76: Front view of the Temple of El-Uksur.

Figure 78: Southern part of the Temple of El-Uksur.

Figure 79: Front of the First Propylon of the Great Temple of El-Karnak.

Figure 77: Great colonnade of the Temple of El-Uksur.

Figure 80: First court of the Great Temple of El-Karnak.

Figure 81: Principal avenue in the great portico of El-Karnak.

On the east of the Great Pyramid are three small pyramids,[1] the middlemost of which is the only monument to which the above passage of Herodotus can be applied. They are all much ruined. The southernmost, which is the least injured, is about 90 feet high. On the same side of the Great Pyramid are three long and deep trenches,[2] very roughly excavated in the rock. One of them is in a direct line with the ruined causeway which I have already mentioned. The object for which they were made it is difficult to conjecture. There are also many ancient tombs on the east of the Great Pyramid; which have been much dilapidated. On the west are others,[3] more numerous and less injured by time or violence: and there is likewise a row of ruined tombs[4] on the southern side of the Great Pyramid. I shall speak of these particularly in another part of this chapter. The Great Pyramid is thus surrounded, on three sides, by almost innumerable tombs. Some persons, who have been unreasonable enough to doubt whether the pyramids are sepulchral monuments, must, I think, be convinced of their error when they learn that I found human bones and mummy-rags in the principal pyramid of Sack'ka'rah.

The Second Pyramid, which is said to have been built by Chephrēn, or Chephrēnes, or Amōsis,[5] (though it is very doubtful who was its author), is 680 feet square. The length of its base is therefore 66 feet less than that of the First, or Great Pyramid.[6] Its site is about 30 feet higher than that of the latter; and its summit, which is nearly entire, is about 10 feet above the level of the summit of the Great Pyramid: consequently its height is about 436 feet; or 20 feet less than that of the latter. Herodotus asserts that it was 40 feet lower than that of Cheops; and it probably was so in his time; for the Great Pyramid wants about 25 feet of its original height; and the Second Pyramid, about 5 feet.—As the place chosen for the site of this Pyramid was a gentle acclivity, rising towards the north-west, the rock has been cut away on the northern and western sides, in order to form a level area round the base.[7] This area, which is nearly 200 feet wide on the northern side, and about 100 feet on the western, is bounded by the hewn, perpendicular face of the rock; which is about 30 feet high at and near the angle; diminishing in height towards the extremities.—The Second Pyramid is not so well constructed as the First. At the lower part, where it has been most dilapidated, and where, consequently, we have a

---

[1]Marked *d, e, f,* in the plan, no. 1, plate 6 [fig. 24].

[2]Marked *a, b, c,* in the plan [fig. 24].

[3]See *g, g,* in the plan [fig. 24].

[4]Marked *k, k,* in the plan [fig. 24].

[5]I believe (for reasons which I shall here after state) that the names of Amōsis and Chephrēn apply to the same king.

[6]According to Diodorus Siculus, the base of the Second Pyramid was 75 feet less than that of the First. This was probably very near the truth when both those monuments were entire.

[7]Revert to plate 20 [fig. 29].

view of its interior composition, we observe blocks of various sizes, piled, one upon another, in a very irregular manner. Higher up, where not so many stones have been stripped down, we see uniform courses. The uppermost part retains its original smooth casing, almost entire, for about a fourth of the way down. It is evident that the whole Pyramid was thus cased. The stone of which the structure is mainly composed is of the same kind as that of the Great Pyramid; and was doubtless supplied by the rock in its immediate neighbourhood; where we find extensive quarries; but what remains of the casing is composed of stones of a more compact kind, which were brought from the quarries on the opposite side of the Nile. To ascend to the summit of this Pyramid is extremely difficult. Even the ascent of the lower part is not easy; the stones being much broken: but when we reach the casing, we find a perfectly smooth surface, with only small holes, which will scarcely admit the fingers and toes, between the several courses. Some European travellers have accomplished the ascent to the summit. The mere contemplation of it affected *me* with giddiness; and I therefore did not attempt it. On each side of this Pyramid is an accumulation of fragments of stone and mortar, composing a very compact mass, in the same manner as the rubbish which has fallen from the First Pyramid. Each of these slopes of rubbish rises to the height of between 40 and 50 feet above the base of the Pyramid.

Until the year 1818, we were entirely unacquainted with the interior of this Pyramid; and were ignorant of its having ever been opened. Herodotus was informed that it had no subterranean chambers; and many modern travellers doubted whether it contained any chambers whatever. Its entrance was discovered, and its interior explored, by the acute and indefatigable Belzoni: and in its principal chamber were found several Arabic inscriptions, in the Nus'khee character, which has been commonly used by the Arabs since the 10th century. It is probable that the period at which it was open and visited by the Arabs who wrote these inscriptions was the 14th or 15th century of the Christian era[1]; and that the entrance shortly after became covered by degrees by the fragments of stone and mortar which fell from the side of the Pyramid.[2]

In the centre of the northern side, are two narrow apertures, which are the entrances of forced passages; one above the other: (see the annexed engraving).[3] The upper passage turns downwards, and communicates with the lower, which continues to the distance of about 100 feet, running towards the centre of the Pyramid; but in a very irregular manner; in some parts, very contracted; in others, wide and lofty. Nearly 30 feet to the left (or eastward) of the two forced apertures, is the true

---

[1] I conjecture so merely from the style of the characters; for we find no date attached.

[2] See *a* in the section, plate 17 [fig. 37].

[3] See no. [8] of the subjects for wood-cuts (among the *mounted* drawings—next to plate 25) [fig. 38].

entrance of the Pyramid. Several of the blocks of granite of which the passage is constructed project beyond the present surface of the Pyramid; a great number of stones having been removed from above and from either side: (see *b* in the section, plate 26†). The passage (*c, c*) is of the same dimensions as that of the Great Pyramid; namely 4 feet high, and 3 feet and a half wide. It descends, also, with the same inclination; an angle of twenty-six degrees and a half. The whole of this passage is lined with granite, cut with great care. At the distance of 108 feet, we find a portcullis of granite (*d*), 1 foot 3 inches thick; by which the passage was closed. Belzoni raised this sufficiently high to allow a person to drag himself through. At the distance of 3 feet and a half beyond it, the granite work ceases; the rest of the passage being cut through the solid rock. From this point, we proceed along a horizontal passage (*e*), 22 feet and a half in length, of the same dimensions as the first. At the end of this is an excavation over head (*f*), turning up to the right: immediately beyond which is a perpendicular descent of 15 feet (*g*). Some stones are piled up below, on the right side, for the convenience of descending. From the bottom of the perpendicular, we ascend a slope of 30 feet (*h*). From the top of this, the passage runs horizontally; of the same width as before, but 6 feet high; the top being even with that of the former horizontal passage, but the floor lower. This passage (*i, i*) is 129 feet long; measured from the top of the slope. At the end of it is the principal chamber (*k*); which is 46 feet 3 inches long, 16 feet 3 inches wide and 23 feet and a half high: (see the annexed engraving).[1] It is exactly under the centre of the Pyramid. At the western end is a sarcophagus of granite buried so that its top is level with the floor. It is 8 feet long, 3 feet 6 inches wide, and 2 feet 3 inches deep in the inside. The lid has not been taken away; but lies obliquely upon the top. Within were found some bones; one of which, when brought to England, was discovered to have belonged—not to a human being, but—to a cow, or a bull; or, in other words, to a representative of the goddess Isis, or of the god Apis, who was the same with Osiris. Whether the sarcophagus also contained a human mummy cannot now be ascertained[2]: but I am inclined to hold the same opinion with respect to this sarcophagus that I mentioned with regard to that in the Great Pyramid; namely, that it covers the mouth of a vault, or pit, or the top of a stair-case. The sides of this chamber are cut in the rock. The floor is paved with large, flat stones; and the roof is formed by long stones, resting their upper ends together, as in one of the chambers in the Great Pyramid. Several stones have been taken up from the pavement, apparently in search for treasure. There are two small holes, one in the northern, and the other in the southern side; like those in the principal

---

†Fig. 37.
[1]See No. [9] of the subjects for wood-cuts [fig. 39].
[2]If the assertion of Diodorus Siculus be true, that the Second Pyramid did not receive the remains of its founder, it may, for that reason, have been made the sepulchre of a god, or, rather, of the representative of a god.

chamber of the Great Pyramid; but higher up. The entrance of the chamber is on the northern side, 8 feet 8 inches from the eastern end. On the southern side, the name of Belzoni is written, in large characters, with the date of his discovery. Several Arabic inscriptions (to which I have before alluded) are scrawled with charcoal upon various parts: most of these were written before the opening of the Pyramid by Belzoni; and are nearly illegible; generally consisting of a single line; and recording the visit of some person or persons. I could not find any date among them. Two lines, at the western end of the chamber, written in the same modern Arabic characters as the others, and with the same material, are not so imperfectly legible. Belzoni particularly remarked these; and took a Ckoob'tee scribe to copy them. This man did not faithfully execute his task: he concluded that the two lines composed one legend (which is not at all certain) and, instead of making a fac-simile of them, presumed to restore them, thus,

و فتحهم المعلم محمد احمد الحجار و ذلك المعلم
عثمان حضرو الملك على محمد اولًا ولغلاك

which Mr. Salam[é] (substituting للغلاق for لغلاك) translates—"The Master Mohammed Ahmed, lapicide, has opened them; and the Master Othman attended this (opening); and the King Alÿ Mohammed at first (from the beginning) to the closing up."—This legend has exceedingly puzzled the learned orientalists of Europe; and great pains have been taken to find out who was this King Alÿ (or 'Al'ee Mohham'mad); and at what period he reigned. Now it unfortunately happens that the first line is almost wholly defaced: a traveller having scribbled his name over it: the first two words, however, have not been written over; and I must pronounce it very uncertain whether وفتحهم (signifying "and opened them") be the correct reading: but the second line, which is the more important, has not been defaced like the first. The following is a copy.

حصر الخلا ل على ر محد او ولا ر الـ الـ الـ

The greater part of this sentence is so plain that we can hardly read it otherwise than thus,

حضر الخليل على بن محمد ————
Hhad'ar El-Khalee'l 'Al'ee Ibn Mohham'mad ————

That is, "El-Khalee'l 'Al'ee, the son of Mohham'mad ——— has been here"; or, in the order of the Arabic words, "Has been here El-Khalee'l 'Al'ee, the son of Mohham'mad ———": but the characters which appear to compose two words at the end I cannot clearly decipher. It is quite evident that the word which Belzoni's copyist has written الملك ("the King") is a proper name. Another inaccuracy in the copy published by Belzoni is the omission of the word ابن (or "son"), which, in the middle of a sentence, is generally written بن [.]—Thus we find that this much talked of inscription (instead of recording the visit of a *King*, or, perhaps, even of alluding to the opening of the Pyramid) is nothing more than the Arabic scrawls which are seen in great numbers on many of the monuments of Egypt. One of my servants, proud of being able to write, often scribbled his name, with a piece of charcoal, on the temples and tombs, thus حضر الحاج حسن البريري "the hha'gg' Hhas'an, the Bur'ber'ee, has been here." The Arabic inscriptions in the Second Pyramid are, however, interesting, as shewing that this Pyramid was open, and visited by the Arabs, or Egyptians, probably in the 14th or 15th century of the Christian era, as I said before.—I now resume my description of the interior of the Pyramid.

Returning to the perpendicular (*g*), we find a passage (*l*) descending with the same inclination as the other sloping passage, and running towards the north, under the passage marked *e* in the section. It is 48 feet 2 inches long. From this runs a horizontal passage (*m, m*), which is 50 feet long. In the middle of the latter, on the left, is the entrance of another descending passage (*n*), 4 feet high, and 3 feet 5 inches wide, running towards the west. It is 22 feet long, and opens in the middle of the eastern end of a narrow, low chamber (*o*), which is 32 feet long, 9 feet 9 inches wide, and 8 feet 6 inches high. This has a pointed roof, like the other chamber; but is altogether cut in the rock. In it, and in the passage which descends to it, are many masses of stone which have been forced down from other parts of the Pyramid. In the horizontal passage marked *m, m*, in the section, opposite the entrance of the descending passage, or rather to the south, is a recess, 5 feet 8 inches deep, and 10 feet 4 inches wide. Proceeding to the end of this passage, we find another portcullis of granite, (*p*), which has fallen, or been forced from its place, and lies beneath. Beyond this is an ascending passage, (*q, q*), which is parallel with that above. This would conduct us out of the Pyramid, just at the base; but the upper part of it is choked with large blocks of stone; and the rubbish outside of the Pyramid covers its mouth.

I have already mentioned the area on the north and west sides of the Second Pyramid, formed by cutting away the rock. Upon the perpendicular face of the rock on the north of the Pyramid, and not far from the angle, is a hieroglyphic inscription, in large characters, of which a copy is here annexed.[1] It contains the name of Rameses the Second, who was also called Sesostris; and therefore affords a proof that the

---

[1] See no. [10] of the subjects for wood-cuts [fig. 40].

erection of the Second Pyramid was at least anterior to the reign of that prince. In the rock on the west side of the Pyramid are several sepulchral grottoes; most of them small and insignificant; with low and narrow entrances. One,[1] which is opposite the centre of the western side of the pyramid, is remarkable as having its ceiling carved so as to represent a roof supported by palm-trunks. The roofs of the huts in Egypt are so formed in the present day.—Besides the enclosure formed by the hewn rock on the north and west sides of the Pyramid, there are remains of several built walls, further distant; as marked by broken lines in the plan, no[.] 1, plate 14.[†]

Before the centre of the eastern side of the Second Pyramid are considerable remains of a large building which has been called "the Temple of the Second Pyramid."[2] The ruins consist of very thick walls, constructed of stones of enormous magnitude. They have no hieroglyphics. The plan and object of this building cannot be ascertained. From its position, it appears that it appertained to the Second Pyramid.

The Third Pyramid, which, according to Herodotus and Diodorus Siculus, was commonly attributed to Mycerinus, the son of Cheops or Chemnis, but by some believed to have been founded by a courtesan named Rhodōpis, is a very noble monument in point of magnitude, as well as in the nature of its construction; though small in comparison with the First and Second Pyramids. Its base is about 300 feet square; and its height about 180 feet. These dimensions agree very nearly with those stated by the above-mentioned historians. There is, however, some ambiguity in a passage of Herodotus on this subject: it is impossible that he could have meant to say that the height of this Pyramid was only 20 feet less than that of Cheops, and yet its base not more than 3 plethra; the latter measure being nearly correct, but the former, egregiously wrong: he is supposed to have written that the Pyramid of Mycerinus was less than that of his father; for that its base was 3 plethra, *minus* 20 feet. This historian and some others have described the Third Pyramid as constructed, to the middle of its height, of Ethiopian stone (that is, granite), but this stone is stated, by several of these writers, to have been *black*; which we do not find the case. The Arabs call this Pyramid *el-Har'am el-Moolaou'wan,* or the Coloured Pyramid. It is constructed with admirable regularity, and mainly with the same kind of stone as the First and Second Pyramids; but it was cased (at least, *partly*) with granite, of a dull red colour intermixed with black particles, like most of the granite of Egypt. It appears to have lost but little more than the casing-stones; and those, not entirely. The courses are very regular; and the stones, well cut, and generally between two feet and two and a half in height; consequently, the ascent to its summit is not difficult. Very

---

[1]Marked *m* in the plan, no. 1, plate 6 [fig. 24].
[†]Fig. 24.
[2]It is seen in plate 11, towards the left [fig. 29]; and is marked *l* in the plan, no. 1, plate 6 [fig. 24].

laborious attempts have lately been made to open it; but the operation seems to have been begun and prosecuted with little judgement; for the workmen began by pulling down the stones so high up in the northern face, that the blocks which they have thrown down compose a heap which rises considerably higher than the spot where the entrance (if we may judge from the First and Second Pyramids) might reasonably be expected to be found. The two tiers immediately above this accumulation of stone have the granite casing remaining, in a very perfect state (as represented in the annexed sketch[†]); and probably all the tiers below are the same. The removal of some of these granite blocks would, doubtless, lay open the entrance; but it would be necessary first to clear away the heap of stones before mentioned, which would be a work of no small labour. Many of the blocks of granite which formed a part of the casing lie around the base; but the greater number have been carried away, to be cut into mill-stones. Opposite the centre of the northern side is a square pit, lined with masonry.[1]—We cannot but regard this monument with peculiar interest; for the pains taken in its construction, and the praises bestowed upon it by ancient writers, justify us in forming grand conjectures respecting its interior. It is said, by Diodorus Siculus, that the name of Mycerinus was inscribed upon its northern face.

Before the centre of the northern [eastern] side of this Pyramid are remains of a building called "the Temple of the Third Pyramid," similar to that of the Second Pyramid; but more extensive; and having a wide and long causeway running up to it, from the east.[2]

Adjacent to the Third Pyramid are three other pyramids,[3] considerably smaller, being from 100 to 120 feet square. The first, or easternmost of these, is of the same form as those already described; but much ruined: the others are built in the manner of steps or stages, like the principal pyramid of Sack'ka'rah, (of which a view will be found in this volume).

There are remains of several walls of enclosure surrounding the Third Pyramid and the smaller monuments above mentioned. They are marked, in the plan, by broken lines.

I now proceed to give some account of *the numerous tombs in the vicinity of the Great Pyramid.*

I have already stated that the Great Pyramid is surrounded on three sides, by almost innumerable tombs. The most interesting quarter of this extensive necropolis is that lying on the west. It is a space larger than the base of the Great Pyramid, containing a vast number of sepulchral monuments[4]; which are low, flat-roofed buildings, constructed of stone; their walls facing the four cardinal points (like the Pyramids), and slightly inclining inwards. Most of them are of an oblong form, and are

---

[†]Fig. 41.
[1]Marked *p* in the plan, no. 1, plate 6 [fig. 24].
[2]See *n, o,* in the plan, no. 1, plate 6 [fig. 24].
[3]See *q, r, s,* in the plan.
[4]See *g, g,* in the plan.

regularly disposed, in rows, from east to west and from north to south: others are placed more or less irregularly.

All of the former (which must be regarded as among the more ancient) and many of the latter appear to be (like the Pyramids) destitute of hieroglyphics; and each of these seems to consist, internally as well as externally, of solid masonry, or internally of hard rubbish: the building itself not containing any chambers: but a square pit, or well, descends from the flat top, or roof, to a subterranean chamber, in which the mummy or mummies were deposited. Some of these monuments are nearly buried in the drifted sand; and many are almost entirely demolished. A view of one of the largest and least injured of them[1] is here annexed; exhibiting the eastern side of the building; with a false door, or niche, designed, apparently, merely for ornament.[2] The walls are double; and constructed with the utmost neatness; but the stones are not generally rectangular; their upper and lower surfaces, only, being parallel. At the north-eastern corner, a portion of the building has been demolished; and here we obtain an insight into the singular mode of the construction of the roof and the interior. We observe that the roof is composed of two courses of stone; and that the blocks of which it consists are wedge-formed. It seems that the builder was acquainted with the principle of the masonic arch; and that he adopted this mode of construction for the sake of greater strength; the main body of the building being composed of rubbish, which might have yielded to the pressure of the roof, had the latter been differently constructed. I was much astonished to find a monument which was evidently built nearly at the same period as the Pyramids displaying such admirable architectural skill and knowledge.[3] A square pit, descending from the roof of this monument to the depth of about 60 feet, has been cleared of the sand and rubbish with which it was filled. The upper part is lined with masonry, as low as the foundation of the building; and the remainder cut through the solid rock. At the bottom of it is a narrow and short passage leading to a chamber, in which is a plain sarcophagus of granite, similar to that in the Great Pyramid. No hieroglyphics are found upon this, nor in any part of the tomb.

Among those monuments which are irregularly disposed, there are some of a different class from those which I have described; and somewhat less ancient. Each of these contains several narrow apartments, about 7 or 8 feet high; from one or another of which, a square pit descends to the sepulchral chamber. In their exterior form, these edifices differ but little from those of the former class. The walls of the apartments of some of them are decorated—not only with hieroglyphics, but also—with painted sculptures, representing various domestic and

---

[1]Plate 27 [fig. 42]. It is marked *h* in the plan no. 1, plate 6 [fig. 24; Mastaba of Duwanera, G 5110].

[2]A part of the Second Pyramid is also seen in this view.

[3]I shall have occasion to make some remarks respecting the antiquity of the Pyramids and the adjacent tombs before I conclude this chapter.

agricultural scenes, diversions, manufactures, &c. These painted sculptures (which must be classed among the most ancient now existing in the world) are executed in very low relief, generally in stucco, and are painted with the most brilliant colours (red, yellow, green, blue, and black) upon a white or yellow ground. One of these monuments is particularly interesting.[1] A plan here annexed[2] shews the disposition of its apartments, or, at least, of those apartments which are accessible; and exhibits, also, the outlines of another and more ancient edifice (B), against which, that particularly alluded to (A) is built. The entrance (*a*), which is on the eastern side, is low and narrow, and half closed by drifted sand. The sand has also penetrated into all the apartments.—I shall not enter into a detailed description of the curious style of painting employed in the decoration of the walls of the apartments of this edifice, and in other ancient Egyptian tombs. The reader may form some notion of the designs from the several specimens contained in this volume; but it is necessary for me to make a few remarks. The figures are generally arranged in horizontal rows. No attempt is made to express the effects of light and shade, or perspective. Men are generally represented nearly naked, and are painted of a deep red colour: women, either the same, or of a yellow tint; as their complexion was somewhat lighter. The dresses are commonly white. Distinguished persons are represented of a larger size than others. Explanatory hieroglyphics, sculptured and painted with the utmost care, and disposed in perpendicular rows, generally fill up a portion of the space over each figure or each groupe.—The painted sculptures on the walls of the apartments of the edifice which I have begun to describe are executed in very low relief. On the left wall of the first of these little chambers (*b*) are represented several persons engaged in various manufactures. They are chiefly carpenters, who are sawing, planing, and chiseling different articles of furniture, &c. On the wall opposite the entrance is pourtrayed an illustrious personage; apparently the individual for whom this tomb was chiefly destined. His name (see no. 1 in the engraving above referred to) is inscribed in hieroglyphics, and distinguished by a royal title: it seems, therefore, that this monument is the tomb of a king, or of a viceroy.[3] He is standing, and leans upon a

---

[1]It is that which is marked *i* in the plan of the Pyramids, &c., no. 1, plate 6 [fig. 24; Mastaba of Iyuery, G 6020].

[2]See no. 12 of the subjects for wood-cuts [fig. 44].

[3]This and the other names to which I shall presently refer are found among the hieroglyphics in other tombs in the neighbourhood, and mostly with royal titles. They were Memphite Kings, or princes; probably of the 8th Dynasty. Major Felix has found (on the rocks of Wa'dee Magha'rah, in the Peninsula of Mount Sinai) the names of several of these princes, in hieroglyphic inscriptions, which state that they were subjugated by a king who (according to the tablet of Abydos) was the last but one before Amos; that is, the last but one of the 17th Dynasty, which consisted of Diospolites, or princes whose capital was Diospolis (or Thebes). See the Supplement to this work.

staff, looking towards a number of other persons, who are leading to him domestic and wild oxen, and birds, of the size of ostriches, but in form resembling a species of crane. The principal personage is represented nearly of the natural size: the other figures above described are very small, and arranged in horizontal rows, one row above another, according to the usual rules of ancient Egyptian art. Behind the chief is another figure, a little inferior in size; perhaps his son: his name (no. 2) is also inscribed in hieroglyphics. Upon the next wall of this apartment are represented several persons carrying various articles on their shoulders and in baskets; and a scribe making an inventory. Of the figures in the lowest row (which are alternately females and males), some have their name affixed: before each of the first two males is the same name (no. 3): before the third male is another name (no[.] 4); and before a female is the name of the principal personage (no. 1). On the fourth side of this little apartment, are represented subjects similar to those on the opposite wall: persons bringing, to their lord, domestic and wild oxen.—The next chamber (*c*) is 21 feet 5 inches in length, and only 5 feet 5 inches wide. It has an arched roof; the stones which cover it extending from side to side, and being cut in the form of the arch. The walls of this narrow chamber (like those of the first) are adorned with painted sculptures; the subjects of which are various, and highly interesting. On the right side is a very curious and animated representation of a fight between some boatmen, whose barks appear to have run foul of each other. (See the annexed engraving).[1] Above these is represented the constructing of boats; which seem to be formed of rushes bound together.[2] To the left of these subjects, various agricultural employments are depicted. First, ploughing; (see an engraving here annexed)[3]: a yoke of oxen drawing the plough; a man guiding it; and another person urging on the oxen. Beneath this groupe are represented four men breaking the clods of the newly ploughed ground with a kind of pick-axe of this form *A* ; the longer end held in the hand, and the shorter end pointed. These four persons are followed by the sower and another man; both with whips, or thongs. Behind these, five rams are treading down the seed. The man who follows the sower is beating the foremost of the rams for stooping his head to eat the seed on the ground. On the left, or opposite side, of this narrow chamber, are represented groupes of cattle, with their young. Among these is a cow suckling her calf (a beautiful design, but, unfortu-

---

[1]See no. 13 of the subjects for wood-cuts [fig. 45].

[2]Herodotus (in lib. II, cap. 96) describes the larger kind of Egyptian boat, called *baris*, which was formed of short planks bound together with ligaments of the plant *byblus*. Pliny, in his Natural History (lib. XIII, cap. 11), gives an account of Egyptian boats which were made entirely, with the exception of the keel, of the papyrus, which was the same plant. The boats represented in the tombs here described appear to be exactly of this kind.

[3]See no. 14 of the subjects for wood-cuts [fig. 46].

nately, much injured); and another calving, with a man receiving the calf. To the right of these are representations of men slaughtering cattle; and of persons feasting,—two men sitting at a tray which is supported by a low pedestal, and loaded with food: one is holding a fowl in his left hand; and, with his right, tearing off one of the wings: the other is holding a joint, and about to bite off a piece. Both of these persons are depicted as almost naked: had they more clothing, the groupe would be a true representation of two modern Egyptians, or Arabs, at their dinner, or supper. Among other figures on the same wall, are several musicians and dancers. At the further end of the chamber, to the left of a door, is a curious representation of the process of making wine, (a copy of which is here annexed).[1] This subject is divided into three compartments. In the first are five persons treading the wine-vat: in the second, the same number of men pressing out the juice, in a very extraordinary manner: in the third, two men pouring the juice into jars.—On the left side of this chamber are three narrow slits (like the loop-holes for musketry in a fortress), to admit light from another chamber (*d*), which is parallel with the former. The latter has no regular door; but an entrance has been effected by enlarging one of the apertures before mentioned. This apartment has three narrow apertures for the admission of light from the exterior. Its walls are without any ornament. Of its use I shall speak presently.—On the right side of the principal chamber is an entrance (*e*) to one or more other chambers; but I found it blocked up with large masses of stone, and was informed that there was nothing worthy of examination within it.—At the end of the principal chamber is a door, through which we pass into another small apartment (*f*), also containing painted sculptures: the subjects similar to those in the first apartment.—It appears that the entrance of the edifice was never concealed. The open chambers were probably destined for the accommodation of the surviving relations, friends and dependants of the person or persons buried beneath, at those periods when they visited the tomb to perform the customary lamentations. We find, in this and several similar monuments in the same necropolis, one or more *closed* chambers; in which statues and other sacred objects were deposited before the building was completed.[2] Though these chambers have no entrances, but such as have been made by explorers, they have one or more narrow apertures in each oblong side, or one at each end, for the admission of light, through them, into the chambers which were left open; and these apertures might also have been intended to allow the visiters a sight of the statues which were placed in them, and which may have been designed as representations of the deceased. Caviglia found several fragments of statues in some of the closed chambers of these monuments.[3]

---

[1]See no. 15 of the subjects for wood-cuts [fig. 47].

[2]The chamber marked *g*, in the plan of the tomb which I have described, is accessible from the roof.

[3]In a short account of these tombs, furnished by Mr. Salt, and published in the

Of all the monuments in the western quarter of the necropolis adjacent to the Great Pyramid, those of the class first described must be regarded as the more ancient: 1st, from their position: the greater number of them being disposed in regular rows, from east to west, and from north to south; while some of the same kind, and *all* of the latter class, are built around the space which the former occupy. 2ndly, we may infer that those first mentioned are more ancient from their being (like the Pyramids) destitute of hieroglyphics, as well as of other inscriptions or ornaments. It is reasonable, therefore, to conclude that they were built soon after the Pyramids; probably by members of the families of those kings who founded the Pyramids. The monuments of the latter class may justly be considered as but little less ancient. I shall endeavour to investigate this subject more fully towards the close of this chapter.

There is a row of monuments of the former class on the southern side of the Great Pyramid[1]: but these are so much ruined that they appear like oblong mounds of rubbish. A hollow is, however, observable in the centre of each, shewing the situation of the mouth of the square pit, or well, which descends to the subterranean apartments. There are also remains of numerous monuments of the same kind on the east and east-south-east of the Great Pyramid. These I regard as the relics of the many "small pyramids of El-Gee'zeh" which (according to El-Muckree'zee and other Arab writers) Ckar'a'ckoo'sh demolished, in the reign of Sala'hh ed-Deen; and the materials of which he employed in the construction of the Citadel and the Third Wall of El-Cka'hireh, the modern Musr. These buildings were, indeed, truncated pyramids; having sloping sides and a flat roof.

There are numerous tombs, but of a different kind, between the Pyramids and the Great Sphinx. Of these I shall give some account; but first I shall describe the Sphinx.

The Great Sphinx[2] is a figure of enormous size, almost entirely cut out of a mass of rock, which, perhaps, originally had somewhat of the same form. This gigantic object is the representation of an animal with the head of a man, and the body of a lion. It faces the east. Its situation is shewn in the plan of the Pyramids, &c., no[.] 1, plate 15.[3] It is called, by the Arabs, ابو الهول *Ab'oo 'l-Ho'l* ("the Father of Terror," or "the Terrific"); which name is by some written ابو الهولى *Ab'oo 'l-Ho'la*. We have the authority of the Cka'moo's (as well as that of El-Muckree'zee

---

19th volume of the Quarterly Review, it is stated that the doors and windows are found invariably on the northern and eastern sides. This remark is incorrect. In the monument which I have particularly described, the apertures for the admission of light are on the *southern* side; and I perfectly remember at least *one* in which they are on the *western* side.

[1]Marked *k, k*, in the plan no. 1, plate 6 [fig. 24].

[2]See plate 28 [fig. 48].

[3][Fig. 24.] It has been erroneously stated, by several travellers, that the Sphinx is directly opposite the centre of the eastern side of the Second Pyramid.

and many other Arab authors, corroborated by the modern pronunciation) for writing the name in the former manner: but some Arab writers assert that the original name was بلهيت *Belhee't*; which, if a Coptic word, signifies "honest," or "guileless."—I have mentioned, on a former occasion,[1] that the Sphinx is believed, by the Arabs, to possess a talismanic influence, preventing the sand of the desert from overspreading the fields between it and the Nile; and have related how it was mutilated by the fanatic sheykh Mohham'mad, who was surnamed Sa'im ed-Dahr.—The greater portion of this singular colossus is now buried beneath the sand: the head, the neck, the upper part of the body, and the hinder part nearly to the base, being alone visible. The face (see plate 28[†]) is much mutilated; the nose being broken off. This loss gives, to the expression of the face, much of the negro character; but the features of the countenance of the ancient Egyptian (as well as the comparative lightness of complexion) widely distinguished him from the negro; and the nose of the former particularly differed from that of the latter; being slightly aquiline, and rather rounded at the end. Notwithstanding the injuries it has sustained, there is yet observable, in the countenance of the Sphinx, a peculiar sweetness of expression which has excited a high degree of admiration in several travellers; and which is extremely difficult to pourtray. Mr. Salt, who says that he "repeatedly attempted a likeness of it with little success,"[2] having never seen any that was correct, was perfectly satisfied with my drawing, which was made with the camera-lucida. The praise is due to the *instrument*, more than to *myself*. The eye-brows are formally outlines, and a border is sculptured round the eyes, and elongated towards the ears. The face was originally painted of a dull red colour (remains of which paint are still seen upon it); and the eye-brows and the border round the eyes, were black: the latter representing the border of *kohhl* which the ancient Egyptians, both male and female, painted round their eyes. The modern Egyptian women, also, blacken the edges of their eye-lids with kohhl; and I have seen Egyptian girls (though not often) with the black line extended to the length of nearly an inch from the corner of the eye (towards the ear), in exact conformity with the ancient custom. It is no longer common in Egypt for *men* to apply kohhl to their eye-lids, though it is in some other eastern countries. The head-dress of the Sphinx, when complete, was not inelegant. Upon the front of it is represented the asp which usually adorns the heads of Egyptian gods and kings.—In the year 1817, Caviglia accomplished the very laborious operation of uncovering the Sphinx to its very base. The form of the whole figure is shewn by the annexed sketch,[3] partly taken from the colossus itself, partly from a comparison of other Egyptian Sphinxes; and the representation of the tablets, &c.,

---

[1]In the 8th chapter of the former volume of this work [chapter eight].
[†]Fig. 48.
[2]Quarterly Review, vol. 19, p. 417.
[3]See no. 16 of the subjects for wood-cuts [fig. 49].

between its fore-legs, from drawings by Mr. Salt.—The head, alone, is twenty feet high. The body is about 160 feet long. The two fore-legs stretch out fifty feet from the breast; and these are constructed of masonry; but as the figure was originally plastered, and painted red, it was not seen that any part was composed of masonry. Upon a pavement between the outstretched fore-legs, Caviglia discovered a large tablet of granite, 14 feet high, placed against the breast; the front of it adorned with sculpture, representing two Sphinxes, seated on pedestals, back to back, and a king standing before each, presenting an offering. The two figures offering are representations of Thothmos the Fourth; his hieroglyphic name being inscribed before them, as well as over each of the sphinxes. Above this design is the winged globe. The lower part of the tablet is occupied by a long hieroglyphic inscription, dated in the reign of the above mentioned king. Two other tablets, of calcareous stone, were placed on the right and left, one against each of the legs. That on the right was found to be thrown down and broken; and the fragments of it are now in the British Museum. Some fragments of the plaited beard, several small figures of lions, and the forepart of a small sphinx (all of which were painted red, like the colossus itself) were also found between the fore-legs[1]; and an altar, which appeared to have been used for burnt offerings.[2] On the paws of the Sphinx were discovered several Greek inscriptions, addressed to different deities. One of these, cut in deep characters, upon the second digit of the left paw, is in verse, and bears the signature of Arrian. It is addressed to the colossus, which is termed the work of the eternal Gods, and the image of the most pure servant of the Goddess Latona. Two other Greek inscriptions, upon small tablets, found before the Sphinx, are now in the British Museum. One of these celebrates the divine virtues of "the Emperor Nero Claudius Cæsar Augustus Germanicus the Good Genius of the World," for having been present at the "lawful rites, and having worshipped the Sun, the overseer and saviour of the world":—the other records the building of "the walls," in the reign of Antoninus and Verus.[3] The latter seems to allude to walls of crude brick, which enclosed the Sphinx, and which were uncovered by Caviglia. Parts of these walls are yet visible above the sand, behind the colossus.—Within a few months after Caviglia had laid bare this colossus to the pavement upon which it is represented as lying, the sand returned, and covered it, nearly to the same height as before. There is still, however, a great hollow in the sand before it, and another behind. The hinder part is yet exposed, nearly to the base; and is seen to be cased with masonry. I saw labourers pulling down some of the stones, to employ them in modern buildings. It is evident that the whole of the colossus—with the exception of certain ornamental parts,

---

[1] These are in the British Museum.

[2] One of the four "horns" of this altar is in the British Museum.

[3] These two inscriptions, and that before mentioned, addressed to the colossus, are published in the 19th volume of the Quarterly Review, pp. 411-415.

and of the eyes, eye-brows, &c.—was painted red. Vestiges of this colour yet remain even upon the face and other parts which have been always exposed. Upon ascending, by means of a ladder, to the top of the head, I found there a hole, four feet wide, and nearly seven feet in depth. I at first thought that this might have been made for the purpose of securing a high cap, such as are seen upon some Egyptian sphinxes, and upon the heads of kings; but the sphinxes represented upon the tablets before this colossus are *without* caps. I am at a loss, therefore, to conjecture for what purpose this large and deep hole was excavated; unless it were made by persons who imagined that a treasure lay concealed in the head.[1]

The beard of the Sphinx shews that the head is that of a *man*, not of a *woman*. Every Egyptian sphinx with a *human* head is a compound of a *man* and a lion, and is without wings: such, at least, are all that I have seen. The sphinx is generally represented with the head of a man, or with that of a ram: the former called *andro-sphinx*; and the latter, *crio-sphinx*. It is an emblem of a *king*. The title of the king of Egypt was *Pi-ra*, or *Phra (the Sun)*; in Hebrew, פרעה *Phrah*, which we improperly write *Pharaoh*.[2] The avenues to temples were often adorned, on each side, by a row of sphinxes, placed at short intervals, side to side; these being emblems of the Pharaohs who built those temples, and, as such, inscribed with their names. The sphinx, it seems, was properly an emblem of the Sun; and therefore used to represent a king; the appellation of both being the same. This explains the inscription recording Nero's worship of the Sun.—It appears that the Great Sphinx was carved either during, or before, the reign of the fourth Thothmos; at least 16 or 17 centuries before the Christian era: perhaps it was begun during the reign of Amōsis, or Amōs, his sixth predecessor[3]; whence might have originated the tradition (which Pliny mentions) of its being the tomb of Amasis. It is strange that Herodotus does not speak of this wonderful work of art, which, even in *his* time, was more than a thousand years old.

There are numerous *Grottoes and Catacombs* in the vicinity of the Pyramids, which require to be noticed.—The rocky ground between the Sphinx and the Pyramids is naturally irregular, and rendered more so by quarries, and by hillocks composed of fragments of stone and drifted sand. In some parts, where the rock rises abruptly, we see the entrances of sepulchral grottoes: in the level parts, deep pits, or wells, of a square form, about four feet or more in width, are cut in the soft rock; and from the bottoms of these, horizontal passages branch off to the chambers of the dead. Most of the pits are filled with sand and rubbish. Around the

---

[1]Mr. Salt and Mr. Briggs generously contributed to defray the expenses incurred by Caviglia in his operations in the Pyramids and the adjacent tombs, and in uncovering the Sphinx; and Caviglia, with equal generosity, presented to the British Museum all the statues, inscriptions, &c., which he discovered.

[2]For this explanation of the title of Pharaoh, we are indebted to Major Felix.

[3]That he was the sixth Pharaoh before the fourth Thothmos is shewn by the tablet of Abydos.

mouths of many of them, and before the entrances of several of the grottoes, lie heaps of bones and rags of mummies, with many limbs, and even whole bodies, upon which the flesh still remains, hard and quite black. Many of the grottoes have sustained much injury from time and from the hand of man: but upon the walls of several of them we still find very interesting sculptures, in a perfect state of preservation.[1] Most of the sculptures which they contain are similar to those which I have already described; executed in very low relief; and considerably smaller than the objects which they represent. All of them were originally painted; and some still retain the colours. One of the grottoes, which is much injured,[2] contains, among the painted sculptures which adorn its walls, a design possessing extraordinary beauty combined with the utmost simplicity and truth; thoug[h] executed (according to the most moderate computation) more than three thousand years ago.[†] The subject is a gazelle suckling her young one. The annexed engraving is a copy of it.[3] Another design which is found here is particularly curious. It represents eleven men endeavouring to pull down an enormous bull. There is another ancient sepulchral grotto which especially deserves to be mentioned.[4] A few years ago, it was the hermitage of a Moos'lim Sheykh, a reputed saint; and is therefore called "the Grotto of the Sheykh." Its entrance (which is at the left extremity of a long, perpendicular, hewn cliff, facing the east) is furnished with a modern wooden door. Over it is an inscription in hieroglyphics. The interior is large and lofty, and divided into several apartments. Upon each side of a low wall which forms a partition between the two principal apartments, are some interesting sculptures, of men and beasts, executed in intaglio. All the other sculptures in this grotto are much defaced.—Another grotto, to the east of the Great Pyramid,[5] seems to have been designed for a person who was rich in flocks and herds. Several rows of cattle, including a numerous stock of asses, are sculptured upon the walls: the precise number of each kind which the deceased possessed is expressed by numerical characters; and the grotto has been called, on this account, "the Tomb of Numbers."—I saw another excavated tomb in the north-west side of the hill upon which the Pyramids are situated, facing the north.[6] At the time that I first noticed it, I had not a candle, with which

---

[1]Of these grottoes I can only speak from memory, for the reason which I have before stated, in the first of the notes in this chapter.
[2]The situation of this tomb is marked *t* in the plan, no. 1, plate 6 [fig. 24].
[†]Tomb of Nebemakhet, LG 86.
[3]See no. 17 of subjects for wood-cuts [missing] (among the mounted drawings next to plate 28).
   (Missing R.S.P.)
[4]Its situation is marked *u* in the plan above referred to. [Tomb of Debhen, LG 90.]
[5]Its situation is marked *z* in the plan.
[6]Marked *aa* in the plan.

to examine it carefully; but I found that it was nearly filled with drifted sand, and that its walls had been decorated with painted sculptures, which were almost effaced. This tomb seemed to me so little worthy of examination that I forgot to revisit it.[†]

With a few words respecting *the History and Destination of the Pyramids* I shall terminate this chapter.

Pliny mentions no fewer than twelve ancient authors who have written of the Pyramids; but states that they do not agree respecting the founders of these monuments. According to Herodotus, the name of the king who built the First Pyramid was Cheops; according to Diodorus Siculus, it was Chemmis, or Chembis. Both these historians agree in stating that the Second Pyramid was generally attributed to Chephrēn; and the Third to Mycerinus; and that Chephrēn was said to be the brother and successor of the founder of the First Pyramid: but Diodorus adds that some called the successor of Chemmis by the name of Chabruis, or Chabryis, and asserted that he was the *son* of the former: likewise, that Mycerinus was also called Mecherinus, or Cherinus. Cheops, or Chemmis, is related to have been an irreligious king, who closed the temples of the gods, and prohibited every kind of sacrifice. His successor (adds the historian) pursued the same wicked course; and such was the hatred in which the memory of these two kings was held, that the Egyptians would not even utter their names: for which reason, they asserted that the Pyramids which they built were the work of a shepherd, named Philitis, who, at the period of the construction of those monuments, pastured his flocks in the neighbourhood.[1] This assertion seems to have been founded on a tradition of the Pyramids' having been built by some of the Shepherd Kings. Diodorus also says that some persons gave different names to the founders of these monuments; attributing the First to Armæus; the Second, to Amōsis, or Amasis; and the Third, to Marōn, or Inarōn.[2] Both Herodotus and Diodorus mention that some persons believed the Third Pyramid to be the tomb of a courtesan named Rhodōpis. Strabo likewise says that this monument was regarded as the tomb of a courtesan, whom Sappho the Poetess calls Doricha, and others name Rhodōpis.—We have a strong reason for believing that the names of Amōsis and Chephrēn, or Chabruis, apply to the same king. In Manetho's Epitome of the Egyptian Dynasties, Amōs, or Amōsis is placed as the first king of the 18th Dynasty; next to him, Chebrōn, or Chebrōs; and then, Amenōphthis, or Amenōphis: but in the tablet of Abydos, and in a list of kings in the Ramessium[3] at Thebes, we find the name (or, rather, the prenomen) of

---

[†]This tomb is not included in the Giza surveys

[1]Herodotus, lib. II, cap. 128.

[2]Stroth (in his Ægyptiaca, part II, p. 129) says, that, in many good M.S.S. of Diodorus Siculus, he finds Amōsis and Marōn for Amasis and Inarōn; and he regards the former as more correct.

[3]This is the edifice which many travellers have improperly called "the Memnonium."

Amonoph placed immediately next to that of Amŏs, or Amōs, or Amōsis: it is not unreasonable, therefore, to conclude that Chebrōn, or Chebrōs, was a second name of Amos, or Amōsis; and the same which the Greek historians wrote Chephrēn, or Chabruis.[1] It is very remarkable that we find the hieroglyphic name of Amōs among some inscriptions in the quarries of Mons Troicus, which (according to Herodotus, Diodorus, and many other ancient writers) supplied stone for the construction of the Pyramids.[2]—What I have here advanced respecting the identity of Amōs, or Amōsis, with Chebrōn, or Chephrēn, almost amounts to a proof that the two traditions mentioned by Diodorus Siculus relating to the Second Pyramid (the one attributing its erection to Chephrēn, or Chabruis, and the other, to Amōsis) had the same origin. The name of Amos being found in the quarries which supplied some of the stones of which the two principal Pyramids were constructed may appear to confirm those traditions; but I would rather say that it may possibly have been one reason for the supposition that one of the Pyramids was built by that King; for I have convincing arguments to offer against that hypothesis.—1st—We find some hieroglyphics round the two doors of a small chamber under the principal Pyramid of Sack'ka'rah: but this chamber is very different from every other part of the catacombs under the Pyramid; and therefore may have been a later work than the monument itself. We also find two short inscriptions, rudely cut (apparently by visiters), in the passage of the Great Southern Pyramid of Dah'shoo'r, just within the entrance. But all the other pyramids in Egypt, excepting some at Thebes (which are constructed of crude brick), are entirely destitute of hieroglyphics and of any sculptures whatever; and even those two before mentioned appear to have been originally so. There must, then, have been some particular reason why the Pyramids of Memphis thus differed from other Egyptian monuments. It might be supposed that their founders were irreligious persons; as Cheops and Chephrēn are represented to have been: but it is scarcely to be believed that all the kings who built pyramids were of this character: it is more reasonable to infer that, at the period when these monuments were constructed, the custom of ornamenting buildings with

---

[1]Manetho relates that "the Shepherds," who had settled in Egypt, and had rendered the upper and lower regions tributary to them, were subdued by an Egyptian king named Alisphragmuthosis (or Misphragmuthōsis), who hemmed them within a place called Avaris, containing 10,000 acres, which they had surrounded with a strong wall; and that Thummōsis (whom he also calls Tethmōsis), the son and successor of the above-mentioned king, compelled them to depart from Egypt. He then gives a list of the kings and queens who succeeded the latter prince; and we find, by comparing this list with that which the same historian gives of the 18th Dynasty in his general list of the Egyptian kings, that Thummōsis, or Tethmōsis, was the same with Amōsis, or Amos.

[2]These quarries are directly opposite the site of Memphis, behind the modern village of El-Ma'asar'ah.

hieroglyphics had not been introduced.—2ndly—Adjacent to the Great Pyramid are numerous tombs (which I have already described) resembling that monument somewhat in form, but particularly in being destitute of hieroglyphics and other sculptures or ornaments; for which reasons, and on account of their situation and arrangement, it is reasonable to conclude that they were built nearly at the same period as the Great Pyramid. Other tombs, around these, differ from them in their internal construction and in their being adorned with hieroglyphics and painted sculptures; and these I have shewn to be less ancient than the former: yet they contain the names of kings who were *more* ancient than *Amos*. It has been shewn, in my description of one of these monuments that the Memphite Kings under whom they were constructed were contemporary with the 17th Dynasty; which consisted of Diospolites, or princes whose capital was Diospolis (or Thebes). In none of them do we find the name of any king of the 18th Dynasty. The painted sculptures which adorn the walls of their apartments are executed in a style resembling the paintings in the Grottoes of Ben'ee Hhas'an (which were also coeval with the 17th Dynasty), rather than any others in Egypt.—The 17th Dynasty consisted, according to Manetho, of 43 Diospolite Kings and 43 Shepherd Kings, who, it appears, were contemporary with each other and also with the Memphite Kings of the 8th Dynasty; by whom, or by whose subjects, it seems, that these sculptured monuments were erected.[1] Therefore, we may infer that the Pyramids, being more ancient, were built during the 4th and 6th Dynasties; these also consisting of Memphite Kings:—the Memphites of the 7th Dynasty reigned only 70 days:—the 5th Dynasty did not consist of Memphites.—Now Manetho says that Suphis, the second king of the 4th Dynasty, "built the largest Pyramid, which Herodotus writes was founded by Cheops"; and adds "he was also called Peroptes; was translated to the Gods; and wrote the sacred book, which, being a most precious thing, I purchased in Egypt." Thus we read in the transcript by Africanus; but in the chronology of Eusebius, the following is given, as from Manetho's work:—"The *third* king" of the 4th Dynasty "was Suphis."—The *second* and *third* had *both* this name.—"He built the largest Pyramid, which Herodotus asserts was founded by Cheops. He *despised* the Gods; but, repenting, wrote the sacred book, which the Egyptians highly value." Suphis the Second was succeeded by Mencherēs. Suphis the First, Suphis the Second, and Mencherēs are called, by Eratosthenes (in his canon of the Kings of Thebes), Saophis, Sensaophis,[2] and Moscheris. These may be regarded, with much probability, as the founders of the three Pyramids attributed, by Herodotus and Diodorus, to Cheops, or Chemmis, or Chembis; to

---

[1]There are no paintings nor sculptures in Egypt more ancient that those of Ben'ee Hhas'an and of the monuments here mentioned.

[2]"Sensaophis" signifies "brother of Saophis." The founders of the two great Pyramids were said to be brothers. (Wilkinson's Materia Hieroglyphica), p. 74.

Chephren, or Chabruis; and to Mycerinus, or Mecherinus. The last of
these names bears a singular resemblance to Mencherēs: but Manetho
says that the Third Pyramid was found[ed] by a Queen, named Nitocris,
who was the last of the Memphites of the 6th Dynasty, and the
handsomest woman of her time. It is remarkable that he attributes the
founding of this Pyramid to a beautiful woman; and that Herodotus,
Diodorus, and Strabo mention a tradition of its having been built by a
celebrated courtesan. I can see no good reason to doubt that Suphis the
First was the king who founded the Great Pyramid. The period of his
accession, I calculate[1] to have been about 243 years after the
establishment of the Memphite Kingdom; about 93 years before the
invasion of Egypt by the Shepherds; and nearly 7 centuries before the
Exodus of the Israelites.[2] This King reigned 63 years: consequently the
Pyramid must have been built about 23 centuries before the Christian
era. That such a structure should have been raised at so early a period
might appear incredible, had not an equally surprising edifice—the
Tower of Babel, which probably very much resembled the Pyramids in
form—been already constructed.—To account for the Pyramids being
destitute of hieroglyphics, I can only repeat my opinion that, at the
period of their construction, the custom of adorning buildings with
sculptures had not originated; for I have clearly shewn that they are more
ancient than any of the sculptured monuments that we find in Egypt.
The Second and Third Pyramids may have been founded by Suphis the
Second, or Sensaophis, and Mencheres, or Moscheris; or the Third
Pyramid, by Nitocris; as Manetho asserts. This historian also states that
Venephēs, the fourth of the Thinite Kings, of the 1st Dynasty, built the
Pyramids near Cochōme. It is uncertain to what monuments he alludes
in this passage. It is said that Homer visited Egypt; and it has excited
some surprise that he did not consider the Pyramids worthy of being
celebrated in his verses. Some persons have inferred, from his not having
mentioned these monuments, that they did not exist in his time. Perhaps
they made as little impression upon him (if, indeed, he ever saw them) as
they do upon some modern travellers.[3]

   Almost the only important and credible fact which Arab authors have
related respecting these monuments—which, they pretend, were built
before the Deluge—is that the Great Pyramid was opened by the
Khalee'feh El-Ma-moo'n, the son of Ha'roo'n Er-Reshee'd. Whether it
had been previously opened and closed again, we are ignorant. Several
Arab writers, of the 3rd, 4th, 5th and 6th centuries after the flight, and
particularly 'Abd El-Latee'f, who wrote his description of Egypt in the
year of the flight 600 (A.D. 1203-4), have likewise stated that, in their

---

[1]See the Supplement to this work.
[2]Which was in 1648 B.C. according to Dr. Hales.
[3]It is asserted by Diodorus Siculus (lib. I, cap. 69 and 96.) that Homer visited
Egypt; but it is not mentioned (I believe) by any other ancient author; and
therefore may reasonably be doubted.

times, there were numerous inscriptions, in unknown characters, on the sides of the two principal pyramids. A considerable portion of the original smooth casing must, therefore, have remained upon both those pyramids at the periods above mentioned. These inscriptions could not have been of very ancient dates; or Herodotus, Diodorus Siculus, and other ancient authors would certainly have mentioned them. They were probably cut by Greek, Roman, and other travellers, to record their having visited these monuments; like those which modern travellers have engraved upon the stones at the entrance and on the top of the Great Pyramid.—Herodotus mentions one inscription upon this monument, stating that 1,600 talents of silver were expended to supply radishes, onions, and garlic, for the workmen. This, he says, was in Egyptian characters; by which is doubtless meant *enchorial*. The same historian describes the Causeway of the Great Pyramid as beautifully constructed of polished stones, and sculptured with the figures of various animals. I cannot but conclude, from the absence of hieroglyphics on the Pyramid itself—a much more important work—, that this causeway was sculptured—not at the period of its con[s]truction, but—several centuries after. Its utility, as forming a communication between the banks of the Nile and the site of the Pyramids, might have been a sufficient inducement to successors of its founder to adorn it in that manner. We find many temples in Egypt founded under one king, and sculptured, or resculptured, under another.

Respecting the destination of the Pyramids, I deem it unnecessary to say many words.—They were evidently designed for *sepulchres*: but it has been supposed that they might *also* have been intended to serve as *temples*. This, I think, is disproved by the fact that not only the passage into the principal chamber in the Great Pyramid was closed by portcullises of granite, but also the commencement of the first ascending passage (if not the entrance itself of the Pyramid) was completely stopped up and concealed. The two descending passages of the Second Pyramid were also closed by portcullises of granite. I therefore regard them as nothing more than tombs.—Natives of Heliopolis, as well as of Memphis, were buried in the catacombs near the Pyramids of El-Gee'zeh. Mr. Salt had several sepulchral tablets, from those tombs, bearing the names of Priests of On.

Note. Nearly two miles to the north of the Great Pyramid, are two long, ancient bridges, called *Ckana'tir El-Gee'zeh* (or the Bridges of El-Gee'zeh). Their history may thus be briefly stated.—When the Emee'r Ckar'a'ckoo'sh was appointed, by Sala'hh ed-Deen, to build the Citadel and the Third Wall of El-Cka'hireh, he demolished many of the small pyramids of El-Gee'zeh (or, as I suppose, the truncated pyramidal tombs around the Great Pyramid), in order to make use of the stones of which they were composed for these new works. To facilitate the transport of the stones to the metropolis, he raised a dike, or causeway, across the cultivated fields, as far as the Nile; for a great part of that tract was before impassable, during several months in the year, on account of the inundation. He constructed the two bridges above mentioned at the same time: the causeway united them, and continued to the shore of the Nile. It was six miles in length; and "resembled a mountain stretching across the country." Some small portions of the causeway still remain; as well as the bridges. The latter are in a state of ruin. They have often been repaired.

Upon a hill called *Ab'oo Roowey'sh* (the situation of which is marked in the map which accompanies the former volume†), to the north-west of the Pyramids of El-Gee'zeh, are remains of another pyramid, and some rudely excavated sepulchral grottoes.

---

†Fig. 2.

Chapter XVI.

The Pyramids of Ab'oo Seer, Sack'cka'rah, and Dah'shoo'r, and the site, remains, &c., of the City of Memphis.

Journey from the Pyramids of El-Gee'zeh to a tomb between Ab'oo Seer and Sack'cka'rah—Pyramids of Ab'oo Seer—Those of Sack'cka'rah—Description of the principal Pyramid of Sack'cka'rah—Smaller pyramids—Catacombs around them—Catacombs of Birds, or Ibis-mummies—Ancient grotto with arched chambers—Southern Pyramids of Sack'cka'rah—Pyramids of Dah'shoo'r—Great Northern Pyramid of Dah'shoo'r—Great Southern Pyramid—Two Brick Pyramids—The site, remains, &c. of the City of Memphis.

My last visit to the Pyramids of El-Gee'zeh was performed in company with another traveller, Mr. Hay, in May 1827. After having stayed in my old quarters six days, we mounted our donkeys, and proceeded towards the Pyramids of Sack'cka'rah; in the neighbourhood of which we purposed spending about a week more. It was rather late in the afternoon when we started, and the night closed in upon us when we had accomplished but little more than half our journey. Two of our servants attended us: the others were with the donkeys which carried our drawing-apparatus and luggage, at a considerable distance behind: we therefore halted for some time, in the hope of their coming up; and shouted to them several times; but in vain. Supposing that they had followed a different track, we proceeded, as well as we could,—sometimes over rough ground, overgrown with high, coarse grass—at other times over deep sands—, until we perceived before us a modern cemetery with several square, cupola-topped tombs of Sheykhs, which generally have an open door. In one of these we proposed to spend the night; for we concluded that the servants who were following us had halted at some village, as they did not know the place of our destination, which was an ancient sepulchral grotto. We looked into one tomb, and dissatisfied with its gloomy appearance, passed on to several others; all of which, at night, looked equally like the habitations of *ghoo'ls*. While we were thus employed, prying into the black interior of one of these tombs, we faintly heard the barking of several dogs, which told us that a village, or a Bed'awee camp, was at no great distance. On one side we could discern the outline of the low Libyan hills; so, turning towards the opposite direction, we proceeded to the cultivated lands, and soon arrived at the village of Ab'oo Seer. We now seated ourselves under some palm-trees, and sent a servant to inquire for the house of the Sheykh, or chief of the village, and to desire him to give us a night's lodging. Our man, liking much better to sleep in a Sheykh's house than in a Sheykh's tomb, performed this order with alacrity. He walked round the village, thumping at the doors of several of the huts; but all the inhabitants had long before retired to rest: some would not even return any answer; though they must have been roused by his calls and knocking; and those who did reply would not give the information required: some said that the Sheykh was absent from the village; others, that they could not give such a direction as would enable the stranger to find the house; and they were afraid to come out and conduct him thither. The village had been attacked, during the preceding night, by a party of Bed'awees, who had driven away several cattle; and the inhabitants, perhaps, suspected that we, also, might be robbers. Finding it impossible to obtain a night's lodging, we determined at least to satisfy our hunger, which had become extremely keen. By means of reproaches and threats, we induced the inmates of one of the huts to get up and make for us half a dozen thin cakes of unleavened millet bread. A fire was quickly lighted, the meal kneaded, and the cakes—being baked in a few minutes upon an iron plate—were dropped down to us from over the wall of a little courtyard adjoining the hut. Having devoured our supper, with no small relish— though the cakes were not of a dainty kind (being very gritty, from an unusual quantity of sand having become mixed with the meal)—we resolved to proceed; lest our servants should have gone on in the hope of overtaking us. We advanced along the narrow, sandy tract between the cultivated land and the low Libyan range, and at length perceived a large mass of white stone, which my friend remembered to have noticed as lying before the ancient sepulchral grotto which we were seeking. The yawning mouth of this cavern we could just discern, half-way up the rocky acclivity on our right; and immediately ascended to it; but the spacious interior appeared so dismal that we preferred lying down to sleep in the sand before the entrance. Scarcely had we composed ourselves to rest when we heard the voices of persons passing by, evidently in no good humour: we hailed them, thinking that they might be the servants with our luggage; which proved to be the case. Our troubles thus ended: our mattresses were spread; and we passed the night very comfortably.[1]—On the following morning we commenced our examination of the Pyramids in the vicinity.—I shall first mention those of Ab'oo Seer.

The Three Pyramids of Ab'oo Seer are inferior in every respect to the Third Pyramid of El-Gee'zeh. They are constructed of stone; but very much ruined; and not one of them is open. There are remains of wide causeways, composed of enormous stones (some of which are upwards of 20 feet long), leading up to each of these monuments, from the east.

---

[1]This grotto is large, and rudely excavated. Its situation is marked *e*, in the plan no. 3, plate 6 [fig. 24].

They are but slightly elevated; the hill having a very gentle acclivity.—
Between the Pyramids of Ab'oo Seer and those of El-Gee'zeh are several
heaps of stone, which are evidently remains of small pyramids.

The Pyramids of Sack'cka'rah[1] are situated (like all the other pyramids
in the neighbourhood of the site of ancient Memphis) upon an elevated
rocky ground, the surface of which is, in some parts, very flat; in others,
undulating; and everywhere covered with sand and pebbles. Its general
height above the level of the cultivated land is from 100 to 150 feet.

The Principal Pyramid of Sack'cka'rah, with three others, is situated
upon a part of the desert which appears to have been the chief burial-
place of Memphis.[2] On every side are innumerable catacombs. It is called
el-Har'am el-Moodur'rag (or the Pyramid of Steps), from its peculiar
form, which is shewn by the annexed view, (plate 20[3]). The stages, or
steps (if so they may be called), are six in number: the lowest is nearly
buried by the rubbish which has fallen down from the upper parts; on
which account, it is difficult to measure the base with much precision.
On the western side I found it to be about 320 feet. The height is about
180 feet. This monument is therefore rather larger than the Third
Pyramid of El-Gee'zeh: but it appears considerably greater; as there is no
other of equal dimensions in its vicinity. The manner of its construction
is singular; for it appears that the work was commenced by raising a very
slender pyramid; around which was then raised a circumstructure about
60 feet lower; around this, another structure still lower; and so on. No
passage or chamber has been discovered in the body of the Pyramid; but
there are several chambers and passages, composing a perfect labyrinth,
excavated in the rock beneath it. Mr. Hay examined these with me; and
we took the plan of them. (See plate 21[†]). The entrance (*a*) was
discovered and opened in 1821, by Baron Von Minutoli. It is a
perpendicular descent in the level rock, about 75 feet distant from the
northern side (*b,b*) of the Pyramid. It is of an irregular form; its width,
about 10 feet by 6 and a half; the depth, 18 feet. From the bottom, a
horizontal passage (*c,c*), 6 feet high and 4 feet wide, runs towards the
Pyramid, in the direction of South 21° West, by the compass, not
allowing for the variation. The sides of the passage are very irregular, in
consequence of the decay of the rock. At the distance of 13 feet and a
half is a small built door-way (*d*), of a compact, white stone, without any
ornament or inscription. The passage continues as before. At the distance
of 103 feet, is an excavation on each side (*e,e*); like the commencement of
a passage; but filled up with rubbish. Proceeding to the distance of 120
feet (from the entrance), we descend 15 steps (*f*). Above these steps, a
wide passage (*g*) branches off to the left. Descending 15 feet from the top
of the stairs, we enter another passage (*h*), running South 20° East, and

---

[1]Vulgarly pronounced *Sagga'rah*, and *Sa'a'rah*.
[2]See *a* in the plan no. 3, plate 6 [fig. 24].
[3][Fig. 50.] Under the letter *a*.
[†]Fig. 51.

sloping gently downwards. It is 27 feet long (including the space occupied by two of the steps, which descend into it). Here we find a second descent of steps, 11 in number; near the bottom of which, 10 feet from the top step, are the entrances of two passages, one above the other. We first follow the lower (*k,k*); the direction of which is South 65° East for half its length, and then South 82° East to the end. The length of this passage (including, again, the space occupied by two steps which descend into it) is 48 feet. We now turn to the right, along a horizontal passage (*l*), of the same dimensions (6 feet high and 4 wide). At the distance of 13 feet from the angle is an aperture (*m*) in the top of the passage, appearing like a chimney. I shall have occasion to mention it again. It escaped my observation the first time I was in the passage above mentioned. This passage is 26 feet 10 inches long, including a descent of five steps at the end (*n*). We then enter a passage (*o,o*), running both to the right and left. We first turn to the left. To the distance of 9 feet 9 inches it is horizontal; and next is a descent of five steps (*p*), which occupy five feet. We then find an aperture on the right, and a descent of 8 feet and a half (*q*), formed by three steep steps. From this runs a horizontal passage (*r*) in the direction of South 11° West, 26 feet long. At the end of this is the great chamber (*s*), which is 23 feet square, and about 70 feet high. It may be described as a great pit; all but the roof being cut in the solid rock. It is exactly under the center of the Pyramid. The light of our candles scarcely enabled us to discern the roof. We found here a great quantity of rubbish, and blocks and small fragments of stone. Where the rubbish had been removed, near the southern side, were seen several long blocks of granite (*t*), well cut, and nicely placed together, side by side. The southernmost had been forced out of its place; but no aperture was seen beneath it. This block I found to be 10 feet 5 inches deep. The others are of similar proportions. Beneath them is a kind of vault, of which they form the roof. We descend to it through a small forced aperture. The interior is 9 feet 10 inches long, 5 feet 6 inches wide, and about the same in height. The sides and floor are also of granite. It is probable that this vault, or chamber, contained the body of the founder of the Pyramid. Whether it was built upon the floor of the great chamber, or sunk into it, I could not clearly perceive; for it was surrounded by rubbish and loose stones. The sides of the great chamber are black, and roughly cut; and have several apertures; some of which are mere niches; others open into intricate passages. In the north side of the chamber, at the height of 31 feet, is a large aperture (*u*), 11 feet wide, which appears to have been the grand entrance; for, from the floor of the chamber to this aperture, it is not solid rock, but masonry. By lighting a large fire of reeds, we were enabled plainly to see the roof. It was formed, originally, of wood. Two large beams extended from north to south; one of which remains. Over these were laid other timbers; but most of these have now fallen, and, with them, many of the stones which were thus supported. The roof, at present, has a concave form; and consists of small and irregular masses of stone, which hold together, although not purposely constructed to support each other. The firing of a pistol might, perhaps, cause many of them to fall.—At the south-east corner of the chamber, is an aperture (*v*), half closed by rubbish; through which we enter a passage that appears to run round three sides of the chamber; but this, also, is much obstructed by rubbish. From it we pass into two small chambers (*w,w*), the walls of which are of masonry. The first is half filled with rubbish: its width is the same as that of the second—5 feet and 1 inch—: the length is probably the same—18 feet 10 inches. The sides of both these chambers have been lined with small, glazed, blue tiles, 3 inches high, and 1 inch wide, arranged side by side, in horizontal rows, with a space of about half an inch between each row. Their form was that of small segments of cylinders. They were cemented in the grooves made to receive them, and further secured by a string, or wire, which passed through the back of each tile, and also, at intervals, through a hole in the wall. I could not find any of these tiles entire; but there were a few fragments remaining in their places. None of them had any inscription or ornament. In no other Egyptian monument have I seen the walls thus cased. But the most curious thing here is a hieroglyphic inscription, beautifully cut, in very low relief, above and on each side of the door leading from the first to the second of these small chambers; with the mystic title of a king, whose name is not found upon any monument. The same is also traced in black lines around the other door in this chamber. A copy of it is here annexed.[1] This is the more remarkable, as no other inscription, excepting the scrawls of visiters, has been found in the chambers, or passages, or on the exterior, of any other pyramid in Lower Egypt: but as these two chambers differ so entirely from every other part of the catacombs under the same pyramid, it is probable that they were constructed at a later period than the pyramid itself. Two passages branch off from the second of these chambers; but they are choked with rubbish.—Of the other passages around the great chamber, an idea may be formed by inspecting the plan. They are very much obstructed by blocks of stone; and it was with difficulty that we dragged ourselves along them. In some of them, we found many fragments of basins and pateræ of alabaster, black basalt, granite, &c. We also saw a few human bones, and mummy-rags; and Mr. Hay found, among the rubbish, a fragment of a painted mummy-case[2]; proving that these catacombs were burial-places; though for what purposes the passages were made thus narrow and intricate, it is difficult to conjecture. The top and sides of many of these passages were thickly incrusted with saline efflorescences of sparkling whiteness, curling into beautiful forms. In exploring the passage marked *x*, we came to a space somewhat wider, and irregular, and saw above us the bottoms of the long granite blocks which form the floor of the vault, or low chamber, before mentioned. They were supported merely by small square pillars, about 3 feet high, formed of three or four blocks of calcareous stone. It is not

---

[1]See No. 18 of the subjects for wood-cuts [fig. 52].
[2]Baron Von Minutoli found a gilded human scull in this pyramid.

probable that these were the original supports of so great a weight; but it may rather be supposed that persons excavating beneath the granite blocks, in search of treasure, placed these pillars as they gradually removed the solid substructure.—There are yet two passages to be noticed; of which the entrances have already been mentioned. That of the first is on the left of the first stairs in the main passage. This passage is about 7 feet wide: its sides are much decayed. From it, another passage (y) turns off to the right. About half-way along the latter, we observe an aperture (z), on the right. At the end, the passage widens on the left, and has a descent of a few feet. The whole of the passage, it seems, was originally of the same width as the end: it has been contracted both in width and height: probably it terminated with a flight of steps, descending to the floor of the great chamber. From the end of it we look down into the great chamber; the bottom of which is 31 feet below us. I mentioned this in describing that chamber.—The other passage which remains to be noticed commences above the second stairs in the main passage, and runs to the aperture marked z. At the end is a well, or square pit (m), communicating with the main passage below. It was the bottom of this well which I mentioned before, as appearing, from below, like a chimney. I had not observed it before, when I was in the lower passage. After having descended this well, which is 25 feet deep, with some difficulty, not having a rope, I was surprised and disappointed to find myself where I had been before.—The labyrinthian nature of the catacombs under this pyramid might lead a person to infer that they were destined for some other object besides the mere sepulture of mummies; but there are many sepulchral catacombs, in various parts of Egypt, in which the explorer might lose himself. The passages were, perhaps, made thus numerous and narrow and intricate to render it more difficult for any sacrilegious person to discover the chambers in which the dead were deposited; for, in several Egyptian catacombs, we find that great pains have been taken to conceal the passage communicating with the place of sepulture.

At a little distance to the south-west of the monument above described, is a small pyramid, very much dilapidated; and to the north-east of the former are two others, in a similar state of ruin.[1] Of these two, that which is nearest to the principal pyramid is the least dilapidated; and this has lately been opened, (I believe by Caviglia). A large cavity has been formed in the northern side, in forcing the entrance. The passage is partly lined with granite, like that of the Second Pyramid of El-Gee'zeh; to which it is also similar in its dimensions and in its inclination. This descends to two small and plain chambers, excavated in the rock, one leading out of the other; and both empty.

Around these pyramids, on every side, are numerous catacombs, which, as I said before, seem to shew that this tract was the principal burial-place of Memphis. The ground is strewed with rubbish taken out

---

[1] All of these are seen in plate 20 [fig. 50].

of the pits, and with vast quantities of fragments of pottery. The pits descending to the catacombs are generally between 6 and 12 feet square, and from 20 to 50 or 60 feet deep. Many of these are filled, quite to the mouth, with sand and rubbish; but most of them have been thoroughly explored and ransacked. Numbers of peasants from the neighbouring villages have, for many years, past, been occupied in clearing out these catacombs, on their own account, in search of antiquities, to sell to the Europeans; and some have been thus employed by travellers and others. In this operation, two pieces of a split palm-trunk are generally laid across the mouth of the pit: some labourers are then let down by ropes; and two others, standing upon the palm-trunks, draw up the rubbish in a basket, and then toss it out by the side of the pit. Young boys or girls are employed to sift this rubbish carefully on the spot, as soon as it is thrown out of the basket; and thus are often found small scarabs and images of stone or blue glazed porcelain, rings, beads, and other objects of antiquity, which were originally placed with the mummies. The traveller seldom sees much to reward him for the trouble of descending these pits. Arrived at the bottom, he enters narrow passages, and chambers without any kind of ornament, encumbered with sand, and with broken mummies, bones and bandages. Some small figures and ornaments of gold and silver having been found in some of these catacombs, the Ba'sha, Mohham'mad 'Al'ee, was excited to imitate the Frank antiquarians; and employed a number of peasants to ransack the tombs of Sack'cka'rah, in the expectation of finding great treasures. By his directions, a very large pit,[1] of the same dimensions as the great chamber of the Pyramid of Steps (i.e. 23 feet square, and about 70 feet deep), was cleared out. But the Ba'sha soon found himself deceived. The Defturda'r Bey has lately followed his example; and has also taken away the sculptured and painted stones with which several of the tombs were lined to employ them in the construction of a new palace. At the period of my last visit to this spot, an Italian was engaged in clearing out a large and very deep pit; and had discovered, in a chamber on one side of it, a granite sarcophagus, covered with beautiful sculptures, representing subjects similar to those which are of most frequent occurrence in the Tombs of the Kings, at Thebes.

In the northern quarter of this great burial-place, nearly half-way between the Pyramids of Sack'cka'rah and those of Ab'oo Seer, to the south-west of the village of the latter name, are extensive *Catacombs of Birds*, or *Ibis-mummies*.[2] We descend to these by a pit, which is about 4 feet square and about 20 feet deep; and then, with lighted candles, creep along low and narrow horizontal passages, half filled with sand and broken pots which originally contained each a single mummy of an Ibis. Considerable numbers of pots are still found entire. They are of a conical form, about a foot and a half in length, and half a foot in width. The

[1]Marked *b* in the plan no. 3, plate 6 [fig. 24].
[2]Marked *e* in the plan no. 3, plate 6 [fig. 24].

cover is cemented with plaster. These pots are arranged in small recesses, like the bottles of wine in our cellars; laid horizontally, one row above another, to the ceiling. The mummies are ill preserved: the plumage discoloured: and the bones black, and often broken. As Ibises are now only found in Nubia and more southern countries, it is probable that these birds were anciently brought to Egypt from Ethiopia, merely as objects of worship; emblems of the God Thoth, who is generally represented upon the monuments with the body of a man and the head of the Ibis.

In the side of the elevated rocky tract upon which the principal pyramid of Sack'cka'rah and others which I have mentioned are situated, facing the plain of Memphis, are several large grottoes, one of which is very remarkable.[1] A view of the interior is here annexed. (See plate 22[†]). At the entrance it is much ruined, large masses of rock having fallen. Just within the entrance, on each side, are small chambers, with walls of masonry. Beyond these is the principal chamber, which had six square pillars, two of which have been broken down. These and the whole of the interior of the excavation were originally lined with masonry; as the rock was not of a sufficiently compact nature for sculpture to be well executed upon it. Much of the casing has lately been removed by the Defturda'r Bey, to be used in the construction of his new palace. The sculptures which remain are chiefly hieroglyphical. Among them we find the hieroglyphic name of Psammitichus the 2nd, very frequently repeated[2]; shewing that the grotto was excavated (or, at least, finished) during the reign of that king; not less than 600 years before the Christian era. What is particularly remarkable in the chamber of which I have given a view is that the ceiling between the two rows of pillars is arched, and lined with masonry, on the perfect principle of the masonic arch. Much of this casing has been torn down. Upon the part which remains, we find the name above mentioned, proving the very ancient construction of this arch.—It must no longer be said that the masonic arch was not invented before the Augustan era. There are tombs, at Thebes, with brick arches, stuccoed and adorned with paintings, the style of which shews them to be as ancient as the times of the 18th Dynasty (15 or 16 centuries B.C.); and among the paintings of these brick arches, Mr. Wilkinson has been so fortunate as to discover the hieroglyphic name of Amonoph the 1st, one of the kings of that Dynasty. In many of those tombs I searched in vain for a name. I have not seen, nor heard of, any stone arch, constructed on the perfect masonic principle, more ancient than that above described.—In the same grotto, beyond the principal chamber, is another apartment, of an oblate form, the ceiling of which is also arched in the manner before described, and quite perfect. The walls here are in like manner sculptured, chiefly with hieroglyphics:

---

[1]Marked *d* in the plan no. 3, plate 6 [fig. 24; Tomb of Bekenrenef, LS 24].
[†]Fig. 53.
[2]A copy of this is given in plate 22 [fig. 53], under the view.

the only subject of a different kind being the representation of a man seated on a chair, and persons bringing to him birds, meat, lotuses, &c. At the left end is a pit, descending to the sepulchral catacombs. Beyond this chamber is another, of smaller dimensions; having a little cell on each side. The walls of all these have been covered with hieroglyphics; and at the end, there has been a statue, which is now destroyed. All the hieroglyphics in this grotto are very beautifully executed, in intaglio.

The more southern Pyramids of Sack'cka'rah require but a brief notice.—Directly to the west of the village of Sack'cka'rah, is a small pyramid, so much ruined that it appears like a mound of rubbish; and there are remains of a wide and massive causeway, running up the sandy slope, from the mounds upon which the village is situated to the base of this pyramid.[1] At about double the distance from the village, in the same direction, is another small pyramid, in a similar state of ruin. At the distance of rather more than half a mile to the south of the latter, is an unfinished pyramid,[2] about 250 feet square, and between 40 and 50 feet high. The Arabs pretend that the ancient kings of Egypt occasionally held their court, seated upon this flat-topped structure, which they therefore call *Mus'tab'at Far'oo'n*, or the Seat of Pharaoh. It is composed of massive stones. At a short distance to the north-west of this is a small ruined pyramid,[3] like those before mentioned. None of these is open.

The Pyramids of Dah'shoo'r are four in number: two constructed of stone; and two, of crude brick. The two former[4] are surpassed in magnitude by the First and Second Pyramids of El-Gee'zeh; but are greatly superior to all besides.

The Great Northern Pyramid of Dah'shoo'r is about two miles and a half distant from the village of Sack'cka'rah, and 1 mile and a quarter from the nearest part of the cultivated land. Its base is nearly 700 feet square; and its height, about 340 feet. The dimensions of its base are therefore somewhat greater than those of the base of the Second Pyramid of El-Gee'zeh; but its height is nearly 100 feet less than that of the latter; and, consequently, its bulk is considerably less. I ascended to the summit in ten minutes with tolerable ease. Portions of the original smooth casing still remain upon this pyramid, near the base and near the summit, as well as upon the intermediate parts; plainly shewing that the whole was once cased. There is a considerable accumulation of rubbish on each side; but, of the casing-stones which have been thrown down, we find few remaining around the base; for the object of removing them was to employ them in modern buildings. The stones of which the Pyramid is mainly constructed are of a dark, sandy colour; and much decayed; being

---

[1] From the top of this ruined pyramid I made the view of the Pyramids of Dah'shoo'r, &c., no. 1, plate 23 [fig. 54, upper].

[2] See *a* in the view above mentioned; and *f* in the plan no. 3, plate 6 [fig. 24].

[3] See *b* in no. 1, plate 23 [fig. 54, upper].

[4] See *c* and *d* in no. 1, plate 23 [fig. 54, upper]—also *a* and *b* in no. 2 [lower], same plate—and *g* and *h* in no. 3, plate 6 [fig. 24].

of a less durable nature than the casing-stones. The latter are also calcareous; but of a lighter colour, and much more compact: doubtless from the quarries of Mons Troicus, on the opposite side of the Nile.— This Pyramid has been opened; probably, many centuries ago. The steep slope of rubbish on the northern side rises only half-way towards the entrance, which is at a greater elevation than that of any other pyramid that has been opened; being about one third of the height up the side. The ascent to it is not difficult. The passage is 4 feet 5 inches and a quarter in height, 3 feet 5 inches and a half in width, and 200 feet long[1]; descending with the same inclination as the first passages of the First and Second Pyramids of El-Gee'zeh. From the end of this, a horizontal passage, 24 feet 4 inches and a half in length, leads to a chamber, which is 27 feet 4 inches long, 11 feet 11 inches wide, and 43 feet 4 inches high. From the height of eleven feet, each course of stone (for eleven together) projects 6 inches beyond that below, on each side of the chamber; in the same manner as the course which form the sides of the grand passage in the Great Pyramid of El-Gee'zeh; so that the dimensions of the chamber gradually diminish towards the top; each course being three feet high. On the right, or west, of this chamber, is a passage 10 feet 4 inches long, leading to another chamber, of the same dimensions. At the end of the latter, 30 feet 10 inches from the ground, is another horizontal passage, 3 feet 5 inches square, and 24 feet long, leading to a third chamber, which differs only from the others in being 1 foot 8 inches wider. Explorers, in search of treasure, have taken up the pavement and several tiers of stone in this chamber, and in the passage leading to it. In the third chamber, probably, was the sarcophagus.

  The Great Southern Pyramid of Dah'shoo'r is a mile distant from the former. It is remarkable for the peculiarity of its form (which is shewn by plate 23[†]), and for its almost perfect state of preservation. The casing has only been broken down to the height of a few feet from the base, and more at the angles: otherwise, it has sustained scarcely any injury; and presents a beautiful, smooth surface. The stones are of a very compact, calcareous nature, and of a whitish colour, similar to those which composed the casings of the other pyramids already described. This Pyramid is 600 feet square, and about 330 feet high. Like the other great monument of which I have just given an account, its entrance has been laid open; probably at a very remote period. This is about 22 feet above the base. Mr. Hay and myself ascended to it; but not without difficulty and danger. The dimensions of the passage are about the same as those of the passages of the two principal Pyramids of El-Gee'zeh; but the inclination less steep. A few feet within the entrance, we found two short inscriptions in hieroglyphics; each a single line; probably cut by visiters in ancient times; without any date or the name of a king. The passage is

---

[1] I give the measures taken by Mr. Davison; as I only took a few rough measures of the *exterior* of this pyramid.
[†] Fig. 54, lower.

clear to the depth of 150 feet, or more; but towards the end it is completely closed by rubbish. In the 17th century, a chamber, to which this passage leads, was accessible, and visited by travellers.

At the distance of about two thirds of a mile, nearly due east, from the monument above described, is a *Pyramid of crude Brick*, overlooking the cultivated plain.[1] It is so much ruined as to appear, from a little distance, like a shapeless heap of black earth. The original form seems to have been similar to that of the principal pyramid of Sack'cka'rah, called "the Pyramid of Steps"; and its base, between two and three hundred feet. Its present height is about 140 feet. The bricks of which it is constructed are composed of mud and chopped straw; such as the Israelites were employed in making during their bondage in Egypt. They are about 14 inches long, 7 inches broad, and 5 inches thick. Most of them appear as fresh as if newly made: the straw not being at all rotten. Asychis, the successor of Mycerinus[,] (according to Herodotus) erected a pyramid of brick, with this inscription.—"Compare me not with the Pyramids of Stone; for I excel them as Jupiter excels the other gods. Men thrust poles into a lake, and, collecting the mud which adhered to them, formed bricks; and thus constructed me[.]"—The pyramid above described is probably that to which Herodotus thus alludes.

There is another *Pyramid of crude Brick* about a mile and a half to the north of the former[2]; of rather smaller dimensions, and in a more ruined state. I easily ran up to the top. Its perpendicular height is about a hundred feet.

The remains of the city of Memphis[3] (or rather such remains as are apparent) are so inconsiderable, that even the *site* of this famed metropolis of Egypt has been a subject of dispute. Dr. Shaw and some other travellers have supposed that the modern town of El-Gee'zeh marks the site of Memphis; but this opinion is founded, chiefly, upon three palpable errors.—1st. That the point of the ancient Delta was the same as that of the present: whereas it was nearly three leagues to the south-east of the present fork of the river; the Canal of Ckalyoo'b being a part of the bed of the ancient Pelusiac branch.—2ndly. That the distance between the town of El-Gee'zeh and the principal Pyramids is about 12 miles: whereas it is only 5 and a quarter.—3rdly. That El-Gee'zeh is situated in the narrowest part of the valley: whereas the tract between El-Menawa't and Meet Rahee'neh is considerably narrower; and is, indeed, the most contracted part of the valley.—From remarks which are found in the works of ancient writers, it appears that Memphis, with its suburbs, extended as far northward as the village of El-Menawa't, or rather further; and somewhat beyond the village of Meet Rahee'neh southward. 1st. Herodotus states that it was situated in the narrowest part of the valley.—2ndly. Pliny says that it was six miles

---

[1] See *e* in no. 1, plate 23 [fig. 54, upper]—and *i* in no. 3, plate 6 [fig. 24].
[2] See *f* in no. 1, plate 23 [fig. 54, upper]—and *k* in no. 3, plate 6 [fig. 24].
[3] Called, in the Bible, *Noph*.

(or, as we read in some copies of his work, 7 and a half) from the Pyramids. This seems to shew that its northern suburb extended a little beyond El-Menawa't. Strabo makes the distance of the Pyramids from Memphis only 40 stadia, or rather more than two geographical miles; which appears to be considerably too little.[1]—3rdly. According to Ptolemy, the difference of latitude between Memphis and Egyptian Babylon was ten minutes: from which it would seem that his observation for the latitude of the former place was made near the spot now occupied by the village of Meet Rahee'neh.

According to Herodotus, Memphis was founded by Menes, the first king of Egypt: according to Diodorus Siculus, by Uchoreus. The former historian states that the founder of this city, by means of an embankment, 100 stadia (or about 5 geographical miles and one third[2]) higher up the valley, diverted the course of the Nile, which originally ran along the side of the sandy hills of Libya, and made it to flow at an equal distance between the eastern and western mountains: that he then built the city of Memphis upon the spot which he had thus converted into dry ground; (or, more probably, between the old bed of the river and the new): after which he made a lake, on the north and west of the city, communicating with the Nile; and founded the magnificent temple of Vulcan. This building (if we may judge from the subsequent descriptions of it given by the same author) must have been very similar to the grand temple of Kur'nak, at Thebes. Mœris added propylæa to it on the north: Sesostris adorned it with several colossi: Rhampsinitus added propylæa on the west; and two colossi, 25 cubits high; one of which, facing the north, was adorned under the name of Summer; while the other, which was called Winter, was quite neglected: Asychis built the propylæa on the eastern side, which were the grandest of all, and profusely adorned with sculptures[3]: Psammetichus added propylæa on the south[4]; and a temple in front of them, in which the God Apis was kept, whenever he made his appearance in Egypt[5]: this was ornamented with colossi 12 cubits high, instead of columns: lastly, Amasis placed, before this superb

---

[1] This calculation is founded on the supposition that Strabo here means *Egyptian* stadia; as he does when he states the distance from Syene to Philæ to be 100 stadia.—See the following note on the Egyptian stadium.—But the *greater* stadia may here be meant; 40 of which were equal to 4 geographical miles.

[2] Herodotus, in lib. II, cap. 9, mentions several distances in Egyptian stadia; among which he states the distance from Thebes to Elephantis (which is about 96 geographical miles) to be 1800 stadia: hence 100 stadia are equal to about 5 geographical miles and one third.

[3] Diodorus says that the *northern* propylæa, which were built by Mœris, were the most magnificent.

[4] Diodorus asserts that Psammetichus built the *eastern* propylæa.

[5] Strabo mentions this temple; its *secos*, or sanctuary, in which the bull Apis, or Osiris, was kept; another secos for his mother; and a court, in which Apis was occasionally brought, to be seen more publicly.

temple, a colossus 75 feet long, in a reclining posture; similar to that at Sais.[1] On the south of this temple, in a quarter inhabited by Tyrians, was an enclosure consecrated to an Egyptian king, whom the Greeks called Proteus, with a chapel dedicated to Venus the Stranger, supposed, by Herodotus, to be Helen, who, with Paris, being driven to the shores of Egypt, by contrary winds, was hospitably received by Proteus. Strabo mentions the temple of the Grecian Venus; but says that some regarded it as dedicated to the moon.—Such were the principal edifices within the city of Memphis.

Not a wall, nor a column, at the present period, rises above the soil throughout the whole extent of the site of this city; but in many parts, we see lofty and wide-spreading mounds of rubbish, chiefly composed of earth and broken pottery and fragments of stone. The public edifices, as Strabo informs us, were erected upon raised ground. These structures were in a state of ruin in the time of that writer,[2] a few years before the Christian era; and since that period, the convenient elevations upon which they stood have been chosen for the sites of villages. Thus the relics of the public monuments of Memphis have become buried beneath the crumbled walls of modern huts[3]; while all the other remains of this city have been covered over by the deposits of the successive inundations: the bed of the river, as well as the whole superficies of the alluvial land through which it flows, having gradually risen. Forests of palm-trees occupy a great part of the site of Memphis; and among these, in the vicinity of the mounds, are several hollow spaces, which, at the period of the inundation, become lakes, and remain so during a considerable portion of the year. Winding dikes, or raised roads, chiefly formed of earth, traverse the plain in various directions, from village to village. Some of these, which are partly broken down, or washed away, and therefore unserviceable as roads during the inundation, might be mistaken for remains of the wall of Memphis. The village of Meet Rahee'neh ميت رهينه is situated upon mounds of rubbish which doubtless cover the remains of some of the principal buildings of Memphis. A little to the southward of the route from that village to El-Bedreshey'n بدرشين are other large mounds, which seem to conceal the remains of the temple of Phthah, or Vulcan. Here, Caviglia has been busy in excavating, and has uncovered a colossal statue of Rameses the 2nd, the Sesostris of the Greek historians; who, according to Herodotus, placed a colossus of himself, and one of his queen, each 30 cubits high, with four statues of their four children, 20 cubits high, before the temple of Vulcan. The colossus discovered by Caviglia seems to have been 45 feet, or 30 cubits, in height. The feet and part of the legs are broken off; but, in its present

---

[1] All the Egyptian colossi that I have seen are either in a standing or sitting posture.

[2] The city yet ranked next to Alexandria in extent and population.

[3] These were constructed of unburnt bricks, and surmounted by pigeon-houses, chiefly formed of earthen pots.

state, its extreme dimensions are nearly 40 feet: it therefore appears to be the identical statue of Sesostris described by Herodotus. The stone of which it is formed is a hard, white chert. It lies prostrate; with the face downwards; but now more than half exposed; and the features are very beautiful; but the head is too large to bear a just proportion to the rest of the figure. It stood in an erect posture; the arms hanging down. The back and arms are much injured; but the front nearly perfect. Close by it, in the same hollow, lay a statue of granite, of less colossal size, almost entirely buried; and at a little distance, the side of a similar granite colossus just appeared above the rubbish. Near these remains is a lake, which, being surrounded by numerous palm-trees, has a very pretty effect. Caviglia had erected a hut in the neighbourhood; and was desirous of prosecuting his researches in this part, in the hope of laying open the ruins of the temple of Vulcan; but was in want of funds. It was from these same mounds, I believe, that the colossal granite fist which is now in the British Museum was removed by the French during their occupation of Egypt. This fragment belonged to a statue which must have been 55 or 60 feet in height.

In the same quarter were doubtless situated the ruins which several Arab writers have described as the remains of *Menf* منف, or Memphis. El-Muckree'zee and others state that Menf was on the west of the Nile, 12 miles above El-Foosta't. 'Abd El-Latee'f, writing in the beginning of the 7th century after the flight (or the beginning of the 13th century of the Christian era), asserts, that—notwithstanding the numerous revolutions to which Memphis had been subject, the repeated attempts which had been made to destroy its monuments, the removal of the stones and other materials of which some of its edifices were constructed, and the mutilation of the statues with which it was adorned, in addition to the injuries which must naturally have ensued during the lapse of more than four thousand years—there were yet found, among its remains, works so wonderful, that they confounded the contemplative mind, and baffled the utmost powers of description.—He particularly mentions a monolithic chapel, or shrine, which was called *El-Beyt el-Akh'dar* (or the Green Chamber), as one of the most surprising of the monuments of Memphis then existing. It was 9 cubits in height, and 8 by 7 in width; and its hollow, or niche, was 5 cubits high, and 4 wide. It was ornamented, both within and without, with sculptures of the sun and planets, and of men and beasts, and with inscriptions in ancient characters; and rested upon a pedestal formed of large masses of granite: but some ignorant persons had undermined it, in the hope of finding a treasure beneath it, which caused it to lean, slightly, and occasioned several small fissures. It was placed in a magnificent temple, which was admirably constructed with stones of enormous magnitude.—El-Muckree'zee, writing rather more than two centuries later, mentions this monolith, and states that it originally contained an idol of gold. He says that it was formed of a green, flinty stone, of so hard a nature that it could not be cut with a tool of iron. He also describes it as ornamented with sculptured figures and inscriptions, and having the representations of serpents, with the breast expanded, upon the front of the door, or *over the door*. The Sabeans, he says, affirmed that this shrine was consecrated to the moon, and that it was one of seven similar shrines which were consecrated to the seven planets; all of which were at Memphis. He adds, that the Emee'r Seyf ed-Deen Shey'khoo (commonly called Sheykhoo'n) broke it in pieces, after the year 750 (A.D. 1349-50); and that some fragments of it were in the convent and mosque which were built by that Emee'r in the quarter, or street, of Es-Salee'beh, outside of El-Cka'hireh; i.e. in the suburbs.[1]—'Abd El-Latee'f speaks also of pedestals upon enormous bases; of walls constructed of huge masses of stone; of a lofty door-way, formed of three stones (one on each side, and one above); and of statues which were remarkable for their number, their colossal size, the beauty of their forms, and the correctness of their proportions. One was more than 30 cubits high, without the pedestal: it was formed of a single block of red granite, and covered with a coat of red varnish, or paint, to which time had only given fresh lustre. He also mentions two colossal lions, placed face to face; but broken; and states that he observed a considerable portion of the wall of the city, built with small stones and large, oblong bricks. He does not describe the situation of this wall.

It is evident that the principal monuments of Memphis (the temple of Vulcan, and other edifices) were in the neighbourhood of Meet Rahee'neh. There are also extensive mounds of rubbish to the north-east of this village; occupying, apparently, nearly the central part of the site of the ancient city. The villages of Oomm' Khana'n امّ خنان and El-Menawa't المناوات are situated upon other large mounds; among which are found fragments of granite, and other materials of ancient buildings. This quarter was probably the site of a northern suburb of Memphis. Where the village of Ab'oo Seer ابو صير is situated, was doubtless another suburb, called, by the Egyptians, Busir (pronounced, by them, Boosee'r, and by the Greeks written Busiris). The village of Sack'cka'rah صقاره and the high mounds upon which it stands, on the skirts of the desert, may be supposed to occupy part of the site of a third suburb, which, perhaps, derived its name from Phtha Socari, the principal God of Memphis.[2] The great canal which flows along the western side of the site of Memphis, and which is a continuation of the Bahhr Yoo'soof, resembles the natural course of a river; and this may be regarded as a confirmation—or as the foundation—of the assertion of Herodotus that the Nile flowed along the side of the Libyan hills before the building of Memphis. It is also probable that a part of this canal or river, widened by art, formed the ancient lake *Acherusia*, over which the

---

[1] I visited the latter of these buildings; but saw not the fragments alluded to, unless they form part of the pavement, &c., which I imagine to be the case. As an Englishman (though in disguise) I did not venture to attract suspicion by inquiring respecting these relics in the mosque.
[2] This was suggested to me by Mr. Salt.

dead were conveyed, in a boat called *Baris*,[1] under the guidance of a ferry-man, who, in the common dialect of Egypt, was termed *Charon*. By this lake was a temple of Hecate; and here, also, were the gates of Cocytus and Lethe (Lamentation and Oblivion); so called, probably, because the dead were borne through them to the lake. Hence Orpheus derived the fables which he propagated respecting Charon, the Styx, Acheron, &c.[2]; though, in the Greek mythology, the names of Cocytus and Lethe are given—not to gates, but—to *rivers* of Hell. It may reasonably be inferred that the lake Acherusia extended along the whole of the western side of Memphis, near the base of the rocky elevation; so that it was absolutely necessary that the dead should be transported across it: and the ferry was, doubtless, directly opposite the principal burial-place (where the Pyramid of Steps is situated), that the bodies might be landed as near as possible to the catacombs in which they were to be interred.—Strabo mentions a temple of Serapis, which was certainly outside of Memphis, and most probably between the lake Acherusia and the elevated part of the desert. He describes it as situated in a desert tract, where the sand was so deep that some of the sphinxes before it were half buried, and others were buried up to the neck. This temple has experienced the same fate as all the other public edifices of that famous city which once rivalled Thebes in the magnificence, if not in the number, of its monuments.

In the Scriptures we find several prophecies of the fate of Memphis: as the following—"Thus saith the Lord God; I will also destroy the idols, and I will cause their images to cease out of Noph; and there shall be no more a prince of the land of Egypt: and I will put a fear in the land of Egypt."[3]—Again: "O thou daughter dwelling in Egypt, furnish thyself to go into captivity: for Noph shall be waste and desolate, without an inhabitant.[4]

---

[1]Herodotus (in lib. II, cap. 96) describes the Egyptian boats to which the name of Baris was given; as I have already mentioned.
[2]Diodorus Siculus, lib. I, cap 96.
[3]Ezechiel, XXX. 13.
[4]Jeremiah, XLVI. 19.

Chapter XVII.

Ordinary circumstances of the Voyage up the Nile.[†]

On the ninth of March, 1826, between five and six months after my arrival in Musr (or Cairo), I hired a boat to convey me up the Nile as far as the Second Cataracts; intending to examine at leisure the most remarkable antiquities of Upper Egypt and Nubia.

The boats of the Nile I have already described. That which I engaged was a moderate-sized ckan'geh (or ckan'jeh). I paid for it twenty-five dollars (or 5l.4s.2d) monthly. It was navigated by seven men, who found their provisions at their own cost; and the Rei'yis (or Captain) was bound by a written agreement; one of the conditions of which was that we should proceed or stop whenever I desired, by night or day. The boat was about 35 feet in length, and 7 in width. The cabin was about 9 feet long, 6 feet wide at the fore part (inside), and 4½ at the end; and between 4 and 4½ in height. I insert a sketch of its interior.[1] It had, on each side, four small windows, with sliding blinds in the inside. I did not encumber it with European furniture; and did not find its small height at all inconvenient; as the Oriental mode of sitting had become more agreeable to me than any other position. The mattress upon which I slept formed, in the day, with the addition of three cushions, a small *deewa'n* (or divan); and the cabin was large enough to contain, besides this, some of my boxes, &c. A small *segga'deh* (or prayer-carpet) served to cover a part of the floor; and was occasionally of use to spread upon the shore. A round tray (*seene'yeh*) of tinned copper, placed on a low stool, formed my table for dinner &c.; my meals being served up and dispatched in the manner of the country. The only utensils for the table and kitchen &c. that I required were a few dishes, basins, spoons and knives, some earthen water-bottles (called *ckool'lehs* and *do'rucks*) with a copper tray to place them in, a coffee-pot and some cups, a mortar for pounding the coffee, two or three cooking-pots of tinned copper, and a basin and ewer (*tisht* and *ibree'ck*) of the same material; the last used for washing the hands before and after every meal. The cook made his kitchen in the fore

---

[†]Lane attached "Introduction" to the title of this chapter because it began the second volume of the multi-volumed work that he expected *Description of Egypt* to be. Lane added a note "The author solicits the reader's attention to the Supplement annexed to this work previously to the perusal of this volume." by which he meant that the Supplement's treatment of ancient Egyptian history and culture would be useful background for the following chapters.

[1]See plate 1 [fig. 55].

part of the boat; imbedding a couple of earthen fire-pots in a plaster of mud.

In making preparations for the voyage up the Nile, the traveller should provide a dozen or more of the earthen water-bottles; for many will probably be broken: more of them may be procured at Ckin'ë where the best are made: they are of a very porous, grey earth; and cool the water most deliciously. A sufficient quantity of water for each day's use may be left to settle in a large jar, which may be placed behind the cabin, and secured with a rope. During the hot weather, a musquito-curtain (*na'moo'see'yeh*) and a fly-whisk (*minesh'sheh*) are indispensable for the traveller's comfort. A pair of saddle-bags will be found useful in short excursions from the river; and particularly a saddle for a donkey; for at most villages donkeys may be hired, but seldom is one to be found with a saddle. A tent may also be a convenience. If the cabin should not be found to afford sufficient accommodation, the traveller may erect an awning of canvas before it; or, if not caring for the neat appearance of his boat, he may construct an additional cabin with palm-branches and matting; the former stripped of the leaves, and bent in the shape of an arch; and the latter forming the covering.

As bread and meat can only be procured at the principal towns, which are few, and far apart, the traveller must lay in a good stock of provisions before he commences his voyage. His live-stock should consist of at least several dozens of fowls, which may be placed in a coop on the roof of the cabin. Two or three lambs or kids may also be taken on board; and a milch-goat will be a useful acquisition; as milk is not always to be procured in the villages. A good supply of biscuit will be necessary for the use of the traveller and his servants when fresh bread cannot be procured; but it is advisable also to take a stock of flour for making bread occasionally in the boat, or in any village that may be at hand. The bread is made in round, flat cakes; with, or without, leaven; and may be baked on an iron plate. The next most important articles of provision are rice, lentils, and clarified butter (*semn*): with these, very good dishes may be made, even without flesh-meat; and such constituted my principal diet. In the metropolis the traveller may procure macaroni, European cheese and pickles (both very superior to those made in Egypt), sugar, honey, excellent preserves (of orange, citron, &c.), the best tobacco*[1] and coffee*, tea, soap*, wax candles,[2] gun-powder*, &c. A stock of amadon (*soo'fa'n*) and matches &c. must not be forgotten here. Dates, onions, and other vegetables, salt, pepper, lamp-oil, charcoal, and firewood may be procured at the market towns in Egypt.—From this list it may be seen that the traveller in Egypt need undergo no great privations; but, on the

---

[1]Of the articles thus marked the traveller will do well to procure an extra stock, for presents; the best Syrian tobacco (*Geb'elee*) for the Turks, and an inferior and stronger sort (*Soo'ree*) for the Egyptians. Good coffee may also be had in the principal towns in Egypt.

[2]These are much more convenient than lamps in examining the catacombs, &c.

contrary, has at his command many luxuries. The greatest of these luxuries in my estimation were the delicious tobacco and coffee fresh from Syria and Arabia. The coffee made in the Eastern manner, very strong, and without sugar or milk, is not only essential to the full enjoyment of the pipe, but it is also, in a great degree, a preventive of thirst. The manner in which it is served in the East, in small china cups, each placed in another cup, which is of silver or brass, is very convenient.

I found my boat very comfortable in most respects; but if I had had more experience in the navigation of the Nile I should have chosen a dahabee'yeh, as more safe; being wider in proportion to its length. Numbers of rats, as usual, took up their quarters in my boat; and several times one of these animals would nestle himself under the edge of my bed-covering. Swarms of flies were also troublesome during the hot weather; and I could not exterminate the spiders. I had some difficulty to induce my servant to kill the spiders which he found in cleaning the cabin: his reluctance to do so partly arose from his doubt of the propriety of destroying animals not of a dangerous nature, and partly from a feeling of gratitude which he, as a Moos'lim, entertained towards the vermin in question for a service which one of their species had rendered to the Prophet of Arabia. Mohham'mad, in his flight from Mek'keh to El-Medee'neh, being closely pursued, sought refuge, with his companion Ab'oo Bekr, in a cave. His pursuers, thirsting for his blood, arrived at the mouth of the cave, and were about to explore its interior when they observed that a spider had woven its web across the entrance, and that a pair of doves had built their nest there, and were sitting over two eggs: whence concluding that no person could be within, they abstained from entering. From this circumstance both the spider and dove are regarded with a degree of religious respect by the Moos'lims in general.

I had with me two servants; a Nubian and an Egyptian: the latter was my cook. My knowledge of Arabic saved me the trouble of an interpreter in Egypt; and my Nubian servant, speaking Arabic as well as the languages of the Koonoo'z and Noo'beh, was my interpreter above the First Cataracts. My crew consisted of two Nubians (the Rei'yis and his brother), and five Egyptians: most of them fine, muscular men. The Rei'yis (who was captain and helmsman) provided the food of his men; deducting the cost from their pay. I had reason to be very well satisfied in general with his conduct, and with that of the whole crew. It was my custom (as it is that of most travellers on the Nile) to give the crew, on arriving at each market-town (which was not oftener, on the average, than about once a week), a sufficient quantity of meat for their supper; and this, with a daily cup or two of coffee to the Rei'yis, and the same occasionally to each boatman, kept them in good humour. I found them always very obliging; and attentive to my orders; excepting on one occasion, when they absented themselves for the greater part of a day, without leave, to make bread; and I prevented a recurrence of such conduct by deducting, in that instance, a day's pay from their wages.

During the month of abstinence (Rum'ada'n) I gave them some meat for their supper more frequently; with a little coffee; and I reaped much advantage from this kind of conduct towards them; for I never had to complain of their being remiss in their work: even when they were fasting from day-break to sunset, I could not prevail upon them to desist from towing the boat in calm and sultry weather.—Travellers about to undertake a voyage up the Nile are generally advised to take the earliest opportunity of inflicting corporal chastisement on the Rei'yis, to inspire due respect; but I think that such treatment will seldom have a good effect: the crew will probably be revenged; having it in their power to retard the traveller's progress even while apparently exerting themselves to the utmost to forward his desires.

One of my crew was skilled in playing on the double reed-pipe called *zoomma'rah*: another accompanied him with the *darabook'keh* (or earthen drum); which is suspended on the left side, and is beaten with the fingers.[1] While my boat was under sail I was often regaled with the rude music of these instruments, and with songs. To convey some notion of the airs sung by the boatmen of the Nile I give two specimens: both of them (as usual) very short; being repeated over and over again; sometimes with the same, and sometimes with different words. The words which accompany these two airs are particularly adapted to the period when the boat has arrived within sight of Musr (or Cairo); but they are often sung on other occasions.

Ya' – sela'm   Ya' – sela' – m   ah!

Ya' sela'm se – l – lim   bel'ed el Ima'–m   ah!
Chorus
"O Peace! preserve the town of the Ima'm[2]!"

ياسلام سلّم بلد الامام

Allah yensoo – – rak   ya' – – Beyh – – we–l Ima'm

---

[1]See plate 6 [fig. 61].

[2]The celebrated Ima'm Esh-Shafe'ee, founder of one of the four orthodox Mohhammadan sects. His tomb is in the southern cemetery of Musr, or Cairo.— "O Peace" means "O God of peace"; and "The town of the Ima'm" is Musr.

we – – llee hhowaleyh   we–l Ima'm wellee hhowaleyh
Chorus
"God protect thee O Bey[1]! and the Ima'm and those around him!"

It is worthy of remark that the Egyptian, in his love-songs, generally designates the object of his admiration by the *masculine* gender; though it is evident that he alludes to a *female* by the description which he gives of her person; as I might prove by many examples. The reason assigned for this strange custom is a desire to palliate the impropriety of making women the subjects of verses which are sung for the amusement of men. The Egyptians, however, are not always delicate in the language of their songs in other respects.—The boatmen of the Nile sing more frequently while rowing down the stream. They have particular chants for particular occasions: one, for instance, which they sing when exerting themselves with the boat-poles to prevent the vessel from running aground: another, when endeavouring to push it off from a sand-bank or from the shore; which they either accomplish with the poles, or by descending into the water and applying their backs and shoulders.—My crew (like the Egyptian boatmen in general) were a very lively set.

When the wind failed (which was seldom the case, and it was more seldom adverse) my crew were always ready to tow the boat; four or five of them at a time performing this arduous work, and each successively coming on board again to rest, while another took his place; the Rei'yis being always at the helm, sitting on the roof of the cabin. This operation in sultry weather is extremely laborious; but the boatmen of the Nile are mostly capable of enduring it, with little intermission, for the greater part of the day.

The crew of my boat were regular in their performance of the five daily prayers. They also fasted during Rum'ada'n; and when the sun had declined behind the Libyan hills I was requested to act the part of a Moo-ed'din, and to inform them, from my watch, when the moment of sunset should arrive, that they might break their fast as soon as possible; the labour of the day rendering the abstinence from drinking more difficult to endure than hunger. Full of religious pride, like the generality of Moos'lims, they seldom wiped from the forehead and nose the dust which adhered in prostration: but with all their zeal, I was surprised to observe how deficient they were in religious knowledge: I often had occasion to correct one or other of them with a quotation from the

---

[1] By the word "Bey" is meant Cka'id Bey, a celebrated Soolta'n, whose tomb is in the eastern cemetery of Musr. The blessing is implored on all those buried around Ckaid Bey and the Ima'm.

Ckoor-a'n or from the traditions. At all times I was careful to do nothing repugnant to their bigoted feelings.

I generally passed the night before a village or town; the boat being made fast to a stake driven into the bank, according to the common custom; for few but the largest vessels are provided with anchors. I always preferred stopping at night, that I might not lose the sight of any part of the country through which I passed; and I should often have done so, at least during the summer, were it only for the sake of eating my evening meal, and sometimes spreading my mattress and quilt, upon the bank. When I slept in the open air, upon the shore, I was particularly careful to cover my head completely over, or to tie a handkerchief over my eyes, as a precaution against ophthalmia: for the night-air is sometimes too cool even in summer; and the moonlight is said to have an injurious effect upon the eyes. The summer evenings in Egypt are most delightful; and in the Sa'ee'd, where no perceptible due [sic] falls at night in that season, sleeping in the open air is quite a luxury. There is little fear of robbers, under the rigorous government of Mohham'mad 'Al'ee[1]; and little chance of the sleeper's being disturbed by passing travellers; for all persons in that sober country retire to rest at a very early hour: but perfect stillness is not always enjoyed: the creaking of the sa'ckiyehs, which ceases in the evening, is succeeded, after the spring has set in, by the continued and unvaried croaking of multitudes of frogs.—As soon as my boat was made fast to the shore the boatmen generally lighted a fire upon the bank, and cooked their supper. Having dispatched their simple (though principal) meal, which usually consisted of bread and lentil-porridge, they remained half an hour or an hour longer; if cold, sitting round their fire, forming a singularly picturesque group, and enjoying the temperate pleasures of smoking and conversation, or amusing themselves with singing, and with the music of the zoomma'rah and the darabook'keh. Before two o'clock (the time being reckoned from sunset) they were generally all asleep: each spread for himself a mat or cloak upon the bank, or in the boat, and slept with little covering, or sometimes, in summer, with none at all.—Long before sunrise, while it was yet dusk, I could faintly perceive the figures of my boatmen in the various attitudes of prayer. Their morning devotions being performed at this early hour, they had leisure for a pipe before the voyage was continued.

When I left my boat for a stroll, or to visit any of the ancient monuments, I was generally armed with a pair of pistols and sabre; and I found, from unpleasant experience, more than once, that it was highly expedient for me always to have arms on such occasions; though it is very rarely that a traveller in Egypt is exposed to any danger; and most improbable that he should be if provided with the means of defence: almost the only risk he is liable to is from meeting with some vagabond

---

[1]There are, however, still some places in Egypt which are notorious for robberies.

Turkish soldier, who does not rate the life of a fellow-creature at the value of a cup of coffee, or his own life at much more.

The fel'la'hhee'n (or peasants) I uniformly found civil and respectful; but often, taking me for a soldier, they fled at my approach, in the fear of being forcibly enlisted in the army: the women mostly retired, covering their faces; or avoided meeting me. The Egyptian peasantry are generally and naturally a cheerful people; but they are often heard to complain of the horrible oppression which they now endure. They are mostly descended from various Arab tribes. About nine tenths of them are Arabs; and all these are Moos'lims: the rest are Ckoobt (or Copts). In complexion they differ considerably in different latitudes: the shades varying from a tawny hue to a deep bronze, or brown, which is the colour of the natives of the more southern parts of the Sa'ee'd. In point of figure they must be pronounced a remarkably fine race: they are not fat; but muscular and strong. Many of them (I here allude to the *men* only) are almost entirely naked; having nothing but a piece of rag to render them at all decent: the rest wear a shirt of blue linen or cotton, or of brown woollen stuff; with a turban, or merely a scull-cap of brown or white felt. The only weapon in general use among them is a thick staff (called *nebboo't*), five or six feet long; which the fella'hh frequently carries when on a journey, and sometimes on other occasions.—The women, until impaired by age, are particularly distinguished by their graceful forms, and erect carriage; and many of them have very fine features; which, however, they disfigure by tattooing blue marks upon the chin, lips, &c.: they also blacken the edges of the eye-lids with *kohhl*, and tinge their nails with the dull red dye of the *hhen'na*. They wear a few trifling ornaments; as necklaces and bracelets; the latter of which are usually simple rings, of blue glass, or of bone; and some of them wear the nose-ring. They are all more fully clad than the men; and always wear a head-veil (a piece of drapery covering the upper part of the head, and hanging down the back), serving, when occasion requires, for a face-veil (which few of them possess); part of it being drawn before the face so as to leave only one eye visible: but they do not all conform with the custom of veiling before men; so that the traveller in Egypt is not always precluded from the sight of a female face; and he may often see a group of girls bathing in the Nile, in parts where they expect to be secure from observation. The children, of both sexes, are generally entirely naked; or if a little girl possess a piece of rag, she hangs it over her head, and often veils her face with it in the presence of men, though her whole body is exposed. Domestic occupations, and the task of bringing water, devolve upon the women. It is, perhaps, to their practice of carrying the large water-pitcher on the head that their upright gait is mainly attributable; for the men, on the contrary, generally stoop a little.—The habitations of these poor people are miserable huts, constructed of unburnt bricks, and seldom containing any other article of furniture (their utensils for food and cooking excepted) than the matting which serves as their bed: but the genial climate renders their privations light in comparison with what they would otherwise be. Their food commonly consists of unleavened millet-bread, dates, milk, new cheese, small salted fish, beans, chick-peas, lupins, onions, &c., and poor pickles. Rice is too dear to be an article of their diet; and flesh-meat is a dainty of which they very seldom partake; but most of them indulge in the cheap luxury of smoking the mild tobacco of the country; though many can afford themselves no better pipe-stick than a door'ah-stalk.

The traveller is limited in his excursions from the river during the autumn by the canals and inundated tracts; and for this reason, and from my love of hot weather, I chose the spring and summer for the period of my voyage. When I set forth on a walk or ride of two or three hours, or more, I generally took with me a servant and one of my boatmen, to carry (besides my apparatus for drawing) a bottle of water,[1] some bread and dates in a napkin, my pipe, a little coffee, a small coffee-pot and cup, and a handful of charcoal. Thus provided, when I felt inclined for rest and refreshment, I ate my meal with a hearty relish, while my servant was lighting the charcoal to boil the coffee, which I afterwards enjoyed with my pipe; leaving enough to satisfy my attendants.

In the course of the voyage up the Nile, travellers are often presented with milk, &c., by a fella'hh; but unless they offer in return something more than equivalent, either money or some other commodity, they will seldom find that the *donor* is very well contented, or that he willingly leaves his *present*. The traveller is also sometimes visited by a Ka'shif or Cka'im-macka'm (a Turkish governor of a town or small district), and by other men in office; some of whom have the impudence and meanness to ask for anything they may happen to see and take a fancy to in the boat; but a proud look is generally sufficient to put a stop to conduct of this kind. Such persons should always be treated as inferiors; and the only compliment that is necessary to be paid them is the offer of a pipe and a cup of coffee. Should the traveller, however, require the services of a Ka'shif or Cka'im-macka'm, or of the Sheykh of a village, on any occasion, a present is expected from him, and should be given; and when he *receives* a present from any such persons he should give in return something of more value: arms, watches, or other costly articles, he is not likely to find requisite for such purposes: Geb'elee tobacco, and fine gunpowder, are generally acceptable to the Turks[2]; and to many of them, brandy, or any liqueur; but to some, the offer of these prohibited drinks would give offence: any article of dress, Soo'ree tobacco, coffee, soap, or money, may be given to a Sheykh, or to any of the fel'la'hhee'n. It is not necessary for the traveller to visit any of these petty governors, nor those of higher rank (as Ma-moo'rs, Na'zirs, &c.), excepting the governor of

---

[1] I first used a zemzemee'yeh (or leather bottle) on these occasions: but I afterwards found that an earthen bottle (which was conveniently carried in a small linen bag) was preferable, from its keeping the water cooler.

[2] The name of *Turk* (or rather *Toork*) is disliked by those people: *'Osma'nlee* is the favourite appellation.

Aswa'n, to whom he should shew his passport, and give some present, before he proceeds into Nubia. In Egypt the tyranny of the subordinate officers of the state is often more severely felt than that of the Viceroy himself.[†]

To show the degree of power which some of the grandees in Egypt are permitted to exercise I may relate two or three anecdotes of late occurrences, of the authenticity of which I have been assured by many persons.

On the first day of the fast of Rum'ada'n, a servant of one of the chief officers of the Ba'sha went into the room where his master was sitting, about half an hour before sunset, and placed the stool, and the round tray upon it, with the bread, ready for breakfast.[‡] —"What are you doing there?" said his master: "do you want to tempt me to break my fast half an hour before the time?"—The servant replied that he was only preparing the repast, that his lord might not have to wait a minute after the call to prayer.—"You rascal!" exclaimed the grandee: "you have put bread before me to tantalize me."—Again the servant denied the charge, with respectful protestations. To these asseverations his lord paid no attention; but looked wildly about, thinking how he might satisfy his rage. A chain, to which a chandelier was to be attached, hanging from the ceiling, attracted his eye, and suggested to him a mode of punishment. Calling to some soldiers in attendance at the end of the room, he said— "take this fellow, and hang him to that chain."—The sentence was immediately executed; and, with the spectacle of the dying man before him, the tyrant waited calmly until he heard the call to prayer; when he arose, and performed the ablution, said his prayers, and broke his fast.

One of the young memloo'ks of the same grandee had taken a basin of *ckish'tah* (or clouted cream) from a man passing by the house, and refused payment. The poor man complained to the memloo'k's master, who happened to be in the court before the house. Being afraid to confess the truth when questioned by his lord, the boy denied having taken the ckish'tah.—"Come here," said the grandee: "we shall soon see whether you have or not."—Instantly drawing his dagger from his girdle, he ripped up the boy's stomach; and the clouted cream was discovered: then turning to the complainant, he said—"if I had not found the ckish'tah in his stomach, I should have served you in the same manner: now take your money, and go about your business."[1]

Six memloo'ks, all of them young men, belonging to another of the Ba'sha's great officers, made their escape from him, and fled through the desert towards Syria; but on arriving at the frontier fortress of El-'Aree'sh, they were seized by the garrison, and sent back. Their master, no longer considering them as property worth preserving,

---

[†] The Pasha, Muhammad Ali.

[‡] I.e., to break the fast that is maintained from sunrise to sunset during the month of Ramadan.

[1] A similar action is related of Ba'yazee'd (or Bajazet).

ordered them to descend into the court, to draw their swords, and fall upon each other, and try who was the best swordsman. Reclining in a corner of his saloon, by a window which looked into the court, he witnessed the cruel combat. In a few minutes, all of them, but one, lay stretched upon the ground, either dead or mortally wounded. The survivor, himself severely wounded, and almost fainting from loss of blood, ascended to the saloon, to kiss the hand, and claim the pardon of his master, who, as the wretched youth approached him, seized a pistol, which lay by his side, and shot him.

Such are some of the persons whom the traveller in Egypt may visit; and from whom he may receive civilities. His bearing before them should be consequential; but his manners, of course, polite.

In the following chapter I commence the account of my voyage from Musr to Thebes; a distance of about 400 miles by the course of the river. The description of Thebes will occupy the greater portion of this volume.[†]

[†]Chapters seventeen through twenty-six.

Chapter XVIII.[1]

From Musr to Ben'ee Soowey'f.

Commencement of the voyage, and state of the river, &c.—Toor'a, and the quarries of Mons Troicus—Memphis—Pyramids of El-Meta'niyeh—Pyramid of Meydoo'm—Ben'ee Soowey'f.

On the 15th of March we set sail from Boo'la'ck; but the wind being unfavourable, made little progress. The river, at this season, is very low; within about five feet of its *minimum*; and for more than three months it will yet continue to decrease: we therefore can now see but few objects from our boat; only the banks of the river, the villages in its immediate vicinity, the sha'doo'fs, sa'ckiyehs, and palm trees, and generally on one side, or on both, the bare, yellow mountains which confine the valley of the Nile. This will not be the case during my downward voyage: I shall then enjoy a less confined prospect from my boat; and can then visit any objects that may have escaped my observation before. (In this copy of my journal I shall incorporate the notes made during my return, and in the course of a second voyage from Musr to the Second Cataracts.)

During the first few hours of our voyage, the scenery which surrounded us was very pleasing: the island of Er-Ro'dah, with the town of Musr 'Atee'ckah, on our left, and El-Gee'zeh on our right, presented an assemblage of picturesque objects. The Pyramids of El-Gee'zeh were also prominent objects in the scene; and those of Ab'oo Seer, Sack'cka'rah, and Dahshoo'r, were seen, beyond the palm groves which cover a great part of the site of Memphis.

In the evening we passed the village of *Toor'a* طرا, on our left; i.e. on the eastern bank of the river. It occupies the site of the ancient town of *Troja*, which was founded by a colony of Trojans. At a short distance behind it is a point of the eastern mountains. A stone wall extends from the village to a fortress on the side of the mountain; barring the approach to the metropolis from the south. This was built by Isma'ee'l Bey, in the year of the flight 1204 (A.D. 1789-90), to prevent Moora'd Bey and his party from returning to the capital from Upper Egypt. The part of the eastern chain stretching towards Toor'a was anciently called *Mons Troiens*. Along its side, facing the Nile, are the extensive quarries from which were taken the stones which were employed in the construction of the exterior parts, and passages, of the pyramids. The principal of these quarries are behind the village of *El-Ma'asar'ah* المعصرة. The rock is calcareous, like that of the western hills; but of a more compact kind.

[1]A map [fig. 56] to accompany this volume [chapters seventeen through twenty-six] is in the larger portfolio.

The stone is cut away in such a manner as to form caverns; according to the general practice of the ancient Egyptians; probably that the workmen might be sheltered from the sun. In these quarried caverns are numerous sculptured tablets; some, with figures presenting offerings to various divinities, and with hieroglyphics; others, with hieroglyphics only; and there are also many other inscriptions in hieroglyphics, and in the enchorial characters. Some of them contain the name of Amos, or Amosis, the first king of the 18th Dynasty (and 40th of my list[†]), with that of his queen: others have the name of Hakor. There are two temples among the remains of Eilethyia; one, and probably both, built by the latter king. His name and sculptures, executed in low relief, are found upon the columns of one of these temples; and a later line of hieroglyphics, with an oval for a new name (but left blank) has been cut over the old sculptures down the front of one of the columns, in intaglio. The original sculptures of the other temple are in the same style as the older sculptures on the columns above mentioned; but the name is erased; and these have, in most parts, been sculptured over in intaglio, in like manner: here, however, the name of the king under whom the temple was resculptured has not been omitted: it is Rameses 2nd (the first king of the 19th Dynasty, and 51st of my list).[‡] It seems then that this Hakor was anterior to the 18th Dynasty; for his name is not found in the lists of that dynasty.[††] He was probably a Memphite prince: perhaps the king whom Diodorus Siculus calls Uchoreus; and to whom that historian (contrary to the opinion of Herodotus) attributes the *founding* of Memphis.—On the ceilings and other parts of the quarried caverns of the Mons Troicus are many enchorial inscriptions, and lines to direct the workmen as to the form and size of the blocks to be cut.[1]

After having passed the village of El-Ma'asar'ah, above-mentioned, we soon arrive opposite the central part of the site of *Memphis*. Not the smallest relics of the monuments of this city, excepting the pyramids on the elevated desert in the distance, are visible from the river. I discontinued my voyage, for two days to visit again the scanty remains of Memphis, and some of the neighbouring pyramids. While I was on the summit of a small, ruined pyramid, behind the village of Sack'cka'rah, a troop of Turkish cavalry, employed in raising recruits for the newly organized army, passed by, and would have taken the donkey-driver whom I had brought with me; but I interposed, and procured his liberation.

On the 18th we continued our voyage. The wind was light; and we

---

[†]Fig. 160.

[‡]Ramses I was the first king of the Nineteenth Dynasty. The dynastic scheme to which writers referred during Lane's time differed slightly from that of the present.

[††]He was a king of the Twenty-ninth Dynasty.

[1]I find that the most interesting of these sculptures and inscriptions has been published (from the drawings of Mr. Wilkinson) by the Royal Society of Literature, in their collection of hieroglyphics.

advanced very slowly; but I did not yet feel my progress tedious. On the eastern side of the Nile, opposite the site of Memphis, there is but a narrow strip of cultivated land, bordering the river. Here is situated the village of Hhelwa'n (or Hhoolwa'n) حلوان ; once a considerable town, celebrated for a Mickya's, or Nileometer (of which there are now no remains), built in the first century of the Mohhammadan era. A little higher up, on the same side of the river, the sands of the desert reach to the water's edge, for a short space: then again we find a narrow cultivated tract along the bank. The two great pyramids of Dahshoo'r have a noble appearance, viewed from the river hereabouts; seeming scarcely inferior in magnitude to the first and second pyramids of El-Gee'zeh. The mountains on both sides of the river are here too low and too distant to give any degree of bold or picturesque character to the scenery.

Early in the morning of the 19th, we passed the village of *El-Meta'niyeh* المتانيه, to the west of which, upon the low Libyan ridge, are two ruined pyramids, appearing, from the river, like rude heaps of stone, or round hills. They are called "the Pyramids of El-Meta'niyeh." We had proceeded about two or three miles further when the wind subsided, and I availed myself of the opportunity to visit a neighbouring village, with the view of purchasing some additions to my live stock; but though I saw numbers of sheep and fowls I could not prevail upon the owners to sell me any, from their fear lest I should not pay them: though I offered the money beforehand, still they feared that I might afterwards make them return it; and I found the same difficulty almost everywhere during my voyage when I wanted to obtain provisions.—The people of this district are reputed to be of a very thievish disposition. During my second voyage up the Nile, while the boat was made fast to the bank, at night, a few miles higher up the river, a man descended into the water, and drew from under the awning in front of the cabin a large pair of saddle-bags, containing a segga'deh (or prayer-carpet) and some other things of less value, which he succeeded in carrying off without disturbing any one on board, though the bags were close to the place where my bed was laid.

During the afternoon of the 19th, a favourable wind enabled us to continue the voyage, and brought us to the large village of *Rick'ckah*, (or *Rig'gah*) رقة . For several miles before our arrival at this place we had a view of the Pyramid of Meydoo'm; a grand object; being little inferior in height to the two great pyramids of Dahshoo'r.

Early on the 20th I set off to visit the Pyramid of Meydoo'm. It is situated on the low Libyan ridge, about three miles and a half to the south-west of Rick'ckah. The large village of *Meydoo'm* ميدوم is rather more than a mile distant. This monument is called *El-Har'am el-Kedda'b*, or "the False Pyramid"; from its having the appearance of a pyramidal building raised on a round hill.[1] Such I thought it to be until I

---

[1]See no. 19 of the subjects for wood-cuts [fig. 57] (among the *mounted* drawings, next to plate 1 of this volume).

arrived quite near to it; when I perceived that the supposed hill was really a part of the structure; and that the materials thrown down from above had accumulated so high as nearly to cover one half of the pyramid. I found some labourers employed in pulling down and removing upon camels some of the stones from the lower part, to employ them in the construction of some new works ordered by the government. One benefit to be obtained from this work of destruction (independent of the use thus made of the displaced materials) is an insight into the manner in which the edifice was constructed. We find it to be similar in construction to the principal pyramid of Sack'cka'rah; but displaying much more care and skill. It appears that a slender pyramid (almost like an obelisk) was first raised. This was then cased, or covered, with a circumstructure of masonry, about sixteen feet in thickness, which rose to within about fifty feet of the top. This again was built around in the same manner; and so on till the work was completed: each circumstructure being about sixteen feet in thickness, and each rising to within about fifty feet of that next within it. The whole must have had the appearance of seven stages of masonry, in the form of truncated pyramids, one raised on the top of another. Of these seven compartments of the pyramid, three are at present nearly covered by the fragments which have been thrown down from above. That part of the structure which formed the fourth step (if I may use such a term) has been pulled down; so that what originally formed two compartments now appears only one; but the line which is seen half-way up this part, all around, shews the height of the fourth step: the remaining half formed the fifth step. The sixth is entire; but nearly the whole of the upper one has been thrown down. I have said that three compartments of the building are concealed by the rubbish, because at the two southern angles, where many of the stones have been pulled down, I observed this to be the case. The stones which compose the exterior of all the several circumstructures are united with such admirable precision, that if their sides were polished the joinings could scarcely be less apparent: and the same skill has been employed even when this careful work was to be concealed by a circumstructure. The stone of which the pyramid is composed is calcareous; of a whitish colour, and very compact. The width of the building, above the apparent hill, is 200 feet; and the height, about 160: the entire height must therefore be about 310 feet; and the base, about 400. These are rough calculations. Two attempts have been made to open it: high up in the northern side a large cavity has been made by some persons who supposed that what appears (without close examination) to be a hill was really so: a smaller aperture has been made in the eastern side. The sides of this pyramid are directed towards the four cardinal points; as is the case with the pyramids of Memphis, &c.

From Rick'ckah we crossed over to the opposite side of the river. Here is a small town called *Atfee'hh* اطفيح , the capital of a province, supposed to mark the site of *Aphroditopolis*, which was the capital of a nome.— The village of *Ez-Za'wiyeh* الزاويه , a few miles higher up the river, and on the opposite side, is supposed to occupy the site of *Iseum*; and to mark the southern limit of the Memphite nome. The next nome on the same side of the river was the Heracleopolite.—Proceeding a little higher, we find the eastern shore altogether desert; and indeed the whole of what constituted the Aphroditopolite nome is miserably destitute of cultivable land. For the space of about ten miles we do not pass a single village or any habitation, excepting a convent, on that side of the Nile.— In the evening we arrived opposite the large village of *Boo'sh* بوش .

Having set sail early on the 21st, we arrived in two hours at the small town of *Ben'ee Soowey'f* بنى سويف . This is the port of the province of *El-Feiyoo'm* الفيّوم, the ancient Arsinoite or Crocodilopolite nome. Here I found a busy scene in the market-place; but great scarcity of provisions: little meat; and no fruit. The situation of this town, as the emporium for the produce of the Feiyoo'm, is very advantageous. It doubtless occupies the site of *Cæne*, the port of *Heracleopolis Magna*. The latter was called in Coptic *Hnes*[1]: the modern village of *Ahna's*[†] اهناس marks its position.

---

[1]Quatremère. Mem. Geogr. et Hist. sur l'Egypte, t. 1, pp. 500 and 501.
[†]Ihnasya el-Medina.

Chapter XIX.
El-Feiyoo'm.

Journey from Ben'ee Soowey'f to the province of El-Feiyoo'm—Pyramid
of El-La'hoo'n—Inquiry respecting the ancient Lake of Mœris—Pyramid
of Häwa'rah, and remarks on the Labyrinth—Medee'net El-Feiyoo'm—
Obelisk of Begee'g—Route to the great lake Bir'ket el-Ckurn—Voyage
on the Bir'ket el-Ckurn—Ckusr Cka'roo'n—Island El-Ckurn—Route
from the lake to Beyah'moo—Return to the Nile.

I visited the Feiyoo'm in the following year (1827) in company with Mr.
Hay.

Having hired two camels for our luggage, and four donkeys for riding,
we commenced our journey from Ben'ee Soowey'f at half past five in the
evening of the 26th of June. The fields had been sown, and the crops
gathered in; and the ground was now in most parts overspread with the
low, thorny, green shrub called *'a'ckoo'l*, which is eaten by the camels.
The route which we pursued was very winding: not along any regular
road; but in parts over ploughed fields, without any beaten track. For a
little way we proceeded along the dry bed of a small canal; where
numbers of rats crossed from side to side, out of one fissure of the
parched soil and into another, at almost every step. We passed by the
village called El-Ko'm el-Ahh'mar (or the Red Mound), and proceeded
to *Bilif'ya* بلفيا, a large village; behind which we pitched our tent a little
after sunset. The number of rats in the fields astonished us; and at night
some of these animals intruded into our tent. A well being near us, we
were also annoyed by frogs; and a large scorpion payed us a visit. We
had chosen a bad spot for our tent.

27th. Bilif'ya has a respectable mosque, and a good market. Here, and
at every village in our route, at this season, peasants were employed in
cutting the straw of the lately reaped wheat, with the machine called
no'rag.[1] Our course this day was circuitous, as before; and the parched
and cracked ground which we had to traverse was very rugged, and
fatiguing to our animals. The opening in the low mountains which forms
the entrance to the Feiyoo'm is visible from Ben'ee Soowey'f: after
passing Bilif'ya we plainly discerned the brick pyramid of El-La'hoo'n, a
dark mass, on the right side of this opening. Proceeding by a village
called Bah'a, and another called El-Hha'gir, we soon after crossed an
isolated desert tract, very little elevated above the surrounding cultivable
soil, but sufficiently so to be above the reach of the fertilizing

---

[1]Described in the 4th chapter of the first volume of this work [chapter four].

inundation. This tract commands an extensive view, in which the pyramid of El-La'hoo'n, appearing like a mound of earth, is a prominent object. To the right of this monument are seen the mounds and village of *El-La'hoo'n* اللاهون; and to the left, an extensive grove of palm trees, surrounding the village of *Häwa'rat El-La'hoo'n* هوارة اللاهون. Another forest of palm trees, further to the left, nearly conceals from our view the pyramid of Häwa'rah; so called from a second village of that name. Continuing our route, we crossed the dry bed of a part of the great canal called *Bahhr Yoo'soof*, and pitched our tent in the afternoon by a new bridge erected, at Häwa'rat El-La'hoo'n, over the branch of the Bahhr Yoo'soof which turns into the Feiyoo'm. The water is retained in this branch throughout the whole year; being necessary for the supply of the inhabitants of the Feiyoo'm, and for the purposes of agriculture. At, or near, the village just mentioned was situated the town of Ptolemais, the port of the Arsiniote nome.

28th. From the bridge by which we had pitched our tent, we rode, in three quarters of an hour, to the Pyramid of El-La'hoo'n.[†] There is an old dike extending from the village of El-La'hoo'n across the cultivated land, towards the slope of the mountain ridge: it is faced with brick on the eastern side, and has been repaired with stone. Our route to the pyramid lay partly along this dike. The pyramid is situated on an irregular, rising ground, near the mountains. It is much ruïned. Its present height is about 70 feet; and its base, about 200. It is constructed of unburnt bricks; strengthened with a few masses of calcareous stone at the lower part. The bricks are about 18 inches long, 9 inches wide, and 5 inches thick. The structure stands upon a hill of rock, which is nearly covered with the rubbish that has fallen, or been thrown down, from the summit and sides of the pyramid; the rock itself only appearing at the angles. The ascent to the summit of the pyramid is not difficult: we commence on the southern side, and then come round to the western. From the top we have a very extensive view towards the Nile; and on the other side we overlook the valley by which we enter the Feiyoo'm. The cultivated land along the middle of this valley is very narrow; and the Bahhr Yoo'soof, to which it owes its fertility, runs through the midst of it. Its verdure has a particularly pleasing appearance, contrasted with the glaring tracts of desert which hem it in on either side. On the south and east of the pyramid are traces of a square enclosure which surrounded it, and other marks which seem to be the vestiges of tombs: there are also, in several places, fragments of pottery and other rubbish. At the distance of about a quarter of an hour's walk from the pyramid, bearing N. 4° W. by compass, is a small sepulchral grotto, excavated in a mass of rock. In this is a pit, which, at the depth of about fifteen feet, we found closed by rubbish and sand.

From the pyramid we turned down towards the cultivated tract in the midst of the valley; passed opposite the village of Dimishckee'n, and

---

[†]The pyramid of the Twelth Dynasty king Senwosret II.

proceeded along the side of the canal (the Bahhr Yoo'soof), towards the
north-west. The thermometer this day rose to 112° in the shade; but I did
not feel the heat oppressive. We halted for the night in a palm-grove
before *Häwa'rat el-Ckusr* هوارة القصر , which is a large village, with two
mosques, and several gardens around it. The place where we pitched our
tent was the bed of a deep and very wide channel for water (but at that
season perfectly dry in almost every part) branching off, to the north,
from the canal which runs through the valley. A long, old bridge, raised
on an embankment which extends across the entrance, admits a flow, or
fall, of water into this deep glen from the higher canal at the season when
the latter is very full. The view of this large, lofty, old bridge, with the
numerous palm trees in the hollow, around our tent, was highly
picturesque. The deep and wide canal here described is doubtless a part
of the ancient channel through which the water of the Nile flowed into
the great lake now called Bir'ket el-Ckurn.

It is impossible to reconcile the various statements of ancient authors
respecting the position and extent of the *Lake of Mœris*. From the
descriptions of some we are led to regard a portion of the Bahhr
Yoo'soof, and the great canal above-mentioned, as the remains of this
Lake; whereas the descriptions given by others seem plainly to apply
either to the Bir'ket el-Ckurn alone, or to that together with the channel
by which it is, or was, supplied. An oblong lake, or wide canal (which
may now form a portion of the Bahhr Yoo'soof), lying nearly in a
direction north and south, before the valley which is the entrance to the
Feiyoo'm, together with the channel by which the water of the Nile
flowed thence to the Bir'ket el-Ckurn, may have been a work of art,
executed by order of Mœris, and therefore properly called the Lake of
Mœris. This opinion is consistent with the description of Herodotus[1];
whose testimony, being most ancient, is most valuable. Persons in later
times were perhaps led to consider the *natural* lake, Bir'ket el-Ckurn, as
the Lake of Mœris from finding the *artificial* channel very much
contracted in width, and nearly filled up by the sediment of its turbid
waters; so as no longer to appear worthy the appellation of a *lake*. Thus
Strabo clearly describes the modern Bir'ket el-Ckurn as the Lake of
Mœris. Pliny speaks of the Lake of Mœris as if it had, in his time, almost
disappeared: for he mentions two pyramids as situated "where *was* the
Lake of Mœris, that is, the *great canal*"—"ubi fuit Mœridis lacus, hoc
est, fossa grandis"—(Nat. Hist. lib. xxxvi, c. 12): again he says—
"between the Arsinoite and Memphite nomes *was* the lake," &c., "called
that of Mœris"—"inter Arsinoiten autem ac Memphitem lacus fuit," &c.,
"Mœridis appellatus"—(lib. v, c. 9): he states it, however to have been 72
miles from Memphis; which must be an error. Herodotus says that this
artificial lake received, by means of a canal,[2] the water of the Nile, which

---

[1]Lib. ii, capp. 149 and 150.
[2]Diodorus, who seems to have copied Herodotus in his description of the Lake
of Mœris, states that the canal which communicated between the Nile and this

flowed into it during six months of the year, and during the other six months flowed back. The water of the Nile might have continued flowing into the lake during the period of the increase of the river; and would have flowed back during the *decrease* of the Nile; but thus it would have been only *three* months flowing in, and *nine* months flowing back. In the case of a *superabundant* inundation, the artificial lake of Mœris served for the purpose of conveying away the superfluous waters into the great *natural* lake (Bir'ket el-Ckurn): in the event of an *insufficient* inundation, its entrance and its outlet being both closed when the Nile was at its greatest height, it was made to retain a vast quantity of water, which was conveyed throughout a large extent of country by numerous small canals, from which a sufficient supply for the purpose of irrigating the fields was raised by means of machines, as in the present day. Herodotus states the circumference of this lake or canal to have been 3,600 stadia; which, he adds,—"is equal to the whole extent of the maritime coast of Egypt": this measure was equivalent to 195 geographical miles; for Herodotus always employed the *smaller* stadia (of three geographical seconds and a quarter) in stating distances in Egypt. Pliny attributes a still greater extent to this artificial lake; asserting its circumference to have been "250 miles; or, according to Mutius, 450." (Lib. v, c. 9). Each of these statements appears to be exaggerated. It is probable, however, that the artificial lake or great canal (fossa grandis) of Mœris extended along the whole length of the Heracleotic nome, and perhaps considerably further southward, and that a large branch of it, "forming an angle to the westward" (as Herodotus says), entered the Arsinoite nome, and communicated with the *natural* lake which in later times received the appellation of the Lake of Mœris, which is now called Bir'ket el-Ckurn: it is probable, also, that the western branch divided into two; for there are still two very wide and deep channels, of which the one terminates in the middle of the southern side of the Bir'ket el-Ckurn, and the other at the eastern point of that lake. Herodotus asserts that the greatest depth of the artificial lake was fifty fathoms; and that there were within it two pyramids; each rising fifty fathoms above the surface of the water, and having as much of their height concealed below; and each surmounted by a statue, seated on a throne.

On the 29th we struck our tent, and in less than half an hour arrived at the Pyramid of Häwa'rah. The first part of our route lay along the bed of the deep channel before-mentioned: we then ascended a slightly rising ground, and leaped across a small canal which runs by the pyramid. This monument[1] is constructed of unburnt bricks of the same kind and size as those of the pyramid of El-La'hoo'n. A considerable quantity of the materials having fallen from the summit and sides, the base is not seen.

---

lake was 80 stadia in length: that is, 8 geographical miles, if the greater stadia be meant; or 4_ if the smaller; both of which measures agree with the distance of the Bahhr Yoo'soof from the Nile at different points.

[1]See plate 2 [missing].

The *apparent* base I measured, and found it to be about 250 feet. The height seemed to be scarcely more than half its base. On the north side an attempt has lately been made by a Frenchman (M. Rifaud), to open it; and a vast quantity of materials removed. With some of the bricks thus displaced the labourers built a number of huts, which now remain (though roofless), and a low wall surrounding them, close to the north side of the pyramid. A small building has also been raised on the *top* of the pyramid; but has fallen to ruin. On the south of the pyramid are some remains of an extensive ancient building, consisting of broken columns, some of which are of granite, and other masses of stone which appear to have been architraves. Adjacent to this site, on the opposite side of the small canal before-mentioned, are the ruins of a small town; the buildings, chiefly of unburnt brick. On the north of the pyramid we observe traces of many structures like the oblong tombs adjacent to the pyramids of El-Geezeh; and the ground is on all sides strewed with broken pottery and other rubbish. [1] On the north-east is seen the mouth of a pit, now filled with rubbish, into which, we were told, persons used to descend with a light, and drink of a spring which is found at a certain depth, and supposed to possess extraordinary healing properties.

The Pyramid of Häwa'rah and the adjacent remains are considered, by some modern travellers, as the relics of the famous Labyrinth; and reasons which scarcely admit of dispute confirm this opinion.—1st. Herodotus says that the Labyrinth was a little above the Lake of Mœris, and not far from Crocodilopolis (or Arsinoë); and that there was at the extreme angle of the building, a pyramid, which measured 40 fathoms. [2] We are not told whether the 40 fathoms was the measure of the height, or of the base: it is considerably more than the *present* height of the pyramid of Häwa'rah; but perhaps not more than the *original* height; and it is less than the *apparent* base. Herodotus adds (in the same place, (lib. ii, c. 148) that the pyramid of the Labyrinth was sculptured with large figures of animals: we must therefore suppose that its *exterior* was of *stone*; but it does not follow that the whole structure was of stone. That there were extensive buildings adjacent to the pyramid of Häwa'rah is evident; and it is said that there are *subterranean* chambers.—2ndly. Strabo describes the Labyrinth as situated near the canal which communicated with the Lake of Mœris (which appellation, as I have already mentioned, he gives to the Bir'ket el-Ckurn, instead of to the canal itself); and adds that Arsinoë, which was formerly called Crocodilopolis, was a hundred stadia distant from it, by water; that is, nearly five geographical miles and a half, supposing the small stadia to be here meant, as in the case where the same author states the distance between Syene and Philæ to be 100 stadia. This is just about the distance,

---

[1] Upon the rocky flat on the north and east I found a vast number of small marine shells.

[2] Strabo says that the base was four plethra (or about 400 feet) and the height the same.

by the course of the Bahhr Yoo'soof, between Häwa'rah and the remains of Arsinoë.—3rdly. Pliny (lib. v, c. 9) speaks of the Labyrinth as being between Memphis and the Arsinoite nome, in Libya (or within the confines of the Libyan desert), near the Lake of Mœris (or great canal). In another place (lib. xxxvi, c. 13) he says that it was in the Heracleopolite nome. The site of the pyramid of Häwa'rah seems rather to have appertained to the Arsinoite than the Heracleopolite nome: but perhaps the valley which connects the Feiyoo'm with the rest of Egypt belonged, at one period, to the Arsinoite nome, and at another, to the Heracleopolite.

The history of the Labyrinth is involved in the greatest uncertainty. Herodotus says that it was founded by the twelve kings, who, reigning conjointly, succeeded Sethon. Diodorus seems to have been misled by three different traditions, which evidently related to one and the same building; and to have concluded that there were *three* labyrinths in Egypt: one constructed by Menes, or Menas (lib. i, c. 89); another, by Mendes, or Marrus (lib. i, c. 61); another, by the twelve kings (lib. i, c. 66). Strabo says that the Labyrinth was constructed by a king named Imandes; and that the pyramid was his tomb. By Manetho (or by his copyists Africanus and Eusebius) it is attributed to Lachares, or Labaris.—Herodotus speaks of the Labyrinth as a structure more wonderful even that the Pyramids. It comprised, he says, 1500 chambers above ground, and the same number below. A wall surrounded the whole. The upper portion contained twelve covered courts; six on the north, and six on the south. The subterranean apartments (which no persons but those who had the care of the place were permitted to see) were said to be appropriated to the interment of the sacred crocodiles, which were particular objects of worship in the Arsiniote nome, formerly called, on that account, the Crocodilopolite nome: and the twelve royal founders were reputed to be buried there. The walls and roofs of the upper apartments were of stone, and adorned with a variety of sculptures; and each court was surrounded by columns of polished white stone. This description of an eye-witness is highly interesting.— Strabo describes the same building as a palace belonging to the governors of the several nomes of Egypt; and therefore containing 27 halls; as there were 27 nomes. In these, he says, the governors occasionally assembled; and each held a court in the hall appropriated to him. A repast was served to the priests and priestesses, and sacrifices were also performed there on those occasions.—Pliny likewise describes the Labyrinth as containing halls called after the names of the several nomes; but states the number to have been sixteen. He adds that the edifice also contained temples of all the gods of Egypt (therefore, when persons from various parts of Egypt collected there, each would find a sanctuary dedicated to the god who was the particular or principal object of worship in his native province). Throughout the greater part of the building the visiter wandered in darkness. The chambers had arched roofs (or were covered with stones cut into an arched form, like some chambers in the great edifice at Abydos[1]). The entrance, according to the same writer, was of Parian marble: the columns in other parts were of syenite; and the edifice was constructed of such large stones that time and the efforts of the Heracleopolites had not prevailed to overthrow it; though that people had much damaged the building; regarding it with dislike. (Nat. Hist. lib. xxxvi, c. 13). It was probably in consequence of their being great venerators of the ichneumon, which was esteemed the chief enemy of the crocodile, that the Heracleopolites abhorred a building where crocodiles were held particularly sacred, and honoured with costly burial.

It is very remarkable that so vast and sumptuous an edifice as the Labyrinth should have been so utterly destroyed, with the exception of its pyramid, that only a few broken columns and architraves (not a single block with hieroglyphics or other sculptures that I could find) remain upon the spot where it is presumed to have been situated. The materials which have been carried away have doubtless been employed in the construction of bridges, dikes, &c., in the vicinity. As to its destination, or use, the account of Strabo seems the most probable. Pliny says that many believed it to be dedicated to the sun; of which, it may here be remarked, the crocodile was a type.

In the evening of the 29th we returned to Häwa'rah. The height of the thermometer in the afternoon of this day, in the shade, was 110°.—On the 30th we proceeded along the left bank of the great dry channel for nearly half an hour: then crossed it. As far as the village of Ckohha'feh our route lay near to the desert. We then forded the Bahhr Yoo'soof, which flows by that village, and made a direct course over the cultivated fields to the *Medee'neh*, or *Medee'net El-Feiyoo'm* مدينة الفيّوم (the City of the Feiyoo'm). Hitherto our expectations of the boasted fertility of the Feiyoo'm had not been fulfilled: but it was the season when the country was most destitute of water, and therefore for the most part destitute of verdure. This morning's journey occupied about two hours. We pitched our tent at a short distance from the town; on the southern side.—Thermometer this day 100°.

Medee'net El-Feiyoo'm is believed, by the Egyptians, to have been founded by Yoo'soof the Just (the patriarch Joseph, the son of Jacob). Viewed from a distance it has a respectable and pretty aspect; but on a near approach the traveller is disappointed. The Bahhr Yoo'soof runs through the midst of it; and contains an ample supply of water for the use of its inhabitants throughout the whole year. On entering the town we found a thronging population, and long soo'cks (or streets of shops), which were covered over; some, with matting, and others, with a more substantial kind of roof: but the shops were, mostly, mean and ill stocked. The town altogether is inferior to most of the chief towns of

---

[1]Strabo says that the roof of each apartment was a single stone. Had it not been for this statement, which is also made by Diodorus, we might have supposed that they were regularly arched roofs, on the masonic principle, like those of the age of Psammetichus 2nd, in a tomb near Sack'cka'rah, which I have described.

provinces in the valley of the Nile. In the construction of its mosques and some of its private houses, materials of the ancient city of Arsinoë have been employed: the remains of that city being contiguous to the modern town. Rose-water is a celebrated produce of the Feiyoo'm: we had already seen large fields of rose-plants. A little wine is also made there. The markets of the Medee'neh are famous for fish: the great lake, Bir'ket el-Ckurn, the water of which is brackish, containing many kinds of fish that are not found in the Nile; and some are much esteemed. They are likewise well supplied with fruit; particularly with very delicious grapes; and prickly-pears; both of which were plentiful at the period of our visit. The north-western portion of the Feiyoo'm, between the Medee'neh and the great lake, is more luxuriantly fertile than any other part of Egypt. Crocodiles are no longer found in this province, where, in ancient times, they were so much favoured. According to Strabo (p. 811) there was a lake here expressly allotted to these animals, which were regularly fed with bread, flesh, wine, and various dainties.

The dialect of the inhabitants of the Feiyoo'm is in some respects much like that of the lower orders in Musr (or Cairo). They suppress the sound of ق in the same manner; or rather are unable to pronounce that letter. Thus, for Ckusr Cka'roo'n, they say 'Usr 'A'roo'n. They have also other peculiarities in consequence of their intercourse with the western Bed'awees; great numbers of whom pasture their camels and sheep in this province.

Mounds of rubbish, about two miles in extent from north to south, and a mile and a half from east to west, occupy the site of Crocodilopolis, or Arsinoë, on the north of the modern town of the Feiyoo'm. The name of Crocodilopolis was changed to Arsinoë by Ptolemy Philadelphus, in honour of his sister and wife. The relics of the old city consist of nothing more than fragments of granite and other stone, broken pottery and glass, burnt and unburnt bricks, and other kinds of rubbish.

July 2nd. In the afternoon we rode to the village of *Begee'g*, or Bejee'j, بجيج , nearly two miles to the south-west of the Medee'neh. On our way thither we passed by some extensive excavations, which, during the season of the inundation, are filled with water. These probably united in ancient times with the great channel before described, and formed a part of one of the branches by which the water of the Nile entered the modern Bir'ket el-Ckurn. They were on the left of our route. The village of Begee'g is situated on high mounds; and has a more naked appearance than most Egyptian villages, from the want of a few palm-trees to encircle it. There is a small group of palms at a short distance, but there are none in the immediate vicinity of the village. Rather less than a mile from this place (bearing W. 1½° N. by compass) is an ancient obelisk, lying on the ground, and broken into two pieces.†We rode on before sunset to view this monument.

---

†The village is now called Abgig. The monument that Lane calls an "obelisk" is a stela. It has been removed to Medinet al-Fayyum.

On the 3rd, after having passed the night in our tent near the village of Begee'g, we visited the obelisk a second time. It lies in the flat, cultivated tract, without any mound or ancient remains in its vicinity to mark the site of a town or temple; but it is probable that the soil, gradually increasing by the successive inundations, has buried some relics of an adjacent edifice. Its form is singular, as my view of it will shew.[1] It is of a dark, red granite; such as is found in the neighbourhood of Aswa'n (the ancient Syene), whence it was probably brought. The length of the upper fragment is 19 feet 7 inches: that of the lower, 22 feet. The width of the front (the upper surface), at the top, is 4 feet 7 inches: at the bottom of the upper fragment, 5 feet 7. The width of the sides, just below the curve at the top, is 2 feet 10; and at the bottom of the upper fragment, 3 feet 5. The upper part of the front is divided into five compartments; one below another. In each of these compartments are sculptured (in intaglio) six figures: the two central figures (which are back to back) each represent the king by whom the obelisk was erected—Osirtesen 1st[†] —adoring, or presenting offerings to, two divinities. The hieroglyphic name of this king (no. 33 in my list) is cut over each of the figures which represent him; and is the same that is found on the obelisk of Heliopolis; in my description of which I have mentioned the king to which this name belongs as the most ancient known Pharaoh of whom any sculptured monuments now remain. This fact gives a high degree of interest to the obelisks of the Feiyoo'm and Heliopolis; and it is remarkable that their sculptures are of the most perfect kind. The lower part of the upper fragment of the obelisk of Begee'g is occupied by a hieroglyphical inscription, consisting of fourteen perpendicular columns; but this is so much injured that little of it can be deciphered. On each side of the upper fragment is an inscription of the same kind as those found on most other obelisks; containing the same name that is sculptured upon the front. The inscription of one side is seen in the view which I have given: that of the other side is exactly similar, with the exception of a few characters immediately following the name. The lower surface appears to be quite plain, as far as we can judge from a small excavation made beneath it. The lower fragment is very rough; and exhibits no traces of sculpture.

On the 4th we proceeded towards the great lake, Bir'ket el-Ckurn. Passing by several encampments of Bed'awees, and by the villages of Dis'yeh and El-Mena'shee, we arrived at *Gar'adoo* جردو . This is a large and respectable village, containing several well built houses, and surrounded by gardens and extensive palm-groves. It is about four geographical miles from Begee'g. We here found the country thickly covered with palm trees, which bounded the prospect in every direction; and we passed by several gardens enclosed by fences of palm-branches. In one hour after having left Gar'adoo we arrived at *El-'Agamee'n*, or *El-'Agamee'yee'n* العجميين , another large village. A market was being

---

[1]See plate 3 [fig. 58].
[†]Senwosret I.

held there at the time we passed through it; and the abundance of excellent grapes, and prickly pears, were exposed for sale. As we advanced from this place to the westward we found the country less fertile; but the palm-trees still very numerous. The land was evidently descending as we proceeded, and slightly undulating; unlike the rest of Egypt, which, as far as the confines of the desert, may almost be said to be as flat as an expanse of water. In another hour we pitched our tent between the villages of *Abshe'y*, or *Absha'y* ابشاى, and *Ab'oo Gen'shoo* ابو جنشو; which are adjacent to each other. A man of the former village was owner of a fishing-boat on the lake. We hired his boat, and engaged him with his men to accompany us for three or four days.

5th. This being the *'Eed el-Kebee'r*, or Great Festival of the Moos'lims,[1] we, for the sake of our attendants, sacrificed a sheep. A sheykh of a branch of the great Bed'awee tribe of O'la'd 'Al'ee, who had come to join with the inhabitants of Abshe'y and others of the neighbourhood in the morning-prayers appointed for that day, afterwards payed us a visit in our tent, to offer us the congratulations of the 'Eed; not knowing that we were Europeans. He took coffee; but did not smoke; and I was rather surprised to observe that he took the cup of coffee in his left hand; though very correct, and respectful to us, in his general behaviour. I afterwards learned that he had lost his right hand: the ample folds of a fine hhera'm and a boor'noos[2] preventing my discovering this. During the struggle between the present Ba'sha of Egypt and the Memloo'k Beys, this sheykh had joined, on one occasion, a party of Memloo'ks; but in a battle which ensued, finding that the other party had the advantage, he employed his men in collecting together, from among his allies, all the horses that had lost their masters, and with these and much other booty he made his retreat. In this affair, though he thus enriched himself, he lost his right arm. During his visit to us he observed a box, belonging to me, bound with iron; and asked me how I could think of carrying about with me such a chest, the strength of which plainly shewed that it contained money. "If any of our people" said he "were to see you with such a box among your luggage they would surely take it from you." I opened the suspicious-looking box, and shewed him that it only contained a medicine-chest, and other things which would be of no value to a Bed'awee. "Al'la'h! Al'la'h!" he exclaimed—"That reminds me of a circumstance that happened to me a little while ago. I was riding with two or three of my people in this province, and met a Turkish soldier travelling with a strong box like that.

---

[1]The day when the pilgrims slay their victims in the valley of Min'a (commonly called Moon'a), on their return from Mount 'Arafa't to Mek'keh. The sacrifice on that day is a *general* custom of the Moos'lims; and the rich kill one or more victims (sheep, goats, kine, or camels) to distribute the meat among the poor; as well as one for their own families.

[2]The hhera'm is a kind of woollen sheet, which is thrown about the body; and the boor'noos is a hooded cloak, generally of fine, white, woollen stuff.

Of course we took it from him; and bade him a safe journey. As we had not the key, I broke in the lid of the box with my battle-axe; and, in doing this, unfortunately smashed some of its contents, which were bottles full of pickles! There was some gunpowder among them; and this would have been very acceptable to me; but it was all wetted and spoiled by the cursed pickles."—After relating some other adventures of a similar kind our visiter took his leave.

As the water of the Bir'ket el-Ckurn is brackish, and we proposed spending two or three days upon it and on its desert shores, we took with us a ckir'beh (or goat's skin) of fresh water for our own use. The fishermen drink the water of the lake. At noon we left Abshe'y; and in a few minutes came in sight of the lake, which appeared like a broad river, of a deep blue colour, bounded by sandy mountains on the opposite side. The country declined very sensibly towards the margin of the lake, and was no longer covered with palm-trees. In one hour and twenty minutes we descended into the dry bed of a very broad and deep channel, called *El-Wa'dee* (or the valley), which extends along the south-west side of the Feiyoo'm, and is about fifteen geographical miles in length. It terminates in the centre of the southern side of the lake. Without doubt it is an ancient work; and probably was a branch of the artificial canal which was called, in the time of Herodotus, the Lake of Mœris. Its south-eastern extremity is now closed by a dike, to prevent its receiving the waters necessary for the irrigation of the adjacent lands; but it serves as a drain to carry of[f] superfluous water; particularly in the event of an excessive inundation. That part of the channel which we traversed was cultivated; chiefly abounding with melons, gourds, and cucumbers. For a little distance our route lay along its bed. After emerging from it we soon arrived at the shore of the lake. The ground over which we passed was thickly overspread with a desert shrub, rising to the height of about six feet. The station of our fishermen (the point of the shore where we first arrived) was opposite the island called *El-Ckurn* القرن , from which the lake takes its name of Bir'ket el-Ckurn.[1] "Ckurn" is a word having many significations; the most common of which is "a horn": but, applied to this island, it signifies "a small, isolated mountain," or "a mountain-top," or "a prominence of a mountain": the island in question being a flat-topped, rocky eminence, rising out of the midst of the bosom of the lake. There are some other islands in the lake; but small and low, and sometimes covered with water, when, during an excessive inundation, the lake receives an unusual supply from the Nile: whereas the Ckurn rises about 200 feet above the surface of the water. The name of this island, in the vulgar dialect of the Feiyoo'm, is pronounced El-'Urn; and that of the lake, Bir'ket el-'Urn; from the inability of the people of that province to pronounce the letter ق . The name of the lake has been improperly written by European travellers "Birket el-Keroun."—Strabo, who considered this as the Lake of Mœris, has truly described it as

[1]See plate 4 [fig. 59].

resembling a *sea* in magnitude and colour and in the nature of its shores. Its length is more than twenty geographical miles; and its greatest breadth, between four and five miles.—We pitched our tent for the night by a little shed, which the fishermen had erected. Their great, clumsy boat lay near. On the opposite shore, to the right of the island, we observed a ruined town, called Deme'y; and looking towards the western extremity of the lake we could just discern the ancient temple called Ckusr Cka'roo'n, the principal monument that remained to attract our curiosity in the Feiyoo'm.—The greatest height of the thermometer this day, in the shade, was 107°.

On the 6th, a strong breeze prevented our commencing the voyage as early as we wished. About four hours after sunset the wind somewhat abated, and we were carried on board. We left our camels and asses, with their conductors, to remain this and the following day at Abshe'y: on the third day they were to await our return at the place of embarcation. We had a voyage of about nine geographical miles to make, if by a straight course, to that part of the shore which is nearest to the Ckusr Cka'roo'n. The bulky boat was of a most rude construction: its short and rough planks were joined together partly by nails and partly by ropes. It was uncovered, with the exception of a quarter-deck, upon which we seated ourselves; and without a sail; having two enormous and shapeless oars, formed of rough pieces of timber; each worked by four or five men, and sometimes by six. Some of these fishermen were horribly picturesque barbarians; quite unlike the Egyptians in general: none of them had any clothing but a few coarse rags to cover their dark and brawny bodies. The owner of the boat was a different kind of person; of respectable appearance, but ignorant, impudent, and troublesome. Suspecting my fellow-traveller and myself to be magicians, he entreated me to write a charm for him, to protect him from the rapacity of the Turkish governor of his province.—By the rude boat which I have described, the scarcely human aspect of some of the crew, the peculiar, melancholy chants with which they accompanied each stroke of the oar, the solitude of the lake, and the barren and desolate character of the shores, we were forcibly reminded (as was Belzoni, during his voyage on this lake) of the descriptions of the boat of the dead, the ferryman Charon, the Styx, and the infernal regions; fables which, however, originated not here, but from the ceremonies of transporting the dead over the Lake Acherusia (which extended along the western side of Memphis) to the catacombs in the neighbouring rocky desert; as we are informed by Diodorus Siculus. The resemblance of the modern name of Bir'ket el-Ckurn and Ckusr Cka'roo'n to Acheron and Charon is singular; but this would be a poor reason upon which to found an idea opposed to the statement of Diodorus; particularly as we do not find any extensive burial-place on the northern side of the Lake of the Feiyoo'm.—As soon as we had embarked the boat was pushed and dragged along for about a quarter of an hour; the water being very shallow; and encumbered with rotten bushes; the withered branches rising two or three feet above its surface.

Having got clear of these bushes, we proceeded tolerably well. The water was now of a light greenish colour; and, the wind being fresh, the boat rolled about as if at sea. There was nothing of beauty in the surrounding scenery: low, yellow mountains on the northern side, with bushes stretching along the shore, bound the prospect in that direction; and on the southern side is a barren expanse of sand and rock. We stopped above an hour on the northern side of the lake while three of the men quitted the boat to cast their nets. In the afternoon we landed a few miles from the western extremity of the lake, and walked to the Ckusr Cka'roo'n.

This ancient edifice is about two miles distant from the shore of the lake, and is situated in a wide, desert plain. The beach where we landed was composed in a great measure of very small spiral shells. About midway towards the Ckusr we passed over a large space in which we found a vast number of stumps and branches of vines, withered and rotten. At one period there were doubtless villages and corn-fields, as well as vineyards, in this now desert and desolate tract[1]; for, on scraping up a little sand and some pebbles, we found, in several parts, a dark, rich soil, probably of little depth, but sufficient for cultivation: it must have been deposited by the waters of the lake when raised by the influx of the muddy water of the Nile during the annual inundation. The ground rises, almost imperceptibly, toward the Ckusr. I made particular inquiry, not only of the fishermen of the lake but also of other inhabitants of the Feiyoo'm, respecting the name of this building; and was invariably told that it was *Ckusr Cka'roo'n* قصر قارون (or, as my informants generally pronounced it, *'Usr 'A'roo'n*), which signifies "the Palace of Cka'roo'n." I met with no one who pronounced the latter word as if it were written *Kha'roo'n* خارون ; which would be the Arabic orthography of the Charon of the Greeks; nor could I learn from any person in the province that any fable similar to that of the ferryman of the Styx was related of him after whom this building is called. In the Ckoor-a'n (chap. 28) the Korah of the Bible (whose story is given in the 16th chapter of Numbers) is called Cka'roo'n. It is a gross mistake of travellers to write the name of the monument here spoken of "Kusr el-Keroun." The place where the Ckusr is situated is called *Bel'ed Cka'roo'n* (or the Town of Cka'roo'n); for there are many remains which indicate the former existence of a town on that spot.—The Ckusr Cka'roo'n has the general characteristics of the ancient Egyptian temples[2]; but was evidently constructed during the period when Egypt was subject to the Romans.[†] It is a plain building, of calcareous stone; and in an unfinished state; having no sculpture, excepting the winged globed [sic] over the entrance. It had a cornice of the usual Egyptian form round the top; now almost entirely thrown down. The front of the building is towards the east-south-east. Before

---

[1] There is not now any village within about ten or twelve miles of this spot.
[2] See plate 5 [fig. 60].
[†] It is a late Ptolemaic temple.

the entrance are remains of a portico; the front of which was formed by
four columns; behind these were four more; and again four other
columns, or rather half-columns, were built against the front-wall of the
temple. The greater portion of one of the half-columns yet remains, on
the right of the entrance. The main body of the building is 96 feet long,
and 65 feet wide. It appears to have been well and strongly built; but the
foundation has sunk towards the back part; causing a considerable
portion of the building to incline a little backwards; and it has been more
injured by the hand of man than by accident or time. At the entrance we
observed the names of Pococke and Paul Lucas: the former regarded this
building as the temple or tomb of the Labyrinth: the latter, still more
erroneously, pronounced it to be the Labyrinth itself; and has given a
very exaggerated description of it. The interior is extremely intricate, and
difficult to describe. Four principal chambers occupy nearly the whole
length of the building; one behind another; receiving light only through
the first door. Over the entrance of each is the winged globe. They are all
much encumbered with sand and rubbish; the walls are quite plain. The
first of these chambers has a small apartment on either side; each leading
to stairs, ascending to the top. The rubbish in the first chamber probably
conceals the doors leading to these side-apartments; which we entered by
forced apertures. In the second of the four principal chambers there is
nothing to notice. The third has a side-chamber, on the left side. The
fourth chamber, which was the sanctuary, has a small niche on either
side; and three deep niches at the end; above which is a forced aperture,
leading into a small cell, which appears to have had only a secret
entrance. To the right and left of the fourth chamber above-mentioned is
a narrow passage, entered from the *third* chamber. Each of these passages
has three small cells on the side next the exterior of the temple.—These
are all the lower apartments of the building.—At the top is a large, open
space, commencing from the front-wall of the building; and on the right
and left of this, and at the end, are many small chambers. The central
chamber of those at the end is the only one that has any sculptures. At
the end of it is a niche; on each side of which is a figure sculptured in low
relief, in the very worst Roman-Egyptian style. That on the right is a
simple human figure: the head had been broken out; and lay beneath: the
eye and eye-brow were formed of some other material, now removed;
probably of bronze. The figure on the left of the niche is that of the
crocodile-headed god, Sovk, or Savak,[1] who was the principal object of
worship in this province, the Crocodilopolite nome. Strabo says that the
sacred crocodile which was kept in a particular lake in this nome, and fed
with various dainties, was called Suchus (Σουχος).—In one of the small
upper apartments of the Ckusr Cka'roo'n, at the right corner of the end,
is a small, square aperture in the floor, have [sic] a ledge all round to
support a stone, which was removed when occasion required. Through
this I descended into a small cell; and thence, by a similar aperture, into

---

[1]This has been mistaken for Kneph, or Chnuphis.

another, which had, on one side, two deep recesses, or holes, one above the other. Beneath this, again, was another cell, or vault, nearly filled with sand and rubbish. It is impossible to give a clear description of the arrangement of the upper apartments of this temple; and it would be difficult to make a plan which would be sufficiently plain without the aid of several sections. Many of the apartments had secret entrances; and in most of these we found deep recesses, or niches, apparently for the concealment of wealth, or of sacred things.—About 1150 feet before the entrance of this building is a small temple, in a state of ruin; having a door at each end, in the direct line of approach to the great temple. It is about 30 feet square; and its sides are formed by twelve columns, connected by a wall. Near it, towards the west, is a small, ruined portal; and about 450 feet distant, towards the south-east, is a small Christian chapel, of a square form, resembling the tomb of a Sheykh; built of unburnt brick, upon a raised foundation of stone; and plastered, within and without, with a cement of great compactness, partly composed of sand. Behind the great temple, 800 feet distant, is a ruin of unburnt brick; and 200 feet from this, a ruined stone arch. Around the Ckusr and the other ruins are many remains of stone and brick; and the ground is strewed with broken pottery.

On the 7th we were occupied in examining the Ckusr, and making drawings, &c. In the morning we found the bushes on the bank of the lake very wet with dew. On the 8th we embarked again. Our ckir'beh was exhausted, and, the heat being sufficiently intense to cause constant thirst (the thermometer at 105° in the shade), we drank freely of the water of the lake, which was very brackish. We landed on the Island *El-Ckurn*. It is about a mile and a half in length, by a mile in breadth; and entirely rock; excepting that it has a scanty alluvial deposit on its sides, and a shallow stratum of soil mixed with pebbles upon its flat top. Detached masses of rock, piled, or, in appearance, thrown together (but evidently not by art), in a great measure compose its sides. We found upon it no ancient remains of any kind; no traces of habitations, nor of cultivation. From the summit of this table-island, about 200 feet above the surface of the lake, we could only perceive one fishing-boat besides our own.

From having drunk too copiously, early in the day, of the water of the lake, I became much distressed by thirst; and continued to take repeated draughts of the brackish water for the sake of temporary relief. On returning, late in the evening, to the place where we first embarked, we were much disappointed at finding that our camel-drivers had neglected to bring any fresh water with them. My thirst was now intolerable. The nearest well being two miles distant, we sent thither immediately; but, dark as it was, it required a full hour to go there and to return; and in the interval I was imprudent enough (as well as my fellow-traveller) to eat some unripe cucumbers, which we found growing near by. These and the brackish water which I had been drinking during the day soon after brought on a dysentery, which was followed by ophthalmia; and before I had quite recovered from the latter painful disease, dysentery returned with tenfold fury. I was ill four or five months; during nearly the whole period of my second voyage up the Nile; and my eyes have never quite regained their original strength; though my sight is uninjured.

On the 9th we returned to Abshe'y, and proceeded thence to *Aboo'kisë* ابو كسا , a rather large village, with pretty environs, nearly two miles from the former place. On the east side of this village is a large reservoir, or tank, lined with brick; at this season nearly dry. We found the desert shrub *'osh'ar* (the Dead-Sea apple) in many parts hereabouts. The next village in our route was *See'naroo* سينرو , about two miles distant. There are extensive gardens in its neighbourhood; but we could procure no fruit there, excepting the prickly-pear; of which there was abundance. Bread we found in very few villages. From See'naroo we proceeded to *Fedmee'n* فدمين , distant about a mile and a half, a large and picturesque village, encompassed by high mounds, which overlook the houses, and surrounded by numerous gardens, containing prickly-pears in abundance, and palm-trees; but little else. Here we pitched our tent, by the side of a canal, in the midst of a grove of palm-trees.

On the 10th, passing by two small villages (Es-Seylee'yeh and El-Kila'bee'yeh), we arrived at *Beyah'moo* بيهمو , a village about five miles from Fedmee'n, and three from the Medee'neh. Near to it, on the west, we crossed a large, deep channel; then dry; probably a part of an ancient branch of the artificial Lake of Mœris. On the same side of Beyah'moo, but immediately adjacent, is a large space strewed with small fragments of granite and other stone, and pottery; evidently the site of ancient buildings. On the north of the village are two ruined pyramids of stone; retaining little of their original bulk or form.[†] Two shapeless piles of masonry, each about thirty feet high, are almost the only remains of these monuments. Some of the stones which compose them are about twenty feet in length, two feet and a half thick, and about four feet broad. The space which the base of each pyramid occupied is shewn by many of the lower stones which remain in their original places to have been about 150 feet square.—About seven geographical miles to the north-east of Beyah'moo is the large village of *Ta'mee'yeh* طاميّه ; from which there is a route, much traversed, to the valley of the Nile, towards the north-east.

From Beyah'moo we proceeded southwards, by the site of Arsinoë, and arrived again at the Medee'neh; whence, after sunset, with the light of a full moon, we returned to Häwa'rat el-C. Starting again early on the 11th, in about six hours we arrived at Ben'ee Soowey'f.

I now continue the account of my voyage up the Nile.

[†]These are two pedestals that originally supported colossal statues of Amenemhet III.

Chapter XX.
From Ben'ee Soowey'f to El-Min'yeh.

Environs of Ben'ee Soowey'f, &c.—Medee'net Gahl—Semeloo't, and the ancient Cynopolis—Geb'el et-Teyr—Et-Tehh'neh (Acoris).

March 21st, 1826. The greater part of this day we spent at Ben'ee Soowey'f. By a valley opposite this place is a route leading to the two convents of St. Anthony and St. Paul (Ma'r Antoo'niyoo's and Ma'r Bo'loos), near the shore of the Red Sea. The ancient town of *Thimonepsi* was situated, according to the itinerary of Antoninus, 24 Roman miles south of Aphroditopolis: consequently opposite Ben'ee Soowey'f.

During the afternoon of the 21st, and the whole of the following day, we advanced very slowly by towing; the weather being perfectly calm.— We still find very little cultivable land on the eastern bank. Just above a village called Nez'let Ab'oo Noo'r, on that side, is a high ridge or point of the eastern chain reaching to the water's edge. Upon this promontory is the tomb of the sheykh Ab'oo Noo'r, after whom the above-mentioned village is named; a small, square building, crowned by a cupola. From this point upwards, the proximity of the eastern chain to the river, in many places, renders our prospect more varied and picturesque. On the 23rd, our progress became still slower; owing to a contrary wind; and for several days we were thus retarded: it was difficult to tow the boat, with both the wind and stream against us; but the crew exerted themselves to the utmost; and never grumbled at their hard work. The eastern hills, extending to the verge of the river, form a high, steep bank, for a short space, opposite the village of *Feshn* فشن, which occupies the ancient town of *Fenchi*. Hereabouts commenced the Oxyrynchite nome, on the western side of the Nile, and the Cynopolite nome on the eastern side. Upon a sand-bank opposite Feshn we saw a crocodile basking in the sun. Such a sight so low in the river is very unusual.

On the 24th I visited the ruins of an ancient town, now called *Medee'net Gahl* مدينة جهل, on the western bank, close to the river. These remains consist of high mounds of broken pottery and other rubbish; among which appear some of the walls of the ancient houses; the whole surrounded partly by ridges of rock, and partly by an enclosure of unburnt brick, about 15 or 16 feet thick, and, in some parts, between 40 and 50 feet high. To the north-east of this is another enclosure, formed by a wall of crude brick. It surrounds an uneven, rocky space, beneath which are some excavated chambers, seen by Hamilton, but now entirely closed up with rubbish. Between this spot and the river (to the north of the town-wall) is the general burial-place of the town. Here I saw four small sarcophagi, of very rude workmanship, and of common calcareous stone: three of them had been broken, and robbed of their contents: the fourth was entire, and the mummy, taken from it, was lying close by, broken in the middle, but otherwise perfect: it was the body of a female; with long, brown, silken hair; probably a Greek. What was the ancient name of this place I do not know. *Alyi*, according to the itinerary of Antoninus, was 16 Roman miles from Thimonepsi, and 40 from Aphroditopolis: it was therefore about 6 Roman miles to the *north* of this place. "Medee'net Gahl" may be interpreted "the city of Ignorance": so this ruined town was called by the inhabitants of the nearest village: the name of "Modn," which Hamilton says was given to it by the people of the neighbourhood, none whom I questioned on the subject knew.

Adjacent to the village of Esh-sheykh M'ba'rak (pronounced Amba'rak), 8 geographical miles (or 10 Roman miles) higher up, on the same side, are some mounds of rubbish, which seem to mark the site of *Hipponon*: for that town, by the itinerary of Antoninus, was 16 Roman miles south of Alyi.—Opposite this place is a large island, called Gezee'ret Shero'neh. Here I accepted an invitation to sup with an inhabitant, a relation of one of my boatmen. A large fire of sticks was lighted in his hut; not for the sake of warmth, but of light; and I sat down with my host and about six other villagers round a large bowl of bread and milk, from which we each helped ourselves with our fingers. After supper we remained until a late hour, smoking and chatting; the burden of the conversation being, as usual, the oppressed state of the peasantry under the present system of government.

25th. To the west of the large village of *Ab'oo Gir'ga* (or *Ab'oo Jir'ja*) ابو جرجا , which we passed this morning, lies the town of *El-Bah'nes'ë* البهنسا , on the skirts of the Libyan desert, occupying the site of the ancient city of *Oxyrynchus*, of which little more than rubbish now remains.[†] The modern town is a poor, and almost deserted, place.

About ten miles higher, on the eastern bank, is the village of Esh-sheykh Hhas'an; where some extensive mounds denote an ancient site. A little above this, the river is divided by a large island called Gezee'ret Seraree'yeh; but the eastern branch is, at this season, dry. Arriving at the southern extremity of this island, we are opposite to the large village of *Semeloo't* سملوط .

This village is situated on the west of the Nile; nearly a mile distant. It is distinguished by a lofty ma'd'neh (or menaret), built by the architect of the great mosque of the Soolta'n Hhas'an, in Musr. I was here informed that the Sooltan above-mentioned, after the completion of his mosque, cut off the right hand of the architect, to disable him from building another ma'd'neh that might rival the great ma'd'neh of that mosque. The injured man, it is said, retired to this place, and here built the ma'd'neh above alluded to; for which, though this work was greatly

---

[†]Out of that rubbish came extraordinary finds of papyrus in the early twentieth century.

inferior to the former one, the Soolta'n deprived him of his other hand. After this, the architect retreated to Asyoo't; where he built another mosque and ma'd'neh; and for this last act, the Soolta'n caused him to be put to death.—Semeloo't is situated on very large mounds, which seem to mark the site of an ancient town, supposed (by M. Jomard) to be that of *Cynopolis*. A part of the Cynopolite nome was on the west of the Nile, immediately on the south of the Oxyrynchite nome. Ptolemy's longitudes and latitudes are little to be relied on; but we may take his observations of the *relative* latitudes of different places with less distrust; and according to that geographer Cynopolis was 20 minutes south of Oxyrynchus. If this were strictly correct, we should look for the site of the former town three or four miles to the south of Semeloo't: but Ptolemy also places Acoris (the site of which is five or six miles further south) in the same latitude as Cynopolis: which statement would lead us to conclude that Cynopolis was directly opposite Acoris. He however draws us again from this point, by speaking of the situation of Cynopolis with respect to *Co*. "Next" he says (after the Oxyrynchite nome) "is the Cynopolite nome, and its *metropolis* Co, 61° 50'. 28° 40': opposite to which, in the island, is Cynopolis, 62° 10'. 28° 30': then, on the east of the river, is Acoris, 62°. 28° 30'." A glance at the map will shew that the relative longitudes here stated are incorrect: for the whole width of the valley in this part is not more than about 10 degrees of longitude. The latitudes are also, doubtless, wrong. It is probable that Co and Cynopolis (particularly as the former is called the metropolis of the Cynopolite nome) were different names, or different quarters, of the same city; the site of which we should fix within ten miles north of Acoris, on the west of the Nile; most probably at Semeloo't. The Nile often changes its course; and has sometimes swept away, by degrees, villages and towns: it may have passed through the midst of the city in question; and gradually assuming a more eastern course may have washed away that part of the city which was on its eastern side. A change equally remarkable has taken place in the neighbourhood of the modern metropolis of Egypt; as I have related in the first volume of this work.

26th. Having passed before Semeloo't, we have before us the long and high cliffs of *Geb'el et-Teyr* (or the Mountain of the Bird), on the left side of the river,[†] which washes their base. Just below these cliffs I landed, on the same side, to visit some ancient quarries and catacombs, not far from the bank of the river. The quarried rock appears, from the river, like a long wall, with many angles and projections. On several parts I saw short inscriptions in hieroglyphics; but so much defaced that they were scarcely discernible. Upon a lower part of the mountain, to the southward, is an isolated mass of rock, in which has been excavated a small chamber, with a portico before it, the roof of which was supported by two square pillars; but one of these has fallen. The remaining pillar is unfinished: its capital seems to be formed for being sculptured in front

---

[†]The right, or eastern, bank.

with the full face of Athor; like many other Egyptian capitals. This portico, which is entirely cut in the rock, faces the south-east; and therefore is not visible from the river. The chamber is 17 feet long, and 9 broad. Its walls are covered with sculptures, representing a king, whose hieroglyphic name shews him to be the immediate successor of Rameses 2nd, presenting offerings to various divinities; from which it would seem that this was a chapel, or place of worship, rather than a sepulchral grotto. At the end are three figures in high relief: these are much mutilated; as are all the sculptures in the chamber. The ceiling is hewn in the form of an arch; and has eight winged globes painted upon it; each extending from side to side. Proceeding to the top of the hill, we find several mouths of mummy-pits: all of them closed with sand. These catacombs seem to indicate the former existence of some large town in their vicinity: perhaps they are the tombs of Cynopolis. *Musæ*, or *Muson*, must also have been situated hereabouts; for, according to the itinerary of Antoninus, it was nearly midway between Hipponon and Speos Artemidos; 30 Roman miles from the former, and 34 from the latter (now Ben'ee Hhas'an).

We now proceed before the high cliffs of Geb'el et-Teyr[1]; upon the summit of which is a Coptic convent, called Deyr el-'Ad'ra (or the Convent of the Virgin), and Deyr el-Bek'arah (or the Convent of the Pulley). On passing this during my downward voyage, two of the monks descended the almost perpendicular cliffs, and swam to my boat for an alms. About three miles higher is an opening in the mountain, called Wa'dee et-Teyr (or the Valley of the Bird).

27th. To the south of the wa'dee the mountains recede, and a tract of cultivated land intervenes between them and the river. A little above this I landed, and walked to the village of *Tehh'neh*; behind which is a valley, running towards the south-east. The foremost mountain at the entrance of this valley, on the right (or southern) side, contains numerous sepulchral excavations; particularly in the side facing the river; and there are many smaller excavations in the sides of the valley.[†] At the foot of the mountain above-mentioned, on the north and north-east, are large mounds, consisting of broken pottery, fragments of stone, crude bricks, &c. They rise to a considerable height up the slope of the mountain, and occupy a large space in the entrance of the valley. These are remains of *Acoris*. Among them are seen the ruins of a small temple; only a few stones appearing above the rubbish. In every part appear ruined walls of crude brick; the relics of the ancient houses. Among the sepulchral grottoes in the side of the mountain, facing the river, is one (a small, square chamber) containing some sculpture of the latest class that I have seen in Egypt: figures of gods are carved round it in relief; and one figure has a dress like the Roman toga. Round the southern angle of this mountain is a small, square bas-relief on the surface of the rock,

---

[1] See plate 6 [fig. 61].
[†] The Fraser Tombs.

representing two Roman figures, each holding a horse; and on the face of the rock between this mountain and the next to the south of it, over a rugged cave or fissure, facing the river, is this inscription.

```
ΥΠΕΡΒΑΣΙΛΕΩΣΠΤΟΛΕΜΑΙΟΥ
ΘΕΟΥΕΠΙ ΑΝΟΥΣΜΕΓΑΛΟΥΕΥΧΑΡΙΣΤΟΥ
ΑΚΟΡΙΣ  ΕΟΣΙΣΙΔΙΜΟΧΙΑ ΙΣΕΩ ΕΙΡΑΙ
```

The K and I in ΑΚΟΡΙΣ are indistinct.—Steps are cut in the rock here, in several places.

Hereabouts commenced the extensive Hermopolite nome, on both sides of the Nile. At the village of Tahh'a el-'Amoo'dey'n (or Tahh'a of the two Columns), opposite the remains of Acoris, mounds of rubbish, and several columns and other relics of ancient buildings, are supposed to mark the site of *Ibeum*; a town where the ibis (the emblem of Thoth, or Hermes) was the chief object of worship; and therefore, doubtless, in the Hermopolite nome.—On the 28th we arrived at *El-Min'yeh*.

Chapter XXI.

El-Min'yeh, Ben'ee Hhas'an, and Antinoë.

El-Min'yeh—Ancient quarries and sepulchral grottoes on the west of the Nile—Grottoes of Ben'ee Hhas'an—Grottoes above Ben'ee Hhas'an—Site and environs of Antinoë.

El-Min'yeh,[1] or *Min'yet Ibn Khasee'b,* منية ابن خصيب , though a small town,[2] is the capital of the middle provinces of Egypt, or of that part which constituted the ancient Heptanomis. It contains several soo'cks (or streets of shops), covered over-head with matting; and its market is pretty well stocked.

30th. A little higher up the river, on the eastern side, is a large village called Soowa'deh, where is a manufactory of sugar. The bank on that side is lined with palm-trees, for several miles; and the mountains, which are low, but steep, are very near to the river. In these, to the distance of about three miles above the village just mentioned, are some ancient quarries and sculptures, representing the processes of agriculture, domestic scenes, &c. These grottoes I did not see; not being aware of their existence; but I noticed an ancient site (indicated by mounds of rubbish) before the more southern of them. Numerous other grottoes are seen a few miles further south, on the same side of the river; but none of them, I believe, contain any sculptures or paintings: the rocky desert here reaches to the water's edge.

A little above these are the very interesting grottoes of *Ben'ee Hhas'an*[3]; so called from two deserted and ruined villages just beyond them. All these grottoes are in the same horizontal line, or stratum of the mountain; their entrances forming one, long row of porticoes and door-ways. To arrive at them we ascend an easy slope, covered with sand and fragments of rock. Here we perceive the remains of roads which lead up from the river to the entrances of some of the grottoes. Two of these roads are seen in the view which I have given: a third is concealed by the irregularities of the slope: they seem to be formed merely by removing the fragments of stone from the way, and placing them in two parallel rows. The grottoes mostly consist of one chamber; with, or without, a portico in front: but some consist of two or three apartments. In the floor of each grotto we find one or more square mummy-pits; by which the bodies were let down into the lower chambers, or catacombs. The

---

[1]More correctly pronounced *El-Moon'yeh.*
[2]See plate 7, no. 1 [fig. 62, upper].
[3]See plate 7, no. 2 [fig. 62, lower].

walls of the upper chambers (which are the only ones generally visited) are covered with paintings of a most interesting nature; representing the sports and diversions of the ancient Egyptians, their domestic and rural occupations, arts, manufactures, &c. The principal subjects are wrestling, dancing, hunting, fishing, archery, agriculture, the tending of cattle, the vintages, the making of wine, feasting, and music. The figures are generally about a foot and a half, or two feet, in height; and are arranged in horizontal rows along the walls of the chambers: but the principal personage (he for whom the tomb was chiefly destined) is sometimes represented of a colossal size. What greatly adds to the interest of these paintings is their very remote antiquity: for we know of none more ancient in all Egypt, and none so old, by many centuries, in any other country of the world. They were executed at about the same period as the painted sculptures which I have described in the monuments adjacent to the Pyramids of El-Gee'zeh. This is proved by our finding, among the hieroglyphics in one of the finest and most perfect of the grottoes, the names of Osirtesen the First, his two next successors, and his third successor; Orirtesen the Second. These names are the 33rd, 34th, 35th, and 36th of my list.[†] The traveller, therefore, here beholds illustrations, the most lively and correct, of the manners, customs, and arts of the people who inhabited Egypt at a period between eighteen and nineteen centuries before the Christian era; probably about the time[1] when the family of Jacob settled in that country; and when Lower Egypt was a distinct kingdom, or tributary to the Diospolite princes. These paintings are indeed wonderful for their antiquity; but still more so for the history they relate, the talent they display, and their almost perfect state of preservation.

To the general remarks which I have just made I may add an account of some of the more remarkable of the grottoes and paintings.—The first of the grottoes which I shall mention is the most perfect of all; and as such I give a view of its interior.[2] It is the second from the north. Before it is a portico with two columns; the form of which shews that the Greeks copied the *Doric* style from the Egyptians; improving, however, upon the original type. The four columns in the interior (one of which is broken—the lower half, or nearly half, still standing, and a small upper portion remaining suspended) are of the same kind. The walls are covered with paintings, such as I have described. In the recess at the end are three mutilated statues, carved out of the solid rock.—Of another grotto I insert an interior view[3]; as it is highly curious, and, though now much injured, has been very handsome.[‡] It has a plain doorway, without a portico. The interior contained six *clustered* columns (four of which

---

[†]Fig. 160.
[1]I adopt Dr. Hales's chronology.
[2]See plate 8 [fig. 63; Tomb of Amenemhet, number 2].
[3]See no. 20 of the subjects for wood-cuts [fig. 64].
[‡]Tomb of Khety, number 17.

have been broken down), supporting the ceiling, which is slightly pointed. These columns, the style of which has long been thought to have originated with *Gothic* architecture, seem to represent four budding lotus-stalks, bound together. Most of the paintings here are effaced. This grotto is the seventeenth from the north. I counted thirty-nine grottoes. Twelve of these contain paintings, or are otherwise interesting, either on account of their size or (if such a term may be used) their architecture. The first, or northernmost (at the left extremity of the general view, plate 7[†]), is quite blocked up. The second I have already described. The third is similar to the second; but the four columns of the interior have been broken down. Its paintings are also very interesting, and well preserved. To these grottoes succeed ten others, of a very inferior kind; small, and without paintings. Next are five large grottoes: the seventeenth, which I have described, being one of them. They have all plain entrances; without porticoes. The remaining grottoes are rather of an inferior kind; but some of them contain paintings.

In the wrestling-matches depicted on the walls of these grottoes much invention is displayed in the variety of attitudes. They are very numerous. I give a specimen: one of the best which I could select.[1] In the dances, the attitudes of the men are far from elegant; but not less so than those sometimes exhibited by modern opera-dancers. In some of the grottoes are represented feats of strength performed by women, raising one another in curious postures; and displaying strange contortions of the body and limbs. Instrumental and vocal musicians are depicted: the former with the harp, flageolet, and other instruments: also women clapping their hands in chorus; like the Egyptians, and more particularly the Nubians, in the present day. In the hunting-scenes, the chief is represented pursuing, over the desert and mountains, gazelles, foxes, lions, &c.: some of the animals are wounded: some caught in a long net which has been spread for them. Fishing with the drag-net is depicted: and the chief is sometimes in a boat, spearing a hippopotamus in the river. The catching of birds in a net is also represented. In the designs illustrative of the various processes of agriculture, the tending of cattle, &c., there is great variety: the implements of husbandry are neatly drawn; and the animals are admirably true to nature; with a degree of elegance very astonishing in works of such remote antiquity.[2] The gathering of grapes, treading the wine-press, or squeezing the grapes, and pouring the wine into jars, are represented. Gardens, houses, and furniture are also delineated; with servants employed in cooking, and other household occupations: others bringing, to their master, viands, fruit, cattle, &c. Among various manufactures, rope-making is well

---

[†]Fig. 62, lower.

[1]See no. 21 of the subjects for wood-cuts [fig. 65].

[2]The agricultural scenes in one of the grottoes of Eilethyia are yet more beautifully executed; and therefore to my specimens of these, in the following volume, I here refer.

depicted: beating the flax, and twisting the cord: also the manufacture of arms: men blowing the fire with a long pipe: bows, arrows, &c. hung up against the wall. In the second grotto are represented three large sailing-vessels, connected together: in the last of these is a corpse, under an awning. Of the middle vessel, which is very perfect in its rigging, I insert a sketch: the apparatus for steering it is particularly curious.[1]

I descended some of the mummy-pits in these grottoes; but found the chambers below choked with stones and rubbish, and, as far as I could see, without any kind of decoration.—On walking round the southern part of the mountain, I found, in a secluded spot, a small enclosure of stones, which appeared to have been the residence of a hermit. An earthen bowl, a water-bottle, and a wooden spoon were lying on the ground within it; and the bones of a goat at the entrance.

Ben'ee Hhas'an evidently marks the site of the town of *Speos Artemidos* (the distance from the site of Antinoë being exactly that which is assigned in the itinerary of Antoninus); but travellers have long looked here in vain for the *speos* from which that town took its name; as there is no evidence of any of the grottoes which I have described having been sacred to the Egyptian Diana.[†]

1st of April. There are several more grottoes, high up in the mountain, a little above Ben'ee Hhas'an. Here is a small tract of cultivated land (on the same side of the river), thickly set with palm-trees; beyond which the mountains again reach to the edge of the river. Along these mountains, for a considerable distance, we see the entrances of small and rude grottoes. A little further, in a grove of palm-trees, is the village of *Esh-sheykh 'Aba'deh* الشيخ عباده, on a part of the site of the ancient city of *Antinoë*, which was founded by Adrian,[‡] in honour of his favourite Antinoüs.[2]

2nd. Scarcely anything but rubbish now remains of the stately city of *Antinoë*. Every piece of masonry has been pulled down, and the materials carried to Asyoo't, for the building of a new palace, or burnt to make lime. Near the water's edge are some small granite columns, lying on the ground. They formed an avenue to the western gate; the principal entrance of the city. This gate was a lofty structure, in the style of a triumphal arch; of an elaborate, but not pure architecture; and all the principal monuments here appear to have been, not Egyptian, but, Roman. Among the high mounds of bricks, broken pottery, and other rubbish, which cover the whole of the site of the city, we trace the two principal streets, which crossed each other at right-angles. A row of

---

[1]See no. 22 of the subjects for wood-cuts [fig. 66].

[†]On the facing page Lane noted: "The Speos was afterwards discovered. I visited it in 1835; and met with an adventure there, which (as well as the Speos) I must describe." Lane's account of the adventure, which he recorded in his diary, was published in Stanley Lane-Poole, *Life of Lane*, pp. 76-79.

[‡]The Roman Emperor Hadrian, r. A.D. 117-138.

[2]Antino[ü]s, it is said, was here drowned in the Nile.

columns, composed of testaceous lime-stone from the neighbouring mountains, extended along each side of these streets: several of them are still standing; and there are four large granite columns lying on the ground. Vestiges of a theatre and of several other public buildings yet remain within the ruined city-wall; which surrounds the site of Antinoë on every side but that of the river; enclosing a space nearly a mile in length, and more than half a mile in breadth. Behind (or to the east of) this space are the remains of a hippodrome, about a thousand feet in length, and two hundred and fifty in breadth; bounded by massive stone walls, which are open at one end, towards the city, and terminate in a semicircular form at the other extremity, towards the mountains.— Adjacent to, or included in, Antinoë was the more ancient town of *Besa*; famous for the oracles of the Egyptian deity so named. On the south of the Roman city are some ruins which are said to be the remains of the Arab city which succeeded Antinoë, and retained a semblance of the same name; being called *An'sin'ë* انصنا . In the neighbouring mountains are numerous grottoes; but none that I saw were worth visiting. During my second voyage up the Nile I made a fruitless search for a grotto which had been described to me as a little above Antinoë, containing a painting representing a number of men drawing along a colossus, placed upon a sledge.[1]

---

[1]The following is the main substance of an account of this and other grottoes from Mr. G. R. Gliddon's MS. journal.—Mr. Harris and Mr. G., proceeding to the northern side of a ravine behind a group of 3 villages called Ed-Deyr, ascended to the commencement of the quarries, which at first present nothing remarkable but abundance of crosses in red ochre. They soon came to a spot where the rock had fallen in, and large masses hid from their view a deep pit. Here they found the remains of three large painted and sculptured tombs, of the most exquisite style, but much broken by a wanton explosion of gunpowder. On the hill above is a very deep pit for mummies. In the first (or northernmost) tomb is a niche beautifully painted, in which was once a figure. This tomb contains no king's name. In the second is the name of Osirtesen 2nd., with designs of birds, cattle, boats, &c., and the colossus above mentioned, beautifully executed, but much injured. The next tomb is smaller, and more injured; not so richly carved, but prettily painted.—Further on towards the ravine is an excavation with a tablet, bearing the name of Thothmes 3rd, and the date of the 34th year of his reign. In another part of the quarries is a tablet with the name of Amenop 3rd.

Chapter XXII.
Hermopolis Magna, &c., to Asyoo't.

Er-Reyremoo'n—Remains of Hermopolis Magna, at Ashmoo'ney'n—
Curious sculpture near Too'na el-Geb'el—Mel'low'ee—Grottoes of
Esh-sheykh Sa'ee'd—Ruined town, and grottoes, at Et-Tell, or
El-'Ama'r'neh—Frontiers of the ancient Thebais, and of the modern
southern division of Egypt—Menfeloo't—Arrival at Asyoo't.

3rd. The large village of *Er-Reyremoo'n* الريرمون , a little above the site of
Antinoë, on the opposite side of the Nile, may be called the port of the
town of Mel'low'ee. Here is the Ba'sha's principal sugar-manufactory
and distillery of rum, where several Franks find employment, under the
superintendence of Sigr. Antonini. It was originally under the direction
of Mr. Brine, an Englishman, who died a few years ago.

From Er-Reyremoo'n I walked to the site of *Hermopolis Magna*,
where the village of Ash'moo'ney'n now stands, about three miles
distant, towards the west-north-west. A great portion of the land over
which my route lay had not been sown, in consequence of the
insufficient inundation of the preceding year; though this is one of the
most fertile parts of the valley of the Nile. The sugar-cane is extensively
cultivated here. Proceeding along a beaten track, I passed by several small
sebee'ls, or receptacles for water, constructed by charitable persons for
the refreshment of passengers, and situated at convenient distances, one
from another. These were small buildings of white-washed brick, about
four feet square, and six or seven feet high; surmounted by a little cupola:
the upper part of one side, directed towards the north, was open; and
below was the trough for water, which was supplied from a well at the
side: a small earthen cup, or bottle, was placed on the edge of the trough.
Sebee'ls of the same or nearly the same description are seen in many
parts of Egypt.

The site of Hermopolis is occupied by high and extensive mounds,
which, in the midst of the flat cultivated land, are seen for many miles
round. Within these mounds, towards the northern side, I found the
ruins of the great temple; but was much disappointed at perceiving that
there remained only four columns of the twelve which I had expected to
see. The eight columns which had disappeared had been employed
chiefly to make lime. The last of these had been blown up with
gunpowder only five days before I visited the spot; and I found labourers
loading their camels with the fragments; while others were commencing
the destruction of the remaining columns. The portico faced the south;
and probably consisted of three rows of columns (or perhaps of four); six
in each row. The four columns which remained at the period of my visit

belonged to one row. They were of the same order as those along the front of the ancient edifice at the ruined village of El-Ckoor'neh, and those in the southern part of the temple of El-Oock'soor (see plates 32 and 20 in this volume†); but of much greater dimensions; their diameter being nine feet, and their height more than forty. The paint with which they were ornamented was still discernible on those parts of the columns which were least injured by time or the hand of man; but the hieroglyphics were so much defaced that I could not, with any degree of certainty, decipher the name of the founder; partly, perhaps, from my being as yet unacquainted with the characters. The name is said to have been that of a Ptolemy; which is singular; for the columns are of an order not seen elsewhere excepting in monuments of the very early Pharaohs. A little to the south of the site of the portico were some large blocks of stone, which perhaps formed a part of a portal before the temple. The main body of the temple has totally disappeared.

Within the mounds, towards the south, is the large village of *Ash'moo'ney'n*, or *Oosh'moo'ney'n* اشمونين ; once a flourishing city; as its ruined mosque and some of the older houses seem to testify. Its name signifies "the two Ashmoo'ns." "Shmoon" is an ancient Egyptian word.[1] To all ancient Egyptian names beginning with two consonants the Arabs add an incipient short vowel; and it is a general rule that the vowel so added shall be as similar as possible in sound to the following vowel of the word: thus Shmoo'n, Khmeem, and Swa'n, they have converted into Ooshmoo'n, Ikhmee'm, and Aswa'n: but in common pronunciation the short vowel *a* (as in *man*) is used in all such cases: therefore, for Ooshmoo'n and Ikhmee'm, they say Ashmoo'n and Akhmee'm.

On the 4th, a violent sand-wind prevailed during the whole of the day, and prevented my going out. Every thing in my cabin was covered with sand; and the finer particles of dust insinuated themselves into my trunks.—On the following day I made an excursion to the western mountains, to search for a curious piece of sculpture which had been described to me, by a friend, as opposite the village of Too'na el-Geb'el, which lies near the confines of the desert, to the west of Ash'moo'ney'n. I hired a donkey at Er-Reyremoo'n, and, accompanied by its owner, proceeded by way of Ash'moo'neyn. As we approached this place, the large mounds appeared to be surrounded by an extensive lake; an illusion caused by the *Sera'b*. Shortly after, we observed a *zo'ba'ah*, or column of sand, of enormous height, whirling rapidly towards us. Though this is not an uncommon phenomenon in Egypt, many of the inhabitants regard it with a degree of terror; believing, as my conductor here said, that it is caused by an *'Efreet* (or Demon), whose flight raises the dust around him. My guide of Er-Reyremoo'n muttered a charm, to divert the

---

†Figs. 90 and 78.
[1]Thoth had the title of "Lord of the Eight Regions"; and "shmoon" signified "eight": hence the name of this city of Thoth, or Hermes.—(See Mr. Wilkinson's Materia Hieroglyphica, p. 34).

course of the zo'ba'ah; and the sprite passed us at a respectful distance.—
The fields through which we bent our course this day presented a lively
appearance, from numerous groups of villagers passing to and fro: it
being market-day at Ash'moo'ney'n. Between this place and the Bahhr
Yoo'soof we found a large encampment of Bed'awees. After crossing the
Bahhr Yoo'soof on the back of an Arab who waded through the stream
(for at this season it contained but little water), we soon arrived at the
village of Too'na el-Geb'el; adjacent to which are vestiges of an ancient
town; supposed to be those of *Tanis*. Strabo says that the canal which
commenced from the Thebaic Phylace (which canal is the modern Bahhr
Yoo'soof) conducted to this place.—We proceeded to the mountains; but
my guide, who pretended to be acquainted with the situation of the
object of my search, misled me; and my trouble was fruitless. After
loitering about until late in the afternoon we turned again towards the
Nile. We chose a more direct route; but the sun set when we were yet
more than three miles from the river; and, in the darkness, we had great
difficulty in finding our way back across the fields.

During my second voyage up the Nile, my fellow traveller[†] and myself
visited the sculpture above alluded to, near Too'na el-Geb'el.[‡] Sigr.
Antonini, of the sugar-manufactory of Er-Reyremoo'n, sent us horses
and a guide for this excursion; and we went by the same route that I had
before followed. The mountains, or rather hills, to the west of Too'na are
low, and rise with a gentle slope: a little southwards, they present, in
several places, a rugged front. On the second of these rugged cliffs is the
sculpture in question; bearing, from the village of Too'na, south 57°
west, by compass. The subject and style are very singular; as the sketch
of it here inserted will shew[1]: quite unlike anything else that I had
previously seen in Egypt: but on the opposite side of the Nile, a few
miles higher up, we afterwards saw sculptures of the same age and style,
and similar in subject. The principal personage here represented appears
to be a king: his queen and two daughters are behind him; and he is
standing before an altar, which is loaded with meat-offerings and drink-
offerings, and adoring the sun; from which numerous rays descend, each
terminating with the form of a human hand. From the disc also issues the
serpent (Uræus) with expanded breast. I am at a loss to account for the
peculiarities in the style of these sculptures. The figures—those of males
as well as females—have a fulness in the lower part of the body, and in
the hips and thighs, which is far too great to be natural even to the
female. The four pairs of figures to the left of the tablet shew this excess
of form more strikingly. I was told that the heads of the larger figures
were sawn off lately by a Frank physician. The hieroglyphics are very
much defaced: particularly the ovals containing the names. These names
are the same as those attached to my sketch of one of the grottoes of

---

[†]Robert Hay.
[‡]Stela A.
[1]See no. 23 of the subjects for wood-cuts [fig. 67].

Et-Tell; of which I shall soon have to speak; and from their being enclosed in ovals, and distinguished with royal titles, they seem to be the names of a king, or prince; but they are not found in any of the royal lists.[1] The rock where this sculpture is executed is a testaceous limestone, abounding with petrifactions in the form of coins. It is, in some parts, of a pinkish colour; but generally white, or greyish; and it is difficult to cut. The mountains on both sides of the Nile are of a similar nature, but more or less compact, in most parts, for several hundred miles from Lower Egypt. About half a league to the south of the sculptured rock above described, there is, we were told, another, similar work; but not so complete; and in the sandy plain before it are some extensive catacombs.[†] We were shown, by Sigr. Antonini, some fragments of the coverings of mummies, and other antiquities, from these catacombs; and the style of them was peculiar: the features of the masks of the mummies had a character somewhat Roman.—On our passing the village of Too'na in the morning of this day, we applied to a Ka'shif of the district, who happened to be there, for some men to clear out the entrance of the catacombs above-mentioned. He invited us to go in and take coffee with him; which we declined; answering that we were then in a hurry, and would pay him a visit on our return. He then sent to inform us that it would not be safe for us to proceed without an escort, for the villagers in the neighbourhood were in a state of insurrection; but we replied that we apprehended no danger to ourselves, as the hostility of the peasants was directed against their Turkish masters, and not against private persons like us; and that we should therefore proceed. We again requested that he would send us some labourers; but he said that he could not do so until the '*asr* (at that season about three hours before sun-set). A little after the '*asr* he came to us, with another Ka'shif and several Arabs, all on horseback. He brought no labourers with him; and on my asking him the reason of his not obliging us by granting our demand, he broke forth with a volley of abuse against us both; called us magicians; and said that we had opened a door in the rock, and, when we saw him coming, had closed it up again, and concealed the treasure which we had obtained. I answered him with a pretty sharp fire of invective; my servant at the same time insinuating to him, in a whisper, that I was a Moos'lim; and he muttered a few apologetic words in Turkish[2]; to which I made no reply. After waiting a few minutes, while my friend was completing a drawing, I drew from under him a small carpet upon which I had at first invited him and the other Ka'shif to sit with me, and we mounted our horses; leaving the two Turks sitting on the sandy slope before the sculptured rock, surrounded by their

---

[1] Mr. Wilkinson conjectures them to be names of a brother of Amonoph 3rd. (See his Materia Hieroglyphica, p. 118, and plate 5 of part 2).

[†] Apparently Stela B, approximately four kilometers south, in a straight line.

[2] In order that his and our attendants might not understand him. He had before addressed us in Arabic.

Bed'awee escort, and wondering at the little awe which they inspired. We were obliged to return without seeing the catacombs; and reached the Nile about two hours after sunset.

Mel'low'ee ملوى is a moderately large and populous town, containing numerous shops and mosques; but situated at an inconvenient distance from the river. About a century ago the Nile flowed close by this town: it is now nearly a mile distant. There is a saying that "the daughters of Mel'low'ee are like her sugar-canes." Whether chance favoured me or not I do not know; but I did certainly see a great number of pretty girls in this town and its neighbourhood. Shortly after I had quitted the town, passing along the bank of the river, I found a group of girls bathing. They were fine illustrations of the popular saying above-mentioned. The moment they perceived me they hastily slipped on their blue shirts, threw on their head-veils, and ran away.—The high mounds of rubbish upon which Mel'low'ee is situated seem to be the remains of an ancient town of considerable size. D'Anville places there the *Hermopolitan Phylace.* The surrounding district is extremely fertile: sugar-canes and cotton are its chief productions.

6th. Within an hour after we had sailed from before the village of Er-Reyremoo'n we stopped on the opposite side of the river, just below a promontory of the eastern chain which reaches to the Nile. This part of the mountains is called *Geb'el esh-sheykh Sa'ee'd.* The ruined tomb of the sheykh after whom it has received this name is on a low point of the rock. A little below it is an ancient wall of crude brick,[1] near, and parallel to the bank of the river. In the hill behind this are many ancient sepulchral grottoes.[†] Only one of these is particularly deserving of notice; and as there is nothing in its entrance to distinguish it from the others, it may be well to mention that it bears due east (by compass) from a gap in the centre of the crude brick wall above alluded to.[‡] It is rather high up the steep; though one of the lowest of the grottoes. It principally consists of a spacious, irregularly formed chamber, much injured, and blackened by smoke; and its walls have been covered with plaster, to conceal the ancient sculptures. Opposite to the entrance is another, but small apartment. To the right of this (in the great chamber) is a wide, arched niche; probably the work of some early Christians, who appear to have made use of the grotto as a church: the plaster with which they covered the walls has almost all fallen off; and the sculptures are again exposed to light; but they are so much blackened and defaced that it is difficult, in many parts, to trace the figures. On the front-wall of the large chamber are represented some agricultural scenes. The figures are small, sculptured in low relief, and arranged in four horizontal rows. In the upper row are two yoke of oxen ploughing: they are followed by the

---

[1] A portion of the Gisr el-'Agooz, or Old Woman's Wall, built, according to Arab historians, by an ancient Queen, named Delookeh (or Delooka?).
[†] The tombs of the Sixth Dynasty governors of the Hare nome.
[‡] Tomb of Werirni, number 2.

sower; and behind him is a flock of rams, driven along to tread in the seed. In the second row are the reapers. In the third is a heap of corn; and some men are represented driving back a number of asses which have brought it. In the lowest row are eight asses treading out the corn: two of these are bending down their heads, and eating; for which, two men are beating them: behind them are some oxen, employed in the same manner as the asses. Upon the right side-wall of the chamber is represented a feast; very much injured. Upon the left wall are some persons dragging a net full of fish; and above this are sculptured some men cutting reeds, and others binding them in the form of a boat; somewhat like the modern *ra'moo's*—a bundle of reeds or door'ah-stalks, upon which the Nubian or Egyptian peasant, sitting astride, crosses the Nile, when there is no ferry-boat to transport him. On the left of these subjects a boat is represented floating in the midst of rushes, or lotus-plants; and in the water are two hippopotami. A niche has been cut in the centre of this piece of sculpture; and the figure of the principal person in the boat thus destroyed: he was probably designed (as in many other instances) in the act of spearing one of the hippopotami. These animals, as here represented, bear a great resemblance to hogs; and have two large tusks in the lower jaw.—Next to this grotto, to the left, is another which deserves to be mentioned.[†] It consists of two apartments. The first of these has six niches around it; each of which had within it one or two figures in high relief, and nearly of the natural size: all of them (nine in number) are now destroyed. Of the sculptures on the walls of this chamber but little remains; and that appears to be unfinished. The subject is a feast. A man and his wife are represented seated together; and before them is a table with viands, &c. In the second chamber is a recess in which are two sitting figures; much injured. In this chamber also is the pit which descends to the sepulchral catacombs; now filled up with rubbish. The catacombs in which mummies were deposited are generally without any kind of decoration.[1]

Beyond the tomb of the sheykh Sa'ee'd, for the space of more than a mile, the eastern mountain, which is steep, but not high, lies close along the edge of the river: it then recedes, and the bank is lined with palm-trees; but the tract of cultivable land is very narrow. Here are two villages: the first (or more northern) of which is called *Et-Tell* (The Hill); and the other, *El-hha'gg Ckandee'l.* These and several other villages on the opposite side of the river are comprised under the general name of

---

[†]Tomb of Serfka, number 1.

[1]Mr. Gliddon mentions, in his MS. journal, that he found in one of the tombs here the name which is read "Pepi" [glyph], and is supposed to be the same as Apappus, or Phiops. In another he found another very ancient name,

partly effaced:

El-Ama'r'neh العمارنه . Adjacent to the village of Et-Tell is the site of a very large ancient town; of which there are considerable remains. M. Jomard believed this spot to be the site of *Psinaula*: Mr. Wilkinson considers it as that of *Alabastron*. This latter traveller, in 1824, discovered the interesting grottoes of this place, of which I shall presently give some account; and, in 1826,[1] he and Mr. Burton found a large alabaster quarry behind those grottoes; which led them to believe the remains in the plain to be those of Alabastron. Pliny mentions this town as situated by the Nile: Ptolemy terms it "an inland city"; as he does also Hermopolis Magna, Lycopolis, &c.; meaning that it was not close to the river. I have mentioned before (in speaking of Mel'low'ee) that the Nile has, within the last century, gradually assumed, hereabouts, a more eastern course: so that the remains at Et-Tell may have been a mile or more distant from the river. The latitude which Ptolemy assigns to Alabastron is 28° 20'; but his latitudes are generally wrong: in many cases egregiously so. I however do not feel quite convinced that the remains at Et-Tell are those of Alabastron.—These remains are very extensive; occupying a space of between two and three miles in length. They consist of ruined walls of houses of unburnt brick, and of several large enclosures. The most conspicuous object among them is a propylæum of crude brick; or two walls, about twenty feet thick, like the propylæum of a temple; facing the river, and forming the front of a spacious enclosure; the other walls of which are of the same kind of material, but less massive, and now ruined. There was probably a temple within this enclosure; but all the temples of the town (for it doubtless contained several) have been destroyed. A long street, running parallel with the river, is plainly traced; as are also several shorter streets, running transversely; and the plans of many of the houses; some of which are very spacious, and with courts or gardens adjacent.

To the north-east of this place, about a mile and a half distant from the central part of the ruins, in the front of the mountains, are the grottoes to which I have already alluded. There is a valley, or opening in the mountains, in this direction; and the grottoes are excavated about half-way up the front of the mountains, to the right and left of this opening. Their entrances are plainly discernible from the site of the ancient town; though they escaped the notice of M. Jomard. I began by examining those to the right, or southward, of the opening above-mentioned; and, proceeding from north to south, first entered several which were merely rude and small excavations.

Beyond these is a grotto of which I insert an interior view.[2] It commences with a passage, or gallery; the sides of which are plastered:

---

[1] Shortly after I had passed this spot for the first time. I visited the ruins and grottoes here in 1827. Previously to my first voyage up the Nile I had not been informed of their existence.

[2] See no. 24 of the subjects for wood-cuts [fig. 68]. [This is tomb number 3, the tomb of Ahmes.]

the left side is decorated with an unfinished design; partly sculptured, and partly outlined with red: the subject is a warrior in his car, with a number of men running before him, in a crouching attitude, bearing spears, shields, bows and arrows, and standards: the opposite wall is quite plain. At the end of this gallery is a chamber of an oblate form, with a pit at each extremity; and behind this chamber is a recess, in which is a sitting colossal figure, representing the person for whom the tomb was chiefly destined. The sculptures in all of the grottoes here are of the same curious character, and of the same age, as that of Too'na el-Geb'el (of which I have given a sketch): the figures have the same peculiar form; and the same emblem of the sun with rays, each ray terminating with a human hand, is common in these tombs, *and is the only divinity that is found represented in them.* The names which occur among the hieroglyphics are in every instance partially or wholly effaced; but by a comparison of several I made out those which are subjoined to the view of the grotto above-described: they are the same as those of the sculpture of Too'na el-Geb'el.—The next tomb is a large one.[†] In its plan, it resembles some of those of Ben'ee Hhas'an. We pass through a small antechamber to the chief apartment, which had four columns; two of which (those on the left) have been broken down: they are of the same order as those of Hermopolis Magna. Behind this chamber is another, which is unfinished. The walls of the former are ornamented with painted sculptures, which are much soiled and broken. On the left side-wall is sculptured a subject similar to that before described; a person in a car, preceded by men bearing standards, &c., and followed by other cars. Over the centre of this device, which occupies the whole of the wall, is represented the sun with rays descending from it. Among the other sculptures there is a subject which, as well as that just described, is found in several of the grottoes here. It is a representation of the estate and possessions of the personage who is the chief in the procession above-mentioned, drawn nearly in the manner of a plan, and exhibiting a number of apartments, courts, large enclosures, with portals and columns, and gardens with avenues of trees, &c. In the houses here delineated we see store-rooms with rows of vases, and various utensils, and provisions. Another subject represented in several of these grottoes is an altar with offerings upon it, and the usual emblem of the sun above it.—A grotto similar, in its plan, to that of which I have given a view is the next.[‡] It is decorated with sculptures of the same kind as those above-mentioned. The colossal figure at the end has been demolished.—A little beyond this grotto is a small, rude excavation; and still further southward, another large grotto. The principal chamber in the latter had four columns; of which the two on the left have been broken down. On the walls are sculptured the same subjects as in the other grottoes at this place. At the end of the chamber is a door-way, in the centre; and there

---

[†]Number 4, the tomb of Meryra.
[‡] Number 5, the tomb of Pentu.

are two other door-ways, which are unfinished; one on each side of the former: that on the left has been converted into a niche, by some early Christians, who made use of these grottoes as places of worship, and, perhaps, as dwellings: we find rude walls before the entrances of several of them, which were probably piled up by the same people. Behind the principal chamber of the grotto which I have partly described is a smaller chamber, with four columns, and a deep recess, as usual, within which was a colossal sitting figure, now broken down.—Besides the grottoes included in the above account, there are two a little to the *left* of the opening in the mountains which are well worthy of examination. The plan of both is the same: each consisting of a chamber with two columns, a smaller chamber, of an oblate form, behind, and a recess. The first[†] (the more southern) is unfinished: but in each, the principal chamber is ornamented with sculptures, of the same kind as in the other grottoes.— Within the valley before-mentioned I saw three small grottoes, rudely excavated. The quarry of alabaster; to which I have before alluded, is a little to the south of this valley; a branch of which runs towards it. Not having been informed of its situation, I could not find this quarry;[‡] nor could I find any person acquainted with it in the village of Et-Tell.[1]

The peculiarities in the sculptures of the grottoes which I have just described, and in that near Too'na el-Geb'el, are very remarkable. The hieroglyphics are the same as we find elsewhere in Egypt; and the costumes are precisely similar to many which are represented on the walls of various temples and tombs of the remote ages of the eighteenth and nineteenth dynasties; but the figures are widely different from any others, in points which I have already mentioned; and a more striking peculiarity in these sculptures is their exhibiting but one object of worship, and that, too, not found elsewhere. Other Egyptian sculptures are distinguished from one another in *style* according to the *different ages* in which they were executed; but not by any *local* style; and in different nomes certain divinities are shewn to have been the *principal*, but not the *exclusive*, *objects of worship*.

Above the villages of El-'Ama'r'neh the Nile is again closely hemmed in by the mountains on the eastern side, for the space of about a mile. Opposite this part is the small town of *Deroo't esh-Sheree'f* دروت الشريف, about a mile distant from the Nile. Here, without doubt, we must place the *Thebaic Phylace*. The Bahhr Yoo'soof branches off from the Nile near this town; on the south-east. A considerable deposit of sand at its

---

[†]Number 2, the tomb of Meryra II. The other tomb is number 1, Huya.
[‡] It is located in the wadi behind number 5.
[1]At the south-eastern extremity of the plain is an opening in the mountains, and close by, on the north of this, is a small ravine, in which is a large tablet sculptured on the rock, similar to that of Toona el-Gebel, and bearing the same hieroglyphic names, but about twice the size of the latter. It was discovered by Messrs. Harris and Gliddon, on the 25th of February, 1840. There are traces of a road leading to it from the remains of the old town.

entrance has rendered it incapable of admitting a sufficient quantity of water during the inundation: a new cut has therefore been made about two miles to the south of the old entrance.

7th. A little higher, on the eastern bank of the Nile, is a large scattered village called *Deyr El-Ckoosey'r* دير القصير , with some low mounds which seem to be the remains of *Pesla*. The mountain behind this village has been extensively quarried; partly externally, and partly by excavation.

About four miles beyond this place, on the western side, and about a mile distant from the river, is a large village called *El-Ckoo'see'yeh* القوصيّه ; near which are some high mounds of rubbish, occupying the site of the town of *Cusæ*. Here terminated the Hermopolite nome. The next nome was the Lycopolite, which (like the former) was both on the east and west of the river.

We now, therefore, enter the *Thebais*. That part of the Sa'ee'd (or valley of Egypt) through which we have passed (the ancient *Heptanomis*) is now called *El-Ack'a'lee'm el-Woos'ta*, or *el-Wus'ta'nee'yeh* (*the Middle Provinces*); and what constituted the *Thebais* is termed *El-Ack'a'lee'm el-Ckiblee'yeh* (or *the Southern Provinces*).

Proceeding two miles further, we find the river flowing nearly east to west, and washing the bases of the steep and rugged mountains on its northern side. These mountains are called Geb'el Ab'oo-l-Fed'a. In one part, at their base, is a narrow strip of land; and on this confined spot stands a little village, or small group of huts, with a cluster of palms and acacias and other trees; among which are two *do'm-trees*. The do'm was anciently called the Thebaic palm; and here, just within the limits of the Thebais, we first meet with it. The little village above-mentioned is called Abra's. A little further we find a continuous narrow strip of cultivated land along the base of the mountains; and in the side of the rock we see many ancient excavations; but those which I examined contained no sculpture or painting, and were generally small, and rudely cut: some of them were inhabited. At an opening in the mountains is a ruined town: the houses are of crude brick; and rise up the slope on each side of the gap. A little beyond this is a ruined Coptic convent, situated behind a projection of the mountain: it is enclosed on two sides by the perpendicular face of the rock, and on the other two sides by high walls of crude brick. The excavations in the side of the mountains beyond this are more numerous: some of them seem to be mere quarried caverns. Where the cultivable land widens on that side a desert tract intervenes between it and the mountains; and in this part are several catacombs in which mummies of crocodiles have been found.[1] It was in one of these

---

[1]Mr. Gliddon visited *the* pit, in 1840. Proceeding from the village of El-Ma'ábideh, he ascended the mountain, and having gone about 2 miles along its summit, to the eastward, arrived at the mouth, a natural hole, about 4 feet square. After passing through a succession of intricate, irregular, natural passages in the rock, which is full of sulphate of lime, to the distance of 438 feet measured by a

that Mr. Legh and his fellow-traveller met with that adventure of which the former has given so interesting a relation: but I was informed here that the principal incident of that story, the death of the guides, was a mere piece of acting, contrived by the crafty Arabs for the purpose of obliging the travellers to give a considerable sum of money to the friends of the supposed victims. These catacombs have since been explored by several travellers; but nothing interesting found in them: I therefore did not examine them.

On the western bank of the Nile, a little further southward, is the town of *Menfeloo't* منفلوط , where we arrived in the evening of the 7th. The inhabitants were looking out for the new moon of Rum'ada'n (the month of fasting); and the sight was soon after announced by the firing of muskets and pistols. I remained here the whole of the following day. Menfeloo't has suffered much from the encroachment of the river, which, year after year, has washed away considerable portions of the high bank upon which it is situated. The front of the town, consequently, consists chiefly of ruined houses, which present a miserable appearance; and beneath the bank are large heaps of bricks that have fallen in successive years, together with the soil: but in the interior of the town we find streets of neat and well built shops, which give to the place an air of respectability that I had not observed elsewhere above the metropolis. On my voyage down the Nile in this same year, I found that this town had suffered much during the inundation: a part of a mosque that was situated close to the high bank had fallen; and many houses had been swept away. The market of Menfeloo't is one of the best in the Sa'ee'd. Most of the honey consumed in Egypt comes from this place. Good honey is seldom to be procured in that country: it is generally very much adulterated. Menfeloo't is mentioned by Coptic writers under the name of *Manbalōt*.

9th. Proceeding slowly on our voyage, in the afternoon we approach the large village of Munckaba't, and the western chain of mountains behind Asyoo't becomes a prominent feature in the landscape. Two of the ma'd'nehs of Asyoo't soon after appear; but as we follow the winding course of the river they are again concealed from our sight. About sunset we arrived at the little village of El-Hham'ra, the port of Asyoo't.

---

roll of twine, he arrived at the depositories of mummies of crocodiles, mixed with those of men and cats, and with date-branches, rags, &c. He was told that Legh's two guides were got out and buried the same day; that the date-branches &c. had been accidentally set on fire, that the fire burned for four years; and that the two men above mentioned were the first who entered after the fire, not knowing of it, and that they died from suffocation. The catacomb is called *Maghárat es-Samoun*. Its proper entrance is not known; for the pit by which it is now entered is evidently not the aperture through which the mummies were introduced.

Chapter XXIII.
Asyoo't, &c., to Gir'ga.

Asyoo't (the ancient Lycopolis), and the grottoes in its neighbourhood—
Cka'oo el-Kebee'reh (the ancient Antæopolis)—Oratory of the sheykh
El-Hharee'dee—Akhmee'm (the ancient Chemmis, or Panopolis)—
El-Menshee'yeh (Ptolemais)—Arrival at Gir'ga.

The sight of its illuminated ma'd'nehs, on the first night of my arrival in
its neighbourhood (it being Rum'ada'n), tempted me to walk to Asyoo't.
The shops, with the exception of those where refreshments were sold,
were closed; and lamps were hung along the streets, which were crowded
with loungers. On my taking a seat among a number of persons before a
coffee-shop, to smoke my pipe, and calling for a cup of coffee, I was
asked, in a whisper, whether I wanted *black* or *white* coffee: by the latter
is meant *brandy*. Not to cast too general a reflection by mentioning this
fact, I must add that I was taken for a Turkish soldier.

10th. *Asyoo't*, or *Oosyoo't*, اسيوط is also called (though rarely)
Sooyoo't سيوط ; whence, a native of this place is termed *Sooyoo'tee*. This
city[1] has succeeded to Gir'ga (or Jir'ja) as the capital of Upper Egypt; or
rather, of the southern provinces of Egypt. It is situated in the midst of a
highly cultivated plain, at the distance of about a mile and a half from the
bank of the river; a winding dike, chiefly formed of earth, leading to it; as
the fields around are subject to the annual inundation. This dike is also of
service in regulating the inundation of the adjacent fields. The city is
built upon low and irregular mounds, occupying the site of the ancient
Lycopolis, which derived its name from the worship of the jackal, the
emblem of Anubis. Of this ancient town there are no remains but
rubbish; and the only antiquities in the neighbourhood are some
sepulchral grottoes in the mountains, to the south-west. Two of the
mosques of Asyoo't have lofty and handsome ma'd'nehs: one of these is
of late erection: the other I have before alluded to in speaking of the
ma'd'neh of Semeloo't. The soo'cks of this city are very extensive, and
well supplied with the various productions of Upper Egypt, and with
merchandize from Musr, and from India and Arabia, brought by way of
Ckin'ë. Asyoo't is also the emporium for the merchandize conveyed to
Egypt by the caravans of Da'r Foo'r; which take their departure from
this place, carrying cotton, linen, and woollen goods, a few striped silks,
segga'dehs (or prayer-carpets), beads and other ornaments, straight
sword-blades of German manufacture, a few fire-arms and a little

---

[1]See plate 9, no. 1 [fig. 69, upper].

gunpowder, razors, copper wares, soap, coffee, sugar, writing-paper, &c.; and bring back slaves,[1] gold-dust, ivory, rhinoceros' horns (for sword-hilts), ostrich-feathers, tamarind (in round, flat cakes), gum-arabic, koorba'gs (or whips) of hippopotamus' hide, and the large water-skins which are borne by camels. The journey is one of great difficulty; the caravan having to go four, five, and even ten days from one watering-place to another in their passage through the desert.—The principal manufactures of Asyoo't are those of cotton and linen cloths, coarse woollen stuffs, and pottery.[2]

The sepulchral grottoes of Lycopolis[3] are about a mile to the south-west of Asyoo't. They are excavated in the sides of the Libyan mountains, which here bound the cultivated land, and face the east; but to the north of this point recede to the westward. In proceeding towards this angle of the mountains from the city, we perceive, within the confines of the desert, on our right, an extensive modern cemetery, where a number of neat, white-washed tombs, crowned with cupolas, and interspersed with acacias, present, on a nearer approach, a pleasing and picturesque appearance.—The traveller who has visited the grottoes of Ben'ee Hhas'an will not be much interested by those of Lycopolis. Several of the latter are very spacious; and have been magnificent; but the sculptures with which they were decorated are almost all effaced; and, from what remains of them, appear to have been not very remarkable. In one grotto we observe representations of the slaughtering of oxen: in another, a procession of warriors, armed with spears and shields: but in none do we find any complete, connected series.[4] Many of the grottoes here are very rudely cut; and evidently have never been adorned with sculptures. Most of the larger excavations contain square pits, descending to sepulchral chambers, which have all been ransacked. At the mouth of one of these I saw several mummies, broken in pieces: they were *human* mummies; and to such, most probably, these tombs were chiefly devoted; but mummies of *jackals* and other beasts and birds have been found in them. Some, and perhaps all, of these grottoes will soon be entirely destroyed. I found workmen employed in blasting the rock, at the entrances of several of the ancient excavations.

'Ab'dee Ka'shif, who was governor of Asyoo't at the period of my visit, was celebrated for his generosity, and was, in many respects, an estimable character. In the Rum'ada'n of the following year, shortly after he had transmitted to the capital the last taxes which had been collected in the provinces under his authority, and was in possession of very little ready cash, a party of Turkish soldiers under the command of Hhosey'n

---

[1]Some of these are emasculated, by Coptic monks, at a village called Za'wiyet ed-Deyr, near Asyoo't.

[2]The pipe-bowls of Asyoo't are the best that are made in Egypt.

[3]See plate 9, no. 2 [fig. 69, lower].

[4]In one is the name marked H in Wilkinson's list of unplaced Kings, "Mat. Hierogl." part ii., plate 5.

Bey, Governor of Ckin'ë, applied to him for their pay, by the Viceroy's order, while he was reposing in his tent, at Menfeloo't: he assured their chief of his inability to comply with their demands, but they disbelieved his protestations; and, after consulting together for a few moments, suddenly cut the tent-ropes: the tent immediately fell: the Ka'shif was unable to extricate himself from beneath it; and five or six of the soldiers at the same time stabbed him through the folds of the canvas with their yatagha'ns. His death was much regretted; for he displayed a degree of clemency in the exercise of his power not common to Turks in his high station.

While my boat remained before Asyoo't my crew continued to observe the fast with the most scrupulous exactness during the appointed hours (from the first dawn of day until sunset), after which they partook of a hasty meal, and then—strange inconsistency!—most of them repaired to amuse themselves in the Khood'a'ree'yeh; which is the quarter inhabited by the courtesans of Asyoo't.—It was truly surprising to witness the fatigue which these men underwent during this month of abstinence, in towing the boat, day after day, during the calms, which were then frequent. Though suffering much from thirst while thus employed, they were always cheerful, and often exerted themselves more than I required.

On the 12th we continued our voyage. A little above Asyoo't commenced the Hypselite nome, on the western side of the Nile, and the Antæopolite nome on the eastern side. The village of *Shootb* شطب is supposed to mark the site of *Hypsele*. We now find the river very shallow, and obstructed by numerous sand-banks, for the space of several leagues; and excavations are again observed in the eastern mountains. In the evening we arrived at *Ab'ootee'g*, or *Ab'ootee'j*, ابو تيج , a small town on the western side, near the bank of the river, occupying the site of *Abutis*. Here we were detained the whole of the following day, by a strong, contrary wind, which rendered it impossible for us to proceed even with the tow-rope.

14th. We still find the river obstructed by sand-banks; upon which we see numerous flocks of pelicans and wild ducks. The village of *Sood'feh* صدفه , which we passed this morning, on the western side, is supposed to occupy the site of *Apollinis Minor Civitas*.

Proceeding about eight miles further, I landed at *Cka'oo el-Kebee'reh* (pronounced *Ga'oo*) قاو الكبيره ; a village in the midst of a grove of palm-trees, on the western bank; occupying a part of the site of *Antæopolis*. It is likewise called *Cka'oo el-Khara'b* (or Cka'oo of the Ruins), and *Cka'oo esh-Sburckee'yeh* (or Eastern Cka'oo) to distinguish it from a village on the opposite bank which is named *Cka'oo el-Ghurbee'yeh* (or Western Cka'oo). This place is no longer interesting to the antiquary or the artist: the picturesque group of columns which formed part of the portico of the temple of Antæus has been swept away by the river, together with the bank on which it stood, and a cluster of palm-trees. Not a single column now remains; and the monolithic pyramidal shrine, which probably stood in the sanctuary of the temple, has been demolished. Upon the frieze of the portico was a Greek inscription, which stated that Ptolemy and Cleopatra, Gods Philometores, dedicated the portico to Antæus and the other Gods of the Temple; and that Antoninus and Verus† restored the temple. As a Ptolemaic structure, we need not regret its destruction so much as we should had it been a Pharaonic edifice: for we invariably find that the temples erected under the Ptolemies are very inferior in interest (though many of them are very majestic and sumptuous monuments) to those of more ancient times.— In the steep sides of the mountains to the north of Cka'oo are several ancient excavations. Some of these are mere quarries: others are sepulchral grottoes, with mummy-pits: in many of them are enchorial inscriptions.

In the evening of this day we arrived before the town of *Tah'ta* طهطا, which is about a mile distant from the river, on the western side. A little below this, on the opposite side of the Nile, the mountains approach very near to the bank; and being steep and rugged, have a picturesque appearance.

15th. There are two islands, abreast of each other, opposite the town of Tah'ta; and behind these is a narrow strip of cultivated land, extending along the base of the mountains, which are high and steep, and bordering the river. Here, behind a village called *Nez'let El-Hharee'dee*, is a long, rugged ravine, which runs upwards, in a very irregular manner, to the top of a mountains [sic]; generally in an eastern direction. Up this ravine I went, with a servant and several of my boatmen, all anxious to visit the celebrated oratory, or sanctuary, of *the sheykh El-Hharee'dee*, which is situated near the upper extremity of the rocky defile. The uneven surfaces of the rocks over which we passed in our winding ascent were polished like marble by the naked feet of the numerous visiters who have repaired to this venerated spot. A person from the neighbouring village (the Nez'leh above-mentioned) followed us, as soon as we were observed, to receive a small donation: for the care of the sanctuary devolved upon him and his fellow-villagers, to whom every pilgrim gives a sum of money. After ascending nearly a quarter of an hour, we arrived at the sanctuary.[1] It is a small building of unburnt brick, plastered and white-washed; exactly similar to the tombs of sheykhs which are so frequently seen in Egypt; and is built against a steep cliff. We entered barefoot, and performed the usual ceremonies; which merely consist in repeating, inaudibly, the *Fe't'hhah* (or opening chapter of the Ckoora'n), walking, at the same time, round the *ta'boo't*, which is an oblong case of wood, about six feet in length, like a large chest; raised, by short legs, about half a foot from the ground, and open at the bottom. A similar ta'boo't, or an oblong monument of brick or stone, is generally placed in

---

†I.e., the Roman Emperor Marcus Aurelius Antoninus and his colleague Lucius Verus.

[1]See plate 10 [missing].

a sheykh's tomb; and the same ceremonies as those above mentioned are performed by the persons who visit those tombs: in the circuit round the ta'boo't (the course of which circuit is always from left to right) the visiters usually either kiss or touch with their hands its four upper corners. The ta'boo't of El-Hharee'dee was placed in the middle of the building; and the floor around it covered with matting. The interior of the building was white-washed, and painted with flowers, in a very rude style; and from a pole which extended across the cupola were suspended three little boats; each about a foot and a half in length: these were votive offerings, presented in gratitude for preservation and good fortune here solicited by boatmen of the Nile: for El-Hharee'dee is considered, by this ignorant and superstitious class of persons as one of their chief patron-saints. A little to the right of this building is a natural cavity in the rock; of which I shall have to speak again; and opposite the sanctuary of the sheykh is another small cavity in the rock, which is regarded as sacred to his son Hhas'an.—I must now mention what I here learned respecting the history of this celebrated sheykh.—The sheykh El-Hharee'dee (said the guardian of the building, who accompanied us) was a *Sahha'bee* (or Companion of the Prophet), and, for his great piety, was translated to heaven. Some centuries since, he appeared in a vision to one of the inhabitants of the village which has received his name, and desired him to build an oratory on the spot which I have described, that people might resort thither to solicit blessings for his sake. His commands were immediately obeyed; and an annual festival was also instituted in his honour. On the occasion of the celebration of this festival, in the Coptic month of Ebee'b, a serpent makes its appearance in the cavity above-mentioned, to the right of the building; and it is believed that the spirit of the sheykh himself animates the body of this reptile. The crowds who resort thither from various parts of the neighbourhood, and even from distant places, are chiefly attracted by the expectation of deriving some benefit from touching the venerated serpent: some of them kiss it; and put it around their necks. It is said to perform astonishing cures; particularly on insane persons; who, on being brought before it, are seized with a bleeding from the nose and mouth, and recover their reason. Another miracle attributed to it is the removal of the curse of barrenness. From the theatre of these pretended wonders we climbed, with little difficulty, over the ridge which separates this secluded spot from the valley of the Nile; and then descended towards the river. The mountains here are between four and five hundred feet in height. They rise at first with a steep slope; above which they present a line of perpendicular cliffs; and in several parts, quarries and sepulchral grottoes have been excavated in them by the ancients. Proceeding along the base of these mountains towards the south-east, we arrive at a group of sheykh's tombs, on the lower part of the slope. A little beyond these, at the foot of the slope, is a high, insulated, perpendicular mass of rock; before which is a mutilated statue, nearly ten feet high, representing a person in a sitting posture, clad in the Roman toga: the sculpture is of a rude style: the material, a hard, calcareous stone: the head, arms, and feet have been broken off. On the steep behind are some mounds of rubbish; supposed to be the remains of *Passalus;* which Ptolemy places midway (in latitude) between Antæopolis and Panopolis.

Hereabouts commenced the Panopolite nome, on the same side of the Nile, and the Aphroditopolite on the western side. The sites of the two cities of *Aphroditopolis* and *Crocodilopolis* (the latter of which, notwithstanding the name of the former, is called by Ptolemy the capital of the Aphroditopolite nome) are not decidedly ascertained: that of the former has been supposed to be at *'Annebee's,* four or five miles to the south-west of Tah'ta; and that of the latter, at *Ad'fa,* about three miles south-west of Soo'ha'g.

17th. After having proceeded very slowly during the preceeding [sic] day and this, we arrived in the evening at the small town of *Soo'ha'g* سوهاج . Just above this town is the entrance of the cut by which the water of the Nile enters, during the inundation, into that great canal which, commencing at Bahgoo'rah (between forty and fifty miles higher up the Nile), runs along by the skirts of the desert, and unites with the Bahhr Yoo'soof. Northwards of Soo'ha'g this great canal is called *Toor''at Soo'ha'g*: southwards, to Bahgoo'rah, *Toor''at Bahgoo'rah.* It is of important utility in facilitating the irrigation of the lands adjacent to it.— The Thinite nome seems to have commenced a little above Soo'ha'g; lying wholly on the west of the river: on the opposite side, the Panopolite nome continued many miles further.

18th. Early in the morning we arrived before *Akhmee'm,* or *Ikhmee'm,* اخميم , a large town on the eastern side of the Nile, on the site of the ancient city of *Chemmis,* or *Panopolis.* A small canal runs, in a straight direction, from the landing-place to the town; a distance of about half a mile; but it only receives the water of the Nile during the inundation. Akhmee'm has of late very much declined, and appears to be but very thinly inhabited. I observed here that the females of the poorer class were generally clad in a dress peculiar to the southern parts of Egypt; consisting merely of a piece of coarse, brown, woollen stuff, nearly square, which is wound round the body, under each arm; the edges being drawn together, and fastened, over each shoulder. There were, however, many women here clothed with the blue shirt; which is a very uncommon dress for females in the more southern provinces, excepting in the towns.—Akhmee'm occupies but a part of the mounds of rubbish which cover the site of the ancient city. Among these mounds, behind the town, is a modern cemetery. Here also we find vestiges of two ancient temples. The site of one of these is shewn by some large blocks of stone, which, composed the architrave of the front of the portico. Other remains of this temple are doubtless buried beneath the rubbish. Upon the side of one of the blocks above-mentioned is an imperfect Greek inscription, containing the name of Tiberius Claudius, and recording the dedication of the temple to the great god Pan, and to the goddess Triphis. A portion of the figure of Pan remains at the left extremity of the inscription; and we see it to be the same god whom the Egyptians called *Khem*: hence the city here situated was called Chemmis, or Panopolis.[1] Herodotus relates that there was at Chemmis a temple dedicated to Perseus the son of Danaë (whose ancestors Danaüs and Lynceus the Egyptians affirmed to have been natives of this city); and that Perseus, visiting Chemmis, instituted there gymnastic games, which (he adds) were not celebrated elsewhere in Egypt: but we have seen (in the grottoes of Ben'ee Hhas'an) that the latter assertion is incorrect.

Proceeding a few miles above Akhmee'm, we find the eastern shore entirely desert. In the evening we arrived at *El-Menshee'yeh* المنشيّه , a small town on the western bank, on the site of the ancient *Ptolemais*, which, in the time of Strabo, was the largest city in the Thebais, and not inferior to Memphis. Mounds of rubbish are its only remains.

19th. A little beyond El-Menshee'yeh, the high mountains on the western side are wasted by the river; and in their sides are some ancient excavations. The stream is here divided by several islands; having passed which, we again find excavations in the mountain on the eastern side, more numerous than those just before mentioned. Opposite the islands above alluded to, on the western bank, is supposed to lie the site of the very ancient city of *This*, the capital of the Thinite nome, and the seat of the Thinite kings, whom Manetho classes as the first and second dynasties of Egypt. Menes, who (according to this historian) founded the Thinite Kingdom, is said to have been the first mortal who reigned in Egypt.

About noon we arrived at Gir'ga, or Jir'ja. A little below this place, in the eastern mountains, are some sepulchral grottoes. Several of these have a sloping passage, with a pit at its extremity; but they are not ornamented with sculptures or paintings.

---

[1]Mr. Gliddon, in 1840, found here a stone lately uncovered, about 14 feet long, 7 broad, and 2¹/₂ deep, on the side of which were the hieroglyphic names of Ptolemy Alexander 1st and Cleopatra Cocce. The other blocks, before mentioned, had been broken up, to build a bridge at Soohág.

Chapter XXIV.
Gir'ga, Abydos, &c.—Den'dar'a.

Gir'ga—Monuments of Abydos—Furshoo't—Hoo' (Diospolis Parva)—
Den'dar'a (Tentyra), and its monuments.

Gir'ga, or *Jir'ja*,[1] جرجا, is still a large and flourishing town; but not so populous or wealthy as it was prior to the fall of the Memloo'ks; for during the period of their ascendancy it was the capital of Upper Egypt. Its numerous ma'd'nehs render its distant appearance rather imposing. Several of its mosques are very well built; and it contains extensive soo'cks. It suffers, like several other towns in Egypt, from the encroachments of the river during every successive inundation; large portions of the bank falling from the violence of the current, and from being saturated with water. There is a large Roman Catholic convent at this place; but only one monk was residing in it at the period of my visit; and there had been none other there for many previous years: he had thrown off his monastic habit, and adopted the common dress of the Egyptian fel'la'hee'n. Few converts to his faith had been gained here; as the Copts are, of all Christians, the most bigoted.[†]

On the 22nd, having hired a donkey, I set off a little before sunrise to visit the monuments of *Abydos*, accompanied by a servant and a guide. The extensive plain over which we passed is one of the richest and best cultivated tracts in Egypt. Where the soil had been lately sown, the peasants were raising the water for irrigation from pits, or wide wells, by means of the sha'doo'f. The plain is interspersed with many palm-groves and villages. After a loitering ride of about three hours we arrived at the ruins.—On a subsequent occasion I chose a better route to this spot; landing at Bel'yen'ë, a large village; from whence to the site of Abydos is a journey of about two hours. Midway in this route, we passed through part of a plantation of sunt-trees, which extends a considerable distance towards the east south-east; occupying (it is said) no less than a thousand fedda'ns (or more than a thousand acres).

The site of Abydos is just within the confines of the desert, behind the villages of El-'Ar'abah and El-Khir'beh. Here we find a vast edifice, of high antiquity, buried nearly to the roof by rubbish and the drifted sand of the desert. It is doubtless the building to which Strabo and Pliny have

---

[1]See plate 11 [missing].

[†]Lane took for granted the reader's awareness that there was no question of the monk's proselytizing among Muslims. Such an effort would have resulted in his expulsion, or worse. Missionaries in Egypt concentrated their efforts on Egypt's Coptic Christian minority.

given the name of Memnonium, or the palace of Memnon. It occupies a space rather more than 350 feet in length; from south-east to north-east. The epithet "El-Med'foo'neh" (or "the buried"), which is sometimes given to the neighbouring village of El-'Ar'abah, more properly applies to this building. No entrance is visible from without; but in two parts, where the roof has fallen in, we may descend into the interior. Here, also, the sand has accumulated so high that we have to crawl for some space on our hands and knees, among the capitals of the columns which support the roof. The shafts of these columns are, at the top, four feet three inches in diameter: the capitals are similar to those of the side-columns in the great portico of Kur'nak.[1] It is very difficult to trace the disposition of the various apartments in this great edifice; but the interior does not seem to resemble very nearly any other Egyptian building: it is very spacious; and contains a vast number of columns; all of which are more or less buried in sand. The sculptures of the columns, architraves, and walls shew that the structure was erected, or at least originally sculptured, under the immediate predecessor and father of Rameses the 2nd. The more ancient sculptures on the walls were in very low relief: these have been planed down, and fresh sculptures executed in their place, in intaglio, by Rameses the 2nd: but the original sculpture on the architraves was in intaglio; and here we find the first name, which is that of the father of Rameses the 2nd, filled up with plaster, and the name of the son cut over it: the plaster, in some parts, has fallen out, and exposed the artifice. The original name is also, in some instances, effaced, without any other being sculptured over it. The sculptures are similar to those which adorn most of the temples of Egypt; being representations of the king in whose reign they were executed adoring and presenting offerings to various divinities. Along that side of the edifice which is towards the mountains (the south-western) we find a row of chambers with arched roofs, extending, side by side, along the whole width of the building. The manner in which the roofs of these chambers are constructed, which is not on the principal of the masonic arch, is shewn by a view which I made.[2] The walls are of a very white and compact lime-stone: the roofs, of sand-stone. The sculptures within are of the more ancient date. The ovals containing the name of the predecessor of Rameses the 2nd, intermixed with stars, decorate the arched roofs. There are remains of a portico (seen in the view above referred to) adjoining the row of arched chambers. The architraves and columns of this bear the sculptures and name of the older king.

At a short distance to the north-west of this great edifice are remains of another building (perhaps the temple of Osiris mentioned by Pliny), not so extensive as the former, and more ruined. Some large blocks of red and black granite, covered with sculpture, the remains of three handsome portals, rise above the sand and ancient rubbish; and some ruined walls,

---

[1] Seen in plate 24 [fig. 82].
[2] See plate 12 [fig. 70].

composed of white lime-stone, and ornamented with painted sculptures, the colours of which are still very brilliant, have been laid bare. Upon these we find the same two names as on the greater edifice; and upon the right side-wall of a small apartment, which is 24 feet and a half in length, and 8 feet 9 inches wide, is sculptured the famous record of the successions of many Egyptian kings, which was discovered by Mr. Bankes, in 1818. This consists of three horizontal rows of kings' names, enclosed, as usual, in ovals; one row below another. Each row original[ly] consisted of twenty-six ovals; but several are wanting at the commencement (which is the right extremity) of each: half of the first row is deficient; and eight names of the second are lost: this is owing to a part of the wall having been thrown down. The remaining names of the first row are of unknown kings. The second row contains the names of some kings of the 17th Dynasty, and a complete list of the 18th Dynasty, and terminates with the name of Rameses the 2nd, who was the head of the 19th. The lowest row merely contains variations of the name of this Rameses; under whose order the sculpture was evidently executed. This record is the principal authority for the most important part of the list of kings appended to the last volume of the present work[†]; and it is confirmed by several other minor lists and legends on various Egyptian monuments.[1]

In the desert, adjacent to the site of Abydos, and in the neighbouring mountains, are numerous sepulchral catacombs; and a large collection of very curious and beautiful relics of antiquity has been made by excavating here; many of them, of the times of the 17th Dynasty.

Abydos was once, according to Strabo, a very great city: it was deemed to have been second only to Thebes; but the author here cited adds that, in his time, it had sunk into insignificance. We are told, also, that it was one of those cities which laid claim to the honour of being regarded as the burial-place of Osiris; and that it was famous for certain very sacred mysteries, and for a highly revered oracle. It was probably the furthest city of the Thinite nome: the next nome on that side of the Nile was the Diospolite (or that of Diospolis Parva).

23rd. Continuing our voyage, from Gir'ga, we find the scenery more varied; do'ms, nubeks, and acacias being intermixed among the palm-trees which, in large groves, here and there line the banks of the river. The houses are generally raised higher than those in the more northern parts of the Sa'ee'd; having an upper story appropriated to pigeons. In

---

[†]Fig. 160.

[1]Upon some remains of another temple, which were being removed for the purpose of building a bridge, Mr. Gliddon found the names of Osiris and Rameses, and also a portion of the name which accompanies the sun at Tell el-'Amárineh, as follows:

the morning of this day we saw three crocodiles basking in the sun, upon a sand-bank; and shortly after, upon another sand-bank, we saw *nine* of these animals, lying asleep, with their mouths wide open.[1] At night we lay near the entrance of the canal of Bahgoo'rah, which flows near the town of *Furshoo't*, or *Firsho't*, فرشوط , about an hour's journey inland, from this point.

Furshoo't was the capital, or chief place of residence, of the famous Hemma'm, Sheykh of the Hawa'rah Arabs, who, in the time of the great 'Al'ee Bey, the Memloo'k, had made himself the absolute master of half of Upper Egypt, from Asyoo't upwards; and also of Nubia, as far as the frontiers of Dun'ckal'ah, or Dun'gal'ah. So great was his power that the Memloo'ks were unable to overcome him: after a vigorous, but vain attempt to do so, they were induced formally to cede to him the provinces of Upper Egypt from the small town of Burdee's, which is just above Gir'ga. In the following year after this treaty, the Memloo'ks, led by the same chief as on the former occasion, Mohham'mad Ab'oo Dah'ab, made another attempt to subdue Hemma'm. They were so far successful as to compel him to retire before them; and this event affected him in such a manner as to bring him to the grave in the course of a few days. He died in Shaaba'n, 1183 (or at the close of the year 1769 of the Christian era). His son Durwee'sh succeeded him; but was dependant on the Memloo'ks.

24th. About three miles beyond the entrance of the canal of Bahgoo'rah, on the same side of the Nile, is the village of *Hoo'* هُو , situated on the mounds of rubbish which cover the site of *Diospolis Parva*. Just above this place, the river flowing nearly from north to south, for the space of a few miles, and the wind being nearly in the same direction, we with difficulty advanced three miles in as many hours; making short and frequent tacks. On our left, near the village of *Ckusr es-Seiya'd* قصر الصيّاد , we observed extensive mounds, which are supposed to occupy the site of *Chænoboscion*. The tract in which these mounds are situated is encompassed on the east, south, and west, by the Nile; and, during a great part of the year, is rendered an island, by a narrow branch of the river, which flows along the northern side, parallel with the mountains, and very near to their base.

25th. Our course up the river this day varied from south-east to north-east. The wind, being from the same quarter as yesterday, was favourable to us; though light. We now found the cultivable land, on each side of the river, very contracted; particularly on the Libyan, or southern side; in one part of which, a slightly elevated tract of desert bordered the stream. We had probably passed, early in this day, the point where the Tentyrite nome commenced, on the Libyan side of the Nile; and the commencement of the Coptite nome on the opposite, or Arabian side. In the evening we arrived within about four miles of Den'dar'a.

---

[1] They are always very numerous in this part of the Nile.

26th. *Den'dar'a* دندرا , or *Den'dar'ah* دندره , is situated on the Libyan side of the Nile, a little below the point where the river changes its course from north to west. Approaching that village, in ascending the Nile, we find the bank on the same side lined with do'ms and date-palms. Den'dar'a derives its name from its being the nearest village to the site of the ancient city of *Tentyra*, or *Tentyris*. The river just before it is very shallow; and at this season nearly half its bed is dry. Over this sandy space I walked to the village, which is surrounded by do'ms, intermixed with the common date-palms, and with tur'fas and nubeks, which compose an agreeable variety of foliage. The plain behind us is, for the most part, well cultivated, as far as the desert; on the boundaries of which, about a mile and a half distant from the river, are the remains of Tentyra. Here, in the midst of extensive mounds, and among the ruined, crude-brick walls of the houses of the last inhabitants of that town, stands the magnificent temple of Athor; one of the most sumptuous monuments of ancient Egypt. The upper part of this building, together with a portal before it, and five remaining columns of a small temple in the same direction, are visible from the cultivated fields over which lies our route.—The great temple of Den'dar'a must attract a high degree of admiration from every traveller by its grandeur and beauty, and because it is the first temple in an almost perfect state that he beholds in his voyage up the Nile. It is to be admired as a monument of architecture, and for the profusion of its sculptures; for the whole of the exterior, and almost every part of the interior, are elaborately ornamented with sculptures: but the style of these decorations (which were executed at the close of the Ptolemaic dynasty, and under several Roman Emperors) is extremely bad: when the traveller has been accustomed to Pharaonic sculptures he will be little pleased with those of Den'dar'a.

On arriving at the mounds, the first object that attracted my attention was a small, unfinished, and ruined temple, before alluded to.[1] It originally consisted of fourteen columns, connected by a wall about half their height: there were four columns in one direction, and five in the other. The capitals, and every other part, are unfinished, and therefore have no hieroglyphics or other sculptures. Between the two middle columns of each end was a door-way, making a free passage through the building, exactly directed towards the front of the great temple; which faces N. 27° E. by compass. Proceeding hence towards the great temple, we arrive at a stone portal, which was built into a great wall of crude brick that surrounded the principal sacred edifices of Tentyra. A portal of this kind is often found forming the entrance of an enclosure of crude brick; but more generally, connecting the two wings of a propylæum. The great enclosure of Den'dar'a is nearly a thousand feet square. The walls, in their present ruined state, rise thirty feet, or more, above the rubbish, in some parts; and are about sixteen feet thick. The bricks are fifteen inches and a half in length; seven and a half, or eight, in breadth,

---

[1] See plate 13 [fig. 71].

and four and a half, or five, in thickness. There are two entrances to the enclosure besides that already mentioned: one is on the east, and has a similar stone portal: the other is in the middle of the southern end; and appears to be merely a breach. About one third of the portal in front of the great temple is buried in rubbish, and a considerable portion of the fore part of it has been destroyed. It is covered with sculptures, which have a rich effect, though their style is bad. The hieroglyphic names attached are those of Domitian and Trajan; who are represented worshipping and offering to Athor and other divinities. Upon Egyptian monuments, the Roman Emperors are never represented otherwise than in the dress, and with the insignia, of Egyptian monarchs; and none of the representations of those kings are portraits, or have any distinguishing physiognomy. The features have a soft and effeminate expression: and so have those of the Ptolemies. The figures and countenances of the kings and others in the more ancient sculptures are of a character both beautiful and manly. In the representations of the Pharaohs of different ages we see certain characteristic differences; but these differences, I think, are rather the results of a progressive improvement, and subsequent decline, in the style of art than of any attempt at individual portraiture.[†] —Passing through the portal above described, we proceed towards the front of the great temple; leaving on our right, just within the great wall of enclosure, a small temple called the Typhonium.

The great temple stands in the midst of the enclosure; and is surrounded by ruined houses of crude brick, and partly buried in rubbish. The portico which forms the front of this edifice has a magnificent appearance:[1] its width is about 135 feet; which is a little more than half the length of the entire building; and it contains twenty-four columns, arranged in six rows. The diameter of each column is seven feet and a half at the base; and about seven feet just below the capital: the capital alone is about sixteen feet high; and the height of the whole column is about forty-six or forty-seven feet. The capitals are very

---

[†]The following passage, written on a separate sheet of paper and inserted further down in the manuscript, may have been a never-completed revision for the preceding passage in the text. "But that the effigies of the Pharaohs upon their own monuments are *generally* portraits, in the common acceptation of the term, I cannot admit: those of *different* Kings are too much *alike*, and too uniformly handsome; and those of the *same* Monarch too often *unlike*. Without any desire to deceive others, a person may single out the most unusual of each of the representatives of the Pharaohs, and give a copy of it as a portrait; and when I consider the high and just reputation, as Egn. antiquaries, of some who have done so, I wish that I could agree with them as to this point. Even the differences which are observable in the representations of different Pharaohs may, I think, be reasonably supposed to be, in some degree, the results of their having been executed by different artists. Of any of the Ptolemies, or Roman Emperors, I do not know a single portrait upon any Egn. monument."

[1]See plate 14 [fig. 72].

singular: they are of a square form; with the full face of the goddess Athor sculptured on each of the four sides. Not one of these faces in the front is entire: but this is fortunate for the general effect; for, from some in the interior that are less injured, we may discover that the expression of the countenance was far from being pleasing: the eyes being very near together; the cheeks broad and puffy: the ears were designed to resemble those of a cow (the emblem of Athor); and seem to be pulled out in an awkward manner. Above this part of the capital is a cubic mass, resembling a little temple; on each side of which is sculptured Athor, nursing Horus, who sits on her knee, and receiving an offering. In the centre of the cornice, over the entrance, is the usual ornament of the winged globe. Above this is a Greek inscription, recording the dedication of the *pronaos* (or portico), by the inhabitants of the city and nome of Tentyra, in the reign of Tiberius Cæsar, to Aphrodite (or Athor) and the other divinities of the temple. This inscription is in three lines: some parts of it are obliterated; but apparently only the name of a person, probably a governor of Egypt, and a few letters at the end, perhaps containing a date. Upon the architrave over the entrance is sculptured the full face of Athor; and on each side of this the same goddess is represented sitting, with Horus behind her, and receiving offerings from a long procession of persons. The columns of the front row are connected, to more than half the height of the shaft, by a wall, which is concealed in the view which I have given by the accumulated rubbish. The entrance, which is between the two middle columns, was furnished with folding doors, turning upon pivots: a block of granite is inserted on each side to receive these pivots: all the other parts of the building are of sand-stone; but the difference in the nature of the stone was not apparent here originally; as every part was painted. The paint still adheres to some parts of the columns and walls; and is seen to have been very brilliant; consisting, as usual, of red, yellow, green, blue, and black, applied upon a white ground. The interior of the portico is extremely grand and beautiful: the highly-finished sculptures on the columns and walls produce a very rich effect, notwithstanding the badness of their style, which is characterized by lumpy forms, faces devoid of any pleasing expression, and figures utterly graceless. The same remarks apply to the sculptures in every part of this temple. The portico was sculptured in the reigns of Tiberius, Caius Caligula, and Nero; and we may conclude hence, and from the Greek inscription before mentioned, that it was built under the first of those emperors. That it was posterior to the main body of the temple is certain: it is plainly seen to be a subsequent addition; and some of the sculptures on the other part have the names of the last Cleopatra and her son Ptolemy Cæsar, or Cæsarion. The temple, therefore, appears to have been founded by this queen: its decorations were continued by Augustus, and later emperors. The subjects of the sculptures on the columns and walls of the portico are offerings, presented, in almost every case, to Athor, by the monarchs above-mentioned; each of whom is distinguished by his hieroglyphic name. The sculptures on the ceiling are very remarkable. The central compartment is ornamented with winged globes and vultures; each alternately. In the compartment next on the right is represented, among many other mystic devices, an eye enclosed in a circle, and supported by a boat: to the left of it are four birds with human heads and hands; and to the right, figures with jackals' heads, in an attitude of adoration. Next to this subject, to the left, is represented another eye in a circle, supported by a crescent, upon a short stem; and fourteen figures are ascending a flight of steps towards this strange object of adoration, which was an emblem, I believe, of the god Khem, or Pan.[1] Processions of men and monsters, apes, jackals, serpents, birds, &c., with several boats, bearing the figures or emblems of gods, are also sculptured upon the ceiling of this portico. The two compartments of the ceiling next the side-walls are occupied by the celebrated zodiac.

It has been supposed that this zodiac was designed to shew the period at which it was sculptured—that the summer-solstice, or the commencement of a particular cycle, or other period, of the Egyptian calendar, corresponded at that time to some part of the sign of Cancer, or of that of Leo; but rather of the former; for the sign of [C]ancer is expressed by two beetles; one at the end of the ascending signs, and the other at the commencement of the descending signs: therefore Leo is only the first *complete* descending sign. We find, indeed, from the Greek inscription on the cornice, and from the hieroglyphic names of Tiberius, Caligula, and Nero, among the sculptures, that the portico was constructed at a period when the summer-solstice was in Cancer, and when the commencement of the vague Egyptian year corresponded to the sign of Leo. But if we adopt either of these interpretations we are at a loss to account for the difference in the zodiac of *Is'na*; in which, though it was sculptured at about the same period as that of Den'dar'a, or rather later, the first of the descending signs is *Virgo*. We cannot reject the proofs of the age of the portico of Is'na afforded by the hieroglyphic names of Roman Emperors found throughout its decorations, and suppose that it was built at a period when the summer-solstice was in Virgo, or when the vague Egyptian year corresponded to that sign. Under these circumstances, therefore, I cannot but regard the representations of the zodiac in Egyptian temples as merely designed to convey some mythological or astrological information.

The main body of the great temple of Den'dar'a, which is proved, by the occurrence of the names of the last Cleopatra and her son Ptolemy Cæsar among its sculptures, to be more ancient that the portico, contains four principal apartments on the ground-floor, and several smaller chambers around those four, and in the upper part. The original front of the temple forms the back of the great portico; but with a small addition on each side and at the top; for the portico is both wider and higher than

---

[1] It is put for Khem in a group of hieroglyphics signifying Egypt, or the Land of Khem.

the rest of the temple. The first apartment behind the great portico has two rows of columns; three in each row; similar to the former columns, excepting that they have the addition of another capital, of a more common form, below that which is ornamented with the face of Athor. This and the succeeding chambers are nearly filled with rubbish: they receive but a feeble light from the entrance, and from narrow horizontal apertures in the sides, and small holes in the ceiling. The second and third chambers are small, but wide. The fourth is an oblong chamber: this was the sanctuary. The walls of all these apartments are decorated with sculptures, representing the usual subjects, of offerings, &c. From the third chamber we pass through a door-way on the right, and ascend, by a handsome, though rather narrow staircase, to the upper apartments. The walls of the staircase are sculptured with figures carrying offerings; on the right side, ascending; on the left, descending. The roof of the temple does not present a uniform surface; for the chambers below are of unequal heights. Next the great portico are six small chambers; three on the west (where is the exit from the stairs), and three on the eastern side. The first of the former has its walls ornamented chiefly with hieroglyphics. The second chamber has a curious device sculptured on its ceiling: a female figure, emblematic of the firmament, is represented stretching (with the arms and legs at right-angles to the body) over a distorted male figure, apparently designed as an emblem of the earth. The ceiling of the third chamber is decorated with similar sculptures. The three corresponding chambers, also, have sculptures of the same kind. In the central one was the circular zodiac, which has been removed to Paris: it occupied half of the ceiling. The sculptures on the walls of the third of these chambers are illustrative of the death and resurrection of Osiris.[1] The greater part of the roof of the temple originally presented an open area, bounded by the exterior walls of the edifice, which rise considerably higher; but this part of the building, and the top of the great portico, are now encumbered with numerous ruined walls of huts, composed of crude brick. At the south-west angle of the roof is a small edifice, resembling a distinct temple, composed of twelve columns, connected by a low wall, and enclosing a square space: the columns are similar to those of the great portico.

The exterior of the temple is profusely decorated with sculptures, which, like those of the interior, are remarkable for little else but bad taste and elaborate finishing. Three figures of demi-lions, in a reposing posture, project from each of the side-walls; and two from the end-wall: each rests upon a corbel; and between the outstretched fore-legs is an aperture perforated through the wall, for the escape of rain-water from the depressed parts of the roof. The eastern side is more than half concealed by the accumulation of rubbish; by which one easily ascends,

---

[1] A copy of some similar sculptures in an upper chamber of the great temple of Philæ, from a drawing by Mr. Wilkinson, has been published in the collection of hieroglyphics of the Royal Society of Literature.

through a forced aperture in the wall, to the top of the roof. Among the subjects sculptured on this wall is a sacrifice of four human victims; and on the same wall is a representation, on a small scale, of several persons climbing up ropes which are attached to a pole fixed in the ground. In the centre of the back-wall of the temple is sculptured a colossal full face of Athor, which is much mutilated.

Behind this great temple of Athor, near its south-west angle, is a small temple of Isis; the regular approach to which is through a stone portal (before alluded to) built into the eastern side of the great crude-brick enclosure. This portal was erected (or at least sculptured) in the reign of Antoninus Pius. On the cornice, on each side, is a Greek inscription, recording that—"under the Emperor Cæsar, God, Son of Zeus Eleutherios,[1] Augustus,—Publius Octavius being Governor, and Marcus Claudius General in chief, and Tryphon General,—the inhabitants of the metropolis and nome (dedicated) the propylon to the most great goddess Isis, and to the other divinities of the temple—." The little temple of Isis faces the back of the great temple of Athor; its left side being directed towards the portal which leads to it.[2] It is about thirty-six feet square; and is divided into four apartments; the first of which is a transverse gallery, of the whole width of the building: the other three are side by side; and the central of these is the sanctuary; and it is therefore the largest. The right side of the building, and part of the front wall, are ruined. The subjects of the sculptures are chiefly offerings to Isis and Horus, who are represented in the usual manner and, in some instances, by the emblems of a cow and a hawk.

The Typhonium[†] (the situation of which I have already pointed out as just within the great crude-brick enclosure, to the right as one enters by the portal before the temple of Athor) is almost entirely buried in rubbish. It is surrounded on either side, and at the back (and was also, originally, in front), by a row of columns, which have a cubic block above the capital, with the hideous figure of Typhon sculptured in relief on each side. The columns are unfinished; and so, also, is the exterior of the body of the temple. The decorations were begun under Trajan, and continued under Adrian and Antoninus. Upon the architraves we find Harpocrates represented, sitting upon a lotus-flower, between two Typhonian figures, male and female. The fore-part (or eastern part) of the temple is much ruined. The roof, and part of the walls, of the first chamber have been demolished. From this chamber we pass to a second and a third. The last is the sanctuary. Here, in the centre of the end-wall, is sculptured a kind of shrine, resembling a false door; and above this, in a small niche, is a figure of Harpocrates, in a standing posture, with his

---

[1] A title of Adrian [Hadrian], the adoptive father of Antoninus Pius.
[2] The hieroglyphic name of the king who is represented upon its walls, both within and without, offering to the Gods, reads merely, "Cæsar (Kaisaros) Ever Living, beloved of Phtha and Isis."
[†] The Roman period birth house.

finger, as usual, placed to his lips. This figure is much mutilated: the god which it represents is the principal object among the sculptures upon the walls throughout the temple: he is generally represented with his mother, or with Athor, who is presenting her breast to him.

Chapter XXV.
Ckin'ë, Ckooft, Ckoo's, &c., to Thebes.

Ckin'ë—Ancient remains at Ckooft (or Coptos)—Ckoo's (Apollinopolis Parva); and the old commercial route thence to 'Eyda'b, on the Red Sea—Arrival at Thebes.

The town of *Ckin'ë* قنا (more commonly pronounced *Gin'ë*, or *Gin'eh*), which occupies the site of the ancient *Cænopolis*, is about four miles above the village of Den'dar'a, on the opposite side of the river. It is inconveniently situated behind a large island, formed on the eastern side by a shallow branch of the river, which is nearly dry during several months of the year, and was so, therefore, at the period of our arrival: we had to walk a distance of more than a mile from our boat to the town, along a dry part of the bed. Egypt receives considerable imports from Arabia by way of *El-Ckoosey'r* القصير and Ckin'ë; but the transport of merchandize between those two countries is chiefly by land or by the port of Es-Soowey's (or Suez), which is the only Egyptian port on the Red Sea excepting El-Ckoosey'r. The route across the desert between Ckin'ë and El-Ckoosey'r lies along a winding valley: the journey occupies three days, at the general rate of caravan travelling; the distance by the usual route being about a hundred geographical miles. Many pilgrims chose this route to Arabia. Ckin'ë, therefore, though not a handsome town, is a scene of bustle at all seasons: we always find congregated there many natives of Arabia, persons from various parts of Africa, and generally some of the dark-complexioned 'Aba'b'deh and Bisha'ree'n Arabs, who inhabit the adjacent desert between the Nile and the Red Sea. As it was the month of Rum'ada'n when I arrived at Ckin'ë, I found many pilgrims there from various parts of Egypt and other countries, on their way to Mek'keh. The soo'cks of this town are abundantly supplied with everything that the pilgrims require, but they have a mean appearance. Much of the trade is engrossed by the Ba'sha: otherwise this would be a very flourishing place. It is famous for the manufacture of the earthen water-bottles (called *ckool'lehs* and *do'rucks*) which are in such general use in Egypt for their cooling property. No clay has been found elsewhere so well adapted for this purpose as that of Ckin'ë. The bottles made there are sent to Musr, and to all parts of Egypt, in great quantities; and some even to Arabia, Syria, and other countries: so highly are they esteemed. There is a large quarter at Ckin'ë, next the river, inhabited solely by courtesans; among whom are many of the public dancers called *Ghäwa'zee* (or *Gha'zee'yehs*).[1] These women (I mean the courtesans in general) are widely distinguished from the rest of their sex by their unveiled faces, their consummate effrontery, their trinkets, and their flaunting dress, which is usually opened wider at the bosom than that of other females. I walked through their quarter at Ckin'ë, and observed several handsome girls there: almost all whom I saw there were handsome in point of figure, if not in face.—A merchant in this town, an old man named the seyd Hhosey'n, had been appointed by our Consul to supply English travellers, particularly those on their way to India, with provisions, &c., and to accommodate them with lodging, and assist them as a banker, if necessary. I twice breakfasted with him (this was after sunset, as it was Rum'ada'n) before the door of his house; and procured from him a stock of provisions for my voyage above this place; but many of the articles that I purchased of him were of a very inferior quality, and the prices most exorbitant.—Near Ckin'ë is the tomb of the most venerated saint in this part of Egypt, the seyd 'Abd Er-Rahhma'n El-Ckinna'wee; in honour of whom an annual festival is held.[2]

On the 4th of May we continued our voyage; but proceeded not more than about two miles. At night we were annoyed by the cries of numerous jackals near us. The weather was now becoming hot: the thermometer, at noon, in the shade, generally rose to 90° or 92°.—On the morning of the 5th we passed before the large village of *Bella's* بلاص on the western side, at a short distance from the river. Here is a great manufactory of pottery; particularly of the pitchers which are called by the same name as this village; and which are generally used by the women throughout Egypt for bringing water from the Nile.

A little higher, on the opposite side of the river, about a mile and a half from the bank, is *Ckooft*, of *Ckift* قفط (commonly pronounced *Gooft*). We find here extensive remains of the great city of *Coptos*, which I did not visit till my return to this part from the upper countries. These remains consist of little more than mounds of rubbish, about three quarters of a mile in length, and half a mile in width, among which are many ruined houses, solidly built, but of unburnt brick. There are considerable remains of walls which surrounded the town; apparently of Arab work: they are of crude brick, well built, about thirteen feet in

---

[1]The distinction between the *Gha'zee'yeh* and *'A'l'meh* I have already explained, in the sixth chapter of the first volume of this work [chapter six].

[2]Burckhardt was present at the festival of this sheykh in the summer of 1813. He says—"Many thousands of the people of the country were assembled on the plain in which stands the saint's tomb, at a distance of one mile from the town. Each person, as he arrived, walked seven times round the small mosque which contains the tomb; and when the new covering intended to be laid over it for that year was brought in solemn procession, the whole assembly followed it seven times round the building; after which it was placed on the tomb." (Travels in Arabia, p. 95).

thickness, and strengthened with projecting semicircular towers. Among the mounds within the walls are remains of two temples. The first at which we arrive (that is the more western) has been converted into a large church, which, in its turn, has fallen to ruin. The two jambs of a granite portal are the only remains of this temple that appear to be in their original position. We find here the name of Nectanebo, and those of several Roman Emperors; but no relics of monuments erected by earlier kings; which is not surprising, as Coptos rose into importance under the Ptolemies. There are many fragments of granite lying on the spot above-mentioned. To the east of this are the remains of the other temple; a Ptolemaic structure. Here are found the lower parts of several columns, and little else.—Around the mounds of Coptos are several villages: none can be called a town. At the south-western angle is a ruined stone bridge, which has been built with the materials of ancient temples. There are also remains of some ancient dikes here, constructed for the purpose of preserving the communication between Coptos and neighbouring places (particularly the adjacent desert and the river) during the season of the inundation. Coptos derived its opulence from the trade which it carried on with Arabia and India, under the Ptolemies, and in later times, by the route across the desert between this town and Berenice. This great commercial route, the length of which is said to have been 258 Roman miles, was established by Ptolemy Philadelphus. In the eleventh century, Ckoo's succeeded Coptos as the emporium of the trade between Egypt and India; and from that period the latter town rapidly declined.

On my return from the ruins of Coptos to my boat, in company with a servant, we were overtaken by a violent semoo'm. We saw its approach, from the south-south-east, like a purple haze, about a quarter of an hour before it reached us in its full force.[1] In less than half an hour it had quite passed over; and all was serene as before: but in the evening we saw very vivid lightning; which is a rare phenomenon in this part of Egypt.

The small town of *Ckoo's* قوص (commonly pronounced *Goo's*) is about five miles above Ckooft, on the same side of the river. I passed before this place, as well as Ckooft, on my voyage up the Nile without landing; but visited it on my return. It is situated at the distance of about a mile from the river, upon extensive mounds of rubbish, which cover the site of *Apollinopolis Parva*. In the time of Ab'oo-l-Fed'a (who was born A.D. 1273) Ckoo's was surpassed in size by no city in Egypt excepting El-Foosta't: it carried on a great trade with 'Ad'an (the principal port of Arabia for Indian merchandize) by the route of 'Eyda'b,[2] and afterwards by that of El-Ckoosey'r. Thus it succeeded Coptos as the chief emporium of the trade with India; and has itself been

---

[1] I have described this remarkable phenomenon in the fourth chapter of the first volume of this work [chapter four].

[2] A town no longer existing; supposed to have been situated in latitude about 22°. It was on the shore of the Red Sea.

succeeded by Ckin'ë. It has not, however, entirely lost the trade with Arabia; for small caravans still pass occasionally between it and El-Ckoosey'r; and there is a dike extending from it to the confines of the desert behind, to maintain the constant communication, as well as to retain the waters of the inundation. But Ckoo's is now half in ruins; as well as much contracted in size. In a large vacant space in the midst of this town is an ancient portal, similar to those at Den'dar'a, buried, to about three fourths of its height, beneath the accumulated rubbish of later buildings of crude brick.[1] It faces west-north-west. Its sculptures, which merely represent offerings and acts of worship, bear the names of Ptolemy Alexander 1st and his mother Cleopatra; and on the cornice is a Greek inscription, of the following purport—"Queen Cleopatra and King Ptolemy, the great gods Philometores.........and their children, to the most great god Aröeris, and the other gods of the temple."—Aröeris was the Apollo of the Egyptians, and the chief object of worship in this city. This portal, even in its present state, has a noble appearance. It is probable that the temple to which it led is not wholly destroyed; and that some remains of it would be discovered by removing a considerable quantity of rubbish two or three hundred feet behind the portal; but perhaps most of its materials have been employed in modern constructions.

Of the route from Ckoo's to 'Eyda'b, and of the town, inhabitants, &c., of 'Eyda'b, El-Muckree'zee gives the following account.[2]

"Know that the pilgrims of Egypt and Western Africa, for the space of more than two hundred years, went to Mek'keh—which may God, whose name be exalted, honour—by no other route than the Desert of 'Eyda'b. They sailed up the Nile from the port of Musr El-Foosta't to Ckoo's; where they mounted camels, and thence traversed this desert to 'Eyda'b. At this place they embarked, and crossed the sea to Jid'deh, the port of Mek'keh. So also the merchants of India and the Yem'en and Abyssinia repaired by sea to 'Eyda'b, and crossed this desert to Ckoo's; whence they proceeded to Musr. Thus was this desert continually frequented by caravans of merchants and pilgrims so numerous that bales of spices, as cinnamon, pepper, and the like, were seen lying in the route, as the caravans passed to and fro; and no person touched them until the owner came and took them away. This route ceased not to be traversed by the pilgrims, in going and coming, more than two hundred years; from the period of 450 and odd years (after the flight) to that of 660 and odd years: that is to say, from the period of the great famine in the reign of the Khalee'feh El-Moostun'sir bi-l'la'h Ab'oo Temee'm Ma'ad'd, the son of Ez-Za'hir, when the passage of the pilgrim-caravans

---

[1]See plate 15 [fig. 73].

[2]This extract has been before translated and published by Quatremère and Burckhardt; but I need offer no apology for introducing it here.

by the land-route[1] was interrupted, until the Soolta'n El-Mel'ik
Ez-Za'hir Beybur's clothed the Ka'abeh, and made a key to it. A caravan
then went by the land-route in the year six hundred and sixty-___.[2] The
passage of pilgrims after that became less frequent through this desert;
but the merchants continued to convey their goods from 'Eyda'b to
Ckoo's until this route was abandoned after the year 760; from which
period Ckoo's began to decline. The journey across this desert from
Ckoo's to 'Eyda'b occupies seventeen days; during which no water is
found for three days, and sometimes for four days together.—'Eyda'b is
a city on the coast of the Sea of Jid'deh: it is without a wall; and most of
its houses are huts of matting. It was one of the first harbours of the
world, on account of the ships of India and the Yem'en which brought
their merchanize thither and then departed with the vessels which
conveyed the pilgrims to and fro; but when the ships of India and the
Yem'en ceased to arrive at 'Eyda'b, the 'Ad'an, in the Yem'en, became
the great port, and continued so until 820 and odd years, when Jid'deh
became (one of) the greatest of the ports of the world; and likewise
Hoor'mooz, which is a fine anchoring-place.—'Eyda'b is in a desert
destitute of vegetation. All its provisions, and even its water, are brought
from other places. Its inhabitants derived incalculable benefits from the
pilgrims: they received an established due upon every loaded camel of a
pilgrim; and they let out vessels to the pilgrims, to transport them across
the sea to Jid'deh, and from Jid'deh back to 'Eyda'b. Thus they amassed
great wealth. Among the inhabitants of 'Eyda'b there was none who had
not one vessel, or more, according to his wealth.—In the sea of 'Eyda'b
is a pearl-fishery, at some islands near the town. The divers repair thither
at a certain period every year, in their boats; and after having remained
there some days return with whatever they have had the good fortune to
find. The water, where the pearls are found, is of little depth.—The
people of 'Eyda'b live like brutes; and in their nature they resemble wild
beasts rather than human beings. The pilgrims, in their sea-voyage in the
vessels of these people, were subject to frightful dangers; violent winds
driving them into desert and distant ports, towards the south: then the
Booja'weh (or people of Booj'ah, or Beh'eh) used to come down from
their mountains to them, and let their camels to them, with which they
travelled without any supply of water; so that most of them, probably,
perished from thirst, and the Booja'weh took their property: others
wandered from the right way, and also perished from thirst; and he who
escaped entered 'Eyda'b appearing like a corpse taken out of its winding-
sheet; so altered in features, and changed in form. More pilgrims perished
at these anchoring-places than elsewhere: some met with favourable
winds, which carried them to the port of 'Eyda'b; but these were
comparatively few.—In the construction of the vessels which transported

[1]That is, by the route lying entirely over-land, by Es-Soowey's (or Suez). This
passage is mistranslated by Burckhardt.
[2]A numeral omitted in my manuscript.

the pilgrims across the sea, no nails were used[1]: the planks were sewed together with the *ckoomba'r*, which is obtained from the cocoa-nut-tree: they calked them with the fibres of the palm-tree; after which they greased them with butter, or with the oil of the *khur'wa'*,[2] or with the fat of the *ckirsh*, which is a large sea-fish, that swallows the drowned. The sails of these vessels were made of matting of the leaves of the *moockl*.[3]— The people of 'Eyda'b behaved in a most shameful manner towards the pilgrims: they loaded their vessels with passengers one above another; and cared not what calamities befel any of them at sea; always saying— 'On *us* the care of the *vessels*, and on the *pilgrims* the care of their *own selves*.' The people of 'Eyda'b are of the Booja'weh race; and have a king of their own tribe. In the town is a governor on the part of the Soolta'n of Egypt. I have seen their cka'dee among us in El-Cka'hireh: he was a man of black colour. The Booja'weh are a people devoid of religion and intellect. Both the men and women are always naked, with the exception of their having a piece of rag round their loins; and many of them have no covering whatever. The heat is very great at 'Eyda'b; and it is subject to burning semoo'ms."

A little above Ckoo's commenced the Theban nome, on the same side of the Nile, and the Phaturite nome on the opposite side. On the latter side of the river, about two miles above Ckoo's, is a small town called *Nacka'deh* نقاده (commonly pronounced *Naga'deh*), situated on the bank of the Nile, and supposed to occupy the site of *Maximianopolis*.

6th. After having proceeded, with a delightful northerly breeze, about six miles beyond the town just mentioned, we found the western mountains of Thebes—those mountains which contain so many wonders—within our view. We shortly after passed the large village of *Ckamoo'la* (or *Gamoo'la*) قمولا , on the western bank; and in another hour were within the limits of the site of *Thebes*. I was asked where I wished first to land: and never did I feel more perplexed for an answer. I looked around me, and saw, a little higher up the river, on the left side, the small town of El-Oock'soor, with the obelisks and propylæum and columns of its grand and picturesque temple rising above the modern houses. On the same side, but directly opposite to me, I perceived the great propylæum of Kur'nak; appearing like a ruined fortress. On my right (that is, on the western side of the river) I could see nothing but

---

[1]This kind of vessel is described by Lobo in a similar manner under the name of *gelve*, which is a corruption of (or improper mode of spelling) *jel'beh* (pl. *jila'b*), the word used by El-Muckree'zee.

[2]The *palma Christi* (or castor-oil-plant); very common throughout Nubia.

[3]Burckhardt rightly conjectured the *moockl* to be the same with the *do'm*. In the Cka'moo's it is stated that the *Mek'keh moockl* (*el-moockl el-mek'kee*) is the *fruit* of the *do'm*; and it is therefore certain that it was the do'm-tree to which the name of moockl was given in the deserts and on the banks of the Nile in Nubia. Moockl was also, according to the Cka'moo's, the name of a medicinal gum yielded by another tree, and of a kind of incense used by the Jews.

bold and picturesque mountains, with the entrances of numerous grottoes in their sides. These are the mountains of El-Ckoor'neh (or El-Goor'neh), a name which is given to the district containing most of the monuments of western Thebes.

Chapter XXVI.
Thebes.[1]

Introductory Observations.

Lamentably scanty are the notices of Thebes contained in the works of
ancient writers; and yet its monuments, even in their present state,
notwithstanding the injuries they have sustained during the lapse of
several thousand years, well deserve to be the subjects of a voluminous
work. The river has raised the surface of the soil above the relics of the
private dwellings of this once mighty city; and Persian invaders, and the
equally barbarous Christian iconoclasts, have employed their utmost
efforts to deface and demolish its public edifices, colossi, and tombs: so
that a traveller, arriving at this celebrated spot, may at first feel some
degree of disappointment: a wide, cultivated plain, intersected by the
river, and partly bounded by mountains, stretches before him; and, as his
eye wanders over it to discover some interesting object, he remarks, in
the distance, here and there, the remains of a temple, which would hardly
be known to be such but for its towering propylæa, or its obelisks. But
as soon as the stranger arrives at one of these edifices, or enters some of
the sepulchral grottoes excavated in the slopes of the mountains, he is
filled with surprise and admiration. When he stands at the feet of the
enormous columns or obelisks of Kur'nak, or by the grand ruins at
El-Oock'soor, or before the two huge colossi seated in the midst of the
western plain, his imagination is utterly confounded in reflecting upon
the art, the science, and the labour employed in the execution and
elevation of such stupendous objects. Wonders surround him on every
side, and if he desire to examine the most remarkable remains of
antiquity throughout the whole of Egypt, and to divide his time
judiciously, he must devote more than half of it to this assemblage of
monuments, which comprises edifices more noble and colossal than any
that exist in the valleys of the Nile, or in its vicinity, excepting the
Pyramids of Memphis. The tombs alone, in their sculptured and painted
decorations, present so vast a variety of interesting illustrations of the

---

[1]See the topographical plan—plate 16 [fig. 74]—(In the larger portfolio.) Those
who desire a more detailed plan of Thebes, will do well to procure Sir G.
Wilkinson's, the accuracy of which is most admirable. It is indeed a surpassing
monument of exactness and of patience; and I state my opinion of it with
confidence as I often watched the progress of its execution, and saw the [illegible]
applied in cases in which most persons would have considered the eye fully
satisfied.

religious and civil history of the ancient Egyptians, that a complete examination of them would be an almost endless work.

"Thebes," or "Θηβαι," is doubtless a corruption of the Egyptian name of "Tápé,"[1] which, in the Memphitic dialect, was pronounced "Thaba."[2] The city and suburbs on both sides of the river seem to have been comprised under this name. The name of "Diospolis," which was given to Thebes by the Greeks, from its being dedicated to the worship of Amon-Ra, whom they identified with their Zeus, or Jupiter, particularly applied to the *city* alone, which was on the east of the Nile.

It is probable that Thebes was founded about twenty-three centuries, or perhaps more, before the Christian era.[3] Of all the remains found there, the most ancient of those that have sculptures to prove their age are of the period of the earliest Egyptian sculptured monuments (between 1800 and 1900 B.C.); and are probably surpassed in antiquity only by the pyramids, and some of the other tombs, of Memphis.

Of all the monuments of Thebes, Herodotus only mentions (and that, merely incidentally) a great hall (probably the hypostyle hall, or great portico, of Kur'nak) into which he was conducted by the priests of Jupiter, and where he was shewn the colossal wooden images of the successive high-priests. (Vide lib. ii, cap. 143.)

The account of Thebes given in the work of Diodorus Siculus (who visited that city in the 180th Olympiad, or B.C. 60-57[4]) is the best that we obtain from any ancient author; though it is far from satisfactory. He states (lib. i, cap. 45) that it was founded by Busiris, and was 140 stadia (or rather more than seven geographical miles and a half[5]) in circuit. This extent its ruins would justify our assigning to it; supposing Kur'nak, Medee'net Hha'boo, the ruined village of El-Ckoor'neh, and El-Oock'soor to mark, respectively, its limits towards the east, west, north, and south: for the town certainly did not extend beyond the second and third of the points above-mentioned; and probably not beyond the first and last. Strabo, in mentioning Thebes, states that the vestiges of its greatness lay in a space eighty stadia (or, if the small stadia be meant, four geographical miles and one third) in length: which remark must refer to the ruins of the temples, &c.; and not to the town itself. Diodorus adds to the passage which I have quoted above that the fame of Thebes was spread through every country, as the most magnificent city

---

[1]That this was the ancient Egyptian name of Thebes has been shewn by Mr. Wilkinson. See his "Materia Hieroglyphica,["] p. 55. See A. Egns. v[.], 60.

[2]Wilkinson's "Thebes and Egypt," page 1.

[3]See the remarks on the first part of the illustration of the chronology and history of the Pharaohs, in the supplement to this work.

[4]I see no reason to doubt this writer's assertion of his having visited Thebes. Some of his descriptions of the monuments of this city are certainly borrowed; but this may be owing to his not having been permitted to enter them.

[5]I conclude that the smaller Egyptian stadia are here meant, equal each, to three seconds and a quarter.

of the world; whence we find it thus mentioned by Homer as having 100 gates, from each of which issued 200 men with horses and chariots. In commenting upon these lines, Diodorus remarks that, it was said, Thebes never had a hundred gates; but it contained many great propylæa of temples; and from these it was called "Hecatompylos," or "the City of a Hundred Gates," meaning "of *many* gates."—(There are no traces either of walls or gates to the city; and it is therefore scarcely possible to believe that Thebes was ever surrounded by a wall.)—The same historian adds that there was no other city under the sun adorned with so many and such magnificent offerings in silver and gold and ivory; nor any that contained so many colossi and obelisks, each of a single mass of stone.

There were four temples (which this author deemed particularly deserving of mention), the most ancient of which (doubtless that of Kur'nak, which contains the oldest remains yet found at Thebes, being of the age of Osirtesen 1st) was thirteen stadia (or nearly four thousand three hundred feet) in circuit.—(This measure agrees, with tolerable exactness, with the circuit of the principal edifice of Kur'nak and the structures more immediately connected with it, from the entrance of the avenue of sphinxes before the great propylæum to the portal, in the great brick wall, directly behind the end-wall of this grand temple.)—The height of the temple thus alluded to is stated to have been forty-five cubits (which agrees with the height of the most lofty part of the great portico of the principal edifice of Kur'nak); and some of its walls (perhaps the propylæa) were twenty-four feet thick. Though this temple was remaining in the time of Diodorus, the silver and gold and ivory and precious stones which it once contained had been carried away by the Persians, when Cambyses burned the temples of Egypt.

The other three temples alluded to by Diodorus are probably that of El-Oock'soor, the great temple of Medee'net Hha'boo, and either the Amonophium, or the Rameséum of El-Ckoor'neh: but the last of these agrees in a very remarkable manner with the description which the same author gives, after his general remarks on Thebes, of a building which he calls "the Tomb of Osymadyas."—According to Strabo, who visited Thebes probably but a few years after Diodorus Siculus, the *city*, which was on the east of the Nile, where Kur'nak is situated, was called "Diospolis"; and either an edifice or a suburb on the western side of the river was called "Memnonium" or "Memnonia"[1]: the latter was perhaps a suburb named after some buildings attributed to Memnon (or Amonoph 3rd), who, we find, was the author of the finest edifice in western Thebes.

It is not improbable that Eastern and Western Thebes were connected by a bridge; for in one of the sculptures of the time of Osirei I., on the exterior of the north wall of the great edifice of El-Karnak is represented a bridge crossing a river, which is shewn to be the Nile by several crocodiles in the river, and by Egn. buildings on each side. I admit it to

---

[1]Vide Strabo, pp. 816 and 813.

be uncertain whether these buildings are designed to represent Thebes; and as the bridge is delineated as seen from above, it is doubtful whether it was constructed with arches or otherwise: but it shows that the Nile was *in some place* crossed by a bridge at that very ancient period, and Sir G. W[ilkinson]. has proved that the Egns. constructed brick arches in a still earlier age, as will be seen in their work. They also constructed stone arches, though not on the masonic principle, in and before the age of Osirei I. The bridge above mentioned may therefore have been constructed with arches, of stone or brick, or with rafters supported by piers or by boats. If a bridge of stone or brick crossed the Nile at Thebes when that city was in its most flourishing state, the annual rise in the bed of the Nile, and the great changes that are continually happening in the river's course may account for its total disappearance.†

Whether the ravages of the Shepherd Kings extended thus far is doubtful, but it is difficult to account for the destruction of some of the edifices erected before the times of the 10th Dyny. without supposing that this was the case. Nebuchadnezzar is related, by many Arab historians, to have laid waste the whole of Egypt; and Thebes may have suffered under him: yet I think it not improbable that the Arab writers may have confounded the acts of Cambyses with those of Nebuchadnezzar.[1] The most lamentable catastrophe that ever befel this great city was that which it suffered under Cambyses, when its most magnificent temples were pillaged, and in part destroyed by fire and other means. Probably the most sacred objects in these temples (and, with them, the wooden statues of the priests which were shewn to Herodotus) were removed and concealed on the approach of this mad barbarian, and replaced when tranquillity was restored. Of the importance of Thebes even in the time of Ptolemy Lathyrus some idea may be formed from the fact that, shortly after the restoration of that king in the year 88 B.C., its inhabitants having rebelled, it endured a siege of three years; which, however, terminated in its capture and pillage.—Some small buildings were erected there even under the Roman Emperors.[2]

---

†This paragraph is a late interpolation, written on a separate sheet of paper and inserted into the manuscript, therefore is not as finely polished as some of the text around it. This is characteristic of the later additions to the manuscript.

[1]Though the latter did certainly conquer Egypt, and I have no doubt that he fulfilled Ezekial's prophecy, chap. xxix, which probably was not meant to be understood in its literal sense.

[2]Here insert article 10 of the supplement, excepting the portion relating to the Tombs. Commence thus—"To the reader who has not visited Egypt, it will not be easy to convey correct notions of the monuments of Thebes without prefacing the description of them by some general observations on Egyptian temples, sculptures, and paintings.["]

[Although other revisions to this chapter are incorporated, this direction for moving text is not, because the Supplement is printed in full in this edition, whereas Lane made this note for his unrealized book about Thebes after he had abandoned hope of publishing his Supplement as part of *Description of Egypt*.]

During my first voyage up the Nile I only spent three days at Thebes (arriving on the 6th of May, and quitting it on the 9th). I hurried away thus speedily as I saw enough in those three days to make me fear that, if I remained much longer, every thing else that I had yet to see in the valley of the Nile would appear insignificant and uninteresting: on my return, however, I remained at Thebes seventy-three days. During this latter period (which was from the 30th of July to the 11th of October) the greatest height of the thermometer, in the afternoon, in the shade, was 108°; and the least, 90°: this was while I was living in a house on the western side, among the tombs, and subsequently in a ruined part of the first propylæum of the great temple of Kur'nak: but in the shade of one of the tombs of the kings in which I stayed for fifteen days it rose no higher than 87°, during three days. On my second voyage up the Nile I spent eight days at Thebes (from the 31st of July, 1827, to the 7th of August); and on my return, forty-one days (from the 1st of November to the 12th of December). The greatest height of the thermometer during this last period was 94° (in the shade); and the least, 74°. The whole time that I spent at Thebes was therefore a hundred and twenty-five days; or more than one third of a year.[†]

Section 1. El-Oock'soor.
The Town and Temple.

On the site of Thebes are several scattered villages, and one small town, which is of sufficient importance to be the station of forty Turkish soldiers. This town is called *El-Oock'soor* الاقصر . Being situated close to the river,[1] and conspicuous for the noble temple which it partly encircles, it is the most remarkable object that the traveller sees from his boat on his arrival at Thebes. It is also called *El-Oock'soor Ab'oo-l-Hhagga'g* الاقصر ابو الحجّاج , or simply *Ab'oo-l-Hhagga'g* (Father of El-Hagga'g); which was the name of a devout sheykh, who, according to the historian Es-Sooyoo'tee, died in the month of Reg'eb 642 (A.D. 1244-5), and is buried here, in a small mosque built in a court of the ancient temple, behind the great propylæum.

By European travellers, this town has generally been called *Luxor*. Burckhardt has asserted that its true name is "El Aksor (or, as I should

---

[†]In a late pencilled addition, Lane wrote here: "Add from last journal, and move in the temperature, the zo'bahs &c." The reference to the "last journal" is unclear. It could mean one of those from his first trip to Egypt or the diary of his second trip, all in the archives of the Griffith Institute; alternatively it might mean a journal no longer extant.

[1]See the topographical plan of Thebes, plate 16 [fig. 74]. (In the larger portfolio.)

write it, El-Ack'soor), an ancient plural of Qaszer" (or Ckusr). The word *Ckusr* signifies "a palace," or "a mansion"; and is often applied to an ancient edifice: thus two ancient buildings on the opposite part of the site of Thebes are called "Ckusr Ed-Dacka'ckee" and "Ckusr Er-Roobey'ck." But the modern pronunciation of the name of the town in question is *El-Oock'soor*; and I have seen it written accordingly (that is with the vowel dum'meh over the incipient El'if) in several Arabic works.[1]

El-Oock'soor, with its venerable and majestic temple, has a very picturesque appearance; particularly when viewed from the opposite bank of the river, a little lower down[2]: the back-ground of the scene is a fine chain of distant mountains. On landing at El-Oock'soor, though less of the temple is then seen, the effect is very striking.[3]

The temple[4] is about eight hundred feet in length. The foremost, or northernmost part (which, though built in the reign of Rameses 2nd, or Sesostris, thirty-three centuries ago, is not the most ancient part) is environed by the crude-brick houses of the modern town. These houses generally have pigeon-towers (as they are called in Egypt), with inclining walls, like the ancient Egyptian temples, upon their roofs. The town stands upon low mounds of rubbish.

An avenue of colossal sphinxes, of which there are now but few remains, led from the avenues of the monuments of Kur'nak directly to the great propylæum of El-Oock'soor, a distance of not less than a mile and a quarter; thus connecting the two principal temples of Diospolis.[5] At present, not only are almost all the sphinxes which bordered this road completely destroyed but in some parts, particularly towards its south-western extremity, the traces of the road itself are concealed by rubbish or soil. We have not now the advantage even of a direct and open approach to the temple of El-Oock'soor: we must wind among the modern houses which partly surround it: but before its entrance there is a vacant space; and here, from a high mound of rubbish, we enjoy a

---

[1]The name of El-Uksureyn (or The Two Uksurs) was formerly applied to the town and village of El-Karnak, conjointly; and the latter was called El-Uksur el-Kadeem (or the Old Uksur). (Add, as a note, no. 3 of the "Addenda." [not found])

[2]See plate 17, no. 1 [fig. 75, upper].

[3]See plate 17, no. 2 [fig. 75, lower].

[4]See [Wilkinson's] T and E., p. 166, note T. It is dedicated to the worship of the Great Triad of Thebes, Amun-Ra, Maut, and Khonso; and the secondary Theban Triad, Amun-Ra-Generator, Tamun, and Harka; each of these Triads consisting of father, mother, and son. (In a note, refer to W. on the subject of the Pantheon, and quote a paragraph commencing in page 105 of vol. iv. of the A. Ens.; to which add a few words on the manifestation of the Deity on earth. In the Egn. worship of a Triad, and in the belief in the manifestation of the Deity on earth, we recognize doctrines of visitation[)].

[5]See the topographical plan, plate 16 [fig. 74].

noble view of the front of the great propylæum,[1] which is two hundred feet in width, the two obelisks before it, which are the finest in Egypt, and one of three[2] mutilated colossi, buried to the breast in rubbish. Another of these colossi is seen on a nearer approach, on the other side of the entrance; but to see the other two we must obtain admission to two of the modern houses, which enclose them. These four colossi are placed against the front of the propylæum. To finish the description of the view from the mound, I must add that through the space between the two wings of the propylæum are seen the upper parts of some enormous columns. The summit of the ma'd'neh of the mosque of Ab'oo-l-Hhagga'g just appears above the left wing of the propylæum.[3]

The attention of the spectator is at first engrossed by the grand and picturesque outlines of the objects before him, and he hardly notices that the whole front of the propylæum is covered with sculptures. These sculptures, which are faintly, but not indistinctly discernible in their present state, from this distance, are executed in intaglio, and represent scenes in a military expedition of Rameses 2nd, under whom the propylæum was built.[4] On the left wing is a battle-scene, executed with amazing spirit.[5] First to the right is seen the foremost line of Egyptian chariots, charging upon the enemy, who appear to be Persians. A little in advance of the former is the Egyptian king, in his car, in the midst of the enemies' forces: he is discharging an arrow: the reins are lashed round his body; and he is represented, as usual, of an enormously colossal size. There is no forced expression in his countenance; but a remarkable simplicity, calmness, and dignity. Above his head is the globe with the two serpents: the figure of a lion is sculptured on his car. Before him is a confused group of warriors, intercepted in their flight by his arrows, and falling from their cars. Beneath the horses' bellies are others falling into a river, which runs in two horizontal, parallel lines along the lower part of the scene; apparently enclosing an island, on which is a long row of the enemies' cars. At a little distance before the Egyptian king is the fortress of the enemy, surrounded by the stream. One fugitive is entering this castle, which is probably designed to represent a fortified town; and another, behind the former, appears to have passed the stream in his chariot. Around the fortress are several companies of the enemy: some are pulling out their comrades who have fallen into the river. Behind the fortress is a person in a car, who appears to be the general of the hostile

---

[1] See plate 18 [fig. 76].

[2] See T. and E., p. 168. [Lane first wrote that there were four of these colossi then corrected to three, hence the discrepency in numbers that follows.]

[3] The square apertures in the two wings of the propylæum were designed for the support of high, pointed shafts, which were generally set up against the front of Egyptian propylæa.

[4] Here quote from C[hampollion]'s Letters, p. 217.

[5] In the following chapter [section] of this work will be found an engraving of a battle-scene on a smaller scale, from a sculpture at Kur'nak.

army, addressing his troops. Along the top of the scene are represented two rows of cars advancing towards the Egyptians; most of them containing three warriors; and the others, two in each: these persons have long dresses: their arms are the spear and shield.

On the right wing of the propylæum a complete subject has been sculptured, and afterwards the work stopped up with plaster: these sculptures being, like the rest, in intaglio. It is singular that this original design should have been cancelled after having been completely and carefully finished: it probably displeased the monarch whose exploits it was designed to record. The plaster has since fallen out, and rendered apparent some parts of the first work. Near the left extremity of the scene the figure of the Egyptian king is perceived, seated on his throne: his face is directed towards the right. A little before this figure the same prince was represented advancing in his car to battle. Some other figures are discernible; but they are not worth mentioning in their imperfect state. We therefore give our attention to the second design, which was sculptured over the first. Towards the left is the figure of the king on his throne. This has partly been cut over the sitting figure first mentioned; but is looking towards the left. In his left hand he holds a sceptre, or long wand: his right hand is extended. Before him are eleven persons; Egyptians, by their dress; not prisoners; nor are they bound.[1] Above them is another Egyptian, standing behind a car; and holding the reins. Below the monarch's feet are two prisoners, being put to death. Behind his throne is represented the enemies' camp: among the tents are several sacks and skins; and some groups of Egyptians putting prisoners to death are here noticed. This appears to me to be the enemies' camp; for the Egyptians are riding into the enclosure, and taking possession of the booty. A lion is in the camp.[2] Above are two lines of chariots, meeting in the centre. Below the camp is another line of cars; and beneath them, the river. In the camp we observe cars without horses, and several asses, or mules.

The vigour and invention displayed in all these sculptures are truly surprising and admirable. Their effect must have been very singular, and perhaps not so pleasing to modern European taste, when the bright colours with which they were painted was yet fresh. Few traces of the paint can now be perceived.

The two obelisks[3] which stand before this great propylæum are not exactly similar to each other in their dimensions: that on the left is about eighty-two feet in height; the other, rather more than seventy-seven feet: the point of the latter is much injured. Each is about eight feet square

---

[1]Mr. Hamilton, generally so accurate, has given an erroneous description of these figures, and, as I think, of almost all the sculptures on this wing of the propylæum.

[2]Sesostris (that is Rameses 2nd, whose exploits these sculptures represent) is said to have been accompanied in his wars by a lion.

[3]See T. and E., p. 167.

near the base: part is buried in the rubbish which has for centuries been accumulating here.[1] They resemble each other in all respects but in their height. Each is a single mass of red granite, brought from the quarries of Syene (the modern Aswa'n), and cut and polished with the utmost nicety. Three perpendicular lines of hieroglyphics, most beautifully sculptured in intaglio, adorn each face of either obelisk. All of these bear the name of Rameses 2nd, and record his dedication of these monuments, and of the propylæum, &c, to Amon-Ra, the chief object of the ancient Theban worship. The middle lines are more deeply sculptured than the others.[2]

From what we see of the three sitting colossi which are placed before the propylæum, it is easy to calculate that they cannot be less than forty feet in height, including the cap, which is ten feet high. Each is a single mass of granite. They represent the king above-mentioned, Rameses 2nd. All of them are much injured: the faces, particularly, are greatly disfigured.

The rubbish of the modern town rises more than twenty feet above the foundations of the propylæum: every house that falls to ruin adds to the height of the site of this town. The upper part of the portal between the two wings of the propylæum has fallen, or been destroyed; and the sides are also much ruined. A modern, brick wall, with a small door, has been built across this ancient gateway.[3]

Passing through the modern door, we enter what was once a vast, open court.[4] This court is now crowded with modern buildings; and here, on our left, is the mosque of Ab'oo-l-Hhagga'g, which has a picturesque appearance: adjoining it is the principal school of the town. Two rows of columns (of the same kind as the smaller columns of the great portico of Kur'nak), now concealed by the modern houses, surround the court, which is bounded in front by the back of the great propylæum; at the other extremity, by another propylæum now for the most part

---

[1]By digging down through the rubbish to the bases of the obelisks (a depth of about 20 feet) the authors of the description of Thebes in the great French work ascertained their entire height to be as above-stated, and that the base of the smaller is raised a little higher than that of the other, to make the difference of their height less apparent: for which reason also the smaller is placed a little in advance of the greater.

[2]It is stated, in the great French work[,] that the sides of these obelisks are not perfectly flat, but slightly convex; and it is supposed that this form was given them because a perfectly flat surface does not appear so to the eye. This peculiarity I did not notice. [The "great French work" is the *Description de l'Égypte.*]

[3]In this gateway, on the left hand, Shebek (who is either Sabaco, Sebechos, or Sevechus), whose name is purposely so far erased as to be scarcely visible, is represented paying adoration to Amun-Generator. He appears to have rebuilt this part. The opposite side is concealed by a modern brick wall.

[4]The first pillar on the left bears, on its plinth, the name of Ptolemy Philopator; and the architrave above was resculptured under this king.

demolished; and on the right and left sides by massive walls. After having crossed a small, open space in front of the mosque, we wind through a narrow lane between low and half-ruined huts, and, approaching thus the end of the court, see before us a grand colonnade, of fourteen enormous columns, in two rows, presenting a most noble appearance, though less than half of them is visible.[1] To the left of the portal at the end of the court, through which we pass to the great colonnade above-mentioned, the upper part of the cap of a colossal statue of granite protrudes above the rubbish; and we may infer that there is another colossus, corresponding with the former, on the right of the portal, as before the great propylæum. The great court which I have described, like the great propylæum and its obelisks and colossi, is of the age of Rameses 2nd, whose name is found everywhere among the hieroglyphics and other decorations of the columns and walls: the rest (or southern part) of the building is yet more ancient; being of the reign of Amonoph 3rd, whom the Greeks and Romans called Memnon.

It is remarkable that the part added by Rameses is not in the same line with the great colonnade; but turning a little to the eastward; and in the same manner, but in a less degree, the direction of the great colonnade deviates from that of the more southern part of the edifice. Perhaps the course of the river at the period when the building was founded, and until it was completed, may have rendered these irregularities unavoidable: the founder probably did not contemplate the construction of the great colonnade until after the more southern part of the edifice had been finished. It is not improbable, however, that the great propylæum was placed in the direction which I have described in order that it might face the monuments of Kur'nak, with which, as before stated, it was connected by an avenue of sphinxes.

The fourteen great columns are buried to the height of about thirty feet in rubbish. They are at least sixty feet high. Their diameter near the capital is about ten feet: at the base it must be more than eleven. These columns are delicately sculptured, in very low relief. Some of them bear the name of Amonoph 3rd, in whose reign they were constructed; and others have the name of the second successor of Rameses 2nd: this name is no. 53 in my list. In some instances the name of Amonoph 3rd has been effaced; and that of his immediate successor, Horus, sculptured in its place. These columns are the largest in any building in Egypt excepting the two central rows in the great portico of Kur'nak, which are still larger.

Next beyond the great columns we find a spacious court, having, on the right and left, a double row of columns, of one of the most ancient orders.[2] The columns or walls which bounded this court in front have disappeared. At the end of the court are similar columns, composing four rows from north to south, and eight in the transverse direction. These

---

[1]See plate 19 [fig. 77].
[2]Some of these, and some similar columns, are seen in plate 20 [fig. 78].

must have formed a very handsome portico. They are all of the reign of Amonoph 3rd.—This court is not so much crowded with houses as the first: some pigeon-towers are built upon its colonnades.—Behind it there appears to have been an open space, with small side-chambers.

From this place, a central door led to one of the principal chambers of the innermost part of the temple: but it has been closed up with masonry by some early Christians, who have made, in its place, an arched niche, apparently for their altar. We enter that chamber by a small door on the side next the river. It contains four columns. We pass through it to a small chamber on the opposite side, containing three columns, in one row. The walls of this side-chamber are adorned with some remarkable sculptures, representing the birth and nursing of Amonoph 3rd, the founder of the building.[1] On the front-wall are represented two processions; each consisting of three persons drawing along a chest, or sarcophagus: behind them walks Amonoph 3rd. There was a chamber corresponding with this on the side next the river; but it has been destroyed.

The next of the principal (or medial) chambers has an isolated chamber in the midst of it. The latter was a sanctuary; and is the least ancient part of the building. On the walls of the former, Amonoph 3rd is represented adoring and offering to Amon-Ra and other divinities. The hieroglyphics of the isolated sanctuary have the name of Alexandros (or Alexander the Great) as their author. Its sculptures, and those of the chamber in which it is enclosed, I could but slightly, and for a few moments, examine; for this part of the temple had been made a receptacle for filth; and the smell was almost suffocating.

Next beyond this part of the building is a wide chamber, having two rows of columns, six in each row, placed transversely. Its sculptures represent offerings and acts of adoration by Amonoph 3rd to various divinities.

Upon the roof of this and some of the former (adjoining) chambers,[2] a modern house has been constructed, which is the residence of the Turkish commander, and most of the forty soldiers under his orders, who are stationed at this place. These Turks we have to blame for the defilement of the adyta of the temple.

There are remains of three chambers behind that last described; and

---

[1] The Queen, his mother, is addressed by Thoth, who appears to be announcing to her that she is about to bear a son. She is then conducted by Kneph and Athor, and seated on a chair, attended by two females. This portion of the sculptures presents an illustration of the 16th verse of the 1st chapter of Exodus, and is the more interesting from its having been executed, according to the opinion which I think best founded, during the time of Moses, and shortly after the departure of the Israelites from Egypt. We afterwards see the little Amonoph nursed, with other children, and presented to Amon-Ra. This is on the wall next the medial chamber.

[2] See plate 20 [fig. 78].

there are still standing three columns and a part of a fourth which supported the roof of the central of these three chambers.

It appears that, from an early period, the temple of El-Oock'soor has been threatened with destruction by the Nile: a strong quay has therefore been constructed, partly of large, burnt bricks, and partly of stone, near the end of the temple, at the part where the river approaches nearest to the edifice. This quay is now in very ruinous state.[1] Near it have been standing, for some few years past, several large statues of black basalt, representing a lion-headed goddess, seated on a throne. They were brought hither from Kur'nak, for embarkation; but appear to be abandoned.

Section 2. Kur'nak.

The Great Temple, and the monuments, &c., connected with it, or adjacent to it.

The great temple of Kur'nak is a little more than a mile distant from the main branch of the river. A long island stretches before it; but when the Nile is low, the narrow branch on the south-east of this island (that is, on the side next Kur'nak) is dry; and the traveller may then cross the island and the dry channel in a direct line towards the front of the temple: during the greater part of the year he must take the route from El-Oock'soor to Kur'nak; the above-mentioned narrow branch of the river being neither dry nor containing a sufficient depth of water for a boat to pass. The great temple of Kur'nak is rather more than a mile and a half distant from El-Oock'soor, towards the north-east. The stranger approaches it in this direction through long avenues of androsphinxes and criosphinxes, or by an avenue of rams, all of colossal size; and is gradually prepared, by an assemblage of other striking objects, for the all-surpassing grandeur of the principal edifice. The regular, or chief approach is, however, that first mentioned.

From the river, or from the island above-mentioned, we see little of the great temple: the front of the right wing of the first propylæum (the left wing being much ruined) is the most conspicuous object; and appears like a large fortress. The square holes through this mass of masonry, which were made to receive the fastenings that secured those high, pointed shafts anciently set up against its front, resemble embrasures for cannon, or the port-holes of a man-of-war. The word *Kur'nak* كرنك , which is the name given to an adjacent village, signifies "an embrasure," "a port-hole," and "a battery"; and was doubtless, originally, here applied to the propylæum, from its resemblance to a fortress with embrasures.

---

[1]See T. and E., p. 171.

The monuments of Kur'nak are situated among a vast expanse of mounds of rubbish; principally consisting of the materials of buildings of crude brick, intermixed with fragments of pottery and of stone. These mounds cover a portion of that quarter of Thebes which the Greeks called Diospolis, and which was the most ancient part. In the time of Strabo, Diospolis was yet a city, when separate villages occupied the rest of the site of Thebes.

I passed several days among the vast monuments of Kur'nak before my admiration and curiosity sufficiently abated to allow me to commence a regular examination, or to make any drawings or notes; and indeed I was almost discouraged from attempting a detailed description. Towering propylæa, forests of enormous columns, obelisks, colossi, and avenues of sphinxes may be accurately measured and described; but it is impossible, in words,—or even by means of drawings, unless on a very large scale,— to convey an adequate idea of the grandeur of the assemblage of wonderful objects here beheld.

A wall of crude brick seems to have entirely surrounded a square space of about one third of a mile in extent, in which all the principal monuments of Kur'nak are situated. Though buried in many parts to the very top of the mounds of rubbish, the whole extent of the wall facing the north-north-east is plainly seen; and so also is that portion which forms the east-south-east side of the enclosure; and half the south-south-west side.—(It will be more convenient to term these the north, east, and south sides; and, having once stated the more exact directions of the walls, to adopt the same plan in describing the great temple, &c.).—This wall is not less that thirty feet in thickness: the bricks of which it is composed are twelve or thirteen inches in length; about six inches in width; and in thickness, nearly the same. From a little distance it appears like a raised road of earth; in consequence of the mouldering state of the exterior.[1]

The great temple of Kur[']nak, the most noble part of which appears to have been designed as a royal palace as well as consecrated to religion, consists of a series of propylæa, courts, porticoes, sanctuaries, &c., constructed in different ages; and is surrounded by other temples, more or less connected with the general plan. It occupies a space of a rectangular form, eleven hundred and eighty feet in length, measured from the front of the great propylæum to the back of the wall which encloses the sanctuaries.

The first propylæum, which is the greatest,[2] faces the west-north-west; and it is from that direction, or nearly so, that we approach it by the shortest route from the river. Directly before it, at the distance of 240 feet, are the foundations of a small building, on which is the hieroglyphic name of the second successor of Rameses 2nd. From this, an avenue of ram-headed sphinxes led to the great propylæum. Most of these sphinxes

---

[1]Many of the bricks may have been used for the construction of modern huts.
[2]See plate 21 [fig. 79].

are now buried beneath the mounds of rubbish which gradually rise from this point towards the propylæum: six, only, being visible on the right side, and four on the left.[1] Around the entrance of the avenue I observed some small broken columns and capitals of Christian workmanship, lying on the ground.

The great propylæum is 360 feet in width, and 42 feet thick, measured immediately above the rubbish; but the dimensions of the base must be a few feet larger. It is one of the later additions to the temple; and is unfinished: the surfaces are not smoothed; nor are the mouldings at the angles made out. As it is without sculpture we cannot discover the age in which it was constructed; but we may safely pronounce it one of the least ancient parts of the temple, from its unfinished state, and from its place in the general plan. The left (or northern) wing is much ruined. Each wing had originally eight of those square apertures which I have before mentioned as designed to receive the fastenings for the securing of the high, pointed shafts which were generally erected against the front of the propylæa. The left wing has only the lower tier of these holes remaining; and three of them, some months before the period of my visit, had been converted into comfortable places of abode, by an English party: the front extremity of each had been closed, with the exception of a small aperture for the admission of light and air, by a wall of crude bricks; and thus had been made three snug chambers, the only inconvenience of which is that they are not quite high enough for a man to stand upright in them: they are entered from the back, by passing over the top of the ruin, the ascent to which is easy. One of these was my dwelling-place during a period of twenty days which I spent in the examination of the various monuments of Kur'nak. Another traveller was my companion on this occasion; and our time passed very pleasantly: the only discomfort which we suffered while we stayed here was the howling of jackals in the night: vast numbers of these animals frequenting the temple and its vicinity.—In each wing of the propylæum is a staircase: the one commences nearly from the north extremity of the north wing, and ascends in a straight direction to the top of the portal, which, before it was ruined, connected the two wings, and formed a communication between the first and second staircase: the latter staircase ascends in the same direction as the first to the top of the south wing. The entrance of the lower staircase is concealed by rubbish: it is probably under the gallery which forms the north side of the court behind the propylæum: with some difficulty I climbed to the entrance of the other, and ascended to the summit of the south wing, whence I enjoyed a most interesting view of all the principal monuments in the vicinity, as well as of the whole of the great temple, which presented a scene of grandeur and desolation utterly indescribable.

---

[1] Of these ten, only four are seen in the view which I have inserted of the great propylæum: the inequalities of the mounds of rubbish concealing the rest from the point whence that view was taken.

Passing through the ruined portal[1] between the two wings of the great propylæum, we enter a spacious court,[2] 330 feet in width, measured from the interior of each side-wall: its extent in the other direction is about 270 feet. Before each of the side-walls is a row of massive, plain columns; which, together with the wall, support a roof, and thus form a covered gallery: these columns are seven feet in diameter; and of the same form as the smaller columns in the great portico of this temple.[3] The opposite end of the court is formed by a propylæum; the fore part of which is in a state of utter ruin; so that its two wings, viewed from the court, appear to be little more than rude heaps of blocks of stone. This propylæum was somewhat inferior in dimensions to the first: its portal, and the view through it, present a grand appearance. Two rows of columns, nearly nine feet and a half in diameter, and about sixty feet in height, formed a magnificent avenue through the midst of the court to the portal just mentioned. Only one of these is now standing: the ruins of five of each row are lying on the ground; and the remains of the others are probably buried beneath the rubbish, which has accumulated to a great height in the fore part of the court. The blocks of stone of which they are composed are much smaller than is usual in Egyptian columns of such magnitude. As the two rows are forty-five feet apart, it is probable that the roof which extended across was of wood.[4]—In the left corner of the court, immediately behind the north wing of the great propylæum, is a temple almost wholly buried in the rubbish. The front, which faces the right side of the court, has three doors; each leading into a separate apartment; but the interior is filled nearly to the roof with rubbish. Among the sculptures of this temple we find everywhere the same name as on the remains before the great propylæum, which is that of the second successor of Rameses 2nd. It is remarkable that the figure of the god in this name (see no. 53 in my list) is almost always erased: but in the interior of this building I found some perfect examples of it.—The great court has an entrance on the north side. This is a large, plain doorway; nearer to the second propylæum than to the first. The stone which forms its lintel is of enormous dimensions—thirty feet six inches long, five feet three inches high, and five feet wide.—On the south side of the great court is another temple built before the court was enclosed. Its front, which is ninety feet wide, projects about fifty feet into the great court; but the greater part of it lies without. It is two hundred feet in length. This temple is a monument of the reign of Rameses 3rd, the founder of the great edifice of Medee'net Hhab'boo. A small propylæum, much ruined, forms its front. On the face of each wing of this propylæum is represented the monarch above-mentioned holding a group of five

---

[1]Before it stood two colossal granite statues.
[2]See plate 22 [fig. 80].
[3]Seen in plate 24 [fig. 82].
[4]The sculptures exhibit the hieroglyphic names of Tirhakah, Psammetichus I., and Ptolemy Philopator.

kneeling captives by the hair of their heads, before the great god Amon-Ra, and about to destroy them with his uplifted mace. Behind the propylæum is a court, surrounded on three sides by square pillars, each of which is ornamented in front by a large Osiridean (or mummy-shaped) figure. Behind the row of square pillars at the end of the court is a row of columns, in four rows; nearly filled to the roof with rubbish; and behind this are some other apartments, quite choked up. The sculptures on the exterior of this edifice are almost entirely concealed by the surrounding rubbish: on the northern part of the western side is sculptured a battle scene; but this is much injured.—The gallery which forms the southern side of the great court is proved, by the manner in which it unites with the temple just described, to be a later construction than that temple; and we may therefore infer the same of the *opposite* gallery: both, we have reason to believe, were built in the reign of Sheshonk 1st; for between the temple of Rameses 3rd and the second propylæum of the great temple intervenes a part of the southern gallery, consisting of two columns and a gateway, ornamented with sculptures, representing the common subjects of offerings, &c., among which we find the figures and names of Sheshonk 1st and Osorkon 1st. These two kings were the first and second of the twenty-second Dynasty; and are called by Manetho "Sesonchis," or "Sesenchosis," and "Osoroth," or "Osorthon." The former is the "Shishak" of the Bible. The gateway is in the wall behind the two columns. On the exterior face of this wall, to the right of the gateway, we find the hieroglyphic names of a great number of prisoners, or of countries or places, subjected by the arms of Sheshonk I. (or Shishak), who plundered the Temple of Jerusalem and the palace of Rehoboam. Each of these names is enclosed in an oval, which is surmounted by the upper quarter of a bearded human figure, with an Asiatic physiognomy, not unlike the Jewish, and with the arms bound together and hanging down behind. As to their total number I am not certain; but in 1835, I found 133 visible, above the rubbish, forming nine rows; five rows, of thirteen each, being represented as led in bonds by the king; and four rows, of seventeen each, led by the goddess whom Sir G. Wilkinson supposed to be Khêmi, of Egypt (See his Anct. Ens., plate 53, part 3), who has a kind of battle-axe or mace in one hand, and a bow, and apparently a quiver, in the other. Before these two is also a group of prisoners. The third name in the third of the rows first mentioned is read, by Champollion, "Ioudahamalek," and interpreted "the Kingdom of the Jews," or "— of Judah": but it is in no way distinguished from the others. Had it been placed at the head of a row, his interpretation would have been more satisfactory.—We now return to the great court.

Before the great portal at the end of the court were two colossal statues of granite, about twenty-three feet high, facing each other, one on either side. One of these, that on the right, is still standing; but much mutilated: the head has been broken off: the attitude is that of walking; the left foot advanced: upon the belt is the name of the king whom it was meant to represent, Rameses 2nd.[1] The fragments of the other colossus are lying on the ground.—The portal of the second propylæum is a most noble object: its height is scarcely less than a hundred feet. Two very massive walls, projecting from it, one on either side, form a sort of vestibule before it. The upper part of the portal has been demolished, or has, perhaps, fallen in consequence of the weight of the enormous blocks of stone of which it was constructed. Both the portal and the whole propylæum were built (partly with materials of a structure still more ancient[2]) by the immediate predecessor (and father) of Rameses 2nd, and the latter added some sculptures; but the portal was repaired, many centuries after, by Ptolemy Physcon; who added to it a new front; covered this front with sculptures; and sculptured afresh the interior of the portal, where it did not require to be rebuilt; inserting his own name with that of Rameses 2nd. These sculptures represent the two kings offering to Amon-Ra and other gods: they are executed in the usual clumsy style which characterizes the Ptolemaic sculptures, and distinguishes them from those of the times of the Pharaohs; particularly of the more ancient Pharaohs.

The view through this portal into the great portico, or hypostyle hall,[3] is one of the grandest scenes that architecture can present. We look up an avenue of twelve enormous columns, the largest in any Egyptian building: there are six in either row: each is eleven feet eight inches in diameter, and sixty-four feet high, without the plinth which surmounts the capital; and with this, more than sixty-eight feet: the capital is nearly eleven feet high; and its diameter, at the widest part, about twenty-three feet. The injuries which these columns have sustained from violence and time render them more picturesque: and an obelisk and two portals beyond terminate the view very finely. The width of the great portico is the same as that of the preceding court,—330 feet; and its length is 170. The great colonnade which I have described extends through the centre of it: the rest of the portico is occupied by smaller columns: yet these are nine feet in diameter, and more than forty feet high. The capitals of the larger columns represent the full-blown lotus; and the architect, with good taste, chose the form of the *bud* of the same flower for the capitals of the *smaller* columns. The number of the smaller columns is one hundred and twenty-two: there are sixty-one on either side of the great colonnade, arranged in seven rows; each row consisting of nine columns, excepting the row next the great columns, where the places of the two

---

[1]On the side of the back support of this statue, facing the great propylæum, is sculptured a daughter of this king; and on the same side of the base is the name of his second successor, Osirei II.

[2]In some of the ruined parts of the propylæum I remarked many blocks of stone bearing sculptures upon one side, which was turned inwards: but I searched in vain among them for a name, by which to ascertain the age of the building to which they had belonged.

[3]See plate 23 [fig. 81].

last columns are occupied by a wall projecting from the propylæum which forms the end of the court. The portico therefore contains the prodigious number of one hundred and thirty-four enormous columns. The intercolumniations of the great columns are each thirteen feet: those of the others, eight feet; with one exception; for in order to form a sufficiently wide *transverse* avenue across the middle of the portico, the fourth and fifth columns in each row are placed twelve feet apart.[1] There is a doorway at each end of this avenue. The portico was entirely roofed with enormous masses of stone. The roof over the great central columns, composed of stones about thirty feet in length, all of which have been thrown down, or have fallen by reason of their great length and weight, was continued in the same level to the top of a row of columns on each side. Each of these windows had stone gratings.[2] The roof over the other columns is lower; being supported immediately by the architraves of those columns. The portico is bounded in front by the back of the second propylæum: and at the eastern end, by a wall built against the front of another propylæum: while the exterior walls of the temple bound it on the north and south sides.

I have now to speak of the sculptures on the columns and walls, and of the history which they convey. It appears from them that this vast portico was constructed during the reign of Osiree 1st, the father of Rameses 2nd. The most ancient sculptures, both on the columns and walls, bear his name (no. 50 in my list); and are executed in very low relief, and with great delicacy. The great central columns, and many of the others, were smoothed down, and sculptured afresh, in intaglio, by Rameses 2nd; and several of the remaining columns were in the same manner partly or wholly resculptured by Rameses 4th; who also caused the conspicuous name of Rameses 2nd, which was cut on the lower part of each of the greater columns, to be filled up with plaster, and his own engraved in its place: but the plaster has fallen out, and rendered this second imposture manifest. The fore-part, and southern part, of the portico is much obstructed by rubbish, which conceals many of the sculptures. The subjects of the sculptures are mostly offerings presented by the kings above mentioned to Amon-Ra (the great god of Thebes), Amon-Generator, or Khem (another form or character of the same), and other divinities. The interior side of the propylæum which forms the front of the portico, is, in comparison with its fore part, but little ruined. Its sculptures are on a colossal scale; but in very low relief; and represent similar subjects to those before mentioned. In some instances here the name of the king under whom the sculptures were executed (the founder of the portico) has been erased; and that of his son and successor, Rameses 2nd, cut in its place. On the interior of the north side-wall of the portico the sculptures are of the age of the former king: upon the other side-wall they are of the reign of Rameses 2nd. Both of these walls

---

[1]See the view of this transverse avenue—plate 24 [fig. 82].
[2]One of them is seen in my view of the transverse avenue—plate 24 [fig. 82].

are much ruined. Among the sculptures on the interior of the south wall is a representation of a net spread among some lotus-plants, and full of water-fowls: the ram-head god Kneph, the king (Rameses 2nd), and a hawk-headed deity are pulling a cord which is to close the net: before them stand Thoth, with extended arms, and the goddess Neith: this design is found in several tombs. We find that the wall which forms the eastern end of the portico bears sculptures of the reign of the father of Rameses 2nd on its northern half, and of the reign of the latter king on the southern half; and that it is built against the sculptured front of a propylæum, now in a very ruined state: the propylæum is therefore more ancient than the portico; and it is also proved to be so by its sculptures: it is of the reign of Amonoph 3rd.

The interior of the great portico suggests some further remarks. This stupendous structure is the most noble part of the principal edifice of Diospolis, and was doubtless the scene of the most magnificent festivals of that city, and of the most splendid displays of Pharaonic pomp. Here its illustrious founder, and his more illustrious son, Rameses 2nd (the mighty Sesostris), celebrated their triumphs, and offered their thanksgivings to the great god of Thebes for their extensive conquests. It is interesting to inquire how and when the extensive injuries which it has sustained were effected. We cannot look round upon its enormous columns, and observe the massive structure of its roof, without being at once convinced that these injuries are more the results of barbarian violence than of natural decay or accident. We find, moreover, that it was in a state of ruin before the times of the Ptolemies: for not only was the great portal which forms its entrance resculptured and in part rebuilt by a Ptolemy, as already mentioned, but many of the great columns were repaired at the same time. To reduce it to such a state as to have needed these extensive repairs must have required prodigious labour; and to none can we attribute the work of demolition with so much probability (seeing that it was done at so early a period) as to the Persians under Cambyses, in accordance with the testimony of respectable historians. It might be supposed that the building had suffered from an earthquake; but there are adjacent structures of equal antiquity and of less solidity which exhibit no sign of such a convulsion. The lower parts of some of its columns and walls are somewhat decayed. This may partly be attributed to the existence of nitre in the rubbish in which those parts are buried, but in a greater degree, perhaps, to damp. It is melancholy to reflect that before the lapse of many centuries this proud portico will, probably, have fallen to utter ruin: successive inundations have raised the level of the surrounding plain above that of the site of the great temple; and though the latter is protected from the influx of the waters of the swollen river by the mounds of rubbish which environ it, yet the water filters through the soil sufficiently to produce a sensible degree of damp at the foundations of the building after the season of the inundation.

On the exterior of the two side-walls of the great portico are some of the finest and most interesting sculptures in Egypt. I begin with the description of those on the *north* wall. Many of the upper ranges of stone along the whole extent of this wall have been thrown down. The face of the wall is divided into three horizontal compartments, each about eight feet and a half in height, containing a series of sculptures representing various events of a war prosecuted by the father of Rameses 2nd. Of the upper compartment nearly the whole is destroyed. Upon a small portion of it remaining at the right extremity is represented a group of defeated soldiers pursued by the Egyptian king in his car, and pierced by his arrows: they have arrived too late at the walls of their fortress; which is situated on a hill surrounded by trees or shrubs. Beneath the fortress is a peasant driving away from the field of battle four oxen, which have the Indian hunch. The piece is imperfect. All the sculptures on this wall are in intaglio; but boldly relieved in the hollow. They represent conquests obtained over the armies of several Asiatic nations.

Of the sculptures of the middle compartment; beginning at the right extremity of the wall, the first subject is a battle-scene: of this I insert a copy,[1] which will serve to convey an idea of the general style of sculptures of similar subjects upon the walls of various Egyptian edifices. The colossal[2] figure of the Egyptian monarch is characterised, as usual, by a remarkable easiness: that of his principal opponent is most admirably delineated: the horses are full of pride and fire, and are richly caparisoned; and the confusion of the routed host is expressed with much invention and ingenuity. The next piece is a spirited group, representing the Egyptian king in the act of slaying one of his foes with a javelin; and trampling on another. We then see him proceeding at a slow pace in his car, preceded by two rows of captives, whose arms are bound in painful attitudes. Next he is represented leading the same captives before Amon-Ra.[3] Then we see him killing a group of these captives before the same god. Here intervenes the door-way which is one of the two entrances to the transverse avenue of the great portico.

Before I describe the sculptures of the eastern half of the wall I shall mention those of the lower compartment of the other half.[4] They are very similar to those above. First is a battle-scene: the enemy, on foot and in cars, and one on horseback, are flying before the Egyptian king; and most of them are wounded. Next, the king is represented stepping into his car, dragging behind him two captives by the hair of their heads, and holding the reins of two cars, in each of which are two men: he is

---

[1]See no. 25 of the subjects for wood-cuts. (among the *mounted* drawings next to plate 24 [missing]). (Not found R.S.P.)

[2]It is only colossal in comparison with the other figures: in reality it is about the size of life.

[3]Behind and below whom are represented six rows of captives, or captured places, in a similar manner to those of Sheshonk, before mentioned.

[4]These were cleared of the rubbish by which they had long been concealed by Mr. Burton and Mr. Hay, some months before the period of my visit.

also preceded, as above, by two rows of captives; whom, in the next piece, he is leading before Amon-Ra.

On the other half of the wall are represented subjects of the same kind. I begin at the left extremity of what is now the upper compartment. The first piece is a battle-scene: the enemies of the Egyptian king are, as usual, overwhelmed, and pierced with arrows, in their flight to their fortress, situated on a hill, at the foot of which several fugitives are crouching down to hide themselves behind some trees; but the trees are represented smaller than the men. Two wounded horses here, one plunging, and the other fainting from loss of blood, are very admirably executed. The Egyptian monarch is next represented in the act of binding a captive: but this design is much injured. We then see him standing behind his car, holding two captives in each arm, and crushing them to death against his sides: this piece, also, is, unfortunately, much injured. The king is next represented leading his captives before Amon-Ra; and then, as before, slaying them with a mace. In the lower compartment of the wall, beginning from the same extremity, we first see the Egyptian king in his car, setting out from a fortress. Then we again see him overwhelming his enemies, who have three fortresses. Next is one of the most interesting of all the historical sculptures now found in Egypt. The same monarch is here represented in his car, returning from a victorious expedition: he is preceded by three rows of miserable captives, and followed by three other captives: all of these have their arms bound together in painful attitudes. The king holds, besides his bow, four cords, which are tied round the necks of the three groups of captives before him and of the group behind his car. He is approaching the Nile; which is represented by a narrow, perpendicular space, within which are several crocodiles; and across it is a bridge. One each side of the river are some edifices, designed, probably, to represent the temples of Thebes. Beyond the river are two groups of Egyptians, coming forth to congratulate their prince on his triumphant return: in the hands of one party, some of whom are standing erect, and some bowing the body, are what appear to be nosegays: the others (the lower group) are represented, some standing, some kneeling, with uplifted hands. We then again see the king leading his captives before Amon-Ra.

Round the left (or eastern) extremity of the wall are two other pieces of sculpture. In the uppermost of these, eight captives are represented employed in felling trees. The Egyptian king is standing before them, at the back of his car, and extending his hand, as if giving orders to the foremost person, an Egyptian soldier, apparently the task-master of the captives.[1] Before the king's car is a fortress; the door of which is falling. Sir Gardner Wilkinson has strong reasons for regarding the sculptures on

---

[1] It has been said that the king is giving money: this is a mistake: the supposed coins are merely chips in the stone.

this portion of the wall as representing events of a campaign in Syria.[1]
The lower sculpture is a representation of another siege, or battle-scene.
The king is pressing upon his flying enemies, who are endeavouring to
reach their fortress: this is situated on a hill: one of the fugitives has
nearly reached the top of the hill, when an arrow strikes him, and he
falls: another receives a wound while in the act of helping up one of his
comrades, who is too weak from loss of blood to climb the steep: even
those at the top of the hill who have as yet escaped unwounded are aware
of their impending fate: one is stretching out his arms, imploring mercy;
and another, behind the former, is breaking his bow against his knee. The
enemy are clad in a close-fitting vest; and are armed with spears, javelins,
and battle-axes.

The sculptures on the exterior of the *south* wall of the great portico are
of a similar nature to those just described: they commemorate the
exploits of Rameses 2nd; and are admirable in point of style; but, as far as
they are now visible, not so interesting as the sculptures of the father of
this king, on the north wall. The divisions of the south wall are similar to
those of the other; and the upper part is, in like manner, ruined. The
whole of the lower compartment, and part of that next above, are
concealed by the rubbish. One groupe I particularly admired: it
represents the Egyptian monarch in the act of binding two captives.
About one quarter of this wall, at the right (or eastern) extremity, is
included in a square court; the walls of which were built at the same time
as the south wall of the portico; as is proved by the construction at the
point where one wall unites with the other: the same name is also found
upon the walls of this side court.[2] This court is approached by four
propylæa, which constituted the grand southern entrance to the great
temple: of these I shall have to speak more particularly hereafter: they are
all more ancient than the great portico.

From the top of the door-way which leads from the side-court above-
mentioned into the great temple I made a view[3] which will convey an
idea of the remains next behind the great portico. The propylæum of
Amonoph 3rd, which forms the back of the great portico, is thrown
down nearly to its base. Upon the back of the northern wing of this are
sculptured, in a very delicate style, in low relief, two large boats; but so
little remains of the structure itself that neither of these sculptures are
entire. One of the boats was above forty feet in length; and a number of
figures are represented on board, employed in propelling it with poles.
The other (which is to the right) is rather more than fifty feet in length:
the body of it is richly carved with representations of the king Amonoph

---

[1]Finding here the names of "Canana" and "Lemanon," which confirm his
opinion, he remarks, on the latter name. A. Ens., i, 62.
[2]On the west side of the west [south] wall are remains of battle-scenes, and a long
hieroglyphic inscription with the names of Rameses I. and his two next
successors. See T. and E., p. 195, first sentence.
[3]See plate 25 [fig. 83].

3rd presenting offerings to the gods: at the prow and stern is a ram's head; and in the middle of the boat is erected a kind of shrine, supporting another boat, to which the king is presenting an offering.

Beyond this third propylæum is a fourth, in a state of ruin. The intermediate space is about fifty feet. Here were two granite obelisks; and behind the fourth propylæum were two others. Of the former, the northernmost has fallen, or been thrown down, and broken in pieces; and the southernmost of the latter has experienced the same fate. The two remaining obelisks are seen in the plate last referred to. Each is, as usual, a single block of red granite. The first, though not equal in dimensions to the other, is six feet square near the base; and, notwithstanding a part is concealed beneath a quantity of rubbish, the height above the ground is at least sixty-five feet: the entire height must be more than seventy feet. There are three columns of hieroglyphics down each side. The middle column is the most ancient: it contains the names of Thothmos 1st; the earliest king, excepting one, under whom any of the existing monuments of Kur'nak were constructed: this name is engraved with some slight variations on the different sides. The lateral lines, or columns, have the name of Rameses 4th; which, however, has been cut over another name.

A part of the left side of the portal of the fourth propylæum remains: upon it are some of the original sculptures, with the name of Thothmos 4th; and some late sculptures, in the Ptolemaic style. Behind this propylæum is a portal without any sculpture. The other obelisk is to the left of this. It is eight feet square near the base; and, though the rubbish around it rises fifteen feet, or more, above the base, its summit is at least eighty feet above the ground; therefore its entire height cannot be less than ninety-five feet, and is probably a hundred: yet this is a single mass of granite, doubtless brought from the quarries of Syene. It is the largest obelisk now in Egypt; and the largest ever known to have been in Egypt, excepting one.[1] It has a single line of very large hieroglyphics extending from the top down each side; and several horizontal lines of smaller hieroglyphics next the base: both the former and the latter contain the name of a personage whom I suppose to have been regent of Egypt during the minority of Thothmos 3rd.[2] On the eastern face of the obelisk this name is found at the commencement of the principal inscription, and that of Thothmos 1st about the middle, and near the end. The upper half of the obelisk is also ornamented with the figures of several kings offering to Amon-Ra: there are eight figures of kings on one side of the great line of hieroglyphics, and a figure of Amon-Ra opposite to each on

---

[1]The Lateran obelisk, which is 105 feet and a half in height. This was removed from Heliopolis to Alexandria by Constantine the father of Constantius; and by the latter transported to Rome.

[2]My reasons for this supposition will be stated in my account of the temple of the As'a'see'f, in the next section of this chapter. The name is no. 44a in my list. [Hatshepsut, of whose existence Lane was unaware.]

the other side. Among these kings are Thothmos 1st and 3rd, and the father of Rameses 2nd, besides the prince by whom the obelisk was erected; and we may therefore conclude that these lateral sculptures were added by order of the father of Rameses 2nd. The corresponding obelisk is broken into many pieces. The part in which the two great obelisks are situated was an oblate court, which seems to have been surrounded by Osiridean pillars: of these there are many remains.

A few feet beyond the great obelisks are ruins of another small propylæum, or of a wall; and a little further are remains of a granite portal. On either side of the altar are ruined walls; mostly with the name of Thothmos 3rd; but on some parts is the name of the second successor of Rameses 2nd (no. 53 in my list). Behind the broken granite portal are two pillars (if such they may be called), nearly in the form of obelisks; but flat-topped[1]: these are of red granite; and monolithic. Upon the front and back of each is represented Thothmos 3rd embraced by Amon-Ra and by a goddess. The sides of each are beautifully ornamented: upon the sides of the left pillars are sculptured, in relief, three lotus-plants; and upon those of the right, three other water-plants. These two pillars are erected before a granite sanctuary, which is open at each end, and consists of two chambers, divided only by a wide door-way. The roof of this building is double: the uppermost roof is of sand-stone: the structure is otherwise entirely of granite; and built with the materials of an older edifice, which had been erected, probably, on the same spot, by Thothmos 3rd, whose name is found on the top of the granite roof-stones. The present building appears, from its sculptures, to have been founded by Philip Arridæus. In two hieroglyphic inscriptions in the second chamber the name of Thothmos 3rd is found together with that of Philip. It was, doubtless, to conciliate the good will of the Egyptians that Philip and Alexander erected sanctuaries in Egyptian temples. The granite sanctuary of Kur'nak is decorated with sculptures within and without; and these sculptures retain in a great degree the colours with which they were originally painted. On the exterior Philip is represented receiving emblems of divinity from the gods: in the interior we see him presenting offerings to Amon-Ra and Amon Generator: here also is sculptured a design which I have mentioned as found on the interior of the south-wall of the great portico; representing the king and two gods drawing a net full of water-fowls. The ceiling is painted with yellow and red stars, upon a blue ground.

There are constructions on each side of the granite sanctuary; but these are in so ruined a state that their plan cannot be completely traced. On the left (or northern) side is a wall facing the sanctuary, with a door-way of black basalt; and on this wall, to the right of the door-way, is sculptured a curious collection of offerings made to the temple by Thothmos 3rd; consisting of two high shafts to set up against the front of a propylæum, two obelisks, and various ornaments and utensils, with the

---

[1]See plate 26 [fig. 84].

number of each beneath. This wall is built close against the sculptured front of another wall, on which is the same name as that in the inscriptions of the great obelisk before described; if we had no other grounds for placing this name before that of Thothmos 3rd this fact alone would be sufficient.

In an excavated hollow behind the granite sanctuary[1] are two blocks of stone, portions of architraves, one of which bears a fragment of the first oval, or prenomen, of Osirtesen 1st, and the other, a fragment of the second oval, or name, of the same king, the earliest known Pharaoh of whom any sculptured monuments now remain. Here, then, was the most ancient part of the temple, or rather the most ancient part of which any vestiges exist. In this same hollow are two large granite blocks, or pedestals, lying one behind the other, in the central line of the general ranges of buidings; and to the left of these is an altar, or pedestal, of black stone.

About a hundred and eighty feet beyond the granite sanctuary is a wide building of very singular construction.[2] It is of the reign of Thothmos 3rd: his name, which is expressed with many variations, being the only one found among its sculptures. The plate above referred to will convey an idea of its exterior appearance. The stones above the lower architraves project nearly nine feet all round the building: their outer extremities must have been supported by a wall, or by pillars. At the back of the building, upon one of the square blocks which support the upper architraves, is a neat hieroglyphic inscription, in small characters.[3] The interior[4] is a hundred and twenty-one feet by thirty-three and a half. The roof, of which the greater part is entire, is supported by two rows of columns; ten in each row. These columns are of a very remarkable description: according to the usual principles of architecture we should call them *inverted* columns; for they increase in size towards the top: their capitals are of a form common in Egyptian buildings, resembling the full-blown lotus; but these, too, are inverted. This portico has been used, some centuries ago, as a place of Christian worship: there are remains of Christian paintings and inscriptions in it. Hieroglyphic legends on the architraves are its only sculptures. It is very remarkable that a building of so fantastic a style should be one of the most ancient in Egypt.

Near the right angle of the front of this building is a small, square chamber, the interior of which is decorated with very interesting sculptures; which have caused it to be called "the Chamber of Kings.["] These sculptures are divided, by a perpendicular line, into two compartments; each of which contains a representation of four rows of

---

[1]See plate 27 [fig. 85].
[2]See again plate 27 [fig. 85].
[3]Containing two variations of the name of King Tacellothis, of the 22nd Dynasty.
[4]See plate 28 [fig. 86].

kings, seated, and every one distinguished by his hieroglyphic name. Thothmos 3rd (who is represented standing, and on a larger scale) is presenting to them offerings, piled upon a table: they are therefore his deified predecessors; but the order in which they are placed appears to be not altogether regular: in the left compartment it seems that we are to begin one series at the right extremity of the bottom row: the first seven in this row, one excepted, I have not met with elsewhere[1]: we then have no. 33 of my list (Osirtesen 1st): this completes the bottom row: then we begin the next row above, from left to right; and find nos. 34 and 35 of my list: the next three are erased; and after these is no. 39 of my list, which is the last of the 17th Dynasty: the names which follow this seem to be a more ancient series.—We are indebted to Mr. Burton or Mr. Hay (I know not which) for the discovery of this "chamber of kings."

Between the wide portico of Thothmos 3rd and the end boundary-wall of the great temple is a space of rather more than a hundred feet; the greater part of which is occupied by buildings, chiefly of the age of the same Thothmos, in a very ruined state, so that it would be difficult to detect their complete plan, and the more so as there is much irregularity in their distribution. Here, to the left of the central line of the great temple, and parallel with that line, is a row of columns of the same order as those in the southern part of the temple of El-Oock'soor. To the right of the same line are two rows of polygonal columns, placed transversely; four in each row; and between these and the end wall of the temple is a series of small chambers, uniting with another series running at a right angle with the former, parallel with the south wall of the temple: the northernmost chamber of the former series appears to have been a sanctuary; and was built, or at least finished, under Alexander the Great: the hieroglyphic name of Alexandros being found throughout, among its sculptures.—Along the interior of the north wall of the temple are also some small, narrow apartments.

The wall which encloses all the buildings more particularly appertaining to the great temple, beyond the great portico, is covered with sculptures of the reign of Rameses 2nd, representing that king offering to the gods. At the back of the temple (placed against the exterior of the boundary-wall, and in the centre) is a monolithic shrine, of the time of Thothmos 3rd, containing two sitting figures, broken off at the waist.

About midway between the end of the great temple and the east side of the crude-brick enclosure, directly behind the former, is a small, ruined temple, of the time of Rameses 2nd, nearly buried in rubbish. It contains several columns almost entire, and two square pillars with Osiridean figures in front. The sculptures present nothing remarkable. Just beyond are five broken columns of Tirhakah, on the right; and on the left, some

remains bearing the name of Ptolemy ⬚𓏤𓂋𓏤 Auletes.—Proceeding in the

---

[1]The third name is found in the list of the Raméseum of El-Ckoor'neh.

same direction from the great temple, we arrive at an unfinished stone portal, which is built into the great crude-brick wall. This bears the name of the supposed Nectanebo.[1]

My slight description of the great temple of Kur'nak is not yet complete. The four propylæa through which we approach the southern entrance behind the great portico properly appertain to this vast temple: so do also, though not exclusively, the grand avenues of androsphinxes, criosphinxes, and rams, on the south-west and south.

In my description of the temple of El-Oock'soor I have mentioned that there are traces of an avenue of sphinxes which appears to have extended from that temple in a direct line towards the monuments of Kur'nak, to the distance of a mile and a quarter. Towards the north-east extremity of this avenue the remains of several sphinxes (which are of the common kind—that is, androsphinxes) are yet seen. From this extremity[2] two other avenues branch off: one, an avenue of androsphinxes, turning off towards the east, and communicating with an avenue of criosphinxes, which leads to the four propylæa above-mentioned: the other is an avenue of rams, leading towards the north, or rather towards the north-north-east.

The latter[3] is a road nine hundred feet in length. From its northern extremity to more than half its length it is bordered on each side by a row of colossal rams, all more or less mutilated, but still presenting a very striking appearance: these two rows were probably continued the whole length of the road: as far as they extend at present, each row appears to have consisted of nearly sixty rams, all of the same dimensions, eleven feet in length: but the series on each side is interrupted in several places by the demolition of one or more of these colossi. They are evidently not criosphinxes which I have here called rams: the fore-legs are folded under the body; and the forms altogether are very true to nature. They are monuments of the reign of Amonoph 3rd. All of them have been wantonly mutilated: the heads have all been broken off.[4] Against the breast of each is sculptured, in high relief, a small Osiridean figure. The material of which these colossi are formed (as well as the sphinxes of all the other avenues here) is a yellowish sandstone, of the same kind as that of which most of the temples are constructed. The pedestals upon which they rest are buried entirely, or almost entirely, in rubbish.

This avenue is terminated, at the northern extremity, by a Ptolemaic portal, of very noble proportions, nearly seventy feet in height, and

---

[1]On the lower part of the sides, under the gateway, this King is represented offering to Amon-Ra, Maut, and Khons: on the eastern face, over the door, is Ptolemy Philadelphus presenting offerings.
[2]See the topographical plan of Thebes—plate 16 [fig. 74].
[3]See plate 29 [fig. 87].
[4]One of these heads was carried off by the French, and is now in the British Museum.

covered with sculptures by Euergetes 1st, carefully finished, but in a clumsy style, like all of that age: much of the paint with which they were adorned still remains upon them. This portal was to have connected the two wings of a propylæum, of which we see the foundations.

The avenue of rams, and the portal just described, form a direct approach to a temple, of more ancient date than the latter, but less ancient than the former. It is most probable, also, that a road branched off from behind the portal, and communicated with one of the southern entrances of the *great* temple. The space between this portal and the temple behind it is about 140 feet. Here are remains of more rams, which composed another avenue, in a line with the former, but about double the width. The propylæum which forms the front of the temple is covered with sculptures representing offerings. All of these bear a name (no. 90 of my list) supposed by Wilkinson (See T. and E., p. 172) to be that of Boccharis, excepting the sculptures round and within the door-way, which has been repaired, and sculptured afresh, under Alexander the Great. Passing through the propylæum, we enter a small court, surrounded on every side except the front by a double colonnade. The columns are of the same order as the smaller ones in the great portico of the grand temple: the walls behind them are covered with a profusion of sculptures; the subjects of which are of the usual kind; merely offerings, &c. Behind this court is a wide but small chamber, with two rows of columns on either side; two columns in each row: those in the two rows next the centre have capitals of that form which seems to be taken from the full-blown lotus: the others are similar to those in the preceding court. The former columns being higher than the latter, the central part of the roof, also, is higher than the portions extending from the side-columns to the side walls; and the light is admitted by stone grated windows over the smaller columns, of the same kind as those of the great temple. This is a more ancient part of the edifice: its sculptures bear the name of Rameses 8th. The remaining part of the temple (the most ancient) is divided into a number of small apartments, nearly filled with rubbish. The oldest sculptures here bear the name of Rameses 4th; but some parts have been sculptured, perhaps a second time, by the Roman Emperor Augustus; whose name in hieroglyphics is merely Autocrator Kaisaros.

Adjoining this temple, on the left (or western) side, is one of smaller dimensions, and of less ancient date; a Ptolemaic structure.[1] The sculptures of the exterior have the name of the Roman Emperor above-mentioned. We enter on the western side, by a high door-way, into a square chamber, with plain, unsculptured walls: it has two columns, with capitals similar to those of the portico of the great temple of Den'dar'a. Beyond this chamber is another, of less dimensions; and there is one on

---

[1]The sculptures within bear the name of Physcon: at the door, we find the name

of another Ptolemy; I believe, Auletes. It is ◗◖

each side of the latter, and a very small one at the end, with a niche for some sacred object: all these are sculptured, with the usual subjects of offerings, &c.—Near these two temples is a small monolithic shrine of sandstone, on the west of the avenue of rams. It is decorated with some ill-executed sculptures, representing offerings, with the name of a Ptolemy.[1]

The avenue of criosphinxes leading to the four propylæa which form the principal southern approach to the great temple is nearly parallel with the avenue of rams, and of about the same length that the latter is supposed to have been when complete; that is, nine hundred feet. These sphinxes are of the reign of Horus (no. 48 on my list), the immediate successor of Amonoph 3rd; and they exceed in size the colossal rams of his predecessor, as well as all the other sphinxes at Thebes: they are about seventeen feet in length[,] four feet six inches in width, and between ten and eleven feet apart: so each row must have consisted, originally, of about sixty of these colossi. Most of them are much mutilated: some are entirely demolished; and others, broken into almost shapeless masses; and their pedestals are mostly buried in rubbish. From the few which are less injured we may plainly see that the body is that of the lion; and the head, that of the ram: both are true to nature. In one part of the avenue is a grove of palm-trees. I have already mentioned that this avenue is connected with that which leads from the direction of the temple of El-Oock'soor (and which doubtless originally extended the whole of the way to that temple) by a transverse avenue of androsphinxes: these sphinxes are of smaller dimensions, and nearer together, than those before described: most of them are much broken; and few, in their places.

The propylæum to which the avenue of criosphinxes leads is much ruined: particularly its left wing; which is almost entirely demolished. It is of the same age as the criosphinxes; for it bears the name of Horus. Its portal is of granite. Before it were two colossal statues; but the base and fragments of only one of these, of grit-stone, are now seen. The propylæum has but little sculpture, excepting on the portal: the subjects are offerings, &c., tendered by King Horus to Amon-Ra and other divinities. The sculptures on the portal are executed with a remarkable delicacy. Behind the propylæum are two colossi, of hard, white chert, like marble. They are in a standing posture; and, when entire, must have been about thirty feet in height: both the heads have been broken off.[2] One of these colossi is nearly buried by blocks of stone which have been thrown down from the propylæum: the other (the western) exposed to the feet: it has, upon the belt, the name of Rameses 2nd, whom, therefore, it is designed to represent; and in the belt is stuck a dagger.— The first propylæum is connected with the second by a wall, now ruined,

---

[1]Philopator.

[2]Each, in its present state, is more than twenty feet high.

on each side, enclosing a spacious square court. On the eastern side of this court is a temple, nearly buried in rubbish: it bears the name of Amonoph 2nd: all that remains of it is a chamber, or portico, with a number of square pillars: before it is one jamb of a granite portal.

The second propylæum is much ruined, like the first. The fragments of its granite colossi are strewed upon the ground in front. This propylæum had the same name as the first, but the name of Rameses 2nd has been cut over it, and is found on many parts of the pile.

The third propylæum and the fourth are parallel with the southern side of the great temple; not with the first and second propylæa; the fronts of which are directed rather more towards the south. The third propylæum is much smaller than the first and second; but it is the most perfect of all. It bears the names of Thothmos 3rd, Amonoph 2nd, of the father of Rameses 2nd, also the name of Rameses 2nd, and that of Rameses 3rd. Under all these kings have its sculptures been carried on; but it was erected in the reign of a yet more ancient king, Thothmos 1st; his name being found on the back. I think, too, that the name of Amonoph 2nd on the front has been altered from that of Thothmos 1st. In front of this propylæum were, or are, four sitting colossal statues; but only two of them are now seen; those in front of the left wing. The colossus next the doorway has been broken off at the waist: it is of red grit-stone, and represents Thothmos 2nd. The other[1] is of hard, white chert: the face is quite destroyed; but the statue is otherwise quite perfect. On each wing of the propylæum is represented a king, to whom the name of Amonoph 2nd is given (but this name is apparently cut over that of Thothmos 1st), killing a groupe of captives, as a sacrifice to Amon-Ra. The subjects of the sculptures on the back are merely offerings. This propylæum was connected with the fourth by two side-walls, which are almost entirely destroyed.[2]

The fourth (or last) propylæum is the most ruined of all; nothing remaining of it but shapeless heaps.[3] The only object worthy of being mentioned here is a granite colossus broken off at the waist, just appearing above the rubbish on the right of the doorway.[4] Behind this propylæum is the court through which we enter the great temple: the entrance is at the end of this court, near the right angle: it is a wide gateway, now almost wholly demolished.—As the latest of the four propylæa which I have just described were built by Horus, they are all more ancient than the great portico of the grand temple.

To the east of the third and fourth of these propylæa is a lake, or large tank, which was anciently cased with stone. It is of a rectangular form;

---

[1]It is of Amonoph 2nd. From the top of the seat to the top of the head, it measures between fourteen and fifteen feet. The former statue is not quite so large.

[2]The right-wall has sculptures of the reign of Thothmos 3rd.

[3]It has no name, but a few sculptured blocks.

[4]Upon a fragment of it is the name of Rameses 2nd.

and about 430 feet in length, by 260 in breadth. The greater part of its bottom is still covered with water, which filters into it from the Nile, and, being stagnant here, becomes very brackish.—Between this lake and the great temple are some ancient remains; among which, near the wall of the temple, is a small building containing some curious sculptures. It consists of two chambers; and in the first (which is the smaller) of these, over the door which leads into the second chamber, is sculptured a tree, beneath which is the hieroglyphic name of Osiris: on the left of the tree is a female discharging an arrow from a bow: on the right, a man casting stones, or round balls. On the left side-wall are some devices which seem to represent a funeral-procession: on the opposite wall, some persons carrying images of gods.—Not far from this little building is a covered passage, inclining gently downwards: at the distance of about ten or twelve feet, I found it closed with rubbish.—There are many other remains around the lake, or tank; mostly, little edifices, or cells, like shrines, for the reception of images.

There are numerous ancient remains on the *north* of the great temple.—Here, within the great crude-brick enclosure are two small ruined temples in this quarter; both nearly buried in rubbish. One of them, the smaller of the two, is near the great portico: it bears the name of Psammetichus 3rd. The other, which is next the great crude-brick wall, was built, or first sculptured in the reign of Thothmos 3rd[1]; and has been repaired under the Ptolemies.

On the north of the great enclosure is a smaller one, formed by similar walls of crude brick. This is entered from the north by a stone portal, nearly sixty feet high, which, standing apart from any lofty ruin, has a fine appearance.[2] It is of the Ptolemaic period, and bears the name of Philopator. A short avenue of androsphinxes, of which there are few remaining, forms a direct approach to it. Within the enclosure, directly behind this portal, are remains of an extensive building of the ages of Amonoph 3rd and Rameses 2nd, repaired or enlarged under the Ptolemies. Among these are numerous columns wholly or almost wholly overthrown, walls destroyed nearly to their foundations, fragments of two granite obelisks, and statues and sphinxes of black granite. This edifice must have been very magnificent.[3]—At the western side of the enclosure are remains of another temple, of the reign of Amyrtæus.[4]

---

[1] It contains also the names of Rameses 2nd, Shebek (who is either Sabaco or Sebechon or Sevechus), Euergetes 1st, Philomator, and another Ptolemy; I believe, Auletes. It is 𓊖 𓄿𓈖𓏏

[2] It is covered with sculptures, partly retaining the colours, by Euergetes 1st and Philopator.

[3] On the east is a small temple of the reign of Hakor. There is also, in the brick wall, a portal bearing the names of Amyrtæus and Nectanebo.

[4] It is very small, and has an ascent of low stone steps to its entrance, which is towards the east.

Near the south-eastern angle of the great enclosure is a small square enclosure, also formed by walls of crude brick, having in each of three of its sides a stone doorway. It surrounds some relics of a small temple, of the age of Rameses 2nd.

There is yet another enclosure to be mentioned: it is one of considerable extent; and formed by walls of crude brick. Its entrance is at the southern extremity of the great avenue of criosphinxes which leads to the four propylæa on the south of the great temple. A little to the left of the entrance are remains of a temple of the reign of Thothmos 3rd; and among these ruins are some broken statues of black basalt. The entrance to the enclosure above-mentioned is a ruined Ptolemaic portal.[1] Immediately within it we find an avenue of sphinxes, and one of rams, running to the right and left. In the former direction are some Ptolemaic remains, unworthy of notice. In the opposite direction are some relics of a temple of a very ancient period: I judge of its age only from the style of its sculptures; for I found no name here, excepting upon some Ptolemaic restorations: the site of this temple is in the north-east angle of the enclosure: before it are two prostrate broken statues of granite. Nearly in the centre of the enclosure which contains these remains is another enclosure, formed by equally massive walls of crude brick, which surround a space about 300 feet in length, and 150 in width. The entrance of this inner enclosure is a stone portal, now ruined, at its northern extremity, directly behind the entrance of the outer enclosure.[2] Immediately before this portal are some Ptolemaic remains[3]; and on the right are several more sphinxes. Entering the inner enclosure, we find it occupied by ruined columns and walls which seem to have composed a considerable temple. Some of these remains are of the reigns of Thothmos 3rd and Amonoph 3rd; others, of the times of the Ptolemies. Among them are many sitting statues of a goddess with the head of a lion, in black basalt.[4] A lake of a horse-shoe form[5] surrounds, on three sides, the southern part of this inner enclosure. Like that near the great temple, this lake receives the water of the Nile by filtration through the soil.—On the west of the horse-shoe lake, just within the outer wall of crude brick, are remains of another temple, of the reign of Rameses 3rd; near which are two broken colossi of granite.[6] Upon its western wall are seen some relics of sculptures representing battle-scenes; but no subject is complete: just enough of these sculptures has been spared to make us

[1]Bearing the name of Philadelphus.
[2]It bears the names of Osirei 2nd and Ptolemy Physcon.
[3]The name upon them is, I believe, that of Auletes. It is ⟨hieroglyphs⟩
[4]The lion-headed statues which are in the British Museum were removed from this place by the French. See A. Ens., iv., p. 276.
[5]See plate 30 [fig. 88].
[6]A door of this temple, ornamented with the winged globe and the name of its founder, is seen in plate 30 [fig. 88].

regret very much the ruin of the temple which they decorated: its remains scarcely shew themselves above the surrounding rubbish.

Section 3. El-Ckoor'neh.

General remarks—Ruined village of El-Ckoor'neh, and ancient edifice there—Mummy-pits, &c.; inhabited grottoes, and the people residing in them—Grottoes and pyramids of the hills nearest to the ruined village—Tombs of the As'a'see'f—Temple of the As'a'see'f—Grottoes of the Hill of the As'a'see'f—Hill of the sheykh 'Abd El-Ckoor'neh, and its numerous grottoes—The Rameséum of El-Ckoor'neh—The two colossi of Amonoph 3rd (or Memnon); the Amonophium, and some adjacent remains—Hill of Mar''ee, and its grottoes—Temple of Athor—Valley of the temple of Athor, and hills behind it—Valley of the tombs of Queens.

A fine, spreading sycamore and a sa'ckiyeh (or water-wheel) mark the landing-place of *El-Ckoor'neh*, or, as it is commonly pronounced by the natives, *El-Goor'neh*: but seldom is any boat, unless it be that of a European traveller, seen at that spot; for the inhabitants of El-Ckoor'neh generally cross over to the opposite side of the Nile from a point higher up the river, by the ferry-boat of El-Oock'soor. The name of *El-Ckoor'neh* القرنه is given to the district which contains most of the temples and tombs of western Thebes. "Ckoor'neh" signifies "a promontory," or "a point of a mountain"; such as the western chain forms at this place, approaching within a mile of the river. The inhabitants of this district live not in houses or huts, but in ancient tombs, excavated in the rock. There is a ruined village here, called El-Ckoor'neh; but without a single inhabitant.

Thebes on the west of the Nile presents to our view monuments even more interesting than those on the east of the river; though its temples are not on so stupendous a scale as the great edifice of Kur'nak. It has no obelisks; but, to compensate for the want of these, it has its peculiar wonders, its unrivalled colossi, and its unnumerable sculptured and painted grottoes. The colossi to which I allude I term unrivalled because they are the largest monolithic statues carved out of hard stone, and transported from a distance: the colossi of Absem'bel (or Ab'oo Sim'bil), in Nubia, are indeed larger; and still more so is the great sphinx near the Pyramids of El-Gee'zeh; but these are carved out of soft rock, and not detached and removed from their natural places: therefore they are not so much objects of wonder as those of Thebes.

The traveller who spends but a few days at El-Ckoor'neh will perhaps prefer to pass the night in his boat, before the sycamore: the creaking of the sa'ckiyeh would annoy him during the day; but he would often find the shade of the sycamore very agreeable. He who devotes a longer period to the examination of western Thebes will find it more convenient to imitate the modern inhabitants of El-Ckoor'neh, and to chose for his abode one of the ancient excavated tombs, in a central situation. I was accommodated for some weeks in a house at the foot of the hill of the sheykh 'Abd El-Ckoor'neh, built and inhabited by a Greek, long employed in excavating for antiquities for Mr. Salt.[†]

In describing western Thebes, I shall begin from the sycamore.

For a few miles below this spot the cultivable land which borders the river is very narrow; but immediately above it (that is, to the south-west) is a wide expanse of fertile land. The greater part of this plain is subject to the annual inundation; chiefly towards the mountains: in the month of December, after the inundation has subsided, it is covered with fresh verdure, and has a very pleasant appearance: it is sown with dor'ah sha'mee, door'ah sey'fee, wheat, beans, cotton, indigo, &c. There are some groups of palms and other trees near the landing-place and the old village; but the rest of the plain is almost wholly destitute of trees.

The plain on this side of the river probably comprised not less than half of Thebes, when that city was in its most flourishing state. In the time of Strabo it seems to have been occupied only by scattered dwellings; or was at least considered but as a suburban district of the "Great Diospolis"; which name was restricted to Thebes on the east of the Nile. The surface of the soil of the plain of Thebes has risen, since that author's time (that is, in the space of a little more than eighteen centuries), about seven feet, by the annual deposits of the inundations: these floods at the same time dissolve the crude-brick walls of the ancient dwellings. No traces, therefore, of any of the houses of the ancient city now remain: but there are a few spots a little above the reach of the inundation, which are overgrown with *hhal'feh* (or coarse grass); and these are evidently ancient sites, raised artificially. The temples are mostly on higher ground; for the Egyptians here as well as elsewhere generally built their temples without the limits of the cultivable soil, to secure them from the inundation; and, for the same reason, excavated their tombs in the rock. The mountains of Thebes on this side of the river are remarkably picturesque, and their two highest summits, which are seen in several of my views, rise about eleven hundred feet above the level of the cultivated plain.

Proceeding from the sycamore towards the old village, we first cross the narrow strip of cultivated land. The track here is hemmed in on each side by a low wall, built to protect the crops from the cattle which occasionally pass this way. On entering the desert beyond (which is of a dazzling whiteness, and covered with small fragments of stone), we have before us the ruined village, partly surrounding an ancient edifice[1]: on our left are several enclosures of low walls, containing palms and other trees: on our right is a modern burial-place, with some tombs of sheykhs. We arrive at the ruined village in ten or twelve minutes: it is just half a mile from the river. This village was reduced to ruin, and its inhabitants

---

†Giovanni d'Athanasi, known as Yanni.
[1]See plate 31 [fig. 89].

fled to the neighbouring grottoes, when the Memloo'ks passed this way in their flight before the troops of Mohham'mad 'Al'ee.

The ancient edifice at the ruined village of El-Ckoor'neh[1] is now called *Ckusr Er-Roobey'ck* قصر الربيق but from what this name is derived I could not learn. It seems to have been a palace and temple: for one part is evidently a temple; but the greater part appears, from its plan, to have been a palace. The front of this building is a wide portico, which originally had a row of ten columns: two of these, at the left extremity, have fallen or been thrown down. The front-wall, architraves, &c., bear the name of the father of Rameses 2nd,[†] the founder of the edifice, and that of the latter king, by whose order its decorations were continued. There are three entrances under the colonnade; one in the centre, and one near each extremity. Through the central doorway (which seems to be the grand entrance of the palace) we pass into the principal apartment; the roof of which is supported by two rows of columns; three on the right and three on the left. These are of the same order as the smaller columns in the great portico of Kur'nak, which was built by the founder of this edifice. The columns and walls are ornamented with sculptures beautifully executed; but the subjects are merely offerings and acts of adoration: these are of the reign of the founder. There are three small, square apartments on either side of this great chamber, and several others at the end; but the latter are for the most part ruined.—By the right-hand entrance of this edifice we enter a roofless and ruined part of the palace: it appears like an open court; but was originally divided into a number of apartments, the partition-walls of which have been thrown down.—The left entrance of the building admits us into the temple, which is distinct from the rest of the edifice. We first enter a square chamber with two columns. Beyond this are three very narrow apartments; the central of which was the sanctuary; and it is wider than the other two: on its end-wall are sculptured two sitting figures, each with the habit and insignia of Osiris, and the name of Rameses 1st, accompanied by the *title* of the god Osiris, which was only given to persons deceased: whence it appears that the founder of this temple and palace dedicated the former to his deceased and deified father.—Among the hieroglyphic inscriptions of this edifice are some which are of importance in confirming the order of the list of kings found at Abydos. On the architrave of the front entrance we find the king who is placed in the list of Abydos as the immediate predecessor of Rameses 2nd called the *father* of the latter king: also, on the right side of the entrance of the sanctuary we find Rameses 1st called the *grandfather* of Rameses 2nd; and there are several other inscriptions there establishing the relationship of these three kings. Over the door of the sanctuary is a disk sculptured in relief: to the right of this are ten ovals, in one line, containing five variations of the nomen and prenomen of Rameses 2nd; and on the left of the disk are the same number of ovals,

[1]See plate 32 [fig. 90].
[†]Seti I.

containing the nomens and prenomens of his father and grandfather, placed alternately.—Among the brick ruins in front of this edifice are remains of a stone portal, exactly before the central door; and at about double the distance are some very large blocks which formed part of a propylæum, or of another portal.

In the desert tract to the north-east of the old village of El-Ckoor'neh are many tombs, excavated in the rock, presenting long rows of doors; but they are very rude, and without sculpture or painting.

In my view of El-Ckoor'neh (plate 31[†]) is seen, to the right, in the distance, the entrance of the long, winding valley which leads to the tombs of the kings, called Beeba'n el-Mooloo'k. In the same view is also seen the general aspect of the mountains to the left of the entrance of that valley.

The tract between these mountains and the cultivable land is rocky, and very irregular, and is strewed with a vast quantity of small fragments of stone thrown up in the excavation of ancient catacombs. In traversing this tract, the glaring whiteness of which is rather distressing to the eyes, we observe almost everywhere near the mountains the mouths of numerous mummy-pits, generally between four and eight feet wide: most of them are more or less filled with rubbish; and around some of them we see the bones and rags of the mummies which have been taken out of the subterranean chambers. In some parts, where the rock has been cut so as to present a perpendicular front, or where it has nearly that form by nature, we see the entrances of ancient sepulchral grottoes. The rock is calcareous, white, compact, rather soft, and easily broken: the fragments are angular and sharp.[1] The grottoes in general have low and narrow entrances, without any exterior ornament. They are most numerous in and near the lower part of the sides of the mountains. Each grotto has one or more mummy-pits within it. The mummies, I believe, were originally deposited only in the chamber or chambers beneath the grotto; and the grotto itself was probably left open, or was opened occasionally, for the accommodation of visiters, and for this reason was decorated with paintings or painted sculptures.

Many of the grottoes in the tract adjacent to the mountains, and many of those which are in the sides of the mountains, but not too high to be easily accessible, are now inhabited; the whole population of El-Ckoor'neh, as I have before mentioned, residing in them. The number of inhabited grottoes in this place is between 130 and 150; and few of these are occupied by less than five or six inmates. There are only two inhabited houses in the district: one is that of the Greek whom I have

---

[†]Fig. 89.

[1]Here insert the portion relating to the Tombs in article 10 of the Supplement. On Mummies, see article 9 of the same, and Wilkinson's Anct. Egns., v., near the end. [Another insertion direction that was probably intended for Lane's never-completed book about Thebes. Like the previous one in this chapter, it is not followed here.]

already mentioned: the other is the residence of an Italian[†] who excavates here chiefly on account of the Swedish consul. The sepulchral grottoes of El-Ckoor'neh are very comfortable habitations; sheltering the inmates from the heat in summer, and from the cold of the winter months, more effectually than do the huts of the villagers of Egypt. Almost all the families here keep dogs to guard them: to strangers, these animals are very savage. The Ckoorna'wees (or people of El-Ckoor'neh) are mostly Moos'lims, but very negligent of the ceremonies of their religion. The nature of their usual occupation has made them remiss in this respect: for they obtain their livelihood chiefly by the sale of the antiquities which they procure by ransacking the ancient catacombs, and rifling the mummies; an employment which a strict Moos'lim would regard with the utmost abhorrence, as subjecting the person to constant defilement, and altogether impious and sacrilegious. Many of them practice much deception in their trade. The occupation of excavating they prefer to agricultural labour; as it is more profitable: they do not, however, appear less poor than the generality of the Egyptian peasants: they do not suffer themselves to appear so; fearing to subject themselves to greater exactions than the other fel'la'hhee'n. Their dress is the same: the men wearing the blue or brown shirt, or only a few rags: the women being clad in the dark brown woollen drapery which I have before described as peculiar to the women of the southern parts of the valley of Egypt: a small piece of similar stuff serves them as a veil for the head and, occasionally, for the face also. Their cows, goats, and sheep are often seen, for lack of proper pasture, stripping off with their teeth, and eating, the bandages of cast-out mummies. Mummy-cases are used for firewood. During my stay at El-Ckoor'neh I could obtain no other wood for cooking; and sometimes my servant brought, for this purpose, cases so beautifully ornamented that I was reluctant to allow the cook to make use of them. The people of El-Ckoor'neh were formerly notorious for their savage disposition towards Europeans; to whom, for their own interest, they now behave with all possible civility. They are as obstinate as the generality of the Egyptian peasants in their attempts to save themselves either in part or wholly from the demands of the collector of the taxes: some of them will suffer a severe bastonading rather than pay the full sum required of them; protesting their inability to pay the whole: some, on the approach of the collector, fly, and hide themselves in some distant grotto; leaving their sheykh to be beaten for their default.

In passing, for the first time, near the irregular and rocky tract beyond the ruined village of El-Ckoor'neh, towards the mountains, nothing so much attracted my attention as the inhabited grottoes which I saw here and there. Some of these, being in depressed parts, I should not have seen, and some I should not have known to be inhabited, had not my approach roused the watch-dogs. Dark-complexioned and wrinkled old

---

[†]Piccinini, whose first name is unrecorded, but who is often mentioned by travelers of the day.

women, like resuscitated mummies, sometimes come forth from their sepulchral abodes to call back these ferocious animals, whose attacks often obliged me to draw my sabre. The men were generally absent, engaged in their usual occupation of excavating.

Few of the mummy-pits which have been examined remain open. I descended several: on reaching the bottom, I generally found, on one side, a small chamber, rudely cut, without any ornament, and containing nothing but dust and broken mummies and fragments of stone. But to see one of these tombs opened is very interesting. It is seldom that a traveller has an opportunity to gratify his curiosity by witnessing such a sight; for the labourers generally ransack the tomb as soon as they effect an entrance. I once saw a tomb of this kind opened and examined, during my first stay at El-Ckoor'neh. The pit was eight feet by four in width, and twenty-five feet deep. At the bottom were two small chambers; one opposite the other: one of these was empty: the entrance of the other was closed by a wall of crude bricks. The latter chamber contained four mummies; each in a chest: it was not large enough to receive another mummy: one of the chests was placed upon two others: the fourth chest was very large; containing another within it. These chests were painted in the ordinary manner; not in an elaborate style. Upon and within them were several little boxes containing various ornaments. The three inferior mummies were broken up on the spot: the other was carried away to be examined more carefully. One of the former was enveloped in a large piece of fringed linen, which was in a very perfect state. Some of the ornaments found with these mummies were of beautiful workmanship.[1]—In many of the tombs of Thebes are found small baskets containing flat cakes of bread, in appearance perfectly fresh; but dry and tasteless: also, dates, raisins, and various other eatables, all in a wonderful state of preservation, after having been buried two or three thousand years: and on many other articles the lapse of so many ages seems to have had absolutely no effect; owing to the extreme dryness of the climate. There are many catacombs here which are the depositories of the mummies of sacred animals. Mummies of cats are particularly numerous, and most of these are enveloped with great care, and in a very tasteful manner; the covering of the head having the features represented upon it, with false eyes and ears attached: the body and limbs are compressed into a cylindrical form.

The traveller will find it expedient to have a guide to accompany him in his examination of the antiquities of El-Ckoor'neh; particularly to point out those grottoes which are most worthy of his notice; for he would find it a tedious task even to number the most conspicuous of these tombs; while on the other hand there are many of the most interesting which, from their situation, or in consequence of their entrances being nearly choked and concealed by rubbish, would

---

[1] A list of the principal antiquities found in the tombs of Thebes and other places in Egypt will be found at the end of the supplement to this work.

altogether escape his observation. Several months would not suffice for him to examine all of them, even in a cursory manner.—After having passed the ruined village of El-Ckoor'neh, the traveller will probably first direct his course to the noble and beautiful structure of Rameses 2nd, which has been improperly called the Memnonium; then to the two colossi sitting in the midst of the plain; and next to the edifices of Medee'net Hha'boo; passing, on his way to the first of these monuments, innumerable interesting objects, which have not the same attractive grandeur: but I need not pursue the like irregular course in my description: I deem it preferable to continue this in the order in which I have begun; combining the archæography with the topography.

In the rugged sides of the hills nearest to the ruined village, to the left of the entrance of the valley which leads to the tombs of the kings, are several grottoes which merit a careful inspection, containing interesting paintings. The ascent of these hills is rendered rather fatiguing by the accumulation of small fragments of stone thrown down during the process of excavating the grottoes. By this rubbish many grottoes are, doubtless, choked up and covered; and in the same manner the entrances of many are concealed from the view of a spectator below. Often the clearing out of one grotto occasions the closing up of another. In one of the grottoes at the part which I have pointed out is a painting of a funeral-procession, of which the engraving here inserted will serve (as far as the outline is concerned) as a specimen.[1] This and numerous other paintings shew that the ceremony of conveying the mummy to the tomb in a boat was practised even where there was no water over which to transport it: for here we see it placed in a boat upon a sledge, and drawn by cattle.—Below the same place are extensive catacombs of mummies of cats, and of cows, and snakes, &c.—Proceeding hence up the steep acclivities, towards the north-west, we find, in a dreary, secluded spot, the ruins of a large Christian settlement; consisting of buildings of crude brick.—In the lower parts of the hills, to the south and south-west of these ruins, are numerous grottoes: several of them contain paintings, and many are inhabited. Here, also, are remains of a small pyramid, similar to some which I am about to describe.

Upon the ridge of a hill a little to the west of the part above alluded to are two small, ruined pyramids of crude brick; and upon a steep which rises considerably higher behind are several more, of the same kind. In the front of the lower hill are many grottoes; and here, too, half-way up the steep, is the house of the Italian whom I have before mentioned. The two pyramids on the ridge of this hill are very conspicuous objects, partly from their dark colour, which contrasts with the whiteness of the rocky eminence on which they are situated; but they are very small, and so much ruined that they retain little of the pyramidal form. I insert a view of the westernmost of these two[2]: it is called *El-Mun'dar'ah*, which

---

[1]See no. 26 of the subjects for wood-cuts [fig. 91].
[2]See no. 27 of the subjects for wood-cuts [fig. 92].

is a term applied to any building commanding an extensive view. This and the other pyramids here are much alike in construction: above every second, or every fourth tier of bricks is a layer of *hhal'fa* (or coarse grass): the interior of each is small; from four to eight feet wide; and has an arched roof. The entrances of these pyramids are generally towards the south, or nearly so: the entrance of that of which I have given a view is towards the south-south-west. I have only marked in my topographical plan of Thebes (plate 16[†]) the positions of the *principal* pyramids. The interior of the easternmost of these is plastered and painted: the stucco is much broken; but enough remains to shew that the subjects of the decorations were the same as are generally represented in the tombs, and, consequently, that these brick pyramids are sepulchral monuments. But the paintings here alluded to are highly interesting and important in another point of view, as shewing the very remote antiquity of the brick arch: unfortunately no name of a king remains upon them; but their style is of a very ancient character; and we certainly cannot be much mistaken in referring them to the times of the Eighteenth Dynasty.[1] There are remains of the paintings on both sides of the chamber of the pyramid above-mentioned: on the right side, Osiris, seated, as judge of the dead, and Thoth writing before him. This pyramid is the largest of all: the base, between seventy and eighty feet: but it is one of the most ruined.—Immediately before it is an extensive excavated tomb, which must have been the finest in this part.[‡] It is the tomb of a priest; and is of the reign of Rameses 2nd. Unfortunately, it is much injured. We first enter a transverse gallery, with a row of Osiridean pillars, twelve in number, and cut out of the solid rock, supporting the roof: all of these are much broken; and several have fallen. At each end of the gallery are four colossal sitting figures; two and two; male and female. The sculptures on the walls chiefly represent the deceased priest, clad in a leopard's skin, presenting offerings. Behind the gallery is a chamber with twelve square pillars, in two equal rows: its walls have been plastered and painted; but they are much broken. Beyond this is a small, rudely excavated chamber, with a recess at the end, and one on either side, and a small, broken, sitting figure lying among the rubbish on the ground.—To the left of this tomb, and a little higher up the steep, is another, of the same kind; but not so large.[††] This, also, is the tomb of a priest; and is of the reign of the immediate successor of Rameses 2nd. It has been very handsome. Before it are two masses of a rude wall, resembling remains of a propylæum of the usual Egyptian form. The exterior of the hewn rock forming the front of the tomb has been

---

[†]Fig. 74.
[1]This opinion is confirmed by a discovery of Mr. Wilkinson: he has found in a building of the same kind (and at the same place), with an arched roof, paintings with the name of Amonoph 1st (no. 41 of my list).
[‡]Tomb of Nebwenenet, TT 157.
[††]Tomb of Thonufer, TT 158.

covered with sculptures, which are almost effaced. The transverse gallery which we first enter is without pillars: at each end of it are two colossal sitting figures, which, though much broken, have a fine effect: they represent the deceased priest and his wife. Opposite the entrance is a long passage, or gallery. The sculptures in this tomb are much injured: among them we find the boat of the ram-headed god Kneph, and other designs similar to some of those in the tombs of the kings.—Before the hill of the pyramids (that is, on the south) is a large space occupied entirely by tombs of crude brick; all of which are much ruined.

Having passed the hill of the pyramids of brick, a wide tract, of the same desolate aspect as that which we have already traversed, opens to our view on the right. It is called *El-As'a'see'f* الاساسيف ; a name perhaps derived from *esee'f* اسيف , which signifies "barren," "unproductive," as applied to land. The tract is, for the most part, surrounded by the mountains, which, at the further extremity, present a boundary of high and rugged cliffs.

In that part of the As'a'see'f at which we first arrive are numerous large buildings of crude brick, and many of smaller dimensions. As we approach these buildings we seem to have before us a ruined town. Of the foremost of them, which is one of the most perfect, I give a view.[1] Like all the rest which we see here, the entrance of this is arched. It is in the centre of a very massive construction, resembling the propylæum of a temple. The rest of the walls have deep channels, and probably were originally ornamented with hieroglyphics, upon a coat of plaster. This building was for some time inhabited by Caillaud; whence it is now called "Deyr See Kayo'," or "the Convent of M. Caillaud": all the brick edifices here being supposed, by the modern inhabitants of El-Ckoor'neh, to have been convents. It was Caillaud who contracted the door-way, in the manner shewn by the view which is given. The building consists of two courts: the latter of these encloses a wide excavation in the rock, which formed an open area before some excavated chambers; but the entrance to these chambers is concealed by rubbish.—Most of the larger buildings in the As'a'see'f are similar to that above-described: each being an oblong enclosure formed by walls of unburnt brick: the front, like the propylæum of a temple: the sides and end, less lofty and less thick: within is a large excavation, or sunken, uncovered court; generally about thirty feet deep; from the end of which we enter spacious excavated chambers, with one or more mummy-pits. Most of these tombs are of the time of the 26th Dynasty. Their hieroglyphical and other sculptures are remarkable for the elaborate manner in which they are finished. The rock here is very compact, and even susceptible of a polish; but it is rather soft, and very liable to crack. Though most of the tombs of the As'a'see'f are of the period above-mentioned, it appears that there were in this tract some buildings of a much more ancient epoch; for Mr. Wilkinson pointed out to me, in 1827,

---

[1]See plate 33 [fig. 93].

a stone lying among some rubbish just before the largest of these tombs with the prenomen of the immediate successor of Osirtesen 1st sculptured upon it.

At a short distance behind the building which I have already described is a similar large building, which, as well as the former, is marked in my topographical plan of Thebes. From the great quantity and variety of antiques found in its excavated chambers this tomb has received the appellation of *"the Ghoo're'yeh"*: this is the name of one of the principal soo'cks (or ba'za'rs) of the modern Egyptian metropolis.

Having passed among many tombs of inferior interest, we arrive at the principal tomb of the As'a'see'f.† I made a view of the exterior of this tomb, and also a plan of it.[1] The brick propylæum and the rest of the brick enclosure are almost entirely demolished. These surrounded two open courts, excavated in the rock. The two courts communicate with each other by a doorway in the centre of a barrier of rock which supported a second crude-brick propylæum. On either side of the second court are galleries excavated in the rock: of these the plan which I have given will convey a sufficient notion: at the end of a gallery on the left is a mummy-pit. The principal excavated chambers and galleries, the entrance to which is in the centre of the end of the second court, are more extensive than those of any other tomb at Thebes. The first and largest chamber contained two rows of square pillars; four in each row; but these have all been broken down; and the walls of the chamber are much injured. The sculptures of this tomb are chiefly hieroglyphics, cut with great nicety in the fine calcareous rock: besides these we find the boat of the ram-headed god Kneph represented upon the walls; and other devices similar to some of those in the tombs of the kings. The second chamber has four square pillars. The third is small: it has, at the end, a niche, which originally contained a statue of the person for whom the tomb was principally destined, or figures of himself and his wife. On the left is another small chamber; and on the right, a long gallery. We must here light our candles, to proceed along the latter. Two passages branch off to the right from this long gallery. In the first of these is a pit, stretching across nearly the whole width of the passage: an incautious person might fall into it unawares: it descends to some sepulchral chambers. Beyond this we find four passages surrounding a solid square. At each angle of this square are two figures (one on either side of the angle, or one at each extremity of each side of the square) with extended arms, fronting and embracing the wall: they represent the goddesses Isis and Nephthys; are in high, or full relief; and resemble persons crucified, excepting that the back is outwards. In the same walls (the sides of the solid square) are many shallow, small recesses, in each of which are sculptured, in relief, small figures similar to the four genii of Amenti (The Egyptian Hades); each having a human body, with the head of a

---

†Tomb of Pedamenopet, TT 33.
[1] See plates 34 and 35 [figs. 94 and 95].

man, an ape, a jackal, or a hawk: in some cases there are twelve of these figures: in some, less: they are generally in three rows; one above another. The hieroglyphics and mystical sculptures of the walls of the four passages which form this square are very neatly executed. On the exterior side of one of the four passages are three small cells.—Returning to the long gallery, and proceeding towards the end of it, we have to descend two flights of steps; each of which has a narrow inclined plane down the middle, probably formed for the convenience of sliding down the mummies. At the extremity of the gallery is a small chamber, in a corner of which is another mummy-pit. From this chamber branches off the second of the two passages before alluded to, leading to another chamber; which is only remarkable as having an oblong mass of rock rising above the floor at the extremity, like a large chest, or pedestal.

A little to the left of this great tomb is one of comparatively small dimensions, but highly interesting.† From the subjects sculptured in it, it has received the name of "the Tomb of Trades." Descending into a small, uncovered, excavated court, nearly filled with crude bricks and rubbish, we find, on the southern side, two chambers; each having its door of entrance from the court, and each communicating with the other by a third door. The principal chamber had three square pillars (one of which has fallen), and two pilasters: the pillars are ornamented on each side with the full face of Athor; and the pilasters have the same ornament. In this chamber, on the wall opposite the entrance, are the sculptures above alluded to: the principal designs are representations of statuaries at work—an artist carving a lion, and another painting a statue which he has made—, boat-builders making or repairing a boat, and shoemakers at work: there is nothing remarkable in the instruments made use of. Here are also, as in many other tombs, representations of dancers and musicians. The name of Psammitichus 2nd is found among the sculptures throughout this tomb. These sculptures are of a good style; though inferior to those of the earlier Pharaohs.

In the tomb next behind the principal tomb of the As'a'see'f are some relics of very delicately finished sculptures; among which are some animals that are executed with remarkable beauty and correctness.‡ I found no name among them; but believe them to be, like most others in this part, of the times of the 26th Dynasty: they are worthy of the best age of Egyptian sculpture: this remark I mean to apply to the animals above alluded to, which are among the sculptures in the open court of this tomb: the other sculptures, however, are all skilfully and very elaborately executed. There are extensive excavated chambers at the end of the court, which have suffered much from violence.

The furthest of the great tombs of the As'a'see'f is remarkable for its great propylæum.†† Of this I introduce a sketch, to shew the perfect and

---

†Tomb of Ihi, TT 36.
‡Probably the Tomb of Harura, TT 37.
††Tomb of Pahasa, TT 279.

firm construction of the arch of its lofty entrance.[†] In the north (or right) wing is a flight of stairs ascending from the north extremity towards the south, and leading to the top.[1] The other brick walls of this tomb are destroyed; and its courts are filled with rubbish; therefore we have no means, in its present state, of ascertaining its age; but it is most probably, like the greater number of the tombs here, of the times of the 26th Dynasty.—This part of Thebes presents to us a number of arches of two widely different epochs: one of a different kind from any that I have yet described I have still to mention; but I must first give an account of a few other remains.

There is a little pyramid of crude brick near the right wing of the great brick propylæum. I have already introduced a sketch of it, with the view of another brick pyramid before described.[2] Its base is about twelve feet square. In its southern side is the entrance; which is narrow, and arched. The interior is of a conical form; with a small square cell beneath. The top of the pyramid is broken and open. We have no evidence of its age; but I should think it not very ancient.

Beyond the tombs of the As'a'see'f which I have described are several wide ridges, composed of rough fragments of limestone, apparently the remains of rude but massive walls, which formed very long enclosures, extending, parallel with one another, towards the west-north-west. I found no sculpture on any of the fragments, which are all much decayed.

On the north-north-east side of the As'a'see'f are remains of a road leading to a very ancient temple, which is under the high cliffs of the mountain. On each side of this road, at equal distances, are patches covered with small fragments of sand-stone (a kind of stone foreign to this part): these are doubtless the remains of sphinxes, demolished by barbarian violence: they are opposite to each other. Behind them, on each side, is a ridge of fragments of stone, which seem to be relics of a wall. The avenue of sphinxes (for such we may certainly call it) was one third of a mile in length. There is a direct approach to it through a hollow (which is, apparently, partly natural and partly artificial) between two ridges of rock.

The temple of the As'a'see'f[3] to which this avenue leads is at the top of a gentle slope, which rises to the foot of the high and rugged cliffs of the mountain. This slope is covered with fragments of stone and pottery: at the bottom, the foundations of stone walls are discovered; but higher up, where a little of the rubbish has been removed, we find the rough surface of the natural rock apparent. The temple is partly constructed of the same kind of stone that composes the mountains here (which is very fine, compact, white limestone); and it is partly excavated in the rock. Some

---

[†]Fig. 96.
[1]Another brick propylæum, a little before this, has a flight of steps in its left wing, entered by a doorway in the back.
[2]No. 27 of the subjects for wood-cuts [fig. 92].
[3]See plate 36 [fig. 97].

crude-brick buildings, probably remains of a convent erected by Christians, are among the ruins of this temple, which, together with these later buildings, is hence called "ed-Deyr el-Bahh'ree," or "the Northern Convent." At the top of the slope is a rectangular space, bounded in front and on the right and left by stone walls, and behind by the face of the rock. In the centre of the front-wall is inserted a small portal of red granite, composed of only three blocks, and adorned with hieroglyphics, beautifully sculptured. On surveying these hieroglyphics I was struck by a remarkable peculiarity[1]: the inscription upon each of the jambs of the portal begins with the square title of the prince who erected the two great obelisks of Kur'nak; and this is immediately followed by the prenomen of Thothmos 3rd. This seems to shew either that the sculptures were begun by the former and finished by the latter, or that the former and latter were one and the same person, or that they were contemporary. The first supposition, however, is very improbable: for had the former only begun the inscriptions by engraving his peculiar title, the latter would surely have erased this, rather than place his own name immediately after. The second supposition is not more tenable: for in this very temple we find the name to which this square title belonged erased, and the name of Thothmos 3rd inscribed in its place. I must therefore hold the third supposition. The former person founded this building; in some parts of which he inscribed his own name alone. As his name is not found in the regal lists of the monuments, we may conclude that he was a viceroy, or regent, during the minority of Thothmes 3rd.[2]—Behind the portal above described are heaps of blocks of stone and rubbish, among which are seen remains of walls covered with hieroglyphics very beautifully executed in low relief, bearing the name of Thothmos 3rd. Another portal of granite is built almost close before the face of the rock exactly behind the former.[3] It is the entrance to the excavated part of the temple; but at the periods of my visits to Thebes it was completely closed with brick-work and rubbish; and I could not see whether there were any interior chambers. The rock on each side and behind, where its surface was uneven, has been cased with masonry.[4]

---

[1]See first copy, page 57 [not extant]. I think that the doubtful personage here mentioned was a Queen-Regent during the minority of Thothmos 2nd and that of Thothmos 3rd. See A. Ens., i., 52.

[2]On the wall to the left of the portal are delicate sculptures of offerings &c., and here we find the names of Rameses 2nd and his immediate successor. The back of the portal is sculptured with hieroglyphics similar to those of the front, exhibiting the same peculiarities of double dedication, and alteration.

[3]On the lintel, the doubtful personage before mentioned and Thothmos 3rd are represented kneeling, and offering to Amon-Ra. This subject is double; the two figures of the god sitting back to back. The doubtful name is altered to that of Thothmos 3rd. The figure of the former is foremost. On the lintel, his name is altered as on the first portal; the original square title remaining.

[4]And in the wall in which the portal is inserted are several narrow recesses, like

Towards the left are two small chambers, adjoining each other. The further of these[1] had an arched roof, not constructed on the regular masonic principle, but nearly in the same manner as the arches of Abydos. The only difference being that here there is a division in the centre; whereas in the arches of Abydos the upper-most stones reach quite across. The manner in which this arch is formed (more plainly shewn by the sketch here subjoined   ) would lead us to con-

clude, were it not for the evidence to the contrary which I have adduced, that, at the period of its construction, the Egyptians were unacquainted with the principle of the common masonic arch.[2] The interior of the chamber which is roofed with this singular arch has been plastered by some early Christians, to conceal the sculptures, which, however, have become again partly apparent. Both in this and the adjoining chamber we find the two names which I have mentioned in speaking of the first granite portal: the former has been erased (but it has become visible again); and the latter put in its place. In 1827, within a few days after my last departure from Thebes, Mr. Wilkinson cleared out the excavated chambers of this temple: he discovered one very fine chamber,[3] and three small ones, roofed in the manner above described, and another (the last) which was of the comparatively late age of Ptolemy Physcon, and which had a flat roof. Some persons had previously supposed that there was a passage through the mountain from this temple to the valley of the tombs of the kings; which idea Mr. Wilkinson's operations have proved to be erroneous.

On the right side of the avenue which leads to this temple are two broken androsphinxes of granite, and several broken Osiridean statues of limestone. They lie in a hollow, into which they appear to have fallen from a higher ground: one of the sphinxes lies upon a higher place than the other fragments. I found no name upon them; but they are evidently very ancient.

---

niches for statues; apparently three on each side of the door. Here the alteration of names may again be traced; and the name of Thothmos 1st is found here: this king being introduced as a deceased ancestor of the third Thothmose.

[1] It is seen in plate 36 [fig. 97], immediately to the left of the granite portal.

[2] The most ancient *stone* arches on the common masonic principle that have yet been discovered are those of a tomb at Sack'cka'rah, described in the first volume of this work.

[3] 29 feet 6 in. long, and 11 feet 2 in. wide. The sculptures represent offerings, and the prevailing name is that of Thothmos 3rd; but that of Thothmos 2nd is also found here, and Thothmos 1st with his Queen Ames and their daughter, represented as persons deceased, receive offerings from the founder and Thothmos 3rd. The front and end of the chamber are much ruined.—The second chamber is 11 feet 6 in. long, and 7 feet 1 in. wide; and is roofed in the same manner. On each side of it is a little chamber, 8 feet long, and 3 feet 7 in. wide; likewise arched. The sanctuary, which is 11 feet 8 in. long, and 6 feet 10 in. wide, has a flat roof, and bad sculptures, of the age of Ptolemy Physcon.

In the steep acclivities of the mountains by which the tract of El-As'a'see'f is bounded on the north and north-north-east are several grottoes, with traces of roads leading up to them. They contain nothing interesting. Up this steep lies a short route over the mountain to the valley of the tombs of the Kings.

On the southern side of the As'a'see'f is a small hill, called the *'Il'wet El-As'a'see'f* (or the Hill of the As'a'see'f), in and around which are many grottoes; some containing interesting paintings. One of these, at the eastern extremity of the hill, is particularly interesting: it is remarkable for its high antiquity, as well as for its very curious paintings[1]; being of the age of Amonoph 1st, who is represented among its paintings, together with his Ethiopian queen Ameri.[†] This grotto (which, for the sake of distinction, we may call "the Tomb of the Sha'doo'f," for a reason which I shall presently state) chiefly consists of an antechamber of an oblate form and a square chamber, immediately behind the former, with four square pillars: at the end of the latter is a recess, in which are two sitting figures, a male and a female, of the natural size, representing the chief person for whom the tomb was made, and his wife; and beneath are sepulchral catacombs. The entrance is much obstructed by rubbish. The paintings which adorn the walls of the antechamber and of the principal chamber are, for the most part, in good preservation, curious in their subjects, and distinguished by an extraordinary degree of talent in composition and expression: but what strikes the stranger more than these, on entering the tomb, is an accumulation of stripped and rifled mummies, taken up from the catacombs, and left here. In the antechamber, and next the sides in the principal chamber, mummies, piled upon one another, have been trodden down into a solid mass. There is not a spot upon which we can set our foot but upon whole or pounded mummies; and the smell of them is disagreeable, as well as the sight. Among the paintings on the walls of the antechamber is the representation of a funeral-procession; a good design; but much injured: the best part of it is a group of wailing women.[2] Persons feasting, dancers, musicians, and servants employed in various domestic occupations are delineated with much natural simplicity. Here, also, are represented several boats, full of passengers: two of them have run foul of each other; and the momentary alarm is well expressed. Beneath these are seen some carpenters at work: also, the preparing of mummies. The decoration of the principal chamber has been left incomplete: the left side is not ornamented with paintings. One of the most interesting subjects portrayed on the opposite wall is a *sha'doo'f*; the machine which is still in most general use in Egypt for irrigating the fields: this is much injured; but enough of it remains to shew the whole process of raising the water; which is just the same as in the present day. On the same wall is a

[1]See T and E.[,] p. 157
[†]Tomb of Neferhotep, TT 49.
[2]See no. 29 of subjects for wood-cuts [fig. 98].

representation of a man weaving: this, also, is much injured: it is on the left of a small door, leading to a side-apartment. Among the other paintings are a herd of cattle, and the wine-press: there is also a representation of a temple, with two propylæa; before each of which are set up the high, pointed shafts, which I have mentioned on more than one occasion.

Between the Hill of the As'a'see'f and the great hill of the sheykh 'Abd El-Ckoor'neh are some tombs similar to those in the As'a'see'f which I have described.

The Hill of the sheykh 'Abd El-Ckoor'neh[1] (*Ckoor'net esh-sheykh Abd El-Ckoor'neh*), which is so called from a sheykh of that name, whose tomb is upon the summit, is one of the most remarkable objects at Thebes, from the great number of grottoes excavated in its sides, particularly in the acclivities overlooking the plain. At its foot, towards the east, is the house of the Greek, before mentioned; neatly built, of sunburnt brick. On entering this house for the first time, I was surprised to see doors, shutters, shelves, &c. formed of the materials of mummy-chests, covered with paintings. In the principal sitting-room was, at one end, a deewa'n, and at the other end, some chairs. My servant sat down on one of these, and it fell to pieces under him: it had been found, a few days before, in an ancient tomb. The servant was not to blame; for the chair appeared perfectly strong: the seat was of thick leather; tightly stretched. Upon a table lay a small basket full of round cakes of bread; also taken from an ancient tomb; and appearing quite fresh. Many other antiquities were in the room.—There are several tombs in the Hill of the Sheykh which are particularly conspicuous; each of them having, in front, a gallery with many entrances, forming a kind of portico. One of these has a gallery with seven entrances (only five of which are seen in my view of the hill): another, a little above the former, has one with nine entrances: a third, in the upper part of the hill, has a gallery with thirteen entrances; and immediately to the right of this is a tomb which has a gallery with seven entrances. There are also two similar tombs in the lower part of the hill, towards the south-east. What I have here called "entrances" may be termed the spaces between square pillars.—The first of the tombs above-mentioned, which has a gallery with seven entrances, is less than half-way up the hill. It is much injured. Behind the gallery is a chamber with six square pillars.—Just above this is the tomb which has a gallery with nine entrances. It has, doubtless, been magnificent, but its paintings are almost entirely destroyed, and the plaster upon which they were executed broken down. Besides the gallery, there is only a passage, behind the central entrance, in which are several mummy-pits. In 1827, I found Mr. Wilkinson residing in this tomb; which, with the help of some crude bricks from ancient ruins in the vicinity, he had made a very comfortable habitation.—A little above this tomb is a grotto consisting of a short passage with a transverse gallery, and a small cell, or recess,

---

[1]See plate 37 [fig. 99].

behind; in the first of which is a representation of what may be termed a feast.[1] As this is a good specimen of a design common in the tombs, I insert a copy of it.[2] The master and mistress of the family for whom the tomb was destined are here represented seated together; with a table before them, covered with viands: a monkey, tied under the seat, is eating fruit, from a basket: before the table stands a priest, clad in a leopard's skin, in the attitude of addressing the master and his wife; and behind him are seated five men and five women; each, with two exceptions, holding either a full-blown or budding lotus, and smelling it, or about to eat it.[3] Just below the tomb which has the most extensive gallery (before the third and fourth of its thirteen entrances, counting from the right, as one faces it), is a grotto containing very curious paintings, of the age of Thothmos 4th.[4] It is a small chamber of an oblate form. On the wall opposite the entrance, is represented the king above-mentioned,[5] with long ranks of archers, spearmen, and standard-bearers, and a trumpeter, before him.[6] To the right of this is represented a chief dragging before the same king two rows of captives, by ropes tied round their necks. Their arms are bound behind them. They are red men (like the Egns.), mostly dressed in a small kirtle or apron; but are so slightly drawn that it is difficult to conjecture to what race they belong. Here also is the name ⟨cartouche⟩. Next are the vintage, and wine-press; the slaughtering of cattle; and

the front of a temple, with the high shafts fixed up before it.[7] The subjects of the paintings on the front-wall are feasting, dancing, and music.[8] At the left extremity of the chamber is represented a confused multitude; perhaps designed to express a muster of troops.—The tomb which has a gallery with thirteen entrances contains no remains of painting. Before the central entrance is a mummy-pit. Behind the gallery is only a passage leading to a small, rudely excavated chamber, in which is another pit. The next tomb to the right, which has a gallery with seven

---

[1] In 1835, I found this much injured. [Tomb of Ken, TT 59.]
[2] See no. 30 of the subjects for wood-cuts. (among the *mounted* drawings, next to plate 37 [missing].) (Not found R.S.P.)
[3] There are also some remains of funeral-scenes, and agricultural subjects.
[4] In 1835, I found these paintings much injured. They are executed on plaster, and all are more or less unfinished. [Tomb of Nehamun, TT 90.]
[5] His figure I found, in 1835, quite effaced.
[6] Also, persons bringing provisions, a bull with a garland round his neck, ducks, &c.
[7] Also the front of an Egn. house, with a door, a window above the door, two other windows, and two malkafs on the roof. Two palm-trees overtop it. Unfortunately, it is much injured in the most remarkable parts. ⟨sketch⟩
[8] There are two women, in transparent dresses, playing on mandolins, and dancing.

entrances, is alike uninteresting.—On nearly the same level with the two tombs just mentioned, to the right (or eastward), are several grottoes with curious paintings. First is a small grotto in a very perfect state[1]; with four sitting figures at the end. It is adorned with paintings, which are remarkable for little more than their freshness; but two harpers may be mentioned, as well drawn.—Just above this is a grotto with much painting[2]: the subjects, music, with dancing; a long funeral procession; fowling, &c. (Here I copied a group of female musicians and dancers; of which I insert an engraving[3]: two of the dancing-girls are naked.)—To the right of this is another interesting grotto: it is a chamber of an oblate form, with a row of four square pillars: also of Thothmos 4th.[†] Here are represented four groups of cattle, designed with an unusual degree of freedom, and with an attempt at perspective: the animals which are meant to appear more distant being a little higher in the picture than those before them; though not smaller. This is now (in 1835) much broken. The greater part of this grotto is unfinished. There is an aperture broken through into another grotto, to the right.—The latter grotto, above alluded to, is decorated with paintings representing several manufactures, &c.: the principal subjects are pottery; the making of a chariot; and a man carving a sphinx: also, a feast, with music and dancing[4]; a visiter coming in his chariot, and his servant knocking at the door.[‡] Here, too, is a view of the front of a propylæum, with two shafts and two colossal statues before it.[5]—There are several large grottoes in the southern part of the hill: the paintings in most of them are much

---

[1] In 1835, I found it much injured.

[2] It consists of a small oblate chamber, with a passage behind leading to an unfinished chamber with four square pillars. The paintings in the first chamber are almost all similar, and similarly arranged, to those in the grotto above described, where Thothmos 4th is represented; as he also is here; and they are similarly unfinished; but more injured. In the passage, on the left wall, is a long representation of funeral ceremonies. Towards the right extremity of this, Horus is weighing the merits of the deceased in a balance (which has a jar on one scale, a feather in the other, and an ape sitting on the fulcrum), in the presence of Thoth and Thmei (goddess of Truth or Justice). To the right of this are four small sitting figures, of Thothmos 3rd, Amonoph 2nd, Thothmos 4th, and Amonoph 3rd, with their names above, in the order of their succession, from right to left. The tomb, therefore, was finished in the reign of the last of these kings. Osiris (a large figure) sits behind them. On the opposite wall are represented fowling, fishing, and feasting. The birds are chiefly ducks: there are also some pelicans, slightly but well drawn.

[3] No. 31, among the *mounted* drawings, next before plate 38. [missing]

[†] Tomb of Thenuna, TT 76.

[4] Here I copied a group of female musicians and dancers: two, naked.

[‡] Tomb of Amenhotp-si-se, TT 75.

[5] The tomb contains several blank ovals for names, and one in which I faintly perceived characters seeming to belong to the name of Thothmos 4th. The entrance looks towards the As'aseef.

injured; but the relics of these, particularly good.—On the acclivities of the hill are some ruined buildings which are very remarkable; being constructed of large crude bricks, stamped with the hieroglyphic name of Rameses 2nd.

To the east of the Hill of the Sheykh are numerous mummy-pits, and several inhabited grottoes. The grotto inhabited by the sheykh 'Osma'n (Sheykh of El-Ckoor'neh) is almost close before the house of the Greek.

To the south-east of the Hill of the Sheykh is the fine edifice of Rameses 2nd which most travellers have miscalled "the Memnonium": we may name it, with propriety, *"the Raméséum† of El-Ckoor'neh."* Behind it, and on its north-east side, are extensive structures of crude brick; consisting of long arches[1]; the directions of which are shewn in my topographical plan of Thebes. They are probably very ancient[2]; but for what purpose they were constructed, no one has been able to discover.

The Raméséum of El-Ckoor'neh is now called, by the people of the neighbourhood, *Ckusr Ed-Dacka'ckee* قصر الدقاقي , or the Palace of Ed-Dacka'ckee; who, they pretend, was a person possessing great flocks and herds, and who, coming to El-Ckoor'neh, took up his abode in this ancient building, and kept up but little intercourse with the other inhabitants of this district. This building[3] is one of the finest monuments of Thebes; but it is, for the most part, in a very ruined state. Under the effect of the morning or evening sun it has a remarkably picturesque appearance; the yellowish hue of the sandstone of which it is constructed softening the sun-light upon its large and elegant columns, and upon its colossal caryatid pillars, and presenting a most beautiful contrast with the deep blue of the sky. The effect of this magnificent ruin is also rendered more striking from its being very little encumbered with rubbish.

The foremost part of the edifice, which is the propylæum, touches upon the present limits of the cultivated plain. The soil of this plain being annually augmented by the inundation, its limits every year become imperceptibly extended; and thus it is now beginning to encroach upon

---

†Lane's orthography of "Raméséum" is ambiguous, often appearing more as "Ramese'um."

[1]See plate 38 [fig. 100].

[2]Mr. Hay informed me, during my second visit to Egypt, of a remarkable discovery that he had made; that many of the bricks were stamped with the name of Rameses 2nd. I have since examined a great number of them: on few was the name very clearly discernible; but I found the above name, and no other; and therefore cannot doubt that these buildings are coeval with the Raméséum. The straw in them has been eaten by worms. The stamped bricks are those which support, and those which cover, the arches: those composing the arches are thinner, and their sides are scored. The former are mostly from 1 foot 3 1/2 to 1 foot 5 long, 7 in. wide, and 5 1/2 to 6 in. thick. Beneath the arches are mummy-pits, of a more ancient period, as appears from their positions. They were opened shortly before I last quitted Thebes.

[3]See plate 39 [fig. 101].

the building which I am describing. The propylæum is 225 feet in width. It is much ruined; as my general view of the building will shew. The back is covered with remarkable sculptures, very much resembling those of the propylæum of El-Oock'soor. The history of the subjects of these sculptures commences upon the south-western wing, which is not so much ruined as the other wing. The Egyptian monarch (Rameses 2nd, under whom all the sculptures of this edifice were executed, and whose exploits and acts of piety they commemorate) is here twice represented standing in his car, and charging into the midst of his enemies: but it appears that the uppermost of these two designs was either sculptured after the other, or that it was the original sculpture, and was afterwards cancelled, and filled up with plaster. The confusion of the vanquished, and the flight of their prince, are well expressed.[1]—Upon the other wing of the propylæum, the Egyptian king (this is always Rameses 2nd, the great Sesostris) is represented seated on a throne, and receiving the congratulations of his people. One figure here has been mistaken for the vanquished monarch; but it is evidently an Egyptian, both in feature and dress: he stands behind a chariot, holding in his hands a bow and arrows. To the left of this subject is a confused scene of plunder: some of the victors are packing up and carrying away the property of the conquered; while others are beating them with staves, or putting them to death. Among these groups are represented carriages of various kinds, several asses, and some oxen with the Indian hunch; and there is a lion in the camp. At the left extremity are some groups of prisoners.[2]

From the extremities of the back of the propylæum extended a wall, on each side: these formed a square court between the propylæum and a wall which is now ruined. Before each of the side-walls were two rows of columns; but these, and the side-walls, have been completely destroyed: the bases, only, of some of the columns remain; and but a small portion of the end-wall of the court is now standing.—The most remarkable object in this part of the edifice is an enormous colossus, thrown down and broken.[3] The fragments extend from the end of the court nearly to the propylæum. This is (or rather was) the largest colossus in Egypt or Nubia of all those carved out of hard stone, or detached from the parent rock. It was composed of a single mass of red granite; and was placed on the left side of the door-way which was in the centre of the end-wall of the court; its back being towards that wall. Of the features of the face not a trace remains; but, in other parts, the work is seen to be of a most finished kind; and the surface, highly polished, though (in accordance with a custom not agreeable to modern taste) it was originally painted. It was in a sitting posture; and from the fragments which remain we may

---

[1]Towards the right is the King holding a group of three prisoners, by the hair of their heads.
[2]At the right are four Egyptians bastinading two prisoners. Along a part of the base of the picture are Egyptian soldiers on their march.
[3]See plate 40 [fig. 102].

calculate that the whole figure was not less than sixty feet in height: yet this was one mass of stone, and doubtless brought from the quarries of Syene, more than a hundred miles distant. The width across the shoulders, in a direct line, is twenty-one feet: the length of the ear, three feet five inches. On the shoulders is cut, in very deep and large characters, the hieroglyphic name of Rameses 2nd, whom this stupendous colossus represented. The pedestal, which is eight feet high, is nearly buried in the ground. This also is a single block of red granite.

The second court[1] was nearly of the same length and width as the first. It was confined on the right and left by two rows of columns and an exterior wall. Parallel with its front-wall was a row of square pillars, each fronted by a colossal Osiridean figure, about thirty feet high including the cap. Before the end-wall was a row of similar caryatid pillars, and behind these a row of columns. The columns and square pillars of the left half of the court have been demolished, together with the lateral wall and the left half of the front-wall: so, also, have almost all the columns, with the lateral wall and end-wall, of the right half of the court.—Upon the interior face of the remaining portion of the wall which separated the first and second courts is sculptured a very interesting and comprehensive battle-scene; illustrating the same campaign as the sculptures of the propylæum above described and those of the temple of El-Oock'soor. The river runs along the bottom of the scene in two parallel branches; and the space between these is occupied by chariots of the enemy. Towards the right extremity of the picture (such it may still literally be termed, for the colours are not effaced) the two branches unite, and turn upwards, towards the top of the scene; and here the river is again divided; enclosing a circular island, on which is a fortress, belonging to the invaded nation. Near the left extremity of the wall, the Egyptian monarch is represented in his chariot, in the usual attitude, discharging an arrow: the reins are lashed round his body, and the horses, in full speed, are bounding over the wounded and slain. Each individual of the routed party has been pierced by an arrow from the bow of the Egyptian king: some of them have fallen into the river; and their friends on the opposite bank are endeavouring to extricate them. Beyond the bend of the river are more of the enemy's forces, drawn up in ranks.[2] The artist has shewn great ingenuity throughout this whole design: the horses are delineated with much spirit; some of them writhing in agony; others expiring. The enemies of the Egyptians are clad in long garments, and mostly armed with spears and shields: few of them have beards: they are evidently Asiatics. Above the battle-scene is represented

---

[1] See plate 41 [fig. 103].

[2] One has been drowned: he has been taken out of the river, and is held with his head downwards, and feet upwards, in order that the water which he has swallowed may run out: one of the persons who hold him is pressing his body: he appears lifeless, and his hair, hanging down, is dripping wet: his arms are hanging down also. This is in the lower part of the scene, at the right extremity.

a procession, consisting of two rows of priests, clad in long, white garments; each row bearing, on the shoulders, a kind of bier, which supports a series of small figures representing statues of kings, placed in the order of their reigns, each with the hieroglyphic name attached. The first appears to be Menes, who is said to have been the first mortal king of Egypt: the second is an unknown king,[†] who is placed in the sculptures of "the Chamber of Kings" at Kur'nak as the fifth before Osirtesen 1st. The rest are placed in the regular and unbroken order of their succession: the third is Amos, or Amosis, the first king of the 18th Dynasty (no. 40 in my list); and the fourteenth and last is Rameses 2nd, the founder of this edifice, and first king of the 19th Dynasty. Thus is presented a complete list of the names of the kings of the 18th dynasty, agreeing exactly with the list of Abydos. The procession is approaching Rameses 2nd. A little to the right we see this king in the act of cutting, with a sickle, a sheaf of wheat.—The second court had a gentle ascent towards the end; as we see by the bases of the side columns. The end of the court was formed by a wall, in which were three door-ways; one in the centre, and one of black basalt, near each extremity. To each of these a flight of steps ascended. Less than half of the wall now remains, on the left of the central entrance. I have already mentioned that there was a row of square caryatid pillars: there now remain, to the right of the centre, three of the columns, and four square pillars; as shewn by plate 41.[‡] The spaces between the pillars and columns before the three door-ways were wider than the other spaces: three square pillars and as many columns intervened between the approaches to the central and minor door-ways. Before the avenue to the central door-way were two sitting colossi of granite; one on either side. Both of these have been thrown down and broken. The head of one, justly admired for its beauty, is in the British Museum; the remains of its body and throne, which are of black granite, lie where they fell. This statue was on the left. The head of the other is still lying in the corresponding place: it is much mutilated. These statues, when entire, were each about twenty-two feet in height. They both represent Rameses 2nd. The head in the British Museum (as the lower part of the colossus bears the name of the king just mentioned) should no longer be called "Memnon"; but it will not be less interesting under its true appellation of "the head of Sesostris."—On the front of the ruined wall at the end of the court (on the left of the central door) are sculptures representing the king offering to various divinities,[1] and receiving the crux ansata (the emblem of life) from the god Ra. The principal object of worship throughout the edifice is Amon-Ra, the great god of Thebes.

Immediately behind the second court is a noble portico, or hypostyle

---

[†]Mentuhotep II.
[‡]Fig. 103.
[1]Chiefly to Amon-Ra, Maut, and Khons, who are seated on three thrones.

hall,[1] which at present contains five rows of columns; but originally it had, apparently, ten rows; each consisting of six columns. Two of these rows form a grand avenue up the centre: they are of larger dimensions than the other columns, and, I think, the most elegant of their kind in Egypt. The views which I have given shew the forms both of these and of the smaller columns: they also shew that this portico, in its roof as well as its columns, resembles the great portico of Kur'nak. The diameter of the larger columns is six feet and a half; and that of the others, five feet nine inches: the height of the former is about thirty-six feet: that of the latter, about twenty-four. All of them are ornamented with sculptures, representing the royal founder of the edifice offering to Amon-Ra, Amon-Generator, Phtha, Ra, and other divinities. The first of the larger columns on the right of a person entering the portico from the preceding court has fallen. Between its base and the column next to it is an oblong, low pedestal, with holes cut in the upper surface for receiving the feet of a colossal statue, which was most probably of wood. There are no remains of any other statue or pedestal corresponding with this.—Upon the interior face of the remaining portion of the front-wall of the portico is sculptured another representation of a battle-scene. The subject of it is not so complicated as that last described; but it is very interesting. The Egyptian monarch is represented, as usual, in his car, pursuing his enemies; his chariot-wheels passing over the bodies of two men, and the horses rearing over another car, in which are two men, about to be crushed to death. The vanquished have fled to the walls of their fortress; but, before they can obtain admission, are pierced by the arrows of the Egyptian king. Below this group are two Egyptians, sons of the King, each in the act of stabbing an enemy. These figures are designed with great spirit. A little further to the right, beneath the walls of the fortress, is a father, with his wife and family and his little property (consisting of a cow, and some vessels filled with provisions), imploring mercy. The assailants are scaling the walls of the fortress, at the foot of which are four sons of the King: some of the besieged are falling from the ramparts: two others are letting themselves down by a rope; and one, at the top, is holding out fire, perhaps as a signal of submission.—Upon the end-wall of the portico are two subjects of sculpture representing the King receiving emblems of divinity from Amon-Ra, behind whom is Maut, on the left half, and Khons on the right. Along the base of the wall are sculptured the children of Rameses 2nd: twenty sons and two daughters on the left half (in which a forced door-way occupies the place of three figures), and twenty-three sons on the other. The latter series is complete. The immediate successor of Rameses 2nd appears to have been his thirteenth son, who is here distinguished by a royal prenomen.

Next behind the portico is a hall containing eight columns, in four rows; two rows on either side, and two columns in each row. These are similar to the smaller columns in the great portico; and are ornamented

---

[1]See plate 41 [fig. 103], before referred to, and plate 42 [fig. 104].

in the same manner. On the front-wall of this hall are sculptured eight groups of priests; each group carrying, on their shoulders, a boat. Of the end-wall, the part to the left of the door is much ruined. Upon the right portion is represented the king seated on a throne under a tree (probably designed for the sacred persea), at the foot of the throne of the god Atmoo. The tree has six oval fruits; upon three of which the god above-mentioned, and the goddess of letters, and Thoth, the god of letters, are inscribing the king's name, which is also inscribed on the other fruits.— The ceiling of this hall is decorated with astronomical or astrological sculptures.

There appears to have been a similar hall beyond that just described; but only the four columns on the right now remain. Upon the back of the remaining portion of the wall between this and the preceding hall, and upon the columns, the king is represented offering to various divinities: on the wall, on the left of the door, he is throwing incense into a censer which he holds over a pile of offerings before the mummy-shaped god Phtha: between the offerings and the throne of the god are fourteen vertical lines of hieroglyphics. On the other side, he is offering a libation and incense to Ra, whose figure is gone, but whose hieroglyphic name remains. In this sculpture there are 19 columns of hieroglyphics between the King and the place where the god was represented. The hieroglyphics, in each case, contain the names of various gods, and commemorate his offerings to them.

On each side of the two halls above-mentioned, and behind the last, were, doubtless, several apartments, the walls of which have been completely destroyed.—The existing ruins occupy a space five hundred feet in length. The length of the entire edifice was probably six hundred feet.[1]

This noble building, which we must regard as both a palace and a temple, seems to be the only edifice at Thebes of which any ancient writer has left us a full description. The following brief statement will shew the points of approximative or exact agreement existing between the Raméseum of El-Ckoor'neh and the description given by Diodorus Siculus of the building which he calls "the Tomb of Osymandyas"; excepting with respect to the measures, which in some cases nearly agree. The most considerable disagreement in the measures is in the extent ascribed to the first court in the description of Diodorus: this being said to have been four plethra (or four hundred feet), while the propylæum was but two plethra; and we may fairly infer that the former measure is incorrectly stated, because we find that the width of a court behind a propylæum is never greater, and generally *less*, that the width of the propylæum itself. The *situation* of the monument of Osymandyas is described as ten stadia distant from the first tombs in which the females sacred to Jupiter were buried: at the distance of ten great stadia from the

---

[1]Close on the right (or northern) side of the great portico are the bases of several columns.

Raméséum are many remarkable tombs (among which are those of the kings, and those of the queens also); or, if the smaller stadia be meant, that distance from the Raméséum will be found to extend to many other important tombs. There is nothing, therefore, in the situation of the Raméséum to disprove its identity with the building which Diodorus calls "the Tomb of Osymandyas."

The Raméséum of El-Ckoor'-neh consists of

The Tomb of Osymandyas is thus described.—It consists—we read—of

1. A propylæum of sandstone, ornamented with sculptures which were originally painted with various colours.

1. A propylæum (or *pylon*) of various-coloured stone.

2. A square court; having originally a gallery on the right and left, the roofs of which were supported by a double row of columns. (The second court has caryatid pillars; but not the first).

2. A square peristyle court: the roofs of the surrounding galleries supported by pillars with images in front.

Before the end-wall of this court, to the left of a door-way which is in the centre, is a broken colossus of granite of Syene, in a sitting posture. It is probable that this, when entire, resembled the two sitting colossi of Amonoph 3rd, in the midst of the adjacent plain; each of which has two colossi, one on the outer side of each leg, in a standing posture, against the front of the throne, reaching nearly to the top of the knees of the greater, formed of the same mass of stone, and representing the mother and queen of Amonoph 3rd.

By a door-way which leads from this into a second court are three colossi, all formed of one mass of stone of Syene.[1] One of the statues of this group (the largest) is in a sitting posture; and represents the king Osymandyas: the other two are by his knees; and represent his mother and daughter. The great statue bears this inscription—"I am Osymandyas, King of Kings: if any one would know how great I am, and where I lie, let him surpass (or destroy) some of my works."

The colossus of the Raméséum is the largest statue in Egypt. The foot, when entire, must have been twelve feet in length.

The sitting colossus is the largest statue in Egypt. The foot is seven cubits in length (i.e. if the Egyptian cubit be meant, about twelve feet; or, if the Greek cubit, ten feet and a half).

As the great colossus is for the most part demolished, there may have been a smaller statue in the same court, though there are now no remains of such.

There was also another statue of the mother of Osymandyas, twenty cubits high.

3. A second, peristyle court. Upon the front-wall are sculptures representing a military expedition of the royal founder of the building. A fortress

3. A second peristyle court. Here is a great variety of sculptures representing the wars of Osymandyas with the revolted Bactrians. On the first wall

[1] According to Wesseling's correction.

belonging to the enemy is surrounded by a river. A rampant lion forms an ornament of the car of the Egyptian monarch. The walls on the other sides of the court are demolished, excepting a portion of the end-wall, on which the king is represented offering to the gods.

At the further end of the court are remains of two colossi, in a sitting posture; each monolithic. When entire, they must have been about twenty-two feet high.

4. A hypostyle hall which was entered by three door-ways. Between two of the columns is a pedestal of stone, with holes cut in the upper surface for receiving the feet of a colossal statue, most probably of wood. The side-walls of this hall are demolished.

5. Remains of two more apartments; besides which there were, doubtless, several more.

That part of the Reméseum where we should look for the place of a calendar such as is described by Diodorus is destroyed; but as several of the Egyptian temples contain representations of the zodiac, it is not improbable that this edifice also contained one, though perhaps only sculptured on the ceiling (like the astronomical sculptures of the hall behind the great portico), and certainly not of the large circumference of 365 cubits.

the king is represented besieging a fortress surrounded by a river. He is aided by a lion, that is fighting with terrible fury.[1] On the other walls are represented the King dragging along some captives; also sacrifices, and a triumph.—In the middle of this court is an hypæthral altar.

Before the end-wall of the court are two monolithic colossi, in a sitting posture; each twenty-seven cubits in height.

4. A hypostyle hall, entered by three door-ways. Here are many statues of wood, representing persons who have law-suits, and looking towards the figures of the judges which are sculptured on one of the walls, and are thirty in number.

5. A large space occupied by various apartments; among which were the sacred library, &c.

Here, upon the roof (or on the ceiling) was a gold circle, 365 cubits in circumference, and a cubit in breadth (or thickness); on which were marked the 365 days of the year, with the risings and settings of the stars, and the astrological deductions, for each day.[2] This circle was carried away by Cambyses.

---

[1] I have mentioned that a lion is represented in the scene sculptured on the north wing of the propylæum.

[2] If so, the circle must have been divided into 365 parts and a quarter (to be true for every year), representing the days of the solar year. Hence it is probable that the historian from whom Diodorus borrowed the description of this circle said, or should have said,—not that it was 365 cubits in circumference and a cubit in thickness, but—that its circumference was divided into 365 parts and a quarter; which divisions might as correctly be termed πηχεις as the measures of verse are called, by Aristophanes, πηχεις επων.

The above comparison shews, I think, beyond all reasonable doubt, that the Raméséum of El-Ckoor'neh is the building called by Diodorus "the tomb of Osymandyas." The trifling disagreements are far outweighed by the many points of exact agreement; and are easily and satisfactorily accounted for, as errors, by the fact that Diodorus describes this building on the authority of others; for he adds "such, *they say, was* the Tomb of Osymandyas"; and he evidently means such it was before the period of the conquest of Egypt by Cambyses. This edifice, however, cannot be regarded as a *tomb*: there can be little doubt of its having been a palace and temple. Of Osymandyas, if he bore no other name, we know nothing but from Diodorus. The fact of a building being called after his name but found to be a monument of Rameses 2nd is a strong reason for supposing the former name to be a corruption of some title of the great Rameses.

On the N.E. of the Raméséum is an extensive crude brick enclosure, with a propylæum of the same material in front (facing the cultivated soil, which is near it), and another similar propylæum dividing the enclosure into two courts. The whole is much ruined. The propylæa are of large stamped bricks, 16 inches long, 7 wide, and between 5 and 6 thick; those of the other bearing, some, that of Thothmos 1st, and some, the emblem of stability ☥. Within are fragments of sandstone; probably the remains of a temple.[1]—On the S.W. of the Raméséum, and almost close to the edge of the cultivable soil, are remains of another propylæum, of crude bricks stamped with the name of Thothmos 4th. Behind it are fragments of sandstone.

Nearly half a mile to the south of the edifice which I have just described, and a little more than the same distance to the eastward of Medee'net Hha'boo, in the midst of the cultivable plain, are the two enormous colossi of Amonoph 3rd (whom the Greeks and Romans called Memnon); each representing that monarch seated on a throne, placed on a pedestal, and facing the east-south-east.[2] The northernmost of these is the famous statue celebrated as "the Vocal Memnon"; from which a sound like the twanging or the breaking of a harp-string was said to proceed every morning, at, or soon after, sunrise. It is remarkable that these two colossi are called by the modern inhabitants of El-Ckoor'neh "the Sel'a'ma't" السلامات , which signifies "salutations"; and are said to hold converse with each other by night! The awful majesty of their appearance, and the solitude of their position, may have given rise to this popular idea; but I think it is more probably founded on an old tradition. These colossi are also distinguished by the names of "Sha'mikh" and "Ta'mehh" شامخ وطامخ ; words which both signify "lofty," or "elate": the latter appellation applies to the northernmost statue. They are annually surrounded by the waters of the inundation, which generally

---

[1]There are remains of another crude-brick propylæum before this enclosure.
[2]See plate 43 [fig. 105].

rise more than half-way up that part of the pedestals which remains above the surface of the soil: for the soil has risen far above the bases of the pedestals: I calculate its rise since the time of Amonoph 3rd to have been nearly thirteen feet.[1] The water does not subside sufficiently for the traveller to approach the two colossi before the month of January. These statues are similar to each other in size; but not so, at present, in all other respects. The southernmost is, with its throne, a single mass of stone; and the other statue was originally so, without doubt; but its upper part, and the back part of the throne and pedestal, have been broken down; and the fragments have since been replaced; or, where they could not be replaced, other masses of the same kind of stone have been substituted. The material of both is a very hard, variegated stone, partly consisting of coarse sandstone of a dull reddish and yellowish colour, and partly of pudding-stone. The height of each statue, without the pedestal, is fifty-one feet, according to my measurement, very carefully made.[2] The pedestal is nearly thirty-five feet long, and eighteen feet wide: it rises about seven feet above the surface of the soil[3]; and this is about half its height. Whence these stupendous masses of stone were brought is unknown. The foundations of both of the colossi have sunk a little; and they incline slightly towards each other and backwards. The features of each of them have been mutilated by barbarian violence; as also other parts of the figures. Both bear, in several parts, the name of Amonoph 3rd. On either side of the throne of each statue are sculptured two figures of the hermaphrodite god Nilus, tying the stalks of water-plants around the stem of a table, or altar. In the centre of the hieroglyphics over this sculpture is the name of Amonoph 3rd. In front of each throne are two female figures, one on each side of the legs of the great statue, about nineteen feet high; and there is a third figure, much smaller, and greatly mutilated, between the legs: each of the former, which are considerably injured, but less so than the latter, has the name of the person whom it represents among its accompanying hieroglyphics: one is the queen-mother of Amonoph 3rd, and the other his queen-consort. Around the upper part of each pedestal is a line of large hieroglyphics, very delicately and beautifully executed; but much effaced.

The foregoing remarks chiefly apply to both the statues: I must now speak more particularly of the northernmost—the Vocal Memnon.— There can no longer be any doubt that this statue is the one celebrated by ancient authors as the Vocal Memnon. 1st. In proof of this may be urged

---

[1] Allowing four inches and a half to a century, agreeably with the data explained in my account of the Nilometer of Elephantine, in the 4th chapter of the third volume of this work [chapter thirty]. The reign of Amonoph 3rd I place immediately after the period of the Exodus; and this period (in accordance with Dr. Hales's chronology) I refer to the year 1648 B.C.

[2] And the space between the two statues is nearly fifty-seven feet.

[3] Six feet 1 inch and a half above the general level of the surrounding plain, measured near the front angle of the north side of the vocal statue.

its appearance and position agreeing with most of the descriptions of those authors. 2ndly. The recent discoveries in hieroglyphic literature enable us to read the name of Amonoph (the 3rd Pharaoh so named) upon various parts of the colossus. 3rdly. The legs and pedestal bear many inscriptions in Greek and Latin, cut by persons in testimony of their having heard "the voice of Memnon": one of these states that he "heard the sounds of Memnon or Phamenoph": the latter name is "Amenoph" with the Egyptian article prefixed; and Pausanias says that the statue which was commonly called "Memnon" the Thebans asserted to be not so, but the figure of a countryman of their's named Phamenoph.—Strabo's description of this vocal statue is very precise; but he does not mention its being called the colossus of Memnon. He says—"At Thebes are many temples; for the most part ruined by Cambyses. Its inhabitants occupy separate villages; partly on the Arabian side, where is the city (Diospolis), and partly on the opposite side, where is the Memnonium. In the latter part are two monolithic colossi, near together: one is yet entire: of the other, the upper part has been broken down, above the seat; they say, by an earthquake. It is commonly believed that, once every day, a sound like that of a slight blow proceeds from the part which remains upon the throne and base. I visited it with Ælius Gallus and the friends and soldiers who were with him; and about the first hour I heard the sound; but whether it proceeded from the base, or from the colossus, or from any of the bystanders, I cannot affirm; and, in uncertainty with respect to the cause, it is easier to believe anything than that stones so constructed should utter a sound."—Pliny mentions "the statue of Memnon" as being in a temple of Serapis; and adds that it uttered a sound every morning when first struck by the rays of the sun.—The great temple of which the principal entrance, or approach, was ornamented by the statue in question and the corresponding colossus was, I believe, consecrated chiefly to the worship of Amon-Ra.—Tacitus mentions the statue of Memnon, and the miraculous sound.—Juvenal alludes to it in the following line (sat. XV)—

Dimidio magicæ resonant ubi Memnone chordæ.

—Pausanias visited this statue, and describes its position as near the Syringes (or Catacombs). He represents it as a sitting colossus; and adds—"many call it the statue of Memnon, who, they say, came from Ethiopia into Egypt, and penetrated as far as Susæ: but the Thebans assert that it is not the statue of Memnon; but of Phamenoph, their countryman; and I have heard it called the statue of Sesostris. Cambyses cleft it in two: the upper part, the head with half the body, is broken down: the remainder is seated; and every day, at sunrise, it utters a sound like the snapping of the string of a harp or lyre." This description plainly applies to the statue which bears so many inscriptions engraved by persons contemporary with this author; in whose time, it appears, the colossus had not been repaired. The temple to which this statue belonged

Pausanias does not mention: it was doubtless in ruins in his time. It is very strange that the Greeks and Romans should have confounded Amonoph 3rd (who died more than four centuries before the Trojan war) with the Memnon of Homer; but he was not the only king whom they erroneously identified with Memnon: the great edifice of Abydos, which was built by the father of Rameses 2nd, is called by Strabo and Pliny a palace of Memnon.—Damis, the disciple and companion of the magician Apollonius Tyaneus, visited the ruined edifice which he calls "the temple of Memnon," and speaks of the vocal statue as perfect; describing the countenance "as that of a man about to speak." He was probably as great an impostor and liar as his master; in whose life, by Philostratus, this account is found: it is, however, worthy of remark that he describes the temple above-mentioned as utterly ruined; presenting an assemblage of remains of columns and of walls, with seats and thresholds and Hermes-statues; and such precisely are the relics of that temple now subsisting, in a direct line behind the two colossi of Amonoph 3rd. The appellation of Hermes-statues, it appears, was given to the Osiridean, or mummy-shaped, figures: we see the fragments of many such among the remains of the temple above-alluded to.

The Greek and Latin inscriptions on the vocal statue of Memnon are very numerous. They are, with few exceptions, on the lower parts of the legs. Many of them are imperfectly legible. They are mostly of the times of the early Roman Emperors. On the front of the pedestal is a Greek epigram, of six lines, superscribed with the name of its author, Asclepiodotus. The following is a translation of it—"Learn, O Thetis, goddess of the seas, that Memnon, who was slain at Troy, yet lives, and utters melodious sounds, under the brows of the Libyan mountains of Egypt, where the troubled Nile divides Thebes, the city famous for its beautiful portals; while Achilles, the insatiable in fight, speaks not in the plain of Troy, nor in Thessaly."—Many of the inscriptions on the legs bear dates: these are of the first and second centuries of the Christian era. The earliest, I believe, is one which is dated in the eleventh year of Nero (A.D. 64). Many of them are of the reign of Adrian; and not a few of these by persons who visited the statue in company with that emperor and the empress Sabina. Perhaps the most remarkable of the inscriptions is that of which the following is a translation, consisting of seven Greek verses, written A.D. 130, on the left leg of the statue—"I, Balbilla, heard the speaking stone, the divine voice of Memnon, or Phamenoph: I came with the beloved queen Sabinna; when the sun was in the first hour of his course; in the fifteenth year of King Adrian; on the twenty-fourth day of Athyr—on the twenty-fifth day of Athyr."—The last date seems to be a correction of the preceding one.—Many of the inscriptions are by military visiters. Most of these and of the other visiters merely record their having heard the voice; generally at, or soon after, the first hour of the day: some allude to the mutilation of the statue by Cambyses: none mention its being repaired. Two inscriptions record that the voice was heard twice; and another, that it was heard thrice, on the same day.

That a sound, or musical note, did really proceed from some part of this statue when first warmed by the rays of the morning sun I do not disbelieve; for I have several times heard a similar sound, doubtless produced by the same cause, proceeding from a stone in the roof, or the upper part, of the neighbouring edifice, the Rameséum of El-Ckoor'neh. For several successive days, during which I was engaged in making drawings and notes in that edifice and its vicinity, I had my dinner brought to me in the great portico, a little after noon; and generally while partaking of this meal, or shortly afterwards, I and another traveller with me heard a single, distinct, musical sound, like that produced by a harp-string, evidently proceeding from some stone above us. This stone, I suppose, became exposed to the sun soon after mid-day; and a sudden expansion of it, resulting from its increase of temperature, occasioned this sound. In the granite sanctuary of Kur'nak, also, several of the authors of the great "Description de l'Egypte" heard (on many different occasions, but always at the same hour, a little after sunrise) a similar sound, like the twanging of a chord, seeming to proceed from one of the displaced stones in the roof: six members of the Institute attest this fact. The sound which is described to have proceeded from the statue of Memnon is said to have been heard generally within an hour or an hour and a half after the rays of the rising sun had fallen upon the colossus. It is a remarkable circumstance (first noticed, I believe, by Mr. Burton) that in the front part of the body of this statue, in the middle of the lowest course of stone, there is a block of stone of such a nature, and placed in such a manner, that, on being struck with any hard substance, it yields a very musical sound. By means of a ladder, I mounted on the lap of the colossus, and satisfied myself of this singular fact. I should have imagined that the sound which of old excited so much wonder might have proceeded from this identical block of stone, did not some of the inscriptions on the legs of the colossus seem to imply that the statue had not been repaired at the period when it attracted so many visiters: the same must also be inferred from the descriptions of Strabo and Pausanias. We are left in ignorance as to the precise period at which the statue of Memnon was repaired: but we must believe it to have been in the third or fourth century of our era, before the final suppression of the ancient religion of Egypt in the reign of the Emperor Theodosius.

The Vocal Memnon and the corresponding colossus appear to have stood before the principal entrance of one of the most extensive and superb edifices of ancient Thebes. This edifice was probably both a palace and a temple; and it was undoubtedly what the Greeks and Romans called the Memnonium, or palace and temple of Memnon: it should more properly receive the appellation of *Amonophium*. The ruins of the main body of the building are nearly a quarter of a mile behind the two colossi, towards the west-north-west; that is, exactly behind the colossi. If a propylæum stood immediately behind the two great statues, which is very probable, it must have been thrown down nearly to its foundations, and its materials must lie buried beneath the soil deposited by the inundations since its destruction.—In the direct line of approach from these huge statues to the principal remains of the edifice we find other colossi, but thrown down, and so much broken as to appear almost shapeless masses. First in the line of approach, at the distance of about three hundred feet, is an enormous mutilated colossus, half buried beneath the annually increasing soil.[1] What appears of it is more than twenty-four feet in length[2]: it is of the same kind of stone as the two great statues which I have described: too little is seen of it to give an exact idea of its entire dimensions; but it seems to be scarcely inferior in magnitude to the two first. There was probably another colossus corresponding with this; and, behind the two, another propylæum. There are fragments of other colossal statues near.—Rather more than three hundred feet further, in the same direction, are some fragments of two sitting colossi of hard, white chert, which seem to have been less than the former.

Arriving within a few paces of the main body of the building in the approach to which so many huge colossi were placed, we find two enormous tablets, of the same kind of stone as the two grand colossi, thrown down, and partly buried. The northernmost of these is much broken: the other is broken in the middle; but otherwise nearly entire. This is more than 31 feet long, and 13 feet 2 inches wide. The top is of a semicircular form. On the upper part of the front are sculptured two similar devices, separated by a double line of hieroglyphics down the middle: on the one side, Amonoph 3rd is represented receiving, from Phtha-Socari-Osiris, the crux ansata, the emblem of life, which is held to his mouth: on the other side he is receiving the same emblem from Amon-Ra. Behind the king, in each of these sculptures, stands his queen; the same whose figure, with that of the mother of this king, ornaments the front of the throne of each of the two grand colossi. Below the sculptures above-described are twenty-four lines of hieroglyphics; which, as well as the other sculptures, are executed in the most beautiful and highly finished manner; notwithstanding the great hardness of the stone. These huge tablets are about two hundred feet before the front of the ruins of the portico of the Amonophium.

The site of these remains is elevated just sufficiently to be above the reach of the annual inundation. The ruins of the great portico were partly cleared of the rubbish with which they had long been encumbered, by Belzoni. The lower parts of a vast number of columns yet remain: these columns are of the same order as those which compose the front colonnade of the edifice at the ruined village of El-Ckoor'neh: they must have formed a very magnificent portico. Here are found several broken colossi of most exquisite workmanship: one is of granite: the others are of the same species of stone as the two grand colossi; and on the belt of

---

[1]See A. Ens., iv., 110—and his [Wilkinson's] Plan—plate 18—also, p. 109.
[2]This is the length of the principal fragment, which appears to have composed the upper half (from the seat to the top of the head) of a sitting figure.

one I found the prenomen of the same king. There are, besides these, a great many broken statues, of the natural size, or a little larger than nature; representing a lion-headed goddess; also some fragments of Osiridean figures; which, I suppose, as I have already mentioned, are those that Damis has alluded to by the term "Hermes-statues," in speaking of the remains of "the temple of Memnon." All the relics of the Amonophium, and the statues which adorned it, seem to be works of the reign of the same king, Amonoph 3rd; and the entire edifice appears to have been even more extensive than the principal edifice of Kur'nak and the structures more immediately connected with it, which rose during the reigns of several successive monarchs: that is, supposing a series of propylæa, &c., to have extended from the two grand colossi to the ruins just described. From the ruins of the Amonophium was brought, by Belzoni, the fine, sitting colossus of black stone now in the British Museum. This also represents Amonoph 3rd; for it bears his hieroglyphic name.

Just within the limits of the desert, between seven and eight hundred feet to the north of the ruins of the portico of the Amonophium, are remains of a temple which was probably connected with that great edifice; being of the same age.[†] These remains consist of large blocks of white calcareous stone from the neighbouring mountains, bearing hieroglyphics, with the name of Amonoph 3rd. Some have the name of the immediate successor of Rameses 2nd, cut over the former. There are also seen here some blocks of sandstone, and some broken colossal statues of hard, white chert, which are of very beautiful workmanship. These, likewise, bear the name of Amonoph 3rd, and the later king's name above-mentioned.—Near these remains, but within the limits of the cultivable soil, lie two colossi, in a standing attitude, now thrown down and much mutilated.[1] They are statues of Amonoph 3rd: are of the same kind of stone as the two grand colossi, and about thirty-five feet in length.[2] They perhaps adorned a northern entrance to the precincts of the Amonophium; or belonged to the neighbouring temple, the remains of which I have just before mentioned.

In a situation which, with reference to the grand portico of the Amonophium, exactly corresponds with that of the remains above alluded to are some blocks of sandstone, probably the relics of another edifice of the same age, but without any name, that I could find, to prove their antiquity. The building of which they formed a part may also have been connected with the Amonophium.

There are many ruins of crude-brick tombs, and other remains, besides those which I have described, in the desert tract between the Reméséum of El-Ckoor'neh and Medee'net Hha'boo. In one part the rock has been cut perpendicularly, as if to form a boundary on two sides of some

---

[†]The Temple of Merneptah.
[1]And broken into several pieces.
[2]One, from the shoulder to the bottom of the fist, measures 14 feet 8 inches.

edifice; or perhaps merely to form the fronts of sepulchral grottoes.

On the north-west of this tract rises an isolated hill, called *Ckoor'net Mar''ee* قرنة مرعى (or the Hill of Mar''ee), on the summit of which is a ruined Christian convent. In the sides of this hill are many ancient grottoes; but not so numerous as those of the hill of the sheykh 'Abd El-Ckoor'neh, nor so interesting. Several of them are large, but rude and much decayed; and few of them contain paintings or sculptures. In one of them, a mummy was lately found with a papyrus in which it was stated that the deceased had desired to be buried behind the Memnon.

Between this hill and that of the sheykh 'Abd El-Ckoor'neh are some tombs of the same kind as those of the As'a'see'f, which I have described; and, apparently, of about the same age; that is, of the times of the 26th Dynasty.

At the north-eastern entrance of the valley behind the Hill of Mar''ee is a small temple of Athor, the Egyptian Venus,[1] built and partly sculptured in the reign of Ptolemy Philopator, and further adorned by Epiphanes and Physcon. It is surrounded by a high wall of crude brick, apparently not very ancient. In the front of this brick wall is a small stone portal, with ill-executed sculptures, representing offerings made to Athor and Thmei, and to Amon-Ra, Maut, and Khons, and other divinities, by Ptolemy Auletes. This portal is directly in front of the temple.—The temple is a plain building, of an oblong form, in the usual Egyptian style. Upon the front, which is plain,[2] but which would have been sculptured had the temple been quite finished, are cut several Greek inscriptions, the work of early Christians, who converted this edifice into a church, and perhaps constructed the crude-brick wall, and made for themselves a convent within it. The temple is now called *Deyr el-Medee'neh* (the Convent of the Medee'neh, or City; that is, of Medee'net Hha'boo; from which, however, it is half a mile distant). The interior of the temple consists of a portico and three small sanctuaries behind. The portico had four columns, in two rows; but the first column on the right has been thrown down, and with it a considerable portion of the roof has fallen. The two further columns, between which is a doorway, are connected, by a wall about half their height, with two square pillars, which latter are united, from the bottom to the top, with the side-walls of the building, so that only three of their sides are exposed; and these sides are ornamented with the full face of Athor, surmounted by a kind of miniature temple, forming a capital similar to those of the columns of the great portico of the temple of Athor at Den'dar'a. The portico is thus divided.[3] Over the door of the middle sanctuary is a

---

[1] See plate 44 [fig. 106].

[2] Excepting immediately around the doorway, where are represented offerings, as on the portal above-mentioned, by a Ptolemy whose ovals are left blank.

[3] Only the front of the second portion, and its interior, are sculptured. The subjects are offerings to the divinities before mentioned, by Philometor.

cornice decorated with the winged globe; and over this is a row of seven heads of Athor. The middle sanctuary[1] and that on the right are ornamented with sculptures representing offerings to Athor, &c. In the sanctuary on the left are some curious sculptures relating to the infernal regions. Here, on the left side-wall, is represented the judgement of a soul before Osiris, who is seated on his throne (at the right extremity), and presiding over the place of departed spirits, called Amenti. A lotus rises at the foot of the throne; and upon this are represented the four genii of Amenti, which are mummy-shaped figures; one with a human head; the second with the head of an ape; the third with that of a jackal; and the fourth with that of a hawk. On a pedestal before the throne is the Egyptian Cerberus; a hideous monster,[2] with a body partaking of the nature of a hippopotamus and of a dog, and with a head like that of a crocodile. The balance by which the fate of a soul just arrived is to be decided is erected; and the Ibis-headed god, Thoth, stands ready to record the result. A small jar, or vase, containing or representing the merits of the defunct, is placed in one scale; and a feather, the emblem of truth or justice, in the other. The hawk-headed Horus and the jackal-headed god Anubis stand beneath the beam of the balance; and an ape sits above the fulcrum. The deceased has been introduced, in his natural form, between two female figures, each of whom has an upright feather on her head; the distinguishing mark of the goddess of truth or justice. Another remarkable group in these sculptures above what I have described, consists of forty-two figures, arranged in two rows, in a squatting posture; some with human heads, and others with the heads of various animals, and each with a feather on its head.—On the right wall of this chamber is represented the sacred boat or ark of Pthah-Sokari-Osiris,[3] and among the other sculptures is remarked a ram with four heads, over the doorway.

In the Valley of the Temple of Athor, and near the spot where that temple is situated, are numerous tombs of crude brick; and in the acclivity on the right (or north-west) are several grottoes of the early ages of the 18th Dynasty. One of these (discovered by Mr. Wilkinson) contains a curious piece of sculpture, representing two long rows of

---

[1]The middle sanctuary is dedicated to all the gods of the temple: the further half of it is sculptured by Philopator, and the front half by Philometor, who are presenting offerings. The sanctuary on the right is dedicated chiefly to Athor; and that on the left, to Thmei: both are sculptured by the latter of the two Ptolemies just mentioned.

[2]with a head partaking of the form of the crocodile's and hippopotamus', and a body like that of a lion, sitting as a dog or cat. Behind him sits Harpocrates, on a crook.

[3]with a kind of cupola in the middle, surmounted by the head of a hawk, over which is a disc; and with a prow ornamented with the head of a capricorn, looking backwards, and that of a bull, looking forwards. It is remarkable that, in Arabic, "saker" and "salk" signify "a hawk," and "sakar" is a name of hell.

kings and queens; each with the hieroglyphic name annexed to it: the first two kings of the 18th Dynasty (Amos and Amonoph 1st) are among these: the other kings are certainly more ancient: they are not placed in the regular order of their succession.[1]

Passing a few steps to the westward of the grottoes above-mentioned, we find ourselves in the upper part of a ravine, which descends in a western direction. Here are some sculptures on the rocks on our left. They have the form of tablets; but each appears to have been the end-wall of a grotto, of which the side-walls and roof have fallen. The names of two kings are found here: nos. 54 and 56 of my list.

Descending this ravine, we arrive at a valley in which are the tombs of several queens. Lord Prudhoe and Major Felix were the first travellers who observed that these were the tombs of queens. The regular and plain approach to the Valley of the tombs of Queens is from the south-east: that is, from the direction of Medee'net Hha'boo; from which it is half a mile distant. The tombs here are very similar to those in the valley of the kings; but not so magnificent; nor, generally, so well preserved. The least injured is that of the queen of Amonoph 3rd, whom I have before mentioned. The sculptures in this tomb are not remarkable; being merely representations of the queen offering to various divinities. They are executed in plaster. The colours are well preserved. This is the only tomb in the valley which is well worthy of examination: most of the others appear to have been injured by fire; and contain but scanty remains of sculptures: several of them have names. Their plans are generally irregular; though that of the one first mentioned is not so. There are also several tombs of another kind in this valley: mere pits.

Section 4. Medee'net Hha'boo, &c.

General remarks—The Smaller Temple—Small Palace—Great Edifice—
The town, its name, &c.—Adjacent remains—Small temple on the
south—Great lake—El-Ba'eera't.

Medee'net Hha'boo[2] مدينة حابو (the City of Hha'boo) is a ruined and deserted town, situated upon mounds of rubbish, the remains, of former

---

[1]Close on the right of this is a steep entrance to a grotto excavated rather deep in the mountain. This tomb is a chamber completely lined and arched over with crude bricks, plastered, and covered with coarse paintings, which bear several ovals containing the names of Amonoph 1st and his Queen, and thus show the very remote antiquity of the arch. This arch is almost entirely perfect: it is semi-circular, and 8 feet 1 inch and a half in width. The paintings are not remarkable. The chamber I found half filled with rifled mummies, forming a heap, over which I had to walk. This most interesting tomb was discovered by Wilkinson. It is lined with brick on account of the crumbling and gravelly nature of the rock.

[2]See plate 45 [fig. 107]. This view shews M. H. as it is seen in approaching from the direction of the 2 great Memnonian Colossi.

habitations, just within the limits of the desert. Its elevated site is chiefly occupied by the ruins of houses of unburnt brick; among which are three very remarkable Pharaonic edifices: two of these were temples, which, perhaps, included royal residences, or partly served as palaces: the third was solely a palace. Each of these edifices fronts the cultivated plain, towards the south-east.

The foremost is the Smaller Temple; which is quite at the south-eastern extremity of the mounds. To the right of this building a low stone wall[1] extends to the angle of the mounds; and probably formed part of an enclosure round the temple. It is of the age of Rameses 3rd. In front of the first propylæum of the temple is a square court, formed by stone walls, having an entrance in the middle of the front, and one on each side. The jambs of these door-ways are ornamented with sculptures, in a bad style (being of a bad age) representing the Emperor Antoninus Pius offering to several divinities. At the end of the court, next the propylæum, two columns are standing; and there are remains of six others, engaged in a wall parallel with the front of the propylæum: these eight formed a handsome colonnade; but they have been left unfinished, without sculpture.[2] The propylæum is a Ptolemaic structure. Its portal is decorated with sculptures representing offerings by Ptolemy Lathyrus (Soter II.), who, among other gifts, presents four bulls to Amon-Generator. The portal is the only part of this propylæum that is sculptured; the rest being unfinished: the back of it has either been left incomplete or has been demolished; and here we observe that a considerable number of the blocks of stone employed in its construction are from a more ancient edifice; being sculptured with hieroglyphics and architectural ornaments. It appears to have been chiefly built of the remains of a temple of Rameses 2nd.

Behind this propylæum is another, of very small dimensions, which had before it a small court surrounded by a wall, with columns engaged in it, now for the most part demolished: the sculptures remaining upon it bear the name of Nectanebo, of the 30th Dynasty. The small propylæum is much ruined: the upper part of the left wing has been thrown down. The oldest name upon it is that of Tirhakah, or Taracos (Tahrak), the Ethiopian king, of the 25th Dynasty: this is on the back: on other parts we find the name of Nectanebo, and that of a Ptolemy.[3] Tirhakah, therefore, was probably its founder: his name has been partially erased.

Passing through this small propylæum, we enter another small court, before the main body of the temple. On the left is a portal, leading to the palace; and on the right is another portal: the latter is of granite. The

---

[1]Seen in plate 45 [fig. 107].

[2]The wall is composed of ancient materials. In the back, on several blocks, are sculptures with the name of Rameses 2nd; and on one, three heads of foreign warriors, with the horned helmet, and round shields.

[3]My notes say Philapator; but according to Sir G. Wilkinson (Thebes and Egypt, page 47) it is Lathyrus.

main body of the temple is of an oblong form: the front and the greater
part of each side are formed by square pillars, supporting architraves and
a cornice, and decorated with sculptures bearing the name of Thothmos
3rd. The front of the building is widened by a wing on each side: that on
the left is a small, plain, unfinished chamber: the right wing is also
unfinished; but larger, and containing two columns. The pillared front
and sides of the main building, together with the chambers at the end,
surround an oblong hall; thus forming a gallery entirely around this hall.
Four columns, of the order from which the Doric seems to have
originated, assist to support the roof of this gallery, near the four angles:
in the placing of these, regularity has been disregarded, because one of
the columns would, if at the angle of the gallery, be exactly before the
entrance of one of the adyta.[1] The hall which I have mentioned has a
door-way at each end. Its walls were originally decorated with sculptures
in the reign of Thothmos 3rd; but it has been repaired and partly
resculptured by Ptolemy Physcon, chiefly in the name of Thothmos
3rd.—The adyta, or chambers at the end of the temple, are six in number.
Their walls are covered with sculptures with the names of Thothmos 1st
(the founder of the temple), Thothmos 2nd, and Thothmos 3rd; of the
usual subjects of offerings, &c.[2] The sculptures on the exterior of this
part of the building are of the reign of Rameses 3rd; cut in intaglio, and
in the very deep style which characterizes most of the sculptures of that
king.—A little to the right (or north-east) of this temple is a square tank
lined with masonry; at one of the angles of which are remains of a black,
sitting statue of a lion-headed goddess, like those which are seen in such
numbers by the horse-shoe lake of Kur'nak.

To the left of the building which I have described above is the Palace
of Rameses 3rd, which is the only Pharaonic edifice now remaining that
appears to have been simply a royal residence. A view which I made of
the front of this building[3] will illustrate the following notes respecting
it.—At the entrance (immediately to the left of the first propylæum of
the smaller temple) are two low structures, nearly buried in rubbish.
Their exterior walls are ornamented with sculptures representing
offerings and acts of adoration: the interior of each is small, and without
any decoration. As there seems to have been a gate between them, they
were probably lodges for the porters or guards of the palace. Behind
these are two higher structures; both connected with a small tower, or

---

[1]On two of these (at the end) I observed the names of a Psammetichus and two
royal females. The blocks bearing these names have been used for repairs, and
two of them are inverted. The oldest name on the columns is that of Thothmos
3rd.
[2]In several places, however, we find the same alterations as at the Temple of the
Asa'seef; showing that the sculptures were commenced by the supposed Queen-
Regent Amun-Neit-Gori, who therefore appears to have been the founder of the
building.
[3]See plate 46 [fig. 108].

square building, behind them. On the front of each of the former
structures are sculptures, in low relief, and on a colossal scale,
representing Rameses 3rd in the act of sacrifising four captives; grasping
one arm of each victim in his hand.[1] At the top of each of these buildings
is a small chamber, to which one may climb; but not without difficulty:
there are no remains of stairs by which to ascend to them. They are both
much ruined: particularly that on the left. In the other are some very
remarkable sculptures, executed in delicate, low relief; and of a different
kind from those of the temples: they illustrate the king's private life and
amusements. On the right side-wall of this little chamber the king is
represented playing at a kind of chess with one of his women, and with
his arm over the neck of another female. I insert a copy of this curious
piece of sculpture,[2] to which the other sculptures in the interior of the
same building are similar in point of style and in the nudity of the
figures. On the back-wall of the same chamber, to the right of a window,
is a female presenting a flower to the king, who is chucking her under the
chin: to the left is the chess-playing again; but this is much injured: there
are here eleven pieces on the board, and one in the hand of each player.—
Passing between the two structures above-described, we find their sides,
also, and the walls which connect them with the square tower behind,
decorated with sculptures, representing the same monarch conducting
groups of prisoners, and presenting offerings to the gods. The six
projections which are seen in the view before referred to[3] are each
formed of the heads, shoulders, and arms, of four prostrate captives,
protruding from the wall, in the attitude of pressing with their hands
upon a ridge like the sill of a window, and painfully sustaining some
heavy superincumbent weight. I can form no probable conjecture as to
what they were designed to support: one has a door, or window,
immediately above it: each is level with that which is opposite to it; but
the pairs are on different levels. There were several chambers and
passages on each side, of which there are no other remains than the walls
already mentioned. On the north-eastern side of the right wall are still
seen some sculptures which were part of the interior decorations of these
chambers: the subject of each is the king seated on a chair, and attended
by three or more of his women. The chambers and passages here were
very small: some of them, or perhaps the passages only, were roofed with
stones cut in the form of an arch.—The small square tower which forms
the principal part of the building (and of which the front is seen in my
view of this edifice) consists of two small chambers, one above the other,
with a gateway beneath, leading directly towards the front of the greatest
of the edifices of Medee'net Hha'boo. This gateway I found filled to the
top with rubbish.[4] The stone floor of the chamber immediately above it

---

[1]Under each of these is a row of captives.
[2]See no. 32 of the subjects for wood-cuts [fig. 109].
[3]Plate 46 [fig. 108].
[4]On each side of the upper window is sculptured a human figure kneeling in an

remains perfect: that of the upper chamber has fallen: this seems to have been of wood. The walls of the latter chamber are decorated with sculptures similar to those of the other upper chamber before described. The top of the tower is surrounded with semicircular-topped battlements, like those represented in many sculptures as crowning fortresses besieged by Egyptian monarchs. From the back window of the lower chamber we look directly to the entrance of the great edifice, to which I have already alluded, 273 feet distant. I introduce a sketch of the view from this window.[1]

The great edifice of Medee'net Hha'boo, which seems to have been a palace as well as a temple, is one of the most splendid monuments of ancient Thebes, and one which has suffered less than many others from violence; but it is much encumbered, both within and without, with the rubbish of crude-brick houses, which must have been built long after the ancient Egyptian worship had been exploded. This magnificent structure appears to have been raised entirely during the reign of Rameses 3rd, whose smaller palace, directly in front of the former, I have just described. This king was a mighty conqueror: his military exploits are commemorated by a series of very interesting sculptures on the walls of this building; the finest of his works.

The great propylæum which forms the front of this edifice is half buried in rubbish, and much ruined. At the base it must be about 200 feet, or rather more, in width. The sculptures upon it, and upon the other parts of the structure, are in intaglio, and very deeply cut. This deep style of sculpture seems to have been adopted by Rameses 3rd to guard against the practise, common among Egyptian kings, of erasing the names and sculptures of one prince, and substituting those of a later king, to make it appear that the edifice in which these alterations had been made was the work of the latter.—On the front of this propylæum is sculptured the same subject as on the front of the palace which I have just described— the king sacrifising a group of captives.[2]

Through the portal of the first propylæum we pass into a square court, occupying the space between that propylæum and the second, which is 110 feet from the former. This court is very much encumbered with ruins of crude-brick houses. On each side is a covered gallery: that on the left has a row of eight fine columns towards the court, and a wall towards the

---

attitude of adoration or supplication, with uplifted hands, towards the window, and having wings, which are extended backwards, and, upon his head, a horn, or perhaps the horned helmet worn by a foreign people who are represented on some blocks already mentioned, and among the sculptures of the great edifice at this place. On the back of the tower, the King is represented in several places, holding prisoners; twice before Amon-Ra.

[1]See no. 33 of the subjects for wood-cuts [fig. 110].

[2]But most of the sculptures are hieroglyphics and offerings. There are stairs in each wing; but they are obstructed by rubbish at the bottom, and the entrances to them are thus concealed.

exterior: the capitals of the columns, only, appear above the rubbish, and one, that next the first propylæum, is entirely concealed. They are of the elegant form imitating the full-blown flower of a lotus, or other water-plant. The gallery on the right presents a strange irregularity with respect to that opposite: it differs from the latter in having, instead of eight columns, seven square pillars; each ornamented in front with a colossal Osiridean figure; of which little is seen but the high cap, with a pair of ram's horns. The space between this row of pillars and the row of columns on the opposite side is 107 feet. The walls, architraves, &c., of the galleries are decorated with sculptures, which, as far as they are visible, present nothing remarkable; but the colours are very well preserved: the plain surface of the walls, &c., is painted white, as usual; and the hieroglyphics and other sculptures are blue, green, yellow, and red.—On the back of the great propylæum is sculptured a battle-scene; of which nearly the whole is concealed by the rubbish: this is on the southernmost wing: the other wing is probably ornamented with similar sculptures, which are entirely hidden by the accumulation of rubbish.— The portal of the second propylæum is of granite, which has been painted like the rest.[1] Upon the face of the left wing of this propylæum is sculptured the king dragging along three rows of captives before the god Amon-Ra. This work is in a bold and correct style: as usual, the god and the king are of a colossal size, and the captives like pigmies. There are stairs in each wing, which are entered by two doors from the roof of the galleries of the great court behind.

Behind the second propylæum is a magnificent peristyle court,[2] 136 feet in width, and 123 feet in the other direction; measured from wall to wall. The roof of the front gallery is supported by a row of square pillars, eight in number: that of the end-gallery, by a row of eight similar pillars, and eight columns, behind the former. The square pillars had each a colossal Osiridean figure in front, like those of the preceding court; but all these figures are partially, or almost wholly, demolished. The galleries on the right and left have each a row of five columns. The walls and columns are richly adorned with painted sculptures, which still exhibit colours of extraordinary brilliancy. In the midst of the court are many small monolithic columns of granite; the remains of a spacious Christian church. There is less rubbish in this court than in any other part of the edifice.—In taking a survey of the sculptures, I begin with those of the front-wall, which is the back of the second propylæum.—A great portion of this is occupied by the display of religious processions and offerings to the gods. A little to the left of the entrance, and in the upper compartment of the sculptures, is represented a procession of nine small figures of kings; each with a staff in his hand, and with his name before him. The name of the first is that of Rameses 3rd, the founder of the building: the other names are those of his predecessors, in the regular

---

[1]Over it is a row of eight sitting apes, much broken.
[2]See plate 47 [fig. 111].

order of their succession—nos. 55, 54, 53, 52, 51, 50, 49, 48, and 47, of
my list. They follow a larger figure of Rameses 3rd, who is presenting an
offering to Amon-Generator. This sculpture is important both as a
confirmation and continuation of the list of kings presented by the tablet
of Abydos, which terminates with no. 51 of my list. A little to the left of
this is a similar subject: three small figures, each with the name annexed,
are represented borne on the shoulders of as many priests: the names
agree with the three first in the former series. Above these are four
similar figures, borne in the same manner, with their names in this
order—55, 54, 51, 52: why they are so arranged I know not: the order in
which they are placed in the first series is proved to be correct by many
inscriptions. What I have here called "names" are the prenomens. At the
right extremity of the wall which is decorated with these sculptures (the
back of the propylæum) is represented a battle-scene. It occupies but a
small space; is very confused; and much injured: the king is without any
covering on his head.[1] To the left of this we see the monarch[2] proceeding
at a slow pace in his chariot, accompanied by a group of captives, who
are bound together, and are walking beneath the horses['] bellies;
apparently assisting in drawing the chariot. Below this is a procession of
soldiers with spears and shields and long daggers. Still further to the left,
the king is represented bringing three trains of captives before the god
Amon-Ra and Maut.—The sculptures illustrative of the conquests of this
prince are continued on the southern (or south-western) side-wall.
Commencing our examination at the left extremity, we see the Egyptian
monarch seated on the back of his car. Four rows of miserable prisoners
are conducted before him: their hands or arms bound together in
distorted and painful attitudes. At the head of each of these four rows is
an Egyptian soldier, throwing at the feet of the conqueror a number of
amputated hands and other members, which some have supposed to be
those of prisoners, but which are more probably merely tokens of the
number of enemies slain in a particular battle or campaign: for it is still a
common custom in the East to bring similar trophies from a field of
battle. Behind each of the soldiers who are throwing down these
members is a scribe, counting and writing down the number of them as
they are added to the pile. The rest of this wall is occupied by religious
processions and by a very long record in hieroglyphics.—The end-wall is
decorated with sculptures representing the homage and offerings of the
king to various divinities for the signal successes which have crowned his
arms. Along the base are sculptured 26 princes. There are five more on
the right wall, and thirteen princesses on the left wall. They are the sons
and daughters of Rameses 3rd.—On the right side-wall is a very

---

[1]His hair is hanging in long plaits. The enemy have beards, and long coats,
mostly blue, bordered with white. They are of light red complexion.

[2]With a whip in his hand.

remarkable religious procession; probably in celebration of the triumphs of the Egyptian monarch. Towards the left extremity, he is borne on a splendid throne in a kind of shrine, or palanquin, on the shoulders of twelve princes, his sons. Officers and priests, with flabella and the King's arms, &c., attend; and behind are six other sons of the King, preceded by 4 priests, and followed by 2 officers, and 8 other persons, 4 of whom carry the steps of the throne, and 4 bear two stools. Above these followers of the shrine are priests and others, with 4 more sons of the King. Before the King are 2 priests burning incense, with other persons, arranged in 2 rows; among them, one reading from a papyrus, and a trumpeter. Next, the King is represented burning incense before Amon-Ra. Then we see twenty-two priests bearing on their shoulders a kind of bier, covered with an embroidered red cloth, which, falling down at the side, conceals their persons excepting the upper part of the head, and the feet. Upon this stands the statue of the god Amon-Generator, attended by bearers of flabella &c. In the representations of this god we generally see two or more trees, resembling cypresses, on an altar or shrine, behind him; and here these emblems, five in number, are borne behind the group of priests who carry his statue. Before the statue of the god walks the king; following a white bull, which was a living emblem of that god. A priest is burning incense before the sacred animal.—Such are the most remarkable of the sculptures which adorn the walls of this great court.

In the middle of the end-wall of the great peristyle court is a large door-way. The edifice continues two hundred feet further, and comprises numerous apartments; most of which are entirely buried in rubbish. Excavation here would probably be rewarded by the discovery of many interesting sculptures.

The exterior of the north-eastern wall of this great edifice,[1] from which the rubbish has been cleared away, is decorated by an extensive series of sculptures, in a very spirited style, presenting the history of many military exploits of Rameses 3rd. The order of these sculptures seems to be from right to left.[2] After contemplating several battle-scenes, we next see the Egyptian monarch, with his troops, proceeding through a rushy country, infested by wild beasts: he is in his chariot; has just transfixed, with his javelins, two lions, and is turning back upon a third. This piece

---

[1] Many doors, or windows, have been cut in this wall by the Christians.

[2] 1st. The King proceeding to battle, twice represented. A repetition of the battle in the great court. The King seated: prisoners brought before him, and heaps of hands &c. thrown at his feet: his car behind him. The King seated, addressing his soldiers on another campaign: arms distributed to them. The King in his car, marching against the enemy, with his troops. A battle-scene. The enemy in great confusion: some in cars drawn, each, by a pair of horses; and some in carts, each drawn by four oxen with the Indian hunch. They are beardless, and with a dress reaching only to the knees. Chiefly

of sculpture is one of the finest and most animated specimens of ancient Egyptian art. The next subject is a naval engagement, either on a sea or river, and is one of the most interesting of the series. The prows of the Egyptian vessels are ornamented each by a lion's head and have several oars, as well as a sail, but the sails of all are furled. These vessels, advancing in regular order from the left, and manned chiefly by archers, have hemmed in between them and the shore the enemies' vessels, which are in a state of disorder. The opponents of the Egyptians appear to be of two different nations, distinguished by their dress and arms: the helmets of the one class have two small horns projecting from them, before and behind; those of the other are ornamented with feathers: both seem to be Asiatics. The Egyptian monarch and four of his sons are standing on the shore, to the right; and are pouring a shower of arrows into the enemies' vessels.[1] Behind the king is his chariot. In the next piece we see the Egyptian king receiving congratulations from his warriors.[2] Lastly, he is represented conducting two rows of miserable prisoners before the god Amon-Ra. Behind him is his empty car.—These sculptures extend to the second propylæum; between which and the first propylæum are other similar sculptures, but almost wholly concealed by rubbish.[3]—The other side of the temple is more encumbered with rubbish than this: it is ornamented with sculptures of which too little is seen to admit of any particular description.

The whole length of this great edifice is about 487 feet. Some of the exploits of its founder, commemorated by its sculptures (particularly the naval engagement), remind us of the acts recorded of Sesostris. As there seem to have been two kings called Sesoosis or Sesostris, perhaps their achievements have been confounded by historians; and some of which the latter should have the credit ascribed to the former. If we are to regard Rameses 2nd as the *great* Sesostris, I am inclined to consider Rameses 3rd as the *second* Sesostris, or Sesoosis 2nd of Diodorus; though the latter was the fourth successor of the former, and not his son, as Diodorus makes him.

The name at present given to the ruined town in which the monuments which I have just described are situated is certainly *Medee'net Hha'boo*; but this may be a corruption of *Medee'net Ab'oo* مدينة ابو . The word

---

[1]He is represented, as usual, of a colossal size, and is trampling upon several prostrate enemies. Thus assisted by their King, the Egns. in the boats have obtained a great advantage over their enemies, and taken many prisoners. The enemy are chiefly the same as in the former battle; but some have a helmet with two horns. See the two heads in first copy, p. 97 [not extant]. Some of each class have shields, of a circular form. The Egn. shields are rounded at the top, and straight at the bottom. One of the enemies' vessels is overturned.

[2]And the lopped hands are counted before him. Behind him is his chariot.

[3]Upon the wall between the two propylæa, and upon the back of a projecting portion of the first propylæum, we see another battle-scene, and the assault of a town or fortress.

Ab'oo ابو has always been used by the people of Egypt since Arabic became the language of the country as synonymous with Αββα and Παπα; titles bestowed on bishops and other Christian dignitaries; and when thus used is *indeclinable*. This word could not be employed in the above name a signifying simply *father*: "the City of the Father" would be written in Arabic "Medee'net el-Ab" مدينة الاب . "Medee'net Ab'oo" would signify "the City of Αββα," or "—— of an Αββα," or "—— Παπα." There is little doubt but that the town in question is that mentioned in the itinerary of Antoninus by the name of *Papa*.[1] In that itinerary it seems (as Hamilton conjectures) that, instead of Papa being placed 8 miles above Contra Copton, and Hermonthis 30 miles above Papa, the distances should be transposed. The ruined town which I suppose to be Papa is only 25 Roman miles from the site of Contra Copton: it is, however, less than 8 miles below Hermonthis. When Thebes became divided into detached towns and villages, what is now called Medee'net Hha'boo was probably the principal town on the western side.

By the northern angle of the mounds of Medee'net Hha'boo are some remains of a temple, consisting of little more than small fragments of stone. Among these are two broken colossi of hard white chert, and of beautiful workmanship, like those of Amonoph 3rd which are found among the blocks of white limestone to the north of the remains of the great portico of the Amonophium.

Adjacent to the southern angle of Medee'net Hha'boo is a small temple, of an age which, in comparison with that of the monuments which I have lately described, must be termed modern; being of the reign of Ptolemy Physcon. It is divided into three small chambers; one behind another; and has remains of a vestibule, or portico, before it. Thoth is the chief divinity of this temple. Thoth is the chief divinity of this temple. The exterior of the building is not sculptured. The first chamber is also without sculpture: in the second, the subjects have been outlined in red; and the sculpture commenced: the third chamber is finished: its sculptures represent Ptolemy Physcon offering to the gods, and performing acts of worship.[2]

A little to the south of Medee'net Hha'boo is an extensive lake; or a shallow excavation which retains the waters of the inundation a month or two longer than any other part adjacent. It is of an oblong, rectangular form: its direction from north-east to south-west. Its width is rather more than half a mile; and its length, twice that extent, or about a mile and a quarter. The earth which was dug up in the process of excavating this great lake is heaped in regular mounds along the margin all round.

---

[1] This opinion (which the correspondence of the words *Ab'oo* and *Papa* suggested to me) has been already advanced by M. Quatremère, in his Memoires Geogr. et Hist. sur l'Egypte, t. i, pp. 248-50.

[2] On the front wall he is represented offering to his four deceased predecessors, each of whom sits on a throne, with his wife standing behind. Their names are imperfectly legible.

Along the north-west side are two parallel ridges of mounds; which seem as if a canal had run between them. I do not suppose that this large lake was designed for any sacred purposes; but rather to drain off the waters of superabundant inundations from the adjacent fields, and to retain water for the purpose of irrigation when the inundation was insufficient. After the waters have sunk into the soil its bed is sown. The French savants regarded this not as a lake but a hippodrome, and a place for military and gymnastic exercises.

Upon one of the mounds on the south-eastern side of this lake is situated the village of *El-Ba'eera't* البعيرات which gives its name to the district next above that of El-Ckoor'neh. It is near the eastern angle of the lake.[1]

Section 5. The Tombs of the Kings.
(Beeba'n el-Mooloo'k).

Introductory remarks, &c.—Description of the principal (or Eastern) Valley, and of the tombs which it contains—The Western Valley, and its tombs.

Among the western mountains of Thebes is the barren and secluded Valley of *Beeba'n el-Mooloo'k* بيبان الملوك , or the Tombs of the Kings.[2] The word *beeba'n* is the plural (or one of the plural forms) of *ba'b* باب , which is the general Arabic term for a *door*, or *gate*: therefore "Beeba'n el-Mooloo'k" might be translated: "the Gates of the Kings": but the term *ba'b* is also commonly used by the modern Egyptians in a different sense, as synonymous with *magha'rah*, signifying a *grotto*, or *hypogeum*.[3] De Sacy has rightly traced the word *ba'b*, having this signification, to the Coptic βηβ[4]: but he is mistaken in supposing that the modern Egyptians apply this term to sepulchral grottoes, or hypogea, merely as referring to the *doors*, or *entrances*, of those tombs: they use it in the sense of *magha'rah*. Quatremère, also, is wrong in thinking that the Coptic βηβ must be expressed in Arabic by *viv*[5] (there is no such sound in Arabic as *v*, but I conclude he means *w*[6]); for there are abundant examples of *b* being used in similar cases; as, for instance, in Ba'belyoo'n بابليون for Βαβυλων . Βηβ might be expressed in Arabic by

---

[1] It has lately been ruined, on account of the refractory conduct of its inhabitants. The name belongs to several villages.

[2] See the topographical plan of Thebes, &c.—plate 16 [fig. 74].

[3] And it is worthy of remark that when it is used by the Modern Egyptians in this sense, its plural is *beeba'n*; whereas the form which they use for the plural of *ba'b*, or door, is *abwa'b*.

[4] Observations sur le nom des pyramides, p. 43.

[5] Memoires geogr. et hist. sur l'Egypte, t. 1, p. 252.

[6] i. e. the letter wä'w, which some Eastern nations pronounce *v*.

ba'b باب or *beeb* بيب. The word *ba'b* I have heard a thousand times used as signifying a sepulchral grotto, or hypogeum. "Beeba'n el-Mooloo'k" is therefore to be interpreted "the Hypogea (or excavated tombs) of the Kings." The Valley of the Tombs of the Kings is, however, called by some of the modern inhabitants of El-Ckoor'neh "The Valley of Ba'b el-Mooloo'k": in which case allusion is made either to that very magnificent tomb discovered by Belzoni, which principally attracts the attention of travellers, or else to the contracted *entrance* of the *valley*. On my first visit to this valley my guide led me directly to the entrance of the tomb above-mentioned, and said هو باب الملوك ها *ha' hoo ba'b el-mooloo'k*—"here is the tomb of the Kings."

The natural road to the Tombs of the Kings is a narrow, long, and winding valley; the entrance of which is about half a mile from the ruined village of El-Ckoor'neh. The sides are steep and rugged; and of a whitish and sandy hue. Not a blade of grass, nor even a noxious weed, is seen throughout the tedious route; which is well calculated to prepare the mind of the traveller for the contemplation of the solemn and mysterious tombs; and seldom is his attention diverted by any living creature inhabiting the valley or its immediate vicinity; though he may see there some flights of rock-pigeons, and a few doves, and sometimes a vulture or two soaring above. The summits and slopes of the rock are strewed with flint-stones, of a dark, reddish colour, and of curious forms: some of them are spherical; others of an annular form, surrounding a spherical mass; and intermixed with these are many petrifactions in the forms of shell-fish; mostly of a bivalve kind, many of which are three inches, or more, in length. High up the mountains on the right, or northern side, is an *'ack'abah*, or mountain-road, leading to Furshoo't. The bottom of the valley is flat; but encumbered with large masses of rock, which have fallen down from the sides: and the rains (which are of extremely rare occurrence, but sometimes, perhaps once in four or five years, very copious) have washed down from the steeps a quantity of small, white detritus, and deposited it along the bottom of their channel, throughout the whole length of the valley.

Proceeding leisurely, we arrive in about forty minutes at a point where the valley divides into two branches. The right (or western) branch contains several tombs; but the eastern is the principal valley. Continuing our route along the latter, we soon come to a very contracted pass, where the rock appears to have been cut through; and here are some traces of rude hieroglyphics, on the left side. From the steep on the right, a little before this pass, I made a view which gives a good general idea of the valley.[1] From the principal, or central branch of this valley (seen in the view above-mentioned) smaller branches turn off to the right and left.

There are shorter routes from the plain of Thebes to the Valley of the Tombs of the Kings: the traveller may ascend the rocky acclivity on the north of the As'a'see'f, either by an easy, or by a steep, ascent; and,

[1]See plate 48 [fig. 112].

passing over the mountain, will find several points at which he may descend into the valley. From the intervening heights he enjoys a most interesting view of the whole site of Thebes; and if he will ascend to the more eastern of the two highest summits of the mountains he will be amply repaid for his toil by the far more extensive view which it commands, comprising both of the valleys of the tombs of the kings.

I spent fifteen days in this valley; from the 17th of August, 1826, to the 1st of September. Mr. Hay (being then at Thebes) made arrangements to go there at the same time; but intending to spend a much longer period there. We occupied the entrance of a tomb, the greater part of which was closed with sand and rubbish. This was the tomb of Rameses 10th; marked no. 18 in my sketch of the plan of the valley. It was necessary for our little party to have watchmen at night; as there are sometimes robbers wandering about the mountains, and our presence in this secluded valley might have attracted them, as well as wolves, hyænas, and jackals. While we were here some robbers came down at night from some part of the mountains to the sa'ckiyeh under the sycamore at the landing-place of El-Ckoor'neh, killed one of the oxen which were employed for turning the sa'ckiyeh, and having roasted and eaten a portion of it, returned before day-break.—While we stayed in the valley, Nile-water was brought to us every morning: no water being found nearer than the cultivated plain. The heat there, in the sun, at that period, was very great; but within the tombs the thermometer did not rise higher than 92°, and three days not higher than 87°.

Strabo's description, stating that the tombs of the kings are above the Memnonium, is a very vague direction to them. That writer affirms that there were about forty of these tombs; and that near them were obelisks with inscriptions recording the riches and power of the kings buried there, and the extent of their empire, which included Scythia, Bactria, India, and Ionia; as well as the amount of the tribute, and the number of their forces, which was about a million. These obelisks are now nowhere seen: but of the tombs, more than half the number which Strabo mentions are known and open. Many of these were discovered by Belzoni. There are sixteen in this valley which contain sculptures, with the names of the kings buried in them: but the whole number of tombs in the valley (not including several which are mere pits descending to catacombs) is twenty-one. Each tomb is a separate excavation; or was originally distinct from any other: there are, however, forced communications between some of them, made by explorers in search of treasure. Each tomb was excavated during the life-time of the monarch for whom it was destined; being a work of much time and labour. The valley is much encumbered with the chips of stone resulting from the excavation of these extensive hypogea. The tombs which contain names are those of kings of the 18th, 19th, and 20th Dynasties: the greater number are of the Rameses family. No order of succession has been followed in fixing upon the spot where a tomb was to be excavated: but the less conspicuous places appear to have been chosen earliest.

I now proceed to give a concise description of each of these tombs, in the order in which they are numbered in the topographical sketch here annexed: but I recommend the description of the 17th tomb to be read first, as it is the most complete: the more brief accounts of the other tombs will then be more intelligible.

In the first of the lateral branches of the valley,[1] which is on the right, is the *First Tomb*, which is that of Rameses 9th.[†] Of this I made a view,[2] in which is seen nearly the whole of the excavation; it being much shorter than most of the other tombs. Its direction, by the compass, is N. 24° W. Above the entrance (which is nearly similar in all) is sculptured a disk, painted yellow, representing the sun, within which is the figure of the ram-headed god Kneph, and behind him is a beetle: the latter was an emblem of the sun; and the former probably here typified the sun in the lower hemisphere[3]; as also when represented in a boat. The title of "Pharaoh" (or "Phra") signifying "the Sun," this great luminary below the horizon, depicted in the manner above-described, appears to be emblematic of the deceased Pharaoh. On each side of the disk is a kneeling figure of the king, in adoration: behind one of these figures (that on the left) stands the goddess Isis; and behind the other, Nephthys. On each side of the door-way is a column of hieroglyphics, containing the name of the king. At the entrances of all the tombs in this valley we find the same devices (if any), or nearly the same, as above described.—The passage slopes gently downwards. The sides are covered with a fine plaster, upon which the sculptures are executed; and all of these are painted with bright colours upon the white ground. Within the entrance, on the left side, the first subject is the king presenting an offering to Ra, who is represented, as usual, with the head of a hawk, and crowned with the sun's disk, round which a serpent, raising its head in front, issues. This is found in the same place, just within the entrance, in most of the kings' tombs.[4] The other sculptures in the passage are extremely curious: they retain their colours.[5] Among them are a row of human figures inverted: others enclosed in ovals, placed in a horizontal position; and others with their arms bound behind them: these exhibit the punishments of guilty souls. The boat of the ram-headed god Kneph is also represented here: the god himself standing in the midst, beneath a

---

[1]See no. 34 of the subjects for wood-cuts [fig. 113].
[†]Ramses VII. As with dynasties, the numbering of monarchs during Lane's time differed occasionally from that of the present.
[2]See plate 49 [fig. 114].
[3]The hieroglyphic of Neb, Nef, or Kneph, is the lower hemisphere.
[4]Facing it is a similar subject, the King offering to the hawk-headed Osiris.
[5]On the left side is a row of men inverted, representing wicked souls. The sun, emblematic of the King, in a boat, with a serpent wreathing round it, arriving at a door guarded by a serpent. Then the boat of Kneph.

canopy, over which a huge serpent curls itself in many folds.[1]—At the end of the passage is the sepulchral chamber; which is 28 feet long, and 17 feet wide. In the middle is a deep lid of granite, like an inverted chest, 10 feet long, 5 feet 9 inches wide, and 4 feet 9 inches deep, placed over a grave cut in the floor, 3 feet deep: nothing but rubbish is within it. The subjects of the sculptures on the walls of the chamber are of a very mysterious kind. Kneph is here again represented in the sun's disk, on each side of which is a figure adoring him. Here, also, we see again the punishment of wicked souls: two figures[2] are sculptured kneeling, with their arms bound together, and a rope tied round their necks: each is held by a person behind. Around the base of the walls is a border composed of similar figures. The ceiling is decorated with astronomical paintings. Two female figures, emblematic of the firmament, are here represented, back to back; their bodies elongated in an unnatural manner, and stretching along the middle of the ceiling, from end to end; and their arms and legs extended at right angles towards the sides of the chamber. In each space thus enclosed is a singular group of figures. Among these is the hideous female personification of Typhon (having the head of a crocodile, the arms and shoulders and breasts of a woman, and the lower parts of a hippopotamus): a crocodile leans over the back and head of this figure. Among the other figures are several signs of the zodiac— taurus, leo, virgo, and scorpio.—At the end of this chamber is a smaller one; at the further extremity of which is a recess; and over this is painted a boat with a pig in it, and an ape before and behind the pig.[3]

The *Second Tomb* is in the central branch of the valley, a little above the entrance of the branch which leads to the first tomb. Its direction is N. 30° W. This is the tomb of Rameses 4th, the son and successor of Rameses 3rd. It is one of the most magnificent, though not one of the most extensive, of the tombs in this valley. Over the entrance is the same device as that which decorates the entrance of the first tomb. The passage, at first, has a gentle slope, and then becomes horizontal.[4] Its sides are plastered, and adorned with painted sculptures, which are well preserved. Next to the usual representation of the king before the god Ra is a device which is also found in several of the other tombs, but here much defaced.[5] It consists of the disk of the sun, with the figures of Kneph and the beetle within it; and a serpent above it; a crocodile below; and at the top and bottom, the head of an animal, resembling that of a cow, but with three horn[s]: the uppermost of these heads is inverted. The crocodile is in a descending posture; presenting an emblem of the

[1] At the end of the passage, on each side, is the King habited as a priest, with a leopard's skin, offering to Osiris, who represents the King himself, having his name.
[2] Now almost white, but retaining remains of black paint.
[3] On each side-wall is the King offering to Osiris.
[4] It had five doors.
[5] A copy of the same device is given with the description of the 17th tomb.

sun descending to the lower hemisphere, and of the Pharaoh entering the infernal regions.[1] The greater part of the walls of the passage is covered with hieroglyphics; after which we meet with subjects similar to some in the first tomb. On the left side is a row of eight decapitated men; four of whom are painted black (to represent their *moral* blackness), and four, red, standing behind three serpents at the foot of the god Kneph. Behind these victims are eight others, bound for the like punishment. On the opposite wall are represented four men painted black, who are also decapitated; and their heads are placed before them: four executioners, with knives in their hands, are standing in front of them.[2]—Some idea of the grandeur of this tomb may be formed from a sketch which is here introduced, taken from a point near the end of the passage; looking into the sepulchral chamber.[3] This chamber is 27 feet 8 inches wide, and 23 feet 10 inches long. In the middle of it is an enormous sarcophagus of granite, 11 feet 7 inches long, 6 feet 9 inches wide, and 8 feet 4 inches high, covered with hieroglyphics and sculptured figures. The lid is 1 foot 4 inches thick: on the top of it is a mummy-shaped figure of the king, in high relief, with the horns of Amon. The lid remains on the top; but it has been broken into two pieces; and the sarcophagus itself is broken a little at the side.[4] On the walls of the chamber are represented the punishments of the wicked, as before, the boat of Kneph, and many strange devices. The paintings of the ceiling resemble those in the first tomb, excepting in some of the details.—Beyond this chamber is another, which is long and narrow, and nearly covered with hieroglyphics; having on each side a narrow cell, the walls of which are painted with mummy-shaped figures; and at the end, another cell. Here we find the following inscription—IANVARIVS P P VIDI ET MIRAVI LOCVM FILEA MEA IANVARINA VALETE OMNES.—There are also several Greek inscriptions scribbled by early Christians on the walls of this tomb.

Opposite the tomb just described is a branch of the valley which turns off to the left. At the entrance of this branc[h], on the left side, is the *Third Tomb*; the direction of which is E. 12° N. This is an unfinished tomb. It was begun for Rameses 3rd,[†] the father of the king whose tomb I have just before described. For some reason the work was stopped, and

---

[1]The crocodile, being an emblem of the sun, was also an emblem of the Egyptian king, whose title was "the Sun" (Phra): hence Ezekiel calls Pharaoh Hophra "the great dragon"—i.e. the crocodile—"that lieth in the midst of his rivers." Ch. xxix, v. 3.

[2]There are also black and red men with their arms bound; some, placed horizontally; others, inverted.

[3]See no. 35 of the subjects for wood-cuts [fig. 115].

[4]On the 2nd of June, 1835, I found a dove's nest, with two eggs, on the top of this sarcophagus.

[†]Lane and his colleagues correctly noted traces of Ramses III's cartouches, but the tomb probably was designed for one of the king's sons. Whether it ever contained a burial is unclear.

a new and very magnificent tomb was excavated and finished for this king higher up the valley. The latter I shall speak of in its place. The third tomb is nearly filled with dust and sand which has been washed in by the rare, but sometimes violent, rains. It consists of several chambers, for the most part in a rough, unfinished state. On the few parts which are sculptured we find the name of the king for whom it was at first designed.

A little further up the same branch, and on the same side, is the *Fourth Tomb*; which is that of Rameses 8th.[†] Its direction is E. 14° N. It is very extensive; but unfinished. It commences with a high and wide passage, sloping gently downwards. The sides are plastered; and, just within the entrance, some designs which were to have been sculptured are outlined in red. On the right side the artist has drawn the king offering to a divinity who has four ram's heads. At the end of this passage is an unfinished chamber, with four square pillars; through the midst of which is a steeper descent. From hence a short horizontal passage leads to the last chamber, which also has four square pillars. In the centre is a large square pit; 11 feet by 15 in width, and 33 feet deep, in its present state; there being large fragments of stone, and a quantity of rubbish, at the bottom of it.—I entered this tomb for the first time very incautiously, without a light. On my visiting it a second time, with a candle, I found that I had, on the former occasion, approached almost close to the brink of the great pit: had I taken another step or two I should certainly have been killed. No one was with me at the time. A traveller should never venture into any Egyptian catacomb in the dark; and should always carry a flint and steel, with some tinder and matches, in order to relight his candle, should it be put out by a flight of bats, or by another accident.— From the very unfinished state of the tomb above-described it is doubtful whether it ever contained the body of the king for whom it was destined.

Returning, and proceeding along the central branch, we arrive at the *Fifth Tomb*,[‡] on the left side; the direction of which is towards the south-east. Its entrance is at the base of the slope, and is surrounded by rubbish which has been taken out. The passage has been quite filled up by detritus washed in by rains, and by fragments of the rock which have fallen in consequence of the damp on such occasions: but a way has been cut through this mass of rubbish and stones; leaving part all along to support the loosened portions of rock above. As we proceed, the destruction becomes greater; and at length it is impossible to trace any plan: nothing is seen but rubbish and fragments of stone, through which a passage has been made with difficulty and danger.

[†]Ramses XI. Lane was correct that the tomb was abandoned by the king, but it had a more complex history than he suspected.
[‡]It has recently been discovered to be an extensive tomb for the sons of Ramses II.

The *Sixth Tomb*, which is that of Rameses 7th,[†] is on the same side, a few paces further, and a little way up the steep. Its direction is E. 42° S. It is extensive and highly interesting. The entrance is nearly closed by fragments of stone and rubbish. Over the door-way is the usual device.[1] Within the entrance, on each side, are two small chambers, without any decoration. As we advance we find sculptures on the walls and ceiling more mysterious than any in the tombs which I have hitherto described.[2] Among other strange devices, on the right side, are inverted figures of men with their arms bound behind them, and of others decapitated, and inverted black birds with human heads: all of which are emblems of wicked departed souls. The subjects on the ceiling are astronomical, or astrological. Proceeding further we observe the progress of the sun in the lower hemisphere represented by Kneph in a boat, and by a crocodile in a boat. On the right side is a very remarkable figure of the Priapian god, Amon-Generator, in a strange attitude, as if falling backwards; his arms uplifted: it is very highly and curiously ornamented; but much injured.[3] At the end of this passage is an unfinished chamber, having no sculpture or painting, excepting a figure on each side of a door at the end, through which we pass into another chamber, also unfinished, with four square pillars, and no decorations. Through this we proceed, down a steep slope, to a third chamber, which is the last. Here we find no sarcophagus, but a large grave cut in the floor, as in the first tomb, but much larger, and now filled with rubbish. The walls and ceiling are covered with mysterious devices, which, for the most part, it is impossible to describe. Three rows of figures extend around the chamber: some are adoring the red disk of the sun: others, worshipping the sun under the emblem of a beetle. Among the decorations of the right side are long hieroglyphic inscriptions. The ceiling resembles those before described; but it is very coarsely painted.

The *Seventh Tomb* is directly opposite to that just described. Its direction is N. 25° W. This is the tomb which was intended for the great Sesostris (Rameses 2nd); but it is doubtful if that king was buried in it; for it appears to be unfinished.[‡] Being at the very base of the slope, it has been filled with rubbish, by torrents, like the fifth tomb. A narrow passage has been cut through the rubbish, along the side; but nothing can be seen of the interior distribution of the tomb: I only remarked that the hieroglyphics at the entrance (among which is the name of the great Pharaoh above-mentioned) are very beautifully sculptured. Had this tomb been finished it would doubtless have been very magnificent.

[†]Ramses IX.

[1]The passage had four doors.

[2]A door is represented on each side, guarded by a serpent.

[3]It has the name of the King, and the face and arms are black. Was he a voluptuous and wicked King? And is he in purgatory?

[‡]Contrary to Lane, evidence indicates that Ramses II was interred there. The tomb's condition prevented proper examination.

Just beyond the tomb last described is a lateral valley, on the same side, in which is the *Eighth Tomb*; that of the son and immediate successor of Rameses 2nd. Its direction is W. 19° N. Over the entrance is the usual device, which is here very perfect. Within the sloping passage we see, as in most of the tombs, the king offering to Ra: this is beautifully executed, and in good preservation. Next is the sun's disk, the crocodile, &c.: then succeed columns of hieroglyphics. After proceeding a little way down we find the slope more steep; and here, steps are cut; but the centre is left plane, for the convenience of sliding down the sarcophagus. Hieroglyphics still occupy the sides, excepting along the top, where are represented small mummy-shaped figures, with human heads or the heads of various animals. As we advance we find the same curious subjects represented on the walls as in other tombs already described, and arrive at a chamber with two square pillars, much encumbered with rubbish: the walls, similarly decorated. On the right of this is a plain chamber, which also has two square pillars. Through the former chamber we proceed down a slope, and a few feet beyond find the passage quite closed with rubbish; so that the sepulchral hall is inaccessible.†

The *Ninth Tomb*, which is that of Rameses 5th,[1] is on the right side of the central branch, just above the entrance of the lateral branch in which is the eighth tomb. It is large and interesting. Its direction is W. 29° N. The entrance is much encumbered with rubbish. Within it, on each side, the king is represented adoring Ra. Advancing along the passage, which is nearly horizontal, we find the same subjects exhibited on the walls as in the first and second tombs; and the ceiling is curiously decorated, as usual. On the left side of the passage, in one part, is represented a scene of judgement. Osiris, the judge of the infernal regions (or Amenti) is seated on his throne. Before him stands a mummy-shaped figure, bearing on its shoulders the scales by which the merits of the deceased are weighed. Nine figures of men, probably representing souls about to be tried, are ascending a flight of as many steps to the platform of the throne. Over these figures is a boat, in which is a condemned soul, in the form of a large pig: an ape stands behind it, in the boat, with an uplifted scourge; and another ape, armed in the same manner, precedes the boat, which is returning from the throne: Anubis is waiting the arrival of the guilty soul. Over the figure of Osiris are four cows' heads, inverted.— This device is also found upon several sarcophagi.—The walls of the tomb which I am describing are, in many parts, wantonly injured. At the end of the passage is a chamber with four square pillars: the walls decorated with designs on a small scale: on the left are boats, and processions of gods, men, and apes: on the right are represented the punishments of the guilty in Hades, with other curious subjects. Passing down a slope through the centre of this chamber, we enter another

---

†Lane descended little more than halfway into the tomb.
[1]Called of Memnon. (Wilkinson) [It was probably designed as a double tomb for Ramses V and Ramses VI.]

passage, sloping downwards: the walls and ceiling sculptured as the first. Over a door at the bottom is an aperture (forced by some explorer) communicating with the twelfth tomb.—We now arrive at the sepulchral hall, which has an arched ceiling, and four square pillars on the side of the entrance. It is 42 feet wide, and 21 feet from the pillars to the opposite wall. In the centre are some fragments of an enormous granite lid, the cover of the grave, which is hollowed out in the floor, as in the first and sixth tombs. The devices on the walls are of the usual kind; for the most part indescribable. A row of kneeling, decapitated figures forms a border round the base. The paintings of the ceiling are like those of the first tomb; but the details more full. Part of the chamber, behind the pillars, is unfinished.

Opposite to the tomb just described is a lateral branch, in which are several other tombs: of these I shall speak after having described the remaining tombs in the central branch. The *Tenth Tomb* is a little higher up, on the left side. Its direction is S. 20° W.[1] It bears the names of Amunrameses, which I have not found elsewhere.[2] This tomb is unfinished,[3] and so much encumbered with rubbish that I was obliged to crawl along it upon my hands and knees. In an unfinished chamber and antechamber at the end is some very coarse painting; and in a side-chamber is an aperture broken through into the next tomb on the right.

The *Eleventh Tomb* is that just alluded to. It is the tomb of Rameses 3rd,[4] for whom the third tomb was originally designed, but afterwards abandoned, as I have already stated. The magnificence of this tomb is worthy of its illustrious author, who is shewn by his great edifice at Medee'net Hha'boo to have been one of the most distinguished of all the Pharaohs. Its direction is S. 7° W. The entrance is peculiar: I insert a sketch of it[5]: on each side are two columns sculptured in low relief, each surmounted with the head of a cow. The passage at first slopes gently downwards. On the left is the usual design of the king adoring the god Ra: next, Kneph and the beetle in the sun's disk, with the crocodile, &c. Then follow numerous columns of hieroglyphics. On each side of this passage is a small, square cell: in that on the left are paintings of a coarse kind, exhibiting various operations of cooking: in the opposite cell are represented several kinds of boats, richly ornamented. A little beyond these the passage becomes horizontal; and in this part are four small cells

---

[1] It was originally destined for a Queen. Her name is no. 2 in the list of unplaced Queens in Wilkinson's Materia Hieroglyphica (part ii, plate 5.)

[2] The name is that of the last King of the 21st Dynasty (marked λμ) in plate ii of the Dynasties of the Pharaohs appended to Wilkinson[']s "Thebes and Egypt." [It is the tomb of the little-known king of the late Nineteenth Dynasty, Amenmesse.]

[3] The sculptures in the passage were on plaster, which has been almost entirely broken down.

[4] See T and E. page 109.

[5] See no. 36 of the subjects for wood-cuts [fig. 116].

(like those above-mentioned) on each side.[1] In one of these are depicted, in a very neat manner, arms of various kinds, with coats of mail, &c.: of some of these I give specimens.[2] In another are highly-finished paintings of elegant furniture, very richly ornamented, consisting of chairs, sofas, foot-stools, and head-rests: also water-jars, baskets, elephants' teeth, &c. In another are the two celebrated harpers, first noticed by Bruce, whose drawings of them were certainly made from the originals, but subsequently altered and beautified in a most unwarrantable manner. An outline of one of them is here inserted.[3]—The other designs represent ploughing, sowing, and reaping; boats, birds, flowers and trees, oxen; &c.—The excavation continues in the same direction a little beyond these cells; then reaching a part of the rock unsuited to sculpture, from its hard, flinty nature, turns to the right; but a few feet beyond this angle it resumes its former direction. Here are some large figures in a very good style; representing the king offering to the gods. Throughout the whole of this tomb the sculptures are in a good state of preservation, with few exceptions; but the brilliant colours with which they are painted are much sullied, apparently by smoke. Where the passage resumes the first direction it is still horizontal: its sides are decorated with the usual mysterious sculptures. By this passage we are conducted to a chamber with four square pillars. Here, on the left side, is a procession of men of four different nations (including Egyptians, who are the hindmost), as in the seventeenth tomb, where I copied one figure of each of these four races. The sculptures in general throughout this tomb are similar to those of the seventeenth tomb. There is another chamber to the right of that last mentioned: its walls are decorated with two rows of figures: in the lower row, opposite the entrance, are figures of men tied by the arms to jackal-headed staves; two to each.—Returning to the former chamber, we pass down a slope in the centre, and descend a sloping passage; then pass through two chambers, and enter the sepulchral hall, which has a row of four square pillars before the wall in which is the entrance, and the same before the opposite wall: the ceiling between these two rows of pillars is arched. The width of the hall is 45

---

[1]Each of these had a door. In the first on the left are a row of gods, each with an ear of wheat on the head, and a row of serpents, clothed. In the first on the right, arms and standards &c. In the second on the left, gods and goddesses of the Nile, carrying lotuses, &c., and a row of figures of the god Nilus along the bottom. In the second on the right, furniture. In the third on the left, sacred oxen &c., with various insignia. In the third on the right, ploughing with two oxen; a calf skipping before them: sowing, reaping, &c. See A. Ens., iv, 48. In the fourth on the left, harpers: one playing before a sitting goddess; the other, before a black god (daughter and son of Ra?): the former is that on the right. On the back wall are two sitting figures, Ra and Atmoo. In the fourth on the right, 12 figures of Osiris, each on a throne.

For the drawing of Harper see 1st copy, p.115. [Not extant.]

[2]See no. 37 of the subjects for woodcuts [fig. 117].

[3]See no. 38 of the subjects for wood-cuts [fig. 118].

feet and a half; and the space between the two rows of pillars is about
half that measure. The sarcophagus has been removed.[1] On the left side-
wall of the hall is a curious representation of the Priapian god, Amon-
Generator, standing on a serpent, and surrounded by stars. On the right
wall is a ram-headed vulture, with extended wings. Here also I noticed
the singular device of the name of the king surrounded by a serpent. The
walls are much sullied, and the painted sculptures consequently
indistinct. There is a small chamber on each side of the sepulchral hall.
The excavation continues a few feet beyond the hall, in the same
direction; but there is nothing remarkable in this part.

The *Twelfth Tomb*, which is a little higher up the valley, on the right
side, is large, but unfinished, and without sculptures. It communicates,
by a forced aperture, with the ninth tomb; as I have before mentioned.

The *Thirteenth Tomb* is under the high cliffs at the end of the valley. It
is without a name; much injured; and nearly filled with rubbish.

The *Fourteenth Tomb*, which is under the same barrier of cliffs, a little
to the left of that just before mentioned, is very long, and is a very
remarkable tomb. It was originally the tomb of a queen, named Taosiri,
probably of the 18th Dynasty; but was usurped by a later king.[†] The
queen above-mentioned is accompanied by a king Se-Phtha, her
husband; whose name is not found in any of the royal lists; probably
because his wife was the heiress to the throne, and was the reigning
queen: in this tomb, at least, she takes precedence of him. The later king
who usurped her tomb was the immediate predecessor of Rameses 3rd:
his name appears to be Amerri, or Ramerri.[‡] This king endeavoured to
give to the tomb the appearance of its having been made for himself; and
throughout the whole of the excavation he either plastered over the
original sculptures of the queen, and had his own sculptures executed on
the coat of plaster, or he altered her figure and name into those of
himself. Over the entrance, the original design (which was of the usual
kind) was covered with plaster, upon which the same device, with the
difference only of the name, was sculptured afresh. Within the entrance,
on the left, we observe the same artifice to have been practised: the
plaster has fallen off, and exposed to view the original sculpture, which is
highly finished, and represents the queen offering to the god Ra. On the
opposite side she is standing behind the king her husband, who is
presenting an offering. Immediately beyond these sculptures we find the
plaster with the sculptures of the later king still remaining on the walls.
The designs exhibit nothing remarkable. The first chamber at which we
arrive is almost exactly similar to that in the tomb of Rameses 3rd—the
eleventh tomb—not only in form but also in its decorations. Beyond this

---

[1]It is at Paris, and the cover at Cambridge.
[†]The tomb was originally designed for the regent Tawosret, the last ruler of the
Nineteenth Dynasty, and her husband, Seti II, but it was completed by
Sethnakhte, the first king of the Twentieth Dynasty, who took it for his own.
[‡]Lane refers to a portion of the throne name of Sethnakhte.

is another chamber, in a very ruined state. Here is a sarcophagus of granite: the lid is entire; and bears the name of the later king; but the sarcophagus itself is broken into two pieces, and its sides are much demolished. The excavation continues a little further, in the same direction.

The *Fifteenth Tomb* is under the same cliffs, a little to the left of the fourteenth. This is the tomb of the immediate predecessor of the later king who appropriated to himself the tomb which I have just described.[†] It is large; but unfinished. The sculptures at the entrance are of the usual kind; and very beautifully executed: the rest of the decorations are, for the most part, merely outlined. At the end of the tomb are fragments of the granite lid of the sarcophagus; with a mummy-shaped figure, in high relief, upon it.—This tomb, as it contained a sarcophagus, and was yet unfinished, seems to shew that the ancient kings of Egypt had their tombs excavated during their life-time; and that when one died before his tomb was completed, his successor did not always cause it to be properly finished.

There are, at the end of the valley, besides the tombs which I have described, three pits, descending to catacombs; but they are obstructed by rubbish.[‡]

The tombs which remain to be described are in the south-eastern part of the valley. Entering the second of the lateral branches of the valley on that side, we arrive before the *Sixteenth Tomb*, on our right. This is the tomb of Rameses 1st; and is the oldest, of all those which have names, in the valley; unless the fourteenth, the age of which is rather doubtful, be more ancient. Its direction is W. 20° S. The entrance is surrounded by heaps of rubbish, by which it is nearly closed. This tomb is small in comparison with most of the others; but it is particularly interesting, from its extraordinary state of preservation. We first descend a steep sloping passage, without any sculpture, and now filled nearly to the top with fragments of stone. Next to this is a descent of steps; the entrance to which was formerly closed by a wall of stone and plaster, now partly broken down. This was doubtless constructed with the view of deceiving any person who might attempt to violate the tomb. At the bottom of the stairs is the sepulchral chamber, which is covered with paintings, in appearance perfectly fresh. This chamber is 20 feet and a half in length, and 17 feet wide. In the midst of it stands a granite sarcophagus, of a plain, oblong, rectangular form, 9 feet long, 4 feet wide, and 5 feet high:

[†]I.e., it is the tomb of Seti II, who was the immediate predecessor of Sethnakhte—disregarding the intervening irregular royal arrangements, of which Lane was unaware—and whose original tomb Sethnakhte appropriated.

[‡]These are shown in Lane's map of the valley. The first two as one moves more deeply into the valley are now numbered 59 (or less likely 26) and 32 (or less likely 31), the original occupants of which are unknown. The one at the extremity of that branch of the valley is apparently the one now numbered 34, the tomb of Thuthmose III, which was formally discovered by Victor Loret in 1898.

it is painted red; and the hieroglyphics upon it are painted yellow, and not cut.[1] The subjects on the walls are of the usual kind; as the boat of Kneph; the adoration of the serpent; &c. Among these are larger figures, representing the king making offerings. The paintings are in very bright colours, upon a grey ground.[2]

A few feet further on the same side of the same branch of the valley is the *Seventeenth Tomb,* which is that of Osiree 1st,[†] the son and immediate successor of Rameses 1st, and father of Rameses 2nd; than whom he was scarcely less illustrious. This tomb was discovered by Belzoni. It is the most splendid, and one of the least injured, of all the tombs in the valley. Its situation is ill chosen; for it is at the bottom of the bed of a small torrent; and though rain is a very rare phenomenon in Upper Egypt it has occasionally done great damage to this magnificent tomb. A rude wall has lately been built to divert this torrent as much as possible. To the entrance (a sketch of which is here introduced[3]) we descend a flight of steps, now much broken. There is no exterior decoration, nor any thing else in the entrance to attract the particular notice of a stranger, excepting a wooden door, made by Belzoni, and furnished with a lock. The key of this, at the period of my first visit to Thebes, was kept by the Sheykh of El-Ckoor'neh, to whom I applied for it. The direction of the tomb is S. 46° W. The passage descends rather steeply. First within the entrance, on the left side, is represented the king standing in an attitude of adoration before the god Ra; and next to this is the other usual device of Kneph and the beetle in the sun's disk, with the serpent, crocodile, &c.[4] The rest of the left side of the first passage, and the whole of the opposite side are occupied by columns of hieroglyphics, very beautifully sculptured, but not painted; this part of the tomb being unfinished. At the bottom of this passage is a descent of several steps. On each side is a row of small, mummy-shaped figures, painted with bright, unfaded colours, upon a yellow ground. The hieroglyphics of the lower compartment of each side here are, for the most part, merely outlined; shewing, again, the unfinished state of the tomb. At the bottom of the steps is a doorway; and over this are the two ovals containing the hieroglyphic title and name of the king; on each side of which is represented a kneeling figure of the goddess of truth or justice, with extended wings. We next descend a short, sloping passage: the sculptures

---

[1]Belzoni, who opened this tomb, found two mummies in the sarcophagus. He also found in this tomb two wooden statues, each 6 feet and a half high, with one arm extended, and the other hanging down: likewise a number of little images of the genii of Amenti, &c.

[2]In the back wall, near the left corner, is a niche, with Osiris represented at the end, Kneph behind him, and a serpent before him. On each side of the chamber is a small cell, without decoration. The roof of the chamber is unpainted.

[†]Seti I.

[3]See no. 39 of the subjects for wood-cuts [fig. 119].

[4]See no. 40 of the subjects for wood-cuts [fig. 120].

on the walls are of the usual mysterious kind: the boat of Kneph is twice represented: among the other devices are several serpents; one with a human head and four human legs; another with three natural heads and with legs like the former, and wings. Lower down are fourteen human heads; each with a disk above it and a star beneath it. At the end of this passage is a large pit, 30 feet in depth, and 14 feet by 12 in width; but it is now filled up to the level of the floor of the passage. The walls above this level are beautifully sculptured and painted with figures of the king presenting offerings to the gods: these figures are brilliantly coloured, upon a grey ground. The tomb had been explored and ransacked before Belzoni reopened it; and the contrivance of the pit, which to most persons would have seemed to terminate the excavation,—for the wall on the opposite side was built up to the ceiling, and sculptured and painted with the same care as the other parts of the tomb,—did not deceive the explorers: they broke through this wall.—Having crossed over the filled-up pit, we enter a fine chamber, with four square pillars, which are decorated on each side with a figure of the king offering to one of the gods. These figures, and those upon the sides of the chamber, are delicately sculptured, in very low relief (like all the sculptures in this tomb), and painted with very bright colours, upon a white ground. They are, for the most part, as well preserved as if they were the work of yesterday; but one of the pillars has been cracked by water which has entered the tomb, and must soon fall. The decorations of the walls consist of three rows of figures. Among these, on the left side, is a procession of persons of four different nations; four of each nation: I insert a specimen of each.[1] The first four are fair-complexioned men, of some northern climate: they have mustaches, and a scanty, projecting beard: their hair is curiously dressed; partly in the modern Nubian manner; and two feathers are stuck in their head: their dress is a long coat, apparently formed of an ox-hide, with the hair on: their legs and arms are tattooed.[2] The next four figures are negroes: they are painted black; and their features characterize them as truly as does their colour: their hair is dressed more simply than that of the figures before described; more precisely in the modern Nubian manner: their dress is simple: and not inelegant. The third race are fair-complexioned men; with a full, plaited beard, and bushy head of hair; much resembling the figures in Persepolitan sculptures: their physiognomy is very like that of the Jews; and they probably represent individuals of that or a neighbouring nation: their scanty dress is very remarkable. The last four are Egyptians, painted red, as usual, to denote their dark brown complexion. The hawk-headed Horus, leaning on a staff, follows this interesting procession.—In another part of the same chamber are

---

[1] See no. 41 of the subjects for wood-cuts [fig. 121].

[2] These four persons are evidently of the same race as a people conquered by Osiree, as represented in the sculpture at Kur'nak of which I have given a copy. [This sketch apparently was never put into the manuscript.]

represented twelve men pulling a rope which is attached to the neck of a standing mummy. The boat of Kneph is again found here. Upon the end-wall is a piece which is remarkable for elaborate execution and brilliant and harmonious colouring. It consists of four figures, of the natural size; the king standing before Osiris, with Athor behind the latter, and Horus behind the former. These figures are painted upon a dull yellow ground; and the whole piece is surrounded by an ornamental border.—To the right of this is a door, by which we pass into a chamber with two square pillars. The subjects here, upon the walls and pillars, are merely outlined: it became necessary to close the tomb before the sculptor had commenced his work in this chamber. The walls having been covered with a fine coat of white plaster, the devices were sketched in red lines, and afterwards more carefully drawn in black. Had they been sculptured, a second very thin coat of plaster, or a white-wash, would have been applied, previously to the painting. They are of the usual mysterious kind, and very beautifully drawn.—We return to the chamber of the four pillars. Here, on the left side, is a wide flight of steps, descending in the same direction as the former passages. At the bottom of this descent is a passage sloping gently downwards. At the entrance are sculptured two large figures on each side, very richly and delicately painted. They represent the king and the goddess Athor. Next, on the left side, we observe the king seated on a chair, or throne: before him stand two priests clad in leopards' skins; one of whom has his back towards him, and faces a small, standing figure of the same prince. Along the upper part of the wall on both sides are several groups of small figures; persons presenting offerings to what appear to be statues of the king: many of the offerers are priests clad in leopards' skins. The space below is occupied by hieroglyphics.—Next is a short passage, into which we descend by eight steps. The subjects represented upon the walls are similar to those in the last before described. At the end of this passage is a small chamber decorated with sculptures of figures nearly of the natural size, representing the king paying his adoration to the gods: they are painted with the brightest colours, upon a white ground. Here we see deplorable damage caused by the entrance of rain-water: the entrance and the left side of the chamber are much injured.—We now enter a portico before the sepulchral hall. It has six square pillars; some of which have been sadly damaged by the cause above mentioned. The sculptures here are painted upon a yellow ground; and have a rich effect: they consist of three rows of figures: in the lowest row is a procession of men prepared for punishment; their arms bound behind them; doubtless designed to represent guilty souls in Amenti. On the left side is a small chamber, in which we observe the boat of Kneph, the adoration of the serpent, &c. Corresponding in situation (on the right of the portico) is another small chamber, in which is sculptured a cow (the emblem of Athor), half the natural size; and several small figures are represented stroking her legs.— The sepulchral hall is a little lower than the portico: that is, its floor is lower. Of its decorations it would be difficult to give a clear description:

they consist of boats and processions of men and gods, with several beasts, as the ape and crocodile; also, the serpent and beetle. The ceiling is of an arched form; and ornamented with representations of several signs of the zodiac, and other astronomical or astrological devices. In the middle of the floor is a hollow, where lay the beautiful alabaster sarcophagus, which has been brought to England. It was placed upon blocks of stone which closed the entrance of a steeply-descending passage, running very far down into the heart of the rock,—no one knows whither,—having, as far as it can be traced, regular steps, with an inclined plane down the middle, for the convenience of sliding down some heavy weight; perhaps, another sarcophagus. Belzoni cleared out this passage to the depth of three hundred feet; but the rock in which it is excavated is, a little below the level of the sepulchral hall, very soft, and crumbles in such a manner that the complete clearing of this mysterious descent could not be accomplished without great danger, unless by placing a frame-work of wood as the labourers proceeded; otherwise, a mass of rock would probably fall, and bar their return. Its direction is not, as some have supposed, towards the plain of Thebes; but the same as the general direction of the tomb; south-west by the compass, almost exactly. It runs far and deep into the heart of the mountains: where it terminates, and for what it was designed, are points of curious speculation. As it was closed at the top with masonry, upon which the alabaster sarcophagus was placed, it could not have been a secret entrance to the tomb. I think it probable that the inclined plane which extends down the middle was made for sliding down a second sarcophagus and one or more mummies. Perhaps the alabaster sarcophagus was placed to deceive any person who might violate the tomb; and the body of the king was in a lower chamber.—On the left side of the sepulchral hall is a chamber with two square pillars, which is surrounded, except on the side of the entrance, by a projection like a side-board. In this lay a vast number of small Osiridean, or mummy-shaped, figures of wood, generally from six to eight inches in length, covered with a black, bituminous varnish, and ornamented with hieroglyphics; many of them bearing the name of the king who was buried in this tomb, and whom they were designed to represent. The floor was covered with these little images, to the depth of about half a foot. The walls of this chamber are decorated with three rows of figures. In the upper row of the front-wall, to the right of the door, are represented three decapitated men, kneeling before a god seated on a throne and overarched by the body of a large serpent, which raises its head before the victims: another serpent, with a human head, is behind the throne; and a cat-headed god brandishes a large knife behind the decapitated men. Besides other psychological sculptures, exhibiting the punishments of guilty souls, &c., we observe, in this chamber, the usual devices of boats and serpents, the crocodile, ram, and lion, and a strange row of monstrous gods, with human bodies and the heads of beast[s] and fishes.—There is also on the left side of the great hall a small cell, in which Osiris is represented. On the opposite side is a small, unfinished chamber. Beyond the great hall is a wide, unfinished room, with three† square pillars, of which the middle one has fallen.¹ This is the last chamber. The whole length of this splendid excavation, not including the secret descent from the great hall, is about three hundred feet. Of the king for whom it was destined we know little more than that he signalized himself by conquests in Asia, as well as by his magnificent monuments. A tradition ascribed to him the expulsion of the Israelites from Egypt; but this event I refer to the earlier reign of Thothmos 4th.²

The *Eighteenth Tomb* is a little to the left of that just described. It is the tomb of Rameses 10th. The entrance is wide; but filled nearly to the ceiling with rubbish and sand, a few paces within; and a little further it is quite closed up. The direction is south.—It was in the entrance of this tomb that I made my abode for fifteen days with Mr. Hay.

The *Nineteenth Tomb* is higher up in the same quarter of the valley, nearly at the foot of the high cliffs which bound the valley on the southeast. Its direction is S. 37° E. The entrance is similar to most of the others; but so much obstructed by rubbish that I could not, without difficulty, force myself through. Having entered, I found a wide passage, filled nearly to the top with fragments of stone and rubbish; but towards the end, where it had been cleared, I saw large figures painted upon the wall, in good preservation, and very well designed. This passage is all that was finished: a little beyond it the excavation terminates. The hieroglyphic name of a "Rameses" is found here; but not enclosed as kings' names, in an oval: I saw none here so enclosed.‡

The *Twentieth Tomb*†† is a few paces to the east of that last mentioned. It is quite different from those which I have described. The entrance is a plain door-way, at the foot of the high cliffs. The passage is narrow, long, and steep; running at first in a straight direction, and then turning gradually to the right. At the end is a wide pit, nearly filled with rubbish washed in by torrents. On one side this rubbish has been dug away; and there I found the pit to be 22 feet deep. I attempted to descend to the bottom; but the rubbish gave way when touched by my feet; and if I had persevered I should probably have been buried. The passage perhaps continues from the bottom of the pit.‡‡

---

†Four.

¹Belzoni found in this chamber the carcase of a bull, embalmed with asphaltum; and also those numerous little wooden images which, when I visited the tomb, had been strewed upon the floor of another chamber, as before mentioned.

²See the Supplement to this work.

‡It is the tomb of Mentuherkhepshef, a son of Ramses IX.

††It is the tomb of Thuthmose I and Hatshepsut. Lane was unaware of Hatshepsut's existence.

‡‡Lane was correct about the continuation, for the "wide pit," which was the extent of Lane's penetration of the tomb, is in fact only the first chamber, less than one-third of the way to the end of the tomb.

The *Twenty-first Tomb* (the last that remains to be mentioned in this valley) is between the two lateral branches on the same side. Its entrance might easily escape observation; being surrounded by a quantity of rubbish taken from the interior. This is one of the tombs opened by Belzoni. It is on the same plan as most of the others; but without any sculpture or other decoration; being unfinished. We first descend a sloping passage, running towards the west; then, a flight of steps, in the same direction; and next, another sloping passage; at the bottom of which is a chamber, with one square pillar of the rock left to support the ceiling. Upon the ground were still lying two female mummies, quite naked.[1] On one side (the same side as the entrance) is another chamber, of smaller dimensions, containing many broken jars.

There are perhaps some other tombs in this valley, yet concealed; though Belzoni carefully examined every part where it appeared there could be any without intersecting some one of those already known.[2]

I have now to describe the tombs in the *Western Valley*. Only four have been discovered here; but it appears that this valley was chosen as the burial-place of kings before that which contains so many tombs. It is not much to be wondered at that we are acquainted with comparatively few of the tombs of the ancient kings of Egypt, when we see how careful they were to choose the most secluded spots in which to excavate their splendid hypogea.

About half-way, or rather more, up the Western Valley (ten minutes' walk from the entrance) is the *Tomb of Amonoph 3rd*,[†] the king whom the Greeks and Romans called Memnon, and whose stupendous colossi and other wonderful works on the plain of Thebes I have already described. The entrance of this tomb faces the west; and its situation is such that a person might pass it without observation; but in returning, he could not fail to see it. The exterior appearance is similar to that of most of the tombs in the other valley; though without any decoration. We first descend a sloping passage, without sculpture or painting; then, a flight of steps, and another sloping passage, like the first: altogether, about a hundred feet. At the bottom of this is a large, square pit, nearly filled with fragments of stone and rubbish. The walls around this pit, above the level of the floor of the passage, are plastered and painted; and here we first find the hieroglyphic name which tells us that the remains of the illustrious Pharaoh above-mentioned were deposited in this tomb, or that the tomb was destined for him. The figures of the king and of the gods before whom he is standing are extremely well designed, and have a boldness and simplicity of style which, to a person conversant with ancient Egyptian art, would plainly shew them to be of most remote

---

[1] As they were found by Belzoni. See his book, p. 228.

[2] While I stayed in this valley, the frequent changes which I underwent in passing from the burning sun, reflected from yellow rocks on every side, to the cool interior of the tombs, affected me with diarrhœa.

[†] Now designated as Western Valley tomb number 22.

antiquity, if the name did not exist to prove their age. On the opposite side of the pit is a door, by which we enter a plain chamber, with two square pillars. The direction of the excavation here changes; the passage being continued towards the left, with the same downward slope. From the chamber we first descend a flight of steps; then, a sloping passage, and another flight of steps; at the bottom of which, the passage widens on the left; forming a small, oblong chamber. The walls of this are adorned with paintings, of the same description as those before mentioned; but they are much soiled; apparently by the bats; and their beautiful execution has tempted some person to cut out several large pieces of the plaster. A door-way at the end of this chamber opens into a large portico and hall of sepulture, which, with several surrounding chambers, are on almost exactly the same plan as was afterwards followed in the most magnificent of the tombs discovered by Belzoni. The portico and sepulchral hall are in the same direction as the first passage of the tomb. The former has six square pillars. The floor beyond these (that is, of the place of sepulture) is a little lower; and we descend to it by steps. This part is much encumbered with fragments of stone and rubbish; among which is a large, granite lid: the sarcophagus to which this belonged has been carried away. Towards the right is a narrow, square pit, nearly filled with rubbish. The walls of the sepulchral hall and of its portico have been much injured, either by violence or by some natural cause, or both. Upon the small portions of plaster which remain are some very beautiful specimens of drawing, executed merely in outline, and some excellent hieroglyphic writing, similar to that of the papyri. There are several doors (two on each side, and one at the end) communicating with other apartments; but none of these are decorated with sculptures or paintings. It is evident that this tomb was not finished; though it received the sarcophagus, and doubtless the body of the king for whom it was destined.

The Western Valley divides, at the end, into two small branches. At the entrance of the right (or western) branch, on the left side, are two tombs, near together. I did not enter them; being informed that they contain no sculpture or painting; and the descent to the door of each of them being difficult, if not impracticable, excepting with a ladder or rope.[†]

A few paces further, on the right side of the ravine, is another tomb. It was opened by Belzoni. The entrance is in the usual style; but quite plain. The passage descends rather steeply, towards the north-west: at the bottom is a flight of steps; and then, another steep passage: this leads to the sepulchral chamber, where we find paintings, with the name of the king for whom this tomb was destined; but wherever it occurs this name has been nearly effaced; evidently by design: it was only from a

---

[†]These are now designated as Western Valley tombs numbers 25 and 24. Number 25 was intended to be the tomb of Akhenaton. The designated occupant for 24 is unknown.

comparison of many examples that I could obtain the whole.[1] Who this king was I cannot say; but from the style of his paintings, which are very coarse, I should judge him to be of very early date.[2] In the middle of the chamber is a granite sarcophagus, without a lid, and one side of it broken: its form is elegant: it has a cornice like that of an Egyptian temple: in the centre of the side is the winged globe; and at the two ends are sculptured Nephthys and Isis, the one at the head and the other at the foot, with extended wings: the hieroglyphics upon it are imperfectly legible.—The walls of the chamber are covered with paintings; all of which are in a coarse style. At one end (immediately on the left of a person entering) is a long hieroglyphic inscription. Above this are two boats; in the first of which are two hawks; and in the other, the god Ra, and other divinities, male and female. The other end of the chamber is divided into twelve compartments; in each of which an ape is represented, sitting. On the side opposite the entrance is depicted the reception of the king by the gods. On the other side, the king is represented in a boat, knocking down birds among some water-plants; which is a subject common in Egyptian tombs, but not in royal tombs. To the right of this the prince appears to have been represented spearing a hippopotamus; but much of this design is effaced. Between these two subjects are the king and his queen: her name, as well as his, almost wholly obliterated.—There is another chamber on the opposite side of this: it is small, rudely excavated, and without any decoration.

These are all the tombs of Egyptian kings now known in the neighbourhood of Thebes. How many more yet remain concealed; and how interesting would be the discovery of one such tomb not previously violated![†] It is remarkable that all the royal tombs discovered by Belzoni had been explored centuries before.

---

[1]It is given in the last of the plates which accompany the Supplement to this work [fig. 160, second column from the right, letter d]. It is the name marked E. in plate V., of the 2nd part of Wilkinson's Materia Hieroglyphica.

[2]Mr. Wilkinson has found him to be anterior to Rameses 2nd. Hence, and from the absence of his name in the lists of the kings of the 17th and 18th dynasties, we might conclude that he was anterior even to those; and consequently that his paintings were the most ancient in Egypt, or nearly so: but this I cannot think: I should rather suppose that for some reason he was excluded from the list of the 18th Dynasty, though belonging to that dynasty. [It is the tomb of Aye, the next to the last king of the Eighteenth Dynasty.]

[†]Lane realized that the tombs had not been seen in their original splendor. His wish for the discovery of an undisturbed one was fulfilled about 100 years later with the discovery of Tutankhamun's tomb.

Chapter XXVII.[1]

Armen't, &c.—Is'na.

Armen't (Hermonthis); the temple, &c., there—The Gebeley'n—Temple a little below Is'na—The town and temple of Is'na (Latopolis)—Temple of Contra Latopolis (opposite Is'na).

May 9th, 1826.—Continuing my voyage up the Nile, from Thebes, in about two hours I arrived before *Armen't* ارمنت, a large village, on a part of the site of the ancient city of *Hermonthis*, the capital of the Hermonthite nome.—The tract on the opposite side of the Nile is a part of the Theban nome.

The modern village of Armen't is about half a mile from the river. The remains of the ancient town which was here situated are very extensive: they consist of mounds of broken pottery, bricks, &c.; among which are an interesting temple, and some other relics. In passing over these mounds, in our route from the river, we first arrive at the ruins of a large church,[2] a hundred and sixty feet long, and eighty feet in width: the greater part has been thrown down nearly to the foundations; and within the ruined walls are many prostrate granite columns, which adorned the interior. This building has been constructed with the materials of an ancient temple: many of the blocks of stone in its walls are sculptured with hieroglyphics. Adjacent to it is a Moos'lim burial-ground, with several tombs of sheykhs. Passing by these, we arrive at the temple above alluded to.

This edifice, in its present ruined state,[3] has a very picturesque appearance. The direction of the front is south 60° west, by compass. This part was never finished: the main body of the building, and probably the whole, was erected under the last Cleopatra, the mother of Cæsarion. There seem to have been two courts before the cella, or the temple itself; one before the other. The first court had two columns on either side, and apparently four in front; with intercolumnal walls, about half their height. In the front, it seems, there were three door-ways, between the columns; and there was also an entrance on either side. The front-walls are much ruined; and all the columns, excepting one, have fallen, or been thrown down. That which remains is unfinished; as are also the walls. Four columns, all of which have been thrown down, divided this court from that next behind, which had, likewise, four

---

[1]There is a map [fig. 122] to accompany this volume [chapters 27–Supplement].
[2]See plate 1 [fig. 123].
[3]See plate 2 [fig. 124].

columns on each side: two of these columns, on the left, have been thrown down. The body of the temple, which is small, was surrounded by a colonnade, with an architrave, cornice, and roof; but only one of the columns now remains, in front of the building. The Ka'shif of Armen't has taken possession of this building (that is, of the *naos* itself), surrounded it, excepting on the left side, by a wall of crude brick, and built a pigeon-house upon its roof. I was unable to examine the interior on my first visit: the Ka'shif being absent, I was not allowed to enter it; but on a later occasion I obtained admission. On the front of the building are frequent representations of Isis with Horus on her lap. Over the entrance are two winged globes. The building is divided into three apartments; one behind another. The first of these is very small: its walls are decorated with sculptures; but exhibit nothing remarkable. On the right of this is a narrow staircase, leading up to the roof. The second, which is the principal chamber, is decorated with very strange sculptures. A considerable part of the left side is divided into small compartments. In one of these is the female personification of Typhon, in the usual monstrous form, preceding sixteen similar but smaller figures, arranged in two rows; eight in each row. In another compartment are seven apes; in another, seven cats; in another, seven serpents; in another, two hawks and two crocodiles; and in another, a crocodile with a hawk's head. Other divinities occupy similar places. The rest of this wall is chiefly decorated with representations of offerings; as is also the end-wall of the chamber. In the centre of the latter is sculptured a shrine, resembling a false door, surmounted by a cornice, with the winged globe. The sculptures on the right side-wall are of a similar nature to those on the opposite side. Among the strange figures here are an ape sitting on a pedestal; an ibis; a turtle; two hawks, two hawk-headed crocodiles; a figure of Typhon, in the attitude and with the characteristics of Amon-Generator, and with the wings and tail of a hawk: also, a cat, and an ibis-headed figure presenting an offering to it. Here is likewise the female Typhonian figure, having, instead of the head of a crocodile, a human female head, surmounted by the disk and horns of Isis and other goddesses. Among the other sculptures is a representation of the statue of Amon-Generator, standing on a frame, borne on the shoulders of twelve priests. On the front wall, over the door, is a figure of Harpocrates, sitting on a full-blown lotus-flower. Behind him are three sitting figures of Isis, with Horus on her knees; and before him, the hawk-headed god Ra, sitting between the horns of a cow, behind which is another Isis, with Horus. Above these figures is a hawk (the emblem of Horus) with outspread wings; with Isis on one side, and Nephthys on the other, in an attitude of adoration. In the end-wall of the chamber which is decorated with these singular sculptures is a door, near the right angle: by this we enter the third chamber, which is very small. The most curious of the sculptures here is a representation of a goddess being delivered of a child (I suppose Isis and Horus). The goddess is kneeling, and with uplifted hands: she is held and supported by a female behind her; while another female, kneeling before her, is receiving the child. The wall is broken here, in one part; and of the child, only a leg remains. The nursing of the young god, by his mother, is also represented here; and in two instances, the goddess-mother has the head of a cow. On the ceiling of this narrow apartment is sculptured a female figure (a personification of the firmament) surrounding, on three sides, some astronomical devices.—The sculptures on the exterior of the temple are chiefly representations of offerings and acts of adoration. Those on the right side are partly concealed by some steps lately built to ascend to the pigeon-house, and partly by *gel'leh*, a mixture of cow-dung and straw, used for fuel, pressed into round, flat cakes, and generally stuck against a wall, or placed on the ground, to dry in the sun. Behind the temple, a small apartment has been built by the Ka'shif, as a hall of entrance to the court-yard of his house; and as the back of the ancient edifice forms one side of this hall, it has been covered with a thick coat of white-wash. The sculptures upon it are thus rendered indistinct; but we may still perceive the principal objects. A beetle is here represented, with its wings extended in the form of a lunar crescent; and above it is a disk. To the right of this beetle are several animals; the most conspicuous of which is a camelopard.—A few paces from the temple, on the right side, is an oblong tank about 100 feet in length, and 75 in width, lined with masonry, and having steps at the four angles, by which to descend to the water: it is an ancient work, and evidently belonged to the temple.

On the opposite side of the Nile, a little above Armen't, is the village of *To'd* طود, situated upon mounds of rubbish, which mark the site of the ancient *Tuphium*. Here are some remains of a little Ptolemaic temple, which I did not see.

A little higher is Es-Sa'limee'yeh, the village of the sheykh Ahh'mad, that bold imposter and rebel who, in 1824, gained to himself a party of between twenty and thirty thousand men (all the fel'la'hhee'n hereabouts), and menaced the Ba'sha with destruction. About one fourth of these misguided men, who regarded their leader as a prophet, and trusted that he would be their political liberator, were massacred by the Ba'sha's regular troops. The sheykh escaped, and has never since been heard of.

There is a bend of the river, forming a right-angle, a little above the place just mentioned; and our course changes from west-south-west to south-south-east. Thence, in less than two hours, we arrive before the *Gebeley'n*, or "two mountains." These are two oblong hills of rock; one of which lies close along the edge of the river, and the other parallel to it, a short distance behind; both on the western side. We found some labourers employed in blasting the rock nearest the river, to make lime for new buildings at Is'na; this being the nearest limestone rock to that town; for above this point, the mountains on both sides of the Nile are of sandstone, throughout the remaining portion of the valley of Egypt and Nubia, interrupted only at the cataracts of Aswa'n and few other places by granite, &c. Here are some ancient excavations; but not worth visiting: they were probably the burial-places of the people of *Crocodilopolis*, which appears to have been here situated.—Hereabouts commenced the Latopolite nome, on the western side of the river; and here now begins the province of Is'na.

About six miles higher, on the same side of the Nile, is a village called *Asfoo'n* اصفون , situated on large mounds of rubbish; the remains of the ancient *Asphynis*.

In the evening of this day we arrived at Is'na; not having landed anywhere: Armen't, &c., I visited on my downward voyage. The height of the thermometer this day, in my cabin, was 94°.

Below Is'na, about two miles to the north-west, and a mile and a half from the river, is a small Ptolemaic temple, in a very ruined state.[†] This I also visited on my return from the upper country. I found there about twenty labourers, who had been pulling down a part of the temple, to employ the materials in constructing a bridge over a neighbouring canal: they had just completed their work, and were carrying away the stones. This ruin is called *Ed-Deyr* (or The Convent); a name given to many ancient temples in Egypt. It stands in the midst of a wide, cultivated plain, without any habitation near it. Its site is but little elevated above the level of the plain; but sufficiently so to be above the reach of the inundation. The front is directed towards the east; that is, towards the river. The building consists of a portico, richly sculptured, and three small, narrow chambers, without any decoration, behind. The portico originally contained eight columns; two of which, belonging to the front row, have fallen, or been thrown down. The capitals are of the bell-form, or lotus-form. The front columns were engaged by a wall about half their height; as in most Egyptian temples of the Ptolemaic and Roman times. This temple seems to have been erected under the directions of Ptolemy Euergetes 1st and his wife Berenice: the decorations were continued under Adrian and Antoninus and Verus. In each of the side-walls of the portico are two secret passages; one above the other. The columns and the walls (both within and without) are decorated with sculptures, upon some of which, the brilliant colours with which they were painted are surprisingly preserved: but the subjects are mostly mere offerings and acts of adoration. Upon the ceiling was a zodiac, similar to that at Is'na, painted upon the roofing between each side-wall and the columns next to it; but the greater part has unfortunately been destroyed; only three stones remaining on each side; containing, together, but four signs. On one of the columns is a Greek inscription; but so much effaced that I could not read it. Upon the exterior of each side-wall is sculptured a figure in the act of slaying a numerous group of kneeling captives, whose hair he grasps with one hand, while the other raises the mace: at his feet is a lion, tearing the arm of one of the victims.—A little in advance of this building are the foundations of a structure which appears to have been a portal, leading to the temple.—The workmen whom I saw here had,

---

[†]The Temple of Khnum at Kom al-Deir, now completely destroyed.

shortly before, found the bodies of two murdered men, thrust into one of the secret passages before-mentioned, and concealed by fragments of stone. The ragged clothes of one of these unfortunate men were shewn to me. Secret murders are of rare occurrence in Egypt; but it not unfrequently happens that people are killed in open feuds, which are generally for the avenging of blood.

The large town of Is'na اسنا or اسنى (which is also, but not commonly, pronounced *As'na*) occupies the site of the ancient city of *Sne*; which the Greeks called *Latopolis*. The latter name it derived from the worship of the fish *latus*; supposed to be the *ckish'reh* (or *perca Nilotica*), the largest, and one of the best flavoured, of the fish of the Nile; said to be sometimes eight feet in length.[1]—This town is situated close to the river on the western side. To a spectator viewing it from the river, it has a very wretched appearance; for the Nile has gradually encroached upon it, and, in successive inundations, washed away large portions of the bank, with many houses. The front, therefore, presents a long row of ruined dwellings: and only one ma'd'neh is seen; though there are several mosques. The northern part of an island extends before the town, and, at this season of the year (the Nile being nearly at the lowest) shuts it out from the river; the intervening bed, or branch, being dry. Is'na is the capital of the southernmost province of Egypt. When the Memloo'k Beys were divided into two or more factions, the weakest party generally resided in this town, and kept possession of the province of which it is the capital. Is'na is also the last Ckoob'tee (or Coptic) bishopric in Egypt: there are about three hundred Ckoobt families residing there. It has extensive and well-stocked soo'cks (or market-streets); being a place of considerable trade. Many gella'bs (or slave-merchants are established there, carrying on a constant trade with Senna'r. Their caravans carry with them cotton, linen, and woollen goods, beads and various other ornaments, soap, straight sword-blades (made in Germany), fire-arms, &c.; and bring back (besides slaves) ostrich-feathers, ivory, gold, gum, tamarind (in round cakes), senna, koorba'gs (or whips of hippopotamus' hide), &c. Their route strikes into the desert from Dera'weh, nearly sixty miles higher, on the eastern bank of the Nile. It is a painful journey which they make: water being scarce and bad. Bruce and Burckhardt traversed the most arduous part of this route, and the former, being ill provided, suffered dreadfully: his mind was affected with a degree of temporary derangement; as his narrative of this journey plainly shews at its termination; and every difficulty seemed to him greater than it was in reality.—Is'na is famous for the manufacture of the blue and white chequered shawl called *mela'yeh*, which is used by such of the women as can afford it, as a covering; and also by men, as an article of dress, thrown over the shoulder, or enveloping the person. Is'na has much declined since the times of the Ghooz'z (or Memloo'ks); but still it is only inferior in commercial

---

[1]The largest that I saw during my stay in Egypt was about four feet long.

importance to Asyoo't and Ckin'ë, of all the towns in Upper Egypt. The traveller who is proceeding to Nubia will do well to lay in a stock of any provisions he may want at this place, rather than at Aswa'n.

In the midst of this town is the portico of an ancient temple, which, until the late discoveries in hieroglyphic literature, was considered one of the oldest monuments in Egypt; though I should have thought that the style of its sculptures (which are elaborate but inelegant) would have convinced any careful observer that the contrary was the case. This portico is, however, a very noble structure. It seems to be the only relic of the temple of which it formed the front. It has lately been entirely cleared out, and converted into a magazine for the Ba'sha's cotton: I was therefore obliged to apply to the superintendent for the key. It is surrounded by modern houses, and so deeply buried in the raised soil and rubbish, that it is impossible to obtain a clear view of it from any direction. The front is towards the north-east, or nearly so:—north 50° east by compass. The south-eastern side, which is plastered over with mud, forms part of one side of a street. The front is screened by a high modern wall, about three yards distant, forming a narrow passage before the portico. To this contracted space we enter by a door, which is generally locked; and a striking view of the front of the portico then presents itself.[1] There are six columns along the front; but the two last of these are concealed from our view by another wall of modern erection. All these columns are buried, in front, to about half their height, and are now connected together by walls of crude brick and mud, which rise nearly to the architraves: a very small space being left at the top for the admission of light. The capitals of the columns are not uniform; but those of the front row differ very little from each other; and all of them are elegant and rich.[2] There are two modern doors by which to enter the portico: both of them generally locked and sealed: a small lump of clayey mud being affixed to the wooded lock, and stamped. Being admitted by the second door (which is in the centre of the front, between the jambs of the ancient door), I descended several steps: for the interior had been cleared, almost entirely, of the rubbish with which it had before been half filled.—Before I continue the description, I should mention that, from a careful examination of the sculptures with which it is adorned, both without and within, it appears that this portico was constructed in the reign of the Emperor Claudius; his being the oldest name found here, except on the wall of the temple itself, against the front of which the portico is built, and which was a Ptolemaic structure; bearing the name of Ptolemy Epiphanes. The decorations of the portico were continued in the reigns of Vespasian, Titus, Domitian, Trajan, Adrian, Antoninus, Marcus Aurelius, Commodus, and Septimius Severus: all these names being found among the sculptures, which generally represent the princes

---

[1]See plate 3 [fig. 125].
[2]It is only in the Egyptian temples of the Ptolemaic and Roman ages that we find varieties of form in the capitals of columns in the same portico or colonnade.

to whom they apply offering to the gods.—On entering this portico I was very much struck with its grand appearance, which is in some degree heightened by the gloom: the sculptures are indeed of a bad style; elaborately finished; but clumsy: they however give a rich effect to the architecture, which is certainly very fine. The portico contains twenty-four columns, arranged in six rows of four each. The columns of the front[1] will convey some idea of the rest. They are lofty and well-proportioned; and very little injured by time or violence. The floor is plain, and neatly paved with bricks; but still a few feet above the level of the original pavement; for the lower line of figures sculptured on the walls have only their heads exposed. The gloom prevents our making a satisfactory examination of the curious sculptures which adorn the walls and ceiling. The shafts of the columns are nearly covered with hieroglyphics, in perpendicular lines; the upper part being decorated with sculptured figures; generally of the ram-headed god Kneph, to whom the temple was dedicated. On one column, Typhon occupies the place of Kneph; and on another we find a scarabæus. Over the door-way which led to the apartments (now destroyed) behind the portico is a figure of Kneph sculptured within a disk, which represents the sun: this plainly shews that Kneph was the principal object of worship in this temple. Upon the interior sides of the walls by which the lower parts of the front columns are connected together are some curious devices. Upon the compartment next on the left of the entrance (the left as a person looks back towards the entrance) is a representation of four rams (the emblems of Kneph) receiving an offering. In the next compartment is a crocodile, seated on a low pedestal: his head is surmounted by a disk, with a serpent; and he is presented with a crux ansata, a sistrum, and the sceptre of a god. Many of the sculptures were concealed, at the period of my visit, by high heaps of cotton, which were piled up in several parts. On a general view of the sculptures, I remarked that Kneph was most frequently represented. The crocodile is also a conspicuous figure, receiving divine honours. Of the curious sculptures on the ceiling—where is the celebrated zodiac,[2] which occupies the space between the second and third rows of columns to the left of a person entering the portico—I could see but little, in consequence of the gloom, and the blackness of the surface. I noticed, among the boats and stars here sculptured, figures of jackals, apes, scarabæi, a ram with four heads, and many other mysterious emblems.—The columns of the second row on the left side are connected together by a low, modern, brick wall, dividing off a part of the portico. Into this part I was denied admission.

On the eastern side of the Nile, opposite Is'na, and about half a mile from the river, is a small temple, situated among low mounds of rubbish,

---

[1]See plate 3 [fig. 125].
[2]See the remarks on the zodiac of Den'dar'a, in the 8th chapter of the preceding volume [chapter 24].

which mark the site of *Contra Latopolis*.[†] It was probably built about the same period as the portico which I have just described; but left unfinished. Some of its sculptures bear the name of the Emperor Commodus. Its front is towards the Nile; or rather, west-south-west. It has been much injured by violence. The fore part of the building is a portico; which has four columns along the front. The two middle columns of these four have capitals similar to those of the great portico of the temple of Athor at Den'dar'a. Between these is the entrance. The two other columns of the front row are connected with these and with the side-walls by a wall about half their height. Within the portico were four more columns; of which I found only two remaining: one of them with the palm-formed capital. Behind the portico we enter a small chamber of an irregular form; wider on the left side than on the right. The end-wall only is sculptured; and this exhibits nothing remarkable. On the left is a small, plain chamber. There was also another chamber, now destroyed, behind that first mentioned. Within the front-wall of the temple is a secret passage, which I found filled with fragments of stone and rubbish.—This ruin, altogether, has a very picturesque appearance; but in no other respect does it much excite admiration.—Heaps of crude and baked bricks are the only remains of the town which was here situated.

[†]The temple of al-Hilla, destroyed soon after Lane visited it.

Chapter XXVIII.
Eilethyia—Ad'foo.

Remains of Eilethyia; its temples; and the sculptured and painted grottoes, &c., in its vicinity—The modern village, great temple, and Typhonium, of Ad'foo (Apollinopolis Magna).

Having remained one day at Is'na,[1] on the 11th we proceeded slowly on our voyage, to the distance of six or seven miles. The height of the thermometer this day, in my cabin, in the afternoon, was 101°.

12th. As we advance, the valley gradually contracts: the mountains on our left are almost close to the river; and in one part, the low, western hills, also, stretch very near to the Nile. A little beyond this point are the remains of the city of *Eilethyia* (Εἰληθυιας πολις), situated on the eastern side of the river, between the villages of Mahhamee'd and El-Hila'l. Some travellers mention an adjacent village called El-Ka'b, and another called El-Hegs: but the peasants whom I met here were, or professed to be, unacquainted with these names.[†] —The space which was occupied by the ancient city is enclosed, on three sides, by a very strong wall of crude brick, still remaining in a very extraordinary state of preservation[2]: the fourth side is bounded by the river. The area thus enclosed is about one third of a mile in width, and rather more (about 2000 feet) in length. The surrounding wall is about 20 feet in height, and of the enormous thickness of 37 or 38 feet. The bricks of which it is constructed are very large—between 15 and 16 inches long, 8 inches broad, and 7 inches thick—and of a lightish colour. Smaller enclosures of the same kind in Egypt generally surrounded one or more temples; but this seems, without doubt, to have been the *city-wall* of Eilethyia. It has ramps within, by which to mount to the top. Within this great enclosure is a smaller space, near the river, towards the left angle, occupied by high mounds and brick ruins, which appear to be the remains of a more modern town: among them are many brick arches. These buildings were probably erected when the inhabitants of Eilethyia were too few to require the larger area. They are also enclosed by a wall, of which a considerable portion remains. The rest of the great area is quite clear of rubbish; and, in some parts, seems to have been cultivated. The ruins of several small temples are still seen there. These are all on the south-east

---

[1] On my downward voyage, I spent four days here and in the neighbourhood.
[†] "El-Ka'b" is the name by which the site is known. It is strange that Lane was unable to elicit the information.
[2] See plate 4, no. 1 [fig. 126, upper].

of the mounds above-mentioned.[1]—The first of the two principal temples here referred to in a note consists, in its present state, of one small chamber, measuring, in the interior, 21 feet 2 inches by 8 feet 3 inches. The original sculpture of this temple was in low relief: the walls, however, were smoothed again, and sculptured afresh, in most parts, by Rameses 2nd. On the exterior of the side next the mountains, upon a pedestal which is represented as supporting a boat, is the name of Amonoph 2nd; but whether the temple was constructed, and the original sculptures executed, in the reign of this king, or under Hakor, who built the other temple above alluded to, I could not ascertain. On the side next the river is sculptured a large, sitting figure of an ape (an emblem of Thoth), upon a low pedestal, receiving an offering. On the other temple to which I have just alluded, of which little remains excepting six small columns, we find the name of Hakor. The three front columns, only, are sculptured. They are decorated with the sculptures of Hakor, in low relief; and a line of hieroglyphics—with an oval for a new name, but left blank—is cut in intaglio down the front of one of them. These hieroglyphics resemble, in style, those of Rameses 2nd, on the other temple; and this king seems to have intended to make both temples appear to be his own work[2]; though they were erected some ages before his time, and are *perhaps* the most ancient sculptured buildings in the valley of the Nile.[3] Several other columns, besides the six above-mentioned, are found here, lying on the ground, behind the latter. The foundations of another temple are also seen, and the remains of a small portal, and some other masses of masonry; but nothing remarkable.

A little to the north of the great enclosure are many very interesting sepulchral grottoes, excavated in a rugged, isolated hill, seen in the view before referred to. There are also some grottoes in the sides of the mountains behind. The distance to the hill here allude[d] to, from the northern angle of the great enclosure, is about one fifth of a mile.—In several of the grottoes here, the first chamber is decorated with painted sculptures, or with mere paintings. From this chamber we pass into one or more without sculptures or paintings, and find a deep well, or pit, of a square or oblong form, at the bottom of which are the sepulchral catacombs: all of these catacombs have been plundered of whatever was valuable or curious among their contents; and are now half filled with rubbish, broken mummies, and rags. The subjects portrayed upon the walls of the upper chambers are the grand objects of interest: the sepulchral catacombs beneath contain nothing worthy of examination.

---

[1]In the view which I have given, the two principal temples are seen: a third, nearer to the eye, is thrown down almost to the foundations.

[2]I have mentioned before (in my account of the quarries of Mons Troicus, opposite the site of Memphis) that Major Felix found here an example of the name of Rameses 2nd cut over that of Hakor, which is thus proved to be the more ancient.

[3]See article 6 of the Supplement to this work.

Several of the grottoes, and probably the greater number, are of very high antiquity: this is proved not merely by the style of their sculptures and paintings but by their exhibiting the names of kings of the 17th, 18th, and 19th Dynasties: as Osirtesen 1st, and others of the 17th; Amos, Thothmos 1st, 2nd, and 3rd, &c. The most interesting is the first to the right in a line of grottoes rather low in the front of the hill (seen in the view already referred to).† The entrance of this grotto is much broken; but the walls within are very little injured, and are ornamented with painted sculptures, even the colours of which are well preserved. The chamber is twelve feet wide, by twenty-five feet nine inches long, and has a low ceiling, cut in the form of an arch. At the end, in a deep recess, are three figures, of the natural size, cut out of the rock, and seated on a bench. The figure in the middle is a representation of the principal person for whom the tomb was excavated: he was a priest; and doubtless a man of great consequence. The two other figures are females; each of whom has her hand placed on the shoulder of the man. On the right side of the chamber is a door, leading into a plain apartment, in which is a pit descending to the place of sepulture; and before the entrance of the grotto is another deep pit. On the right side-wall of the first (or principal) chamber is represented a banquet, much resembling that of which I have given a copy in a tomb at Thebes. At the left extremity are the chief personage and his wife, seated on a couch, facing the guests. (The former are nearly of the natural size: most of the others, as usual, considerably smaller: all are sculptured in low relief, and painted, upon a white ground: the men are of the usual deep red colour: the women, of a dull yellow.) A green monkey is tied to one of the legs of the couch, beneath which he is sitting, pawing a basket of grapes. Before the master and mistress stands a priest, clad in a leopard's skin. Behind this figure are the guests; the foremost of whom appear to be two men with their wives; each couple seated on a couch. These, according to the ordinary system of the ancient Egyptian artists, are on a smaller scale than the principal personages; but larger than the other guests. The latter are arranged in four rows; the two uppermost of which are men; and the others, females: they are all seated on the ground; and each is holding a lotus to the mouth, as if eating it. At the head of the lowest row are three females, kneeling, and clapping their hands: next behind them is a female playing upon a double reed: then follows a small figure dancing, with a kind of wand in each hand: next is a female playing upon a harp. Among the guests are several domestics, offering bottles, bowls, and dishes: and behind the lowest row are some servants bringing fresh dishes, and others cutting up two oxen. At the right extremity of the wall are four females; each holding a sistrum; and a male figure holding three lotuses. Offerings of various kinds are piled up before them; and before the offerings stand the master and his wife, in an attitude of adoration. We now turn to the opposite, or *left* side of the chamber. Beginning our

---

†The Tomb of Paheri.

examination from the left, we first see the master represented walking. Four servants, behind him, are carrying a stool, a water-bottle, and other things for his refreshment. To the right are labourers, engaged in agricultural employments. Here are depicted the processes of ploughing, sowing, reaping, treading out the corn, and winnowing it; after which we see it deposited in the granary. The plough is of the form of the hieroglyphic called the *hieralpha*: it is drawn by oxen; being attached to their horns: men precede it, breaking up the parched ground with implements of a similar form; and before the plough passes the soil, the sower throws the seed. Of this subject I insert a copy.[1] There is also represented a plough drawn by four men; with a fifth guiding it, and another throwing the seed. The reapers seem to be employed in cutting barley and wheat: their sickle is similar in form to our own; excepting in the handle: they cut merely the ear; leaving the long straw; and the ears are gathered into baskets by children. Of this subject, also, a copy is here introduced[2]: one of the reapers, it will be observed, is resting from his labours to drink. We likewise see the gathering of flax; which is pulled up by the roots, and bound in small bundles, to be soaked. The treading out of the corn is performed by six oxen, unmuzzled; and it is winnowed by being let fall through the air: before it is carried to the granary, a clerk notes the quantity. Of the representation of the treading out and winnowing I insert a copy.[3] The next subject is the vintage; and of this, too, I introduce a copy.[4] The vines are trained upon a frame, not too high for a person to reach the fruit: the grapes, being gathered, are thrown into the wine-press; where six men, each holding a rope which is tied to a cross pole at the top, express the juice with their feet.[5] Below the subject above described we see (beginning again from the left) the flocks and herds of the same proprietor, and a clerk seated, and writing down their number. They consist of oxen, asses, pigs, and other animals, arranged in four rows. Next is represented the lading of boats with stores, which are previously weighed: the weight being in the form of a sheep: the stores are of an annular form; and seem to be biscuits: they might be mistaken for weights; but this cannot be the case; for they are also piled up on shelves. One of the boats has a high cabin, and above it, a large sail, of a square form; having a wheel attached to the lower yard and resting upon the roof of the cabin: it is steered by a large paddle. A second boat is similar in form; but dismasted; as if for the purpose of descending the river; as is the practice in the navigation of the Nile in the present day. Above these are other boats, of a more ordinary kind. We next see a

---

[1]See no. 42 of the subjects for wood-cuts—(among the mounted drawings next to plate 4 [missing]). (Not found RSP.)

[2]See no. 43 of the subjects for wood-cuts (among the *mounted* drawings [missing]). (Not found R.S.P.)

[3]See no. 44 of do. [missing]. (Not found R.S.P.)

[4]See no. 45 of do. [missing]. (Not found R.S.P.)

[5]Wine, it is said, was forbidden to the vulgar, but not to the priests.

representation of fishing and fowling. The fish are caught in a large net, carried away in buckets, cut, salted, and hung up. One of the fishermen is employed in making a net; the corner of which is attached to his toe.[1] In the fowling-scene, the net is placed among some water-plants; and is full of birds: a man is giving a signal, and his companions are pulling the cord which closes the net. The birds are then prepared and potted. We have now to contemplate the end of the individual whose pleasures and wealth we have seen portrayed in so lively a manner. The representation of the funeral-procession occupies the end of the wall; and is arranged in five horizontal lines. Commencing our examination at the top of the wall, we first see the embalmed body placed upon a couch, on the top of a mummy-chest, in a canopied boat-sledge, drawn by men and oxen. Before and behind the sledge is a female mourner, wringing her hands. In the second line is something like an upright chest, in a sledge, in which are also two sitting figures: the sledge is approaching a small temple; behind which are two figures dancing. Next are four men, bearing a chest on their shoulders. In the third line is a sledge suppporting a mummy-chest, and bearing three figures: before and behind the mummy-chest is a female wringing her hands, like those above. Next is a priest presenting an offering to a jackal lying on a pedestal. Beyond this is another sledge bearing an upright chest, in front of which is a kneeling figure, very indistinct. Before this sledge is a hawk, raised upon a high perch. Next are three men, drawing a smaller sledge, in which is something of an oval form, like a bundle: it is preceded by two men, bearing each a torch, or a standard. In the fourth line we see the mummy-chest under a canopy in a sledge drawn by two men: it is approaching some trees, beyond which are ten narrow shrines; three of which are open: two of these contain each a human figure; and in the third is the jackal-headed god Anubis. In the lowest line are four small figures enclosed in a square: next is a figure of Osiris, the judge of the dead: then are two females, kneeling: lastly, there is a figure representing the deceased, with his arms extended, as if in anxious supplication, kneeling before Osiris, who is seated on his throne, holding the crook and the flagellum.—Such are the varied and interesting subjects delineated on the walls of this small grotto; which I consider unrivalled, in its kind, by any other that I have seen in Egypt. In their style, the sculptures of this grotto much resemble those in one of the truncated pyramidal tombs adjacent to the first and second pyramids of El-Gee'zeh; and they are nearly of the same age.—I must mention some of the other grottoes of Eilethyia; though none can be compared with that just described.—The second to the left of this contains similar sculptures; but not so well executed; and much injured. The right wall is decorated with a subject almost exactly the same. The greater part of the surface of the left wall has fallen off.—Proceeding a little further to the left, after having passed several grottoes which are not worthy of remark, we arrive at another which is very interesting. At the end of this is a

---

[1] The *modern* Egyptians employ their toes in many operations.

mutilated figure, seated in a deep recess. On the right wall is represented the funeral; and on the left, feasting, and agricultural employments. The sculptures are very well executed; but the walls are much injured by the falling of portions of the rock.—Some of the grottoes have horizontal cavities in the walls, in which, it seems, mummies were deposited. I often found that mummies were placed in the decorated chambers of grottoes, as well as in catacombs at the bottom of pits; but this was not generally the case: for the ornamented grottoes seem mostly to have been designed for the accommodation of mourners, on particular occasions.—There are many other grottoes in the vicinity of those which I have described: some in the back of the same isolated hill; and others in the sides of the mountains behind: but among these I found none worth visiting.

About one third of a mile from the walls of the town, bearing N. 25° W. by compass, is a small temple of high antiquity, consisting only of one chamber, which measures, in the interior, 25 feet 8 inches by 10 feet 5 inches.[†] It is of the reign of Thothmos 3rd. It was surrounded by a low wall; upon which were square pillars, very near together, supporting an architrave, cornice, and roof; and so forming a gallery all round; the greater part of which is ruined. Upon the square pillars is represented, on each side, a deity embracing the royal founder, who is distinguished, as usual, by his hieroglyphic name. One of these sculptures occasioned a learned and judicious traveller to form a natural but erroneous hypothesis, founded on the idea that the figure of the king was that of Osiris: our present knowledge of hieroglyphics refutes this. The sculptures of this little temple are in very delicate relief, and in the most pure style. On each side-wall, in the interior, the king is represented making offerings to the boat of the god Ra. Among the sculptures of the exterior we find Thoth and a hawk-headed deity pouring *cruces ansatæ* (the emblems of life) over the king.—This little temple is interesting by its simplicity and the good style of its sculptures: in other respects it is not particularly remarkable.

There are also in the neighbourhood of Eilethyia two small temples which I did not see.[‡] Mr. Hay visited them; and from him I learned the following particulars respecting them. They lie at the entrance of a valley, or opening in the mountains, about a mile, or a mile and a half, to the right (or eastward) of the isolated hill in which are the principal grottoes. One of them is a small, square building, consisting only of one chamber. It is of the age of Rameses 2nd. The sculptures are not remarkable, excepting that among them is the ape; as on the first of the two ruined temples within the great wall of the city. This little temple lies exactly before the other above-mentioned; which consists of a small chamber excavated in the side of the hill on the left side of the opening of the mountains; having before it two courts; one within the other; formed by an enclosure of pillars, with a wall of engagement. The columns are

---

[†]This Chapel of Tuthmosis III is now destroyed.
[‡]The 'desert temples.'

broken down as low as the top of this wall. A flight of steps leads up to the first court. The sculptures in the chamber are almost entirely destroyed: they bear the name of Ptolemy Physcon.—I made but a hasty visit to the monuments of Eilethyia on my voyage up the Nile; but spent two days in examining them on my return.

On the western side of the Nile, opposite the remains of Eilethyia, is an extensive mound of rubbish, called *El-Ko'm el-Ahh'mar* (or The Red Mound), which probably marks the site of *Hieraconpolis*, the City of the Hawk. The Apollinopolite nome seems to have commenced a little below this.—The young women of the village of El-Bus'alee'yeh, and of other villages in this part, are reputed to be mostly of loose character. Having occasion to go once a week to Is'na, to market; they are unable to return the same day; the distance being nearly twenty miles: they therefore pass the night at Is'na, away from their husbands.

Having proceeded a little above the site of Eilethyia, the two lofty towers of the propylæum of the great temple of *Apollinopolis Magna* become visible. About three hours after our first sight of these remarkable objects we arrived before *Ad'foo*, a village which occupies a part of the site of the City of Apollo. I made a view of Ad'foo and its great temple from the opposite bank of the Nile.[1]

The name of this place ادفو is commonly pronounced *Ad'foo*; but the literati of Egypt, for the sake of assimilating the incipient and final vowels, make it *Ood'foo*. The Coptic name was *At'bo*. It is a large village; the residence of a Ka'shif. It is situated at the distance of about a mile from the river, upon the front slope of a long and high ridge of mounds, the remains of Apollinopolis Magna. The village contains a mosque with a ma'd'neh; and extensive groves of palm-trees adjacent to it give it a pleasing appearance. The propylæum of the great temple rises above it like a fortress. A part of the village is built upon the roof of this temple. There is also a second temple among the mounds, behind the village. At Ad'foo, the manufacture of pottery employs many families. There are a few Ckoobt families here; but above this place no Christians are found, excepting a very few at Aswa'n.

The great temple is situated at the north-western part of the village; and so crowded in front (that is, on the south), and also on the western side, by modern huts, that it is impossible to obtain a good view of it from either of these directions: but the modern huts are not the only objects which obstruct the view of this fine building; for it is, in some parts, buried nearly to the roof in rubbish. Though raised in the Ptolemaic period, when the arts of architecture and sculpture had much declined in Egypt, it is a very noble monument.[†] The great propylæum,[2] which forms the front, has a particularly grand appearance: each wing is

---

[1]See plate 4, no. 2 [fig. 126, lower].

[†]The monument contains dynastic elements, but the rubbish and his cursory examination may have prevented Lane from seeing them.

[2]See plate 5 [fig. 127].

above a hundred feet in breadth, and the same in height. The temple seems to have been founded, and partly sculptured, by Ptolemy Philopator—his being the oldest name found upon it—but the decorations were continued under several of his successors—Philometor, Physcon and Cleopatra, and Ptolemy Alexander 1st and Berenice. The propylæum was decorated by Philometor. The front is adorned with three rows of sculptured figures, representing this king offering to, and worshipping, various divinities, at the head of whom is always Aroëris, the god to whom the temple was chiefly dedicated: he generally has the head of a hawk: being identified with the Greek Apollo, the ancient town here situated was called Apollinopolis Magna by the Greeks because this god was the chief object of worship in the place. The figures of the lowest row of sculptures on the front of the propylæum are about thirty feet high; but little of them is seen; for the rubbish rises nearly to their heads. The king is here represented in the act of slaying a group of prisoners before the principal god of the temple; behind whom stands Athor. These figures are in a very bad style; greatly inferior to the sculptures executed under the Pharaohs. In the two upper rows, the same king is represented offering to several series of sitting deities; at the head of whom is Aroëris. The back and sides of the propylæum are similarly decorated.—Passing through the portal of the propylæum, we enter a spacious court,[1] bounded on the right and left by a wall fronted by a row of columns, twelve in number. Eight other columns extend along the back of the propylæum. The capitals are not uniform; but most of them are rich and elegant; and they produce, altogether, a fine effect. The walls behind the columns are decorated with sculptures, representing the usual offerings to the gods. This noble court is now used as a granary. It has been cleared of much of the rubbish by which it was encumbered; and a few heaps of corn, the property of the government, give less offence to the eye of the traveller.—A fine portico, which forms the front of the main body of the temple, is at the end of the court. It contains eighteen columns; six in front, and three deep. The capitals of these, also, are not all uniform; but those which correspond in situation are similar to each other: thus the two between which is the entrance are of the same form; the two next to these are also similar to each other; and so are the two extreme columns. Upon the architraves of the front columns are sculptured several rows of monkeys and men adoring the winged globe and the scarabæus: this insect is represented with his ball, and with his wings expanded; and is frequently seen here, being a particular object of adoration: it was an emblem of the sun; of which Aroëris was one personification. The interior of the portico is filled nearly to the roof with rubbish; therefore little can be seen of its sculptures; but some of those which remain visible are serious, and deserve to be mentioned. On the upper part of the left side-wall is represented a boat-sledge drawn by four jackals: Harpocrates is seated on the prow; and the boat contains

---

[1]See plate 6 [fig. 128].

several other gods. Before this curious procession are four monsters, each of which has the head of a jackal, the hands and arms of a man, and the body of a bird: the hands are raised in an attitude of adoration. Upon the opposite side-wall is another boat, supporting a circle, in the centre of which is an eye, and above and below the eye is a row of small sitting figures.—The entrance of the apartments behind the portico is entirely closed with rubbish. Upon the cornice above this entrance is the winged globe; and below this is a scarabæus enclosed in a circle, and supported by a boat. In the upper cornice is represented the same insect, also enclosed in circle, and with two heads; the head of the hawk, which is common to Aroëris, and that of the ram, which distinguishes Kneph. This device of the beetle with the heads of a hawk and ram is a common ornament on the cornices of the temple. The roof of the interior apartments, as well as that of the portico, is covered with modern huts; most of which are inhabited. Under one of these huts is an aperture by which we may descend into one of the inner chambers. It was pointed out to me by an English traveller[†] whom I met here on my return from the upper country; but I believe it is generally shewn to travellers: I had not seen it; for I had not completed my examination of the temple. We descended together; and found ourselves obliged to worm along in a prostrate position for several feet: the rubbish, at the part where we entered, rising nearly to the roof. We observed that the chamber contained four rows of massive columns; three in each row; and that some of the capitals which were not covered by the rubbish were rich and elegant in form: of the sculptures we could scarcely see anything excepting the hieroglyphics on the architraves. This chamber we found to be the one next behind the great portico: there are several smaller apartments beyond it. On our egress from it, the inhabitants of the hut through which we had passed asked us for a present.—The whole of the exterior of the temple is covered with sculptures; as is also a high wall which surrounds the whole of the main body of the building, and of which the two side-walls of the great court form parts. This edifice is, upon the whole, a stupendous and elaborate work.—Each wing of the propylæum has a well-built flight of stairs by which to ascend to the summit. We enter each stair-case by a door in the back of either wing of the propylæum. In ascending the stairs, we pass, successively, the entrances of a series of apartments, of which, half the number lie on the eastern, and half on the western side. These chambers were perhaps destined for the accommodation of the priests. They have no decoration. For the admission of light, they have narrow apertures, like the loop-holes for musketry, but horizontal instead of being perpendicular.—The whole length of the temple is about 450 feet.

At a short distance from the south-western angle of the propylæum of the great temple is another Ptolemaic temple, almost buried among the

---

[†]Richard Robert Madden.

mounds of rubbish.† This is a monument of Physcon; but the sculptures are partly by a later Ptolemy; supposed to be Lathyrus. It is a small edifice; consisting only of two chambers, and surrounded by a colonnade. High blocks (higher than they are wide) are interposed between the capitals and the architraves, and have a figure of the pigmy monster Typhon, carved in high relief, on each of their four sides. Hence the temple has been called the Typhonium of Ad'foo. Of the cornice, little remains. The sculptures on the interior face of the architraves in front are remarkable: two rows of figures are here represented meeting together in the centre: they are all armed with various instruments of destruction; and each procession commences by a human figure with the head of a lion. The interior of the temple is more than half filled with rubbish. We enter first a small apartment. The principal object in the sculptures is Horus, or Harpocrates, who is generally represented seated on the knees of his nurse Athor, on the walls of the second chamber, which is longer than the first. This chamber contains a single column; opposite the entrance: there was probably another column behind it, corresponding in situation; but it has been thrown down; and the fragments are either buried in the rubbish or have been removed. On the left side-wall of the second chamber, Athor is represented seated on a throne, from which lotuses are springing out in every direction.

I spent three days at Ad'foo on my return from Nubia. The Ka'shif, a young Turk, of agreeable manners, was very polite to me: he accompanied me about the great temple and the village, with several of his soldiers; and I accepted an invitation to sup with him. After my meagre diet for several months, the supper which he gave me appeared magnificent. A Turkish officer of some consequence, sent by the Ba'sha to inspect the state of the cotton throughout the southern provinces of Egypt, was another guest; but not so civil to me as our host. On my being introduced to him as an Englishman, he muttered something about infidels: I reproved him rather intemperately; though from the Ckoor-a'n; and made him beg God's pardon; but not mine. After supper, an interesting council of the sheykhs of the neighbouring villages was held. This ended, the great visiter attacked me again on the subject of religion; it having been whispered to him that I was thought to be a Moos'lim. He questioned me as to the nature of Christ. Wishing to make him ashamed of himself, I argued merely on Mohhammadan principles; and replied that He was the Word of God, and a Spirit proceeding from God; and that He was born of the Virgin Mary, without any natural father, but by a miraculous act of God. What Christian might not thus express himself? But this is the language of the Ckoor-a'n. My adversary, however,—being, as I had suspected, very ignorant of the principles of the religion which he professed,—denied the truth of my assertions; while the Ka'shif, highly amused, sided with me; saying "good! Efen'dee! good! the truth is with you!" But the former could not believe that the

---

†The Birth House, or Mammisi.

expressions which I had used were to be found in the Ckoor-a'n, until he had called in one of his own soldiers, a man who, he said, was very learned in the law: this person immediately confirmed what I had said, and thus I made the great man take to himself the epithet of infidel which he had bestowed upon me. After having again begged God's pardon, he requested me to recite some passages of the Ckoor-a'n—those which almost every Moos'lim has by heart—and was much surprised at my being able to do this.—I mention this anecdote as it presents a true portraiture of many Turkish officers of middling rank.

Chapter XXIX.

Geb'el es-Sil'sil'eh—Ko'm Oom'boo, &c., to Aswa'n.

Scenery, &c., above Ad'foo—Geb'el es-Sil'sil'eh; its grottoes, sculptures on rocks, &c., and quarries—Ko'm Oom'boo (Ombos) its temples, &c.—Dera'weh and the 'Aba'b'deh—Scenery between Dera'weh and Aswa'n—Arrival at Aswa'n.

13th. On the eastern side of the Nile, a little above Ad'foo, is the village of *Er-Redesee'yeh*الردسیه; where is a settlement of 'Aba'b'deh Arabs, who bring charcoal, senna, &c., from the desert.

Advancing a few miles higher, we find the valley very contracted, and thinly inhabited, partly by 'Aba'b'deh Arabs from the adjacent desert on the eastern side. The Egyptians in these southern parts are nearly as dark in complexion as the 'Aba'b'deh, who are of a deep brown colour. The valley here has exactly the same aspect as throughout the greater part of Nubia between the first and second cataracts: and we even find a few Nubians among the inhabitants of this part; and more as we approach nearer to their own country.

At the distance of about 23 miles above Ad'foo, the Nile is hemmed within a narrow channel (about 2,000 feet, or about three furlongs, in breadth) by the low, sandstone mountains on each side.[1] This part of the mountains is called *Geb'el es-Sil'sil'eh* جبل السلسله (the Mountain of the Chain); from a tradition that a chain of iron was anciently stretched across the Nile at this point. A mass of rock, to which the chain is said to have been attached, on the western side of the river, is called *Hhag'ar es-Sil'sil'eh* (or the Rock of the Chain). This name has given rise to the supposition that a town called *Silsili* was situated hereabouts. A little below the most contracted part, there are vestiges of an ancient site on both sides of the Nile: perhaps of *Thmuis* and *Contra Thmuis*; the latter of which is mentioned in the Itinerary of Antoninus. Ptolemy places a town called *Phthontis* 20 minutes south of Apollinopolis Magna: consequently just below Geb'el es-Sil'sil'eh. This natural boundary was probably the division between the Apollinopolite nome and the Ombite, the last nome of Egypt.

Geb'el es-Sil'sil'eh is remarkable for containing many sepulchral grottoes, and other excavations which seem to have been dedicated to worship, and for the extensive quarries from which were taken the

---

[1] See plate 7, no. 1 [fig. 129, upper].

materials for the construction of most of the great edifices of the Thebais. The grottoes, and numerous inscriptions and other sculptures, as well as some of the quarries, are upon the western side of the river: the largest quarries are upon the eastern side.—I commenced my examination upon the western bank.

The first object which attracted my notice on approaching Geb'el es-Sil'sil'eh was an excavated temple[†] near the water's edge, on the western side.[1] It has a long, low front, with a door-way in the centre, and four larger apertures; two to the right and two to the left of the centre. The interior consists of a long, transverse gallery, with a small chamber, or sanctuary, behind it. The gallery is 77 feet long, and ten feet and a half in breadth: its ceiling is cut in an arched form. It is decorated with sculptures of the reign of the successor of Amonoph 3rd, or the Horus of Manetho's list;[‡] and with other sculptures executed under succeeding kings; particularly Rameses 2nd. Most of these sculptures occupy a series of distinct compartments, or tablets, along the back-wall of the gallery: each surmounted by a winged globe. There are also many figures carved in niches. The most interesting of the sculptures is at the left extremity of the back-wall of the gallery. It represents a triumphal procession of King Horus. The monarch is seated on an elegant throne, or chair, borne upon the shoulders of twelve men. He is preceded by a number of captive negroes, whose arms are bound together in various distorted attitudes. Thus these sculptures, which are worthy of the highest admiration for their style and natural truth, inform us that Horus made a successful expedition into Ethiopia; a fact which, I believe, is nowhere else recorded. The other sculptures are mostly representations of Rameses 2nd and other kings making offerings to one or more gods. We find here the hermaphrodite god Nilus, who was particularly worshipped at these *straits* of the Nile, and the crocodile-headed god Sovk, or Savak, the principal deity of the Ombite nome, which was adjacent to (if it did not include) this spot. The small chamber which was the sanctuary of this temple is directly behind the central entrance. It is only eleven feet wide and thirteen feet and a half in length. At the end of it are six small, standing figures, and a sitting figure of the same proportions in the midst of them: all much mutilated.

Proceeding southwards, along the side of the river, we pass several sculptures on the rocks, very well executed; some consisting wholly of hieroglyphics, and some having also other sculptures, of offerings; and bearing the names of several Pharaohs of the Rameses family; proving the remote periods at which the neighbouring quarries were worked. At short intervals we find also small sepulchral grottoes, in all, a considerable number, facing the river. They all appear to be of most remote antiquity: many of them bearing the names of Pharaohs of the

---

[†]The Speos of Horemheb.
[1]It is seen in plate 7, no. 1 [fig. 129, upper].
[‡]Horemheb.

Thothmos family. They are mostly from five to ten feet in length, and rather less in width; having small entrances, with little or no exterior sculpture. At the end of each, with few exceptions, we find a small figure sitting on a bench: sometimes a male; sometimes a female: or two such figures; a male and a female: or three; a male between two females: the females having one hand resting on the shoulder of the man. These are the images of the persons who were buried in the grottoes; which have not places of sepulture excavated beneath like most other grottoes. In many of them the walls are not sculptured. In one of them, which bears the name of Thothmos 1st, we find represented, on the right side-wall, a banquet, nearly similar to the device of the same subject found in many other tombs; and seen in several other grottoes here; but not so well executed. Two sitting figures are represented, a male and a female, with a table before them loaded with fruit and flowers; and persons are bringing them additional supplies: others are sitting before the two chief personages; each having before him a table loaded with provisions, and two jars of wine; and each holds a lotus to his mouth. This grotto is one of the more southern: it is rather difficult of access; unless from a boat, when the river is high. When the Nile is at its highest point, the water enters this grotto; as it does, also, several others. Here, then, we have another proof of the rise of the *bed* of the Nile, as well as of the whole of the cultivable soil of Egypt, by the deposits of the turbid waters during successive inundations: for the ancient Egyptians certainly would not have excavated sepulchral grottoes on a level which the inundation reached in *their* times. I was at first rather doubtful respecting the object for which these grottoes were excavated; from my not finding any catacombs beneath them: but in the last which I entered (I believe it was the southernmost) I found three graves hollowed out in the floor: one of these was of a rectangular form: the other two were nearly of the form of mummies: but all of them too small for full-grown persons. It is evident, then, that the grottoes here were intended for places of sepulture.

A little beyond the tomb last mentioned is the mass of rock to which, it is said, the chain was fastened which extended across the river, and obstructed the navigation.[1] A few paces further are three small chapels, or open recesses, hewn in the rock.[2] The first of these is of the reign of the son and immediate successor of Rameses 2nd; the second is of the reign of Rameses 2nd; and the third bears the name of this king's father and predecessor, Osiree 1st. The last is almost wholly destroyed. The sculptures in both the others are similar. Two figures of the king are represented making offerings to six deities; among whom is the god Nilus. Beneath this sculpture are many lines of hieroglyphics. On the left side-wall of each is the hideous female Typhonian figure, having the usual monstrous body, but a human head and arms: the head is surmounted by the disk and horns of Isis and other goddesses; and in

---

[1]See plate 7, no. 2 [fig. 129, lower].
[2]Two of these are seen in the plate above referred to.

each hand is the *crux ansata*, not held in the ordinary manner, but by the end. Other divinities are sculptured on the same and on the opposite wall, receiving the usual homage. Between these chapels and "the rock of the chain" is a tablet of hieroglyphics bearing the name of Rameses 3rd.

The more extensive of the quarries of Geb'el es-Sil'sil'eh, which, as I have already mentioned, are on the eastern side of the river, are well worthy of the traveller's attention. I landed on that side immediately opposite to the excavated temple which I first described. Here are seen the foundations of a temple, near the river; and near the same spot, towards the south-east, are several rude catacombs, excavated in a low stratum of rock. The mountains beyond contain some extensive caverns, formed by quarrying the rock. They are in few places more than twenty feet in height in the interior; and have large, square masses left to support the superincumbent rock: if they were more lofty, the effect which they would exhibit would be very grand; for they are, in some parts, from two to three hundred feet in extent. Most of the quarries are open to the sky. The first few that we see in proceeding from the northward are comparatively small: they are very near the river; and mostly have a road cut through the rock, by which the blocks were conveyed for embarkation. Upon the higher parts of the rock, above these quarries, are many hewn blocks of stone; and in one place I observed a colossal sphinx; the length of which was seventeen feet. Many other masses of stone I saw lying in various places, partly sculptures with hieroglyphics or architectural ornaments. Continuing our route to the southward, we arrive at the largest of all the quarries. It is entered by a long, winding passage, about 20 feet wide, and 300 feet long, cut through the rock: at the end of this road is an irregular space, of which the greatest extent is nearly six hundred feet: the sides are cut perpendicularly. Another quarry, to the south of that just mentioned, has a straight road, or passage, cut through the rock; but shorter and narrower than the last. In various parts of these quarries we find inscriptions, rudely cut, in Coptic, Greek, and Arabic: but I saw none of any interest, unless among the first, of which I could not judge. There are also a few rude sculptures of implements used by the workmen; with some other scratches, which appear to have been done in sport.

Proceeding above Geb'el es-Sil'sil'eh, we find the river, in some parts, bordered by a scanty strip of cultivated land: in other parts, the sands of the deserts on the east and west reach to the water's edge. At the distance of about eleven miles, is a large, fertile island, called El-Mun'soo'ree'yeh; opposite which, in the eastern side of the Nile, is *Ko'm Oom'boo* كوم انبو (the site of the ancient city of *Ombos*), a rocky hill, overspread with sand; high and steep; particularly towards the river, which washes its base. Upon the summit of this hill[1] are the ruined temples of Ombos, which was the capital of the southernmost nome of Egypt. "Ko'm Oom'boo" signifies "the Hill of Oom'boo," or "— Ombos." The upper

---

[1]See plate 8 [fig. 130].

part of the hill is surrounded, excepting on the side next the river, by a very high and thick wall, composed of large, strong bricks, which appear to have been half burnt. As the surface upon which it rests is irregular, this wall is not of uniform height throughout: in some parts it is fifty feet high; and in one part, considerably more. In many places, only the top appears above the drifted sand, which has nearly buried all the remains of the ancient town, and almost filled the sacred enclosure. The town was probably situated on the slopes, around the wall; where ruins of brick buildings are still seen. There are also some brick ruins within the wall; but they are probably of a later date. At the southern angle of the great enclosure, next the river, is one remaining side of a lofty and handsome Ptolemaic portal[1]: the other side has fallen down the steep. It is richly sculptured; and bears the name of Philometor. Near this is a small, but very ancient portal of stone, built into the exterior side of the great brick wall. It originally formed an approach to an equally ancient (or more ancient) temple, no longer existing; and may afterwards have become one of the gates of the sacred enclosure; but the passage within it is now closed by loose bricks and rubbish. The lintel and cornice have been sculptured by a Ptolemy, whose name is illegible; but upon the front of the two jambs is sculptured a figure of Thothmos 3rd, standing in an attitude of adoration, with one hand uplifted. Beneath his feet is a short record in hieroglyphics; containing the prenonomen [sic] of the great personage who, as I have stated in my account of the temple of the As'a'see'f, in western Thebes, seems to have been regent of Egypt during the minority of Thothmos 3rd:[†] he often associated his name with that of Thothmos 3rd, as in this case; and here the hieroglyphics tell us that he erected, or dedicated, "the portal" before "the abode (or temple) of Sovk (or Savak)," who is here represented by a crocodile, upon a low pedestal. This was the great god of the Ombite nome: his usual form is that of a human figure with the head of a crocodile; which animal was an object of particular veneration in this nome. We learn by the hieroglyphic record above mentioned that there was, at least, one Pharaonic temple at Ombos; and that it was dedicated to the great god Sovk. The greater of the two ruined temples now remaining within the enclosure (both of which are Ptolemaic buildings) probably occupies the site of the older building above alluded to.

The great temple of Ombos is one of the most picturesque ruins on the banks of the Nile. The sanctuaries seem to be of the age of Philometor[2]: the sculptures bearing his name: the other parts were built, or at least decorated, under Physcon and a later Ptolemy, whose name I copied, but I do not know to whom it applies.[3] It is accompanied by the name of a

---

[1]Seen in plate 8 [fig. 130].

[†]Hatshepsut.

[2]Champollion also found the older name of Epiphanes.

[3]Mr. Wilkinson, I find, conjectures it to be Philometor 2nd. (See his Materia Hieroglyphica, part ii, plate 4.)

Cleopatra. To the great portico which forms the front of this temple, and to each succeeding apartment of the building, there are two entrances. The right half of the temple was dedicated to Sovk: this is shewn by its sculptures: the left half to Aroëris; as is proved by a Greek inscription, as well as by the hieroglyphic sculptures. The front of the temple is towards the river. The great portico contains five rows of massive columns. Each row originally consisted of three columns; but the foremost column of each side-row has been thrown down; and the front, therefore, is formed now by three columns, instead of five. The drifted sand has buried those columns to about half their height; and rises still higher in other parts of the temple. The winged globe is sculptured on the cornice over each of the two entrances: a gateway between the columns formed each of these entrances; and the other intercolumnal spaces in the front were closed, to about half their height, by a wall. The capitals of the columns are not uniform; but, as in similar cases, they produce a grand and rich effect. The shafts of the columns are six feet ten inches in diameter, at the middle. They are fully sculptured; as is also the wall behind them. The width of the portico is 83 feet: its depth, 46 feet. The length of the whole building, in its present state, is 148 feet. Two doorways, corresponding with the two entrances before mentioned, lead, or rather *did* lead, from the first into a second portico, immediately behind, but this portico is much lower than the first, and not so large in any respect. The sand rises to the lintels; and we now enter the second portico from the side; for the side-walls are ruined. It has five rows of columns; two in each row. Of these, only the capitals are seen; as the sand rises nearly to the roof. The sculptures here are of the reign of Physcon: in the apartments beyond, they are of the time of Philometor. There remain the partition-walls, but not the side-walls, of three chambers behind the second portico; one behind another. Two doors lead into the first of these. On the cornice over the left door is a line of hieroglyphics; and beneath this is the Greek inscription before alluded to; which informs us that the left half of the temple, or the sanctuary to which that door led, was dedicated to Aroëris. A copy of it is given in Hamilton's work. The following is a translation of it.—"During the reign of the divine king Ptolemy and queen Cleopatra, his sister, the gods Philometores, and their children, the infantry and cavalry and others stationed in the Ombite nome (dedicated) the sekos to Aroëris, the great god Apollo, and to the other gods of the temple."—In the back-wall of the last of the three apartments above mentioned, there are also (as in the preceding walls) two doors, which led into two distinct sanctuaries; that of Sovk on the right, and that of Aroëris on the left. The side and back walls of these are destroyed; but remains of the partition-wall between the two sanctuaries are still seen: whether they had a door of communication does not appear. None of the preceding chambers are divided.—Among the sculptures, we find the crocodile-headed god, Sovk, frequently represented; and among the hieroglyphics, the crocodile itself, as the chief emblem of that god, frequently occurs.

Upon the edge of the steep, above the river's side, is a small and much ruined temple, which appears to have been chiefly dedicated to Athor.[1] It was built and decorated under Physcon and the later Ptolemy before alluded to. The side of the building is towards the river (the front being towards the south-east); and it seems that the great ruined portal which I have already mentioned led directly to this small temple. The entrance to this building was through a portico, which consisted of four columns; three of which remain: their capitals are ornamented with the full face of Athor, like those of the portico of the great temple of Athor at Den'dar'a and are painted with brilliant colours. On the front of the body of the temple we find Athor represented with the young Horus, or Harpocrates, upon her knees, receiving offerings, which appear to be a sphinx, with the disk and horns which are usually on the head of the goddess, and a kind of sistrum. Behind the king (Physcon) who presents these offerings is a female playing upon a harp, and there are three others following her, with tambourines. The body of the temple is so much ruined that its plan cannot be made out; but it appears to have consisted of at least four or five apartments.

In the side of the hill, above the reach of the water, are some covered passages, which were perhaps constructed for the convenience of landing. The accumulation of sand and rubbish above makes them appear like subterranean passages; but it seems they were not so originally; for in one which is near the foundations of the temple of Athor there are apertures, of the usual form, for the admission of light, in the sides and roof. This passage is about nine feet high, and three feet and a half in width. At the distance of about fifty feet, I found it closed with rubbish.[2]

The crocodile, being the emblem of the chief god of Ombos, was held in great veneration here; while the inhabitants of the neighbouring nome of Apollinopolis Magna, as Strabo informs us, were hostile to this animal. Of the catacombs of crocodiles, near Ko'm Oom'boo, visited by Hamilton, I could obtain no information. On my return from Nubia, I found, at this place, a large party of 'Aba'b'deh Arabs, making a lamentation for a friend who had been carried off by a crocodile, two days before, from this spot. Such an occurrence is very rare in Egypt: but the women seldom go down to the river to fill their pitchers, or to wash their clothes, alone; for fear of becoming the prey of a crocodile. This animal generally retreats at the approach of a single person; and is always frightened away by the passing of a boat near to it.

A little above Ko'm Oom'boo, and on the same side of the Nile, is

---

[1]This temple, I learn, was washed away by the inundation of 1829, which was unusually high, and very destructive.

[2]In the adjacent desert is the burial-place of Ombos; and Mr. Gliddon states, that by a sycomore[*sic*]-tree, about a mile from the temple, to the south-east, is the mouth of a large crocodile-pit, from which he procured "a small crocodile, out of a large number broken about, as well as heads of cranes, cats, and, what is very curious, that of an ichneumon."

Dera'weh دراوه , the principal abode of the 'Aba'b'deh Arabs who have settled near the river. It is also the place whence the caravans of Shen'deh and Senna'r generally start; striking off from this point into the desert: and hither the 'Aba'b'deh frequently bring, for sale, camels, sheep, senna, and charcoal. Dera'weh consists of several villages, or groups of huts, near together. Almost all the inhabitants are 'Aba'b'deh.[1] These people, mostly, are of a deep brown complexion; much like the Nubians; but with more of the general Arab physiognomy. Their women grease their crisp, black hair, and twist it, in the same manner as those of Nubia; and in like manner, the young unmarried girls wear nothing but the leather fringe round their loins. Behind Dera'weh is an extensive, sandy plain, between the cultivated land and the mountains.

Above Dera'weh, as far as Aswa'n, the valley of the Nile is very contracted; and its aspect, in every respect, is very like the Nubian valley from Debo'd to Wa'dee es-Sooboo'a: the resemblance, too, is made more striking by the inhabitants of the small and scanty villages being either Nubians or 'Aba'b'deh; for the greater number, nearly black. The mountains throughout this portion of the valley of Egypt are very near to the river, low, and rugged: in some parts they reach to the water's edge: excepting at these points, a narrow strip of verdure, generally door'ah sey'fee, borders the river.

In the evening of the 13th, having availed ourselves of a fine breeze, and landed at few of the places which (from notes made on my return) I have described in this day's journal, we arrived at Aswa'n. As we approached this place, and passed along the side of the verdant isle of Elephantine, which is opposite to it, the Nubian children ran along the bank in crowds, attracted by the sounds of our darabook'keh and zoomma'rah, and the singing of the boatmen. Most of these children were naked: some had a piece of rag tied about them. Sometimes they were joined by women, who, at frequent intervals, raised their shrill zugh'a'ree't, or quavering cries of joy.—The greatest height of the thermometer this day, in my cabin, was not more than 92°.

---

[1] *'Aba'b'deh* is the plural of 'Abba'dee. An Arab of this tribe is always called 'Abba'dee.

Figure 82: Transverse avenue in the great portico of El-Karnak.

Figure 83: Obelisks &c. behind the great portico of El-Karnak.

Figure 85: View from the
roof of the Granite
Sanctuary of El-Karnak,
looking towards the portico
of Thothmes III.

Figure 84: The Granite Sanctuary of El-Karnak, with other remains.

Figure 86: Interior of the portico of Thothmes III., El-Karnak.

Figure 87: The Avenue of colossal rams at El-Karnak.
a, Southern Temple. b, Temple of Isis. c, Propylon of the Great
Temple. d, Ancient monolith. e,f,g,h, The four southern propyla.

Figure 88: Horse-shoe lake at El-Karnak, Ancient Temple, and Colossi.

Figure 89: El-Kurneh.

Figure 91: Funeral-procession—from a tomb at El-Ckoor'neh.

Figure 90: Ancient edifice at the ruined village of El-Kurneh.

Figure 92: [Brick Pyramidal Structures in the Asasif, Thebes.]

Figure 93: Ancient brick buildings in the Asáseef, El-Kurneh.

Figure 94: Great tomb in the Asáseef.

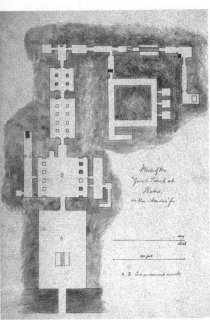

Figure 96: Brick Propylæum
in the Asasee'f.

Figure 95: Plan of the Great Tomb at Thebes, in the Asasee'f.
A B Two uncovered courts.

Figure 97: Temple of the Asáseef.

Figure 98: Wailing women—from one of the tombs in the As'a'see'f.

Figure 99: Hill of the sheykh 'Abd-El-Kurneh.

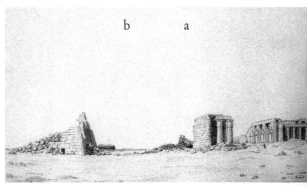

Figure 101: The Raméséum of
El-Kurneh. a, Great broken
colossus. b, Medeenet Haboo.

Figure 100: Ancient brick arches
adjacent to the Raméséum of
El-Kurneh. a, Part of the Raméséum.
b, Hill of Mar'ee. c, Temple of Athor.

Figure 102: Great broken colossus in the Rameséum.

Figure 103: Second court, and portico,
of the Rameséum.

Figure 104: Interior of the portico of the Raméséum,
from a door-way at the end.

Figure 105: The two colossi of Amonoph III. (or Memnon).
The nearer is the "Vocal Memnon." b, Medeenet Haboo.

b

a

Figure 107: View of Medeenet
Haboo from the east.
a, The smaller temple. b, Small
palace. c, Great edifice.

Figure 106:
Temple of Athor: Thebes.

c

Figure 108: Front view of the small palace of Medeenet Haboo. a, Part of the first propylon of the Smaller Temple.

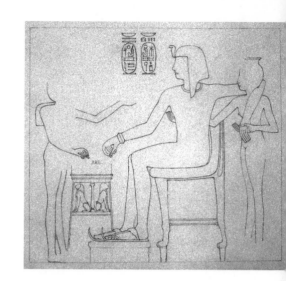

Figure 109: Sculpture in the Small Palace of Medee'net Hha'boo.

Figure 110: Front of the Great Edifice of Medee'net Hhab'oo, from a back window of the Small Palace.

Figure 111: Peristyle court of the great edifice of Medeenet Haboo.

Figure 112: The Valley of the Tombs of the Kings, at Thebes.

Figure 114:
The First Tomb
in the Valley
of the Kings.

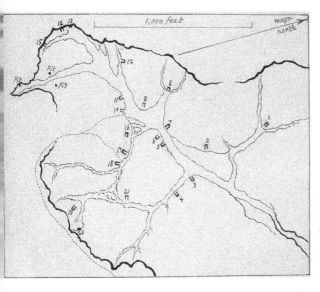

Figure 113:
Beeba'n el-Mooloo'k.
Topographical sketch,
shewing the situation
of the tombs.

Figure 116: Entrance
of the Eleventh
Tomb—that of
Rameses 3rd.

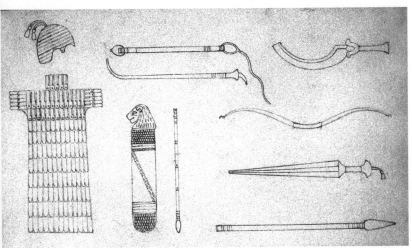

Figure 117: Ancient Arms, from the [Eleventh] of the Tombs of the Kings.
[Lane originally wrote "seventeenth" according to the numbering system
that he used before Wilkinson's system became established.]

Figure 115: Interior of one of the Tombs of the Kings (No. 2 in the Plan).

Figure 118: One of the Harpers in the
[Eleventh] of the Tombs of the Kings.

Figure 119: Entrance of the Seventeenth Tomb—That of Osiree 1st—
The great tomb opened by Belzoni.

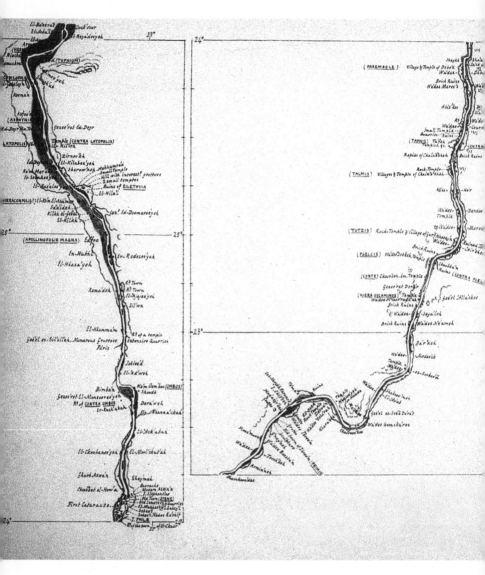

Figure 122: Map of the Valley of the Nile from Thebes to the Second Cataracts. The tint shews the extent of the cultivable land.

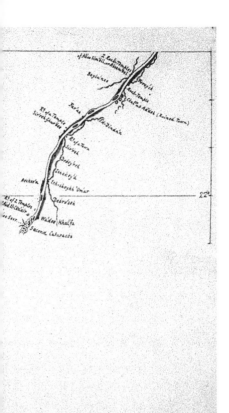

Figure 120: Design sculptured within the entrance of the Tomb opened by Belzoni, and in several other tombs.

Figure 121: Figures from the Tomb opened by Belzoni.

B   C   A

Figure 123: Ruined church (A), modern tombs (B),
and ancient temple (C), at Arment.

Figure 124: Temple of Arment (front view).

Figure 125: Front of
the portico of Isna.

Figure 126: First view, Eilethyia. Second view, Adfoo.

Figure 127: Front of
the great temple of Adfoo

Figure 128: Court of the great temple of Adfoo.

A A

Figure 129: View of Gebel es-Silsileh.
Rock-chapels of Gebel es-Silsileh (AA), and "Rock of the Chain" (B).

B

Figure 130: Kóm Umboo.

Figure 132:
The old Arab
cemetery
of Aswán.

Figure 131: Aswán, and part of the island of Elephantine, from a rock near the eastern bank.

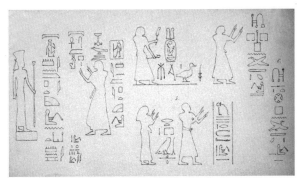

Figure 133: Sculptures on the rocks of the Island of Sahey'l.

Figure 134: The First Cataracts.

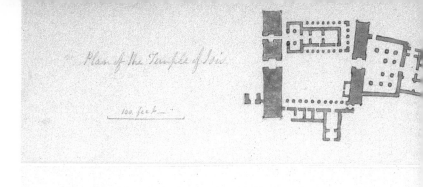

Plan of the Temple of Isis

100 feet

Figure 136:
General view of
the great temple
and other
monuments of
Philæ.

Figure 135: View of the Isle of Philæ, from the east. Plan of the Temple of Isis, on the Isle of Philæ.

Figure 137: The Temple of Dabód.

Figure 138: The Temple of Kardáseh.

Figure 139: In the Quarries of Ckurda'seh.

Figure 140: Táfeh.

Figure 141: Temple at Táfeh.

Figure 142: Front view of the great temple of Kaláb'sheh.

Figure 143: Court and portico of the great temple of Kaláb'sheh.

Figure 144: The Temple of Dendoor.

Figure 145: Exterior view of the Rock-Temple of Garf Hoseyn.

Figure 146: Interior of the Rock-Temple of Garf Hoseyn.

Figure 147:
The Temple of Dakkeh.

Figure 148: Sculptures on a ruin at M'hhar'ruck'ah.

Figure 149: The Temple of Wádee es-Subooa.

Figure 150: The Temple of Hassáyeh, or Amada.

Figure 151: The Rock-Temple of Ed-Dirr.

Figure 152: The old town
of Ibreem.

Figure 153: Aboo-Simbil,
or Absembel.

Figure 154: The great temple of Absembel.

Figure 155: Head of the northernmost of the four colossi
in front of the great temple of Absembel.

Figure 157: Wádee Halfa.

Figure 156: Interior of the great temple of Absembel.

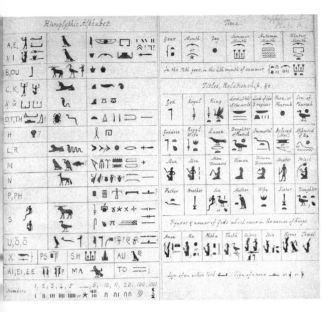

Figure 158: Hieroglyphic Alphabet.

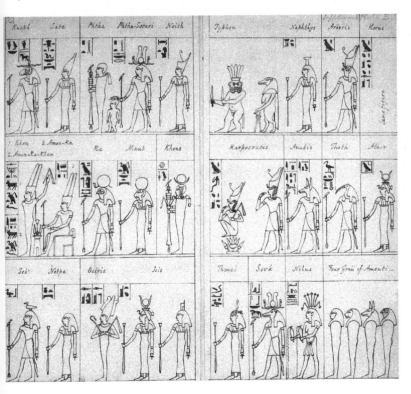

Figure 159: [Egyptian Deities.]

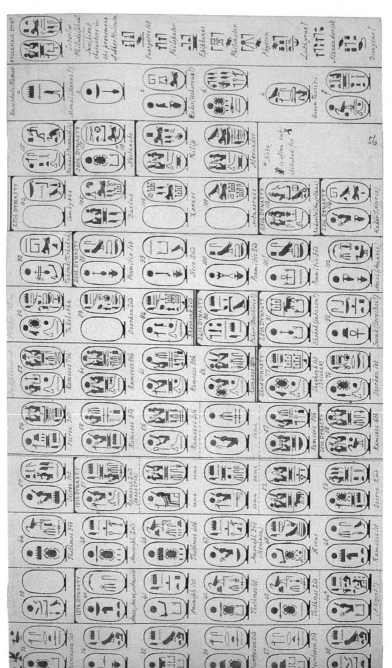

Figure 160: [List of Ancient Egyptian Kings.]

Chapter XXX.
Elephantine, Aswa'n, the Cataracts, &c.

Scenery of the environs of Aswa'n—The Island of Elephantine—The Nilometer and other remains there—The modern town of Aswa'n—Old Aswa'n and Syene—The Temple of Syene—Remarks on the Tropical Well—Old Arab Cemetery—Quarries—The usual land-route from Aswa'n to the bank of the Nile opposite Philæ—Description of that part of the Nile between Elephantine and Philæ—The Island of Sahey'l, and its sculptured rocks—The Cataracts.

The approach to Aswa'n is certainly picturesque; particularly when contrasted with the scenery below. Upon the summit of a mountain of the western chain which closely hems in the river is a Sheykh's tomb; a small, white-washed, square building, surmounted by a cupola: it is called *Ckoob'bet el-How'a* (or the Cupola of the Wind). Upon a lower eminence of the same mountain, about half the height, is a ruined convent; and in the side of the rock, immediately beneath this, are some rude, ancient, sepulchral excavations, having square pillars of the rock left to support the ceiling. The sand which covers the side of the mountain on almost every part probably conceals the entrances of many more excavations, the burial-places of the ancient inhabitants of Syene. Some smaller tombs of this kind in the lower part of the mountain are still open; but are not worth visiting. To some of the higher sepulchres, the remains of roads are observable; running up the slope.

The river, a little higher, is divided by the fertile island of *Elephantine*; now called *Gezee'ret Aswa'n* (or the Island of Aswa'n); which extends before the modern town, and partly before the ancient town also. On entering the channel between Aswa'n and this island, we enjoy a very pleasing view. The modern town of Aswa'n is, for the most part, screened from our view by numerous palm-trees. In the bed of the river are many granite rocks; several of which, when the water is low, appear above the surface. From the summit of one of these I made a view,[1] which comprises the site and ruins of the old town, the old pier, and the most remarkable part of the island of Elephantine. Of the various objects which here surrounded me, I shall first describe the island.

The whole of this island is flat (being mainly composed of cultivable soil, the deposit of the river), excepting at the southern end, which is higher than the rest. Around its sides, in many parts, granite rocks, which form its basis, protrude from the soil, and serve to defend it

---

[1]See plate 9 [fig. 131].

against the force of the stream during the inundation. The island is nearly a mile in length, and about a quarter of a mile in breadth; contracting towards the northern end. In contains two considerable villages, and other groups of huts, all inhabited by Bara'b'reh (or Nubians); who are nearly black, and scantily clad: the young, of both sexes, generally quite naked. Here I may mention that from this point, excepting in the town of Aswa'n, we find no Egyptians among the inhabitants of the valley of the Nile; and that the race of Nubians hereabouts are darker than those a hundred miles further southwards. The island of Elephantine abounds with palm-trees; but has very little variety of foliage: I only observed two or three sycamores, a few seya'lehs and sunts, and some hhen'na-trees, among the green corn which covered the soil: the other varieties were too scanty to add at all to the picturesque character of the landscape. The southern end of the island is high and rocky; and this natural elevation in increased by immense quantities of broken pottery and other rubbish, covering the site of the ancient town of Elephantine; which was a place of considerable importance, and, according to Strabo, the station of a Roman cohort. This elevated part is strengthened, on the eastern side (the side facing the ruins of the old town of Aswa'n) by two high and massive walls of masonry, raised perpendicularly before and above the rocks of granite which form the foundation and heart of this part of the island. The southernmost of these walls, which is divided from the other by a bold mass of rocks, has, in the upper part, several blocks sculptured with hieroglyphics; some of which are inverted: it is evident, therefore, that it is no very ancient work; or that it was heightened in later times. There are several hieroglyphic sculptures on the granite rocks here. The other wall seems to have had a row of windows, two of which yet remain, along the top. It contains a well-built stair-case.

This stair-case was the *Nilometer* of Elephantine. We enter it, when the river is low, by a door at the base; and immediately turn up to the left, and ascend a flight of about fifty steps, running parallel with the exterior face of the wall. The steps were mostly covered with soil deposited by the river; and therefore I could not ascertain their exact number. From the top, another ascending stair-case turns off to the right, at a right angle. The lower stair-case was originally roofed entirely over; but most of the covering has fallen, or been removed. It received light by apertures on the side next the river (the left side to a person ascending the stairs); and the water enters by these apertures when the Nile is nearly at the highest.—In ascending this stair-case, we observe, on the right-wall, successively six Nilometric scales: the bottom of each succeeding scale being exactly on a level with the top of that next below. The graduations of these are, in some parts, very indistinct; and a person might pass them unnoticed. M. Girard, I believe, was the first who observed them in modern times; but he saw only the three lower scales. The lowest of these seems to consist of three cubits (or certainly more than two): the second and third are of two cubits each; and each of the other three scales consists of only one cubit: thus, altogether, they compose ten cubits.

Each cubit, or peck (πηχυς) is twenty English inches and two thirds in length; and is divided into fourteen parts: each of these parts being half a palm (παλαιςη). The numbers of the cubits are marked, on the left side of the scales, by Greek letters: as KA (21). The first scale consists of the 18th, 19th, and 20th cubits: the second, of the 21st and 22nd: the third, of the 23rd and 24th: the fourth, of the 25th: the fifth, of the 26th: and the sixth is the 27th cubit. It seems that it was deemed unnecessary to have a lower scale than the first of these, as the river scarcely ever failed to attain to the height of 17 cubits (or 29 feet 4 inches and three quarters). To the right of several of the scales are Greek inscriptions, rudely cut, and much obliterated, in consequence of the wall having been, during the course of many centuries, annually soaked by the waters of the inundation, and then subjected to the extreme of dryness. It is wonderful that, under such circumstances, they have not wholly disappeared: much of them, indeed, is quite lost.—To the lowest scale there seem to have been no inscriptions.—On the right of the upper part of the second scale (i.e. against the upper part of the 22nd cubit) is a Greek inscription, much effaced; and to the right of this is another small scale, not continuing the graduation, but corresponding with nine divisions of the 22nd cubit. The inscription above mentioned contains the name of Trajan, the rest, excepting the preceding word, KAICAPOC, is illegible: it evidently alludes (like others which will be mentioned here) to the Nile having risen to the corresponding cubit; that is, to the height of 22 cubits (or 37 feet 10 inches and two thirds) during the reign of that Emperor.—To the right of the upper part of the next scale (the third—i.e. against the upper part of the 24th cubit) are several inscriptions. In these we read the following records: but in none of them can we perfectly decipher the dates of the reigns; and in some, the heights of the river are illegible. In the first we read "....... of Augustus Cæsar ......" in the second, "....... of Trajan Cæsar ......" The third is almost wholly effaced. In the fourth we read "....... of Nero ......" in the fifth, "...... of Tiberius Cæsar ......" in the sixth, "....... of Tiberius Cæsar, 24 cubits (KΔ) ......" in the seventh, "....... of Domitian, 24 cubits ......" in the eighth, "....... of Augustus Cæsar, 24 cubits, 4 palms, 1 digit": in the ninth, "....... of Nero Cæsar, 24 cubits, 4 palms, 1 digit": (this measure is written thus ΠΗΚΔΠΑΔΔΑΔ: the ΠΗΧΥΣ being expressed by ΠΗ; the ΠΑΛΑΙΣΤΗ, by ΠΑ ; and the ΔΑΚΤΥΛΟΣ , by ΔΑ). The digit is the fourth of the palm. Between these inscriptions and the scale to which they refer are distinguished some words of four other lines; in the first of which we read "....... of Tiberius Cæsar, ... cubits ...."; and *below* the former inscriptions we find the following.

ΛΟΥΚΙΟΥCΕΠΤΙΜΙΟΥCΕΟΥΗΡΟΥ
ΕΥCΕΒΟΥCΠΕΡΤΙΝΑΚΟCCΕΒΑCΤΟΥ
ΤΟΥΚΥΡΙΟΥΕΠΙΟΥΛΠΙΟΥΠΡΙΜΙΑΝΟΥ
ΤΟΥΛΑΜΠΡΟΤΑΤΟΥΗΓΕΜΟΝΟC
ΠΑΛΑΙCΤΟΙΔΔΑΚΤΥ Β

"(In the .... year) of Lucius Septimius Severus Pius Pertinax Augustus, the Sovereign, and under Ulpius Primianus, the most illustrious Governor, (...... cubits), four palms, two digits." The number of cubits here should, it seems, be 23; for the inscription appears to correspond with the 23rd cubit.—Against the fourth scale (or 25th cubit) are a few short lines; in one of which we read the words "...... in the reign of Lucius ......" and in another, "....... of Antoninus Cæsar ......"—On the right of the fifth scale (or 26th cubit) are also a few short lines. In one of these is the name of Nero: in another, that of Lucius Septimius (Severus).—The sixth (the last) scale (or 27th cubit) has no inscriptions.—An interesting inquiry is suggested by these inscriptions; and has been ably pursued by M. Girard; but this savant was unacquainted with many of these records which afford better data for the inquiry. The inscriptions, we have seen, are commemorative of the heights which the Nile attained in the reigns of certain Emperors. We find that it rose to the following points of the scale of this Nilometer in the reigns of the undermentioned Emperors, whom I place in the order of their accession: the exact years we are not acquainted with; but this is of little consequence in the investigation; or rather of no consequence at all.

In the reign of	Cubits.	Palms.	Digits.
Augustus	24.		
and	24.	4.	1.
Tiberius	24.		
Nero	24.		
and	24.	4.	1.
and	26.		
Domitian	24.		
Trajan	22.		
and	24.		
Antoninus	25.		
Septimius Severus	23.	4.	2.
and	25.		
and	26.		

Thus we find that about 18 centuries ago the Nile attained to the 24th cubit. This seems to have been the standard of a good inundation at that period, in the southernmost part of Egypt. The inscriptions recording that height cannot, I think, be commemorative of unusually high inundations; for in the reign of Nero, it appears there was a rise as high as the 26th cubit: this is the highest recorded here. Now we know that those unusually high inundations, which, when they do happen, cause dreadful devastation, are scarcely ever higher than about two of these cubits above the standard measure of a good inundation. We have, then, strong reasons for concluding that the 24th cubit of this Nilometer was the mark of a good inundation about 18 centuries ago. But the Nile now rises, in good years, about 4 cubits (of the same scale) higher; that is, one cubit above the highest marked on the scale.[1] Thus it appears that the bed of the river has risen four cubits of the measure of the Nilometer, or nearly seven feet (more correctly 6 feet 10 inches and two thirds), in 18 centuries; which is at the rate of increase of the cultivable soil throughout the whole of Egypt: for I have shewn, in a general physical sketch of the country, that the bed of the river and the whole soil of Egypt rise together, and at the same rate. To verify this estimate, the *exact* height which the Nile attains at Elephantine should be carefully ascertained: but the above calculation probably approximates very nearly to the truth.— From the data which the Nilometer furnishes we may also make a rough calculation of the period at which it was constructed. The true height of the river at this place (as appears from modern observations of its rise) must have been scarcely more than 40 feet when it attained to the 24th cubit of the Nilometer here, about 18 centuries ago: 24 cubits of that scale are equal to about 41 feet and one third: therefore the bed of the river must then have risen somewhat more than one foot since the construction of the Nilometer; and thus we may conclude that a little more than three centuries was the interval between its construction and the period of the earlier of its inscriptions. This calculation refers its construction to the first age of the Ptolemaic Dynasty; and there is nothing in its appearance to lead us to regard it as the work of a more ancient period.—I think no one will doubt but that this is the Nilometer of Elephantine mentioned by Strabo. The two earliest of the inscriptions above-quoted bear the name of Augustus, with whom Strabo was contemporary. This writer describes the Nilometer by the term φρεαρ, which commonly signifies a *well*; and which would certainly lead one to look for a perpendicular pit, rather than a stair-case: but as the Nilometer which I have described existed in the time of Strabo, I cannot think that the geographer alluded to any other; or he would have mentioned that there were two. Casaubon, in his notes on Strabo, has satisfactorily shewn that, instead of the expression συν μονολιθω (which would imply that the Nilometer was a monolithic work), we should read συννομω λίθω; which signifies that it was constructed of well-joined, or well-cut stone.

Before I quit the subject of this Nilometer, I must remark that M. Jomard, who has written an admirable memoir on the ancient Egyptian measures, has shewn that the cubit of this monument is of most remote antiquity: that it was the measure employed in constructing the Pyramids of Memphis. On referring to my measurements of the First and Second Pyramids of El-Gee'zeh, I find a great many of them to be very nearly divisible into these cubits: but I often disregarded a fraction of an inch in measures which were not very small[2]; not imagining that I should ever

---

[1] I was not at Elephantine at the proper period to ascertain this by actually witnessing the fact; and therefore rely upon appearances and the information of others.

[2] I took these measures *exactly* during my last visit.

want to refer to them for such a purpose as that here explained; and hence there is a trifling difference discovered in reducing them to the ancient cubits: the near degree of coincidence is, however, very remarkable. For instance:—the great chamber of the Great Pyramid is, by my admeasurement, 17 feet 2 inches in width; or 10 ancient Egyptian cubits *minus*, by that admeasurement, two thirds of an inch; and it is twice that measure in length:—the short passage leading to that chamber is 2 cubits wide, or 3 feet $5^{1/3}$ (3 feet $5^{1/2}$ by my admeasurement):—the great gallery is 4 cubits wide, or 6 feet $10^{2/3}$ (6 feet 10 by my admeasurement):—the stone benches which extend along each side of that gallery are one cubit square, or 1 foot $8^{2/3}$ (1 foot $8^{1/2}$ by my admeasurement)—I might give many other instances, were it necessary.

I observed many blocks of stone, with hieroglyphics, to the south of the Nilometer. They had belonged to ancient edifices; and had been employed by the Romans in the construction of later buildings. In the ruined walls of a quay here were two stones which were each sculptured with a reclining figure of a river-god, in the Roman style, and ill executed.

Upon the mounds of rubbish which cover this end of the island were two small ancient temples, which have lately been demolished, and their materials employed partly in the construction of extensive barracks behind the town of Aswa'n, and partly for some other modern buildings. One of these was dedicated to Kneph (or Cnuphis); and the other to Amon-Ra, or to Amon Generator: both were monuments of the reign of Amonoph 3rd; and were decorated with sculptures in the usual pure style of that remote period. Strabo mentions a temple of Cnuphis here: there were two, on this island, dedicated to that god, who was the principal divinity of Elephantine. The other temple of Kneph is also entirely destroyed; but the two jambs of a granite portal which formed an approach to it yet remain. Its sculptures bear the hieroglyphic name of Alexandros (Alexander the Great).—On the lower part of the mounds, towards the north, is a granite statue of a king, with the crook and flail of Osiris, in a sitting posture, rather above the natural size, and much mutilated. It bears a name, almost effaced, which appears to be that of the immediate successor of Rameses 2nd.

The granite rocks at the southern extremity of the island have many circular perforations, like wells; some of which seem like the work of nature; but others are so regularly formed as to leave little doubt that they are artificial, or that they have been widened and deepened by art. Most of them I found more or less filled with rubbish; and around the mouths of some were heaps of dried and broken human bodies, and rags. That these are the remains of ancient Egyptians is probable; but not certain; as will appear from the following fact. Another traveller pointed out to me a narrow, horizontal cavity made in a thick wall of crude brick on this island, among the mounds. This cavity was in the side of the wall; and was closed in front by bricks; a few of which being removed, we perceived that human bodies were placed in this narrow space: they were enveloped in linen; and appeared, to both of us, to be mummies; but on my friend endeavouring to remove one of them for examination, some of the inhabitants of the island came running to us, and crying out that [we] were disturbing the remains of Moos'lims.

Above Elephantine, the river is divided by numerous granite islands and rocks. At the distance of between three and four miles above Aswa'n are the Cataracts. Of these, and of one of the islands about midway between them and Elephantine, I shall give some account after I shall have taken a survey of the modern town, and of the ruins, &c., on the eastern side of the river, from Aswa'n to the neighbourhood of Philæ.

Aswa'n (or, as it is sometimes pronounced, *Ooswa'n*) اسوان is a place of importance as the frontier town of Egypt towards Nubia; but it does not now mark the limit of Mohham'mad 'Al'ee's government. Little of it is seen from the river, or from the island; the greater part being concealed by palm-trees, which line the shore: it therefore appears, when viewed thus partially from the river, little more than a village: it is, however, pretty extensive; though its market is very ill supplied. It is said to have been founded in the time of Selee'm, the Turkish Soolta'n who conquered Egypt. (The *old* Arab town of Aswa'n occupied the site of the ancient Egyptian city which the Romans called Syene). Many of its inhabitants are Nubians. The trade of the place is chiefly in the dates of Nubia. All merchandize from that country is landed on the eastern bank of the Nile opposite to the island of Philæ, nearly two miles above the Cataracts, and conveyed by land to Aswa'n; excepting when the river is very high; at which period, loaded boats sometimes descend the cataracts, or rather rapids.

On my arrival at Aswa'n, I first repaired to the house of the A'gha, to shew my passport. The A'gha himself was at a country-house, a little lower down the river, confined by an attack of ophthalmia; to the great satisfaction of the people of the town; by whom he was much disliked. Aswa'n is the only town in Egypt where it is absolutely necessary for the European traveller to call upon the governor, and to exhibit his passport. A Dutch traveller arrived at Aswa'n about two months before me; but proceeded on his voyage up the Nile, above the Cataracts. The A'gha, irritated at this traveller's not having called upon him, nor sent him any present, took advantage of his being unprovided with a passport, pretended to believe that he must be a person who had committed some offence for which he was obliged to fly from Egypt, and dispatched a messenger on a dromedary, a few days after, to bring him back to Aswa'n. The traveller was overtaken beyond Ed-Dirr, more than a hundred miles above Aswa'n; and not only compelled to return, but shamefully pillaged.—I was received by the A'gha's lieutenant and a group of his forty soldiers. As my luggage was to be conveyed by land to a village above the cataracts, I requested to be accommodated with camels; which were promised to me, with an intimation that I was not to pay any hire. This intimation was not necessary; for I could hardly prevail upon the Sheykh of the camels to accept a small present; and when he had accepted it he sent me a sheep, of nearly equal value. As the A'gha was a sportsman, I sent him, as a present, a canister of fine gunpowder. This governor, who was properly styled 'Al'ee A'gha, was nicknamed Ab'oo Turboo'sh; from his habitually wearing a turboo'sh (or red cloth scull-cap) without the shawl wound round it. He and his M'al'lim (or Ckoob'tee scribe and tax-gatherer) were very unpopular: the former, on account of his severity; particularly in bastonading, and beating people, with his own hand, with an iron mace: the latter was probably hated merely on account of his office, or his talents for extortion. Some wit of this place had composed a song, the burden of which was a prayer that the plague might take Ab'oo Turboo'sh and his M'al'lim together. The boatmen here did not scruple to sing this song, even in the hearing of the Turkish soldiers: it was also a favourite with the boatmen throughout Nubia.

After my visit to the house of the A'gha, I had to make a bargain with the Rei'yis esh-Shila'l (or Captain of the Cataracts) for drawing up my boat. This man—an old Nubian, short, nearly black, with a remarkably cunning physiognomy, and a beard composed of a few grey hairs—is exceedingly troublesome to travellers, by his exorbitant demands, and his delays. He came to my boat with several friends to assist him in making a good bargain; and, after many compliments, told me that my boat should be drawn up the cataracts on the following day; and that whatever I might think proper to give him he was sure would be sufficient: but on my offering 100 piasters, he said "no"; that he should do it for nothing; for there was a pleasure in doing a service gratis; but that, if he were paid, he must be paid fairly. The sum I intended to give was 125 piasters; and this I afterwards offered; being a liberal remuneration. Much wrangling ensued; and the old man seemed resolved to reject this offer. At length, the proposal to recite the *fe't'hhah*,[1] as conclusive of the bargain, silenced both him and his party. On my commencing the recital, he hesitated for a moment, and then joined with me; as did also all present. It was then settled that I should pay 70 piasters on ascending, and the remaining 55 on my return.

The modern Aswa'n has been in a more flourishing state than it is at present; though it has been founded little more than three centuries. This is evident from the extent of its cemetery, which is immediately behind the town: it contains many tombs of sheykhs and persons of some distinction.—It was at Aswa'n that Mohham'mad 'Al'ee's first regiments of regular troops (Niza'm Gedee'd) were organized, in 1822. These were chiefly composed of natives of Koordoofa'n, Senna'r, and Nubia. To the east of the town are extensive barracks, enclosing a square court, which were built for these troops, partly with the materials of the temples of Elephantine.

Aswa'n is frequently visited by 'Aba'b'deh Arabs; and occasionally, by

---

[1]The opening chapter of the Ckoor-a'n; by the recital of which, the Moos'lims generally conclude an important bargain.

Bish'a'ree'n, who inhabit various parts of the desert between the Red Sea
and Nubia; chiefly near the sea-coast. The 'Aba'b'deh, for the most part,
dwell in the more northern districts of the desert. The Bish'a'ree'n bring
to Aswa'n, from their deserts, camels of the finest breed existing, sheep,
charcoal, the best senna, and ostrich-feathers. They are of a very deep
brown complexion: some of them nearly black: and in physiognomy,
they greatly resemble the Abyssinians. The men generally dress their hair
like some of the Nubians: very thick and bushy at the sides, and stiffened
with grease. The women also arrange their crisp hair nearly in the same
manner as those of Nubia; but part it into smaller strings. Some of the
men shave the head, and wear a white scull-cap; but few wear turbans.
Their costume consists of a shirt (if they can afford it), or of any ragged
piece of linen, covering a part of their bodies, and confined by a girdle.
The young women are celebrated for their beauty: many of them wear
nothing but the leather fringe round the loins, reaching half-way down
the thigh. I visited an encampment of Bish'a'ree'n at Aswa'n, on my
return from Nubia, as well from motives of curiosity as for the purpose
of purchasing some charcoal, of which they had brought a great quantity.
These people were living in small, low, square tents, of matting. A very
handsome girl, sitting with an old man in one of the tents, and with no
other clothing than a small strip of rag, attracted my notice; and after I
had passed on, she sent her brother to me, to say that she would pay me
a visit, but that her father (the old man who was with her) was so angry
at my having stopped before the open front of his tent without saluting
him, that he swore he would thrust his spear through her body if she
went to me: the old man added that if I had paid him the least
compliment he would not have objected to her visiting me. This
anecdote is not worth committing to paper, but as illustrating the
character and manners of this singular people. The Bisha'ree is the least
civilized of the Bed'awee tribes between the Nile and the Red Sea.

   Immediately on the south of the modern Aswa'n are the ruins of the
old Arab town, which bore the same name, and which was built on the
same site as the ancient Egyptian city of *Syene*, the frontier town of
ancient Egypt, and the place of Juvenal's banishment. Before the point
where the modern town stretches over a part of the ancient site, a brick
pier juts out into the river. This has been mistaken for remains of a
bridge.[1] It has the appearance of being a Roman work; but may perhaps
have been constructed by the early Arabs. The name of *el-Mickya's* (or
the Nilometer) is given to it by the modern inhabitants of Aswa'n. It
contains some stuccoed apartments, and a square well, which is said to
descend to the foundations, in the foremost part of the structure. This, I
have little doubt, is the Nilometer which, as El-Muckree'zee relates,
'Amr Ibn El-'A'see built. I believe that Burckhardt erred in attributing
this to the Khalee'feh El-Mo'a'wiyeh. El-Muckree'zee states that a
nilometer was built by this prince; but it was at An'sin'ë, the ancient

---

[1] It is seen in plate 9 [fig. 131].

Antinöe. In the building at Aswa'n we do not find any graduated scale
now remaining. The nilometer of which Heliodorus gives an account
(lib. ix) seems to be that of Elephantine, described in similar terms by
Strabo.

A grove of palm-trees extends, from the pier above described, before a
part of the ruined town, which is slightly elevated: the southern part is
much higher. The most conspicuous ruins are on the irregular summit
and slopes of a hill of granite rocks, overlooking the river, which washes
the side of this rocky eminence.[1] There are some rude sculptures on the
front of the rocks here: they are of very ancient date; bearing the name of
Amonoph 3rd: there are two similar subjects; a person kneeling, in
adoration, before the god Ra, who is seated on his throne. The ruined
houses of the old town are constructed of crude brick: all the roofs have
fallen; and likewise many of the walls; but some portions of considerable
height yet remain standing; though built of such frail materials that a few
heavy showers of rain would completely dissolve them.—I met with a
disagreeable adventure among these ruined houses. On my return from
Nubia to this place, just after my boat had been made fast to the bank
before the town of Aswa'n, two Turkish soldiers (one of them a sheree'f,
as appeared by his green turban) seated themselves on the bank near by.
One of my servants, who had learned a little Turkish (having been in the
service of an 'Osma'nlee) happened to sit within a few feet of them; and
overheard a conversation which passed between them. He remained until
they rose and went away, that they might not suspect his having
understood them; and then came and informed me that they had been
laying a plot to rob and murder me. The sheree'f, he said, remarked to
his companion that European travellers generally carried a good sum of
money about them; and that it would be well for them to lie in wait for
me in the ruined town; as every traveller visited it. I regarded this as an
idle tale; the mere fabrication of the servant; made him rather angry by
my incredulity; and thought no more about it. A little while after, I left
my boat, alone and unarmed (contrary to my usual custom) and
ascended to the highest part of the ruined town. The servant, hearing that
I had gone thither, ran to recal[l] me, if possible: but I had arrived in the
midst of the ruins when he overtook me; and immediately after, we
observed the two Turks before-mentioned, lurking about, and were seen
by them. One of them, the sheree'f, was very near to us; and the other, at
no considerable distance. The former instantly came up to me, and stood
with his back towards me: his object seemed to be either to provoke me
to insult him, or else to keep near me till his companion could join him. I
retreated with my servant behind a mass of ruin; and we quickly
determined to attempt our escape by dodging among the ruins, and
taking care that we were not both exposed to the aim of the villains at the
same time, since, if one of us escaped it would be fatal to them, and
therefore they were not likely to attempt the life of one without being

---

[1]See again plate 9 [fig. 131].

sure of the other. This we did; and in this manner we happily regained the boat. There I found my good friend the Sheykh of the camels, whom I have before mentioned. He seemed delighted to see me; and wished to make a private communication to me. On my promising secresy [sic], he told me that he believed my life to be in danger from a certain soldier; whom I might know by his wearing a green turban; as he was the only sheree'f among the Turkish soldiers there. He assured me that this man had murdered several persons at Aswa'n; and that the governor overlooked his atrocities. My kind friend was not much surprised when I told him that I had just encountered and escaped the danger of which he warned me. On the following day I went again to the ruined town; but not unarmed: I wore my pistols and sabre; and my servant carried my gun. There again I found the two villains loitering: but on seeing me armed, they immediately retreated. I knew their disposition; and that I was not thus exposing myself to danger.

The only monument of the ancient Syene that is found among the ruined houses is a small temple, which has, most unreasonably, been regarded as the observatory of Syene. It is situated in the lower part of the ruined town, behind the grove of palm-trees which extends along the side of the river from the pier of the Mickya's, southwards. It is surrounded by rubbish and ruined walls of houses rising to its roof. We descend into two small chambers, without any sculptures, excepting some hieroglyphics round the entrance of the first, containing the name of the Emperor Nerva (Autocrator Nerva); proving (as the style of the building, and that of the hieroglyphics also shew) that this is one of the least ancient of the temples of Egypt. It faces the east. There was a portico before it; with four columns along the front; two of which have been partly thrown down. The first chamber is 12 feet wide, by 8 feet 1 inch and a half: the second is of the same width, by 6 feet 10 inches. The entrance of each is a little removed from the centre: between five and six inches nearer to the left side than to the right. The first chamber has a side-door, on the left. At the end of the second chamber, which was the sanctuary, is sculptured a kind of shrine, like a false door, surmounted by the winged globe: before this, was probably placed a monolithic granite shrine. There seem to have been other chambers on each side of the two above described. In both of these, the walls have been broken at the joints of the stones, for the purpose of taking out the cramps, which were probably of metal. There are apertures of the usual form for the admission of light.—As I had some difficulty in finding this temple, I took a bearing from it of the large sycamore on the island of Elephantine. This tree is just opposite, bearing W. 2° N. by compass.—Among the palm-trees just below the little temple, towards the south-west, are three granite columns, remaining erect, and what appears to have been a jamb of a granite door-way. There are also several fragments of similar columns close by. These certainly belonged to no very ancient building.

Travellers have searched in vain, among and near the remains of Syene, for the well in which the sun was seen reflected on the day of the summer solstice. I cannot regard as a fable the account of the Tropical Well of Syene; though this place is now more than 37 minutes to the north of the tropic. It has been calculated that the obliquity of the ecliptic diminishes at the rate of about one minute in 120 years: therefore Syene was under the tropic about forty-four centuries and a half ago. That period, if the chronology of the Hebrew bible were correct, was about two centuries and three quarters before the Deluge: but according to the chronology of the Septuagint, which is now generally preferred, it was five centuries *after* the Deluge. I suppose that, at that remote period, or somewhat later, the accidental observation of the sun's disk reflected in the bottom of a deep well at Syene, on the day of the summer solstice, excited surprise, and caused this well to be made use of afterwards, every year, for the purpose of making the same observation: but if the well continued to be so used, like an astronomical instrument, we must conclude that, as the obliquity of the ecliptic diminished, the diameter of the well was gradually enlarged.

We find no mention, in the works of ancient authors, of any other monuments for which we should look among the remains of Syene: but under the vast accumulation of crumbled walls, some relics of temples, beside that which I have described, are probably concealed. By digging among the rubbish, Arab coins, chiefly of copper, and Arab weights, of glass, are often found; as well as glass beads, &c. By sending a servant to many of the shops of the modern town, to offer new money for old (the old being used as weights by some of the trades people of Aswa'n), I procured three small copper coins, and eight specimens of the glass weights; all with inscriptions in the Koo'fee (or old Arabic) characters; but few legible. One of the coins is inscribed, on one side, "There is no deity but God, alone"; and on the reverse, "Mohham'mad is God's Apostle": one of the glass weights bears this inscription—"In the name of God. The weight of half ....." The last word is doubtful.

The ruins of the Arab town do not cover the whole of the space which was occupied by the city of Syene. They are surrounded by a thick wall of crude brick, with square towers; of which much yet remains in a very entire state. This town was celebrated for its extensive commerce, and for the fertility of the soil adjacent to it. It suffered much during the frequent wars between Egypt and Nubia.

The old Egyptian city of Syene is mentioned in two passages in the prophecies of Ezekiel (xxix, 10, and xxx, 6); but in our common translation, those passages are incorrectly rendered: instead of "from the tower of Syene" we should read "from Migdol to Syene." It was to this place that the poet Juvenal is said to have been banished by Domitian, with the title of governor of this frontier.

On the south of the ruined town is the old Arab Cemetery; which presents a striking scene.[1] It is very extensive; occupying an irregular, rocky tract: the hollow places among the rocks, which are of granite,

---

[1]See plate 10 [fig. 132].

being partly filled up with dark, granite sand, and rubbish; and the eminences of the rocks shewing themselves in many places among the tombs. By the modern inhabitants of Aswa'n, this is called the cemetery of the Sahha'beh (or Companions of the Prophet); and this appellation has probably not been given to it without reason; for doubtless many "companions" were buried here; soldiers of the first Arab army which took Syene, and founded the town of which the ruins have been described: and besides these there must have been many "companions" among the Moos'lims who first settled, and engaged in commerce, at Aswa'n. I could not, however, distinguish the tombs of any of these revered individuals. This cemetery must also contain the remains of many whom those of the same religion regard as martyrs; many who fell in the contests with the Nubians: for the latter, before their conversion to the Mohhammadan faith, often attacked Aswa'n. The tombs are constructed with crude brick, with few exceptions; and are, or have been, plastered and white-washed. Many of them are surmounted by cupolas. They are mostly very small; and much ruined. Among them are many small tablets, or tomb-stones, from a foot to three feet high, inscribed in the Koo'fee (or old Arabic) characters: generally in the *flexuous* style which came into use in the fourth century of the flight, and which has been improperly called, by European orientalists, "the Karmatic character." These inscriptions mostly begin with sentences from the Ckoor-a'n: next to which is generally added "O God! bless our lord Mohham'mad, and his pure family, and his companions": then follows the name of the deceased, and the date of his death. The dates of a great number (most of those that I examined) are between the years of the flight 410 and 430 (A.D. 1019-1039). I observed a great many of the inscriptions to begin with the short, but highly esteemed chapter called the Sum'adee'yeh (the 112th):—"In the name of God! the Compassionate! the Merciful!—Say, He is one God; God the Everlasting: He neither begets; nor is He begotten: and there is not any equal unto Him."—These tomb-stones are very numerous in the souther[n]most quarter of the cemetery. I saw a few of marble: but almost all of them are of sandstone. It would be difficult for a traveller to carry away one of them: for the people of Aswa'n regard them with the utmost reverence. One was pointed out to me bearing the mark of a bullet: I was told that a Turkish soldier, a short time before, had fired at it, and had dropt down dead immediately after the sacrilegious act.—On the hill to the west of this cemetery are several large sepulchral mosques.

The tract in which the cemetery lies is bounded on the east, as well as on the west, by granite hills. The hills on the eastern side are about a mile distant. They are quarried in numerous places. In one part is an unfinished obelisk, of large dimensions; and in many places are seen unfinished sarcophagi, columns, &c. It is probable that almost all the obelisks, granite colossi, &c., which adorned the temples of Egypt were from these and the neighbouring quarries. The granite rocks nearer to the Nile, towards the Cataracts, have also been quarried; but not so extensively as those just mentioned. Most of the granite is chiefly composed of red feldspath, intermixed with black mica, and bright, glassy quartz. Some is very dark, from the greater quantity of mica; and some is of a very coarse grain, black and white: the general colour is a dull red.

Through the old Arab cemetery lies the most frequented route towards Philæ; or rather to the place (to the north-east of the island of Philæ) where boats bound to the southward, or arriving from the south, receive or land their cargoes, which are conveyed by land from or to Aswa'n. About half-way from the modern Aswa'n to that place is a small *sebee'l*; a square building, with a large water jar within it, which is daily replenished from the Nile, for the sake of the passengers. Before and beyond this, we observe, on the left of the route, considerable remains of a very thick, but low wall, of crude brick. At first sight, one would imagine that this was designed to defend the land-communication between Egypt and Nubia from the wandering tribes of the eastern desert: but in some parts we find that the wall has a slope on the eastern side; and further southward, it is built sometimes close to the western hills; not leaving a passage on its western side. It is difficult, therefore, to decide for what purpose it was constructed. The people of Aswa'n call it *Hha'it El-'Agoo'z* (or "the Wall of the Old Woman"[)]. It is mentioned by Arab writers as the work of Deloo'keh, who was surnamed *El-'Agoo'z* (or the Old Woman[1]), a queen of Egypt before the Deluge! It is said to have surrounded Egypt. In several parts of the valley of Egypt, on the eastern side of the Nile, are seen remains of similar walls, which are likewise called Hha'it El-'Agoo'z, and are supposed to be portions of the same wall.—After proceeding a little beyond the small sebee'l above mentioned, we enter a narrow valley, running in an irregular course, and bounded on each side by rugged granite rocks, like the more open tract through which we have passed. The old wall continues nearly the whole of the way; but is broken at intervals; and in some parts it is on one side of the road, and in other parts on the other side. The hearting of this wall is of unhewn granite blocks: the rest, of large crude bricks. On the rocks, in various parts, are several rude inscriptions in hieroglyphics, and other designs which I need not particularize, as I shall presently give specimens of some similar sculptures, but more worthy of notice, on the rocks of an island, called Sahey'l, between Elephantine and the Cataracts. About midway in the contracted valley which I have described is a second sebee'l, which was built by 'Ab'dee Ka'shif, in gratitude for his safe return to Egypt from Senna'r. This is neat building, larger than the first, surmounted by two cupolas, and having an apartment on its north-eastern side, open towards the north-west, for passengers to rest and pray in: a niche in the back wall of this apartment shews the direction of Mek'keh.—On reaching the bank of the Nile at the end of the valley, we

---

[1] '*Agoo'z* properly signifies "an old woman"; but the modern Egyptians apply this word to an old *man*; and an old *woman* they call '*agoo'zeh*.

enjoy a striking view of the island of Philæ, which I must not yet describe: I have first to give an account of the islands and cataracts and banks of the Nile between Elephantine and Philæ.

Throughout this part of the river are numerous granite islands and small rocks; many of which become covered by the rising Nile. The mountains, or rather hills, on the eastern side of the river are also of granite; presenting many picturesque forms. Here and there, on this side of the river are a few palm-trees, and Nubian huts, with a small patch of door'ah. The bright verdure seen at these spots forms a singular contrast with the dark granite rocks. A quantity of grey, drifted sand lodges in the hollows, and around the bases of the rocks. The hills, or low mountains, on the western side of the river are of sandstone: their sides and bases covered with bright yellow sand. The few inhabitants of these parts are exclusively Nubians; and almost an amphibious race: many of them have no other employment than that of drawing boats up the cataracts. They are in general the most uncivil of any tribe of Nubians that I have met with. On my taking a walk to view the cataracts, one of these barbarians[1] accosted me, and demanded if I were the Frank whose boat was about to be drawn up the cataracts. I replied that I was an Englishman: not a Frank. "God curse the English and the Franks too," said the fellow: "it will not be thus when Mohham'mad Ba'sha is dead: if any of you then dare to come into our country, they will have our daggers in their bodies."—The Nubian generally has a small dagger attached to the left arm, a little above the elbow; and a very slight provocation induces him to draw it.

At the distance of about a mile above Elephantine, or a mile and a half from the modern town of Aswa'n, is an inhabited island, of rather less extent than Elephantine, near the eastern side of the river. It is opposite to a small village, or group of huts, on that side, called *El-Mahhat't*; which name signifies "a place where one halts on a journey, or unloads." This spot is so called because boats sometimes unload here when they have to ascend the cataracts: the cargo being conveyed along the bank, by camels, to the first port above the cataracts. The island above mentioned is called *Gezee'ret Sahey'l*, or *Soohey'l*, which might be interpreted "the Island of the star Conopus"; for *Soohey'l* is the name which the Arabs give to that star: but the ancient name of the island appears, from hieroglyphic inscriptions on its rocks, to have been *Sate*, or *Sete*. The god Kneph and the goddess Sate were the chief objects of worship in this part: the latter presided over the lower hemisphere; and perhaps Canopus, that most beautiful star of the southern hemisphere, was an emblem of her.—The island of Sahey'l, like the other islands in its vicinity, is mainly composed of heaps of granite rocks, which appear as if they had been thrown together by some convulsion of nature. Upon one

---

[1] The term *Bur'ber'ee* (in the plural *Bera'b'rah*, for *Bera'bireh*), which, in Egypt, is always applied to a Nubian, is also the appellation of a people of Northern Africa, and is the origin of the term *barbarian*.

of these natural piles of granite rocks, at the southern end of the island, are many hieroglyphic inscriptions and other sculptures, rudely and slightly cut; but in a good style. They are very ancient. Among the names which they bear are those of Osirtesen 3rd, Amonoph 2nd and 3rd, Rameses 2nd and 5th, Osiree 2nd, and a few others. The figures and hieroglyphic characters appear like paintings, rather than sculptures; being much lighter than the uncut surface of the rock. I insert copies of some of them, which will serve as specimens of their general nature and style.[1]—This island contains a little cultivable soil. Towards the western side are some relics of a temple, which, from the style of the hieroglyphics upon some of the overthrown blocks, appears to have been a bad Ptolemaic or Roman work: so little of it remains that it is impossible to judge of its plan: but it seems to have been small: I could find no name among its hieroglyphics.

Proceeding about a mile above this island, we arrive at the commencement of the cataracts. From some spots, at the distance of nearly two miles, I heard the roaring of the cataracts; but in proceeding up the bank of the river, I did not hear their sound until I had arrived within about half a mile. The cataracts are called in Arabic *esh-Shila'l*; and the same term is applied to them by the Nubians: it signifies merely "the rapids." I insert a view which embraces the principal falls,[2] and shews the operation of drawing up my boat. At the moment when I began to sketch the boat, she had arrived at the second fall, and the men having slightly relaxed in their exertions, the violence of the current had turned her from the right course, and a great effort was required to bring her head to meet the stream. In spite of all the force that was applied by nearly seventy men, the boat remained, apparently, perfectly stationary long enough for me to sketch it in leisurely with my camera.[†] It required no less than six hours to draw up the boat from El-Mahhat't to the first village above the cataracts. The river was nearly at the lowest at the period when my view was taken. The lower the river, the more considerable, of course, are the falls. The river has no perpendicular fall; but it shoots down at an angle of twenty or thirty degrees between the masses of rock; and the length of the descent is sometimes as much as about thirty feet. During the period of the inundation, boats may, with a strong northerly breeze, sail up the rapids, which then merely foam, and form eddies, but have no perceptible fall. We cannot but wonder at the exaggerated descriptions of these "cataracts" which we find in the works of some ancient authors; but our wonder is somewhat diminished when we reflect that the bed of the river has risen about seven feet during the last eighteen centuries; and that these falls were, therefore, far more considerable than they are now. We may presume that, after the lapse of eighteen more centuries, the bed of the river will have risen so much that

[1]See no. 46 of the subjects for wood-cuts [fig. 133].
[2]See plate 11 [fig. 134].
[†]I.e., with his camera lucida.

there will be scarcely any fall of water here. We are told by Cicero (Somn. Scip.) that the noise of the cataracts was so great that the people residing in the neighbourhood were, in consequence, deaf. The present Ba'sha of Egypt proposed to cut, through the rocks of the cataracts, a passage which should be easily navigable during the greater portion of the year; and I was informed that a few masses of rock were removed; but nothing more was done.

The first port above the cataracts, or the first convenient place for landing and embarking, is about a mile higher, on the eastern bank. A small village is there situated; with a few palm-trees. It is called *El-Mo'rideh*, or "the landing-place." The boats which ascend the cataracts generally reload here. From a point about half a mile further, we have a view of the isle of Philæ.

While my boat was made fast to the bank, one evening, hereabouts, on my return from the south, a party of women who had composed the hharee'm of Mel'ik Nimr (King[1] of Shen'deh), and who had been sent from the Turkish army in Senna'r to be sold as slaves in Egypt, but liberated and sent back by Mohham'mad 'Al'ee, came to me begging alms, and shewing their long fingers to prove their high birth.

---

[1]The title of Mel'ik (or King) is applied to the independent chiefs of several small districts in Nubia.

Chapter XXXI.
Philæ, and its environs.

General remarks—Roman gateway—Peristyle temple—Ruins of the town of Bila'ck—Small temple of Athor—Galleries before the great temple— Description of the great temple, and other monuments—Island of Big'eh—Sculptures, &c., on the eastern bank of the Nile.

The isle of Philæ is a magnificent and most picturesque object, from whatever direction it is viewed: but the traveller is most forcibly struck with its majestic appearance when he first beholds it after winding along the narrow valley which I have described, or along the rugged bank of the river. Φιλαι and *Plilæ* are the names by which this little island, the generally-reputed burial-place of Osiris, was [were] known to the Greeks and Romans. The ancient Egyptians probably called it, like the later Ckoobt (or Copts), *Pilakh*. In the works of Arab authors, it has the name of *Bila'ck* بلاق. At present it is called by several different names:— *Gezee'ret el-Ckusr* (or the Island of the Palace); *Gezee'ret el-Bir'ba* (or the Island of the Temple); and *Gezee'ret En'es el-Woogoo'd*, or— *Woojoo'd* (which has been supposed to be derived from a tradition of its having been a place devoted to the social pleasures of a king named El-Woogoo'd).

This island is a quarter of a mile in length, and rather less than half that measure, or about 500 feet, in width. A much larger island lies on the west of it; and to the west of the latter is another still larger. Both of these are, like Philæ, composed of granite rocks, with a few small tracts of alluvial soil deposited by the river. The eastern shore of the Nile stretches round Philæ in a semicircular form. From this bank I made a view of the island,[1] shewing all its most remarkable monuments, and, in the distance, part of the island of Big'eh, which is the island next to Philæ, on the west.[†]

In this view, towards the right, is seen a ruined structure resembling a triumphal arch. It is evidently a Roman work; and was probably merely an ornament of the principal landing-place.

Proceeding hence to the southward, along the bank of the island, we arrive at a handsome peristyle temple; a rich and elegant building, though

---

[1]See plate 12. no. 1 [fig. 135].

[†]The island of Philae is almost entirely submerged now. The temple has been resited on the nearby island of Agilkia, just north of Biga island. Agilkia was originally the northern part of Biga island, but became separated from it after the construction of the dams Aswan.

of Roman times, and unfinished.[†] The front of this temple, which is towards the river, is 48 feet wide: the length is 63 feet. Before it is a platform of stone, strongly built; and in front of this is a little port, in which my boat lay. I generally slept upon the stone terrace during my stay here; the night-air being then very mild and pleasant. The temple consists of fourteen columns, connected by a wall of half their height, excepting at each end, where there is a door-way between the two middle columns. Besides the four columns at the angles, there are two at each end, and three others in each side. The capitals are very rich, and of different forms, with small volutes: those which are in corresponding situations are similar to each other. Above the capital of each column is a mass of almost a cubic form; but its height is rather greater than its breadth: each of these, had the temple been finished, would probably have been sculptured with the figure of Typhon; as at Den'dar'ah and Ad'foo. In the interior, the sculpture has been commenced, on the intercolumnal walls on the left (or southern) side; and is of the most elaborately finished kind; and in some respects very tasteful. Here we find the name of Trajan, and (if I have not mistaken one of my notes) that of Augustus also. There are cavities at the top of the architraves on each side, apparently for rafters, to support a roof of wood. The building could not have been roofed with stone, unless pillars, or a chamber, had been erected in the interior. I should think, however, that it had been designed to construct a sanctuary within it. As it is, there being a clear way through it, this edifice seems like an appertenance to the great temple.

From a high mass of granite rocks, at the south-eastern angle of the island, we have a fine view of the great temple and the structures connected with it.[‡] Of this scene I made a drawing.[1] The whole intermediate space is covered by the ruined walls and rubbish of crude-brick houses; the remains of the town of which El-Idree'see, El-Muckree'zee, and other Arab authors speak. The former of these writers mentions Bila'ck[2] (i.e. Philæ) as a town situated between two branches of the Nile; and adds that the boats of the negroes descended the Nile thence to the cataracts, which prevented their entering Egypt. El-Muckree'zee (in whose time the town of Bila'ck had become the residence of Moos'lims) says "Bila'ck is the last place that belongs to the Moos'lims: it is an island near the cataracts, surrounded by the waters of the Nile: it contains a large and populous town, with fine palm-trees; and

---

[†]The Kiosk of Trajan.
[‡]This "high mass of granite rocks" is the only portion of the island that remains above water.
[1]See plate 13 [fig. 136].
[2]In the printed editions erroneously written Ialac and بلاق. The printed text and translation of this author abound with errors.

a congregational mosque, with a pulpit."[1] At present, instead of containing a populous town (which, we see, covered the greater part of the island) Philæ has no other inhabitants than a single family, consisting of two old women and two young girls: but it is occasionally visited by people from the eastern shore, who carry away the rubbish of the old houses to use as manure. The traveller, therefore, may examine its monuments in agreeable solitude: he is not annoyed by the old women until he is about to quit the island; when he is solicited for a present.—In the view above mentioned is seen, at the right extremity, a part of the peristyle temple which I have already described: beyond the brick ruins are the great temple, the galleries before it, &c. In the distance is seen, between the first propylæum of the great temple and the left extremity of the view, a part of the high and rocky island of Big'eh, with a ruin of a temple.

The first six columns that are seen at the left extremity of the view just described, do not form a part of the long colonnade which extends nearly to the first propylæum of the great temple, but belong to a small temple of Athor, the Egyptian Venus. This ruin bears, among its hieroglyphics, the name of Nectanebo, as its founder. This king was the last king of Egypt, or the last but two, before the second conquest of that country by the Persians: but his was the oldest name that I found at Philæ. All the monuments on the island, excepting this little edifice and a portal of the great temple (between the two wings of the first propylæum) are of the Ptolemaic or Roman times: but Philæ certainly contained more ancient monuments, which were probably destroyed by the Persians. The little temple of Athor is situated almost close to the south-western angle of the island. The six columns which remain erect formed, together with intercolumnal walls about half their height, the western side of the temple. Six other columns formed the eastern side; and the extreme columns of each of these sides with two others between them formed the front and the back. The front was towards the north: that is, towards the great temple. The capitals of the columns are rich and varied; and each is surmounted by the high block with the full face of Athor carved on each of its four sides. On a stone wall, which encases the bank of the island on the south of this little temple, were two small obelisks; each in a line with the oblong sides of the temple; but at unequal distances; the wall not being parallel with the back of the little temple. One of these obelisks only remains; and its pyramidal top has been broken off. It is of sandstone; and, probably, of no very ancient date; being without hieroglyphics. Several Greek inscriptions have been engraved upon it: among these is the *proscynema* of King Ptolemy Dionysus Philopator

---

[1]Burckhardt says (see his Travels in Nubia, &c., p. 533) "It might be supposed that Belak (or Bila'ck) was upon the island of Philæ, but in that case there is no place, one mile in advance of Philæ, where we can place El Kaszer" (or El-Ckusr). The remains of El-Ckusr are, however, recognized a mile above Philæ: they were not seen by Burckhardt; as he passed over the mountains behind that spot.

and Philadelphus, and of his children, to the goddess Isis and the cotemplar divinities.

From the little temple of Athor commences a handsome gallery, which extends to the length of about 250 feet along the western side of the island, towards the front of the great temple; thus bounding the approach to that temple on the left side. A wall of stone, which encases, and defends from the inundations, that side of the island, is built up so as to form the back of the gallery. The front is composed of a fine row of columns; and long stones extend from the architraves of the columns to the top of the back-wall; forming the roof of the gallery. Thirty columns yet remain. Almost all of these have capitals of different forms; some of them, rich and beautiful, others, rather inelegant; but the colonnade altogether has a very handsome appearance. The back-wall has ten windows, at unequal distances from one another. From these we have an agreeable view of the stream below, and of the rocky island opposite. The whole of the interior of the wall is decorated with sculptures, which bear the names of Tiberius, Claudius, and Nero. These emperors are represented offering to various divinities. A part of the wall, about the middle, has fallen down; and many of the roof-stones have also fallen. A stair-case, constructed beneath the gallery, near the middle, leads down, in a transverse direction, to the river.

Opposite this gallery is another, of similar construction; but not so long; consisting of only sixteen columns in front; and in a very unfinished state. It is not parallel with the other; being 56 feet distant at the southern end, and 78 at the northern. The long, narrow court between these two galleries is encumbered with the ruined walls of houses of unburnt brick; like all the rest of the southern part of the island. This formed the principal approach to the great temple; but is not directed towards the centre of the propylæum.

Between the end of the eastern gallery and the front of the propylæum is a portal, forming a side entrance to the area before the temple. The sculptures of this bear the name of a Ptolemy, supposed to be that of Philadelphus. On the inner side is also the name of Tiberius Cæsar.

The general plan of the great temple,[1] with its two propylæa, exhibits remarkable irregularities, which are thus accounted for.—There was an older temple, nearly on the same site, anterior to the second invasion of Egypt by the Persians, who, it appears, destroyed this temple, with the exception only of one portal, which is that to which the two wings of the first propylæum have been added. Ptolemy Philadelphus began the temple now existing; and perhaps intending to pull down the portal above mentioned, did not found his new building with reference to this portal, so as to make the latter in the direct line of approach to the temple. All that he built was the main body of the temple; or the sanctuaries; which formed a complete edifice. Epiphanes next

---

[1]See plate 12, no. 2 [fig. 135, inset].

constructed the temple of Athor[1]; a distinct building, at a little distance before the former. Physcon then built the portico of the first temple; and its portal; and he deviated from regularity in the plan evidently in order to make this portal nearly in a direct line with that which the Persians had left standing: doubtless intending to add the wings to each of these portals. These wings, forming the two propylæa, were perhaps constructed in his reign, and left unsculptured: their sculptures were executed in the reign of a later Ptolemy, whose name I copied, but I do not know to which of Physcon's successors it applies.[2]

The first propylæum, which is the greater of the two, has two door-ways; the portal between the two wings, and a smaller door-way nearly in the middle of the left wing. Before the principal entrance were two obelisks, of small dimensions; both of which have been removed: one of them is now in England: Belzoni removed and embarked it for Mr. W. J. Bankes. There were also placed before the entrance two granite lions, in a sitting posture: they are lying on the ground among the rubbish: the heads, broken off. The portal between the two wings of the propylæum is seen, at a glance, to be more ancient than the structures connected with it. Its sculptures, which are much defaced, yet partially retain the paint with which they were adorned. They bear the name of Nectanebo; the founder of the little temple of Athor already described. The propylæum is 122 feet wide. It is covered with colossal sculptured figures, in a very bad style, which detract very much from the grandeur of the effect of this noble pile, when viewed on a near approach. The Ptolemy under whom these sculptures were executed is here represented sacrificing a numerous group of captives, whom he holds by the hair of their heads, before Isis; the goddess to whom this temple was chiefly dedicated. The sculptures on the upper part of the front of each wing, which are on a less colossal scale, exhibit the same prince presenting offerings. There are also, on the front of this propylæum, several Greek inscriptions, of the times of the Ptolemies and Roman Emperors. Some of these were engraved before the sculptures which I mentioned previously. To the right of the portal, for instance, are some Greek inscriptions which are interrupted by the figure of Isis: they commence a little to the left of this figure; and the continuations of several of the lines are seen upon those parts of the body of the goddess which are in the same plane with the face of the structure: the figure being (as are all the others) in relieved intaglio. They merely record acts of worship to Isis.

The portal between the two wings of the first propylæum leads into a court between the two propylæa; and the door in the left wing of the first propylæum leads directly to the temple of Athor which extends along the left side of that court. On entering the court, the traveller is particularly struck with the irregularity of the plan.—On the right (or eastern) side is a gallery formed by a row of columns in front of a

---

[1] A *little* temple of Athor, before described, is not the building here alluded to.
[2] Supposed, by Mr. Wilkinson, to be Dionysus.

structure which consists of a series of small cells, with a side-entrance to the court. The sculptures bear the name of the same Ptolemy who is represented on the propylæa. The small cells here mentioned were probably lodgings for the priests.

The Temple of Athor, which extends along the left side of the court, appears to have been built by Ptolemy Epiphanes, and finished by Physcon and the later Ptolemy above alluded to, and Augustus. The front[1] is towards the back of the western wing of the first propylæum of the great temple; and the door-way, or passage, through that wing leads directly to its front-entrance. Within this passage are some curious sculptures. On the left side, among other subjects, is a female playing on a harp, before Athor, and a row of females beating the tambourine. Upon the opposite side are eight apes, arranged in two rows, adoring this goddess; and along the base are figures of the hermaphrodite god Nilus; each carrying some offering: one of them bears a small figure of an elephant: this is the only case in which I have observed this animal represented on an Egyptian monument; and it has been remarked as singular that it should only be found on an island the name of which bears so near a resemblance to the Arabic name of an Elephant, which is *Feel.*—The fore part of the temple to which this passage is directed is a small portico. The front is formed by two columns; and two other columns, within, support the roof. They have, above the capital, the high block with the full face of Athor sculptured on each of the four sides. This portico is in an unfinished state; but those sculptures which have been completed are painted, with brilliant colours. From it we pass into the main body of the temple; which consists of three sanctuaries; one behind another. Over the door leading to these chambers is a Greek dedicatory inscription, as follows—ΒΑΣΙΛΕΥΣ ΠΤΟΛΕΜΑΙΟΣ ΚΑΙ ΒΑΣΙΛΙΣΣΑ ΚΛΕΟΠΑΤΡΑ Η ΑΔΕΛΦΗ ΚΑΙ ΒΑΣΙΛΙΣΣΑ ΚΛΕΟΠΑΤΡΑ Η ΓΥΝΗ ΘΕΟΙ ΕΥΡΓΕΤΑΙ ΑΦΡΟΔΙΤΗΙ—This dedication of Physcon is also sculptured along the upper part of the walls, in hieroglyphics.—The walls of the three sanctuaries are so blackened, and bedaubed with mud, that the sculptures are almost concealed. Upon the end-wall of the last chamber is represented Athor sitting upon her heels, with the young Horus on her lap; and above this piece is sculptured a large hawk, an emblem of Horus.—The main body of this building, being narrower than the portico, is surrounded by a covered gallery, the roof of which is supported by columns. Upon the upper part of the exterior of the right (or eastern) side-wall of the portico is a hieroglyphic inscription of "Ptolemy and Cleopatra, the gods Epiphanes," with a corresponding inscription in the enchorial characters. Large figures, subsequently sculptured, unfortunately interrupt this interesting record in several parts. The other side of this temple, which faces the river, is in an unfinished state. Opposite this side is a small, unfinished portal.—On the roof of the temple above described are ruins of crude-brick houses; and

---

[1]See, again, the plan, plate 12, no. 2 [fig. 135, inset].

there are similar ruins on the roof of the structure on the opposite side of the court between the two propylæa.

On the back of the first (or great) propylæum are sculptures of the same age and kind as those on the front. The sculptures on the front of the second propylæum are also of the same age as those on the first: the subjects, merely offerings. A considerable portion of the front of the left wing of this propylæum is concealed by the temple of Athor. At the base of the right wing is a small chamber, or cell, with a door surmounted by the winged globe. Its hieroglyphics bear the names of the Emperor (Autocrator) Cæsar, Domitianus Sebastos, and the Emperor Cæsar, Trajanus Adrianus. This small structure is built close against the front of the propylæum, to enclose, or screen, a sculptured granite rock, which forms a part of the foundation of the propylæum; existing there, apparently, by nature; the heart of the island being entirely of granite. The front of this mass of rock has been cut smooth, and sculptured with a row of figures along the upper part, and several lines of hieroglyphics beneath. The subjects of the former are offerings to the deities of the temple. The inscription bears the names of Ptolemy Physcon and his wife Cleopatra; and is dated in the 24th year of the reign of that prince. This mass of granite appears like a tablet set up against the wall: its top is of an arched form; and is ornamented with the winged globe: its length is fifteen feet and a half.

Through the portal of the second propylæum, built by Physcon, we pass into the portico, or pronaos, which was also constructed under the same Ptolemy; his name being found among all its sculptures. This is the most beautiful part of the temple. It contains ten columns; eight at the end, and one other on each side: the space between these two, and between the back of the propylæum and the columns at the end, being open to the sky. There were originally intercolumnal walls, which divided the portico into two parts; but these have been cut away. The columns are constructed of the remains of an older building; for in one of them we find a block with inverted hieroglyphics, which had been concealed by an intercolumnal wall. The sculptures here have all been painted with the most brilliant colours, which, in some parts, appear almost fresh; particularly on the capitals of the columns: these are painted chiefly with light green and blue; and have a very beautiful effect; their forms being rich and tasteful: one of them, an imitation of the head of the palm-tree, is remarkably elegant. The subjects of the sculptures on the walls are the usual offerings: but some of those on the ceiling, between the architraves of the columns, are very curious. In the easternmost compartment of the ceiling are represented two female figures, with their arms and legs extended at right angles with the body: they are emblematic of the firmament; and are bending over a male figure, an emblem of the earth, lying in a strange, distorted attitude. The other compartments of the ceiling are occupied by representations of boats, winged globes, scarabæi, and birds: in each of the boats is a circle, within which is the figure of some divinity.—The exterior of the portico is also sculptured; and bears the name of Tiberius Cæsar.—The portico has a side-entrance, on the left (or west), next the back of the propylæum.

Immediately beyond the portico is the most ancient part of the temple, built in the reign of Philadelphus. It is divided into many small chambers; all of which are sculptured; but the walls of most of them are much blackened and defiled by bats. In the first of these chambers we observe, among the sculptures on the left side, Thoth and a hawk-headed deity, each pouring a stream of alternate *cruces ansatæ* and sceptres (the emblems of life and power) over the Ptolemy. The figures of the gods are much blackened, like many of the other sculptures in this chamber; but enough of the paint is seen to shew that the former was green, and the other either the same colour or blue: the colour of the king is, as usual, red. An ingenious interpretation of this sculpture has been formed on the supposition that the two figures of the gods were of a *black* complexion. On the same side of this chamber is a minor entrance to the temple, crossing a narrow passage, from which a flight of stairs ascends, northward, to the roof. On the *right* side of the first chamber is a small apartment; the partition-walls of which, both towards the former chamber and towards another small apartment on the north, are broken down. At the end of the second of these small apartments is a narrow passage, with stairs descending to a little square chamber below.— Beyond the chamber which is next behind the portico are three others; one behind another; but the walls are so black and defiled by the bats that it is almost impossible to see the sculptures; the light being only admitted by the door-ways. There are smaller apartments on each side of these. From the second of the three central chambers we enter two other chambers, on the right and left of the third of the former. In that on the right is a monolithic granite shrine, placed upright at the end, in the right-hand corner. It is 7 feet 6 inches high, and 2 feet 8 inches wide. In the upper part is a square niche, 2 feet 10 inches high, 1 foot four inches wide, and 2 feet 6 inches deep. In the central sanctuary, on the lower portion of a similar shrine, lying among the rubbish on the ground, are three ovals which contain the names of Ptolemy and Berenice.— Ascending the stairs before mentioned, we arrive at a small chamber, about 6 feet and a half in length, and 4 feet in width, the walls of which are covered with mysterious sculptures, representing the death, embalming, and resurection, of Osiris. On the left and right walls, the sculptures, which are arranged in three horizontal rows, exhibit, in the first and second rows, a king (the oval for his name left blank) offering incense and paying worship to a series of gods, almost the entire pantheon, some with the heads of frogs, serpents, &c. The lowest row of sculptures on these two walls consists of representations of standards, mostly surmounted by the figures of birds and beasts, and held, alternately, by *cruces ansatæ*, and sceptres, each with human hands and arms. On the end-wall is represented the embalming, with the funeral-ceremonies, &c., of Osiris. In the middle row of sculptures here we see the god stretched on a lion-shaped couch, and shewing signs of animation and vigour: Nep[h]thys is at the head, and Isis at the feet, bewailing. Next to this are two females, who seem to be removing the intestines. Then the god, as a mummy, with a hawk's head, is borne by the four genii of Amenti. In the lowest row, Osiris, still as a mummy, is laid upon a lion-shaped couch; beneath which are the four jars mentioned, and which contain the intestines of the deceased: the hawk-headed Horus is at the head, and Isis, with the head of a cow, at the feet. Next, the mummy is represented placed on a bier, among some water-plants. Then, again, we see it on a lion-shaped couch: Anubis standing by. On the front-wall of this little chamber are sculptures of a more mysterious nature. In the lowest row is a tree enclosed in a shrine; and two figures are worshipping it.

The interior of Egyptian temples was generally sculptured first. The exterior of the main body of that which I am describing is sculptured; and bears the name of the Emperor Augustus (Autocrator Cæsar). The exterior of the portico, I have already mentioned, was sculptured in the reign of Tiberius. These exterior sculptures merely exhibit the princes under whom they were executed presenting offerings to Isis and other divinities.

In the interior of each of the two propylæa are stairs, by which we ascend to the summit. The view of the temple, of the whole island and its other monuments, and of the surrounding scenery, from the top of the great propylæum is of a very remarkable, wild, and grand character. The cataracts are not distinguished from this point; but their murmur, on a still day, is distinctly heard.

On the west of this temple, directly before the side-door of the portico, and close to the wall which encases that side of the island, is a small, unfinished portal, with two walls forming a passage from it towards the temple. On the interior sides of these two walls are some very curious sculptures. On the left, as one goes from the temple, over a small side-door, is represented a mummy on the back of a crocodile, which is crawling among the rushes of the Nile: above is a circle, in which are seated two figures, much defaced; the foremost is Harpocrates; the other has his arm raised behind him in the attitude of the Priapian god: to the left of the circle is a figure of Isis; much injured; and over the whole is a row of stars, with the sun at one end and the moon at the other. This design seems to relate to the death of Osiris; and, if so, aptly found on this island, his reputed burial-place. On the same wall are represented several small shrines, in the form of portals; to each of which, offerings are presented. These sculptures are carefully finished, and have been delicately coloured. On the opposite wall is a remarkable representation of the masculo-feminine god Nilus, encircled by a serpent; above which is a high pile of granite rocks, with a hawk and a vulture perched upon it. This device, at the spot where the Nile passes the high piles of rocks above the cataracts, is very appropriate and striking. Along the cornice of each of these walls is a series of ovals containing the titles and names of the Emperors Marcus Aurelius and Lucius Verus.

On the east of the great temple is a small chapel dedicated to Asclepius. It was built, or at least sculptured, under Ptolemy Epiphanes. On the front is the following inscription.

ΒΑΣΙΛΕΥΣΠΤΟΛΕΜΑΙΟΣΚΑΙΒΑΣΙΛΙΣΣΑΚΛΕΟΠΑΤΡΑ
ΘΕΟΙΕΠΙΦΑΝΕΙΣΚΑΙΠΤΟΛΕΜΑΙΟΣΥΙΟΣΑΣΚΛΗΠΙΩΙ

Over this is a long line of hieroglyphics. The sculptures exhibit nothing remarkable.

A little to the north are some ruined stone walls, probably the remains of a church or mosque.

The Island of Big'eh, or Bij'eh, بجه , on the west of Philæ, is much larger than the latter isle, and high and rocky. On its eastern side is a ruin of a temple; the position of which is seen in my general view of the great temple of Philæ. It consists of little more than a portal and two columns with a door-way between them. This edifice appears to have been built in the reign of the latest of the Ptolemies who added to the great temple of Philæ. An arch has been built in the portal in later times.—Upon the granite rocks of this island are several hieroglyphic inscriptions, similar to those of the island of Sahey'l.

On the bank of the river, to the north of the isle of Philæ, is a singular granite rock, or cluster of rocks, called *El-Koorsee*, or "The Chair." Upon it are several hieroglyphic names and other inscriptions. The most conspicuous of these is the name of Psammitichus 1st: the two ovals containing it are enclosed in a square.

Behind the strip of cultivated land which borders the Nile to the east of Philæ are several rudely-excavated mummy-pits. These are the only ancient tombs that have been discovered near Philæ.

During four days which I passed chiefly at Philæ before I proceeded on my voyage to the southward, the greatest height of the thermometer, in the shade, was 97°. Its greatest height during eight days which I spent at this island on my return, in July, 108°.

Chapter XXXII.
The Nubians.

Section I. General description of the country between the First and Second Cataracts; and history of the Nubians to the period of the last invasion of their country, by the troops of Mohham'mad 'Al'ee.

El-Muckree'zee gives the following correct description of the country between the First and Second Cataracts, extracted from the history of Nubia written by Ibn Selee'm El-Aswa'nee.

"This district is narrow, and very mountainous; extending but little from the Nile. Its villages are far apart, one from another, on each bank. Its trees are the date-palm and the *moockl*.[1] The higher parts of this district are wider than the lower; and in the former, the vine is cultivated. The fields are not naturally irrigated by the Nile: being too elevated: the inhabitants sow by the fedda'n,[2] or two fedda'ns, or three[3]; and employ cows to raise the water from the river by means of wheels. Wheat is scarce among them: barley is more plentiful; and *soolt*.[4] They cultivate and sow the land a second time (every year); on account of its being so confined. In the summer, after having manured it with dung and earth, they sow dookhn,[5] door'ah,[6] ja'wur's,[7] sim'sim,[8] and loo'biya."[9]

From the following passages in the work of Ibn Selee'm, it appears that the whole of the country which we call Nubia was formerly inhabited by two races, the *Noo'beh* and the *Moock'rah*. These names were also given to their respective districts.

"The *Noo'beh* النوبه and the *Moock'rah* المُقْره (or, according to the Cka'moo's, the *Moock'ra* المُقْرى) are two different races, with two different languages; both inhabiting the banks of the Nile. The Noo'beh,

---

[1] This (as I have shewn in a note to an extract from El-Muckree'zee following my remarks on Ckoo's, or Goo's) is another name for the do'm-tree.

[2] The *fedda'n* is now equal to about an acre and one tenth: it was formerly a little more.

[3] This seems to have been (as conjectured by Burckhardt) the extent of land irrigated by one sa'ckiyeh.

[4] A kind of barley. (Burckhardt.)

[5] A small kind of millet.

[6] Millet.

[7] Another kind of millet.

[8] Sesame.

[9] Kidney-beans.

who are also called the *Meree's*,[1] border on the country of the Moos'lims (or Egypt); and between their first town (El-Ckusr[2]) and Aswa'n is a distance of five miles. It is said that Sel'ha, the forefather of the Noo'beh, and Moock'ra (or Moock'ree), the forefather of the Moock'rah, were natives of the Yem'en; and likewise that the Noo'beh and Moock'rah were descendants of Khem'yar: but most genealogists agree that both are descended from Hha'm the son of Noo'hh (Ham the son of Noah). It is said that there were frequent wars between the Noo'beh and the Moock'rah, before the introduction of Christianity among them. The district of the Moock'rah commences at a town called Ta'feh, a day's journey from Aswa'n; and their capital is Bejra'sh, which is less than ten days' journey from Aswa'n. It is related that Moo'sa (or Moses), upon whom be the blessing of God, before his mission in the days of Pharaoh, waged war with these people, and destroyed Ta'feh: they were then Sabæans, worshipping the stars to which they erected idols. In later times they embraced Christianity; both the Noo'beh and Moock'rah."

From a statement in the foregoing extract it would seem that the Noo'beh occupied but a small district in comparison with that of the Moock'rah, which is there said to have commenced at Ta'feh, one day's journey, only, above Aswa'n: but El-Muckree'zee gives another extract from Ibn Selee'm's work which states that the district of the Meree's (that is, of the Noo'beh) extended beyond Sa'y, and near to Dun'ckal'ah, or Dun'gal'ah; and that from their southern frontier commenced the district of the Moock'rah, which included Dun'ckal'ah.[3] Above the district of Dun'ckal'ah and the territory of the Sha'ckee'yeh or the Sha'gee'yeh Arabs is a district still called *Moockra't*.

The inhabitants of Nubia followed the example of the Ckoobt (or Copts) in embracing the Eutychian doctrines. They were rendered tributary to the Moos'lim Arabs in the same year in which the latter conquered Egypt, or in the year following.—The subjoined extract from the work of Ibn Selee'm is quoted by El-Muckree'zee.

"The *buckt*[4] was received from the Noo'beh at the town called El-Ckusr, between Bila'ck (or Philæ) and the country of the Noo'beh. The imposts of El-Ckusr belonged to the province of Ckoo's. The buckt of the Noo'beh was first instituted during the government of 'Amr Ibn El-'A'see, who sent 'Abd Al'lah the son of Saad the son of Ab'oo Sarhh, after the conquest of Egypt, to the country of the Noo'beh, in the year 20 or 21 (A.D. 641-42), at the head of 20,000 men. He remained there a long time, until 'Amr wrote to him, and commanded him to return. At

---

[1] A little above Debo'd is a tract still called Meree's, with a ruined town at (or near to) its northern extremity.

[2] See the map [fig. 122].

[3] The Koonoo'z, another tribe, now inhabit a part of what belonged to the Noo'beh; from Aswa'n to Wa'dee es-Sooboo'ă.

[4] The buckt was an annual tribute of slaves, which the Noo'beh, as Christians, paid to their Moos'lim conquerors.

the death of 'Amr—God be well pleased with him—The Noo'beh broke
the treaty of peace which had been concluded with them by 'Abd Al'lah
Ibn Saad, and made many incursions into the Sa'ee'd, laying waste and
ruining the country. 'Abd Al'lah Ibn Saad Ibn Ab'ee Sarhh attacked
them a second time; he being then Governor of Egypt, in the reign of the
Khalee'feh 'Osma'n—God be well pleased with him—in the year 31. He
besieged them very closely in the city of Dun'ckal'ah, and launched
stones into the town with catapults; machines with which the Noo'beh
were unacquainted; and thus his soldiers shattered the church. This
terrified the Noo'beh; and their king, whose name was Ckaleedoro't,
demanded peace. He came forth to 'Abd Al'lah with every sign of
weakness and misery and humility. 'Abd Al'lah met him, and raised him
up, and caused him to approach, and concluded a treaty of peace with
him, on condition that he should pay a tribute of three hundred and sixty
head of slaves every year. 'Abd Al'lah also promised to send him grain;
as he (the king of the Noo'beh) complained of scarcity of provision in his
country. A writing was then drawn up, of which the following is a copy.

"After the bismi-l'lah—'This is a treaty granted by the Emeer 'Abd
Al'lah Ibn Saad Ibn Ab'ee Sarhh to the chief of the Noo'beh and to all
the people of his dominions; a treaty binding on the great and the small
among the Noo'beh, from the frontier of Aswa'n to the frontier of
'Al'weh. 'Abd Al'lah Ibn Saad establishes safety and peace between them
and the Moos'lims who are their neighbours in the Sa'ee'd, as well as the
other Moos'lims and their tributaries. Ye people of Noo'beh, ye shall be
in security, under the safeguard of God and his Apostle, Mohham'mad
the Prophet—God bless and save him. We will not attack you, nor wage
war with you, nor make any incursions against you, as long as ye shall
abide by the conditions now settled between us and you. When ye enter
our country, it shall be only as travellers; not as settlers; and when we
enter your country, it shall be only as travellers; not as settlers. Ye shall
protect those Moos'lims, or their allies, who arrive in your country and
travel there, until they quit it. Ye shall give up the slaves of Moos'lims
who seek refuge among you, and send them back to the country of the
Isla'm; and likewise the refugee Moos'lim who is at war with the
Moos'lims; ye shall expel him from your country to the country of the
Isla'm: ye shall not embrace his cause; nor prevent his being seized. Ye
shall not put any obstacle in the way of a Moos'lim; but shall render him
assistance until he quits your country. Ye shall take care of the mosque
which the Moos'lims have built in the suburb of your city; and not
prevent any one from praying there: ye shall clean it, and light it, and
honour it. Every year ye shall pay three hundred and sixty head of slaves
to the Ima'm of the Moos'lims (the Khalee'feh), of the middle class of
slaves of your country, without bodily defects; males and females; but no
old men, nor old women, nor young children: ye shall deliver them to
the Governor of Aswa'n. No Moos'lim shall be obliged to repulse an
enemy from you, or to attack him, or hinder him; from the province of
'Al'weh to that of Aswa'n. If ye receive a Moos'lim's slave, or kill a

Moos'lim or an ally (of our's), or attempt to destroy the mosque which the Moos'lims have built in the suburb of your city, or with hold any of the three hundred and sixty head of slaves, this promised peace and security will be retracted from you, and we shall return to enmity, until God shall judge between us; and He is the best of judges. For our performance of these conditions we pledge our promise in the name of God, and compact and faith, and our faith in the name of his Apostle Mohham'mad—God bless and save him—and for your performance of the same ye pledge yourselves by all that ye hold most sacred in your religion; by the Messiah, and by the Apostles, and by all whom ye revere in your religion and your faith: and God is witness of these things between us and you.—'Amr the son of Shoorahhbee'l wrote (the above) in Rum'ada'n, in the year thirty-one.'

"The Noo'beh had paid, to 'Amr Ibn El-'A'see, the buckt agreed upon by treaty before their infringement of the peace; and they gave, to 'Amr, forty head of slaves besides; but he would not accept this present, and returned it to the chief officer of the buckt, who was called Ckumsoo's: he bought with them provisions and wine, which he sent (to the Noo'beh). Also 'Abd Al'lal Ibn Saad sent to them the corn which he had promised; wheat and barley and lentils; and likewise clothes and horses. This remained a regular custom for a long time: they received these provisions at the time of their payment of the buckt, every year: and the number of forty slaves which had been offered to 'Amr was regularly taken by the Governors of Egypt."

It is related, by El-Mekee'n, that, in the reign of the Khalee'feh Hisha'm Ibn 'Abd El-Mel'ik (who ascended to the throne in the year of the flight 105, and died in 125), a Nubian king, named Kiryakoo's, hearing that the Coptic Patriarch had been thrown into prison in Egypt, invaded that country, at the head of 100,000 horsemen, and approached the capital. The Egyptian Governor, 'Abd El-Mel'ik, alarmed at this formidable attack, desired the Patriarch, whom he had then liberated, to write to the King of the Noo'beh, and request him to return to his dominions. The Patriarch did so; and the Nubian King retired with his forces.

In the year 345 (as related by the same historian), the King of the Noo'beh attacked and pillaged Aswa'n, massacred many of its inhabitants, and took many prisoners. The Governor of Egypt dispatched an army against him, which repulsed the invaders, and made a considerable number of them prisoners. The Egyptian army pursued their enemies into Nubia, and took the fortified town of Ibree'm.

In 351, the King of the Noo'beh again entered Egypt, and penetrated as far as Akhmee'm; massacring multitudes of Moos'lims, and pillaging and burning the houses on his way.

Go'har, the general of the forces of the Khalee'feh El-Mo'ez'z, after his conquest of Egypt, sent an embassy to the King of the Noo'beh, to endeavour to persuade him to embrace the Mohhammadan faith: but without success.

(Quatremère's Memoirs on Egypt, &c., contain some further accounts of the history of the Noo'beh, derived from various Arab authors, the leading particulars of which I must here mention.)

The tribe of El-Kenz الكنز , descendants of Rebee''ah the son of Niza'r the son of Ma'ad'd the son of Adna'n, who originally resided in the province of El-Yema'meh, had entered Egypt in the time of the Khalee'feh El-Mootawek'kil 'al'a-lla'h, about the year of the flight 240 (A.D. 854-5), and dispersed themselves throughout that country. Some of them settled in the upper parts of the Sa'ee'd; and succeeded in repressing the incursions of the Booja'weh, who inhabited the desert between Nubia and the Red Sea. Afterwards, they contracted alliances, and intermarried, with these people; possessed themselves of some gold-mines in the mountain of 'Alla'ckee, in the territories of these their allies; and became very wealthy and powerful.—In the year 397, the rebel Ab'oo Rek'weh, who had raised a formidable faction against the Egyptian Khalee'feh El-Hha'kim, and made himself master of a great part of the Sa'ee'd, was taken prisoner and sent to the Khalee'feh by the chief of the Kenz; for which act, this chief received the title of Kenz ed-Do'leh; and this title became hereditary in his family.

A Kenz ed-Do'leh (probably son of the chief above mentioned), in the reign of the Khalee'feh El-Moostun'sir, rendered himself independent in the Sa'ee'd, and took Aswa'n. Bedr El-Gema'lee was dispatched against him, defeated him, and compelled him to retire into Nubia; but he was brought back; being delivered up by the King of the Noo'beh; and taken to El-Foosta't, where he was put to death.

After the overthrow of the dynasty of the Fawa'tim in Egypt, the Noo'beh frequently broke the treaty into which they had entered with the Moos'lims. It is related that, in the year 568, in the reign of Sala'hh ed-Deen, the Noo'beh and their slaves, composing a great army, made an incursion into Egypt. The Emee'r Kenz ed-Do'leh (the chief of the Kenz), then residing at Aswa'n (of which place he was probably Governor), sent to demand aid of the Soolta'n, who dispatched, against the invaders, an army under a commander named Shooja'à. On arriving at Aswa'n, Shooja'à found that the Noo'beh had retired. He pursued them, in company with Kenz ed-Do'leh; and came to an engagement with them, in which many were killed on both sides; after which he returned.—Sala'hh ed-Deen then sent his brother Shems ed-Do'leh, with a numerous army, to prosecute the war. This general found that the enemy had, as before, retired into their own country; and he pursued them. He penetrated as far as the castle (or fortified town) of Ibree'm, which is situated on a hill of rock, close on the eastern side of the Nile. This place he took, after a siege of three days; pillaged it; and made slaves of all its inhabitants; men, women, and children. There was a fine church there, which he also plundered; and he tortured the bishop, to make him confess and give up the wealth which he was presumed to possess; but in vain; he therefore took him into slavery, with the other inhabitants. He returned to Egypt; but gave the command of Ibree'm to one of his chiefs,

Ibrahee'm El-Koor'dee,[1] who, with a number of other Koor'dees in his service, retained possession of it for the period of two years. This chief and his troop made frequent marauding expeditions, and acquired vast booty; but at last, he and several of his men were drowned in the Nile, in crossing over to the island of Dinda'n; and those who escaped on this occasion returned to Ibree'm, carried off every thing valuable that was portable, and retired to Egypt.

Two years after Shems ed-Do'leh's expedition (that is, in the year 570), the chief of the Kenz, then resident at Aswa'n, rebelled against the Soolta'n. This Kenz ed-Do'leh, having assembled a vast number of blacks and slaves, and avowed his object to be the conquest of Egypt, and the reestablishment of the dynasty of the Fawa'tim, was joined by many of the people of Egypt, and found himself at the head of a numerous army. With this force he marched to the province of Ckoo's; and massacred all the persons in authority in that part. Sala'hh ed-Deen sent his brother El-Mel'ik El-'A'dil, at the head of a large army against these rebels. The Egyptian commander assaulted and took the village of To'd (a little above Thebes), and slew its inhabitants, who had sided with the insurgents. He then proceeded against Kenz ed-Do'leh, whom, after several engagements, he completely defeated and put to flight; killing or making prisoners all who were with him: the rebel chief, also, being pursued, was killed; and all of his party who escaped were obliged to fly from Aswa'n. The Kenz were highly extolled, by several poets of this age, for their generosity.

(The following is a translation of an extract from the Kita'b el-Footoo'hha't of El-Bela'diree, quoted by El-Muckree'zee.)

"In the year 674, Da'oo'd, the King of the Noo'beh, did much mischief. He attacked Aswa'n; and, in his way thither, burned many sa'ckiyehs; after having pillaged the town of 'Eyda'b. The Governor of Ckoo's marched against him, and pursued him; but not being able to overtake him he made prisoners "the Lord of the Mountain"[2] (Sa'hheb el-Geb'el) and a number of other Noo'beh, and took them to the Soolta'n El-Mel'ik Ez-Za'hir Beybur's El-Boondoockda'ree, at the Citadel of El-Cka'hireh, and they were severed in two. After this, Sheken'deh, the son of a sister of the King of the Noo'beh, came to complain of the tyranny of his uncle Da'oo'd. The Soolta'n sent with him the Emee'r Shems ed-Deen A'ck Soon'ckoor El-Fa'ricka'nee, the Oostoda'r, and the Emee'r 'Ezz ed-Deen Ey'beck El-Af'ram, the Emeer Ja'nda'r, with a numerous army composed of the regular troops and those of the provinces and the Arabs of the southern parts of Egypt and lancers and archers and boatmen. They commenced their march from El-Cka'hireh on the 1st of Shaaba'n, and proceeded to the country of the Noo'beh, where the enemy met them, mounted on dromedaries, and armed with spears and with black coats of mail. A sanguinary conflict

---

[1] "Koor'dee" signifies "native of Koordista'n."
[2] The Governor of Ed-Do; now called Ckal"at Ad'deh.

ensued; and the Noo'beh were put to flight. El-Af'ram then besieged the castle (or fortified hill-town) of Ed-Do[1]; and here he killed many, and took many prisoners. El-Fa'ricka'nee proceeded up the country of the Noo'beh by land and by the river; killing and making prisoners on his way; and driving away with him an innumerable multitude of cattle. He alighted at the island of Meeka-ee'l, at the entrance (or head) of the (Second) Cataracts; and caused the boats to retire from (or pass up) the Cataracts: the Noo'beh fled to the islands. He then wrote a promise of security to Ckumr ed-Do'leh, the Viceroy of Da'oo'd the King of the Noo'beh, who swore allegiance to the Sheken'deh, and brought back the people of Meree's, and other fugitives. El-Af'ram next forded to a tower in the river; assaulted and took it; killed, in it, two hundred men; and took prisoner a brother of Da'oo'd: but Da'oo'd himself fled; and the invading army pursued him for three days; killing and making prisoners on the way, until the people submitted. Sheken'deh was then confirmed in his stead; and he bound himself to pay an annual tribute of three elephants, three giraffes, five female fahds (or lynxes), a hundred bay camels, and four hundred head of choice cattle; and it was agreed that the (produce or revenues of the) country of the Noo'beh should be divided into equal parts; one of which should be the property of the Soolta'n, and the other be appropriated to the cultivation of the country; but that the district of the Cataracts (between the First and Second Cataracts) should belong wholly to the Soolta'n, on account of its proximity to Aswa'n; and this was about one fourth of the country of the Noo'beh: also that he (the Soolta'n) should receive the dates and cotton of this district, with the customary dues which had been paid in former times; and that the inhabitants should pay tribute as long as they should remain Christians, for every grown person among them, every year, the sum of one deena'r. A form of oath respecting these conditions was written, to which King Sheken'deh swore; and another was written, to which the people swore. The two Emee'rs destroyed the churches of the Noo'beh; and carried off whatever they found in them. They also seized about twenty of the chiefs of the Noo'beh; and liberated those Moos'lims of Aswa'n and 'Eyda'b who were captives in the lands of the Noo'beh. Sheken'deh was crowned, and seated on the throne of the kingdom, after he had taken the oath. He was obliged to send to the Soolta'n the property of Da'oo'd, and that of all those who had been killed or made prisoners, whether it was money or cattle, with the customary buckt, which consisted of four hundred head of slaves every year, and a giraffe: of these slaves, three hundred and sixty were for the Khalee'feh, and forty for the Soolta'n of Egypt; and this was on the condition that, on the full receipt of the buckt, there should be given to them (the Noo'beh) 1000 ardeb'bs (or 500 bushels) of wheat, for their king, and 30 ardeb'bs for his envoy."

---

[1]Or Ckal''at Ad'deh, which is close on the east of the Nile; and like Ibree'm; but less lofty, and not so large.

[1]In the reign of the Soolta'n Ckala-oo'n, Nubia was twice invaded by the Egyptian forces. The first expedition was in the year 686. Its object was to reduce to submission the Nubian king Shemamoo'n. The Egyptian army came to an engagement with the forces of this king before his capital Dun'ckal'ah; made a great slaughter; put the king to flight; pursued him five days' journey above his capital; and made prisoners one of his cousins, and "the Lord of the Mountain" (the Governor of Ed-Do), whom the king had summoned to his assistance. The Egyptian commander then gave the kingdom to a nephew of Shemamoo'n; reinstated the Lord of the Mountain in his government, as subject to the new king; and, leaving some of his troops to defend these chiefs, returned to Egypt with immense booty, consisting of slaves, horses, camels, oxen, &c. But as soon as Shemamoo'n heard of their departure, he returned to Dun'ckal'ah, and recovered his kingdom.—The deposed king and the Lord of the Mountain repaired to make this known to the Egyptian Soolta'n, who immediately dispatched another army to Nubia; and the ex-king and the Lord of the Mountain accompanied this expedition; but the former, on his arrival at Aswa'n, died. The Soolta'n, informed of this, sent a nephew of King Da'oo'd to be placed on the throne of Nubia; and with him the Egyptian army proceeded. Throughout the district of the Lord of the Mountain, or Lower Nubia, the inhabitants every where tendered their submission, and were not molested; but higher up the country, the invading army found that most of the natives had fled. They massacred those who had remained; seized their property; fed their horses in the corn-fields; and burned the water-wheels and houses. On arriving at the city of Dun'ckal'ah, they found that here also all the inhabitants had fled, excepting one old man and an old woman; who informed them that the King had retired to a large island, three days' journey in length, and five days' journey above Dun'ckal'ah. The Egyptians pursued, and the King, soon after their arrival opposite this island, fled to Abwa'b, three days' journey higher up the river, and beyond the limits of his dominions: but his officers and troops and priests surrendered themselves; and gave up to the Moos'lim general, the crown, and a cross of silver, which were the insignia of royalty. The Egyptian army then returned to Dun'ckal'ah; where the nephew of Da'oo'd was, as the Soolta'n had appointed, proclaimed king: his subjects were made to take the oath of allegiance to him; and he pledged himself to remit the buckt to Egypt as in former times. Some troops, under the command of Rookn ed-Deen Beybur's (the same, I suppose, who was afterwards Soolta'n, the second of that name), were left to support the new king; and the rest of the Egyptian army returned to the Soolta'n, with large booty. Shemamoo'n, however, as soon as they had quitted Dun'ckal'ah, returned, and a second time recovered his kingdom; forcing Beybur's and his troops to withdraw to Egypt. Having seized the king whom the Moos'lims had elevated in his stead, he caused him to be

---

[1]Here, again, I make use of the work of Quatremère.

bound to a stake with strips of the hide of a newly-slaughtered bull, which by contracting as they dried, caused his death. He also put to death the Lord of the Mountain; and then wrote to the Egyptian Soolta'n, soliciting his favour, and promising to remit the accustomed buckt, with an additional tribute. This proposal was backed by considerable presents, including a great number of slaves; and Shemamoo'n was suffered to remain in peaceful possession of his kingdom to the reign of El-Mel'ik El-'A'dil Ket'boogh'a, in the year 694.

In the year 716, the Soolta'n Mohham'mad Ibn Ckala-oo'n dispatched an expedition to Nubia to depose Kerem'bes, the King of that country, and to elevate in his stead a grand-nephew of King Da'oo'd, named 'Abd Al'lah. From this name it would appear that this person had embraced the Mohhammadan religion; and probably many of the Noo'beh had now done so. Kerem'bes sent the chief of the Kenz to intercede for him; but this envoy was thrown into prison by the Soolta'n. On the approach of the Egyptian army, Kerem'bes fled from Dun'ckal'ah, with his brother Ibrahee'm; but both were taken, and sent to El-Cka'hireh, where the Soolta'n cast them into prison.—The Kenz ed-Do'leh (the chief of the Kenz) who had been sent by Kerem'bes to the Soolta'n, was soon set at liberty, and, returning to Nubia, he collected a considerable force, deposed and put to death King 'Abd Al'lah, and usurped his throne. The Soolta'n, hearing of this, released Ibrahee'm from prison, and promised him that, if he would send to him Kenz ed-Do'leh bound, he would set at liberty his brother Kerem'bes. Ibrahee'm repaired to Dun'ckal'ah; and on his arrival there, Kenz ed-Do'leh voluntarily gave himself up to him: but three days after, Ibrahee'm died; and the Noo'beh restored Kenz ed-Do'leh to the supreme authority.—In 723, an Egyptian army was dispatched to reinstate Kerem'bes, who accompanied them. Kenz ed-Do'leh fled from Dun'ckal'ah on their approach; and Kerem'bes was restored to his kingdom; but as soon as the Egyptian troops had quitted Nubia, Kenz ed-Do'leh returned to Dun'ckal'ah, and recovered the throne.—Native princes, it appears, afterwards obtained the kingdom.

In 767, the Kenz and the Ak'rem'ee Arabs plundered Aswa'n and Sawa'kin (on the shore of the Red Sea). The Kenz made themselves masters of the province of Aswa'n, the desert of 'Eyda'b, and the Interior Oases; and, having contracted alliances by marriage with the Kings of Dun'ckal'ah and the chiefs of the Al'rem'ee tribe, had acquired great power.

At the same period, Nubia was a scene of civil war, and a prey to the tribes above mentioned, and to other marauding Arabs; and the interference of the Egyptian Soolta'n, El-Mel'ik El-Ash'raf Shaaba'n, was solicited, to restore peace and tranquillity: a considerable force was accordingly dispatched thither from Egypt. The commander of this Egyptian army, on arriving at Ckoo's, sent to Aswa'n, to exhort the chiefs of the Kenz to submit. After halting six days at the former place, he proceeded with his troops; and near the opening in the mountains opposite Ad'foo he met the Koonoo'z[1] chiefs, and received their profession of submission. He continued his march in company with these chiefs; on whom he conferred robes of honour, with every mark of respect. The King of the Noo'beh was besieged by Arabs in the fortified town of Ed-Do (or Ckal'’at Ad'deh). Advancing thither, with a division of his army, the Egyptian general was joined by the King, and by many of the chiefs of the Ak'rem'ee tribe, and other chiefs of the Kenz, or Konoo'z. He now, in concert with the King of the Noo'beh, seized the chiefs of both these tribes; and one of his officers, with the King, proceeded against another party of the Ak'rem'ees, and killed or made prisoners the greater number of them. The fortified town of Ed-Do was made the capital of the King of the Noo'beh; as Dun'ckal'ah was depopulated, and more exposed to the attacks of the Arabs. Having confirmed this king in his government, the Egyptian commander returned with his troops and the captive chiefs to Aswa'n; where many slaves of the chiefs of the Kenz were severed in two, to revenge the oppression which the people of that place had suffered from the said chiefs. The captives were then conveyed to the Egyptian metropolis, and there cast into prison; but they were shortly after sent back to Aswa'n, with a new governor appointed over that town. This governor, on arriving at Ckoo's, caused each of the captive chiefs to be nailed upon a plank of wood; and in this state they were carried to Aswa'n, and there severed in two. The families and slaves of these miserable victims, incensed at such barbarity, made an attack upon Aswa'n, defeated the troops of the new governor, wounding the greater number, and wreaked their vengeance on the inhabitants of the town: they burned the houses, killed vast numbers of the people, and carried off their women as slaves.

In 780, the heads of eleven chiefs of the Kenz, together with 200 persons of the same tribe, were sent from Aswa'n to El-Cka'hireh, where the heads were suspended at the Ba'b Zoowey'leh, one of the principal gates of the city.—In the following year, two men of the same tribe were nailed upon boards, and carried thus through the streets of El-Cka'hireh and El-Foosta't; after which, they were severed in two.

In 787, this tribe attacked and plundered Aswa'n; slew the greater number of its inhabitants; and compelled the governor to fly. Another governor was sent thither; but about three of four years after, the Kenz overran and pillaged the whole province.—In 798, they again attacked Aswa'n, and sacked it, in conjunction with the Ahh'med'ee Arabs.

In the calamitous year 806, there ceased to be a governor on the part of the Soolta'n at Aswa'n. In this year (as El-Muckree'zee mentions, in his Account of the Sa'ee'd), Egypt was afflicted by a dreadful famine; by which there died at Ckoo's 17,000 persons; and at Asyoo't, 11,000, of

---

[1]Here we find the name of *"Koonoo'z"* applied, by El-Muckree'zee, from whom these historical notices are derived, to the Kenz. The descendants of these people, together with those Noo'beh with whom their race has become blended, are now distinguished by the name of Koonoo'z.

those who were regularly washed and buried; and at Hoo, 15,000.

In 815 (as related by El-Muckree'zee, in his Account of Aswa'n), the Hawa'rah Arabs attacked Aswa'n, put to flight the Kenz, and killed many of them. They made slaves of all the women and children whom they found there, and carried them away. Having destroyed the walls of the town, they departed with their captives; leaving the place in ruins, and without inhabitants.

At the period of the conquest of Egypt by the Turks under Soolta'n Selee'm, in the year of the flight 923 (or A.D. 1517), the whole of the country between the First and Second Cataracts had (as its present inhabitants relate) become subject to the authority of the Jawa'bireh, or Gawa'bireh, and the Ghurbee'yeh, two Arab tribes. These tribes had long been at war with each other; and the latter, which was the weaker, sent to solicit the aid of the Turkish Soolta'n, who availed himself of this opportunity to annex Nubia to his own empire. A chief named Hhas'an Koo'sa, with several hundred Booshna'cks, or Bosnians, accomplished this object in conjunction with the Arabs who had sought his sovereign's interference, and compelled the other tribe, with the exception of a few peaceable persons, to take refuge in Dun'ckal'ah; where they remained. With his troops he garrisoned the fortresses of Aswa'n, Ibree'm (which became his principal place of residence), and Sa'y; all of which he rebuilt or repaired; and, as viceroy of the Soolta'n, he regularly transmitted the annual *mee'ree*, or land-tax, to the Ba'sha of Egypt. Descendants of this chief (for he and his soldiers intermarried with women of the country) successively held the same power, or, perhaps, a more limited sway; and the descendants of his troops possessed lands exempt from taxation.

These foreigners and their posterity had been thus established in Nubia about two centuries and a half, when Hemma'm, the famous chief of the Hawa'rah Arabs, after having made himself master of the half of Upper Egypt, from Asyoo't upwards, extended his authority as far as the frontiers of Dun'ckal'ah; but after his death, which happened in Shaaba'n 1183 (or at the close of the year 1769 of the Christian era), the government of Nubia reverted to the descendants of Hhas'an Koo'sa; and so it remained until the forces of the present Ba'sha of Egypt took possession of that country and of Senna'r, in 1820; when Turkish governors were placed in the principal villages, and Nubia was reduced to the same state as Egypt.

Section II. The modern Nubians—Nubian agriculture, &c.

In taking a general survey of the present population of Nubia, we perceive some differences in the shades of their complexions (varying from a deep brown to nearly black), but not much difference in their other physical characteristics: they are nearly the same in manners; and profess the same religion; being all Moos'lims, very ignorant, and great bigots; boasting that there is not a single Christian among them. Regarded as one nation, they are known among the Egyptians by the general name of *Bera'bireh* برابره (commonly pronounced *Bera'b'rah*—in the singular, *Bur'ber'ee* بربرى); but they are divided by their languages, and, among themselves, by distinctive appellations. The names of the two grand divisions are the *Koonoo'z* and the *Noo'beh*; the latter people are the more numerous: with both are interspersed many small tribes of Arabs.

The *Koonoo'z* كنوز (in the singular *Ken'zee* كنزى) occupy that part which extends from Egypt to Wa'dee es-Sooboo' ă. They differ somewhat, both in their physical characteristics and in their language, from the Noo'beh, or more genuine Nubians; though in both these respects they bear such a degree of resemblance to that people as is alone sufficient to shew that they are partly descended from the same stock. The country which they inhabit was gradually taken possession of by the Arab tribe called Koonoo'z, as before related. As it is by this name that the present occupants of this part of Nubia distinguish themselves, we might be led to refer their origin more to the Koonoo'z Arabs than to the Noo'beh; but as the modern Koonoo'z speak a language which very much resembles that of the Noo'beh (a great proportion of the words in both those dialects being almost exactly the same) and quite different from Arabic, it is more reasonable to infer that the Arab conquerors were very inferior in number to the people among whom they settled, and for this cause were unable to introduce their language, though they gave their name to the country and its inhabitants. Other Arab tribes also settled among the same people, and intermarried with them, at various periods. The modern Koonoo'z must therefore be regarded as a very mixed race; though principally descended from the Noo'beh. They are divided into a great number of small tribes; most of which have given their names to their respective districts. Thus, for instance, the wa'dee, or district, of the tribe of Koonoo'z called El-Mooba'raka't is named Wa'dee El-Mooba'raka't. I have before had occasion to mention that many of the Koonoo'z have settled in the district of Egypt between Aswa'n and Ad'foo.—At what period the Nubians embraced the Mohhammadan faith is not certainly known. Their conversion from Christianity was probably very gradual; and seems hardly to have commenced earlier that four centuries ago.

Next above the country of the Koonoo'z is the district called Wa'dee es-Sooboo' ă; and next to this, another district called Wa'dee el-'Ar'ab; the former of which is inhabited by Arabs of the tribe of 'Aleycka't, or 'Aleyga't; and the latter, by Arabs of the same tribe, and by others of the tribe of El-Ghurbee'yeh, before mentioned. They have all preserved their original Arabic dialect, though dwelling between the countries of the Koonoo'z and the Noo'beh, who speak different languages. Most of them, however, the women excepted, are acquainted with both these languages. The Nubian 'Aleycka't, as Burckhardt informs us, belong to the tribe of the same name who dwell in the desert of Mount Sinai.

Immediately above the districts of these Arabs commences the country of the *Noo'beh,* نوبه , extending to the furthest limits of Dun'ckal'ah. Many Arab tribes have settled among these people, and contracted marriages with them; but the Noo'beh seem to have been less blended with foreigners than the Koonoo'z. Their features partake less of the Arab character. We find among them Arabs of the Ckoorey'sh and other tribes who have preserved their race in a great measure distinct from the Noo'beh. At the town of Ed-Dirr, and in the villages of Ibree'm, are many descendants of the Booshna'cks, or Bosnians, whom Hhas'an Koo'sa brought thither.

The Nubians in general are remarkably well made from the waist upwards; particularly in the chest and shoulders; but their legs are disproportionately thin. Their stature is rather low. In their features, they bear the greatest resemblance to the ancient Egyptians as represented by the sculptures on the walls of the temples and tombs, and by the statues. Their countenances have a mild expression, little agreeing (more particularly in the case of the Koonoo'z) with their dispositions. The nose and lips are rather thick; but very different from those of the negro; especially the nose; which is rounded a little at the end, and in many instances rather aquiline. The generality of the Nubians have but little mustache,[1] and less beard, which is, in most cases, only on the chin.—The dress of the men, or rather of those who can afford any dress, is generally a blue or plain white or brown shirt; with a turboo'sh, or a felt cap, or (more commonly) a white cotton cap, and sometimes a turban, which often consists only of a piece of ragged cotton or woolen stuff.[2] Some wear a long piece of drapery wound about them, over the shirt, if they have the latter, or over the otherwise-naked body. The greater number, however, have no article of clothing but the white scull-cap, and one small piece of rag, which is passed between the thighs and attached before and behind to a string tied round the loins. Some of them still dress their hair in the thick, frizzled, bushy form (copiously greased) which was more generally the fashion among them a few years ago, and is still the mode followed by most of the Bish'a'ree'n and 'Aba'b'deh Arabs; and they stick a porcupine's quill, or a skewer of wood, through it, to be always handy for scratching the head. These wear no cap like the rest, who shave their heads. Some of them divide their hair into small twists (which is the universal custom of the women), exactly in the manner which we so often see represented in the sculptures of the ancient Egyptians, some of whom shaved their heads, while others wore their hair, and dressed it in this manner. The hair of the Nubians is quite black, and very crisp and curly; but not woolly. In this respect, and in the superior fineness of the skin, as well as in their complexion and features, the Nubians are widely distinguished from the negroes. I never

---

[1]Burckhardt has erroneously asserted that they have none.
[2]See illustrations of the Nubian costumes in plates 14, 16, 17, 18, and 33 [figs. 137, 140, 141, 142, and 157].

saw a Nubian absolutely black. The Nubian generally wears a short dagger, or knife, either straight or curved, in a leather scabbard, attached to the left arm, a little above the elbow, by a plaited leather string; and many also wear, on the same part, amulets, or charms written upon paper, generally rolled up, and enclosed in leather cases. The spear or lance, and the shield, and sword, are not so generally possessed as they were a few years ago. The spears are mostly about five feet, or six, or six and a half, in length; very slender; with an iron point and barbs, and bound with iron at the bottom. The shields are mostly of hippopotamus' hide; some, of the crocodile's skin: both kinds proof against the lance and sword. They are generally of an oval form, with an indentation at each end, in the edge, and a boss in the centre, formed by pressing out the skin before it is dry, so as to make a hollow, in which is fixed the handle. The shield is always held in the hand; and not attached to the arm: the length is generally from one foot six inches to one foot nine. The larger shields mentioned by some travellers, I never saw. The sword is a straight, double-edged blade, about an inch and a half, or a little more, in width; and about three feet in length without the handle; and it is of German manufacture. It is not usually worn by the side; but hung over the left shoulder. Very few of the Nubians possess fire-arms. The long staff called *nebboo't* is much used by them, as in Egypt.

The Nubian women mostly have pleasing countenances, at least when young; and some are really beautiful. Their breasts are very small; and soon become pendulous and flat; assuming an angular form.—The dress of the women of the Koonoo'z consists of a piece of dark, brown, woollen stuff, of coarse texture, wrapped round the body; the upper edge being passed under the right arm (so as to expose part of the right breast), and the two upper corners attached together over the left shoulder: it reaches to the ankles.[1] Instead of this, some wear a shirt. The women of the Noo'beh mostly wear a pair of full drawers, and a piece of cotton cloth or linen thrown about the body, leaving much of the person exposed.[2] All the Nubian women divide their hair into small twists, profusely greased or oiled; and they anoint their persons in the same manner; this being a luxury in their hot climate. Those of the Koonoo'z generally suffer their hair to reach to their shoulders; but the women of the Noo'beh more commonly cut it straight round a little below the ears, exactly in the manner represented by many ancient Egyptian statues. Some of the Nubian women wear upon their heads a piece of linen: others have the head bare: and they are not so scrupulous to cover their faces as are the Egyptian women; though they are far more modest than the generality of the latter. They wear necklaces of glass beads, coral, &c., and ear-rings and glass or bone bracelets; and a few wear anclets. The young girls, until they are considered marriageable (that is, till the age of between ten and twelve years), wear nothing but the fringed girdle

---

[1]This dress is represented in plates 14 and 17 [figs. 137 and 141].
[2]As represented in plate 33 [fig. 157].

called *raht*, composed of small strips of leather, and usually ornamented with a few cowries: it is tied round the loins; and reaches rather more than half-way down the thighs.[1] A custom described by Strabo (p. 824) as practised upon the female children in Egypt still prevails throughout Nubia, as well as in Upper Egypt.[†]

In their manners and customs, the Nubians differ in some respects from the Egyptian peasants; but their life is much the same; and so, at present, is their political condition. Few of them are taught to write or read, or even to say their prayers in a proper manner. As Burckhardt has remarked, the only prayer generally known among them is the exclamation of Alla'hoo Ak'bar, or God is most Great! If they have any one to act as Ima'm, they perform the regular attitudes with him, though, in words, they can only join with him in this exclamation. They are of the sect of the Ma'likees; which is one of the four orthodox sects of the Moos'lims. I never saw any writing by a Nubian, excepting in Arabic; and if any Nubian ever writes in his own dialect, he must use the Arabic characters; having none of his own.

The huts of the Koonoo'z are very small, and mostly built of rough fragments of stone; the sides of the sandstone mountains being covered with such fragments, detached by nature, and ready for their use. The dwellings of the Noo'beh are larger; and generally neatly built, of crude brick. The huts are roofed with split palm-trunks, and with the branches and leaves of the same tree, or with door'ah-stalks. They are mostly built in small groups, and seldom on a spot capable of cultivation; as the cultivable land is so extremely narrow. Through out the whole of the country of the Koonoo'z we find these groups of huts generally on slight eminences of the rock, or at the base of the mountains; and, from the narrowness of the valley, necessarily near the river. Two or three vessels of a round form, contracting a little towards the top, two feet or more in width at the bottom, and about five feet high, composed of mud and chopped straw, and standing outside the hut,[2] serve to contain the provisions of the family. A few vessels of baked clay, consisting of pitchers, bowls, and dishes, with an iron plate for baking the bread, a hand-mill to grind the corn, and a few baskets or trays of palm-leaves, compose the household utensils. Mats of palm-leaves are used to sleep upon.

The bread of the Nubians is made of door'ah (i.e. door'ah sey'fee, or millet), and generally in very thin, round cakes, like pan-cakes, without salt, and usually without leaven. It is baked insufficiently on the iron plate. This bread, broken up into a bowl of fresh or sour milk, sometimes with a little butter floating upon the surface, constitutes their principal dish. Flesh-meat, they seldom taste. Their dates are remarkably fine; particularly those of the southern districts: most of them are exported to

---

[1]See plates 14, 17, and 18 [figs. 137, 141, and 142].

[†]Female circumcision.

[2]See plate 17 [fig. 141].

Egypt. They often indulge themselves with *boo'zeh*; of which they are very fond; and sometimes with date-wine, and with brandy; which latter they also obtain from dates. Smoking is a general custom among them, as in Egypt. They grow their own tobacco; which is rather strong: it is dried in the sun; retains its pale green colour; and is merely broken up for use. They also make of it a powder like snuff, by pounding it, and mixing a little nitre with it; and this powder they put into the mouth, between the lower lip and the gums. The women perform all the household business; as grinding the corn (which is done every morning), making the bread, &c. Some of them likewise weave coarse cotton and woollen stuffs; and many make mats, and small baskets, &c., of palm-leaves; often in a very neat manner.

As there are very few boats in Nubia, the inhabitants generally cross over the Nile upon a bundle of door'ah-stalks tied together, called a *ra'moo's*; or upon a piece of the trunk of a palm-tree.[1]

The men employ themselves in agriculture. The climate of Nubia is extremely hot, but favourable to vegetation, very dry, and particularly healthy. The greatest heat that I experienced in that country in the hottest season of the year was $114°$ of Fahrenheit, in the afternoon, and in the shade. The usual summer heat is from $105°$ to $110°$, at the same time of day, in the shade. It is often $90°$ at sunrise, $110°$ in the afternoon, and $107°$ or $108°$ at sunset. The thermometer has been known to rise as high as $100°$ in the month of December; and in summer, to $130°$, and even higher. But though the heat is so intense, I never felt much oppressed by it; which I attribute to the extreme dryness of the air. Rain is almost a prodigy in this country: I, however, once witnessed here a shower of rain, accompanied by lightning. The Nubians therefore depend solely upon the river for the fertilization of their fields. In their country, the Nile does not rise sufficiently high to overflow the narrow tracts of cultivable soil which border it; nor does it sink so low as in Egypt; as the water is in a great measure retained by the rocks of the First Cataracts. There is rather more cultivable land on the eastern than the western side; but, if we may judge from the remains of antiquity, the most considerable ancient towns were on the western side. The land is irrigated by means of sa'ckiyehs. Generally one sa'ckiyeh belongs to more than one person. For each sa'ckiyeh is paid an annual tax of fifteen dollars (or 3*l.*2*s.*6*d.*) as land-tax; but if it is not worked, the proprietor pays nothing. One of these machines serves to irrigate four or five fedda'ns, or rather more than so many English acres.[2] In the end of September, when the river begins to subside, the land is irrigated: the

---

[1]As represented in plates 33 and 12 [figs. 157 and 135].

[2]Burckhardt estimated the number of sa'ckiyehs between Aswa'n and Wa'dee Hhal'fa at about six or seven hundred; from which it would appear that the whole of the cultivable soil is not more than about three thousand acres; and this along a tract of country about 190 geographical miles, or 220 British miles, in length.

seed is then sown. The grain most commonly cultivated is *door'ah sey'fee* (or millet). The seed is cast upon the unploughed ground at the period above-mentioned; and the harvest is in December. A smaller kind of millet, called *dookh'n*, is also much cultivated. After this crop of door'ah or dookh'n has been gathered in, the land is again irrigated, and barley, or sometimes wheat (but very little of the latter), is sown; and the crop is reaped in March. After this, in some parts, a second crop of door'ah is raised. Ba'miyeh, and a few lentils, kidney-beans, peas, and a little cotton are also grown. Tobacco is cultivated in abundance. At Ed-Dirr, a few water-melons and cucumbers are raised. Senna, of a poor kind, grows wild in many parts: so, also, does the colocynth.—Among the trees of Nubia, the most numerous and valuable are the date-palms. They are all taxed, at the rate of twenty fud'dahs, or pa'rah's, each tree. The dates of Ibree'm are much celebrated; but those of the more southern districts are larger, and finer in flavour. The do'm-palm is less abundant. The tur'fa (or tamarisk), and several kinds of acacia (the sunt, seya'leh, &c.), in many parts, border the river; and, though less common, the khur'wa' (or castor-oil plant), the oil of which is used by many of the Nubian women for anointing their hair. Along the skirts of the desert, the plant 'osh'ar (the Dead-Sea apple) is often seen.—The Nubians possess cows, sheep, goats, and a few asses. I never saw a buffalo in their country; I was told that there were none. There are but few camels; and those mostly belonging to Arabs; and of a fine breed; such as should rather be called dromedaries. Gazelles are common in the adjacent deserts; and come down to the Nile at night to drink, and to feed upon the herbage growing on the banks. Hares, also, are not unfrequently met with. The most common birds are wild geese, pelicans, the vulture rukh'um (or vultur perenopterus), herons, and multitudes of sparrows, which last are very mischievous in devouring the ripening corn. I saw but one crocodile in Nubia; and not one hippopotamus; though the latter is not uncommon there: it rises from the river in the night; and feeds upon the young door'ah on the banks. Beetles (the scarabæi held sacred by the ancient Egyptians, as emblems of the sun) are very numerous in the deserts. Locusts not unfrequently commit dreadful havoc in this country. In my second voyage up the Nile, when before the village of Boosta'n, a little above Ibree'm, many locusts pitched upon the boat. They were beautifully variegated: yellow and blue. In the following night, a southerly wind brought other locusts, in immense swarms. Next morning, the air was darkened by them, as if by a heavy fall of snow; and the surface of the river was thickly scattered over by those which had fallen and were unable to rise again. Great numbers came upon and within the boat, and alighted upon our persons. They were different from those of the preceding day; being of a bright yellow colour, with brown marks. The desolation which they made was dreadful. In four hours, a field of young door'ah was cropt to the ground. In another field of door'ah more advanced, only the stalks were left. No where was there space on the ground to set the foot without treading on many. A field of cotton-plants was completely stripped. Even the acacias along the banks were made bare, and palm-trees were stripped of the fruit and leaves. In the preceding evening, we heard the creaking of sa'ckiyehs, and the singing of the women driving the cows which turned them: now, not one sa'ckiyeh was in motion; and the women were going about howling, and vainly attempting to frighten away the locusts. On the preceding day, I had preserved two of the more beautiful kind of these creatures with a solution of arsenic: on the next day, some of the other locusts *ate* them almost entirely, poisoned as they were, unseen by me until they had nearly finished their meal. On the third day, they were less numerous, and gradually disappeared. Locusts are eaten by most of the Bed'awees of Arabia, and by some of the Nubians. We ate a few, dressed in the most approved manner; being stripped of the legs, wings, and head, and fried in butter. They had a flavour somewhat like that of the woodcock; owing to their food. The Arabs preserve locusts as an article of provision by parboiling them in salt and water, and then drying them in the sun.

The above notes may suffice to convey a notion of the modern Nubians, their life, condition, and country.

The character for kindness and honesty given by Burckhardt to the Nubians in general rather applies, I should say, to the Noo'beh. From my own experience, I should describe the Koonoo'z as a very savage, extortionate, and dishonest race. In their district, attempts were often made to extort money from me for my visiting the antiquities; which they called their property;—conduct which I never met with from any of the Noo'beh;—and my life was more than once threatened by individuals of the former race. I could also mention several instances of theft committed by Koonoo'z, within my own knowledge. Petty tribes among them are often at war with each other. When a man is killed, which does not often happen, his family receive, from the homicide, the fine for his blood. The Nubian women are justly celebrated for their chastity: there is not a single prostitute among them: whereas in Egypt there are great numbers. They are kept in a state of greater subjection than the Egyptian women. If a Nubian has reason to suspect his wife of infidelity towards him, or his sister or daughter of incontinence, he slaughters her, and throws her into the river. Some of the Nubian boatmen (who are mostly employed in Egypt, as there are few boats in Nubia) have two, three, or even four wives; generally in different villages. Many Nubians obtain their livelihood as boatmen; and many go as servants to Musr; but most of these are constantly sighing after their native wa'dee; to which they generally return after a few years, when they have amassed a small sum of money, notwithstanding the comforts and luxuries which they enjoy in the Egyptian metropolis.

Chapter XXXIII.
Debo'd, and Ckurda'seh, &c.

Remains of the town of El'Ckusr—Scenery between Plilæ and Debo'd—
Temple of Debo'd—Remains in Wa'dee Sahda'b—Temple, Quarries, &c.
of Ckurda'seh.

18th of May. In the afternoon, with a gentle breeze, we continued our
voyage. The thermometer, suspended in my cabin, rose to 105°.

About a mile above Philæ, on the eastern side of the river, are two
ruined mosques, and the remains of a town, which, I have no doubt,
mark the site of El-Ckusr, once the frontier town of Nubia.[1] El-Ckusr,
according to Ibn Selee'm El-Aswa'nee (quoted by El-Muckree'zee) was
five miles above Aswa'n (i.e. Old Aswa'n), and one mile from the isle of
Bila'ck, or Philæ: but El-Mes'oo'dee states, more correctly, that its
distance from Aswa'n was *six* miles. The ruins in question are about six
miles from Old Aswa'n, and, as above stated, one from Philæ. As this
was the first town of Nubia above Egypt it was necessary to defend it on
the Egyptian side; and accordingly we find a thick wall extending up the
upper part of the slope, and along the summit, of the mountain
immediately on the north. The two mosques above-mentioned are
absurdly supposed, by the modern Nubians, to have been built by Bila'l,
the Prophet's Moo-ed'din, who died at Damascus, in the 20th year of the
flight.

After having advanced above the island of Beg'eh and the more
extensive island which lies on the west of the former, we find the valley
of the Nile very contracted. The dusky mountains on either side are
almost close to the water's edge. A very narrow strip of alluvial soil has
been deposited along the bases: but in some parts, this scanty strip of
land is interrupted; and the bases of the mountains are washed by the
stream. We stopped for the night before a little village, or group of huts,
perched (like most others in the district of the Koonoo'z) upon a rocky
eminence: the little adjacent patch of cultivable land being too valuable to
be built upon. This was the village of my rei'yis; who, shortly after our
arrival, brought me a present of a sheep, and a bowl full of milk, with
some thin cakes of unleavened bread, of door'ah, broken into it.
Burckhardt justly says, of this common dish of Nubia, that, from the
door'ah being badly ground, it is very coarse food, and he adds that
nothing but absolute hunger could have tempted him to taste it: I did not
dislike it at first; but I soon became tired of it.

---

[1] I have already explained the cause of Burckhardt's erroneously placing the town
of El-Ckusr on the isle of Philæ.

19th. We now find the western mountains nearly covered with drifted sand, of a bright yellow tint, exhibiting a strong contrast with the dark hue of the tops of the hills, which, with the rugged prominences on their sides, alone remain uncovered. About five miles above Philæ is a sharp turn of the river, occasioned by the mountains. The course of the river there, for the space of one mile, is from west to east: above that bend, as below, its course is towards the north. About three miles further, within the district called *Wa'dee Debo'd* وادى دبود is an ancient temple, on the western side of the river.[†]

The mountains at this part recede a little from the river, which is bordered by a narrow strip of cultivated land. The temple above mentioned[1] marks the site of *Parembole*. It is situated behind the cultivated tract, in the midst of a sandy plain, about six or seven hundred feet from the river; which it faces. On the bank of the river, directly before the front of the temple, are remains of a stone causeway, which led to the entrance of it. The temple is enclosed within a low and ruined wall of roughly-hewn stones. Before it are three portals, in the direct line of approach. The foremost of these is in the front wall of enclosure. All of them are unfinished; but the second is less so than the others: it has the winged globe upon the cornice; and, above this, part of a Greek inscription, which states that the temple was dedicated by Ptolemy Philometor and Cleopatra to Isis and the contemplar divinities. Wings were to have been added to each of these portals; in consequence of which, their sides were left in an unfinished state. The foundations of the wings of the second portal are seen. The whole space within the enclosure is very little encumbered with rubbish or ruins. In one part, between the first and second portals, we discover a pavement. The age of the temple cannot be exactly ascertained; but it is evidently not much anterior to the times of the Ptolemies. Its sculptures were commenced by an unknown king; probably an Ethiopian; and continued, but not completed, under Augustus and Tiberius. The front of the portico is formed by four columns; of which the two next the sides are unfinished. To the right and left of the entrance, the columns are engaged by a wall about half their height, decorated with sculptures. The interior of the portico is only partially sculptured. The intercolumnal walls to the north of the entrance are sculptured; but not the corresponding walls; and the decorations of the two side-walls and of the back-walls are confined to the lower part. Upon one of the intercolumnal walls is sculptured a subject similar to one which I have mentioned at Philæ: a hawk-headed god and the ibis-headed god Thoth are pouring streams of alternate *cruces ansatæ* and sceptres (the emblems of life and power) over the

---

[†]The sites of this and most of the other Nubian monuments that Lane described are now beneath the surface of Lake Nasser, formed by the construction of the Aswan High Dam. Many of the major monuments of Nubia, though by no means all, were resited before the lake filled.

[1]See plate 14 [Fig. 137].

emperor Tiberius Cæsar. The same wrong inference has been drawn respecting this piece of sculpture as in the case of that above-alluded to at Philæ. Here not a vestige of paint remains upon the figures. Mr. Hamilton is generally so accurate that I think he must have confounded this sculpture with the similar one at Philæ, in which the figures of the gods are blackened by dirt, while the colour of the king is plainly seen to be red.—On the left of the portico of the temple of Debo'd is a door leading into a small chamber which is built out at the side, and spoils the uniformity of the edifice. The pavement in this side-chamber has been removed; apparently in search of treasure. The walls are not sculptured.—Behind the portico is a small chamber; the walls of which are decorated with ordinary sculptures. This chamber is the oldest part; and originally formed a temple of itself. On the right of it is another apartment, without sculptures; to which we also enter from the portico; and on the left is a space of the same extent, part of which is occupied by a narrow, dark apartment, and the remaining part by a flight of stairs ascending to the roof. Beyond the first central chamber is one much smaller; from which we pass into three others, occupying the end of the building. All of these have plain walls. In the central chamber (of these three) were two monolithic granite shrines, like that at Philæ. One of them has been removed: the other I found in the chamber before, thrown down, and broken in two. It bears the hieroglyphic name of a Ptolemy; very indistinct; probably the same mentioned in the Greek inscription; namely Philometor.—No part of the exterior of the building has any sculptures; excepting the front.—There are some catacombs in the neighbourhood; and some trifling antiquities, none of which seemed very ancient, were brought to me. The inhabitants of the neighbouring huts begged for a few fud'dahs from me, for the sight of the temple. The Egyptians seldom do this: but the Koonoo'z Nubians generally make a demand on the traveller for viewing the ancient monuments: when money was thus *claimed* from me, I invariably refused it; though not when it was civilly asked.—The thermometer this day, in my cabin, rose to 110°.

20th. Continuing our voyage, we pass some small islands, and shortly after observe, upon the western side of the river, on a hill near the bank, a ruined town. This is about three miles above the temple of Debo'd; but apparently not quite so far from the southern limit of the site of Parmebole: it may therefore be *Izijzi*, which is placed, in the itinerary of Antoninus, at the distance of two miles above Parembole. The ruins are of crude brick. A little above this spot are remains of a pier, jutting out into the river; and about two miles (geographical miles) higher is an island, upon which are some crude-brick ruins. The western side of the river here is called *Wa'dee Meree's*; and the opposite side, *Wa'dee Seya'leh*. The next district is *Wa'dee Dihmee't*. The mountains, which are low, and of sandstone, are, on both sides, very near the river; and the tracts of cultivable land along the banks, consequently very narrow. The sa'ckiyehs are constantly in motion; and no portion of the soil is left uncultivated. The district above Wa'dee Dihmee't, as far as Ta'feh, is comprised under the name of *Wa'dee El-Mooba'raka't*; being inhabited chiefly by a tribe of the Koonoo'z of that name: but it is subdivided into several small wa'dees. The Mooba'raka't are a most uncivil race.

A little above Wa'dee Dihmee't, in a tract called *Wa'dee Sahda'b*, on the east of the river, is a small, ruined temple. I could not find any perfect specimen of the name it bears: it is one of the Ptolemies. The building is almost entirely destroyed. There are some huts on the north and south of it, which have the name of Ckum'leh. Here I first saw Nubians with frizzled hair: the Nubians, now, generally shave their heads, and wear a white cotton cap.

On the opposite side of the river, a little higher up, are relics of another small temple: a solitary column remaining erect.

The valley continues very contracted: and the strip of cultivated land on either side of the river, extremely narrow. About two miles higher, on the west of the river, within the district called *Wa'dee Ckurda'seh* (or *Gurda'seh*) وادى قرداسه , is a small, picturesque, ruined temple,[1] situated on the low ridge of sandstone rock which bounds the valley on this side; a few paces behind the narrow strip of alluvial soil, which I found overgrown here with senna and colocynths. This little temple originally had twelve columns; but only half that number are now standing. The entrance is towards the north; between two columns with square capitals ornamented on each side with the full face of Athor. The other spaces between the columns are closed, to half the height of the shafts, by walls. Of the stones which formed the roof, only one remains; stretching across from side to side. The style of this temple shews it to be one of the least ancient on the banks of the Nile; but we cannot ascertain its exact age: it never was finished: no name is found upon it; and it has no hieroglyphics or other sculptures, excepting a figure offering to Athor, which is sculptured upon one of the columns.

Walking along the side of the rocky ridge to the distance of about a furlong south of the temple above-described, we arrive before the entrance to some extensive quarries. It is a short road, cut through the sandstone rock, which leads to them. On entering these quarries, we observe a number of Greek inscriptions, cut on the perpendicular, hewn surface of a mass of rock which appears like the front of a temple; having a recess, in the form of a door, surmounted by the winged globe. Within this recess is a bench, or pedestal; apparently for a statue. On each side, but higher up, is a bust, of rude workmanship, cut in high relief; each within an arched niche. There are also, near the base of the rock, some little figures of Athor or Isis, carved in the same manner. The inscriptions are commemorative of the pious homage of certain individuals, each of whom styles himself ιερευς γομου, "priest of *gomos*." This word γομος signifies "a cargo." It would seem, therefore, that the persons here named had each conveyed a boat-load of stones (and some,

---

[1]See plate 15 [fig. 138].

five and eight boat-loads) for the construction of temples in the neighbourhood of these quarries, or between this place and the Cataracts; and that the priests were ambitious of performing this meritorious act; or that the title of priest was conferred upon those who did this gratuitously. The sculptors of sacred subjects were certainly of the order of the priesthood; and perhaps also stone-cutters for the temples. I insert a copy of one of the inscriptions and of one of the two busts before mentioned, beneath which it is cut.[1] We find, among them, inscriptions dated in the reigns of Gordian and Philip. They all appear to have been executed at periods between the latter part of the second, and the middle of the third, century of the Christian era. Probably the neighbouring temple which I have described was constructed in this age.

About a mile higher, on the same side of the river, is a large, oblong enclosure of ruined stone walls, above 300 feet in length, and scarcely less in breadth. The walls are about ten feet thick, and about fifteen feet high where they are least ruined. There is a gateway in the northern side, and another in the southern; and there may have been others. In the interior are some remains of stone buildings; but whether there was a temple within it does not appear. It has been inferred, from the thickness of the walls, that this enclosure was designed as a military defence: it is, however, similar to the enclosure of the great temple of Ckala'b'sheh.— In August, 1827, on my second voyage up the Nile, I witnessed here an extraordinary phenomenon; a shower of rain, accompanied by lightning.

---

[1]See no. 47 of the subjects for wood-cuts [fig. 139].

Chapter XXXIV.
Ta'feh and Ckala'b'sheh.

Monuments to Ta'feh (the ancient Taphis)—Rapids between Ta'feh and Ckala'b'sheh—Temples of Ckala'b'sheh (the ancient Talmis).

Above Wa'dee Ckurda'seh the valley widens, for the spaces of about three miles; and the tract of cultivable land on each side of the river is not so narrow. In this comparatively open district, on the west side of the river, are situated two small temples and numerous other monuments of the town of *Taphis*. The name of *Ta'feh* طافه, which is also pronounced *Te'feh*, and *Tey'feh*, is still given to this district, and particularly to a village which occupies a part of the site of the ancient town. Adjacent to this village are numerous ancient edifices of a very singular construction. From one spot I counted more than twenty of them. They are built of stone; and, in their present state, most of them appear merely like square enclosures. They are mostly between 40 and 50 feet square. Their walls are constructed in a very remarkable manner; having the form of the portion of an inverted arch; as shewn by a view which I made.[1] This peculiarity is not the effect of a sinking of the foundation: all are the same. Perhaps this mode of construction was adopted with the view of giving greater strength to the edifice. The space which these buildings occupy is covered with broken pottery and fragments of stone, which shew the extent of the ancient town. In that which is seen in the view above referred to, and in many others, are several fallen blocks which formed cornices, lintels, &c. These shew a strange mixture of Egyptian and late Roman ornaments. On many blocks we find the winged globe, and, above the cornice, a row of asps; as over the doors of many temples. All the ornaments are in very bad taste. In some of these buildings which are less injured than the rest, we find one or two small doors, and the interior divided into apartments by one or more walls. I cannot conjecture any use for which they could have been designed, unless as guard-houses: Taphis, being situated at one of the natural divisions of the country, just below the spot where the Nile is hemmed in on either side by granite mountains, which leave no road along its banks, was a fit place for a military station.

There are also, at Ta'feh, two small temples; both, evidently of the period of the Roman domination. One of these is at a short distance to the south of the village: the other is within the village in the northern quarter; and the back of it is seen in the view before referred to.—The

---

[1]See plate 16 [fig. 140].

former of these[†] consisted of a portico, with a small chamber behind it. The two side-walls and the back of the portico are nearly entire; and two columns remain in the interior. There were two more columns, originally, in the interior, and two others forming the front. The interior (which, as well as the exterior, is without sculpture) has been painted by early Christians; but their work is now scarcely visible. At the end are some late Greek inscriptions, written on the wall with red paint, and now, for the most part, illegible. Above them is part of a Greek-Egyptian calendar; but the writing of this, also, is almost effaced. Behind the portico are the ruined walls of the sanctuary; which was very small; and without any sculpture. The temple was enclosed by a wall, of which little remains.

The other temple,[‡] within the village, is in a better state of preservation, but half concealed by the huts which surround it.[1] It is of a most irregular and strange construction; and apparently still less ancient than that which I have just described. The front has two columns, between which is the principal entrance, now closed with dry mud and stones. On the right of this is a smaller door. The part corresponding with this latter entrance is a blank wall. The building is nearly square; consisting only of one chamber; and not exactly rectangular. In the interior are four columns, supporting the roof; which is entire. Neither within nor without are any sculptures, excepting the winged globes over the doors, and the few usual architectural ornaments. On the top of it are remains of a modern building.

In my view of the little temple just described is seen one of the huts of the village. In the interior is a hand-mill, of the usual form, composed of two stones; the lower stone attached to the floor; with a rim of mud-plaster round it. In the same view are seen two of the common receptacles for corn; in the form of truncated cones; composed of mud and chopped straw; and left to harden in the sun. These are also common in Egypt.

Ta'feh is one of the largest villages in Nubia. The inhabitants of the western quarter of this village (the furthest from the river) distinguish themselves as Arabs; and speak both Arabic and the language of the Koonoo'z. Their dress and manners are the same as those of their neighbours; excepting that they are a more brutal set. I was informed that they sometimes make trading expeditions to Koordoofa'n, for slaves. European travellers often meet with much incivility from these people; and I was not without my share.—The bushy, frizzled hair is still seen here.

To the west of this village, in the midst of a desert plain, is an old Arab cemetery, with many tomb-stones inscribed in the Koo'fee characters, like those of Aswa'n. The dates of these are between the middle of the

---

[†]The South Temple, which disappeared, perhaps in the late nineteenth century.
[‡]The North Temple.
[1]See plate 17 [fig. 141].

fourth and the beginning of the sixth centuries after the flight. They are mostly ill cut. All that I saw were of Moos'lim Arabs. They are curious historical monuments; and I can only account for their existence here and being of such an age by supposing that, when Ka'foo'r El-Ikhshee'dee, the Governor of Egypt, after an incursion of the Nubians into his territories, sent an expedition which penetrated as far as Ibree'm, and took that place, in the year of the flight 345, some of the Arab soldiers remained at Ta'feh, and their posterity likewise for many years.—There is also here the tomb of a sheykh, which is much respected.

Upon the summit of the foremost of the rugged granite mountains on this side of the Nile, to the south of the village and ruins which I have described,[1] are two small buildings. The upper part of each is of crude brick, and rests upon a foundation of stone; the materials of which were perhaps taken from the ruins on the plain below. On some of the blocks on the ground are ancient architectural ornaments; as the winged globe. I cannot conceive the purpose for which these buildings were erected on a site so difficult of access: they may have been similar to the larger edifices on the adjacent plain; and the brick superstructure raised in later times; but I rather incline to the opinion first suggested.—I examined these on my first arrival at Ta'feh. The ascent to them being difficult, I did not encumber myself with arms. Arriving at the summit, I found that a Nubian, bearing a musket, had followed me unperceived; and when I was about to descend, the fellow prevented me; threatening to shoot me if I did not give him a small sum of money. The answer that I had none upon my person did not satisfy him; and he still detained me. Finding him resolute, I offered, if he would descend with me to my boat, to give him some powder and balls. This he at first declined to do; but on my solemnly assuring him that I would give him what I promised, he consented. Still, however, he mistrusted me; and presently stopped me again, and made me repeat "by God!" that I would fulfil my promise. On arriving at my boat, I desired him to wait on the bank while I got ready the present for him: then, taking my pistols, I offered him their contents. The fellow sculked away; grumbling a warning to me not to land again at Ta'feh. I was not, however, molested here on my return; nor did I see this person again: but a few miles below, I was treated with more serious hostility, for suffering a lamb, one of my live-stock, to eat a few kidney-beans on the bank. Several armed men followed and kept pace with my boat for about an hour, until it was dark, running along the bank, and shouting and vowing vengeance. My boatmen thought it necessary to continue our course during the night; contrary to my usual custom.

In the plain on the east of the river, opposite the remains of Taphis, the site of the town of *Contra Taphis* is denoted by quantities of broken pottery and stones, covering the soil. Here, also, are remains of two

---

[1] Seen in plate 16 [fig. 140].

buildings of the same singular construction as those which are so numerous on the west.

The mountains of granite which confine and contract the bed of the Nile immediately above Ta'feh have a bold and picturesque appearance. Proceeding a little way up this narrow strait, we find the stream obstructed yet more by numerous rocky islands, which are also of granite. These, when the river is low, form rapids, which are termed the *Shila'l of Ckala'b'sheh*. On the two largest of the islands are crude-brick ruins; and upon a hill of rock upon the eastern bank, just below these, are similar remains. Here and there we see a little patch of verdure; presenting a pleasing contrast with the high, dark, craggy hills of naked granite. At the distance of about three miles above the first granite hills, we again find the river free from islands and sunk rocks. The valley then widens a little; and is again bounded by sandstone mountains. This district is called *Ckala'b'sheh* (or *Gala'b'sheh*) قلابشه.

The principal village of Ckala'b'sheh, one of the largest in Nubia, is on the western bank. It occupies the site of the ancient *Talmis*; and lies partly on the north and partly on the south of a large temple, which, though one of the least ancient class, is a very fine structure. An embankment of stone supports and lines the shore before the village and great temple; which are nearly concealed from the view of a person approaching by the river by do'ms and date-palms. A causeway of stone, twenty-five feet broad, and a hundred and sixty feet long, with a flight of steps at the end, leads from the river to a terrace extending along the front of the temple; of which I made a view, from this causeway.[1] The causeway had a parapet-wall on each side, composed of two courses of stone; but almost all the stones of the upper course have been thrown down. The front of the temple is formed by a fine propylæum, a hundred and fifteen feet wide. There is a remarkable irregularity in the disposition of this propylæum: it is not parallel with the front of the portico; nor at right-angles with the causeway leading to it. Much of the upper part of each wing has been thrown down; and the displaced materials nearly cover the terrace. The propylæum being the least finished part of the structure, it has not been sculptured. Passing through its portal, we enter a court[2] encumbered with a vast accumulation of blocks of stone; the ruins of the propylæum and other parts of the edifice. On each side is a wall, extending from the propylæum, and forming an enclosure round the portico and the main body of the temple; and without this is a second wall of enclosure. The court had originally a row of columns on the right and left, and along the back of the propylæum. Only one of these is standing; on the left side. Amazing pains have been taken to destroy this edifice. The front of the portico forms the end of the court. In each of the side-walls of the court are four small, narrow cells; of which it is difficult to divine the use; and on the right side is also a door; opposite to which is

---

[1] See plate 18. The tree on the left is a do'm-palm [fig. 142].
[2] See plate 19 [fig. 143].

a small portal, in the outer wall, forming a side-entrance to the temple. Each wing of the propylæum has a door at the back, 7 stairs ascending to the summit.—The front of the portico has four columns. The entrance is in the middle. To the right and left of this, the columns are engaged to about half their height; and this part of the building is in a very unfinished state. Here we find several votive inscriptions, in Greek, in honour of Manduli, the principal god of the temple, and one of the representatives of the sun: in one we read παρα θεω μεγιςω μανδυλι: in another, παρα τω χυριω μανδυλι. There is also an inscription in the enchorial characters; very neatly cut; and a remarkable Greek inscription; which I copied. Of the latter, the following is a translation.

"I, Silco, prince of the Nubians and of all the Ethiopians, have penetrated to Talmis and Taphis; waging war against the Blemmyes. I conquered them in a former war, by the aid of a god. The second time also I conquered them, and took their villages. I rested with my forces. The first time that I conquered them, they sued for peace. I made peace with them; and they swore (to observe the treaty) by their gods; and I believed their oath, thinking them a good people: and I retired to the upper region of my country. Being a king, I was not inferior to the other kings; but I surpassed them: for those who opposed me I left not unpunished, unless they implored forgiveness (and called me Mars). In the lower provinces of my kingdom I am a lion; and in the upper parts, Mars. I have waged war with the Blemmyes from Primis to Talmis. The other nations dwelling above the Nubians, I have ravaged their country, because they (opposed me). The chiefs, also, of other nations who contended with me I have not suffered to repose at their ease in the shade; (but have driven them from their houses to be scorched all day by) the sun .... even their women and children."

Within the portico there were originally eight columns; of which, only two remain: the fragments of the roof and of the other columns which supported it cover the floor to a considerable height. This part of the edifice, also, is unfinished, and without sculpture, excepting at the end: the central part of which (that is, the part that formed the front of the main body of the temple, which was more ancient, and considerably less wide, than the portico) is surrounded by a torus, and surmounted by a cornice; and it is covered with sculptures representing the usual offerings, in a very bad style. The sculptures of the interior of the building bear the name of Augustus (Autocrator Cæsar), in whose reign the main body of the edifice was probably constructed. The sculptures before mentioned only bear a mystic name, which is also found on the propylæum.—The first chamber, immediately behind the great portico, is decorated with sculptures of the same description; but the hieroglyphics are not finished; some of them being merely drawn in red lines. Some parts of the walls retain the plaster with which they were covered by early Christians, who concealed the sculptures probably in the fear that the people might relapse into that idolatry from which they had lately emerged. This is much narrower than the portico. On the left side are two doors; from the first of which, a staircase ascends to the roof: the second door only communicates with the space under the stairs. On the same side, higher up, is a small chamber, to which we descend by stairs from the roof of the temple.—Next behind the chamber first described is another, similar to the former. Here, also, are two doors on the left; each leading into a small, narrow apartment. The sculptures in this chamber are finished and painted; but of the same kind as those before mentioned; and partly covered with plaster.—The third (and last) chamber is wider than the others: no space being parted off on the left. The sculptures are similar to those in the two former chambers; and the execution as bad. The colours upon them, in most parts, are remarkably fresh in appearance; and very brilliant; but they have not that beautiful harmony which is observable in all the more ancient Egyptian paintings and painted sculptures. Here, and here only, I observed a violet-colour much used. The decorations altogether are vile; but the temple itself is certainly a noble structure.—Between the two enclosing walls, to the right of the court behind the propylæum, is a small, sculptured chamber: the decorations are on a small scale; and presenting nothing remarkable. The outer enclosure is partly formed, at the western extremity, by the hewn, perpendicular face of the rock (the temple being at the base of the hills); and at the end, towards the left corner, is a small, square, excavated chamber. There are some remains of an unfinished building before its entrance; but the chamber has no sculpture, nor any decoration.

In the rocky acclivity behind the temple and the scattered village are the excavated tombs of the ancient inhabitants of Talmis; appearing almost like natural cavities; and containing nothing but a few rough sarcophagi, and the bones of the dead. The steep is covered with small fragments of stone, and a vast quantity of broken pottery. In many parts, it is extensively quarried.

Proceeding along the slopes of the hills, from the great temple northwards, we pass some quarries, and in a quarter of an hour arrive at a most interesting rock-temple, of the time of Rameses 2nd (or Sesostris); now called *Da'r el-Wa'lee*, or *Beyt el-Wa'lee* (the House of the Magistrate). This temple[1] is excavated in the upper part of an angle of the mountains; between which and the river is a small tract of cultivated land. From the plain below, it is concealed from observation by some ruins of crude brick in a narrow court before it. This court, or avenue, is forty-four feet in length, and twenty in width. The sides, which are formed by the hewn rock, are six feet high. Early Christians converted this temple into a church, and made of the court a covered hall, by raising a wall of crude brick across it, increasing the height of the sides with the same material, and then arching it over. The whole of the arched roof has, however, fallen; and only the walls remain. The hewn sides of this court are decorated with beautiful and very interesting sculptures. The left wall is divided into two equal compartments. In the first of these

[1]See plate 20 [missing].

(commencing our examination from the left extremity) we first see a confused group of negroes flying before the chariot of the great Sesostris, and the hindmost of them trampled upon by his horses: the Egyptian monarch, as usual, represented as of a colossal size in comparison with the other figures. Behind him, to the right, are two other chariots. The subjects of the other compartment of this side are particularly curious. They exhibit the spoils and tribute brought and presented to the Egyptian king after the conquest. Of the most interesting portion of the sculptures of this compartment I insert a copy.[1] Here are represented, as some of the fruits obtained by the expedition into Ethiopia, various productions of art and nature:—four elegant chairs, two fans, or shades, logs of wood (probably ebony), elephants' teeth, ostrich-feathers and eggs, a lion, a beautiful antelope with straight horns, oxen with the tips of their horns cut into the form of human hands, and with the figure of a human head between their horns, a man bearing a log of some precious wood and the skin of a small animal, a group of captives clad in leopards' skins: there are also a kind of panther, several monkeys, a giraffe, other oxen with the peculiarity above-described, Ethiopian women and children (one woman bearing two children in a basket on her back), a gazelle, an ostrich, and another animal of the panther kind. The king, seated on a throne, views these curious objects.—The opposite (or right) side-wall illustrates another of this prince's conquests. In a compartment at the centre we see again the king in his car, pursuing and riding over the fugitives, who are stout, bearded men; probably Persians, or Assyrians. The monarch, stooping in his car, has seized two of his enemies by the hair of the head, and is about to destroy them. To the right of this piece is represented a fortress, before which stands the Egyptian king, nearly twice the height of the fort (for it was the universal practice of the ancient Egyptian sculptors to distinguish the most important objects by superior relative magnitude). An enemy of the same colossal size raises his head out of this diminutive fortress, which is scarcely large enough to contain his body: he is grasping a broken bow; and is about to perish by the hand of his too powerful opponent, who has seized him by the hair of the head, and is ready to inflict the fatal blow. Next to this, the victorious prince is represented holding three kneeling captives by the hair: he has his battle-ax upon his shoulder; but not in the attitude of striking: a person approaching him is dragging along three more captives, who are hand-bound, and tied together by a rope. This is at the right extremity of the wall. To the left of the central subject (which commences the history of the war) the king is portrayed in the act of slaying an enemy. Next to this, at the further extremity of the wall, we see the monarch seated on his throne: a person brings before him three captives; and below these is represented a party of Egyptian warriors, approaching to congratulate their prince.—The front of the temple, at

---

[1]See no. 48 of the subjects for wood-cuts (one of the mounted drawings, placed next to plate 20 [missing]). (Not found RSP.)

the end of this narrow court, has three entrances.[1] It is decorated with sculptures representing the same Egyptian king offering and paying homage to Amon-Ra, and other divinities. The two lateral entrances have been made at a later period; for they interrupt the sculptures. The chamber to which these entrances admit us is of an oblate plan; being 34 feet in width, and only 14 feet from the front to the back. It has two thick, polygonal columns, without capitals; the types of the Doric order. At each extremity of the front-wall we find the king represented in the act of slaying a kneeling captive, whom he holds by the hair. The victim on the right is a negro; and that in the corresponding piece, of the same nation which I have supposed to be Persian or Assyrian. The other walls are decorated with representations of the king offering to and worshipping the gods. They have been covered with a coat of white-wash; but in most parts we may discern the brilliant and harmonious colours with which they were painted. In the back-wall are two recesses; in each of which are seated three small figures—the king between two deities.—A door opposite to the central entrance leads us into the sanctuary; which is 12 feet long, and 9 feet wide. At the end is a recess, like the two before mentioned; but the figures which were within it have been destroyed. On each side of the door, within the sanctuary, is sculptured the king, Rameses 2nd, as a youth, standing, and receiving nourishment from the breast of a goddess—of Isis in the one case, and of Anouke in the other. The side-walls of the sanctuary are occupied by sculptures representing offerings.—This rock-temple, from the style and subjects of its sculptures, must be pronounced one of the most interesting of Egyptian monuments.

That Talmis was a very considerable town, we may infer from the magnitude of the temple which I first described: that it was also a very ancient town is shewn by the other temple.—On the opposite side of the river are some mounds of rubbish which mark the site of *Contra Talmis*.

---

[1]See, again, plate 20 [missing].

Chapter XXXV.
Dendoo'r, Gur'f Hhosey'n, Dek'keh, &c.

Scenery above Ckala'b'sheh—Temple of Dendoo'r—Rock-temple of Gur'f Hhosey'n—Temple of Dek'keh—Remains opposite Dek'keh—Little temple of Ckoor'teh—Ruins of M'[h]har'ruck'ah—Scenery between M'hhar'ruck'ah and Wa'dee es-Sooboo'ä.

After a short visit to Ckala'b'sheh, which made me look forward with much pleasure to the examination of its monuments on my return, we continued our voyage; having a fresh and favourable breeze. Immediately above Ckala'b'sheh, the mountains on both sides are very near the river: so much so that, for the space of a mile and a half, I saw not the smallest patch of verdure on either bank. We then find a little border of cultivated land both on the east and west; though the valley is scarcely less contracted. This part is called *Ab'oo Ho'r* ابو هور : the name applies to both sides of the river, and to a few groups of huts there situated, on the lower parts of the rocky slopes.—We made fast to the bank for the night about three miles within the tropic.—The greatest height of the thermometer this day was 106°.

21st. The next district, or portion of the valley, above Ab'oo Ho'r is *Wa'dee Dendoo'r* وادی دندور. On the western side (Ghur'b Dendoo'r) is a temple, of small dimensions, and of the same age as the main part of the great temple of Ckala'b'sheh; the reign of Augustus. I landed before this temple early in the morning. It is situated almost close to the river; only a very narrow strip of cultivated land intervening; which, when I visited the spot, was covered with senna and the creeping colocynth. The temple is built on the irregular slope of the low, rocky ridge; which is here strewed with detached masses of stone, intermixed with broken pottery, indicating that a small town stood here. My view of this edifice[1] is taken from the direction in which it is seen in ascending the valley. It has, in front, a small portal; before which is a square enclosure, formed by well-built walls of stone. The front-wall of this enclosure has a singular peculiarity: its exterior face being slightly concave, or curved inwards. As the temple is unfinished, we may suppose that this enclosure was to have been filled up, so as to form a platform: indeed it is partly so filled. The portal is decorated with sculptures of the usual kind, representing offerings, &c.; but with only a mystic name, similar to that which I have mentioned in describing the great temple of Ckala'b'sheh; so that it is uncertain when the sculptures were executed. The space between this

---

[1]See plate 21 [fig. 144].

portal and the temple itself is covered with fragments of stone; some of which formed parts of the temple, and perhaps of the two wings of a propylæum connected by the portal above mentioned. Among them I observed a small figure of a hawk; the head of which was broken off.— The portico of the temple has two small columns; between which is the entrance. The front and the interior are sculptured, with the usual subjects of offerings &c., and bear, throughout, the hieroglyphic name of the Emperor Augustus (Autocrator Cæsar). The exterior of the temple is also similarly sculptured. The interior has been plastered and painted by early Christians: but their work has almost entirely perished. Behind the portico is a little chamber, without any sculpture, excepting round the door through which we pass into the sanctuary. This is almost as small as the former chamber, and, like it, without decoration, excepting at the end, where is sculptured a shrine, in the form of a door, in which is represented the king offering to Isis.—A few feet behind the temple, but not exactly in a direct line with the axis of the building, is a small, square chamber, excavated in the rock. Before the door of this was a little porch of masonry, which is now nearly demolished.

Proceeding about six miles higher, through the district of *Wa'dee Meree'yeh* وادى مريّه, we arrive at *Wa'dee Ckir'sheh* (or *Gir'sheh*) وادى قرشه, which comprises both banks of the river. Here, on the eastern side, are the remains of a considerable town, situated on a slope of rock, close to the river, and consisting of ruins of crude brick and fragments of stone. The Nubians call it *Sebagoo'ra*; and say that a king of that name reigned there.

On the opposite side of the river is a small village called *Gur'f Hhosey'n* (or *Jur'f Hhosey'n*) جرف حسين.[1] Here is a large rock-temple, of the reign of Rameses 2nd. It is excavated in the upper part of the rocky barrier of the valley; which is here at a short distance from the river: a small strip of cultivated land intervenes. There must have been a flight of steps leading up to this temple; and an avenue of sphinxes; of which several are lying, much broken, at the bottom of the steep. At the spot where, I suppose, the avenue commenced is a mutilated statue of the king; like those which are seen in my view of the temple of Wa'dee es-Sooboo'ă. Before the temple was a peristyle court[2]; the two sides of which consisted each of four square pillars, fronted by Osiridean figures of the king, of rather clumsy proportions: all of these are much injured; and some, almost wholly demolished. There was, along the front of this court, a row of four columns; only two of which remain. Perhaps there was also a propylæum in front of the court. On each side, behind the square pillars, was a wall, partly formed of the solid rock; little of which

---

[1]In Burckhardt's work, this name is written *Djorn Hosseyn*: in his notes it was probably only written in Arabic; and in copying, the final letter of the first word was, I suppose, mistaken for ن . It has been variously misspelled by other travellers.

[2]See plate 22 [fig. 145].

now remains. The rock has also been cut parallel with these two walls. The face of the hewn, perpendicular rock which forms the front of the temple has been decorated with sculptures, which are now almost wholly effaced. We still trace, on the upper part, on each side of the centre, the figure of the king sacrificing some captives. Of the sculptures on the lower part, not a line can be discovered, excepting near the base, to the left of the door; where the feet, only, of some figures are discernible. The two side-walls, outside the square pillars, have also been sculptured; apparently with battle-scenes; for, on the lower part of that on the left is a row of men with shields. At the end of each of these walls are sculptured three figures, in high relief, in a recess; representing the king between two deities: but, as the upper part of the walls is destroyed, the figures here mentioned are not entire.—The interior of the first or great chamber[1] has a very grand and striking effect. Standing at the entrance, we behold before us on either side three colossal figures, each about twenty feet high, cut out of the rock. They are clumsy and ill-proportioned; and there is some slight irregularity in their heights; but we have not so much fault to find with the expression of the faces; all of which are, however, much injured. The hands are crossed upon the breast; and hold the flail and crook of Osiris: and on the belt of each is the hieroglyphic name of Rameses 2nd; whom they represent in the character of a god. They are much blackened; as is also every part of the interior of the temple. Each stands upon a square pedestal, before (and uniting with) a square pillar of the rock left to support the roof. The walls of the chamber are so black and so much injured that the sculptures with which they are decorated are very obscurely seen: but they merely exhibit the usual offerings, to Phtha, the chief god of the temple, and to other divinities. In each side-wall are four square recesses, in each of which are three figures, like those of the side-walls of the court, mentioned before; representing the king between two deities. The paint is discernible on some parts; and red and yellow appear to have been the predominant colours.—Behind the great chamber is a second, of an oblate form; having two square pillars: its walls are decorated with sculptures similar to those of the first, and equally black and indistinct. From this chamber we enter five other chambers; one on either side, and three behind. The two side-chambers are of an oblong form; and each of them has, at the end, a wide bench of rock.—Of the three chambers at the end, the central is the sanctuary of the temple. This is a small chamber. In the centre of it is a plane altar; and at the end are four figures, of colossal proportions, sitting on a bench, in a recess. The first to the left represents the chief god of the temple; Phtha. Over his head is sculptured a large scarabæus (his particular emblem), with extended wings, which droop downwards, in the form of a crescent. It is much mutilated. The second figure is that of Amon-Ra. The third is the king, Rameses 2nd, with his name on either side. Next to him sits Isis, having

---

[1]See plate 23 [fig. 146].

her right arm passed behind his back, and the hand upon his right shoulder. On each side-wall is sculptured a boat; before which stands the king, presenting an offering.

Gur'f Hhosey'n corresponds with the situation pointed out, by the itinerary of Antoninus, as that of *Tutzis*; being 20 Roman miles above Talmis, the modern Ckala'b'sheh.—There are here several sheykhs' tombs, and a long dyke, or break-water, of stone, which is only seen when the river is low.

Proceeding rather more than two miles higher, we arrive at the district of Wa'dee Ckoostem'neh (or Goostem'neh) وادى قستمنه , which comprehends both sides of the river. On the western side is a low, flat desert, in which no mountains are visible from the river; and there is, on this side, only one small patch of cultivated soil in this wa'dee. On the opposite side is a narrow strip of verdure all along the bank; and the mountains on that side are low, and near the river. Approaching *Wa'dee Dek'keh* وادى دكّه , we observe, on the western, desert bank, some ruins of crude brick.

Dek'keh is remarkable for a temple of Thoth, or Hermes; a fine monument, though one of those of comparatively late times. It is about six miles above Gur'f Hhosey'n, on the western bank of the river. Here, probably, was situated the ancient town of *Pselcis*: for though Pselcis is placed in the itinerary of Antoninus at the distance of twelve miles above Tutzis, yet Contra Pselcis is stated to have been only twenty-four miles from Contra Tammis: therefore I infer that the former statement is incorrect. At Dek'keh was evidently a very considerable town, which I cannot suppose would be omitted in the itinerary. Also, Pselcis was four Roman miles below Corte; and there is a village now called Ckoor'teh, with a small temple, about that distance above Dek'keh.—Behind a narrow strip of cultivated land, which borders the river, stands the temple of Dek'keh, in a wide, sandy plain, a great part of which was formerly cultivated. There is still a small verdant tract in the midst of the sand, somewhat remote from the river; and here, and for the space of several miles southward, are many wells, which were used for the purpose of irrigating the plain: the water being raised by sa'ckiyehs. The natives affirm that there were 1600 of these wells.—The direction of the front of the temple is about north 20° east. The propylæum[1] is eighty feet wide; of good proportions; and little injured; but unfinished. It has no sculpture, excepting within the portal; where, on the left side, are some figures presenting offerings; and on the back of the portal; where are some other, small figures. On each side of the portal, and within it, and likewise on the back of the propylæum, are numerous inscriptions in Greek; merely recording that certain individuals had visited the temple and worshipped "the most great god Hermes." Two of these, I observed, were dated in the reign of Tiberius; and one, in the reign of Adrian. Each wing of the propylæum has a staircase by which to ascend to the summit.

---

[1]See plate 24 [fig. 147].

The entrances to the stairs are in the back of the propylæum.—The front of the portico is forty feet behind the propylæum. Behind the portico is a small chamber: then, the sanctuary, which is the oldest part of the building: and behind this, another chamber. The portico has only two columns; between which is the entrance. The front is sculptured with the usual offerings, and over the entrance, on the front of the architrave, is a Greek inscription; but the stone is much broken; and very little of the writing remains. It records the dedication of the temple by "Ptolemy and Cleopatra, the gods Euergetes." The interior of the portico is decorated with sculptures, of the same description as those of the front; excepting some parts of the walls which have not been finished; and on these plain parts, figures of apostles and saints have been painted by early Christians. The sculptures are bad in point of style; but very carefully finished. There are here two remarkable figures, on the interior sides of the two columns: one is a monkey, the emblem of Thoth, standing, and holding with both hands something in the form of a sceptre surmounted by the head of Athor or Isis: the other is a sitting figure of Typhon, playing on a kind of harp, of a triangular form.—The door which leads into the chamber immediately behind was originally an isolated portal before the sanctuary. The end of this chamber is formed by the front of the sanctuary; and the other sides have no sculptures. Even the sculptures on this front are unfinished. They bear the names of Ptolemy Euergetes and Berenice, and of Philopator and Arsinoë. The interior of the sanctuary is decorated with sculptures representing the usual offerings; and these bear the name of the king by whom the sanctuary was built. His name may be read *Arkamen,* or *Alkamen.* Being anterior to the Ptolemies above-mentioned, and yet not found in Egypt, he was doubtless an Ethiopian king, and probably Ergamenes. The walls of the sanctuary are much blackened. Between the sides of this chamber and the outer walls of the temple a small space intervenes, both on the right and left. In the former are stairs, leading up to the roof. In the corresponding space we find some curious sculptures: at the end is represented a lioness, with a globe and serpents above her head; a vulture, with a palm-branch in its talons, hovering over her; and a monkey standing before her, in an attitude of adoration. Beneath this piece are two lions, sitting face to face.—The northern end of the last chamber is formed by the back of the sanctuary; upon which, over the door, is sculptured a scarabæus with expanded wings; and on each side of this, four monkeys are represented with their hands raised in adoration. The other sides of the chamber are also sculptured. At the base, all round, are figures of the masculo-feminine god Nilus, in the act of pouring water from two jars.—Over a door in the western side of this temple is an inscription in hieroglyphics, with another, occupying about the same space, beneath it, in the enchorial characters.—The exterior of the temple has no sculptures, excepting those already mentioned on the front of the portico, and some on a part of the western side; where is a row of small figures of deities, near the base. On the east and south and part of the western side are remains of a stone wall which surrounded, on those three sides, the main body of the temple; uniting with the portico: and there are, on the east, a small, ruined portal, and some remains of a second wall of enclosure, which appears to have united with the propylæum. All round the temple are traces of extensive constructions: and there seems to have been an avenue of sphinxes leading to it, in front. Close by the propylæum, towards the east, are some fragments which belonged to another temple; and the name of Thothmos 3rd is upon one of these stones. It appears, then, that Pselcis was a town of high antiquity: all its more ancient monuments were probably destroyed by Cambyses.

Opposite Dek'keh is a village called *Ckoobba'n* (or *Goobba'n*) قبّان ; and a little above this, by the river, is a square enclosure, formed by very thick walls of crude brick, surrounding the remains of a small town; doubtless *Contra Pselcis*. Close to the walls, towards the south, are some remains of a temple, with the name of Rameses 2nd, and some relics of sculpture, of no importance. Here we certainly have to regret the destruction of an interesting monument. Some of the sculptures formed part of the representation of a battle-scene.

On the western side of the river, about three miles and a half above Dek'keh, is the village of *Ckoor'teh* (or *Goor'teh*) قرته ; the situation and name of which prove it to mark the site of the ancient *Corte*. There is here, at a short distance from the river, a little temple, of the least ancient class; consisting only of a small, square chamber, with a second and third, both of the same size, but smaller than the first; one behind another. The lintel of the first door is the only part that is decorated with sculptures.

On the east of the Nile, opposite Ckoor'teh, is part of a range of mountains called Geb'el 'Alla'ckee (or 'Alla'gee), reported, by the Arab geographers, to contain gold. A wide, sandy plain, without any border of cultivable soil, intervenes between them and the river.

A little above Ckoor'teh is a well-cultivated island, Gezee'ret Dera'r, about two miles in length. Here I passed the night of the 21st. The height of the thermometer this day, in the afternoon, was 105°.

22nd. Above the island of Dera'r commences the district called *Wa'dee M'hhar'ruck'ah* (or *M'hhar'rug'ah*) وادى محرّقه . Here, very near to the bank of the river, on the western side, is a ruined temple, of the least ancient class. I roughly calculated its distance from Ckoor'teh at three miles and a half. It evidently marks the site of *Hiera Lycaminos*, which is placed, in the itinerary of Antoninus, at the distance of four Roman miles above Corte. The temple above-mentioned is built upon a massive foundation of masonry. The southern wall, which formed the front, has fallen, all at the same time; and its materials are lying in regular layers upon the ground, just as they fell. The building is also rent and shattered in other parts; apparently from a sinking of part of the foundation. It is entirely without sculpture or decoration of any kind; and even the capitals of the columns are unfinished. Though we do not find upon it the name of its founder, we may safely pronounce, from the style of its architecture, that it is one of the least ancient monuments in the valley of the Nile. Within it is a row of columns, six in number, on the southern side: there is another row of the same number on the corresponding side; and there are two more columns on the western side, uniting with the other two rows. In the north-east corner is a winding stair-case, by which to ascend to the top of the building. The columns of the southern row are united by a wall about half their height, excepting the two central columns; between which is a door-way. The principal entrance to the temple was, doubtless, directly before this door-way. There is an entrance also on the eastern side, towards the river; and there is a smaller one at the opposite extremity, and another at the right corner of the northern side. Early Christians, who converted this temple into a church, have painted, upon the interior of the north-wall, the history of the fall of man: the groups representing the different events are arranged in one line, like a procession of men and angels. There are also here many Christian inscriptions.

Almost close to this building, towards the river, are remains of another temple, of small dimensions. The whole has fallen, or been thrown down, excepting part of one wall, upon which is some curious sculpture, which I should think the latest specimen of the kind now existing on the banks of the Nile in Nubia or Egypt.[1] On the upper part, Isis is represented sitting on the ground, under a tree resembling the Indian fig; and before her stands the young Harpocrates, offering her a vase: both these figures are designed with a front face, contrary to the common rule of the ancient Egyptian artists: but the sculptor of this piece seems to have been so well pleased with his clumsy composition that he has made a copy of it on a smaller scale, upon the same wall; or perhaps this was the work of some other admirer. In the former sculpture, over the head of Harpocrates, are three small figures: one of them, Amon, in his Priapian character: the other two are of Roman style. Isis is again represented three times, in a standing posture; extremely clumsy; and likewise the god Thoth. The sculptor, I think, must have been a Roman.

Hiera Sycaminos was the last town (though not the last point) of that part of Nubia which, from its length of twelve schœni, was called Dodeca-s[c]hœnus.

A little above the remains just described we find the sands of the western desert reaching to the water's edge. On the opposite side, the river is bordered by a narrow strip of cultivated land. As we advance, we again find the prospect bounded on the western side by a low, sandstone rid[g]e, upon which we observe the ruins of a small town. This low mountain-ridge extends for several miles, almost close to the river, and only in one part do we see the least border of verdure, or of cultivable soil. A similar line of mountain commences on the opposite side, a little above the former. Here, also, is very little cultivable soil. The first district above M'hhar'ruck'ah is *Wa'dee Seya'leh* وادى سياله . In the next, *Wa'dee*

---

[1] See no. 48 of the subjects for wood-cuts [fig. 148].

Ne'ameh وادی نعمه , the mountains on the western side are washed by the river. On a point of this range are the ruins of another small town. The same description applies to the district of *Ba'r'deh* بارده . From this part, for some miles, including the whole of *Wa'dee Medee'ck* (or *Medee'g*) وادی مدیق, there is scarcely any cultivable land along the narrow tract between the river and the eastern mountains. On the opposite side is an open, low desert; where at first we see a scanty strip of cultivated soil, but none beyond for several miles; though, on removing a little sand, we find a rich alluvial stratum, the deposit of the Nile.

Chapter XXXVI.
Wa'dee es-Sooboo'ă, Hhassa'yeh, and Ed-Dir'r.

Districts inhabited by Arabs—Temple of Wa'dee es-Sooboo'ă —Great bend of the river—Temple of Hhassa'yeh, or Am'ada—Town and rock-temple of Ed-Dir'r.

Wa'dee Medee'ck is the last district of that part of Nubia which is inhabited by the Koonoo'z. In the two next districts, Wa'dee es-Sooboo'ă and Wa'dee el-'Ar'ab, the inhabitants are Arabs. Some of these people carry on a trade with Senna'r, in slaves, &c. They travel, in small parties, across the desert on the east of the Nile, nearly in a direct line, to Bur'bar'ah and Shen'deh.

Wa'dee es-Sooboo'ă وادى السبوع derives its name, which signifies "the Valley of the Lions," from two rows of sphinxes which form an avenue to a large temple here situated.—I must remark here, that the correct plural of *seb'ă* سبع, "a lion," is *siba'ă* سباع; but *Sooboo'ă* سبوع is the plural commonly used, not only by the inhabitants of this wa'dee but also in Egypt.—The temple of Wa'dee es-Sooboo'ă[1] is at a short distance from the river, on the western side, in the midst of a sandy desert. Before it, at the distance of 193 feet, are two granite statues; each ten feet high; in an erect posture, with the left leg advanced. They have the usual royal cap, and, on the belt, the name of Rameses 2nd, whom they represent, and in whose reign the temple was constructed. Down the back of each is an inscription in hieroglyphics, with the same name. These two statues are at the entrance of an avenue of sphinxes with human heads; each ten feet in length. All of these excepting the first three on the right side and the first two on the left are wholly buried beneath an accumulation of sand and fragments of stone. Their heads were surmounted by the royal cap; but all the caps have been thrown down: each of them having been formed of a separate block of stone. The material is sandstone. By measuring the distances between two, I calculated that there must be, or have been, eight sphinxes in each row. Proceeding along this avenue, we arrive at the propylæum. Before the door-way are two statues, like those already described; one on either side; but thrown down. The propylæum is eighty feet wide. The stones of which it is constructed are very roughly cut; particularly at their sides: the interstices having been filled up with mortar; most of which has crumbled away. On the front of each wing of the propylæum the royal founder is represented in the act of slaying two captives, whom he holds by the hair of their heads, as a sacrifice to

---

[1]See plate 25 [fig. 149].

Amon-Ra on the one side, and to Ra on the other; but the rough surfaces and edges of the stones confuse the sculpture so much that, at a little distance, it is very imperfectly seen; though the figures are colossal. Passing through the door-way of the propylæum, we enter a court half filled with sand. On either side is a gallery, formed by the side-wall, with five square pillars before it: each of which pillars has an Osiridean figure of the king in front of it; like those of the temple of Gur'f Hhosey'n. All of these figures are much broken; and the last two pillars of each row are entirely buried in the sand. The back of the propylæum, and the side-walls of the court, which are much ruined, are sculptured: the subjects are offerings presented by the king to various deities. On the architraves, also, are hieroglyphics; but in a great degree effaced. There is a door in the back of the north wing of the propylæum, above the top of the side-gallery of the court: by this we enter a horizontal passage leading to the top of the portal between the two wings; whence a flight of stairs ascends through the southern wing to the summit. There is a second court immediately behind the first. I found it filled with sand to the top of the walls; but at the end, where some of the sand had been removed, there appeared the upper part of a door-way, which is the entrance to several apartments excavated in a stratum of rock that rises to the same height as the walls of the two courts. Having caused some of the sand to be removed, I crawled through. The first of these chambers, which is nearly filled with sand, is of an oblate form; and its walls, which have been covered with plaster to conceal the sculptures, shew us that this temple, like so many others, has been made use of, by early Christians, as a church. In some few parts, where the plaster has fallen off, or been removed, we see that the sculptures are well executed. This chamber has five doors, communicating with as many other chambers; one on each side, and three at the end. Each of the two side-chambers has, at the end, a bench of rock. The walls are sculptured with representations of the usual offerings: the figures painted merely with yellow and black. Of the three last chambers, that in the centre is the sanctuary. It is very small; its ceiling is cut in the form of an arch; and at the end is a square recess, within which were, originally, three sitting figures; but these have been cut away; and upon the plain and white-washed surface, above the bench, the figure of St. Peter has been painted. Above the recess is sculptured a boat, in which is seated the ram-headed god Kneph. On the left side of the chamber is the boat of the same god, with a ram's head at each extremity; and on the opposite side is the boat of Ra, having, at either extremity, the head of a hawk. The chamber on the left of the sanctuary is nearly filled with sand, which has fallen through a crevice in the rock above. The chamber on the other side of the sanctuary has been whitewashed; but the sculptures are not concealed. The subjects are offerings, of the usual kind. At the end of this little apartment, in the right-hand corner, is a square well, or pit, which, being like a mummy-pit, probably descends to some sepulchral chamber, perhaps the depository of the mummies of sacred animals which were objects of worship in this temple: but this pit, at the depth of eight or nine feet, I found to be closed with rubbish.

On the same side of the river, a little higher, some mountains rise very near to the bank; and at this part there is a little cultivated land by the river; but beyond this, there is none for the whole extent of Wa'dee es-Sooboo'ă; nor in Wa'dee el-'Ar'ab, excepting in one short space. On the opposite bank, however, the river is bordered by a strip of cultivated soil throughout the whole of the former of those districts, with one little interruption, and along part of Wa'dee el-'Ar'ab also. The mountains, on the latter side, lie very near to the river. *Wa'dee el-'Ar'ab* وادى العرب derives its name from its being inhabited by Arabs. At the southern part of this district the eastern mountains are, for the space of about two miles, quite close to the river; not admitting of camels passing. This part of the eastern chain is called Geb'el es-Seb'a Do'ra't. Hence commences *Wa'dee Sooncka'ree* (or *Soonga'ree*) وادى سنقارى . Our course here gradually bends to the westward: the shore on our left is narrow, but well-cultivated: on our right is a mountainous desert. At *Ckooroos'koo* (or *Gooroos'koo*) قرسكو , the next place on the southern bank, the cultivation improves a little, and there are many palm-trees. Here, on my return, I found a large slave-caravan, from Senna'r. The slaves were mostly children. Having just reached the banks of the Nile, after their long and fatiguing journey through the desert, they all seemed highly elated: some were reclining in the shade of the palm-trees; and many, playing and laughing. I never saw a more happy-looking set.—From Ckooroos'koo to the town of Ed-Dirr, the capital of Nubia, the navigation is troublesome and tedious, at most times; the river running from the north-west, and the wind being almost constantly in the same, or nearly the same, direction: it is therefore generally necessary to tow the boats.—The height of the thermometer, in the afternoon of the 22nd, was 105°.

23rd. The wind having fortunately subsided, we proceeded easily this day with the tow-rope. Since the time of the expedition to Senna'r, it has been the custom to take the peasants from the sa'ckiyehs on the north-eastern bank,[†] at this bend of the river, and compel them to assist in tracking the boats. They now make no objection to this laborious task, which is particularly tiresome on account of the bank being bordered by acacias. The land on that side is sandy and mountainous, with the exception of a few narrow patches of cultivated soil along the side of the river, which are irrigated entirely by sa'ckiyehs; the inundation never reaching their surface. On the opposite side, from Ckooroos'koo as far as Ed-Dirr, a narrow tract of well-cultivated land, backed by low mountains, and rich in palm-trees, extends uninterruptedly; and acacias skirt the river. Along this tract are many villages. The huts are larger, and better built, than those in the more northern parts (the country of the Koonoo'z): and this we remark throughout the whole of the country of the

---

[†]The left bank, because the river flows toward the southeast at this point.

Noo'beh. Among the villages in the tract above-mentioned is one called Khara'beh, where, according to Burckhardt, are some heaps of hewn stones, the remains of ancient edifices; whence this village takes its name.

On the north-eastern side of the river, at a spot called *Hhassa'yeh* حساية, or (according to some travellers) *Am'ada*, is a very ancient and interesting temple,[1] situated in the desert, on a slightly-elevated stratum of rock, very near the bank. It appears to have been founded by Thothmos 3rd. Its sculptures, which are remarkable for their elegance and exquisite finish, were begun in the reign of that king, and continued under the two next Pharaohs, Amonoph 2nd and Thothmos 4th. The building is small, and half buried in sand. Upon the roof is a small, ruined cupola, of crude brick, the work of early Christians, who converted this temple into a church, and covered the beautiful sculptures with a coat of plaster, upon which they executed rude paintings. It is built of yellow sandstone, containing veins of red, resembling brick. The exterior, which has a very ancient appearance, is without sculpture, excepting on one of the architraves. It is much encumbered by ruined brick walls and fragments of stone. On a door-way at the entrance we find the names of Rameses 2nd and his father, who was his immediate predecessor. Through this door-way we enter a portico, or pronaos; the roof of which is supported by four rows of square pillars; three in each row. Behind the four last pillars are four columns, of the kind from which originated the Doric order. The spaces between the pillars at the two sides are closed by walls; the inner surfaces of which are sculptured; as are also the pillars and architraves, internally. The portico is half filled with sand.[2] The main body of the building is divided into six small apartments; all of which are much encumbered with sand. The first of these is of an oblate form; and occupies the whole width of the building. Its walls are decorated with beautiful sculptures; the more to be admired for their execution, and brilliant colouring, than for their subjects, which are of the ordinary kind, the presentation of offerings, &c. These sculptures are, in many parts, covered by the plaster and white-wash of the Christians; and those in the other chambers, more so. In the back-wall of the first chamber are three doors. The central of these is the entrance of the sanctuary; which is a small, narrow apartment. The walls are here decorated with very beautiful painted sculptures, like the rest, in low relief. Among the objects represented as offerings, two small birds are particularly remarkable for the natural and highly-finished manner in which they are sculptured and painted. Three hideous heads, at the end of the chamber, designed to represent our Saviour between two angels, cover some sculpture over a long hieroglyphic inscription, from which the plaster has been removed. On either side of the sanctuary is an apartment yet narrower, each having, at the end, a little, square chamber, communicating with the sanctuary. The sculptures in these are similar to

[1]See plate 26 [fig. 150].
[2]In it Mr. Gliddon found the name of Osirtesen 3rd, *under* that of Thothmes 3rd.

those in the other chambers.—Between this beautiful temple and the river are the foundations of another stone building; perhaps of a propylæum or other structure in the approach to the former.

Leaving this place, we were soon able to avail ourselves of a northerly breeze which had sprung up; and in about an hour, arrived before the town of *Ed-Dirr* الدّر, the capital of the country. This name has been supposed to be a corruption of "Ed-Deyr," or "the Convent." The town consists of low huts, built of rough fragments of stone, and mud; not connected, one with another, so as to form streets, but scattered among the palm-trees which line the shore. The inhabitants of this place are mostly descendants of the Booshna'cks (or Bosnian soldiers) who were sent into Nubia by the Turkish Soolta'n Selee'm, and who established themselves at Ibree'm, Aswa'n and Sa'y. They are distinguished by their light brown complexion from the other Nubians, who are almost black. There is, thus, a mixed race, between the Booshna'ks and Noo'beh, in the places above mentioned, and in the neighbouring villages; but we find most of this race at Ed-Dirr. As the capital of Nubia, Ed-Dirr must be called a town: otherwise we should designate it as a mere village. Its population probably does not exceed one thousand. It is a place of some little commerce; chiefly in the dates of Ibree'm and the more southern parts of Nubia; which are very highly esteemed: most of them are conveyed to the Egyptian metropolis, during the period of the inundation. At the time of my arrival at this place, a wide, sandy space intervened between the river's edge and the town. The lower parts of this sand-bank, near the water, were covered with cucumbers and water-melons; and behind each cultivated patch was erected a little shed of tattered matting, under the shade of which lay a group of boys or girls, to watch the produce.—A Turkish Cka'im-macka'm presides here. I was informed that there were no prostitutes in any part of Nubia, excepting at this place; where there were a few females of that class from Senna'r and Abyssinia, originally slaves: I did not see any.

Close behind the town is a temple of the age of Rameses 2nd, excavated in the low ridge of rock which confines the cultivable land. At this part, the narrow strip of cultivable soil is wholly occupied by the town. The exterior appearance of this temple is shewn by a view here inserted.[1] We first enter what was once a portico; for the most part cut in the rock, which still forms a wall on either side and in front. Here are remains of eight square pillars, which, being not more than a quarter of the original height, appear like altars, or pedestals. They are hewn out of the solid rock. Before the principal chamber, which is at the end of this portico, is a row of four square pillars, with an architrave, all cut from the live rock. These pillars were ornamented in front with colossal statues, carved in high relief; all of which have been hewn down as low as the hips. The roof which covered the space between this row of pillars and the wall behind has fallen. The two sides of the court were decorated

---

[1]See plate 27 [fig. 151].

with sculptures representing battle-scenes; which, unfortunately are so much defaced that we can but faintly perceive the principal and boldest figures. On the left side we discover the chariot and horses of the Egyptian king (Rameses 2nd) rushing among a confused group of his enemies. Next to these is a party of captives; and beyond them, at the right extremity of the wall, the king is represented paying homage to the god Ra. The sculptures of the right side-wall are yet more injured: we can just trace the wheels of the car, and the horses rearing over the fallen foes of the Egyptian monarch: to the left of these is a group of prisoners, as on the opposite wall. The end-wall has a large central door-way, much broken, and now obstructed by some large masses of the rock which have fallen down from above. On each side of this door, the king is represented in the act of sacrificing four captives, whom he holds by the hair of their heads; to Ra, on the one side (the left of the door), and to Amon-Ra on the other. In the latter instance, a lion is rushing on to devour the captives. This animal is said to have been the constant companion of Sesostris (or Rameses 2nd) in his military expeditions; and I have seen no other Pharaoh represented so accompanied.—We enter the first or principal chamber by a small door at the left corner: the great entrance being obstructed, as before mentioned. The roof of this chamber is supported by two rows of square pillars, three in each row (longitudinally). The chamber is not exactly rectangular: it is about forty feet square. The sides of the pillars are decorated with sculptures representing the king offering to the gods: so, also, are the walls, which are much blackened and defiled by bats. The offerings are mostly to Amon-Ra, Amon-Generator, and Ra. In one instance, the king is represented standing before or under a tree, and offering to the second of the above-mentioned personifications of the deity: this is on the left side-wall. In each side of the chamber are two large, oblong holes, near the ceiling, which interrupt the sculptures. At the end of this chamber are three doors; each communicating with a small, narrow apartment. These three apartments are sculptured; but much injured. The central, which is the largest of them, is the sanctuary. At the end of it were four sitting, colossal figures; as in the temple of Gur'f Hhosey'n; but these have been broken down. In the left side are two square holes, roughly cut, and evidently in comparatively late times; and in the right side is another similar hole. The left side-chamber has a bench of rock extending along the right and left sides and at the end, and an oblong excavation in the floor, filled with rubbish.—This temple has, altogether, an appearance of more remote antiquity than most of the monuments of the reign of Rameses 2nd; owing to the rude style of the execution. The sculptures yet retain a little of the paint with which they were originally adorned. A little to the left of this temple, in a higher stratum of the rock, is a small excavated chamber; but it has no sculptures, nor inscriptions, excepting some modern Arabic writing. There are also some other small excavations.—The greatest height of the thermometer on the day of my arrival at Ed-Dirr was 107°.

Chapter XXXVII.
Ibree'm, &c.—to Ab'oo Sim'bil.

24th. A grove of palm-trees extends along a well-cultivated, though narrow tract on the southern side of the river, immediately above Ed-Dirr. The shore opposite Ed-Dirr is rocky, but not much elevated: a little higher, the rocky barrier on that side diverges from the river, and leaves a wide, cultivated plain. This district is called *To'ma's* توماس .

On the side opposite To'ma's, the low mountains reach to the river, for a short space; leaving no road but over their flat top. They then recede, and again extend to the river at the distance of about five miles. In the intermediate space is a wide, cultivated tract. This is the chief part of *Wa'dee Ibree'm* وادى ابريم . Before it lies an island, called *Ckit'teh*, or *Git'teh*. The cultivated plain contains several villages, and is rich in palm-trees; the fruit of which, called *bel'ahh Ibree'mee*, is much esteemed.

At the base of the mountain-range behind is a small grotto, excavated in the reign of Thothmos 3rd. It has many sculptures; but they are uninteresting, and much defaced. Within it, at the end of a wide recess, are three small, sitting figures. On the exterior are several inscriptions in hieroglyphics; but very indistinct and imperfect. This grotto, which few would think worth visiting, is behind a group of huts, among which is a whited mosque, with a small ma'd'neh. The place is called Agaïr'keh.

The villages of Wa'dee Ibree'm are recovering from the pillage which they suffered under the Memloo'ks in 1812; when these refugees were defeated by Ibrahee'm Bey (now Ibrahee'm Ba'sha); and forced to fly to Dun'ckal'ah. They are stated (by Burckhardt) to have taken from this district about 1200 cows; and to have exacted upwards of 100,000 Spanish Dollars as ransom for the persons whom they imprisoned. From a dreadful famine, which the Memloo'k marauders contributed to effect, the people of this part suffered yet more severely, in common with the whole population of Nubia.

The north-western shore, opposite the isle of Ckit'teh, is a sandy plain, without a spot of verdure, or any object to attract attention, excepting some brick ruins, said to be the tomb of a sheykh. There are several isolated hills at a little distance inland. A little higher there is a small patch of verdure along the bank, with palm-trees, and a group of huts, called Mug'asir'keh. In the desert behind this spot, at the distance of about half an hour's walk, is a small, isolated mountain, in which is excavated an ancient sepulchral grotto, facing the river. This grotto has a small, plain door. The interior consists of a narrow chamber, 19 feet by 9, in length and width, and 5 feet and a half in height, having a recess behind, with a bench at the end, on which were to have been sculptured three sitting figures; but these are unfinished. The principal part, or chamber, in which is a sepulchral excavation, is decorated with painted sculptures, coarsely executed, but the colours well preserved. These sculptures are similar to those of many of the smaller grottoes at Thebes and other places in Egypt; representing the ceremonies and mysteries of a funeral, together with agricultural scenes.[1]

A little higher, the mountains on the opposite side of the river close upon the stream, and terminate that fertile part of Wa'dee Ibree'm which I have already described. Upon the top of an isolated mountain of this range, rising nearly perpendicularly from the water's edge, stands the old, ruined town of *Ibree'm*.[2] In the front of the mountain next below this, high up the steep, and quite inaccessible, is a small grotto, with a plain entrance. From below, it appears that the interior is unfinished and rough.—The mountain which is crowned by the old town of Ibree'm rises to the height of about 300 feet, or nearly so, above the level of the low Nile.[3] Like the adjacent mountains, it is of sandstone. The old town is now entirely deserted. It is surrounded by a wall of rough masses of stone, now, in many parts, thrown down nearly to the base. On entering the place, at the north, the first object that attracted my notice was a small temple, without any inscription or sculpture to prove its age; but evidently one of the latest monuments of the ancient religion of Egypt. This at once informs the traveller that he is on the site of a town anterior to the Christian era; and other monuments shew that this was a town of very high antiquity. Its modern name, and its elevated and strong position, are good reasons for believing it to have been the *Primis*, or *Premnis*, of ancient geographers, which Strabo describes as a town fortified by nature. The ruined houses are similar to the mean abodes now seen in the lower parts of Nubia; being merely small enclosures of rustic stone walls. In the midst of the town is a large building, on arches, which appears to have been a church. Small granite columns are found in many parts, placed as the thresholds of doors; and a few granite capitals, in very bad taste, with the cross among their ornaments, are lying near the building just mentioned. The town is very small. It was, for several centuries, the principal fortified town of Nubia. The Memloo'ks sustained a siege in it in 1812, and since their flight to the upper country it has been without inhabitants.—On the side of the mountain which is

---

[1] This grotto I did not see: the situation of it had been incorrectly described to me; and I had not with me Burckhardt's book, in which it is noticed. During my second voyage in Nubia I was very unwell; and could not walk so far from the bank of the river.

[2] See plate 28 [fig. 152].

[3] The river was nearly at the lowest when my view of this mountain was taken.

next the river are remains of steps, cut in the rock, which led up to the summit.—Towards the right extremity of this side are four small grottoes, of very remote antiquity.[1] The first two are difficult of access; but one of my boatmen succeeded in climbing up to them, and took up a rope, by means of which I ascended. Each consists of one little chamber. The interior of the first is sculptured; but the walls are much injured; and the name, wherever it occurs, is almost entirely effaced.[2] At the end are three small, sitting figures. The second grotto has four small, sitting figures at the end; and around them, a few hieroglyphics, with the name of Thothmos 2nd; but it has no other sculptures. The third has three figures at the end, resembling those in the first and second; and bears the name of Rameses 2nd. The fourth is similar to the third; but bears the name of Thothmos 3rd. I should not have thought that these grottoes were places of sepulture; but the difficulty of access to them makes it improbable that they were designed for any other purpose.—In the valley above and below this mountain are seen the tombs of the late Moos'lim inhabitants. It is a perfectly desolate place; not only without an inhabitant but without the least vegetation. The opposite shore too is a dreary desert, with only a few little patches of cultivated soil, at wide intervals, along the bank, and low acacias skirting the stream.—On the front of the mountain next above that on which the ruined town is situated is sculptured a tablet commemorative of a conquest by Osiree 1st, the father of Rameses 2nd. The king is represented in the act of spearing a captive; and beneath this design is an inscription in hieroglyphics. The whole of this piece of sculpture is much injured.

A little above the old town of Ibree'm, the mountains on that side recede a little, and the bank is cultivated, and has a grove of palm-trees. Part of this cultivated strip, along which are several villages, is included in the district of Ibree'm. G'ney'neh (or J'ney'neh—"the garden") is one of the principal villages here; and is prettily situated. The more southern part is called *Wa'dee Boosta'n* وادى بستان ; which name bears a similar meaning. On the western shore, opposite to the district just mentioned, a small tract of cultivated land, with a village called Moos'moos, interrupts the general sterility.—We stopped for the night at a little village of Wa'dee Boosta'n, called 'Am'keh, where one of my servants (a native of Nubia) went to visit a sheykh who had educated him; that is, taught him to read and write. The sheykh brought me, as a present, a kid and a dish of bread and milk.—The greatest height of the thermometer this day was 110°.

On the 25th, having no wind, and the weather being extremely hot, I would not employ my crew in tracking; and therefore remained the greater part of the day where I had passed the preceding night; my servant's sheykh keeping me company, and amusing me with stories. In the evening, a light breeze sprang up; and we proceeded. The next district

---

[1]Their entrances are seen in plate 28 [fig. 152].
[2]According to Champollion, it is Amonoph 2nd.

is *Wa'dee Toosh'keh* وادى تشكه ; which comprises a small tract of cultivated land on each side of the river: that on the south-eastern bank is backed by low, rugged hills; and here there are some rude excavations, without any sculpture. In this district, the Nile is obstructed by reefs of rock, which, when the river is low, render the navigation rather difficult.—The greatest height of the thermometer this day was 107°.

26th. Favoured by a fresh breeze, we advanced rapidly; passed by the districts of *Armin'neh* ارمنه and *Foorckoon'dee* (or *Foorgoon'dee*) فرقندى, and in three hours arrived at that of *Ferey'ck* (or *Ferey'g*) فريق . Each of these districts consists of a narrow strip of cultivated land on the south-eastern bank only, backed by low mountains, which, in some parts, reach to the river; interrupting the tract of soil. The north-western shore, opposite the first two districts above-mentioned is a sandy plain, without a spot of cultivation, nor any shrubs, excepting a few acacias along the bank.

Chapter XXXVIII.
Ab'oo Sim'bil, or Absem'bel.

The two rock-temples, &c.

Opposite Ferey'ck, or Ferey'g, is a chain of mountains, which, for the space of about a mile, or more, lie close along the bank of the river. In two prominences of these mountains are excavated the two magnificent temples of *Ab'oo Sim'bil* ابو سنبل or *Absem'bel* ابسنبل . The former of these names is the more common; though the latter, if I may rely upon the assertion of a sheykh of the opposite district, is the more correct. In ascending the river, I first perceived the front of the great temple from the distance of about three miles, with a telescope. Before the opposite shore is a long sand-bank, which at the season of my arrival was dry: from it I took a view of the two temples,[1] &c. A torrent of sand has poured over the mountains, and, nearly filling the space between the two prominences in which these temples are excavated, has half concealed the front of the greater temple.—I shall first describe the northern, or smaller temple.

From a distance, this temple has an imposing appearance; but it loses somewhat of its grandeur on a near approach; there being not much to admire excepting the colossal size of the six figures in front; and even these, though thirty feet high, appear almost insignificant when we turn aside our eyes to the enormous and majestic statues before the great temple.—To form the front of the smaller temple, the surface of the rock has been cut in a sloping direction; receding a little from the base upwards. In this plane surface have been cut six niches, which are considerably deeper at the bottom than at the top; so that the projections of the rock which are left between them have the form of buttresses. The central projection is wider than the others; and through this is cut the entrance to the temple. Over the door are two ovals, containing the titles and name of the illustrious Rameses 2nd; in whose reign this and the neighbouring temple were excavated. The rest of the front of this central projection is sculptured (as are also the others) with hieroglyphics, very deeply cut. In the niche next the entrance on either side is the colossal figure of the king above-named, hewn out of the rock: his name is on his belt. He stands in a firm attitude; with the left foot advanced, and the arms hanging straight by his side. The expression of the face is mild, but not manly; and the head is rather too large for just proportion; in consequence of which, the whole figure has a somewhat boyish

---

[1]See plate 29 [fig. 153].

493

appearance. The two statues bear a close resemblance to each other. The second niche from the door on either side is occupied by a colossus of the queen, as Athor, the goddess to whom the temple was principally dedicated. Her head is surmounted by the disk and horns, with two high feathers. In the third, or extreme niche on each side is a colossus of the king: but these two colossi differ in some respects from those next the entrance: that on the left is habited in the same manner; but is considerably higher: that on the right has the head-dress with which Phtha-Socari is usually represented. Each of these six colossi is accompanied by two figures of about the natural size; one on either side: these represent the sons and daughters of the king and queen: some of them have the hair distributed in a peculiar manner; being short on the left side and hanging down in a large mass on the right side.—Within the entrance, on the left, the king is represented making an offering to Athor; and on the right the queen is presenting to the same goddess. The first, or principal chamber has six square pillars, in two rows, extending longitudinally. On the front of each is carved, in low relief, the full face of Athor, on the upper part: the other sides are decorated with representations of various divinities, sculptured, and painted with yellow and black. Looking back towards the entrance, we see, on either side of the door, the representation of the king slaying a captive, as a sacrifice. The victim has a pointed beard; and is probably an Assyrian. He is kneeling, with his head turned back, and his hand raised in supplication to his destroyer. The king holds him by the hair of the head; having his bow in the same hand; while in the other hand, which is extended behind him, he holds the knife. These groups are executed with simplicity and spirit. The other sides of the chamber are decorated with sculptures, painted only with yellow and black, representing the monarch and his queen offering to various divinities. The temple seems to have been designed as a monument of the piety of this queen, rather than of the king.—At the end of the chamber which I have just described are three doors; all of which communicate with one apartment; a transverse gallery. On the walls of this apartment are sculptures similar to those already mentioned. On either side is a small, square chamber, without any decoration; and behind is the sanctuary. This is very small. Its walls are decorated with sculptures of a similar kind to the others; but on a smaller scale. At the end is a mutilated figure, which appears to be surmounted with the head of a cow, and to represent Athor, the principal divinity of the temple. The cow's head is here crowned with the usual head-dress of that goddess. Among the sculptures in this sanctuary is one remarkable subject, not often met with: it is the king, with his name inscribed as usual, offering to a sitting figure with the same name, behind which sits the queen: the monarch thus intending to signify his own divinity.

This temple would attract more admiration were it not for that far more wonderful work in its vicinity. Besides, its extreme proximity to the river prevents its being viewed to the greatest advantage, unless from the river during the season when the water reaches nearly to the level of the base of the temple. The indefatigable Burckhardt was the first of modern travellers who visited this and the neighbouring temple, and made them known to the European world. The greater temple was then so much concealed by sand, that it had nearly escaped his notice. Belzoni cleared away a great quantity of this sand from the front, and laid open the entrance; assisted by Captains Irby and Mangles.

The view to which I have already referred shews the situation of the Great Temple, and the singular manner in which it has become obstructed by the sand, pouring over the summits of the mountains. Within three hours after sunrise, I found this sand almost too hot to tread upon; and in ascending from the smaller temple to the greater, I was obliged frequently to stop, and empty my shoes, and give a respite to my feet by throwing myself down upon my back.

The general appearance of the exterior of the great temple is shewn by a view here inserted[1]: but in this view the perspective is rather violent, from my position being too near the object; and this I could not avoid. The front I found to be about 120 feet wide at the lowest point then visible: at the base it must be somewhat more. What most contribute to (or, indeed, almost solely constitute) the external grandeur of this most stupendous and unrivalled monument of Egyptian art are four enormous colossi, hewn out of the rock, and sitting upon thrones against the front of the temple. One of them is now headless;[†] but the faces, and almost every part, of the others are fortunately perfect. They represent that most illustrious of all the Pharaohs, Rameses 2nd: his hieroglyphic name is carved upon each of the arms, near the shoulder, in large and deep characters. They are about sixty-five feet high, including the cap; and about twenty-five feet across the shoulders. The faces are seven feet in length, from the line of the head-dress to the bottom of the chin. The expression of the countenances is most sublime and beautiful. They resemble each other as nearly as the sculptor could make them. The northernmost (the furthest to the right) appeared to me the finest of all; and I bestowed great pains in making a drawing of it, which I will venture to pronounce a very close resemblance[2]: I made it with the camera-lucida; and introduced the figure of one of my boatmen, to shew the proportion. The southernmost figure is most exposed; and has more than once been cleared nearly to the base; but when I saw it, the sand reached almost to the knees. Mr. Bankes cleared away the sand from the lower part of this and the next colossus; and found, on the left leg of the latter, a Greek inscription, in large characters, with the name of King Psammitichus. Each of these two figures has been found to resemble those of Amonoph 3rd, on the western plain of Thebes, in having a female colossal figure on each side of the legs, against the front of the

---

[1]See plate 30 [fig. 154].
[†]The fallen head was completely covered by sand.
[2]See plate 31 [fig. 155].

throne, and a smaller figure *between* the legs. These probably represent
the queen and daughters of the monarch. The other two colossi
doubtless correspond with these in every respect. The beards are of a
formal shape, like those of many Egyptian statues. On the fore part of
the cap is an asp, with the breast erect and expanded, and the rest of the
body small and coiled. There are still some traces of the colours with
which these colossi were originally painted; as red, yellow, and blue. The
faces, as usual, were painted red; the eyes, of the natural colours, and
bordered with black, as the ancient Egyptians applied *kohhl* to their eyes,
in the same manner as the women of Egypt at present: the eye-brows
were also painted black. But now the faces have the natural colour of the
sandstone rock (a brownish yellow), which is more agreeable to modern
European taste. The head of the colossus on the left of the door appears
to have fallen by its own weight; probably in consequence of an inclining
vein of the rock: had it been broken by the violence of man, we should
doubtless find the other statues mutilated.[1] In a high niche, over the
entrance, is a figure of the god Ra, with the head of a hawk, as usual,
surmounted by a disk (representing the sun) with an asp issuing from it.
He holds, in each hand, a *crux ansata* (the emblem of life): beneath his
right hand is a jackal-headed sceptre; and beneath his left hand stands a
little figure of Isis or Athor. On the surface of the rock, on each side of
the niche, is sculptured a figure of the king presenting an offering: his
outer garment is transparent; shewing his legs through it. The front of
the temple is surrounded by a torus, over which is a cornice; and above
the cornice is a row of sitting apes, apparently about six feet high, which
have a grotesque effect: many of them have been demolished; probably
by masses of the rock falling from above; and the cornice is much
broken. A dedicatory line of hieroglyphics, with the name of Rameses
2nd, extends along the upper part of the front, beneath the cornice and
torus. The cornice is ornamented with the same name, in perpendicular
ovals, with an asp on each side.—The door-way is about twenty feet
high. I found it closed by the sand, with the exception of a small space,
just large enough for me to crawl through. All within the entrance at first
appeared to me quite dark; and the heat of the confined air was almost
insupportable. The thermometer without, in the shade of one of the
colossi, was at the height of 105°: this I had remarked; and I was curious
to observe its height within; where the heat was quite overpowering;

---

[1]When Belzoni commenced his operations here, only the head and shoulders of
the southernmost statue, and the caps of the others, appeared above the surface of
the sand. He commenced his arduous work in the autumn of the year 1816; but
not being able to obtain sufficient assistance, was soon obliged to suspend his
labours, and return to Egypt. In the summer of the following year, the upper part
of the entrance was laid open, by the exertions of Belzoni, Captains Irby and
Mangles, Mr. W. Beechy, and their servants and boatmen, but little assisted by
any others. Still the northernmost head remained buried: this was shortly after
uncovered.

which was not the case without: to my surprise, it sank to 82°. I repeated this experiment several times, with the same result. I cannot account for the oppressive heat of the air within, unless by supposing it to be damp: yet the freshness of the colours with which the sculptures of the interior are painted seems to shew that they have not been exposed to any great degree of damp.—Just within the entrance, I observed, on either side, a large oval containing the peculiar titles of Rameses 2nd. The darkness prevented my seeing anything more than these hieroglyphics of the door-way, until my eyes had become a little accustomed to the gloom: I then faintly perceived two rows of colossal figures, facing each other, four in each row, forming an avenue through the first to the second chamber.[1] A quantity of sand, which had poured in through the door-way, formed a steep slope between the colossi to the floor of the chamber, towards the end. Having caused several small fires to be lighted in parts of the temple where I could not see the flames when sitting at the entrance, I enjoyed a most magnificent sight: it was altogether like a grand and solemn scene of enchantment. A small, glimmering fire upon an altar in the sanctuary faintly illumined four colossal figures (of the king and three gods) seated at the end; and produced a very striking effect of religious grandeur. It was only by lighting fires and candles that I was enabled to make a view of the interior. With several wax candles tied to a long palm-stick, I proceeded to examine the first or great chamber. It is fifty-seven feet long, and fifty-two feet wide. Eight square pillars of the rock are left to support the roof; and the eight colossal figures which I have already mentioned are represented as standing against these pillars. They are statues of the king, the great Rameses, in the character of Osiris; having his arms crossed upon his breast; and holding the crook and flagellum which are generally seen in the hands of that deity. Some of these colossi are much broken. The two last pillars on the left side are connected together by a wall about half their height; and from the last pillar, a wall of the same height extends to the side of the chamber. On the front of the former wall is a long inscription in hieroglyphics, dated "in the 35th year" of Rameses 2nd. Above this inscription is represented the king in the act of slaying three captives before Phtha-Socari: and the whole is surmounted by the winged globe, and a cornice above. All the walls of the chamber are decorated with painted sculptures, of a very interesting nature, and in a remarkable state of preservation. Looking back towards the entrance, we see, on each side, a representation of the king in the act of sacrificing (to Ra, the chief god of the temple, on one side, and to Amon-Ra on the other) a group of captives, negroes and Asiatics; whom he holds with one hand by the hair of their heads, while with the other hand he wields the knife. The victims are raising their hands in supplication to the god and to the prince. After admiring these spirited designs, I next examined the left (or southern) side-wall. This side of the chamber is divided into two compartments, by

[1] See plate 32 [fig. 156].

a horizontal line passing along it from end to end. Beginning our examination from the left extremity of the lower compartment, we first find a representation of the storming of a fortress. The Egyptian king is standing in his car, and advancing to the siege. As usual, he is of a colossal size. One of the besieged, kneeling at the base of the fortress, raises his hands, imploring mercy. Next to this piece, we behold the monarch slaying a hostile chief. This is an almost exact copy of a sculpture on the exterior of the northern wall of the great portico of Kur'nak; in which the hero is the father of this king. Rameses is here represented trampling upon a prostrate foe, while he thrusts his spear into another: both are of the same race, with small and pointed beards; and evidently of some Asiatic nation. The dress of the Egyptian king is close-fitting; as suits a warrior, but richly ornamented; and what is very remarkable is that he is represented as having a beard of only a few days' growth, and a scanty mustache. This group is designed with much spirit. Next we see the king again in his car; but proceeding at a slow pace. The wall before mentioned which connects the last of the left-hand pillars with the side of the chamber here interrupts the design; but on going round to the other side of it, we find that the prince is preceded by a number of captive negroes and other African prisoners, arranged in two lines; one above another. These captives are painted black and dark red; and the character of each countenance is admirably portrayed. Their hair is dressed in small twists, in the present Nubian fashion. This triumphal procession terminates the lower compartment of this side of the chamber. In the upper compartment, beginning again from the left, we see the king making offerings to the gods for his success. Then follows a representation of the king kneeling under, of before, a small tree, and presenting an offering to Ra, who stands on the right of the tree. Behind the king is the god Thoth. Next to this the king is represented offering to Amon; before whose throne a large serpent raises itself erect. This is the last sculpture on this side of the chamber. We now turn to the *right*, or *northern* side. Here is represented, in a very bold style, an interesting battle-scene, which occupies the whole of the wall. The history of the war commences at the lower corner of the left extremity. We here see the Egyptians drawn up in order for the fight: the infantry, with their high shields, placed in ranks; and the riders standing in their chariots, ready for the onset. Before them is their camp; comprising a strange, confused group; among which are animals of various kinds intermixed among the chariots of the Egyptians. Below this group is a line of chariots proceeding to the battle. Next we behold the monarch seated; and his attendants bringing him his chariot. Below him is a line of smaller figures; among which we see some disorderly soldiers, or deserters, undergoing a bastonading with staves. The remainder of the lower compartment of the wall is occupied by a representation of the commencement of the battle. The Egyptians, in their cars, are charging furiously upon their enemies, who are represented as in the utmost confusion, and falling from their chariots in various attitudes. Above the groups which have been just described is a line of figures extending along the wall, representing the combatants of each party rushing together, and meeting in the centre. Over this is depicted a narrow stream, running horizontally along the whole length of the wall, and enclosing a small island, upon which is a fortress rather to the left of the centre of the picture. Above the river, we see, towards the left extremity of the wall, the Egyptian king, in his chariot, proceeding to the battle; the representation of which occupies the next place. The Egyptians overwhelm their opponents, who are falling, wounded, into the river, or rushing into the stream in their chariots. Beyond this scene of confusion and bloodshed, we again behold the victorious monarch seated in his chariot. His people are bringing before him some of the captives, and cutting off their hands, which are thrown in heaps before his feet. This is the last sculpture upon this side-wall. Upon the *end-wall* of the chamber, the king is represented, on each side of the central door-way, making offerings to the gods for his success. All these sculptures are painted: red, yellow, and black are the predominant colours. In boldness of design, and in invention, they are equal to any in Egypt.—There are three door-ways at the end of the first chamber. The central door-way admits us into the second chamber. This is thirty-seven feet in width, and twenty-six feet in the other direction. Four square pillars of the rock support the roof. The right side of the door-way is much broken; and so also is the first pillar on the right. The walls are decorated with sculptures; but these are not of an interesting description; representing offerings, &c.— Through this chamber we pass to the third, which is a transverse gallery, measuring 37 feet by 10.—Crossing this, we enter the sanctuary, which is 12 feet wide, and 23 feet and a half in length. In the centre is a plain altar; on the front of which were some hieroglyphics, cut (I believe) in plaster, which had fallen off when I visited the temple: they were merely two ovals containing the titles and name of Rameses 2nd, with a column of other hieroglyphics on each side. At the end are four colossal figures, seated on a bench, side by side. The first to the right is the principal god of the temple, Ra, with the head of a hawk, surmounted by the disk which represents the sun, with an asp issuing from it. The next is the king, Rameses 2nd, with the two ovals containing his titles and name over his head. He has a high helmet; with an asp in front. The third is Amon-Ra, with the high head-dress peculiar to him, and his name by the side. The fourth is Phtha, with his name over his head. He holds, with both hands, a staff, which bends in the directions of his thighs and legs, and terminates in a forked form just above his feet. All of these have suffered somewhat from decay and violence. The sides of the sanctuary are sculptured and painted; but in a state of decay: a very small portion of the painted surface is now seen. The ceiling was adorned with white stars, painted upon a dark ground: but these, also, are only discernible on one part.—There are two little chambers, without any decoration, on the right and left of the sanctuary, entered from the preceding gallery.— Other chambers yet remain to be mentioned, which are entered from the first, or principal chamber of the temple. In the right side of this are two doors, each leading into a long, narrow apartment. The walls of these two apartments are decorated with sculptures; but inferior in execution to those which I have described. The second has a bench of rock at the end.—There are no apartments on the opposite side of the great chamber, to correspond with these; but at each extremity of the end of that chamber is a door which leads into a small and narrow apartment, with a bench of rock at the end. Each of these apartments has, on one side, two doors, by which we enter two other apartments, long and narrow, like those on the right of the great chamber; but surrounded with a bench of rock; and one of these, the first of those on the south, has six small, square niches, along the left side above the bench, and two of the same kind at the end. The walls of these apartments are likewise decorated with sculptures of coarse execution, and uninteresting.—The number of chambers in this magnificent temple is fourteen. In several of the chambers is a quantity of bats' dung, strewed on the floor: for the temple was tenanted by bats before it became quite closed by the sand. A few detached pieces of sculpture were found within it by Belzoni. Among these were two small, hawk-headed sphinxes, an ape broken in two, and a kneeling female figure holding an altar on which was a ram's head; and part of a brass socket which received a pivot serving as a hinge for one of the doors was lying on the floor. I entered the temple six times; and after having remained in it about three hours each time, was compelled to return to the pure air without, which seemed quite cool when the thermometer was at 105° in the shade. I took off all my clothes excepting my shirt and drawers on entering; but on coming out, I found it necessary not only to put on the clothes which I had left at the entrance but a cloak also, and to sit in the sun, to avoid taking cold. It was quite a luxury to me to breathe again the fresh air, and gaze on the magnificent colossi.

Before the great temple are two masses of unburnt brick, which appear above the sand, near the bottom of the slope: they seem to be the ends of walls, enclosing, on either side, a court in front of the temple. They are seen in plate 29.†

Upon the face of the mountain, to the left of the great temple, and likewise to the right of the smaller temple, are several sculptures, in the form of tablets, representing offerings and other subjects, with hieroglyphic inscriptions below. Most of them are shallow, square recesses; and of the same age as the two temples: the style of the sculptures, slight, but good.

A little below (or to the right of) the smaller temple, is a niche, or recess, high up in the face of the rock; and within it, a figure of rather colossal size, in a sitting posture, clad in a long dress, reaching to the ankles. This figure is of a somewhat clumsy character, and much injured. It represents Rameses the Second; whose name we may plainly

---

†Fig. 153.

distinguish among some hieroglyphics above the niche, for the most part effaced. On my second visit to this spot, in September 1827, I found that the river, then nearly at the highest, had reached the feet of this statue.

Chapter XXXIX.
From Ab'oo Sim'bil to Wa'dee Hhal'fa.

Rock-temple opposite Beyla'nee—Ckal''at Ad'deh—Far'as—Ruins of a temple at Sir'reh Ghur'bee—Remains of two temples a little below Wa'dee Hhal'fa—Wa'dee Hhal'fa and the Second Cataracts, &c.

There is no village adjacent to the temples of Ab'oo Sim'bil, nor even space for a small town; but a little above this spot, the mountains on the same side recede a little from the river, and there is a narrow tract of cultivated land along the bank, with a village called *Beyla'nee* بيلاني . Opposite the part where the mountains on that side recede from the river, those on the opposite side *approach* the stream, and, at a short distance further, leave no road along the water's edge, excepting when the Nile is low, and even then camels cannot pass, but are obliged to ascend an *'ack'abah*, or road over the mountain. Here, in the front of the mountain, is excavated a small temple, presenting externally only a small and plane door-way, about twelve feet above the highest point that the river attains. It is even more ancient than the temples of Ab'oo Sim'bil; being of the reign of King Horus, the third predecessor of Rameses 2nd. A sculpture at Geb'el es-Sil'sil'eh, which I have described, acquaints us with the fact of this king's having made a victorious campaign in Ethiopia: it was probably on his journey thither, or on his return, that he caused this rock-temple to be excavated.—The entrance admits us into a square chamber, having four columns, hewn out of the rock. A low and narrow bench of rock surrounds the chamber. The walls have been plastered over by early Christians, and covered with paintings of saints, &c.; among which is St. George and the Dragon: all of these are vile dawbs: the ceiling also is similarly painted. In some parts, where the plaster has fallen from the walls, we discover the ancient Egyptian sculptures; but no subjects of interest. The columns are nearly similar to those along the front of the ancient edifice at the ruined village of El-Ckoor'neh; only the shafts are not reeded.—At the end of this chamber we ascend four low steps, and enter the sanctuary, a small apartment, in which is an oblong excavation, communicating with a lower chamber, or chambers, now filled with rubbish, probably destined for the sepulture of sacred animals.—There is also a small, narrow apartment on the right and left of the first chamber.

On the same side of the river, a little above the temple just described, are the remains of a small town, crowning an isolated hill of rock, and called *Ckal''at Ad'deh* قلعة ادّه (the Castle of Ad'deh). It resembles the old town of Ibree'm; but is smaller, and less elevated. The houses are constructed partly of stone and partly of crude brick; and there are remains of a wall which surrounded the town. Just below it is the burial-place of the former Moos'lim inhabitants.—Beyond it, on the side of another isolated hill, I observed a small piece of sculpture, similar to those on the mountains of Ab'oo Sim'bil; but I neglected to examine it.—Opposite this spot is the cultivated island of Beyla'nee; so called from a village already mentioned.—A little above Ckal''at Ad'deh, the mountains on that side of the river are of strange and picturesque forms. There are many isolated mountains here, some of which resemble pyramids; and many small mounds that appear to be artificial; but I doubt whether they be so.

Just above the island of Beyla'nee, the shore on either side is a low desert. A little above this, there is a narrow strip of cultivated land along the south-eastern shore, with a large village called *Ed-Dinda'n* الضنضان , which gives its name to the wa'dee, or district. Opposite this is a cultivated island.

A little higher, a promontory on the south-eastern side reaches to the river. Upon it is a ruined convent or mosque. On the other side of the river, directly opposite this promontory, is a village called *Far'as* فرس . At this place, a narrow tract of cultivated land borders the river. At the distance of nearly an hour to the north of Far'as are some Christian ruins; and a little further are some grottoes, rudely excavated, in which are many Greek inscriptions of Christian times.—Throughout a space of about seven miles (composing the districts of Far'as and Sir'reh Ghur'bee) the north-western bank is bordered by a strip of cultivated soil. Opposite the upper part of the district of Far'as is a small, fertile island, of the same name. On the opposite bank of the river there is a more scanty cultivation; and in some parts, none at all.

On the north-western shore, a little below the first village of *Sir'reh Ghur'bee* سرّه غربى , are remains of a temple of the age of Rameses 2nd, situated very near the river, close behind the narrow strip of cultivated land.[†] Both without and within it is partly buried in rubbish; at some parts, quite to the top of the ruined walls; and at others, to within three or four feet of the top. Superstructures of brick, partly crude and partly burnt, have been raised upon the ancient stone walls. The entrance faces the river. Through this we pass into what was a court, 53 feet in length, and 50 feet in width; with a row of square pillars along the front and along each side, which doubtless supported the roof of a gallery: the central part of the court appears to have been uncovered. The walls are so much ruined, and so little of them is exposed, that we find no subject entire among the sculptures with which they are decorated: but sufficient is seen of these to shew that they are in the very best style.[1] On the interior surface of the front wall, the king by whom the temple was

---

[†]Serra West.

[1] I am astonished Burckhardt thought otherwise: he always admired most the latest sculptures, which are frequently remarkable for their elaborate finishing, but in other respects are, to the eye of an artist, most displeasing.

founded (Rameses 2nd) is represented sacrificing captives. This subject is twice sculptured; on each side of the entrance: in one case there are three captives; and in the other, but two. On the left side-wall, we see a portion of the representation of a siege; and on the opposite wall are similar sculptures. On the latter, an Egyptian is represented driving along a number of captives. The end-wall appears to have been decorated with figures of the king offering &c. There were several chambers behind this court; but their walls are so much ruined and buried in rubbish that I could not make out their dimensions or plan, excepting those of the first, which is small, and presents nothing interesting.—Before this ruined temple, the ground is strewed with fragments of pottery, &c., which mark the site of a small, ancient town.

Another promontory of the range on the south-eastern shore reaches to the river opposite the district of Sir'reh Ghur'bee. On its slope, near the water, is a small, ruined town, composed of houses of crude brick; with a thick wall of the same material surrounding it.[†] —Above the district of Sir'reh Ghur'bee, the shore, on that side, is a low desert, without any cultivation for several miles; but on the other side of the river is a tract of fertile soil, wider than any above Wa'dee Ibree'm to this point, and well cultivated. The first and finest district on this latter side is that of *Sir'reh* سِرّه. It is rich in palm-trees; the dates of which are of a very fine kind both in size and flavour. The large village of Sir'reh is near the river. Here one of my servants landed, to visit his mother, whom he had not seen for many years, and who could hardly be persuaded that he was her son. Within a few minutes after he had entered the village, the air resounded with the zugh'a'ree't of the women, and a crowd of men collected round him to embrace and kiss him.—I remained here for the night, and during part of the following day.—The height of the thermometer in the afternoon of the 26th was 110°.

27th. From Sir'reh, throughout the district of *Debey'reh* دبيره , and that of *Ishckey'd* اشقيد , extends an uninterrupted tract of cultivated land, with numerous palm-trees, and many scattered houses, besides two large villages of the above names. On this side, and on the low, desert shore opposite, I observed, at frequent intervals, ruins of crude brick, which are distinguished from the houses of the modern inhabitants by the greater thickness of the walls. The modern houses are, however, very superior to those of Lower Nubia, the country of the Koonoo'z. Many Arabs, among whom are some of the Prophet's tribe (the Ckoorey'sh) have settled in these parts, with the Noo'beh. Here, as in some other parts of Nubia, I saw women with no other clothing than a piece of ragged stuff tied round their loins; and men quite naked, working on the banks of the river. Under an acacia, on the desert western shore, we saw, as we slowly sailed almost close along the bank, a young woman, perfectly naked, sitting, with an infant asleep by her side, and an earthen bowl upon a fire before her. The only piece of clothing that she

---

[†]Serra East.

possessed she had extended, and fastened to the boughs of the tree, to shade her: for an acacia gives very little shade. As we passed before her, she threw up both her arms, and exclaimed "Hhaba'bak" (Welcome), and did not rise, nor attempt to conceal herself. How powerful is the influence of custom! This woman, I doubt not, was as modest as most of the Nubian females, who are celebrated for their chastity.

A promontory, reaching to the river, terminates the district of Ishckey'd. Upon its slope is the tomb of a sheykh, the sheykh 'Om'ar. From this point, for a short space, the bank on this side is perfectly barren; and for about the same space on the opposite bank, extends a narrow strip of cultivated soil, with three small villages, called *Arckee'n* (or *Argee'n*) ارقين . Just above Arckee'n is a small, cultivated island. A narrow, fertile tract, which borders the river on the eastern side as far as the northernmost island of the Second Cataracts, commences a little below the island above mentioned. The two principal villages in this tract are *Debro'seh* دبروسه and *Wa'dee Hhal'fa* وادى حلفا . Along this shore are numerous palm-trees. The opposite shore is a low desert: no more cultivation does the traveller see on that side until he has passed the cataracts; but the bank is, in many parts, lined with acacias.

A little below Wa'dee Hhal'fa, I landed on the western bank, to see the remains of two temples, very near the river. These ruins are partly buried in sand: only the lower blocks of some columns and square pillars, and some portions of the walls, rising two or three feet above the surface. Upon these parts of the edifices, and upon other parts from which I removed the sand, I found no hieroglyphics to prove their age: but as the columns are of the order resembling the Doric, which are only seen in the most ancient temples in Egypt, we may reasonably refer them to a very remote period.[1] There are constructions of crude brick within and around these ruins.—The height of the thermometer in the afternoon of the 27th was 110°.

28th. At the village of Wa'dee Hhal'fa,[2] forty soldiers are stationed; and granaries and store-houses have lately been erected there for the supply of the troops in the upper countries.—A little higher, in the middle of the river, is a cultivated island, with many palm-trees; but the bed on the east of it is, at this season, dry. Beyond this are several other islands, and numerous small rocks. Some of the islands here alluded to are cultivated; and upon one of them are ruins of crude brick, which seem to have been the work of early Christians.

To the west of these islands, at a short distance from the river, is the tomb, or monument, of a sheykh, picturesquely situated (as sheykhs' tombs generally are) on the point of a low, flat hill[3]; appearing like a

---

[1]Champollion's party cleared much of the sand from these ruins; and found upon one the name of Thothmos 3rd; and upon the other, the names of Amonoph 2nd and Rameses 1st, with that of Osirtesen: the last two names were on two stelæ.

[2]See plate 33 [fig. 157].

[3]Seen in plate 33 [fig. 157].

small tumulus. The name of the sheykh to whom it is consecrated is 'Abd El-Cka'dir; and it is said to be his tomb; but one person assured me that this saint was the famous sheykh 'Abd El-Cka'dir El-Gheela'nee: if so, we must regard this little structure merely as dedicated to that person; in the same manner as the oratory of the sheykh El-Hharee'dee is dedicated to the saint whose name it bears. It is constructed in a singular manner. Rough, unhewn stones are piled one upon another, without regularity; and upon this heap is built a small, round cell, in the same manner, roofed with old mats, and open on the southern side. My crew were urgent with me not to omit performing a pious visit to this monument, as a duty which would call down a blessing on my whole party; and, as usual in such cases, I was to recite the Fe't'hhah. Having climbed up the heap of stones forming the basis of the monument, I entered the little cell, which is about six feet in width, and four in height. Upon the floor was an old, yellow flag, upon which was worked the name of God. Several old pieces of linen were thrown upon it; and at the side of this heap were a number of earthen vessels, wooden bowls, and pieces of rag. With these memorials, left by pious visiters, was a camel's saddle; and in one of the earthen bowls was an offering of a small coin, of five fud'dahs.[1] On the hill, around the monument, I found a vast number of small heaps of stones, either raised like little pillars or in the form of cones. These are also memorials of the numerous visiters who have offered up their prayers at this highly venerated spot. The camel's saddle and some of the other articles in the cell were probably votive gifts.

Returning to the river, I pursued my way along the bank, which is lined with seya'lehs, sunts, and do'ms. Beyond the series of islands before mentioned, the river is divided by innumerable masses of rock, black and highly-polished; forming a strong contrast with the glaring colour of the sand with which, at this season, many of them are surrounded. These rocks are chiefly of green-veined porphyry: the shores, of sandstone, strewed over with pieces of granite, mica, &c. The eastern shore is low; but mountains are seen in the distance on that side. I continued my walk very leisurely; my attendant, a Nubian, being much oppressed by the heat, which was greater than I had yet experienced; the height of the thermometer being 112° in the shade of a rock. The heat affected me but little; excepting that it burnt my arms through my thin shirt-sleeves: for, besides my shirt and drawers, I only wore a cotton vest, without sleeves. Small blisters were raised all along my arms; and in the evening they irritated me so much that I was obliged to open them with a pen-knife. My feet were also burnt a little by the hot sand, which filled my shoes almost immediately after I had emptied them.—In rather more than an hour after I had quitted the monument of the sheykh 'Abd El-Cka'dir, I arrived at a high, rocky point, on the bank of the river, called the mountain of *Ab'oo Seer* ابو صير , overlooking the whole district of the cataracts. This rock rises abruptly from the edge of the

---

[1]Equivalent to a farthing and two thirds.

river. The view from its summit is of a very singular nature. The bed of the river is very wide, and so thickly interspersed with rocks that, excepting in the parts very near to the observer, little water is to be seen; at least when the river is low, as at the period of my visit. Opposite to the rock of Ab'oo Seer were several falls (if so they may be called), where the river shot down with great velocity between the rugged rocks; not perpendicularly, but with a slight slope. The sound heard from the rocky point where I stood was little more than a confused murmur, like that which is heard when standing near a water-mill. Looking north and south, I saw, for a considerable distance, a wide bed of rocks; upon many of which were a few seya'lehs and sunts, springing from a very scanty deposit of soil around the edges of these isles and in the hollows of the rocks. Continuing my route along the western bank, I found the scenery the same; but the falls more considerable. Throughout this whole district, the appearance of the river alters with the seasons of the year: as it rises, some of the falls gradually disappear; and others are formed where, before, the water had no passage. Upon the whole, the falls are more considerable, as well as more numerous, than those of Aswa'n.—After scrambling about among the rocks wherever I could pass, taking a meal, and watching a net spread across one of the falls, I returned along the bank to my boat; at which I arrived in the evening, after having walked the whole of the day.

I had attained the limit of my voyage. Few travellers have proceeded higher; as the passage of the second cataracts is very difficult.—While I was absent on the excursion above described, my boat was undergoing the necessary preparation for descending the river. The almost-constant prevalence of northerly winds renders sails generally useless in the downward navigation of the Nile. The main-mast and yard were removed, and placed along the centre of the boat: one end resting on the roof of the cabin, and the other being lashed to the foremast. The *tarankee't* (or fore-sail) remained as usual.

Supplement.
On the Ancient Egyptians.

1. Their origin and physical characteristics.

That the Egyptian nation derived its origin solely from Mizraim the son of Ham or Cham may reasonably be doubted: the branch of the posterity of Cush which peopled Ethiopia (super Ægyptum) may have spread thence from Egypt; and Phut, or Put, may also have contributed to people the valley of the Nile. Lower Egypt, or that part of Egypt which constituted the Memphite Kingdom, is named in the Bible "the land of Mizraim," and "the land of Khem," or "Khemi." The "No," or "No Amon," of the Scriptures was, it appears, the Theban Kingdom, or Thebes itself: of No Amon the prophet Nahum says (iii, 8 and 9) that Cush and Mizraim (Ethiopia and Lower Egypt) were her strength: Put and Lubin were her helpers.

Of the physical characteristics of the ancient Egyptians we may give a very exact description. Some writers have imagined these people to have been Negroes; founding their opinion upon an expression of Herodotus, which designates them as μελαγχροες και ουλοτριχες (ii, 104). These words have been rendered "of *black* complexion and with *woolly* hair," but the former will bear, and the latter demands, a different interpretation: the two words should be rendered "of *dark* complexion and with *crisp* hair." Ammianus Marcellinus terms the ancient Egyptians "subfusculi, et atrati." Let us view them, however, represented upon the walls of their temples and tombs, and by their statues, and we shall discover how widely, and in what respects, they differed from Negroes.

The eyes are elongated: the nose is rounded a little, or somewhat aquiline, and rather thick: the lips are thicker than those of the natives of more northern countries; but considerably less thick than those of the negro: the forehead slopes a little backwards: the head is rather long; in some instances shaven, and in others not; and in the latter case the hair is divided into a number of small twists, in the same manner as is seen in the present day among the Nubians, whose hair is *crisp*, but not *woolly*. If we look at the paintings, or painted sculptures, we see the flesh-colour of the *men* (of all classes—kings, priests, soldiers, artisans, &c.) represented by a dull red; indicating that they were of a dark or swarthy complexion: that of the *women*, generally by yellow and in some cases by pink; shewing that they were of a lighter complexion than the men, from their being less exposed to the sun; and the same difference we observe in the complexions of the male and female Egyptians of the present day, unless the latter are equally exposed to the scorching rays of the sun. The eyes are painted of the natural colour: the cornea, black. The hair is also painted black.

It may, however, be objected that the colours of these paintings and sculptures were not meant to represent the complexion, any more than were the black, yellow, and red colours of the figures on Etruscan and Greek vases; and also that the Egyptian artists were unable to delineate with correctness the negro countenance. Both these objections must fall to the ground. We find negroes as well as Egyptians among the paintings and sculptures: the former are painted *black*; and their features are very different from those of the Egyptians; presenting as faithful and exact representations of the negro countenance as if they were the works of modern European artists. Let the reader here turn to one of the engravings in this work; an exact copy in outline of four figures in a procession in the great royal tomb at Thebes (the tomb of Osiree 1st, the father of Rameses 2nd) which was discovered by Belzoni[1]: they are four natives of different countries; and among them are an Egyptian and a Negro: the former is painted red; and the latter, black. Let him also turn to another engraving, from the sculptures of the rock-temple of Ckala'b'sheh, in Nubia; in which he will observe how faithfully the countenances of the captive negroes are portrayed, and how differently from those of the Egyptians.[†] Nothing then can be more certain than that the ancient Egyptians differed widely in countenance and complexion from negroes.

It has been supposed that there was a race in Egypt resembling the negroes in *complexion*, though not in *features*; and that this was a race of aboriginal Egyptians. This opinion is urged by the learned Heeren. It is founded upon the singular fact that, in some of the tombs of the Kings at Thebes, decapitated Egyptians are represented painted black, while their executioners are painted red. But these sculptures undoubtedly exhibit the punishments of the damned in Hades, who are painted black to represent their moral darkness: if not, why do we not find black Egyptians represented any-where else than in these tombs?—why not among the paintings or painted sculptures illustrative of the social life of the ancient inhabitants of Egypt? Heeren concludes that the black figures above-mentioned are those of a very dark race in Egypt, over whom the lighter race obtained authority; and he thus draws the inference that the ruling race was of a lighter colour than the aboriginal Egyptians, though he afterwards, from other considerations, brings the former from a more hot climate—from Ethiopia. I am acquainted with only one instance of a person with Egyptian features being represented of a black colour to denote a black complexion. This is the daughter of Amos, or Amosis (the head of the 18th Dynasty): she was the wife of Amonoph 1st, the successor of Amos, and was doubtless an Ethiopian.—This leads me to speak of the Great Sphinx near the Pyramids of El-Gee'zeh; the features of which bear a somewhat nearer resemblance to those of the negro than do the lineaments of most other Egyptian heads. The loss of the nose

---

[1]The drawing is no. 41 of the subject for wood-cuts [fig. 121].
[†]Lane refers to his missing illustration of Beit al-Wali near Kalabsha.

partly accounts for this; but certainly not wholly. Sphinxes were designed as emblems of Kings; and I have mentioned the probability of the Great Sphinx being of the reign of Amos: if so, the peculiarity above-mentioned is entirely accounted for; as Amos appears to have been an Ethiopian: the face of this colossus was, however, painted *red*.

The Ethiopians frequently intermarried with the Egyptians; and individuals of the former race, in more than one or two instances, raised themselves, or were raised, to the throne of Egypt. In features the Ethiopians differed little from the Egyptians; but they were of a darker complexion. Here I should remark that "Ethiopia" is rather a vague term, being sometimes applied to Upper Egypt; but it was generally and more correctly given to the country above Egypt; i.e. south of Syene.

Respecting the colour of the ancient Egyptians I must further observe that we cannot suppose the red pigment to have been used by their artists as very nearly resembling the complexion of the men, and the yellow or pink as representing with the same degree of correctness the colour of the women; but rather that these colours were thus employed in accordance with prescribed rules, or because the painters were little acquainted with [the] art of mixing colours. Nor can we suppose the complexion to have been the same in every part of the country; but that it was lighter or darker (as in the case of the modern inhabitants) in different latitudes; being of a deep bronze colour in the more southern parts, and much lighter towards the Mediterranean.

2. Origin of the civilization of Egypt.

In proceeding to take a general view of the religious and political state of the ancient Egyptian nation, our attention is first directed to the origin of their civilization, which I must ascribe to the aboriginal natives of Egypt alone. Thus again, I find myself obliged to oppose a commonly received opinion, which is that of the Ethiopian descent of the religion and arts of Egypt. This opinion has received the sanction of several learned men, in consequence of their not possessing that sufficient acquaintance with the monuments of Egypt which can only be acquired by a visit to that country, and by the aid of the important lights derivable from the late discovery of the phonetic system of hieroglyphics.

The most antient of all the monuments along the whole tract of country watered by the Nile, from the furthest parts of Ethiopia to the Mediterranean are in *northern Egypt*. I allude to the Pyramids of Memphis. The small pyramids of Ethiopia have been regarded as the types of those stupendous edifices of Egypt; but they are proved by their hieroglyphics to be comparatively modern; which even their structure might lead one to imagine.—The monuments of the next class in point of antiquity are found in the same part, and there only. These are the edifices destitute of sculptures and of painting adjacent to the First and

Second Pyramids.[1]—The monuments of the third class in the order of antiquity are in the same and other parts of Egypt; and one monument of the same age is found in *Lower* Nubia, or *Lower* Ethiopia. These are of the period of the last Memphite Dynasty, and of the Diospolite kings of the 17th Dynasty. The most remarkable of them are the sculptured and painted tombs near the principal Pyramids, the obelisk of Heliopolis, that of the Feiyoo'm, and the grottoes of Ben'ee Hhas'an, in Middle Egypt. They are the earliest monuments ornamented with hieroglyphics, paintings, and sculptures.—The *later* monuments, *and these only*, are found in *Upper* Ethiopia, in common with the lower countries.

It may perhaps be urged that, though architecture had attained to a wonderful degree of excellence in Egypt before any monuments of a durable kind were constructed in Ethiopia, yet, as one of the earliest sculptured monuments is found in Lower Ethiopia, the Egyptian religion and the sciences connected with it may have originated with the Ethiopians. To this I would reply that, if the case were so, monuments of the same antiquity at least, of which there are so many in Egypt, would undoubtedly have been found in that part of Ethiopia where the capital, Meroë, was situated, and not merely in the contracted valley of *Lower* Ethiopia: therefore it is more reasonable to infer either that, in the times of the 17th Dynasty, that part of Ethiopia had been conquered by the Egyptians, or that an Ethiopian seated himself on the throne of the Thebais, and was the means of introducing the religion and arts of Egypt into his own country.—From the period when the Memphite Kingdom became annexed to the Diospolite, which happened (as hereafter will be shewn) at the close of the 17th Dynasty, or the commencement of the 18th, the head of which was Amos the Ethiopian, the kings or queens of Egypt were for several descents and probably for some centuries, partly of Ethiopian origin: for Amos the Ethiopian left a daughter who married his successor Amonoph 1st, an Egyptian; and we have reason to believe that many succeeding kings, or their queens, partook of Ethiopian blood. An influx of Ethiopians, to aid the Thebans in subjugating the Memphites, and the intermixture of Ethiopian with Egyptian blood in the princes who ruled over Egypt after it had thus been reduced to one kingdom, might be supposed to have given rise to the tradition related by Diodorus Siculus (iii, 3) "that the Egyptians were a colony of Ethiopians": but this tradition is to be explained in a more satisfactory manner: the term "Egypt" was restricted, by many ancient writers to *Lower* Egypt (or the Memphite territories), while *Upper* Egypt was confounded with Ethiopia: hence the people termed Egyptians in this restricted sense might be called a colony of Ethiopians because their ancestors had first settled in Upper Egypt: the first kingdom that was founded on the banks of the Nile is said to have been the Thinite, in Upper Egypt; and in very ancient times Lower Egypt was a mere swamp. Diodorus moreover says, in another place (i, 10) that the Egyptians

---

[1]The proofs of their being of this age are given in my description of them.

asserted the first men to have been born in *Egypt*: and as to Osiris (whom some affirmed to have come from Ethiopia) the Egyptians also asserted, according to the same historian (i, 13), that he was one of their own native gods and kings.

3. On Hieroglyphics.

The Egyptians could have made but little progress towards civilization until they were able to commit their ideas to writing; and as we find no inscriptions in their country so ancient as those in hieroglyphics, we are justified in referring the origin of the hieroglyphic system to the infant age of the nation. We may safely state the age of the earliest hieroglyphic inscriptions yet discovered to be between 18 and 19 centuries anterior to the Christian era, or about 7 centuries subsequent to the period when Egypt was first inhabited, and between 4 and 5 centuries later than the foundation of the Great Pyramid; but as these inscriptions are of a nature not less perfect than those of much later ages, they prove that the hieroglyphic system must have been previously very long in use, though not before applied to the decoration of monuments. The same was the case with the Egyptian sculptures and paintings of every kind: the most ancient specimens of these are of the same age as the earliest inscriptions: they accompany the latter, and are of the same perfect description. We may infer, then, that, in the more remote ages, the inscriptions and paintings were executed on very perishable materials.—The principles of the hieroglyphic system discovered by Dr. Young, after having been buried in oblivion for many centuries and since more fully investigated by Champollion and others, require at least a brief notice in these pages, particularly as enabling us to decipher the names of the most unobjectionable sources of information respecting the religious and political state of the Egyptians in general.

The ancient Egyptians used three modes of writing—1. The Hieroglyphic, which was employed for inscriptions—2. The Hieratic, which was the writing of the priests, and but rarely used for inscriptions—3. The Enchorial, or Demotic, the writing of the people in general.—The second of these was derived from the first; and the third, from the second.

Hieroglyphics are of three kinds—1. Figurative—2. Emblematic, or Symbolic—3. Phonetic, or Alphabetic.—In the first, the hieroglyphic is a representation of the object itself: in the second, it is an emblem of the object: in the third, it represents a sound, or letter.—The hieroglyphic alphabet is appended to this volume.

In hieroglyphic inscriptions some words or objects are represented by their figurative signs; others, by their emblems; but the greater proportion, by phonetic characters, combined in the same manner as in other alphabetic modes of writing; and the characters are arranged in perpendicular columns, or in horizontal lines, and read in some cases from right to left, and in others, from left to right: when to be read from right to left, the figures of animals which are introduced always look to the right; and the same rule is observed in other characters: the reverse is the case when the inscription is to be read from left to right. Every phonetic hieroglyphic expresses the sound of the initial vowel or consonant of the name of the object of which it is the image: thus the sun, being called Ra, or Re, expresses the sound of R. Every vowel and consonant may thus be represented by several different characters; but particular characters are generally used, in preference to others which are synonymous, in particular words. In words formed of phonetic characters, the intermediate vowels are often omitted: in proper names, almost always. The phonetic characters composing the name of an object are often followed by the figure of the object itself.—The names of Egyptian kings are contained in two ovals; sometimes placed perpendicularly; sometimes horizontally; according to the text in which they occur. The first oval, or *prenomen*, contains a title derived from the name of some god; and enables us to distinguish between two or more kings whose *nomen*, or second oval, is the same: for we find several kings with the same nomen, but no two with the same prenomen, excepting only, I believe, Osirtesen 1st and Nectanebo: hence the prenomen, or distinguishing title, is often found without the nomen. The first character in the prenomen of every Pharaoh is the disk of the sun, called Ra, or (with the article) Phra, the Phrah, or Pharaoh, of the Scriptures.[1] The original characters of a prenomen, or those distinguishing it from other prenomens, are never altered, but other characters are often added. The nomen, like the prenomen, is generally derived from the name of some god, as Thothmos, or Thothmes, "begotten of Thoth": the characters composing it are in some instances all phonetic; in others, partly phonetic and partly figurative, or partly emblematic. The prenomen is generally preceded by a group of hieroglyphics which Horus Apollo translates "King of an obedient people": the nomen, by a goose and the disk of the sun, signifying "Son of the Sun," or "—— of Phra," or "—— Pharaoh." As an example, the titles and names of Rameses 2nd may be rendered

King of an obedient people (Pharaoh, Approved of Thmei and Ra)

Son of Pharaoh (Amon-mai Rameses)

On many monuments we find the name of a king altered to that of a later king; and sometimes, when the prenomen of the latter is nearly the same as that of the former, the nomen only is altered. It has been clearly established, by Mr. Wilkinson,[2] that the square (containing several hieroglyphics, the first of which, in most cases, are a bull and an arm) having a hawk and disk above it, and generally commencing the

---

[1] Major Felix's Notes on Hieroglyphics.
[2] "Extracts from several Hieroglyphical subjects" &c., p. 7.

inscriptions on obelisks, presents a title of the king whose name follows it. When the name is altered, this square title is also generally altered to that which in other instances accompanies the substituted name.—The names of private individuals are not enclosed in ovals: they are followed by a figure of a man, or woman.

The Hieratic style was a short-hand mode of writing the hieroglyphic.

The Enchorial, or popular writing, was a more simple system, with few emblematic, and still fewer figurative signs.

4. Religion and Laws.

The Egyptian priests alone were acquainted with the mystical, or recondite sense of their mythology. Their religion appears to have been founded upon the worship of the supreme power of nature—of one spiritual being, the author of the universe, adored under different names and forms, according to his different attributes and operations. The belief in the supreme being seems to have been the grand ἀπόῤῥητον of the priests: but the vulgar regarded his different names and personifications as belonging to distinct gods; and seem to have been taught (probably on account of their being obstinately addicted to the worship of their deceased ancestors) to identify these supposed distinct gods with their great progenitors Noah, Ham, and others. Thus the great first cause was called No Neb (or No the Lord), a name which, coupled with the fact of his being often represented in a boat, was sufficient to induce the popular notion of his identity with Noah. The generative power was always represented by a figure bearing the name of Khem, of Amon-Ra; exhibiting a remarkable agreement with Cham, or Ham, the progenitor of the Egyptian nation.—The following were the principal names and characters of the deity, or, according to the popular notions,—of the gods.

Kneph, or No-Neb—Sate.

Kneph, Cneph, Nef, or No-Neb (i.e. No the Lord), called also, by the Romans, Cnoubis, and Jupiter Ammon Cenubis, was the chief title of the supreme being, or great first cause. The hieroglyphic of Neb, or Nef, is the lower hemisphere; and by this name the deity seems to have been distinguished as presiding over the invisible world. According to Porphyry, cited by Eusebius, the author of the world, whom the Egyptians worshipped under the name of Kneph, was represented by a human figure, with a dark blue complexion, bearing a feather on his head, and emitting an egg from his mouth: this was the chaotic egg, of which was formed the world. On the monuments, however, we do not find Kneph thus represented; but by a human figure with the head of a ram: besides the ram's horns he bears another pair of horns, from between which issues an asp, his emblem. He is often represented in a boat, which frequently has the form of a snake; and a snake curls over him. He is also depicted as standing in the midst of the sun's disk, with a beetle, which was an emblem of the sun, behind him. Thus, and in the boat, he represents the sun in the lower hemisphere. The ram-headed figure had sometimes the title of Amon[1]; which may account for his being called Jupiter Ammon Cenubis.—The deity under the name of Kneph was perhaps the chief object of worship throughout Egypt at the earliest period; or throughout Upper Egypt, where the first kingdom, the Thinite, was established; and hence it was, perhaps, that Upper Egypt was called the land of No. According to Plutarch, the inhabitants of the Thebaid refused to contribute to the maintenance of the sacred animals, because they only worshipped Kneph, who was uncreated, and immortal: but the most ancient temples of Thebes now remaining were dedicated chiefly to the worship of Amon-Ra, or Khem. Kneph and Sate were the chief objects of worship at Elephantine, Syene, and the Cataracts.

Sate was the feminine character of Kneph. Her figure, which is that of a woman, wearing the cap of the lower regions, and generally with a pair of cow's horns, always accompanies that of Kneph. According to Horapollo, Sate presided over the lower firmament, as Neith over the upper.

Phtha—Neith.

Phtha was the masculine title of the Demiurgus, or creative power, described as emanating with the egg, or chaos, from Kneph. Horapollo states that Phtha was both masculine and feminine. He seems to have been the deity presiding over the visible world; as Kneph over the invisible. By the Greeks and Romans he is identified with the Vulcan of their own mythology. He is generally represented by a mummy-shaped figure, holding the emblems of life and power and stability. The beetle was his particular emblem.—Phtha-Socari appears to have been the name under which the Demiurgus was worshipped at Memphis. He is generally represented by the figure of a man, with the horns of Kneph, surmounted by a disk and two feathers: also, by a dwarf, with a beetle on his head.[2]

Neith was the feminine character of Phtha; and is generally represented by the figure of a woman, wearing the cap of the upper regions, perhaps to denote the character of president of the upper firmament, or visible heavens, as mentioned in speaking of Sate. Neith was the principal object of worship at Sais; and was thence introduced into Greece (where she became Athena, or Minerva) by Cecrops, the founder of Athens. The statue of Neith at Sais is said to have borne this remarkable inscription— "I am all that has been, and that is, and that shall be; and no mortal has ever penetrated my veil."

---

[1]But only (Mr. Wilkinson observes) as Amon-Ra with the attributes of Kneph.
[2]Mr. Salt once mentioned to me that he conceived the name of the modern village of Sack'cka'rah, which stands on a part of the site of Memphis, to be derived from Phtha-Socari.

Khem, Amon-Ra, Ra—Maut, Koht, Tafnet.

The generative power, or the deity in the office of presiding over generation and vegetation, is represented by a remarkable figure, which in some instances bears the name of Khem, and in others, that of Amon-Ra, and has behind it a small altar, or shrine, crowned with trees or plants. Khem was regarded by the Greeks as the same with their Pan. The city of Chemmis (or Panopolis, as it was called by the Greeks) derived its name from its being chiefly devoted to the worship of Khem; and "The land of Khem," or "—— Cham," or "—— Ham," was the ancient name of Egypt.—Amon-Ra (also sometimes called simply Amon), as the power both of generation and vegetation, was not only represented by the figure of Khem, with the name of Amon-Ra-Khem, or Amon-Khem, but also, sometimes, by the usual figure of Ra, and that of Kneph; and had other forms besides these; generally the simple human form, with a peculiar, high head-dress. This character of the deity was the principal object of worship at Thebes. The Greeks, identifying Amon-Ra with their Zeus, or Jupiter, hence called Thebes "Diospolis."—Ra particularly represented the deity as presiding over the sun, the great cause of vegetation; but was perhaps regarded by the vulgar as the sun itself. The usual form of Ra is a human figure with the head of a hawk, surmounted by a disk (the sun), from which issues an asp. The hawk and the beetle were emblems of the sun and of Ra.—The figure representing the generative power has not only the combined names of Amon-Ra-Khem, but sometimes the name of Ra. Thus we find the same emblematic representation, the attributes of which cannot be mistaken, with the names of Khem, Amon-Ra-Khem, and Ra. Amon-Ra seems to have been a more comprehensive title of the deity than Khem; being given even to the figure of Kneph; and Ra, an abstraction of the same.

Maut represents the same power of the deity in a female character; and generally has the form of a woman with the head of a lion, above which is the disk of the sun, with an asp issuing from it. This figure often accompanies Amon-Ra. Precisely the same figure occurs also with a name which is read "Koht," and again with the name of "Tafnet."[1] It is probable that this figure, in these three different cases, represented the same power with only different names; and was also the "Triphis" of the Greek inscription of the temple of Chemmis, or Panopolis, which inscription records the dedication of that temple to Triphis and Pan, or Khem. When the generative power in a male character was worshipped under the name of Khem, it seems that the same power in a female character was called by the Greeks and Romans "Triphis"; but whether called by the Egyptians Maut, Koht, or Tafnet, is doubtful: when this power in the former character was worshipped under the name of Amon-Ra, it was in the latter character under the name of Maut. Probably Maut was synonymous with the Buto or Latona of Greek and

---

[1]See Mr. Wilkinson's Materia Hieroglyphica.

Roman writers; and Koht, or Tafnet, with Triphis. The vulture was the chief emblem of Maut.

Khons.

Khons is generally found accompanying Amon-Ra and Maut; and is represented by a mummy-shaped figure, similar to that of Phtha, holding the emblems of Phtha, and of Osiris, or the palm-branch of Thoth; or by a human figure with the head of a hawk: the head, in both cases, crowned by the moon (a crescent enclosing a disk) which is also characteristic of Thoth.

Seb—Netpe.

Seb, called in hieroglyphics the father of Osiris, and identified with the Saturn of the Greeks, is represented by a human figure, sometimes with a goose, his chief emblem, on his head.

Netpe, who is termed the wife of Seb, and identified by the Greeks, with their Rhea, is represented by a female figure, sometimes with a vase, which is the initial hieroglyphic of her name, upon her head. The figure of Netpe is also represented in the midst of a sycamore, pouring water from a vase.

Osiris—Isis.

Osiris, in mythological language termed the son of Seb and Netpe, was a personification of the deity in the double character of dispenser of fertility (and as such typified by the inundation of the Nile, and by the sun) and as the judge of mankind, or the dispenser of rewards and punishments after death. He is generally represented by a mummy-shaped figure, holding a flail and crook (the emblems of fertility and authority), and sometimes also with the sceptre and crux ansata (the emblems of power and life); wearing upon his head the cap of the lower regions, with a feather attached to each side of it. He is likewise represented by a front view of a figure combined with the emblem of stability, the upper part of which rises above his head; and crowned with the usual head-dress of Phtha-Socari, represented in my figure of that character of the divinity. Osiris corresponded both with the Bacchus and Pluto of the Greek mythology.—The fable of the manifestation of Osiris upon earth,—of his acquainting mankind with all useful arts and sciences, and particularly enabling them to cultivate the earth,—of his death (being shut up in a chest by Typhon), his burial, resurrection, &c.—is said to have been an allegory representing the overflowing of the Nile, and its fertilizing the soil of Egypt, —its subsiding, and leaving the earth naked, and destitute of herbage (when the *aphanism*, or disappearance of Osiris was solemnly celebrated by the priests),—of the absorption of the waters which had overspread the soil, and of the sowing of the seed (at the period of which the *burial* of Osiris was celebrated),—and of the latent moisture manifesting itself by the springing up of the herbage. A ceremony in celebration of the search of

Isis after the remains of Osiris was solemnized at the winter solstice; and the discovery of the remains was celebrated, it would appear, on the 19th of the following month, *Tobi* (and *not Athyr*, as seems to be implied in the account of Plutarch), when great rejoicing was manifested.—As *judge of Amenti*, or Hades, the most awful character of the deity, Osiris is represented in his most usual form, seated on a throne: a lotus rises at the foot of the throne; and upon it stand the four genii of the infernal regions, who will hereafter be particularized: on a pedestal, or shrine, before the throne, sits the Egyptian Cerberus, who resembles, in his body, the hippopotamus and the dog, and in his head, the crocodile: sometimes behind this monster is Harpocrates, seated on a crook of Osiris: Thoth stands next, to write the result of the judgement of each soul; the fate of which is decided by a balance erected behind him: a small jar, or vase, containing or representing the merits of the deceased, is placed in one scale; and in the other, a feather, the emblem of truth or justice: Horus and Anubis stand beneath the beam of the balance, and an ape (cynocephalus), the emblem of Thoth, sits above the fulcrum.— Many of the Egyptians, from feelings of awful veneration, abstained from even mentioning the name of Osiris.—As every mummy bore the *form* of Osiris, so also it received this *name*.—The title of Serapis, or Sarapis, was applied to Osiris in the character of judge of Amenti; but the Serapis latterly worshipped by the Greeks was a distinct deity.—The bulls Apis and Mnevis were regarded as manifestations of Osiris.

Isis, was termed the sister and wife, and sometimes also the daughter, of Osiris, and was a female personification of the deity in corresponding characters. As Osiris was the power which held dominion over the causes of fertilization; so Isis presided over all that received his blessings: as everything that contributed to fertilize was emblematic of the former; so was the fertile land, of the latter: the sun was an emblem of Osiris; and the moon, of Isis. The most common representation of Isis is the figure of a woman, crowned either by a pair of cow's horns, between which is a disk, or by a throne, which was her chief emblem and the principal hieroglyphic of her name. The form of a vulture with outstretched wings often covers the upper part and back of her head. Sometimes she has the head of a cow; and is often depicted in the act of suckling Harpocrates or Horus: she is also represented with wings. Isis corresponds with the Ceres and Proserpine of the mythology of the Greeks.

Typhon—Nephthys.

Typhon is called the brother of Osiris, and was a personification of the opposite character of the deity, the enemy and vanquisher of Osiris, the power presiding over, or influencing, the destructive operations of nature. The southern blasts which parch the soil of Egypt, the season which succeeds the inundation, the desert which encroaches upon and confines the cultivable soil, and the sea which swallows up the fertilizing Nile were considered as under the dominion of Typhon. The maleficent deity is generally represented by the figure of a hideous dwarf; and by another figure, having the head of a crocodile, the arms and shoulders and hanging breasts of a woman, and the lower parts of a hippopotamus.

Nephthys, who is termed the sister and wife of Typhon, was directly opposed to Isis. Barren land was an emblem of her, and under her dominion; as whatever tended to effect sterility was under the sway of Typhon. Isis and Nephthys are called by Plutarch the beginning and the end, and the upper and visible parts of the world and the lower and invisible. Nephthys was considered as holding authority in the infernal regions, or Amenti. On sarcophagi and mummy-cases Isis is sculptured or painted at the feet, and Nephthys at the head. The usual form of Nephthys is that of a woman, crowned with a throne surmounted by the lower half of a disk, or the lower hemisphere, which compose her chief emblem.

Aroëris.
Aroëris, or the Elder Horus (designated the brother of Osiris), was a personification of the rays or light of the sun; and was identified by the Greeks with their Apollo. The portal of a temple of Apollinopolis Parva bears a Greek inscription recording the dedication of that temple to Aroëris; and in another Greek inscription, in the great temple of Ombos, this deity is called "Aroëris, the great god Apollo." His form is that of a human figure with the head of a hawk, crowned with the combined caps of the upper and lower regions.

Horus.
Horus (the *Younger*), sometimes confounded with Aroëris, or the *Elder* Horus, was termed the son of Osiris and Isis; and was a personification of the power which renovates nature by overcoming Typhon. From this character of renovator of nature he has been confounded with Priapus. He is represented by the same figure as Aroëris,—the hawk-headed figure, wearing the double cap,—or by a hawk alone, his chief emblem. Together with Anubis, he had the office of weighing the merits of the deceased, before Osiris, in Amenti.

Harpocrates.
Harpocrates, or Hor-phoerat (the lame Horus), was said to be the son of Isis, by Osiris, but born after the death of the latter. The first shooting up of esculent plants, brought forth by the soil of Egypt (the emblem of Isis), presents an emblem of Harpocrates, and was considered as under his influence. Harpocrates is represented by the figure of a youth, generally with his finger to his mouth, wearing the double cap, and having a thick, plaited lock of hair curling round his ear, and hanging down to the bottom of his neck. He is often depicted as sitting on a lotus, with the fore-finger of one hand to his mouth, and in the other hand the flail and crook of Osiris. He is also frequently represented as suckled by Isis or by Athor; on whose lap he is seated. Athor being his nurse, he is sometimes called her son.

Anubis.

Anubis is termed the son of Osiris and Nephthys. When the overflowing Nile (which is emblematic of Osiris) extends over a tract of desert (or enters the dominion of Nephthys) it produces a short-lived vegetation between the fertile soil and the regions of sterility (or gives birth to Anubis), and presents a type of the intermediate state between life and death, or between light and darkness. According to some Egyptian writers, as mentioned by Plutarch, the division between the visible and invisible world was considered as representing Anubis. We find that Anubis presided over the departure of the soul; and he is thus represented standing by a bier, upon which lies a person just expired; the soul hovering above, in the form of a bird with a human head. His other office in Amenti, as superintendent of the balance, has been already mentioned. His form is that of a human figure with the head of a jackal, which the Greeks and others in later times mistook for the head of a dog; whence the city where Anubis was chiefly worshipped was called by the Greeks "Cynopolis."

In the various characters of the deity already mentioned a certain connection is observed; but I am unable to discover an affinity in some of those which I have yet to notice with any of the former.

Thoth.

Thoth is called by the Greek and Roman writers "Hermes" or "Mercury"; and was a personification of the deity presiding over letters, and over the moon. According to Horapollo he was the president of the heart, or of wisdom, of which the heart was regarded as the seat. His office of registering the fate, or the actions, of men, in Amenti, I have before mentioned. He is represented by the figure of a man with the head of an Ibis, his chief emblem; and sometimes crowned with a crescent and disk: in one hand he holds a pen; and in the other, a palm-branch, to the bottom of which are attached a frog (the emblem of man in embryo) and, beneath this, the emblem of life: or, instead of the palm-branch, he holds a tablet. He is also represented by a cynocephalus. The title of "Lord of the eight regions" is often given to him.[1] The first month of the year received his name.

Athor.

Athor was called by the Greeks "Aphrodite," or Venus; and seems to have been a personification of one of the properties of Isis; like whom she is represented as the nurse of Harpocrates, or Horus. Plutarch says that Athyri was a name of Isis; and signified "the mundane habitation of Horus"; and we find that the hieroglyphic name of Athor represents "the abode of Horus." Athor generally bears the usual form of Isis; with the

---

[1] Mr. Wilkinson observes that this title gave origin to the name of Hermopolis Magna. The Egyptian name of this city was Shmoun, which, in Coptic, signifies "eight"; and the place is still called Ashmoo'ney'n, or "the two Ashmoo'ns."

disk and horns upon her head, but never with the throne. She is represented also by the figure of a cow, with spots and marks in the form of crosses. Strabo mentions that the inhabitants of Aphroditopolis (the city of Venus, or Athor) kept a white cow, which they regarded as sacred; and he says the same of the people of Momemphis, who also worshipped Venus. Another form of Athor is that of a woman with the head of a cow. She is likewise represented in a persea (a tree sacred to her), pouring water from a vase; as Netpe in the sycamore.

Thmei.

Thmei, or Thme,—as the name is written by Champollion, but its orthography is doubtful,—was a personification of Truth, or justice; and is represented by the figure of a woman with a feather upon her head.

Sovk.

Sovk, or Savak, seems to be a character of Ra; and is generally represented by a human figure with the head of a crocodile. The crocodile was an emblem of the sun. Sovk was the chief object of worship in the Crocodilopolite, or Arsinoite, and Ombit nomes, and in several other parts. His great temple at Ombos was shared by Aroëris.

Nilus.

Nilus, or Hapi-möon, represented by a hermaphrodite figure, crowned with lotuses, and generally pouring water from two vases, was a personification of the power presiding over the Nile; which was also one of the characters of Osiris. I have only seen him receiving offerings or worship at Geb'el es-Sil'sil'eh; but his figure is very frequent in the temples.

The four Genii of Amenti.

The four genii of Amenti are represented standing on a lotus before Osiris as the judge of Amenti. They are four mummy-shaped figures; the first with the head of a man; the second with that of a cynocephalus; the third with that of a jackal; and the fourth with that of a hawk. Four funeral jars, which have been called *canopuses*, with covers in the forms of these four heads, were used as depositories of the intestines of embalmed bodies.

There were many other names and forms of the objects of worship, which, as they are of less common occurrence, I omit.

Of Animal-worship.

Numerous animals, noxious as well as harmless or useful, were worshipped by the ancient Egyptians, as emblems of the deity. The sanctuary of the temple, we are informed, contained, instead of an image of the deity, his living emblem. Particular animals were chief objects of worship in particular nomes; and it was lawful to sacrifice or kill, in some nomes, animals which were held sacred in others. Thus, in the Mendesian nome, sheep were sacrificed, but goats were held especially sacred: at Thebes, on the contrary, it was held unlawful to slaughter sheep, and goats were offered on the altar of the Theban Jupiter.[1] Again, the crocodile was the animal chiefly worshipped in some nomes, while the Tentyrites destroyed it. It is difficult to account for this disagreement. If an Egyptian designedly killed a sacred animal (that is, one held sacred in his own nome), he was put to death: if accidentally, a fine was exacted from him; unless the animal killed was an ibis or a hawk,—or, according to Diodorus (1, 83) a *cat* or an ibis,—for in these cases his death was the inevitable penalty.[2] When a cat died in a house, every inmate shaved his eyebrows, but at the death of a dog, he shaved his whole person.[3] The animals which were the chief objects of worship were bulls (the most celebrated of which were the Apis, worshipped at Memphis, and Mnevis, at Heliopolis,—both black, but distinguished by particular marks, and both believed to be Osiris), cows, jackals, dogs, wolves, cats, rams, goats, apes, the ichneumon, the mygale (or shrew-mouse),—the crocodile, the hippopotamus,—the hawk, vulture, ibis, and goose,—serpents,—the beetle (scarabæus),—the oxyrynchus, and lepidotus. The bodies of the sacred animals were embalmed; generally with great care; and vast numbers are still found in good preservation in various parts of Egypt; particularly ibises, in catacombs near the Pyramids of Sack'cka'rah, and mummies of cats, very neatly enveloped, at Thebes. Some plants, and even stones, were also objects of worship.

Of Sacrifices, &c.

Offerings are represented upon the walls of most of the temples. They are generally fruits, flowers, incense, and libations; but in many sculptures of the very early, as well as later, ages, we see sacred animals laid upon the altars; particularly geese and bulls; and not only the body and legs of the latter, but also the head; disproving the statement of Herodotus (ii, 39) that the head was loaded with imprecations, and sold to some foreigner, or thrown into the river; and confuting the assertion of Macrobius (i, 7) that, in ancient times, it was not lawful for the Egyptians to propitiate the gods with sheep and blood, but only by prayers and incense: but it was doubtless unlawful to sacrifice in a particular temple, or nome, an animal there held especially sacred. Bullocks that were entirely red, and none others were sacrificed by the Egyptians; as the red heifer without spot or blemish was by the Jews. In many of the sculptures we see prisoners of war immolated before a god. Swine were sacrificed, says Herodotus (ii, 47), only to Bacchus (or Osiris) and the Moon (Thoth); that is, to the Judge and Registrar of the fate of departed souls. A pig seems to have been an emblem of a damned soul; and is sometimes represented as conveyed in a boat from the scene

---

[1] Herodotus, ii, 42.
[2] Herodotus, ii, 65.
[3] Herodotus, ii, 66.

of judgement, under the custody of two cynocephali, the emblems of Thoth.

Of the principal religious festivals which were celebrated in Lower Egypt, an account is given by Herodotus (ii, 59-64, and 40). At the most magnificent of these, which was that of Bubastis (or Diana), at the town of that name, not fewer than 700,000 persons were usually present, besides children: they repaired thither by water, testifying their rejoicing by singing, clapping the hands, and playing upon pipes and tabors: when they passed before villages, the female pilgrims indecently exposed their persons: arrived at Bubastis, they sacrificed numberless victims; and consumed more wine than during all the rest of the year.—At the festival of Isis, at Busiris, after fasting and prayer, an ox was sacrificed; and the assembled multitudes whipped themselves; while some Carians who had settled in Egypt distinguished themselves by inflicting gashes on their foreheads.—The festival of Minerva (or Neith) at Sais was celebrated by night; and the inhabitants, and the Egyptians of other places, hung lamps round their houses.—At the festivals of Heliopolis and Butos, only a sacrifice was required.—At that of Mars at Papremis, a statue of the god, having been brought out in the evening before, was placed in a gilded shrine on a four-wheeled chariot, and at the approach of sunset was drawn towards the temple: a number of priests, armed with clubs, opposed its admission; and a confused multitude, armed in like manner, contended with them, and cleared the way for the god: many heads were broken, but the Egyptians asserted that no lives were ever lost on these occasions.

Oracles were delivered in many of the Egyptian sanctuaries. The most famous of them, according to Herodotus (ii, 83 and 150), was that of Butos.

Of the state after death.

The Egyptians, as we are told by Herodotus (ii, 123), were the first who asserted the immortality of the soul; holding the doctrine that, on the dissolution of the body, it transmigrated successively through the various beasts of the field, the birds of the air, and the inhabitants of the waters, and after the revolution of three thousand years again entered a human body. But the information which this historian obtained from the Egyptian priests must always be received with much distrust. The testimony of the monuments must of course be preferred. These, however, convey to us but little intelligence respecting the doctrine of the state of the soul after death. The soul is represented by a bird with a human head, or by a simple human figure, sometimes painted *black* to denote a *depraved* soul. The judgement of departed souls, by Osiris, is depicted (in the manner which I have already had occasion to describe) in many ancient sculptures, and in drawings on papyri; and in the tombs of the kings at Thebes we find representations of a state of rewards and punishments; the latter perhaps purgatorial, and both preparatory to perfect fruition to be enjoyed by the soul when reunited to the human body which it had formerly occupied on earth. The region of departed souls was called Amenti, or Amenthes; a name which Plutarch (De Iside et Osiride, cap. 29) interprets as signifying "the receiver and giver": for it received the soul and sent it forth again to reanimate the body. I can hardly think that, in employing so much care and expense in embalming the dead, and bestowing so much labour on their sepulchres, the Egyptians were activated by the belief that the continuance of the soul depended upon the preservation of the body; but rather that they embalmed human bodies for the same reason that they did cats and other animals; that is, as emblems of the deity; particularly as every mummy bore the form and name of Osiris. This idea appears to me to be strengthened by the statement of Diodorus (i, 92) that, before the Egyptians could commit a corpse to the sepulchre, a solemn council was summoned to judge whether the deceased was worthy of the honour of burial.

Of the Laws.

The Egyptians, as we are informed by Diodorus (i, 75), had a code of laws, in eight books. Some of these laws which have been considered particularly deserving of record are of considerable interest, as enabling us to judge of the degree of civilization to which the Egyptians had attained in early ages.—Perjury was punished with death.—False accusers were to suffer the same punishment as those whom they accused would have undergone if convicted.—If a person chanced to see another violently assaulted, he was bound, on pain of death, to assist him, if able: if not able to do so, he was required to discover and prosecute the offending party, on pain of being scourged, and being confined without food for three days.—Every Egyptian was bound to make a report, in writing, of the means by which he obtained his livelihood, to the governor of his province, and he who gave a false report, or was found to have followed an unlawful occupation, was put to death.—The murder of a freeman and of a slave were alike punished with death.—Parents who killed their children were not punished with death; but were compelled to hug them for three days and nights.—Parricides were tortured, and burnt alive.—A pregnant women convicted of a capital crime was not to be put to death until delivered of the child.—A cowardly or mutinous soldier was disgraced; but might retrieve his rank.—If a soldier was guilty of treachery his tongue was cut out.—Forgery was punished by cutting off the hands of the offender.—Rape and adultery were severely punished.—Usury was allowed; but with this limitation—that the capital could only be doubled.—The goods of a debtor might be seized by the creditor, but not his person.—Thieving was a lawful occupation; but the thieves composed a distinct class, having a chief to whom they brought their plunder, and who was bound to return the stolen goods to the person robbed, on receiving from the latter a fourth part of the value.[1]—It was a law among the Egyptians that a man might marry his sister; and the wife, in every case, enjoyed authority over her husband, who was bound to obey her in all things.[2] The priests were restricted to one wife; but other men might have as many wives as they pleased.—The children of the wife and those of the bondswoman enjoyed equal rights.[3]

We are further informed by Diodorus[4] that the Egyptians had a judicial assembly, consisting of thirty judges, who were chosen from among the most eminent persons (doubtless priests) of Heliopolis, Thebes, and Memphis. These elected from among themselves a president, or chief judge, and supplied the place thus vacated by another person from the city to which the newly-elected president belonged. They were paid by the king. The president wore round his neck a chain of gold, to which was suspended an image formed of precious stones, the emblem of truth. No cause was argued by lawyers before this august assembly; but the complaint and the defence were submitted to the court in writing; and the plaintiff might reply, and the defendant rejoin, in the same manner; after which the judges decided.

5. The Priesthood.

The priests were the most honorable class in Egypt; and appear to have been, as a body, more powerful that the king; over whom they exercised an almost absolute sway. From the tradition that gods reigned over Egypt before mortal kings, we may suppose that a hierarchy was the first form of government established in that country; and with such power as they possessed over the minds of the people the priests might undoubtedly have retained the government entirely in their own hands: but they found it necessary to have a king as the leader of their armies. They composed a distinct caste; the sacerdotal office invariably descending from father to son; and with them probably originated, with most other institutions of a political as well as religious nature, the similar division of the rest of the nation into castes, and the division of the country into nomes; each nome being named after its particular object of worship[5]; and each being a separate hierarchical state.

Under the kings, the independence of the priests appears not to have been infringed. Exemption from taxation and every kind of contribution

---

[1]it is very remarkable that in the *modern* metropolis of Egypt the thieves have a sheykh, or superintendent, who is often required to recover stolen goods, and to bring the offenders to justice.

[2]Diodorus, i, 27.

[3]Diodorus, i, 77-80.

[4]Lib. i, 75 and 76.

[5]Diodorus, however, refers to the division of Egypt into nomes to the time of Sesostris. (i, 54). The number of nomes, and consequently the extent of some of them, varied at different times.

to the state was their privilege. They were the principal proprietors of land; and when, under the management of Joseph, all the rest of "the Egyptians" (or the inhabitants of *Lower* Egypt) "sold every man his field,"[1] the priests retained their possessions. The more eminent among them were the king's privy counsellors; and their sons were his companions from his youth. From their own revenues, according to Diodorus (i, 73), they provided sacrifices, &c. They were, however, maintained by the king. This, we learn, was not only the case in Lower Egypt during the famine in the time of Joseph, but also throughout Egypt in the time of Herodotus. They were supplied, says this historian (ii, 37) with the sacred meats, with geese and beef, and with plenty of wine.[2] To the rest of the Egyptians, wine was forbidden. The priests payed great attention to cleanliness: they were all circumcised: they shaved the head and the whole person every third day; and bathed twice in the day, and twice again at night. They wore a loose dress of linen, which was frequently washed, and shoes of the *byblos* (or papyrus). So says Herodotus (ii, 37). Pliny also mentions (xix, 2) that garments of the Egyptian priests were made of cotton. Woollen garments they never wore; but in sculptures and paintings we often see a priest represented clad in a leopard's skin.

Every temple had a body of priests devoted to its service, who must have been numerous, as there are many different offices to be performed by priests of different ranks; but the number must have varied, since the dignity was hereditary. The Egyptian priests were the monopilizers of science: they were legislators, judges, soothsayers, astrologers (and probably magicians), physicians, embalmers, architects of temples, sculptors and painters. Of the several orders of the priesthood, the most distinguished, or the most frequently mentioned by historians, were the Soothsayers, or Prophets, who seem to have held the highest authority,—the Stolistæ, whose office it was to select the victims for sacrifice,—the Hierogrammatists, or sacred scribes,—and the Astrologers. It was perhaps the office of the hierogrammatist to trace out the hieroglyphics and other devices upon the walls of the temples and tombs &c.

Of the sciences of the Egyptian priests, the most important was astronomy. Their calendar and the monuments prove that they attained a high proficiency in this study, which was intimately connected with their theology. Astrology was a science which they much cultivated, as giving them great influence of the vulgar; and it regulated their practice of medicine. Herodotus (ii, 84) bears testimony to the great skill of the Egyptian physicians. Geometry was of indispensable utility in Egypt, on

---

[1] Genesis, xlvii, 20.

[2] From the frequent representations of the vintage in tombs of very early, as well as later, ages, it appears that wine was always allowed to the priests; though Plutarch says that this allowance was only made at the time when the Greeks had introduced many innovations and much laxity of manners among the Egyptians.

account of the changes effected by the river; and must have engaged attention in the earliest ages. The science of magic was probably confined to the priests; and, unless we reject the testimony of the Bible, we must allow that great wonders were worked by its means.—Of sacred architecture, sculpture, &c., I shall speak hereafter.

What is termed "the period of the reign of the gods" is beyond the limits of authentic information: we may therefore proceed to consider the history of the kings.

6. The Kings.

Introduction.

Several ancient records of the early dynasties of Egypt, more or less complete, have been rescued from the fate which other portions of the works of their compilers have experienced by being quoted in the writings of later chronologers; but only one of these receives general confirmation, as far as we are able to compare it, from the royal lists presented by existing sculptured monuments of very remote times and therefore this, only, can be regarded as generally correct. The record here alluded to exhibits a list of all the Egyptian dynasties from the most early period to the conquest of Egypt by Alexander the Great. It is an extract from a celebrated history of Egypt composed by Manetho, who was "a high-priest and scribe of the sacred adyta in Egypt, by birth a Sebennyte, and a citizen of Heliopolis": these are his own words, in a dedicatory epistle addressed by him to his sovereign Ptolemy Philadelphus. Syncellus has transmitted to us this list, from a transcript by Julius Africanus. A less complete and less correct transcript of the same list (probably made from a very imperfect copy of Manetho's work) is found in the writings of Eusebius. Of Manetho's history of Egypt there remain also two extracts relating to "the Shepherd Kings" and the Israelites, preserved in the treatise of Josephus against Apion.

It is stated by Manetho, and confirmed by other historians, that the Israelites were expelled from Egypt by one of the kings of the 18th Dynasty: therefore the first seventeen dynasties must have ruled in Egypt within the period between "the confusion of languages" and the era of the Exodus. The copies of the Hebrew Bible now existing have been clearly shown to be very incorrect in the chronology of this period: the existing copies of the Samaritan Pentateuch and of the Septuagint agree in assigning 1106 years to the interval in question; and according to the able investigation of Dr. Hales, this period at least exceeded 900 years. Now, that the first seventeen dynasties followed one another in one long and regular order we cannot admit, without presuming that Manetho or his copyists grossly exaggerate their duration, and even discrediting a statement of Manetho which shews that there were several kings ruling in different parts of Egypt at the same time: for this historian speaks of the insurrection of the *Kings of the Thebais* and of *other* parts of Egypt against "the Shepherds," whose *Kings* still ruled in Lower Egypt, and are included in Manetho's dynasties. Here we have a distinct assertion of the fact of there having been more than three contemporary dynasties in different parts of Egypt.—This is also asserted by Artapanus, an Egyptian Jew, quoted by Eusebius (Præp. Evang. ix, 27), and was the opinion of Eusebius himself,[1] and of several later chronologers.

The Thinite Kings were the *first*, and perhaps for some years the *sole* monarchs of Egypt. Their capital, *This*, appears to have been situated a little below the modern town of Gir'ga, or Jir'ja, which was lately, under the Memloo'ks, the capital of Upper Egypt. Soon after the establishment of the Thinite Kingdom, Lower Egypt became an independent state, and Memphis was its capital. Before the expiration of three centuries after this period, both the Thinite and Memphite Kingdoms appear to have been dismembered by the establishment of the Elephantinite, Heracleopolite, and Diospolite Kingdoms. To the last of these, the Thinite and Elephantine dominions soon became united. At a later period, another kingdom, the Xoite, seems to have been founded, in Lower Egypt. Soon after the foundation of the Diospolite Kingdom, a warlike Eastern tribe of pastors, to whose successive chiefs the Egyptians gave the appellation of "Shepherd Kings," invaded Egypt, and, favoured by its divided state, conquered the whole country, made all the native princes tributary to them, and settled in Lower Egypt. These and succeeding tribes of pastors of different races retained considerable possession in the eastern part of Lower Egypt during a period of 511 years.

The arrangement presented by the following table of the various dynasties which governed Egypt during the divided state of that country rests, particularly, on these grounds.—The *Diospolites* of the 17th Dynasty are placed by Manetho with the *Shepherds* of the 17th, who were finally *expelled* from Egypt by a prince of the 18th Dynasty.—I shall hereafter be able to shew that the *Memphite* Kingdom was subverted under the 17th Dynasty.—The arrangement of three columns of the table I consider as thus established.—The *Thinite* Kingdom cannot be supposed to have commenced long before the Memphite.—The *Elephantinites* (or 5th Dynasty) could not, I think, have succeeded the 4th Dynasty, and have ruled in Memphis, as the Thinite Kingdom was between Elephantine and the Memphite dominions.—The *Heracleopolites* and the *Fourteenth Dynasty* were, I suppose, among "the kings of other parts of Egypt" alluded to in the passage of Manetho above-mentioned.—Lastly, the space of time within which the first 17 dynasties are thus brought is perfectly reconcileable with the Scripture Chronology of this early period as deduced from the existing copies of the Samaritan Pentateuch and of the Septuagint; and agrees very nearly with Dr. Hales's computation of the same period derived from those and other sources.

---

[1] In the Armenian version of his Chronicon, pp. 201-2.

Thinites		Memphites		Elephantinites		Heracleopolites		Diospolites		Xoites?		Shepherds	
Dyny.	Years	Dyny.	Years. Ds.	Dyny.	Years	Dyny.	Years	Dyny.	Years	Dyny.	Years	Dyny.	Years
1st.	253	3rd.	214										
2nd.	302	4th.	284	5th.	248	9th.	409	11th.	59			15th.	
		6th.	203			10th.	185	12th.	160			16th.	} 511^c
		7th.	___ 70					13th.	184	14th.^b	184 or 284	17th.^a	
		8th.	146					17th.	151				
	555		847.70		248		594		554		184 or 284		511

^a The 17th Dynasty consisted of 43 Diospolites and 43 contemporary Shepherds.

^b In the transcript of Africanus, this is wanting: I have inserted it on the authority of Eusebius.

^c Why I have assigned this period instead of the sum of the durations of the three dynasties will be stated in my remarks on the 18th Dynasty.

Tables of Dates.

I. Dates from the Pentateuch, &c., according to Dr. Hales's Chronology.

Abraham goes into Egypt (430 years before the Exodus) .... B.C. 2078
The Israelites go into Egypt.. 1863
Moses born.. 1728
The Exodus 1648
Solomon died (in the reign of Shishak, King of Egypt) 990
Capture of Jerusalem by Shishak 986
Compact of Hoshea with So, King of Egypt 726
Tirhakah's war with Sennacherib... 711
Josiah killed by Pharaoh Necho 608
Onaphris, Apries, or Hophra, dethroned by Nebuchadnezzar 570
Conquest of Egypt by Cambyses 525

II. Dates of accession of Egyptian Dynasties, deduced from Manetho, and calculated upwards from the first date in table III.

Diospolites.	Memphites.
	3rd Dyny. .... 214 years. ...... B.C. 2585
11th Dyny. ..... 59 years. B.C. 2292	4th................. 284*.....................2371
12th 160 2233	6th................. 203...........................2087
13th 184 2073	7th................. ___ 70 days.
17th 151 1889	8th................. 146........................ 1884

*The duration of this dynasty I have reckoned 284 years as that is the sum of the reigns, instead of 274 as cast up in Manetho's list.

III. Dates of accession of Egyptian Dynasties, &c., continued.

18th Dynasty... 263 years .... B.C. 1738
19th.. 210 1475
20th.. 135 1265
21st.. 130 1130

22nd (beginning with Shishak) 120 1000
      Capture of Jerusalem, by Shishak. B.C. 986
23rd 89 880
24th (Bocchōris) 44* 791
25th. Sabbacon 8 747
      Sevechos 14 739
        Compact of Hoshea with So, or Sevechos 726
      Tarocos (or Tirhakha) 20* 725
      His war with Sennacherib 711
26th. Ammeris 12* 705
      Stephinates 7 693
      Nerepsos 6 686
      Nechas 8 680
      Psammitichus 54 672
      Nechas 2nd 17* 618
        Killed Josiah 608
      Psammuthis 6 601
      Ouaphris (Apries, or Hophra) 25* 595
      Dethroned by Nebuchadnezzar 570
      An interregnum .... $0^{1/2}$* 570
      Amosis (Amasis) .... 44 .... 569 or 570
      Psammacherites (Psammenitus) .... $0^{1/2}$ .... 525 or 526
      Conquest of Egypt by Cambyses 525

I have deduced from Manetho's lists of the dynasties, as given by Africanus, all the periods in the foregoing table, with the exception of those marked with an asterisk. The periods thus marked I have adopted as corrections, not merely because the dates of certain events in Egyptian history derived from the Bible are thus made to agree with the Egyptian chronology, but for other reasons also. These reasons I shall state in ascending order; as the dates in this table are calculated upwards, from the period of the conquest of Egypt by Cambyses, which is well ascertained to have taken place in the year 525 B.C.—First, I have introduced an interregnum of half a year after the dethronement of Onaphris, Apries, or Hophra, by Nebuchadnezzar; making with the 44 years' reign of Amasis and the half-year's reign of Psammenitus a period of 45 years. This is on the ground of probability, and to avoid a fraction.—Next, I have made the reigns of Apries and Necos, or Nechao 3nd, respectively, 25 years and 17 years (instead of 19 and 6). For both of these I have the authority of Herodotus: for that of Apries, I have also the authority of the transcript of Manetho by Eusebius; which, it may be added, makes the sum of the two reigns of Nechao 2nd and Psammuthis the same as in my table; the periods being reversed by Eusebius. With these two alterations the chronology presented by this table from the accession of Psammitichus[1] to the conquest by Cambyses agrees exactly

---

[1] The *first* Psammitichus of the monuments.

with that given by Herodotus; who must reasonably be allowed to be the best authority we have for *this* period: the lengths of earlier reigns he has seldom ventured to state.—Ammeris I have inserted from the copy of Eusebius; being omitted by Africanus.—The reign of Taracos, or Tirhakah, I have stated to have lasted 20 years (instead of 18) because a date in the 20th year of this prince has been found[1]; and Eusebius makes his reign 20 years.—Lastly, to the 24th Dynasty (i.e. to Bocchōris) I have assigned 44 years (instead of 6) on the concurrent authority of Eusebius and Syncellus and "the Old Chronicle."

According to the transcript of Manetho's list by Eusebius, the duration of the nine dynasties comprised in the preceding table was 199 years; and according to "the Old Chronicle," 1223 years: the former, therefore, would refer the commencement of the 18th Dynasty to the year B.C. 1724; and the latter would refer it to the year 1748: the one date 14 years later, and the other 10 years earlier, than that which I have adopted.

Chronology and History of the Kings derived from Manetho and the sculptured monuments.
Period of Contemporary Dynasties. Part 1st.

Date	Thinites.		Diospolites.	B.C.	Memphites.	
unknown	1st Dynasty.			2585	.... 3rd Dynasty.	
	Menes is said to have been				Necherophes. 28 years.	
	the first mortal who reigned in Egypt.				Tosorthrus. 29	
	His reign lasted 62 years. The succeeding				Tyris. 7	
	kings of the 1st Dynasty were				Mesochris. 17	
	Athothis. 57 years.				Soiphis. 16	
	Cencenes. 31				Tosertasis. 19	
	Venephes. 23				Achis. 42	
	Usaphædus. 20				Siphuris. 30	
	Miebidus. 26				Cerpheres. 26	
	Semempsis. 18			2371	.... 4th Dyny.	
	Bienaches. 26				Soris. 29	
	2nd Dyny.				Suphis. 63. Founder of the	
	Boethus. 38	2292	.... 11th Dyny.		Great Pyramid	
	Chæachos. 39				Suphis 2nd. 66	
	Binothris. 47	2249				First Race of
	Tlas. 17	2233	.... 12th Dyny.			Shepherds
	Sethenes. 41				Mencheres. 63	(Phœnicians,
	Chæres. 17				Rhatæses. 25	or Arabs)
	Nephercheres. 25				Bicheres. 22	
	Sesochris. 48				Sebercheres. 7	
	Cheneres. 30				Thamphthis. 9	
		2087			End of the	
					4th Dyny.	

[1] See Mr. Wilkinson's Materia Hieroglyphica, part 2, plate 3.

At what period the *first Egyptian kingdom*, namely the *Thinite*, was founded, we cannot ascertain; but it could not have been many years anterior to the foundation of the Memphite Kingdom.—Menes has been supposed, by many chronologers, to be another name of the Mizraim of the Bible. According to Herodotus, Menes was the founder of Memphis; and if we may credit a tradition mentioned by Diodorus Siculus, he introduced sumptuous furniture, and many luxuries, on account of which a curse was imprecated on him by Tnephachthus, the father of Bocchōris the Wise, and was registered on a pillar in the temple of Jupiter (or Amon-Ra) at Thebes. It cannot be expected that we should find any monuments that may be recognized as belonging to his age.—From Manetho, or his copyists, we derive the following notices respecting some of the Thinite kings.—Menes made warlike expeditions into foreign countries. He was killed by a hippopotamus. Athothis built the palaces at Memphis; and wrote anatomical books.—In the reign of Venephes a great plague raged throughout Egypt. This king built the pyramids near Cochome.—In the reign of Semempsis a terrible pestilence afflicted Egypt.—During the reign of Boethus, or Bochos, an earthquake near Bubastis destroyed many people.—In the time of Chæachos, or Choos, the bulls Apis, in Memphis, and Meneus (or Mnevis), in Heliopolis, and the Mendesian goat, were appointed to be gods.—In the time of Binothris, or Biophis, it was ordained that women might hold the monarchical power.—Lastly, we read—in the reign of Nephercheres the Nile flowed with honey eleven days.—From one of these traditions, and from that quoted before from Herodotus, it would appear that though *This* (which was not far from Abydos) in Upper Egypt was the seat of the Thinite kings, the dominions of these kings originally included Memphis, and that this city was founded by one of them.

The duration of the *Memphite Kingdom* may be a little exaggerated; and, consequently, its commencement referred to a period a few years too remote. By Manetho, or his copyists, we are told that in the reign of the first Memphite king, Necherophes or Nacherochis, the Libyans revolted from the Egyptians; but that a portentous increase of the Moon terrified them, and induced them to return to their allegiance.—Also, that the next king, Tosorthrus or Sesorthos, was called, in Egypt, Asclepius, for his medical knowledge: that he built a house of hewn stones, and greatly patronized writing.—Soris, Suphis, Suphis 2nd, and Mencheres correspond with the Bïyris, Saophis, Sensaophis, and Moscheris of the list of Eratosthenes. Soris, or Bïyris, may be the Busiris of Diodorus, who says that Thebes was founded by this king. According to the foregoing table, the Diospolite, or Theban, Kingdom commenced only half a century after the reign of Soris. In his time Thebes may have been founded.—Of Suphis, it is stated in the list of Manetho that he built the Great Pyramid; and (as we read in the transcript of that list by Africanus) that he was called Peroptes; was translated to the gods; and wrote the sacred book: it is said, however, in the copy of the same list by

Eusebius, that he *despised* the gods; but, repenting, wrote the sacred book, which the Egyptians highly value. Herodotus says that the founders of the First and Second Pyramids (whom he calls Cheops and Chephrenes) were impious tyrants: he also says that they were brothers: hence we may infer that Suphis 2nd (or Sensaophis, which means "brother of Saophis" or Suphis) built the Second Pyramid. We can discriminate no monuments as being certainly coeval with these pyramids.

Of the first fifteen princes of the *Diospolite Kingdom* we know not even the names. The 11th (or first Diospolite) Dynasty is said to have consisted of 16 kings; the last of whom was named Ammenemes. The 12th is filled up, in Manetho's list, with seven names; some, and probably *all*, of which are taken from other dynasties. Among these misplaced names is that of Sesostris, who was the first king of the 19th Dynasty.

An inquiry into the history of the *Shepherds* will be pursued in some subsequent pages.

Period of Contemporary Dynasties. Part 2nd.

B.C.	Diospolites.	Memphites.	Shepherds.
2087	... (Part of 12th Dyny.) ..	.... 6th Dyny.	
		Othoes—(30 years.)	
2078			Abraham went into
2073	.... 13th Dyny.		Egypt, on account of a
		Phius. 53	famine in the eastern
		Methusuphis. 7	countries, which perhaps
		Phiops. 100	also occasioned the
		Mentesuphis. 1	settlement of the Second
		Nitocris. 12	Race of Shepherds in
1889	.... 17th Dyny.		Egypt.
1884	.... 7th and 8th Dyns.		
1863			The Israelites (or Third
	(The Orirtesens, and		Race of Shepherds) entered
	other kings).		Egypt, and settled there.
1738	End of the 17th Dyny.	End of the Memphite	Subjugation of the Third
		Kingdom.	Race of Shepherds (or
			the Israelites).

Continuation of the history of the Memphite Kingdom.—Soon after the commencement of the 6th Dynasty, in the reign of the first king of that dynasty, according to the preceding table, the Patriarch Abraham visited Egypt, as described in the Bible, which seems to represent Lower Egypt or the Memphite dominions, under the name of Mizraim, as, at that period, a great and wealthy kingdom, and the granary of the surrounding countries. The First and Second Pyramids had already been built, and perhaps some of the oblong, unsculptured tombs, in the form of truncated pyramids, adjacent to those two stupendous structures. As to the other monuments of the same and earlier ages and of the times of the 6th Dynasty,—for there must be many of these ages,—we doubtless see some of them among the inumerable unsculptured grottoes and catacombs in the mountains which hem in the valley of Egypt: but we find no monument with sculptures, nor any of masonry, that can be regarded as equally ancient with the pyramids; and when we consider that in the times of the 18th Dynasty sculptured monuments were destroyed, and their materials employed in new buildings, the non-existence of unsculptured edifices coeval with the pyramids and the tombs above alluded to need not excite our surprise. The times of the 6th Dynasty perhaps embrace the period of the first sculptured monuments. Phiops and Mentesuphis agree in place and in the length of their reigns with the Apappus and Achescos Ocaras of the list of Eratosthenes; and the latter may be the Uchoreus to whom Diodorus ascribes the founding of Memphis; as Mr. Wilkinson conjectures, and the Hakor of the monuments, whose hieroglyphic name is found upon the ruins of a temple of very ancient appearance on the site of Eilethyia, and in the quarries in the eastern mountains opposite the site of Memphis: if so, we may suppose (Eilethyia being to the south of Thebes) that at this period the Memphite Kings enjoyed ascendancy over the Diospolites, and that for this reason it is that several Memphite princes are included by Eratosthenes in his list of "Kings of the Thebans." Nitocris, we are told in Manetho's list, was a very handsome woman, of a yellowish (ξανθή) complexion; and it is added that she built the Third Pyramid. Herodotus, who ascribes the building of this pyramid to a king named Mycerinus, also mentions a tradition of its having been founded by a courtesan, very celebrated for her charms: he mentions Nitocris too; but merely to relate a strange story of her punishing the murderers of her brother, who was her predecessor.—I shall have occasion to allude to some of the later Memphite Kings in the following paragraph.

The advancement of the Diospolite Kingdom, its ascendancy over the Memphite, and the fall of the latter, are now to be considered.—The 13th Dynasty is said to have consisted of 60 Diospolite kings, whose names are lost: the number is probably exaggerated; for their duration is stated to have been only 184 years. The next Diospolite kings were those of the 17th Dynasty. Of this dynasty we are merely informed by Manetho's list, as given by Africanus, that it consisted of 43 Diospolites and 43 "Shepherds of another race"; that is, different in origin from the former Shepherds. I think I shall be able to give satisfactory reasons for identifying the Israelites in Egypt with Manetho's "Third Race of Shepherds": but at present I shall only remark respecting these foreign settlers that we are warranted by Manetho in regarding them as contemporary with the Diospolite kings with whom they are placed by him.—I shall now give some account of these Diospolite kings. As their *names* are not stated in Manetho's list, we cannot place much dependance on the statement of their *number*; which is probably much exaggerated. But we are not left wholly in ignorance respecting them; for their age is within the period that is enlightened by sculptured monuments yet remaining in Egypt. At this early age the hieroglyphic system had been brought to great perfection; and it had become a general custom to decorate the walls of temples and tombs with hieroglyphic inscriptions and other sculptures and paintings, which always in the case of temples, and often in the case of tombs, present the name of the king in whose reign they were executed. In my list of the hieroglyphic names of the Pharaohs, deduced from the monuments, no. 39 is the last of the Diospolites of the 17th Dynasty; and the preceding names (from no. 33 inclusive) are most probably of the same dynasty.[1] No. 33 is the name of Osirtĕsen 1st; the earliest *known* Pharaoh of whom any sculptured monument now exists. The obelisk of Heliopolis, and that of the Feiyoo'm are of his reign; and shew how far his influence, if not his dominion, extended: and the very interesting grottoes of Ben'ee Hhas'an are of the times of this king and his successors of the same dynasty. These grottoes are not only remarkable for their very high antiquity, but also as containing a vast variety of paintings, executed with surprising skill and in a most wonderful state of preservation; and moreover as presenting the prototype of the *Doric* column, and examples of the *clustered* column. They are monuments not of the infancy, but of almost the maturity, of Egyptian art; and yet there are only a very few remains of sculpture or painting (as those of Hakor, before-mentioned, and some of the sculptured and painted tombs near the Pyramids of Memphis) that we can regard, with any possibility of our opinion being right, as more ancient; and the date of these is *uncertain*. There are other monuments of Osirtesen 1st besides those above-mentioned: the most ancient remains within the precincts of the great temple of Kur'nak bear the name of this king as their author. His name has also been found on a mountain in the Peninsula of Mount Sinai: this is a remarkable fact; as the Egyptians seldom quitted their country except on warlike expeditions.—Nos. 34, 35, and 36 are found at Ben'ee Hhas'an. Of another king of this dynasty I have to speak in the statement which I must now offer of my reasons for placing the termination of the Memphite Kingdom as coeval with the termination of the Diospolite 17th Dynasty.—At, or soon after, the period when (according to Manetho, as copied by Africanus) the said Diospolite dynasty terminated—that is, 738 years before Shishak,

---

[1]In my list the first name is numbered 33 as being that which must have occupied the 33rd place in the list of Abydos; supposing the second line in this ancient record to be a continuation of the first line. The order of nos. 33 to 36, inclusive, in my list is proved by sculptures in one of the grottoes of Ben'ee Hhas'an; nos. 35 to 51, by the list of Abydos; nos. 40 to 51, also by a list in the Raméséum of El-Ckoor'neh; nos. 44 to 48, likewise by another list in the same edifice; and nos. 47 to 55, by a list in the great edifice of Medee'net Hha'boo. These are confirmed by many less important inscriptions. The order of the names succeeding no. 55 is derived partly from my own notes from various monuments; but chiefly from the works of Major Felix and Mr. Wilkinson; from which some of the names themselves are taken.

Sesonchosis, or Sheshonk, or about 1738 B.C.—the oppression of the Israelites commenced,[1] when, we read (in Exodus, i, 8) "there arose up a new king over Egypt, which knew not Joseph," or one whose predecessors, we may infer, were under no obligation to that patriarch. This alone affords reasonable ground for the supposition that the first king of the 18th Dynasty, descending from his hereditary dominions (or Upper Egypt), made himself master of Lower Egypt, by putting an end to a Memphite dynasty under which the Israelites had lived on terms of amity, and in the enjoyment of large possessions. But we are not left to mere conjecture on this subject. As I have stated in my description of the Pyramids, &c., Major Felix has found, on the rocks of Wa'dee Magha'rah, in the Peninsula of Mount Sinai, hieroglyphic inscriptions containing the name of the last but one of the Diospolites of the 17th Dynasty, together with the names of several Memphite princes which we find in many of the tombs near the First and Second Pyramids; and these inscriptions record the subjugation of the said Memphites by that Diospolite king. We may conclude that these Memphites were of the 8th Dynasty not only because this was the *last* Memphite dynasty but from another consideration: for the tombs above alluded to I have shewn, in my description of them, to be of a later age that the Pyramids; which, according to Manetho, our best guide, were built under the 4th and 6th Dynasties. But very soon after the above-mentioned subjugation of the Memphites,—perhaps almost immediately (only one reign intervening),—a new dynasty commenced. From this fact, and from the coincidence of the date of the accession of Amos, the first king of the new dynasty, with the period when the Israelites began to be oppressed by a new and strange king, after they had enjoyed remarkable privileges under many Egyptian princes, who were doubtless Memphites (for we find that Memphites *were* ruling at that time) I infer that the Memphite kingdom was not wholly subverted until the reign of Amos. The justice of my referring the prosperous period of the abode of the Israelites in Egypt to the times immediately antecedent to the commencement of the 18th Dynasty rests in a great measure upon the reasons which I shall have to adduce, a few pages further, for identifying the Israelites with Manetho's "Third Race of Shepherds," independently of the evidence in favour of the same position derived from a comparison of Dr. Hales's with Manetho's chronology, and from other considerations.

18th Dynasty.

A Diospolite King having put an end to the dominion of the Memphite princes, and subjugated the foreign settlers in the eastern parts of Lower Egypt, as above related, the whole of Egypt becomes one great monarchy, and continues so under him and his successors. Thus

---

[1] The period of the commencement of this oppression is not determined with exactness; but in placing it at, or within, ten years before the birth of Moses I cannot greatly err.

commences the 18th Dynasty. It is important to compare Manetho's list of this dynasty, as given by Africanus, with that derived from the monuments: both these lists are therefore subjoined. The lists presented by the monuments omit the names of female sovereigns, and of mere regents.

B.C.	From Manetho.	From the Monuments.
1738	Amos, or Amōsis— (or) Chebrōs, or Chebrōn. 13 years	40.[1] Amos, or Ames
——	.... The Israelites first oppressed.	
1728	....Moses born.	
	Amenophthis. 21	41. Amonoph 1st
	Queen Amersis, or Amesses. 22 ⎫ ?	42. Thothmos 1st (and 2n. Ames)
	Misaphris. 13 ⎬	43. Thothmos 2nd
	Misphragmuthosis. 26 ⎭	44. Thothmos 3rd
		45. Amonoph 2nd
	Tuthmosis. 9	46. Thothmos 4th
1648	Exodus of the Israelites (or expulsion of the Third Race of Shepherds).	
	Amenōphis (Memnon). 31	47. Amonoph 3rd (Memnon)
	Horus. 37	48. Horus
	2n. Acherres, or Achencheres. 32	
	Rathos, or Rathotis, or Athoris. 6	
	Chebres, or Achencheres. 12	
	Acherres, or Achencheres. 12	
	Armeses, or Armaïs. 5	
	Rammeses. 1	49. Rameses 1st
	Amenoph, or Menophis. 19	50. Phtha-mai Osiree (Osiree 1st)
1475	.... End of the 18th Dynasty.	

With the 18th Dynasty commenced the most splendid period of ancient Egyptian History. The greatest, and the most beautiful, of all the Egyptian monuments are of the times of this and the next dynasty; and several of the Pharaohs of this period are immortalized by sculptures commemorating their conquests of many and far distant nations.

Manetho, according to Africanus, states the duration of this dynasty to have been 263 years: but it will be observed, in his list, that this period does not exactly agree with the sum of the several reigns. It will also be observed that no period is added, in this list, to the name of Amos; which may, perhaps, be accounted for by what I shall presently have to state respecting that king. There is likewise another list of this dynasty, taken from Manetho, in the writings of Josephus; assigning 333 years as its duration: but I assume the former period of 263 years to be more correct, because in the latter list we find the name of a king, with 66 years assigned as the length of his reign, placed between the last but one and

---

[1]The names are numbered here as in my hieroglyphic list.

the last of the princes in the lists which I have given; whereas it appears from the monuments that no king intervened between those two: this misplaced king evidently belonged to the next dynasty. The list of Eusebius, which gives 348 years to this dynasty, presents the same error, and other inconsistencies. Now, if we subtract the misplaced reign of 66 years from 333, we find the period thus reduced to be nearly the same as that first mentioned; exceeding it only by four years.

Amos, or *Ames*, the first king of the 18th Dynasty, appears to have been an Ethiopian; for his daughter, who married his successor (Amonoph 1st, an Egyptian), is represented *black*, in tombs at Thebes. In the list from the monuments we have no king corresponding with Chebrōs; Amonoph 1st immediately succeeding Amos; and in my remarks on the history of the Pyramids I have given other reasons for considering the names of Amos and Chebrōs, or Chebrōn, as applying to one and the same king. This may account for the fact of no period being added to the name of Amos in the list from Manetho which I have given, but a period of 13 years added to the name of Chebros. It is true that in the list which Josephus gives 25 years are assigned to Amos, and 13 also to Chebros, or Chebron; but, from one inconsistency which I have already pointed out in the latter list, I prefer that given by Africanus.— My chief reasons for referring the period of the commencement of the oppression of the Israelites in Egypt to the reign of this king have already been stated; and other reasons for this may be derived from some subsequent pages. The birth of Moses I refer to the reign of the same Pharaoh.[1] The Pharaoh's daughter who found Moses is called by Josephus "Thermuthis"; but by Artapanus, "*Merrhis*"; and it is remarkable that *Ameri* was the name of a daughter of Amos according to the monuments; and this daughter was his heiress, and apparently his only child.[2]—We find the name of Amos in the quarries of Mons Troicus, opposite the site of Memphis. It is probable that this king, having made himself master of Memphis, adorned that city with some new public edifices.

Amonoph 1st, in the list from the monuments, corresponds with the Amenophthis of the list from Manetho. He was a Theban, or at least an Egyptian, and acceded to the throne of Egypt by his marriage with the Ethiopian princess, the daughter of his predecessor Amos, before-mentioned. His name is often found at Thebes; but there are no great

---

[1]Syncellus says that in the reign of Amos, Moses was educated in Egypt.

[2]Major Felix has mentioned this in his "Notes on Hieroglyphics."—Artapanus says that the king who began to oppress the Israelites was Palmanothes (probably meant for Amenophis, or, with the article, Phamenophis) and that his daughter Merrhis, who adopted Moses, married a Theban king named Chenephren, or Chenebron (that is, Chebron): but the monuments teach us to *reverse* this statement; for Amonoph 1st married Ameri, or Merrhis, who was the daughter of Amos, or Chebron. (See Eusebius, Præp. Evang. ix, 27, and Clemens Alex. Strom. i). The wife of Amos, however, also bore the name of Ameri.

monuments of his reign. In his time, brick arches were built, on the regular masonic principle; as I have stated in my description of the brick pyramids at Thebes.

Thothmos 1st is shewn, by the monuments, to have been the next king: but Manetho places a Queen Amersis, or Amesses, next to Amenophthis, or Amonoph 1st; and in the list copied by Josephus, the said Amesses is stated to have been the *sister* of her predecessor. This queen, it might be thought, was the *wife* of Amonoph 1st (from the name of the latter being Ameri); and that she was called the *sister* of that king as being the daughter of his predecessor. We find, however, that Thothmos 1st had a queen whose name was *Ames*[1]; and who is called "royal sister," as well as "royal wife"; and in the sculptures of a tomb opened by Mr. Wilkinson, at Thebes, she is placed among the family of Amonoph 1st: I therefore can have no hesitation in concluding her to be the Amesses or Amersis of Manetho. As Thothmos 1st appears not to have been the son of his predecessor, I suppose that his queen is placed by Manetho in his stead, as being the heiress to the throne, and as having survived her husband. I do not regard Misaphris, or Mephres, as as [sic] the same with this king, but rather as his successor; because, if the former were the case there would be no king in Manetho's list corresponding with Thothmos 2nd; since Misphragmuthosis (for two reasons which I shall have to state) seems to correspond with the 3rd Thothmos of the monuments. If, then, Ames, or Amesses, survived her husband, she probably shared the throne during a part of the reign of his successor. I make these remarks because I consider the chronology of the period between Amos and the "Tuthmosis" of Manetho as of particular importance, with reference to the eras of the birth of Moses and the Exodus of the Israelites.—The name of Thothmos 1st is found on few monuments. He erected the two smaller obelisks of Kur'nak, and founded the older temple at Medee'net Hha'boo.

Thothmos 2nd is but little known. His name is found, with that of his predecessor, among the sculptures of the temple above-mentioned; shewing that he continued its decoration.

Thothmos 3rd follows next in the regular lists of the monuments, and appears to correspond with the Misphragmuthosis, or Mephramuthosis, of Manetho:—1st, because his prenomen and nomen together may be read "Mephra-Thothmos," or "Mera-Thothmos"; and "Mephramuthosis" is probably a corruption of "Mephratuthmosis":—2ndly, because the period assigned by Manetho to the reign of Mephramuthosis, or Misphragmuthosis, agrees very nearly with the longest date of Thothmos 3rd yet observed (28 years); while that assigned to "Tuthmosis" falls short by more than two thirds of the 3rd Thothmos' reign.—Thothmos 3rd was, I believe, during his minority, under a regent. The personage whose name (marked 44*a* in my hieroglyphic list) we find in the principal hieroglyphics of the great obelisks of Kur'nak seems to have

---

[1]Her name is given in Mr. Wilkinson's "Materia Hieroglyphica," part ii, plate 1.

enjoyed the supreme authority during this period. My reasons for thinking so I have stated in the description of a temple at Thebes (the temple of the As'a'see'f) founded by this person, who is always distinguished by a royal title, and was probably a member of the Thothmos family.—Thothmos 3rd was, if we may judge of the monuments of his reign, a very magnificent monarch. Among these monuments may be mentioned a large portico at Kur'nak (which is a fine building, though its style is very whimsical—the form of the columns being like an inverted shaft, thicker at the top than at the bottom, surmounted by an inverted capital): also, other additions to the great temple of Kur'nak; several small temples in various places, with peculiarly beautiful sculptures; and the obelisks at Alexandria, which were doubtless taken from Heliopolis.—From his prenomen of Mera, or Mephra, Thothmos 3rd has been supposed to be the same with Mœris, or Myris. Another reason also my be adduced for identifying him with this celebrated king: Diodorus states that Sesoosis (Sesostris) was the seventh king after Myris (or Mœris); and in the lists from the monuments Rameses 2nd (or Sesostris) is placed as the seventh after Thothmos 3rd.—I shall soon have to mention this Thothmos again, in speaking of the expulsion of the Israelites.

Amonoph 2nd was the son and successor of Thothmos 3rd. He is not mentioned in the list of Manetho; and his reign was probably very short. He continued the sculpture of the temple of Hhassa'yeh, or Am'ada, which was founded by his father.

Thothmos 4th succeeded his father Amonoph 2nd.—I refer *the Exodus of the Israelites* to the reign of this Pharaoh; and as this is a very important point for decision, I must fully state the reasons which have brought me to the conclusion above-stated. First it is necessary to revert to the first incursion of "Shepherds" into Egypt.

Manetho (as quoted by Josephus) relates that, during the reign of an Egyptian king named Timaus,[1] the gods were displeased with his nation; and a people of obscure origin entered Egypt from the East, and subjugated it without opposition. They burned towns, destroyed temples, and treated the natives with the greatest cruelty; slaying multitudes of men, and making slaves of the women and children. One of their own tribe, whose name was Salatis (probably the Philitis of Herodotus—for my calculation makes him contemporary with the supposed builder of the Second Pyramid), they chose as their king. This chief, it is said, resided at Memphis (as Philitis is related to have done by Herodotus); and exacted tribute from the upper and lower provinces. He also fortified a city called Avaris, which occupied ten thousand acres, on

---

[1] He is not mentioned in Manetho's list of the Dynasties: perhaps he was a petty king ruling in that part of Lower Egypt where the Shepherds first established themselves, on the east of the Delta.

the east of the Bubastic, or Pelusiac branch of the Nile[1]; and thither he
went, in summer, to distribute to his people the corn which he received
as tribute, and to exercise his troops, who, in number 240,000 men, were
stationed there to defend his territories against the Assyrians. This Salatis
is said to have reigned 19 years; after him, Bœon, 44 years; then,
Apachnas, 36 years and 7 months; next, Apophis, 61 years; after whom,
Iamias, 50 years and 1 month; and then, Assis, 49 years and 2 months.
These six princes carried on a continual war with the Egyptians, and they
and their descendants are said to have reigned 511 years.—Josephus adds
that, in one copy of Manetho, he finds "Hycsos," the term by which
these people were designated, translated "Shepherd Kings"; "Hyc" being
said to signify "a king," and "Sos," "a shepherd"; but that in another
copy the same term is translated "Shepherd Captives"; "Hyc" or "Hac"
signifying "captive."

Here we observe that the Shepherds who are said to have held
dominion in Egypt during a period of 511 years are described as of one
race; but in Manetho's list of the Dynasties, as given by Africanus, the six
princes above-mentioned compose a distinct dynasty,—the 15th. They
are followed by a dynasty of a different race: it is said "of Greek
Shepherds"; but it is supposed that for "Greek" we should read "other."
Then follows a *third* race, "of *other* Shepherds." The duration of the
First Race is said to have been 284 years; that of the Second, 518; and that
of the Third, 151. If the three races were consecutive, these numbers
would refer the arrival of the First Race in Egypt to a period anterior to
the commencement of the Memphite kingdom: I therefore conclude that
they were not consecutive; also, that the duration of the Second Race, at
least, is incorrectly stated; and that 511 years, as first stated, was the
period during which the eastern provinces of Lower Egypt were partly
(as they have been of late) in the undisputed possession of tribes of
pastors from the East.

As Manetho thus distinguishes "the Shepherds" into three different
races, evidently entering Egypt at different periods, and establishing
themselves in the same part of the country, we are not, of necessity, to
conclude that, because the First Race was a horde of powerful
conquerors, the Second and the Third were also of the same description.
Either Manetho or his copyist Africanus says that the First was a race of
Phoenicians; and in the extract given by Josephus, Manetho mentions, in
allusion to the Shepherds in general, that some asserted that these people
were Arabs. The Second Race may have been a people who entered
Egypt at, or about, the same period as Abraham; and who were, like him,
induced to go thither on account of a famine in their own country. They
were probably Philistines. The third race I consider as the Israelites.[2]

---

[1]This description exactly applies to "the Land of Goshen" afterwards occupied
by the Israelites.
[2]Allusion is probably made to *two* of the three races of Shepherds who settled in
Egypt in the following words—"Have I not brought up Israel out of the land of

During the period of their independence in Egypt, the Israelites were contemporary with the Diospolites of the 17th Dynasty, with whom the Third Race of Shepherds are classed by Manetho. They were only allowed to settle in a frontier province *because they were shepherds*;—in the same province which had been occupied by the First Race of the Shepherds; in remembrance of whose tyranny, shepherds (evidently those of foreign countries[1]) were then held by the Egyptians as "an abomination." It is true that a period of 151 years is assigned to the Dynasty of the Third Race of Shepherds; whereas the Israelites abode in Egypt certainly not so long as 135 years before they were reduced to a state of bondage[2]; but the term of 151 years may be designed as shewing the duration of the *Diospolites* of the 17th Dynasty; with whom the Third Race of Shepherds may be associated merely as having been contemporary during the greater part of the period of their independence.—It is said that after the lapse of 511 years after the first incursion of Shepherds into Egypt, the kings of that country threw off the yoke of these foreign invaders: I therefore place the period of the incursion of the First Race of Shepherds 511 years before the termination of the 17th Dynasty; for then, according to Manetho, ended the power or authority of the Third Race of Shepherds; and this is about the period at which I calculate the oppression of the Israelites to have commenced.

Without losing sight of the presumed identity of the Israelites and the Third Race of Shepherds, let us now consider two traditions preserved by Josephus from the writings of Manetho; and let it be allowed as not improbable that the vanity of the Egyptians might induce them to represent the expulsion of the Israelites as a martial exploit.—Manetho states that after the expiration of 511 years from the first incursion of the Shepherds, the kings of the Thebais and of other parts of Egypt threw off the yoke of these foreigners, and a long and fierce war was carried on with them, till, under an Egyptian king named Misphragmuthosis (by a mistake of a copyist written Alisphragmuthosis), they were defeated, and confined within their city of Avaris, where Thummosis, or Tethmosis, the son of the above-mentioned king, besieged them, with an army of 480,000 men, and forced them to enter into a capitulation, according to the terms of which they departed from Egypt, in number 240,000 men, together with their cattle and other property: travelling through the desert, they went towards Syria; and built a city to which they gave the name of Jerusalem.—Manetho, having related as above, proceeds to

---

Egypt, and the Philistines from Caphtor, and the Syrians from Kir?" (Amos, ix, 7). Caphtor is stated by the Jewish writers to have been an eastern province of Lower Egypt; in which part of Egypt the "Avaris" in which the Shepherds first established themselves, and "the land of Goshen," were situated.

[1]Many of the Egyptians themselves were shepherds.

[2]The Israelite government in Egypt must however be reckoned from the period when Joseph was made "ruler over all the land of Egypt" (or Lower Egypt); that is, about nine years before the arrival of his father and brethren in that country.

mention the names of the kings of the dynasty to which this Tethmosis belonged; and in this list we find the name of the king just mentioned put in the place of Amos, or Amosis, as head of the dynasty. This I cannot but regard as an error; probably the fault of a careless copyist. I have no hesitation in concluding that the Tethmosis to whom the expulsion of the Shepherds is attributed was a later king of the same dynasty; that he was the king whose name is written in the transcripts of Manetho's list by Africanus and Eusebius "Tuthmosis," and in the extract given by Josephus, "Thmosis"; and I conclude so for the following reasons.—1st. This is the only king of that or any similar name in Manetho's list as copied by Africanus and Eusebius.—2ndly. Manetho places this king as the immediate successor of a king named Misphragmuthosis; and the latter is the only one of that name in the list.—3rdly. It is said that a long and fierce war was carried on from the period when the Egyptians put an end to the dominion of the last dynasty of Shepherds to the period when the latter were expelled.—4thly. The uncertainty of the lengths of the reigns in this dynasty, as stated in Manetho's list, admits of our referring the period of the Exodus to the reign of the said Tuthmosis, the 4th Thothmos of the monuments; whereas we cannot refer that event to the reign of Amos without greatly reducing the duration attributed by Manetho to this and the three following dynasties.—Unfortunately the monuments do not give us the name of the predecessor of Amos; though they do his prenomen[1]: we may conclude, however, that he was not Misphragmuthosis who is mentioned in the account of the expulsion of the Shepherds, from the mere consideration that if Manetho had known that this was the name of the last Diospolite of the 17th Dynasty, and that the head of the 18th was Tethmosis, he certainly would not have omitted the former in his list of the dynasties, nor would he have called the latter "Amos" or "Amosis," which, indeed, the monuments prove to have been his name.[2] One authority, only, induced me, for a moment, to waver in my conclusion respecting this point: I allude to the assertion of Apion the grammarian, who cites Ptolemy, a priest of Mendes,[3] in proof of the statement, that Moses and the Israelites were expelled from Egypt by Amosis. This statement may have been deduced from a corrupted copy of Manetho's celebrated history; or, as Amos (according to my computation) was the first king who *oppressed* the Israelites, and reduced them to a state of bondage, he may on that account have been confounded with the king who *expelled* them: but in either case this

---

[1]This cannot be read *Mephra*, or *Mera*, like that of Thothmos 3rd; whose name I suppose to have been originally written by Manetho "Mephra-Tuthmosis," and afterwards, by ignorant and careless copyists "Mephramuthoses," as we find it in Josephus, and "Misphragmuthosis," as in the transcripts of Manetho's list by Africanus and Eusebius.

[2]The hieroglyphics of the name of Amos may, *perhaps*, be also read *Thothmos*; but we have no proof of the incipient character being ever read *Thoth*.

[3]Quoted by Eusebius, Præp. Evan. x, 11.

assertion confirms the identity of the Israelites with the Third Race of Shepherds. I need hardly add that the reasons which I have adduced for my referring the commencement of the oppression of the Israelites to the reign of Amos are strongly confirmatory of those which attribute their expulsion to "Thuthmosis," the 4th Thothmos of the monuments.

Josephus, having quoted the account of the Shepherds, of which I have given an abstract, and having maintained that it refers to the Israelites, and their expulsion from Egypt, adds another tradition, from the same work; stating it to be, by the admission of Manetho himself, a mere story which was current among the vulgar.—According to this tradition, a certain king of Egypt, named Amenophis, being desirous to see the gods, was advised, by a priest of the same name, to propitiate them by ridding his country of all lepers and other diseased persons. Eighty thousand of such he accordingly collected, and sent them to work in the quarries on the east of the Nile; but afterwards he gave them, as a place of residence, the city of Avaris, which had been vacated by the Shepherds whom Tethmosis had expelled. Here they rebelled, and called to their aid, from Jerusalem, the Shepherds above-mentioned; upon the arrival of whom in Egypt Amenophis, the king, fled to Ethiopia; and there remained thirteen years; the priest, his namesake, having prophecied that the injured people whom he had confined in Avaris would conquer Egypt, and retain possession of it for that term of years. The priest, fearing to communicate this prophecy to the king, had committed it to writing, and destroyed himself. The diseased Egyptians and their auxiliaries perpetrated the most flagrant cruelties and sacrilegious acts. The had chosen for their chief and law-giver a priest of Heliopolis, whose Egyptian name was Osarsiph, from Osiris, the god of Heliopolis; but he afterwards changed his name, and called himself Moses. Amenophis, it is related, after the predicted period of his privation had expired, returned, with an army, from Ethiopia, and, with his son Sethos (to whom he also gave his father's name of Rameses) attacked the diseased people and the Shepherds, expelled them from Egypt, and pursued them to the confines of Syria.—This story, which Josephus condemns as a falsehood designed to injure the reputation of the Jews, is little more than a repetition of the former tradition with some additions, mostly fabulous. Both traditions relate the expulsion of the same race of people from Egypt. The only essential point in which they differ is respecting the king who expelled the foreign aggressors; and even in this point there appears to be a similarity of foundation in either story: for, in the latter, a prince who took a leading part in the expulsion of the foreigners and their confederates is called a son of Amenophis: in the former, the ejectment of the Shepherds is said to have been effected by Tuthmosis, who (though called by Manetho the son of Misphragmuthosis, to whom he is accordingly placed next in the list) appears, from the monuments, to have been son of Amonoph 2nd. The tradition first mentioned bears the stamp of authenticity, and is certainly more conformable with the Scripture history of the oppression and expulsion of the Israelites than the latter, in which the oppressed people are represented chiefly as *Egyptians*, who, in their revenge, perpetrated acts of which it is difficult to believe that Egyptians could have been guilty. The expulsion of the Israelites may have been ascribed to the predecessor of Rameses 2nd and to this latter king in conjunction with him because both of them were celebrated for their victories over some nations of Asia: that they were so, their monuments afford ample proof; and both may, at the outset of their expeditions, have met with and dispersed tribes of Arab pastors in the eastern part of Lower Egypt; for that part, bordering on the deserts of Arabia, was, doubtless, in almost every age, as it is at present, frequented by hordes of Arabs, for the sake of pasture. Rameses 2nd (the Sesostris of the Greek and Roman historians) may have passed through Palestine (though it is not quite certain that he did), and probably, if so, marched along the sea-coast, without interfering with the Israelites, who were, without doubt, too much occupied in their contests with the natives, under whom they were often in a state of servitude, and too painfully impressed with the knowledge of the sufferings which their ancestors endured under the Pharaohs, to throw themselves in the way of the Egyptian host. The silence of the Jewish history respecting this great conqueror need not therefore excite our surprise.—Chæremon relates, nearly in the same manner as Manetho, the tradition ascribing the expulsion of the Israelites to a king named Amenophis and his son; but calls the latter "Messenes."—Lysimachus presents us with a tale the same in its leading particulars; but says that the king who drove out the Israelites was Bocchoris: an assertion which bears its own confutation.— Tacitus repeats the same story, with some additions.—In a fragment of Diodorus Siculus we find an account of the expulsion of the Israelites more consistent with the Scripture narrative. This author relates that, in ancient times, Egypt was visited by a plague, which was attributed to the anger of the gods on account of the multitude of profane foreigners who had settled in that country; all of whom were therefore expelled: the most noble and courageous of them went to Greece, under Danaus and Cadmus; but the greater number repaired, under the conduct of Moses, a very wise and brave leader, to Judæa; and, having conquered that country, built the city of Jerusalem. Diodorus adds an account of the excellent religion and laws which Moses instituted.

Several of these traditions suggest the inference that Amonoph 2nd, whom the monuments shew to have intervened between Thothmos 3rd and 4th (the Misphragmuthosis and Tuthmosis of Manetho, who represents the latter as the immediate successor of the former), particularly signalized himself in the oppression of the Israelites: also, that the Second Race of Shepherds, mentioned in Manetho's epitome of the Dynasties, were yet in Egypt, or had made another incursion into that country, and were expelled at the same period as the Israelites. In Exodus, chapter xii, verses 38, 44, and 45, we are told that "a mixed multitude went up also with them," besides their numerous flocks and herds; and "servants bought with money," and "foreigners," and "hired servants," are mentioned. "The mixed multitude that was among them" is again mentioned in Numbers, chapter xi, verse 4.

Respecting Thothmos 4th, we derive but little information from the monuments in Egypt. If he were drowned in the Red Sea, in pursuit of the Israelites, it would be strange if his tragic death were recorded by sculptures. But we have no direct evidence in the Bible of Pharaoh himself being drowned with his host; unless the 15th verse of the 136th Psalm be admitted as such: this may be misinterpreted; and it is uncertain when, and by whom, this psalm was written. In Genesis, chapter xiv, verse 28, we are told that "the waters returned, and covered the chariots and the horsemen and all the host of Pharaoh that came into the sea."—Under Thothmos 4th the sculptures of the temple of Hhassa'yeh, or Am'ada, were completed; and the great tablet placed against the breast of the Sphinx of the Pyramids bears the name of this Pharaoh.

Amonoph 3rd was son and successor of Thothmos 4th. Mr. Wilkinson has ascertained that the mother of this Amonoph reigned during his minority; and that an elder brother, of the same name, afterwards reigned conjointly with him for some years. Amonoph 3rd has left many very noble and beautiful monuments. He was the king whom the Greeks and Romans called Memnon. This is proved by the famous "vocal statue" (at Thebes), which bears the hieroglyphic name of this king; as does also its companion. Many Greek and Latin inscriptions upon the legs of the former of these stupendous colossi announce it to be "the Vocal Memnon." But the tradition which identifies this Pharaoh with the Memnon of Homer is confuted by a wide anac[h]ronism: for Amonoph 3rd died more than four centuries before the Trojan war; if the period to which I have referred the accession of this king, and the date commonly assigned to the Trojan war, be correct.—A magnificent temple, in the approach to which the two colossi above-mentioned were placed, now, unfortunately in a state of utter ruin, was constructed under this king. The oldest part of the temple of El-Oock'soor, and several noble works at Kur'nak and elsewhere, are also monuments of his splendid reign. The sculptures of these monuments are of a very beautiful style; and are all the works of the same age, whether figures in relief or statues. The tomb of Amonoph 3rd, which is a very fine excavation, is in the long valley to the west of the principal valley of the Tombs of the Kings at Thebes. This is the most ancient royal tomb yet discovered; perhaps excepting one in the same valley, of unknown, or uncertain age.

Horus, according to Manetho, was the name of the successor of the above. His hieroglyphic name contains a hawk; the emblem of the god Horus. A propylæum with a granite portal, and an avenue of criosphinxes leading to it, at Kur'nak, are his works. We also find, at Geb'el es-Sil'sil'eh, an interesting memorial (in an excavated temple) of this king's having carried his victorious arms into Ethiopia; and there is a rock-temple of his reign nearly opposite Absem'bel, or Ab'oo Sim'bil.

After the name of this king there follow five names in Manetho's list which have none corresponding with them in any of the lists which the monuments present: Horus being in each of the latter lists immediately succeeded by Rameses 1st. The first of the five sovereigns whom Manetho makes to intervene between these two may have been omitted in the lists of the monuments as being a queen; and the last of the five seems to have been the brother of Sethos, or Rameses 2nd; and if so he is misplaced here. The three other names (of the five above-mentioned) may be of queens or mere regents.

Raměses 1st reigned for too short a period to admit of his leaving any great monument. A chapel, which is included in the edifice at the ruined village of El-Ckoor'neh, was dedicated to him by his son and successor. His tomb is in the valley of Bee'ba'n el-Mooloo'k; is small, but beautiful; and in a wonderful state of preservation: it appears to be the most ancient of the tombs in that valley; excepting, perhaps, the tomb of a Queen named Taosiri.

Phtha-mai Osiree, or *Amon-mai Osiree* (*Osiree* 1st), who is called by Manetho "Amenoph," or "Amenophis," or "Menophis," was the son and successor of Rameses 1st, and last king of the 18th Dynasty. He closed this dynasty most gloriously; for he was one of the greatest of all the Pharaohs. He built the grand, unrivalled portico of Kur'nak; but its sculptures were not completed during his reign. He also built the edifice at the ruined village of El-Ckoor'neh, above-mentioned, and the great edifice of Abydos. The sculptures on the exterior of the left side-wall of the great portico of Kur'nak, which are among the finest in Egypt, shew him to have been a great conqueror in Asia; and that he was scarcely surpassed by his son Rameses 2nd, or Sesostris. His tomb (which was discovered by Belzoni), in the valley of Beeba'n el-Mooloo'k, is the most splendid, and one of the least injured, of all the tombs in that valley.

19th Dynasty.

The 19th Dynasty is said to have lasted 210 years, and to have consisted of seven princes, whose names are here subscribed from Manetho's list, with the corresponding names obtained from the monuments.

B.C.	From Manetho. years	From the monuments.
1475	Sethos, or Sethosis, or Ramesses. 51	51. Raměses 2nd (Sesostris)
	Rhapsaces, or Rhapses. 61	52. (Name not certainly deciphered)
	Ammenephthes. 20	53. Osiree Men-Phtha
	Rameses. 60 ....,	54. Amerri, or Ramerri
	Ammenemnes. 5 \...................	55. Rameses 3rd (Mai-Amon)
	Thuoris. 6	56. Rameses 4th
	Alcandrus. 7	57. Rameses 5th
1265	End of this dynasty.	

The most splendid period of the history continued with the 19th Dynasty; but appears to have terminated with the reign of Rameses 3rd, if we may judge from the fact that the monuments of the ages posterior to the reign of this king are inferior in grandeur and in the style of their sculptures to those of his predecessors of this and the preceding dynasty. All the kings of the 19th Dynasty seem to be of the Rameses family. The first of them was the son of the last king of the preceding dynasty.

Rамĕses 2nd (*Amon-mai Rameses*), who is called by Manetho "Sethos," "Sethosis," "Ramesses," and Ægyptus," is undoubtedly the same with the "Sesoosis" of Diodorus Siculus, and the great "Sesostris" of Herodotus and other writers; and well do the monuments of his reign, both in Egypt and Nubia, attest his preeminent glory. By Manetho, or, more probably, by one of his copyists, the name of Sesostris is placed in the 12th Dynasty, with a notice of the great conquests of this prince; but in an extract from the same author, preserved by Josephus, these great acts are ascribed to the true Sesostris, the head of the 19th Dynasty.[1] From various ancient historians, and from the monuments of this Pharaoh, we learn that, either during his father's life or during his own reign, he carried his arms into Ethiopia and the negro countries. This was probably his first expedition. He is also said to have conducted a maritime expedition, the object and end of which was the conquest of Cyprus; to have fitted out a navy on the Red Sea; to have conquered Phœnicia, Assyria, Media, Persia, part of India, Bactria, Scythia, and Thrace. Respecting the supposed passage of his forces through Palestine I have already had occasion to speak. Sesostris is said to have been accompanied, in his military expeditions, by a lion; and it is a remarkable fact that among the sculptures of the temple of Ed-Dirr, in Nubia, Rameses 2nd is represented in the act of slaying four captives, and a lion is rushing on to devour them. The most remarkable of his monuments, which are unequalled in number, and some of them unrivalled in grandeur,[2] by those of any other Pharaoh, are the two rock-temples of Absem'bel, or Ab'oo Sim'bil (one of which is the finest monument of the kind in the valley of the Nile, and perhaps the most imposing of all Egyptian monuments),—the rock-temple of Ed-Dirr,—the temple of Wa'dee es-Sooboo'ă (which is in part an excavation),—the rock-temples of Gur'f Hhosey'n and Ckala'b'sheh (the historical sculptures of the latter of which are among the most beautiful of all Egyptian works of art),—the Rameséum[†] of El-Ckoor'neh (the grand and elegant building which travellers have improperly called "the Memnonium"),—and the great propylæum and beautiful obelisks and first peristyle court of El-Oock'soor. He founded many other temples, in various parts of

---

[1]In the notice which follows the misplaced name of Sesostris in the 12th Dynasty it is said that the Egyptians supposed this king to have been the first after Osiris: the monuments shew that Rameses 2nd was the son and successor of a king whose name appears to have been Osiree.

[2]I allude here to some of his colossi; particularly those of the great temple of Absem'bel, or Ab'oo Sim'bil: for among *architectural* monuments, his father's great portico at Kur'nak is quite unrivalled.

[†]Here Lane's orthography looks more like "Ramese'um," as it does in some other instances.

Egypt and Nubia; and made considerable additions to the magnificent temple of Kur'nak. The representations of battle-scenes which adorn the walls of several of the buildings and excavations above-mentioned exhibit more boldness of design, and more invention, than the sculptures of any other Pharaoh. There is an unfinished tomb which was intended for this prince in the valley of Beeba'n el-Mooloo'k: it is doubtful whether he was buried in it.

Of the next three kings no remarkable monuments remain, excepting their tombs, which are in the valley of Beeba'n el-Mooloo'k, and an avenue of crio-sphinxes before the great propylæum, and a small temple in the first court, of Kur'nak, which are of the reign of the first of these princes.

Rameses 3rd (*Mai-Amon Rameses*) is shewn by the monuments to have been the fifth king of this dynasty; but seems to be the same with the Rameses who is placed by Manetho as the fourth; while the fifth in the list of this historian perhaps agrees with the fourth in the list from the monuments. Remeses 3rd was, if we may judge from the sculptures which adorn the walls of the great edifice created under his orders at Medee'net Hha'boo, almost as great a conqueror as Rameses 2nd (or the great Sesostris). In my description of that building I have ventured to suggest that this king may have been the *second* Sesostris, or Sesoosis 2nd of Diodorus, though called, by Diodorus, the *son* of the great Sesoosis, or Sesostris. Various countries of Asia were the scenes of his principal military exploits; and it is remarkable that among the sculptures above alluded to there is a representation of a naval engagement between an Egyptian squadron and the combined fleets of two Asiatic nations. These sculptures are among the finest specimens of Egyptian art: the hieroglyphics are cut in a peculiarly deep style. Rameses 3rd built, in front of the great edifice above-mentioned, a beautiful palace; and the exterior sculptures of the adyta of the smaller temple adjacent to the latter building were executed in his reign. He also built two temples at Kur'nak. His tomb, in the valley of Beeba'n el-Mooloo'k, is very magnificent.

Rameses 4th is memorable for his tomb, which is very grand, in the same valley.

Rameses 5th also excavated for himself a large and handsome tomb in that valley.

It is stated that the capture of Troy took place in the reign of the last king of this dynasty, but the date commonly assigned to that event is B.C. 1183, or 82 years later than the period to which I have referred the termination of the dynasty.

Between Sesostris, or Sesoosis, and Sabacon, Herodotus and Diodorus insert the names of several kings, not one of whom excepting Bocchoris, in the list of Diodorus, we can decidedly recognize among those with which the monuments acquaint us. Both these historians have fallen into the extraordinary error of introducing in this period the builders of the three most celebrated pyramids of Memphis.

20th Dynasty.

Of this dynasty it is merely stated, in Manetho's epitome, that it consisted of twelve Diospolite kings, who reigned 135 years. From the monuments we obtain the names of the first five of these kings; all of whom appear to have been of the same family as those of the preceding dynasty; for they all bear the name of Rameses. The tombs of all but the first of these five kings are found in the valley of Beeba'n el-Mooloo'k; and excepting these tombs there are, I believe, no important monuments of their reigns.

1265 and 1130 B.C. appear to be the dates of the commencement and termination of this dynasty, the last of the great Diospolite families.

21st Dynasty.

In Manetho's list it is stated that this dynasty consisted of seven kings, of a Tanite family, who reigned 130 years. Their names, in that list are as follow.

1130	B.C.	Smedes, or Smendis. 26 years
		Psusenes, or Psusennes. 46
		Nephelcheres, or Nephercheres. 4
		Amenophthis. 9
		Osochor. 6
		Pinaches, or Psinaches. 9
		Susennes, or Psusennes. 30
1000		End of the Dynasty.

From the monuments we do not obtain the name of any king certainly belonging to this dynasty.

22nd Dynasty.

In Manetho's list it is stated that this dynasty consisted of nine kings, of a Bubastite family, who reigned 120 years. From this author we obtain only an imperfect list of these kings; and from the monuments we derive another, also imperfect: both are here subjoined.

	From Manetho	From the monuments.
1000	Sesonchis. (Shishak). 21 years	77. Amon-mai Sheshonk 1st
986	Capture of Jerusalem by Sheshonk, or Shishak.	
	Osoroth, or Osorthon. 15	78. Amon-mai Osorkon 1st
	3 Kings. 25	
	Tacellothis. 13	82. Amon-mai-Se-Isi-mai Takelothe
	3 Kings. 42 (or 46?)	83. Amon-mai Osorkon 2nd
		84. Amon-mai Sheshonk 2nd
880	End of the Dynasty.	

I have placed the accession of Sheshonk, or Shishak, in the year 1000 B.C. according to the calculation in the third table of dates inserted in the introduction to this account of the Egyptian dynasties. Jeroboam the son of Nebat fled for refuge to Shishak before the death of Solomon, which happened in 990 B.C. There is no doubt of the identity of this Sheshonk with Shishak. On the exterior of the southern side of the great temple of Kur'nak, to the right of a gateway which he built, is a remarkable piece of sculpture representing 39 captive chiefs, led in bonds by this king, distinguished by hieroglyphic names enclosed in ovals, and characterized by a countenance considered by some perfectly Jewish.—Of the other kings of this dynasty no monuments remain.

23rd Dynasty.

Manetho gives the following list of this dynasty, which consisted of Tanite kings, and is said to have lasted 89 years.

880	B.C.	Petubates, or Petubastes. 40 years
		Osorcho, or Osorthon. 8
		Psammus. 10
		Zet. 31
791		End of the Dynasty.

The monuments do not give us the name of any king known to be of this dynasty.

24th Dynasty.

B.C.	
791	Bocchōris the Saite (by Diodorus called Bocchōris the Wise,
to	the son of Tnephachthus) reigned 44 years; and with this
747	reign began and terminated the 24th Dynasty.

I have assigned 44 years to the reign of this prince for reasons stated in the remarks subjoined to the third table of dates before referred to. Mr. Wilkinson conjectures that the hieroglyphic came of a king which reads "Amon-se Pahōr" is that of Bocchoris: Pahōr being pronounced in the Memphitic dialect Bakhōr. The sculptures of the propylæum of a temple at Kur'nak bear this name. Bocchoris was dethroned (and, it is said, burnt alive) by the Ethiopian conqueror Sabbacon.

25th Dynasty.

This dynasty consisted of three Ethiopian kings. I subjoin their names from Manetho, and from the monuments. It is uncertain whether the first and second of the names from the monuments should stand as they are placed below, or be transposed.

B.C.	From Manetho.	From the Monuments.
747	Sabbacon. 8 years.	91. Shebek
739	Sevechos (or So). 14	92. Savak, or Sovk
726	Compact of Hoshea, King of Israel, with So, or Sevechos.	

725	Taracos (or Tirhakah). 20	93. Tahrak
711		His war with Sennacherib, King of Assyria.
705		End of the Dynasty.

Egypt is said to have been in a turbulent state when it was invaded and conquered by the Ethiopian king Sabbacon, or Sabacon: perhaps the Anysis of Herodotus had usurped the government of Lower Egypt while Bocchoris ruled over the upper country. I have placed the name of Shebek, in preference to Savak or Sovk, as corresponding with Sabbacon, because the latter (which is also the name of the crocodile-headed god) seems to agree better with the Sevechos of Manetho; though it *may* be read, also, Sabac. My computation makes Sevechos the So of the Bible, with whom Hoshea made a league: some writers have identified So with Sabbacon.—I have assigned 20 years to the reign of Tirhakah for the reasons given in the remarks added to the third table of dates above-mentioned. In the reign of this king, Sennacherib conducted a numerous army against Egypt, and met with that miraculous defeat which is related in the Bible and, though rather differently, by Herodotus. According to this historian, Sethon, a priest of Vulcan, was king of Egypt at this time; from which we might infer that Tirhakah made Thebes his seat of government, and that Sethon was his viceroy in Lower Egypt. The name of Tirhakah is found on a small propylæum at Medee'net Hha'boo.

26th Dynasty.

This dynasty consisted of Saite kings, with the exception of the first, who is said to have been an Ethiopian. I subjoin a list of these kings from Manetho, with several corresponding names from the monuments.

B.C.	From Manetho.	From the Monuments.
705	Ammeris. 12 years*	
693	Stephinates, or Stephanathis. 7	
686	Nerepsos, or Nekepsos. 6	
680	Nechao 1st. 8	
672	Psammitichus 1st. 54	98. Psamitic 1st.
618	Nechao 2nd (Pharaoh Necho). 17*	99. Neco 2nd.
608	Josiah killed in battle with Necho.	
601	Psammuthis, or Psammitichus 2nd. 6	100. Psamitic 2nd
595	Ouaphris (Apries, or Hophra).25*	101? Psamitic 3rd
570	Dethroned by Nebuchadnezzar.	
—	An Interregnum. $^1/_2$ year.*	
570 } 569	Amosis, or Amasis, 44 years	102. Amos, or Ames.
526 } 525	Psammacherites (or Psammenitus) $^1/_2$ yr.	
525	Conquest of Egypt by Cambyses.	

(Respecting the periods marked with an asterisk see the notes following the third table of dates).

If we were to follow Herodotus and Diodorus, we should strike off the four first names in the foregoing list: but I consider the authority of Manetho as of far greater weight; though these names have not yet been found in any hieroglyphic inscriptions. The first event that we find recorded of the times of this dynasty is the division of Egypt into twelve states, each governed by an independent king. One of these kings, the first Psammiticus, soon obtained the ascendancy; and under him Egypt became again united into one kingdom. The period of the dodecarchy is probably comprised in the 54 years assigned to the reign of this king. A tradition ascribed the building of the labyrinth to the twelve contemporary kings: perhaps this edifice was repaired or enlarged by them. There are few remarkable monuments of the times of Psammitichus 1st and the succeeding kings of the same dynasty excepting several fine tombs excavated in and near the tract called El-As'a'see'f, at Thebes: the walls of these tombs are decorated with beautiful and most elaborate sculptures.[1]—Neco 2nd, the Pharaoh Necho of the Bible, is well known by the Scripture account of his expedition against Assyria; in the course of which Josiah, King of Judah, opposing him, was slain in battle.[2] Jehoahaz the son of Josiah succeeded to the throne of Judah; but he was deposed by Neco, and carried captive to Egypt, where he died: his territories became tributary to Egypt; and his brother Eliakim was made king in his stead by the conqueror, and his name changed to Jehoiakim. But Judæa was soon after snatched from the grasp of Egypt; "and the king of Babylon (Nebuchadnezzar) had taken from the river of Egypt unto the river Euphrates all that pertained to the king of Egypt."[3]—Psammuthis, or Psammitichus 2nd, was the Psammis of Herodotus. There is a remarkable monument of the reign of this king: it is an excavated tomb, at Sack'cka'rah, with chambers arched with stone, on the regular masonic principle; presenting the most ancient specimens of *stone* arches of that kind yet found.—The Onaphris, or Vaphris, of Manetho (the Apries of Herodotus, and the Pharaoh Hophra of the Bible) was the next king. He was, perhaps, the third Psammitichus of the monuments. He is said to have invaded Cyprus and Phœnicia; and to have taken Sidon and other towns of the latter country. After a prosperous reign of 25 years, he was dethroned by Nebuchadnezzar, who, according to several Arab historians, ravaged the whole of Egypt, and reduced it to a state of desolation, which lasted forty years; as Ezekiel (chap. xxix, v. 8 to 12) had prophecied.—Amasis, the successor of Onaphris or Apries, was probably merely a viceroy under the Babylonian monarchs; and afterwards under Cyrus, who, according to Xenophon, made himself master of Egypt. Even without the authority of

---

[1] In the reign of Psammitichus 1st foreign merchants were first allowed free access to Egypt.
[2] This expedition is also recorded by Herodotus (ii, 159); but Megiddo is changed by him into Magdolus.
[3] II. Kings, xxiv, 7.

Xenophon as to this latter fact we might infer that Cyrus, having possessed himself of the Babylonian kingdom (which he did about the year 536 B.C.) succeeded to that authority which the kings of Babylon had enjoyed in Egypt. The Egyptians, however, threw off the Persian yoke, certainly before the accession of Cambyses, and most probably on the death of Cyrus, forty years after their subjection by Nebuchadnezzar; in accordance with the prophecy of Ezekiel above alluded to; which is thus confirmed in its general import, though not in its minute particulars, perhaps not intended to be interpreted literally. This may explain the assertion of Herodotus as to the little respect which Amasis experienced from his subjects at the beginning of his reign, and the subsequent prosperity of himself and his country. It appears that Nebuchadnezzar led into captivity many Egyptians (perhaps as hostages), who returned at the close of the reign of Cyrus, or immediately after the death of that prince, to their native land.—Amasis was the first Pharaoh who gave encouragement to foreign merchants to settle in Egypt. He was the author of several remarkable monuments; but none of these are now remaining.—The invasion of Egypt by Cambyses terminated the six months reign of Psammenitus, or Psammacherites, the son and successor of Amasis.

27th Dynasty.
Eight Persian Kings.

B.C.	
525	Cambyses (in the 5th year of his reign over Persia). 6 years.[1]
519	Darius the son of Hystaspes. 36
484	The Egyptians revolt from the Persians, in the last year of Darius:
483	Xerxes the Great. 21 years. In his second year he reduces Egypt.
462	Artabanus. 7 months
—	Artaxerxes 1st (Longimanus). 41 years.
460	? The Egyptians again revolt from the Persians, at the instigation of Inaros, a Libyan prince.
454	? Egypt is reduced; and Inaros, put to death; after a war of six years.
421	Xerxes 2nd. 2 months.
—	Sogdianus. 7 months.
420	Darius 2nd (Nothus). 19 years (of which, 14 over Egypt).
406	Termination of the 27th Dynasty; referred to this period by taking the date of 332 B.C. as well ascertained to be that of the conquest of Egypt by Alexander the Great, and adding together the years of the last four dynasties, according to Africanus.

Cambyses is said to have obtained his first victory over the Egyptians, at Pelusium, by placing a number of cats and dogs at the head of his

---

[1] I continue to follow the transcript of Manetho by Africanus, in preference to that by Eusebius.

army: the Egyptians, refraining from the contest in the fear of killing animals which they regarded as sacred, were, by this stratagem, easily overcome. Memphis soon after submitted to the Persian monarch, and the whole of Egypt was ravaged by him: many temples, particularly at Thebes, were partly or wholly demolished by his order; and various sacrilegious and inhuman acts are recorded to have been perpetrated by him: he ridiculed the pigmy-image of the principal god of Memphis; burnt several other sacred images; and an Apis happening to be born while he was at Memphis, he stabbed the bull-god with his dagger. The dethroned Egyptian king, Psammenitus, was at first treated by Cambyses with humanity; but afterwards, being convicted of plotting a revolt, he was compelled to drink bull's blood, which killed him. The hieroglyphic names of Cambyses, Darius, and Xerxes are found in an inscription upon a rock on the route from Ckin'ë to El-Ckoosey'r,[1] sculptured in the 12th year of the last of these kings, and recording the lengths of the reigns of the two former monarchs; the first, 6 years, and the second, 36, as in the preceding table. The name of Cambyses in hieroglyphics reads Canbosh.—Darius, in his government of the Egyptians, made some amends for the grievous [sic] wrongs which they had suffered under his predecessor Cambyses: we are informed by Diodorus (i, 95) that he paid the utmost respect to their religion; and was so much honoured in return that he received from them the title of a god. Yet, in the last year of his reign they revolted.—His successor Xerxes, in the second year of his reign, reduced Egypt, and constituted his brother Achæmenes its governor.[2]—Early in the reign of Artaxerxes Longimanus, the Egyptians, instigated by Inaros, a Libyan prince, whom they chose for their ruler, and encouraged by the troubles which the death of Xerxes occasioned in Persia, again revolted. Having obtained the aid of an Athenian fleet, they carried on an obstinate war with the Persians. The first expedition that was sent against them, under the command of Achæmenes, failed: the second, commanded by Artabazus and Megabyzus, succeeded in reducing the whole of Egypt excepting the marshy district next the Mediterranean, where Amyrtæus, who at a later period became monarch of all Egypt, continued to defy the Persian army, and arrogated to himself the title of king. Inaros was taken and crucified. The war which he had excited thus terminated in the sixth year after its commencement.[3]—During a further period of nearly half a century the Egyptians were subject to Persia: towards the close of the reign of Darius Nothus they obtained their independence; and Amyrtæus, having come forth from his retreat among the marshes, became the first of a new but short series of native kings of Egypt.

---

[1]Given in Mr. Burton's Excerpta Hieroglyphica, plate 8.
[2]Herodotus, vii, 7.
[3]Thucydides, i, 104, 109, 110.—Diodorus, xi, 20, 21.

28th Dynasty.

B.C.

406	Amyrtæus the Saite, who reigned six years. Being followed
to	by a prince of a different family, his reign alone is registered
400	as the period of a separate dynasty.

A magnificent sarcophagus, now in the British Museum, bears the name of this king throughout its hieroglyphic sculptures: it is probably that which received his corpse. There are also in the British Museum two small, broken obelisks of black basalt, which are monuments of his reign.

29th Dynasty.

B.C.	This dynasty consisted, as Manetho informs us, of four Mendesian kings.
400	Nepherites (or Nephreus). 6 years.
394	Achoris, or Acoris (Nakori). 13
381	Psammuthis (Psamaut). 1
380	Nephorotes, or Nepherites 2nd. 4 months.

Diodorus mentions a Psammitichus, descended from Psammitichus 1st, as king of Egypt before Nephreus or Nepherites, at the period of the contest between Artaxerxes Mnemon and his aspiring brother Cyrus the Younger: this was the period to which I refer the close of the reign of Amyrtæus; of whom Diodorus takes no notice.—Nothing important is recorded of Nephreus; nor do we find any monuments of his reign.— Acoris made great preparations for a war with Persia; enlisting under his banners a great number of Greeks and other foreigners; while Artaxerxes did in like manner[1]; but this projected war was not commenced until after the accession of the next Egyptian dynasty.

30th Dynasty.

This was the last native Egyptian dynasty. It consisted of three Sebennyte kings.

B.C.

379	Nectanebes (or Nectanebo 1st). 18 years.
361	Teos, or Tachos. 2
359	Nectanebes (or Nectanebo 2nd). 18
341	Egypt conquered by Artaxerxes Ochus.

Early in the reign of the first king of this dynasty, Artaxerxes Mnemon dispatched, by sea and land, to Egypt, an army of 200,000 Persians under the command of Pharnabazus, and 20,000 Greeks commanded by Iphicrates, an Athenian general; but, in consequence of a dissension between the two leaders, this formidable expedition failed; and Egypt remained in tranquillity during the rest of the reign of Nectanebo 1st.—

---

[1]Diodorus xv, 29.

His successor, Tachos, or Teos, having raised an army of 80,000 Egyptians, together with 10,000 Greeks under the command of the Spartan king Agesilaus, and having prepared a fleet of 200 sail, marched against Persia: but shortly after he had quitted his dominions, a member of his family, named Nectanebus, or Nectanebo, aspired to his throne, and seduced the Egyptian troops to espouse his cause. Diodorus relates that Tachos, abandoned by all but Agesilaus and his Greek troops, sought and obtained the pardon of Artaxerxes Mnemon, and, upon the death of this prince, which happened shortly after, returned to Egypt, and recovered his throne by the aid of his faithful allies: but another account represents Agesilaus as having joined the rebels, and set up Nectanebo; and the short reign of Tachos renders this more probable.— In the reign of this second Nectanebo, Artaxerxes Ochus twice invaded Egypt: on the first occasion, eight or nine years after the accession of the Egyptian king, he was unsuccessful; but on the second, he accomplished his object; Nectanebo fled to Ethiopia; and, as Ezekiel had prophecied (xxx, 13), there was "no more a prince of the land of Egypt."

Nectanebo 1st or 2nd built a small temple of Athor on the Isle of Philæ, the portal of the first propylæum of the great temple of Philæ, and another portal at Kur'nak.

31st Dynasty.
Three Persian Kings.

B.C.

341	Artaxerxes Ochus (in the 20th year of his reign over Persia). 2 years.
339	Arses. 3
336	Darius Codomannus. 4
332	Conquest of Egypt by Alexander the Great.

The Egyptians experienced from Artaxerxes Ochus a repetition of the sacrilegious outrages of Cambyses: their temples were pillaged, and the walls of the principal cities demolished. This second Persian domination was so oppressive that they hailed the Macedonian conqueror as a deliverer.

Alexander the Great.

332 B.C. to 323.—This monarch rendered himself highly popular in Egypt by flattering the superstitions, and protecting the religion of the country. The granite sanctuary of Kur'nak, founded by Thothmos 3rd, was rebuilt, apparently, either at the expense of Philip, the father of Alexander, or by Alexander for his father: the hieroglyphic name of Philip is annexed to the figures representing the king for whom, or by whose order, the building was erected; and the name of the founder of the original structure also occurs among the sculptures. Alexander added another sanctuary to the great temple of Kur'nak; built one also in the temple of El-Oock'soor; and erected a granite portal, which led to a temple of Kneph, on the Island of Elephantine. The sanctuaries above-

mentioned were dedicated to Amon-Ra, whom the Greeks and Romans identified with Jupiter Ammon; and Kneph was also called Jupiter Ammon Cenubis. Hence, probably, and from his terming Amon-Ra "his father," in conformity with the custom of the Pharaohs in dedicating and offering to that god, he acquired the title of "Son of Jupiter Ammon."— The building of Alexandria, and the establishment of a Greek dynasty, effected great changes in the arts, as well as in the political state, of Egypt.

Ptolemaic Dynasty.

B.C.	
323	Ptolemy Soter, or Lagus, 39 years.
284	——— Philadelphus. 38
246	——— Euergetes 1st. 25
221	——— Philopator. 17
204	——— Epiphanes. 24
180	——— Philometor. 11
169	——— Philometor with Euergetes 2nd, or Physcon. 6
163	——— Philometor again alone. 18
145	——— Euergetes 2nd, or Physcon, alone. 29
116	——— Lathyrus, or Soter 2nd, with his mother Cleopatra 1st. 10
106	——— Alexander 1st with Cleopatra 1st. 18
88	——— Lathyrus again, alone. 7
81	Cleopatra 2nd, 6 months: with Ptolemy Alexander 2nd, 19 days.
80	Ptolemy Alexander 3rd. 15 years.
65	——— Auletes. 14
51	Ptolemy Dionysus with Cleopatra 3rd. 5
46	Cleopatra 3rd with Ptolemy Junior. 3
43	Cleopatra 3rd alone. 13
30	Egypt reduced to a Roman province by Augustus.

Under the Ptolemaic dynasty (the history of which is too generally known to need any repetition of it here), and under several of the Roman Emperors, many temples were erected in Egypt to the ancient objects of worship: others were repaired, enlarged, or decorated with new sculptures. Some of the Ptolemaic monuments, as the great temples of Philæ, Ombos, Ad'foo, and the main part of the principal temple of Den'dar'a, are very noble structures: so also are a few of the Roman-Egyptian buildings, as the portico of the great temple of Den'dar'a, and that of Is'na: but the sculptures of all (both the former and latter) are very inferior in style to those of the earlier times.

Concluding remarks respecting the ancient kings.
Concerning the condition and privileges of the kings of Egypt we obtain some scanty information from Herodotus and Diodorus; and this subject is further illustrated by the monuments.—The king, in most instances, probably derived his origin from the military caste; but was evidently

admitted a member of the sacerdotal order; though to what extent he was initiated into the mysteries of the religion we are ignorant. The regal dignity generally descended from father to son: sometimes to a younger son: in this case it is doubtful whether the successor was appointed by his father or chosen by the priests. If a king left only female issue, the crown usually devolved to the daughter's husband, who was probably of the same race, or descended from a former royal family. The legitimate line of succession was often broken by usurpation.—In the battle-scenes sculptured on the walls of the temples, the king is invariably placed at the head of the Egyptian armies; and in the other sculptures, which are the more common, the king under whom these sculptures were executed, and generally he only, is represented offering to the gods, or leading victims before them, or worshipping them, or receiving their blessings.— The power of the king was not despotic: his judicial authority was limited by the laws. In the distribution of his time, in his diet, and even in his amusements, he was obliged to conform with rules prescribed by the priests. Early in the morning he transacted his affairs of state: this done, he attended certain services of the temple.—The king, the priests, and the soldiers, were the only landed proprietors in Egypt, excepting in very early times. Before the time of Joseph there were *private* proprietors of land, at least in Lower Egypt; but "Joseph bought all the land of Egypt (or of the Memphite dominions) for Pharaoh; for the Egyptians sold every man his field, because the famine prevailed over them: so the land became Pharaoh's." (Genesis, xlvii, 20).—"Only the land of the priests bought he not; for the priests had a portion assigned them of Pharaoh, and did eat their portion which Pharaoh gave them: wherefore they sold not their lands. Then Joseph said unto the people, Behold, I have bought you this day and your land for Pharaoh: lo, here is seed for you, and ye shall sow the land. And it shall come to pass in the increase, that ye shall give the fifth part unto Pharaoh, and four parts shall be your own, for seed of the field, and for your food, and for them of your households, and for food for your little ones." (Ibid, 22-24). "And Joseph made it a law over the land of Egypt unto this day, that Pharaoh should have the fifth part; except the land of the priests only, which became not Pharaohs." (Ibid, 26).—Sesostris, according to Herodotus (ii, 109), divided his land, or let it out, equally among his subjects; allotting a square piece of ground to each individual; and exacting a tribute for it.

7. The Military Caste.

The Military Caste was next in rank to the Sacerdotal. We learn from Herodotus (ii, 164-168) that, in his time, the military caste was divided into two great tribes, called Calasirians and Hermotybians; the former consisting of 250,000 warriors, and the latter, of 160,000. They were, like the priests, great landed proprietors; each soldier having twelve acres of land, measuring each, in length and in breadth, one hundred Egyptian cubits, exempt from tribute or taxation. One thousand men, selected annually from each of the two tribes, constituted the king's body-guard: and received, during their service in this capacity, besides the produce of their land, an allowance of bread, beef, and wine. The profession of arms was strictly hereditary. The soldiers engaged in none of the meaner occupations of life; and their estates were probably farmed out. In the reign of Psammitichus 1st, 240,000 Egyptian soldiers revolted, and migrated into Ethiopia.[1]

8. The Inferior Castes.

The Inferior Castes are divided by Herodotus (ii, 164) into Cowherds, Swineherds, Tradesmen, Interpreters, and Navigators: by Diodorus (1, 74), into Agriculturists, Herdsmen, and Artisans. I shall consider them under the following heads—Agriculturists, Herdsmen, Tradesmen and Artisans, Navigators, and Interpreters.—The occupation of each caste was hereditary.

The Agriculturists must have composed the most numerous caste. The land, being the exclusive property of the king, priests, and soldiers, was let out to the agriculturists, at an easy rent.[2] Thus the state of this caste was similar to that of the Fella'hhee'n of Egypt in the present day.—The Herdsmen in general are not mentioned by profane writers as a class held in abhorrence by the rest of the Egyptians; nor is it likely that they were so regarded: therefore when it is said in the Bible (Genesis, xlvi, 34) that tenders of cattle, and shepherds, were "an abomination to the Egyptians," we may infer that those pastors are alluded to who led a nomad life; and that such the Egyptians abhorred in consequence of the ravages committed by the "Shepherd Kings" and their savage hordes. The swineherds, however, were considered unclean: they were not allowed to intermarry with with [sic] any other class, or to enter the precincts of a temple.—The Tradesmen were, it seems, included in the same class with the Artisans, and composed with them one caste; but this caste must have been subdivided into many minor ones; for the son was obliged to follow the trade, or manufacture, of his father[3]: whence, it is said, a high degree of perfection was attained in every branch of handicraft; the son benefiting by the experience of his father, and being better instructed than he would otherwise have been. Many articles of ancient Egyptian manufacture still exist, and display extraordinary skill and taste.—The Navigators must have composed a very numerous caste; for, although the Egyptians had scarcely any sea-navigation in the times of the Pharaohs, vast numbers of boats were employed on the Nile. Besides the vessels which the internal commerce of Egypt required, many were probably used only as passage-boats. We are told of 700,000 persons repairing by water to the annual festival of Bubastis.—The

---

[1]Herodotus, ii, 30.
[2]Diodorus, i, 74.
[3]Diodorus, i, 74.

Interpreters, who composed a distinct caste, were the descendants of some Egyptians whom Psammitichus 1st committed, when children, to the care of some Carian and Ionian settlers, to be instructed in the Greek language.[1]

9. General manners and customs, &c.

The Egyptians pertinaciously adhered to the customs of their ancestors; and it seems to have been chiefly owing to their dislike of innovations that they refused, for so many ages, to allow foreigners to settle on the banks of the Nile. Even though the Israelites were favourably received in Egypt they were only permitted to reside in one province, bordering on Arabia; and were debarred the privilege of eating and drinking with the Egyptians. The Ethiopians appear to have been the only people with whom the Egyptians intermarried, and whom they held in estimation; their religion and manners and customs being the same.

A common dress of the higher classes (kings, priests, and soldiers) was a long linen gown, drawn tight round the body, but loose below, and having full sleeves, reaching only to the elbows. Some of the gowns of this kind were of a very thin stuff, through which the limbs were apparent. Herodotus states (ii, 81) that the linen gowns of the Egyptians were called "calasires"; and from wearing these, probably, the military body called "Calasirians" derived their name. The same historian adds that a white woollen cloak was worn over the gown; but that it was considered profane either to enter the precincts of a temple or to be buried in a woollen garment; and therefore I am not surprised that I have not recognised this cloak in the sacred sculptures and paintings. A priest is often represented clad in a leopard's skin. The general dress of the inferior classes appears to have been a piece of linen wrapped round the loins, and only descending to the knees; all the rest of the body being bare; or, instead of this article of dress, a pair of linen drawers was worn. The hair of the head was always divided into a number of small twists. The beard was wholly shaven; or a small portion, only, left under the chin, and cut into a short and formal shape. The practise of blackening the edges of the eyelids with kohhl appears to have been very general with the men as well as the women; and the black border not only surrounded the eye but was extended about half-way towards the ear. In the sculptures and paintings, the Egyptians are generally represented as barefoot; but some wore sandals; and shoes have been found in many tombs, very neatly made.—The women were clad in a long but scanty gown; and wore various ornaments, as necklaces, bracelets, armlets, and anclets. Their hair was dressed like that of the men; but in longer twists. Most of the children, as remarked by Diodorus (i, 80) went barefoot and naked; the climate being so warm.

The private dwellings of the ancient Egyptians appear to have been

---

[1] Herodotus, ii, 154.

very similar to those which we see in Egypt in the present day; constructed of crude brick: consequently few vestiges of such buildings now remain; and these are little more than the foundation-walls; enabling us merely to trace the plan or disposition of the apartments. The crude-brick buildings at Den'dar'a, Medee'net Hha'boo, and other places, are evidently of an age posterior to the overthrow of the ancient religion of Egypt; and are scarcely better than the huts of the modern Fel'la'hhee'n. Diodorus remarks (i, 51) that the Egyptians considered their houses as the lodgings of travellers; but their tombs, as eternal abodes; wherefore they paid but little attention to the construction of the former, while they bestowed excessive labour and expense upon the latter. According to Herodotus (ii, 36), they housed their cattle with themselves, in the same apartments; as do many of the modern Egyptian peasants. Many of the temples appear to have served, in part, as palaces; but there remains only one building (at Medee'net Hha'boo) which seems to have been designed solely as a royal residence.—The furniture in the houses of the wealthy was of a very tasteful description: their chairs and couches were particularly elegant: but the generality of the people sat on the ground, like the modern Egyptian. In sleeping, they used a small head-rest; nearly in the form of a Y; but the upper part semicircular; the back of the neck resting upon it. Head-rests exactly similar to those found occasionally in Egyptian tombs are still in general use among the Nubians, the Bish'a'ree'n, and other tribes above Egypt. The ancient Egyptians slept upon the house-top, or under a net, to protect them from the gnats, &c.[1] Musquito-curtains are still used in Egypt; and many persons sleep upon the house-top.

In their diet, the Egyptians bore the character of a very temperate people; and their regard for health induced them, for three successive days in every month, to use purgative medicines, emetics, and injections; though they were esteemed the most healthy people in the world, excepting only the Libyans.[2] In the sculptures and paintings they are represented at their meals sometimes seated on chairs or stools, and sometimes on the ground; with their food placed on a low table, or on a tray supported by a pedestal, and helping themselves with their fingers only, in the same manner as the modern Egyptians and other Eastern nations. Herodotus (ii, 36, 77, and 92) gives an account of their food. Their bread they made with olyra, or zea; reproaching those who ate what was prepared of wheat or barley; and they kneaded the dough with their feet. Their beverage was prepared from barley; but Herodotus is wrong in assigning as a reason of this that the vine did not grow in Egypt; for we see vines, and the process of making wine, represented in the most ancient sculptures and paintings. They ate fish either dried in the sun or salted; and quails, ducks, and other birds, preserved with salt, but with no other preparation: other animals, excepting those esteemed

---

[1]Herodotus ii, 95.
[2]Herodotus, ii, 77.

sacred, were used for food, boiled or roasted. The lotus, and other aquatic plants, also afforded them food.

By a vast variety of sculptures and paintings we are presented with illustrations of the different employments of the ancient Egyptians in agriculture and every kind of manufacture. All manual labour seems to have been performed by the men, sometimes assisted by children. It is stated by Herodotus (ii, 35) that the women were employed in commercial business (that is, I suppose, they sold the produce of the husband's labour), while the men stayed at home to weave, &c. He adds that the son was not bound to maintain his infirm parents; but that the duty of doing this was incumbent on the daughters, however unwilling they might be.

The principal diversions and sports of the ancient Egyptians were music, dancing, wrestling, the chase, fowling, and fishing. Of musical instruments we find, from the sculptures and paintings, that there was a great variety: the most usual seem to have been harps, lyres, pipes, and tambourines. Female dancers and musicians are sometimes represented in a state of nudity. The modern Egyptians indulge in exhibitions of a similar kind, but less indecent.

The funeral-ceremonies of the ancient Egyptians were very remarkable, and in some respects similar to those practised in modern Egypt. In the funeral-scenes depicted on the walls of ancient tombs the mummy is often placed in a sledge of the form of a boat, drawn by oxen, and followed by wailing women and other mourners, as is the bier of a modern Egyptian.—Different processes of embalming are described by Herodotus (ii, 86-90), and by Diodorus (i, 91); but we obtain more correct notions on this subject from the examination of mummies, many of which are still found untouched; as almost all would be but for modern plunderers, who have taken most of them from the catacombs, and strewed them about upon the ground above. There were several different modes of embalming, more or less expensive.[1] In the more expensive modes, an incision, two or three inches in length, was made in the left side, above the groin, for the purpose of removing the intestines, which were separately embalmed, and placed in four jars, called Canopuses[2]; or, as Porphyry states (De Abstinentia, iv, 10), put into a vessel, and thrown into the river: the cavity of the body was then filled with resinous and aromatic substances, or with asphaltum or bitumen. The head was filled in like manner; the brains being removed through the nose, which we generally find, in consequence, disfigured and distorted; as also, though in a less degree, the other features; but the hair remains in a state of wonderful preservation; not excepting the eye-lashes: the teeth,

---

[1]Mummies represented Osiris, as I have before mentioned, and bore that name of the divinity, which was also used in hieroglyphic inscriptions to signify "deceased."

[2]Mentioned in speaking of the four Genii of Amenti, in the 4th article of this supplement.

also, are well preserved: the skin is dark and tough, like tanned leather; sometimes nearly black, and varnished; and some mummies have the skin tense and hard like parchment; doubtless the effect of their having been dried in nitrum, or natron. The face, and some other parts of the more expensively prepared mummies were gilded, and sometimes the whole body was thus ornamented. Bandages of linen, dipped in melted resin, were wound round the body and each limb separately; and were disposed with much art. Other bandages were wound round the whole figure; sometimes ornamented with hieroglyphics and drawings; and between these and the first bandages were often placed small figures of precious metals, bronze, blue glazed earthenware, or wood; with ornaments, &c., and one or more small rolls of papyrus, inscribed with hieroglyphics and drawings or paintings, generally deposited between the thighs, or under one of the arms. The face and head were covered with a kind of mask, composed of several pieces of linen gummed one over another, overspread with a thin coat of plaster, presenting the exact form of the human face, which was either painted in imitation of nature or gilded. The neck and chest were often ornamented with necklaces and a kind of net-work of beads and little tubes, or bugles, of glass or blue earthernware [sic], intermixed with other ornaments of similar materials, or of curious stones, and some of gold, representing sacred objects, &c.; and upon the breast was placed the figure of a scarabæus, with the wings of a vulture extending from it, formed of blue earthenware or of lead. The mummy thus bandaged and ornamented was enclosed in a case of the same form, composed of pieces of linen gummed one over another; the exterior thinly coated with plaster; decorated with hieroglyphics and figures of gods &c., which were painted with bright colours in the usual style; and having the human features also represented upon it. This again was enclosed in a case of the same form and decorated in the same manner; generally of sycamore-wood. Some mummies had one or even more cases besides these: the outer one of the same form as the others; or only resembling them in the upper part, or front; or having simply the form of an oblong chest: the goddess Isis is usually found painted at the feet, and Nephthys at the head. The mummies of kings, and of some other great persons, were placed in sarcophagi, generally sculptured with hieroglyphics, &c.—The inferior classes were embalmed with little expense. The intestines were cleansed, or perhaps dissolved, by the injection of a caustic liquid; and their place was filled, in the same manner, with a bituminous matter; after which the body was dried in a heap of nitrum, or natron. The bitumen of these mummies has been, in late times, collected as an article of commerce; being used in medicine and in painting. The mummies thus prepared are the most abundant: they are blackish and hard; and have a rather pungent and disagreeable smell. Some were prepared in a still more simple manner: they appear to have been merely cleansed out, and dried. All were bandaged.—With the more expensively embalmed mummies were often deposited articles of dress and of furniture, various ornaments placed in little boxes, musical instruments, tools, &c., indicative of the occupation of the deceased; also, bread, and other kinds of food, in small baskets; and sometimes the four jars or vases called Canopuses (already mentioned) containing the intestines. The mummies were always placed *horizontally* in the tomb; though one might be led to imagine otherwise from a remark of Herodotus (ii, 86); but the passage here alluded to only refers to the mummies which were kept in the *house*, for want of a sepulchre; and these were placed erect against the wall of an apartment destined for that purpose; as Diodorus (i, 92) more plainly states.

10. Sacred Architecture, Sculpture, &c.

The professions of sacred architecture, sculpture, and painting, and even the manual labour in those arts, were confined to priests. The principal characteristics of the sacred architecture of Egypt are grandeur, solidity, and profuse decoration. Every part of a temple, unless left unfinished, was ornamented with sculptures, mostly representing the conquests of the royal founder, or his acts of worship, and offerings, to the deity: the king being almost everywhere conspicuous: the priests, but seldom: hieroglyphics accompany these subjects, and ornament the architraves, &c. Every part was painted; and so also were the sphinxes, obelisks, colossal statues, &c.; whether formed of common stone, or of granite or basalt, &c.: whenever hard stone was employed it was for the sake of its superior durability, and not for the beauty of the material; for not the smallest part was left unpainted. The colours were blue, green, yellow, a dull red, and black, applied upon a white ground; the white ground predominating. At present the colours have almost entirely disappeared from most of the monuments; or at least from the parts most exposed to the weather (mild and dry as it is); and particularly from the granite, basalt, &c.; scarcely a vestige remaining; while upon parts which are somewhat sheltered they are in some instances, partly or almost wholly preserved. In many of the tombs, even in some of the most ancient, the colours are still as bright, apparently, as when first laid on; and, being generally applied with much judgement, produce a harmonious and pleasing effect.

Most of the principal edifices of Thebes, and some of those elsewhere, appear to have been designed and used both as temples and palaces; the innermost part being the temple. These edifices agree in most particulars with the following description.

We first find (but not before *every* great temple) a *dromos*, or avenue of sphinxes, leading to a propylæum. Sphinxes are of various kinds: 1st, the androsphinx, or lion with a male human head,[1] and sometimes with human hands and arms (presenting an offering) instead of the fore-legs of

---

[1] I never saw an Egyptian sphinx with a female human head or breasts, excepting in the zodiac of Is'na, where a sphinx is represented with a female head and head-dress: nor have I ever seen one with wings.

the lion: 2nd, the criosphinx, or lion with a ram's head: 3rd, the hieracosphinx, or lion with a hawk's head. The sphinxes were emblems of kings, and of the sun (Ra, or Phra, whence the title of Pharaoh). The most ancient that I have seen with a name to prove their age are of Thothmos 3rd.

Almost every great temple has one or more propylæa. The finest specimen of a propylæum is that of the temple of El-Oocksoor. Before it are two magnificent obelisks; and nearer to it, four[†] granite colossi, in a sitting posture, placed in a row, with their backs towards the front of the propylæum. Obelisks are seldom found in any other situation than before a propylæum: most of them are upwards of 70 feet in height; and each of these is formed of a single piece of red granite: they are sculptured on each side with one or three columns of hieroglyphics, in intaglio; generally recording little more than their presentation to the temple by a certain king. The colossal statues before a propylæum represent the king by whom they were placed there. As the grandest of the very ancient temples were built under kings renowned in war, the propylæa of those temples are generally chiefly sculptured with representations of battle-scenes. Against the front of each propylæum were originally placed two or four or eight lofty shafts, like masts, apparently of wood, tapering to a point, rising considerably higher than the propylæum itself, and ornamented with a kind of pennant near the top: square holes in the propylæum received pieces of timber by which the shafts were secured in their erect position. Propylæa with these shafts are represented in the paintings of several tombs at Thebes.

Passing through the portal of the propylæum (or through that of the first propylæum if there is more than one), we enter a spacious court, of nearly the same extent in length and breadth, bounded on the right and left by a covered gallery, formed by a wall towards the exterior, and by one or two rows of columns or square pillars towards the interior, with flat stones extending from the top of the architraves of the columns or pillars to the top of the wall. Sometimes a similar gallery extends also along one or both *ends* of the court. At the further end of the court is another propylæum, or a wall, with a portal in the centre. Some temples have a second court, similar to the first. The sculptures of the courts of the finest and more ancient temples represent, in most instances, battle-scenes and offerings.

Beyond the court, or courts, is the great portico, or hypostyle hall. That of Kur'nak is the most magnificent in Egypt; containing 134 enormous columns; the architraves supporting, as usual, flat roof-stones. In the great porticoes, as well as in the courts, of some of the finest temples, and upon the exterior of the walls of both, we find sculptures representing battles, the slaughtering of captives, and the presentation of offerings: the royal founder being always the principal actor in these scenes.

[†]Lane did not alter the number here to accord with his correction from four to three in his chapter about Thebes.

In the most important of the edifices, the court, or courts, and the great portico, seem to have constituted that part which was appropriated (though perhaps only on grand occasions) to the holding of political assemblies, the councils of the king and his ministers, thanksgivings for victories, &c., as well as ordinary religious ceremonies; and hence they are decorated, both within and without, by appropriate sculptures, and ornamented by colossal figures of the founder.

Beyond the great portico is that part of the building which was more particularly, if not exclusively, dedicated to religion; and the sculptures here are chiefly of a religious character. This part consists of a variety of apartments; generally decreasing successively in size towards the end: the first apartment, in some temples, is a smaller portico. One of the inner apartments is the sanctuary; generally either at or near the end: it is a small chamber, receiving no light but from the doorway, or, in some cases, from small apertures in the roof or at the end: it contained, according to several ancient writers, not a statue of the deity but his living emblem; as a serpent, or a hawk, or some other animal.

All the inner apartments are very gloomy; some receiving light only through the doorway; some having small apertures in the roof or walls. The apertures in the walls for the admission of light are formed so as to interrupt as little as possible the exterior sculptures: they are narrow, horizontal slits, widening inwards and downwards. It has been imagined that these apertures were thus contrived for the purpose of astronomical observations; as a person can only look through them at the heavens; but if so, the observer would have to go from one chamber to another to view different parts of the heavens; and even thus could not see a heavenly body above a certain elevation; nor do I know of any one instance of these apertures being directed towards the cardinal points.— No doors remain, but we see the holes which received the pivots that served as hinges.

Many temples, originally small, received great additions at different periods. Thus to a temple consisting at the first only of a sanctuary with a few other small apartments, were added, at one or more periods, a great portico, a fore-court, propylæa, colossal statues, obelisks, an avenue of sphinxes. To some temples were added side-approaches, with courts, propylæa, &c. Several structures of different ages, the monuments of the piety of several kings, thus formed one grand temple. Kur'nak affords the most remarkable example of this, as well as of the mean practices of several kings, in causing the sculptures and names of their predecessors to be effaced, and fresh sculptures to be executed in their stead, with their own names: or, which is more deceitful, altering the name alone.

Some temples, as well as tombs, are partly constructed of masonry and partly excavated in rock: some are wholly excavated.—Of the smaller temples, the views and descriptions given in the course of this work will convey a sufficient idea.

It has been conjectured that the Egyptian architects, in some instances, borrowed from the Greeks; but the reverse was certainly the case if either nation was thus indebted to the other.—At Eilethyia, for instance, is (or was; for I believe it has been destroyed, with other monuments at [illegible])† a small temple of the age of Thothmos 3rd, consisting of a cella surrounded on the four sides by square pillars; and from Egyn. edifices of this kind may have originated the Greek peripteral temples. We find the apparent prototypes of the Doric column in grottoes at Ben'ee Hhas'an, of a still more remote age, namely that of Osirtesen I. At Ben'ee Hhas'an we also find *clustered* columns, like those of Gothic architecture, of the same early age.

As the roofs of the Egyptian edifices are, in almost every instance, flat, it has been supposed that the Egyptians were not acquainted with the principle of the arch before other nations; but this is an error. There are, at Thebes, arches of crude bricks, constructed in the same manner as our modern brick arches, of the time of Amonoph 1st, the second king of the 18th Dynasty, about 17 centuries before the Christian era.[1] There are stone arches little less ancient in the temple of the As'a'see'f, at Thebes; and in the great edifice of Abydos; both described in this work; but these are not constructed on the regular masonic principle: the most ancient stone arches in Egypt so constructed that have yet been discovered are those of a tomb at Sack'cka'rah, perfect masonic arches, of the age of Psammitichus 2nd, about six centuries anterior to the Christian era.

The Tombs of the ancient Egyptians are excavated in rock, either in the sides of the mountains or in the level rock at their feet; always beyond the reach of the inundation. The most interesting are generally those in the sides of the mountains; and nowhere are these so numerous as at Thebes. In general, a tomb of this kind consists of a small grotto, or chamber, with one or more rectangular pits, from four to twelve feet wide, and mostly from twenty to fifty feet deep, descending from it to the chambers in which the mummies were deposited. The traveller who visits these tombs should be provided with a wax candle; as the grotto only receives light through the doorway; and he must be on his guard lest he fall into one of the pits. The entrance is generally small and plain. The chamber into which it admits us is also small, and narrow: its plan, oblong, or oblate: its height, about seven or eight feet: the ceiling, cut into the form of a low arch. The walls are ornamented with paintings, or painted sculptures, representing funeral-ceremonies, feasting, dancing, performances of vocal and instrumental music, the processes of agriculture, the tending of cattle, hunting, fowling, &c., domestic and wild animals, arts and trades, boats, houses, gardens, furniture, and other subjects. The ceiling is painted with various ornaments, generally in small squares. Some grottoes consist of two or more apartments; the first being a transverse gallery, and the principal chamber, in many instances,

---

†This and some other entries in this section are rough and incomplete, probably added for the contemplated book about Thebes, into which this passage was to be inserted.

[1]This I have mentioned in my description of the brick pyramids of Thebes.

having square pillars to support the roof of rock: so also has the gallery, if large enough to require them; and here the pillars are either along the middle of the interior or along the front; in the latter case, forming an open-fronted portico. In many grottoes we find, at the further extremity, opposite the entrance (or, in some large grottoes, at each end of the transverse gallery), a sitting figure, carved out of the solid rock, of the natural size or larger than nature, representing the chief occupant of the tomb. In some tombs we find thus placed a male and a female (husband and wife); and in others, a male between two females. The situations of the pits are different in different grottoes: the sepulchral chambers to which these descend are roughly excavated, and without decoration; and generally these chambers, and the pits also, are filled with rubbish and fragments of rifled mummies. It is probable that the grottoes were left open, or opened occasionally,[1] for the reception of the surviving relations of the persons buried in the catacombs beneath; and that the paintings or painted sculptures were designed to remind them, during their visits of pious mourning, of the various habits, occupations, pastimes, &c. of the deceased. That the mummies were not meant to remain exposed, when deposited in the tomb, to the view of relations and friends seems to be evident from the fact that, in most cases, the only access to them was by deep pits. In a tomb which I saw opened, the entrance of the sepulchral chamber at the bottom of the pit was walled up with crude bricks.—Most of the tombs excavated in the rocky plains adjacent to the mountains are nothing more than square pits with small chambers opening from them; like those of the grottoes. Around the mouths of many of these pits, which are more or less filled with rubbish, are heaps of black and broken mummies, taken up by modern plunderers.

The sacred Sculptures and Paintings of the ancient Egyptians, upon the walls of their temples and tombs, were executed according to a system conventionally formed. In representing the figures and insignia of gods and kings, &c., the sacerdotal artists were particularly obliged to follow prescribed rules; and if we make due allowance for the restrictions under which they laboured, we shall perceive much to admire in their works. They had two styles of sculpture,—low relief, and relieved intaglio. The figures of gods and men are, with very few exceptions, represented in profile; but the shoulders are turned as they would appear if the *front* of the figure were directed towards the spectator; and so are those ornaments upon the head, &c., of which the forms can only be seen in a front-view: thus also the eye is represented. The rule which requires the shoulders to be thus turned has this result; that when a figure is represented facing the right, and holding out before him a sceptre, &c., which should be in his right hand, it is his left which is thus extended: so also a figure facing the left, and discharging an arrow, or uplifting a weapon with his arm thrown back, appears left-handed. In many of the

---

[1] This must at least have been the case until the catacombs were filled with dead.

profile figures on the walls of the tombs the shoulders are not turned in this manner, but represented as they would be viewed in true profile. The artist had but little scope for the exercise of his imagination excepting in the battle-scenes, and in the sculptures and paintings of the tombs. In the former, much energy, though combined with a perfect calmness of countenance, is displayed in the figure of the Egyptian king, who is represented of colossal size; and the confusion of the routed host is well expressed. The figures on the walls, &c., of the temples, are, in some instances, of colossal dimensions; in others, of the natural size, or smaller that nature. Gods and kings are represented of the same size. In the tombs, the size of the principal figure or figures is, in some instances, colossal; but in most cases considerably less than the natural size, and yet colossal in comparison with the figures of inferior importance, which are generally disposed in horizontal rows. One striking peculiarity of Egyptian figures is that the legs are rather too long for just proportion: another is that the car is placed too high.[†] The colours most used by Egyptian artists were red (of a dull hue), green, and blue: with these were also employed black and yellow; and sometimes pink. These colours were applied, in most cases, upon a white ground; in a few cases, upon a ground of yellow. The complexion of the men (as I have before had occasion to mention) was represented by red; and that of the women, by yellow, or pink. Blue, green, and other colours, distinguished most of the gods.[‡]

The general style of the sculptures executed before the reign of the last king of the 18th Dynasty is a very low relief; and these sculptures (allowing for the restrictions imposed on the artists) display an admirable simplicity, delicacy, and grace.[1] The two colossi of Amonoph 3rd (or Memnon), on the plain of Thebes, are magnificent monuments of the arts of this epoch; and the countenances of some less injured colossi of the same king, as well as those of most of the statues, and figures in relief, executed in the times of the 18th Dynasty, are characterized by a manly expression with almost feminine beauty. Not less remarkable for their beauty are the *female* countenances in the works of that age.—Under the last Pharaoh of the 18th Dynasty, relieved intaglio became the prevalent style for historical sculptures (having before been employed chiefly for obelisks), and was generally adopted under his son and successor Rameses 2nd (or Sesostris). The sculptures executed in the reigns of these two kings, and in that of Rameses 3rd, excel the earlier works in boldness

---

[†]On the facing page at about this point, Lane wrote: "A specimen of Egyptian paintings to be added."

[‡]At the end of this paragraph, Lane wrote as a note for futher composition: "The representations—Beasts, birds, &c—, often very true to nature."

[1]The earlier sculptures and paintings of the 18th Dyny., are considered by Mr. Bonomi, whom I regard as the best authority in this case, the purest sample of all the specimens of Egn. art. The most beautiful in my opinion are paintings in some tombs of the time of Amunoph II.

of design, and are the finest specimens of Egyptian art. The historical sculptures of Rameses 2nd are the finest of all; equalling those of his father in elegance, and surpassing them in vigour. The hieroglyphics of Rameses 3rd are distinguished by their great depth.—Under the 26th Dynasty, low relief became again a very common style. The sculptures of this period are generally characterized by exquisite finish and richness; but they are inferior to the earlier works in elegance.—The sculptures of the Ptolemaic ages, which are mostly in low relief, are remarkable for elaborate finishing; but the figures, both male and female, are lumpy and altogether inelegant; the countenances of the male figures have an effeminate expression; and the hieroglyphics are of a clumsy style.—The sculptures executed under the Roman domination are even worse.

11. Agriculture, &c.

The processes of agriculture were almost exactly the same in ancient as in modern Egypt. The lands which were subject to the annual inundation were sown as soon as the water had retired; and required no preparatory labour, nor any subsequent, but that of covering up the seed: those tracts which were above the reach of the natural inundation were irrigated artificially. In the paintings of a tomb of the reign of Amonoph 1st, in the As'a'see'f, at Thebes, we find a representation of the process of irrigation by means of the machine which is still in most general use in Egypt, and called *sha'doo'f*. The plough was of a very simple form; without wheels; and drawn by a pair of oxen. A kind of pickaxe was used, previously to the ploughing, for breaking up the ground. The sower was generally followed by a flock of rams, to tread in the grain.

From a remark of Herodotus, that the bread of the Egyptians was made of olyra, or zea, we might infer that this grain was what was chiefly cultivated in Egypt; but I have not recognized it in the sculptures or paintings; while wheat and barley are frequently represented; as well as flax; and these, together with rye are mentioned in the Bible (Exodus, ix, 31, 32) as having been cultivated in Egypt before the departure of the Israelites. The corn was trodden out by oxen. The cultivation of cotton in Egypt is mentioned by Pliny.[1] The lotus, papyrus, and some other plants which afforded food, were spontaneous productions. The date-palm, Thebaic palm (or *do'm*), sycamore, and persea were the principal trees of Egypt.

The common domestic animals of ancient egypt were oxen, sheep, goats, swine, horses, and asses. The horses (if we may judge from the representations of them on the monuments) were of a very fine breed: they were used for drawing chariots; but seldom for riding. Solomon had horses brought for him out of Egypt.[2] From a passage in the Bible (Genesis, xii, 16) it would appear that camels were bred in Egypt in the

---

[1] Nat. Hist. xix, 2.
[2] II. Chronicles, ix, 28.

time of Abraham; but we do not find them represented on the monuments. Some travellers have mistaken, among hieroglyphics, the head of another animal with a long neck for that of the camel.

12. Manufactures and Commerce.

1. The manufactures of ancient Egypt are among the principal subjects represented by the sculptures and paintings of the tombs; and a great variety of articles of dress and of furniture, implements, utensils, ornaments, &c., have been found deposited with the mummies. Thus we have abundant evidence of the skill of the Egyptians in various manufactures; and we find that they attained, in very remote times, a high degree of excellence in every branch of handicraft.

Of the process of weaving we have many illustrations; and the splendid dresses of some of the kings and others depicted in the tombs present beautiful specimens of this art: some are of various colours, in chequers, stripes, &c.; and others are of so delicate a texture that the limbs are seen through. "Fine linen with broidered work from Egypt" is alluded to by Ezekiel (xxvii, 7); and if any further proof were required of the fine quality of the ancient Egyptian linen, it is afforded by the bandages of some of the mummies: most of these appear to be of linen; but some, of cotton. Woollen cloth was not so much used as linen and cotton: never for enveloping the dead; probably for the same reason that persons wearing woollen garments were prohibited entering the temples.

In their works in metal, the Egyptians displayed great skill. There can be little doubt that they made use of iron (though Agatharchides says that they had none) in working granite, &c.[1]: but most of their implements and their weapons were of brass or bronze: so also were a variety of vessels for sacred and common purposes, and numerous other articles. According to Herodotus (ii, 37), the drinking-vessels of the Egyptians were of brass; and cups of this material are still used in Egypt. Vast numbers of small bronze images of gods have been found in the tombs. These and similar images of silver and gold, and, more particularly, small ornaments of the precious metals found with mummies, are of most exquisite workmanship.

Not less worthy of admiration are many of the articles of wooden furniture which have been discovered in some of the tombs. They are remarkable for the beauty of their shapes, and the richness, or delicacy, of their ornamental carvings. The paintings of couches and chairs in the tomb of Rameses 3rd, in the valley of Beeba'n el-Mooloo'k, at Thebes, have served as models in modern times; and afford striking evidence of

---

[1]There are mines of iron and copper in the mountainous desert between the valley of Egypt and the Red Sea. The existence of iron-mines in this district was unknown, I believe, in modern times, till discovered by Mr. Burton. There are also gold-mines in the Nubian desert east of the Nile, which were probably worked by the Egyptians under the Pharaohs.

the luxury which prevailed among the great in Egypt above three thousand years ago. Among other examples of the skill of the ancient Egyptians in the art of carving wood, may be mentioned their musical instruments, some of their mummy-cases, and numerous sacred images.

Their vases, pateræ, &c., of various kinds of stone, exhibit much taste. Many of the receptacles for pigments, ointments, collyrium, &c., and of the vases called Canopuses (before-mentioned) were of stone, particularly of alabaster. Various ornaments, scarabæi, &c., were made of lapis lazuli and other hard stones; in the cutting of which, as in almost every other art, the Egyptians excelled in a surprising degree.

Their works in baked earth chiefly consist of pottery, sacred images, and ornaments for the person. In their pottery we find a vast variety of beautiful shapes; some of which are not less elegant than those of the finest specimens of Etruscan or Greek art. They are generally of a dull red colour, and quite plain; but some are ornamented with hieroglyphics, &c.; and most of these are of a light blue, or greenish colour, and glazed. Some of the vases called Canopuses are of earth. On all the sites of ancient towns in Egypt we find an amazing quantity of broken pottery. Most of the utensils of the inhabitants were of earth: every family must have had several pitchers for bringing water from the Nile or from the canals or wells; and perhaps they used earthen pitchers or jars in the construction of pigeon-houses, like the modern Egyptians. Thus we may easily account for the great quantity of broken pottery among the ruins.—The sacred images of earthenware are of the blue, glazed kind. With many mummies were deposited several small images of this kind, representing the deceased in the form of Osiris; that is in the usual form of a mummy. Various other sacred images of the same material were also buried with the mummies; some of them strung on necklaces. Scarabæi of this material are frequently found in the tombs: the smaller of these (from a quarter of an inch to an inch in length) appear to have been generally used as the ornaments of finger-rings: each is pierced longitudinally; and the lower, flat, oval surface bears, in general, the hieroglyphic name of the king in whose reign it was made: the greatest number of the time of any one king are those which bear the name of Thothmos 3rd. All the ornaments of earthenware are of the same kind in material and colour as the articles above-mentioned. These consist of beads, and various appendages of necklaces, representing sacred objects, or of merely fanciful forms; together with finger-rings, &c.—Burnt bricks seem not to have been used in Egypt in very early times. Unbaked earth was the common material of the ancient Egyptian bricks. They were composed either of mud alone or of mud and chopped straw. Those of the walls of towns, of the enclosures of temples, and of other massive constructions, were generally of large dimensions; from 12 to 18 inches in length; from 6 to 9 in width; and from 5 to 8, in thickness; and merely dried in the sun. Some are found at Thebes stamped with the hieroglyphic name of Rameses 2nd.

Glass was manufactured by the Egyptians at a very early period; and they had the art of imparting to it a variety of beautiful and brilliant colours, of which some of the necklaces of mummies afford fine specimens. It constituted a portion of the tribute which Augustus exacted from Egypt.

The Egyptians made various useful articles in basket-work; chiefly of the leaves of the palm-tree. Many very neat specimens of these have been found in tombs, containing bread, fruits, and other eatables. They are exactly similar to baskets commonly made by the modern Nubians.

Leather was used by the ancient Egyptians in the manufacture of sandals and shoes, the seats of chairs, &c., which are among the antiquities occasionally found in the tombs of Thebes. The shoes are generally right and left; and are extremely well made.

2. The internal commerce of Egypt must have been considerable at all periods. This is proved by the variety of their manufactures, which could only be required by a high degree of civilization and luxury. But it can hardly be believed that its commerce with other nations was very great until the age when foreign merchants were allowed access to Egypt, in the reign of Psammitichus 1st, between six and seven centuries before the Christian era; or till the time of Amasis, a century later, when foreigners were freely permitted to settle in Egypt. Before these periods, gold, ebony, ivory, and many other productions of foreign countries, were brought into Egypt; some, as tribute: but others, doubtless, to be exchanged for Egyptian productions, and particularly for corn. The warlike expeditions of Sesostris (or Rameses 2nd) and other early Pharaohs seem not to have had for their object the reduction of foreign nations to permanent subjection, but merely the acquisition of empty renown, or the punishment of aggression; and probably checked, rather than extended, the commerce of foreigners with Egypt. The Egyptians then, and for many ages, held no intercourse with foreign countries by sea; which was partly owing to their religious prejudices and partly to their having no wood proper for the construction of vessels for the sea[1]; and we cannot suppose that they journeyed into any of the neighbouring countries, except Ethiopia, for the purposes of trade; the deserts on the east and west of Egypt being almost impermeable to any but nomad tribes, such as in the present day conduct the caravan-trade with that country. The liberal policy of Amasis, allowing foreign merchants to settle in his dominions, rendered the latter part of his reign the era of the greatest prosperity of Egypt; and the subsequent establishment there of a Persian dynasty served to extend the intercourse of its inhabitants with other nations. Herodotus mentions (ii, 112) a settlement of Tyrians at Memphis as existing in his time, about three quarters of a century after the invasion of Egypt by Cambyses.

---

[1]The fleets of Sesostris were probably of foreign construction.

Illustrations

---

†Captions enclosed by brackets are supplied by the editor.

Bibliography

Edward William Lane did not prepare a bibliography for his *Description of Egypt*. It would have been unusual to do so in those days, and it would in any case have been largely superfluous since many of the works to which he alluded were well known and readily accessible to readers. But much time has passed since Lane composed this book. Many of those works have faded into obscurity, while others remain known chiefly to specialists. And even the specialist in Egyptology, for example, may be puzzled by some references to medieval Arab authors, just as an expert on nineteenth-century travel literature may not be familiar with the works of classical writers, while few experts in any field today remember people like the German scholar of ancient history A. H. L. Heeren or the British chronographer William Hales, both famous during their moment but now nearly forgotten. This bibliography is therefore offered as a reference tool for identifying works that Lane mentions in his text, often in passing and with incomplete bibliographic information.

As a bibliography it must bear some peculiarities, ambiguities, and shortcomings. I have not been able to locate the Alexandrian publication by Giovanni Battista Caviglia mentioned in chapter two. Occasionally, as in the case of Jeronymo Lobo, it is impossible to tell which edition or translation Lane used, therefore several are given here. An author like George R. Gliddon presents numerous difficulties, for while Lane may have seen one of Gliddon's books before adding annotations from it to the *Description* manuscript during the 1840s, he read at least some of Gliddon's work in manuscript and doubtless drew on material from his conversations with Gliddon in London before leaving for Egypt in 1842. Not necessarily all works by pertinent authors are listed. To give just one example, Henry Salt wrote a treatise about Egyptian hieroglyphs, but since Lane did not mention it, it is not included here although other works by Salt are listed. References that Lane made to authors cited within other works are so indicated.

Wherever possible, full bibliographic information is provided for modern published works. Classical works are given by author and title only, with the title either in English translation or in Latin or Greek, as it is better known. Arabic works, usually consulted by Lane in manuscript but occasionally in published editions, are provided by author and title, both transliterated into English without diacritical marks. Lane's spelling of Arabic names is standardized: hence his El-Mes'oo'dee is rendered into al-Masudi, his El-Gebur'tee into al-Jabarti, etc. Biblical and Qur'anic references are not included in this bibliography.

Jason Thompson

'Abd al-Latif. See Silvestre de Sacy, *Relation de l'Égypte, par Abd-Allatif* and White, *Abdollatiphi historiæ.*

Abu'l-Farag. See al-Isfahani, Abu'l-Farag.

Abu'l-Fida, Ismail. *Descriptio Ægypti Arabie et Latine, ex codice Parisiensi editit, Latine vertit, notas adjecit Joannes David Michaelis.* Göttingen: Dieterich, 1776.

Africanus, Julius. *Chronicle.* (Lost, but extracts and fragments are preserved in Eusebius and Syncellus, q.v.)

Agatharchides. *Peri tas Heruthras Thalassas.* (Lost, but extracts are preserved in Diodorus Siculus, q.v.)

Ammianus Marcellinus. *Rerum gestarum libri.*

d'Anville (see Bourguignon d'Anville, Jean Baptiste).

Aphthonius. Cited in Silvestre de Sacy, *Relation de l'Égypte, par Abd-Allatif,* q.v.

Apion. Cited by Eusebius in his *Praeparatio Evangelica,* q.v.

Artapanus. Cited by Eusebius in his *Praeparatio Evangelica,* q.v.

al-Aswani, Ibn Sulaym. Cited in al-Maqrizi, q.v.

al-Baladhuri. Cited in Maqrizi, q.v.

Bankes, William John. *Geometrical elevation of an Obelisk . . . from the Island of Philae, together with the pedestal . . . first discovered there by W. J. Bankes . . . in 1815: at whose suggestion & expense, both have been since removed . . . for the purpose of being erected at Kingston Hall in Dorsetshire.* London: John Murray, 1821.

Belzoni, Giovanni. *Narrative of Recent Operations and Discoveries within the Pyramids, Temples, and Tombs, and Excavations in Egypt and Nubia.* London: John Murray, 1820.

Bourguignon d'Anville, Jean Baptiste. *An Atlas of Antient Geography.* London: R. H. Laurie, 1821.

————. *Mémoires sur l'Égypte Ancienne et Moderne, suivis d'une Description du Golfe Arabique ou de la Mer Rouge.* Paris: Imprimerie Royale, 1766.

Bruce, James. *Travels to Discover the Sources of the Nile, in the Years 1768, 1769, 1770, 1771, 1772, & 1773.* 5 vols. Edinburgh: G. G. J. and J. Robinson, 1790.

Burckhardt, John Lewis. *Travels in Arabia.* London: Colburn, 1829.

————. *Travels in Nubia.* London: John Murray, 1819.

Burton, James. *Excerpta Hieroglyphica.* Cairo: by the Author, 1825-8.

Cailliaud, Frédéric. *Voyage à Méroé, au Fleuve Blanc.* 4 vols. Paris: Imprimerie Royale, 1826.

Casaubon, Isaac. *Strabonis Rerum geographicarum.* Paris: Typis Regiis, 1620.

Caviglia, Giovanni Battista. See anonymous, "Observations relating to some of the Antiquities of Egypt . . ."

Chaeremon. (His *Hieroglyphica* and *Egyptian History* are lost, but fragments are preserved, especially in Porphyry, q.v.)

Champollion, Jean François. *Lettre à M. Dacier, Secrétaire Perpétuel de l'Académie Royale des Inscriptions et Belles-Lettres.* Paris: Firmin Didot, 1822.

———. *Lettres écrites d'Égypte et de Nubie, en 1828 et 1829.* Paris: Firmin Didot, 1833.

———. *Panthéon Égyptien: Collection des Personnages Mythologiques de l'Ancienne Égypte, d'après les Monuments; avec un Texte Explicatif par M. J. F. Champollion le Jeune, et les Figures d'après les Dessins de M. L. J. J. du Bois.* Paris: Firmin Didot, 1823.

———. *Précis du Système Hiéroglyphique des Anciens Égyptiens, ou Recherches sur les Élémens Premiers de Cette Écriture Sacrée, sur Leurs Diverses Combinaisons, et sur les Rapports de ce Système avec les Autres Méthodes Graphiques Égyptiennes.* Paris: Imprimerie Royale, 1824.

Cicero. *Somnium Scipionis.*

Clarke, Edward Daniel. *Travels in Various Countries of Europe, Asia, and Africa.* 6 vols. London: T. Cadell and W. Davis, 1810–1823.

Clement of Alexandria. *Stromateis.*

Coutelle, Jean-Marie-Joseph. "Observations sur les Pyramides de Gyzeh, et sur les monumens et les constructions qui les environnent." In *Description de l'Égypte,* "Antiquités, Mémoires," vol. 2, pp. 39–56.

Cyril of Alexandria, St. Cited in White in his *Ægyptiaca,* q.v.

Davison, Nathaniel. (Journals and observations on the Pyramids and Catacombs of Alexandria published by Robert Walpole, q.v.)

Denon, Dominique Vivant. *Voyage dans la Basse et la Haute Égypte, pendant les campagnes du Général Bonaparte.* Paris: P. Didot l'Ainé, 1802.

Description de l'Égypte. See Jomard *et al.*

Diodorus Siculus. *Library of History.*

Elmacin, George. *Historia Saracenica.* Lugduni Batavorum: Typographia Erpeniana Linguarum Orientalium, 1625. (English translation: *The Saracenical Historie.* London: Henry Fetherstone, 1626.)

Eratosthenes. (His king list is preserved in Syncellus, q.v.)

Eudoxus. Cited by Plutarch in his *De Iside et Osiride,* q.v.

Eusebius. *Chronica.*

———. *Ecclasiastical History.*

———. *Praeparatio Evangelica.*

Felix, Orlando. *Notes on Hieroglyphics, with plates lithographed at Cairo.* Cairo: by the author, 1830.

al-Firuzabadi, Abu-l-Tahir Muhammad. *al-Qamus.*

Girard, P.S. "Mémoire sur le Nilomètre de l'île d'Éléphantine, et les mesures Égyptiennes." In *Description de l'Égypte,* "Antiquités, Mémoires," vol. 1, pp. 1–48.

Gliddon. George R. *Ancient Egypt: A Series of Chapters on Early Egyptian History, Archaeology, and Other Subjects Connected with Hieroglyphical Literature.* New York: J. Winchester, 1843.

———. *An Appeal to the Antiquaries of Europe on the Destruction of the Monuments of Egypt.* London: James Madden, 1841.

————. *Otia Ægyptiaca: Discourses on Egyptian Archæology and Hieroglyphical Discoveries.* London: James Madden, 1849.

Hales, William. *A New Analysis of Chronology and Geography, History and Prophecy: In Which Their Elements Are Attempted to Be Explained, Harmonized, and Vindicated, upon Scriptural and Scientific Principles; Tending to Remove the Imperfection and Discordance of Preceding Systems, and to Obviate the Cavils of Sceptics, Jews, and Infidels.* 2nd rev. ed. 4 vols. London: C. J. G. & F. Rivington, 1830. (The first edition was published in 1809–12.)

Hamilton, William Richard. *Remarks on Several Parts of Turkey. Part I. Ægyptiaca, or Some Account of the Antient and Modern State of Egypt, As Obtained in the Years 1801, 1802. Accompanied with Etchings, from Original Drawings Taken on the Spot by the Late Charles Hayes of the Royal Engineers.* 1 vol. text and 1 of plates. London: Payne, 1809–1810.

Heeren, Arnold Hermann Ludwig. *Historical Researches into the Politics, Intercourse, and Trade of the Principal Nations of Antiquity.* 3 vols. Oxford: D. A. Talboys, 1833.

————. *A Manual of Ancient History, Particularly with Regard to the Constitutions, the Commerce, and the Colonies, of the States of Antiquity.* Oxford: D. A. Talboys, 1829.

Heliodorus. *Aethiopica.*

d'Herbelot, Barthélemy. *Bibliothèque orientale, ou dictionnaire universel, contenant généralement tout ce qui regarde la connoissance des peuples de l'Orient, leurs histoires et traditions, leurs religions et leurs sectes. Leurs gouvernements, politiques, loix, Coûtumes, Mœurs, Guerres, & les Révolutions de leurs Empires (etc.).* Paris: Compagnie des Libraires, 1697. With a Supplement, 1780, by C. Visdelou and A. Galland.

Herodotus. *The Histories.*

Homer. *The Iliad.*

Horapollo. *Hieroglyphica.*

Horus Apollo. See Horapollo.

al-Idrisi, Abu 'Abd Allah. *Kitab nuzhat al-mushtaq fi 'khtiraq al-afaq* (also known as *Kitab rudjar*).

Irby, Charles Leonard and James Mangles. *Travels in Egypt and Nubia, Syria, and Asia Minor; during the years 1817 & 1818.* London: White, 1823.

al-Isfahani, Abu'l-Farag. *Kitab al-aghani.*

al-Jabarti, 'Abd al-Rahman. *'Aja'ib al-athar.*

Joannes the Grammarian. Cited in Abu'l-Farag al-Isfahani, q.v.

Jomard, Edmé François. "Mémoire sur le système métrique des anciens Égyptiens, contenant des recherches sur leurs connaissances géométriques et les mesures des autres peuples de l'antiquité." In *Description de l'Égypte*, "Antiquités, Mémoires," vol. 1, pp. 495–794.

————. "Psinaula (aujourd'hui el-Tell)." In *Description de l'Égypte*, "Antiquités, Description," vol. 2. (It is in pp. 13–15 of chapter 16,

"Description des Antiquités de l'Heptanomide," of which it forms part of a section.)

Jomard, Edmé François et al. *Description de l'Égypte: ou Recueil des observations et des Recherches qui ont été faites en Egypte pendant l'expédition de l'Armée française, publié par les ordres de Sa Majesté l'empereur Napoléon le Grand* 9 vols. text, 11 vols. plates, and 3 oversized volumes including an atlas. Paris: Imprimerie Imperiale/ Royale, 1809 (1810)-1828. (Lane mostly used the second edition of *Description de l'Égypte* [Paris: Imprimerie de D. L. F. Panckoucke, 1821–1829], which was published in a different format.)

Josephus. *Contra Apionem.*

Juvenal. *Satires.*

Legh, Thomas. *Narrative of a Journey in Egypt and the Country beyond the Cataracts.* London: John Murray, 1816.

Lobo, Jeronymo (Jerome). *A Short Relation of the River Nile, Of Its Source and Current; of Its Overflowing the Campagnia of Ægypt, till it runs into the Mediterranean: And of other Curiosities: Written by an Eye-Witnesse, Who Lived Many Years in the Chief Kingdoms of the Abyssine Empire.* Sir Peter Wyche, trans. London: John Martyn, 1669.

———. *Voyage historique d'Abissinie (en 1621).* Traduite du Portugais; *continuée et augmentée de plusieurs dissertations, lettres et mémoires, par Le Grand.* 2 vols. Paris: P. Gosse and J. Neaulme, 1728.

———. *A Voyage to Abyssinia.* trans. London: A. Bellesworth and C. Hitch, 1735.

Lucas, Paul. *Voyage de Sieur Paul Lucas au Levant.* 2 vols. Paris: Chez Guillaume Vandive, 1704.

———. *Voyage du Sieur Paul Lucas, Fait par Ordre du Roy dans la Grèce, l'Asie Mineure, la Macédoine et l'Afrique.* 2 vols. Paris: Chez Nicolas Simart, 1712.

———. *Troisième Voyage de Sieur Paul Lucas, Fait en M. DCCXIV, &c. par Ordre de Louis XIV. Dans la Turquie, l'Asie, la Sourie, la Palestine, la Haute et la Basse Egypte, &c.* 3 vols. Rouen: Chez Robert Machuel, 1719.

Lysimachus. *Aigyptiaca.*

Macrobius. *Commentarii in Somnium Scipionis.*

———. *Saturnaliorum Conviviorum.*

Madden, R. R. *Travels in Turkey, Egypt, Nubia, and Palestine, in 1824, 1825, 1826, and 1827.* 2 vols. London: Henry Colburn, 1829.

al-Makin b. al-'Amid, Jirjis. *al-Majmu' al-mubarak.*

Malcolm, John, Sir. *The History of Persia, from the Most Early Period to the Present Time: Containing an Account of the Religion, Government, Usages, and Character of the Inhabitants of That Region.* 2 vols. London: John Murray, 1815.

———. *Sketches of Persia, from the Journals of a Traveller in the East.* 2 vols. London: John Murray, 1827.

Manetho. *Aigyptiaca.* (Lost, but excerpts from it are preserved in Africanus, Eusebius, Josephus, and Syncellus, all cited elsewhere in this bibliography. The "Old Chronicle," mentioned in the Supplement, is a corrupt version of Manetho preserved in Syncellus.)

al-Maqrizi, Taqi al-Din Ahmad. *Kitab al-mawa'iz wa'l-i'tibar fi dhikr al-khitat wa'l-athar.*

al-Mas'udi, Abu'l-Hasan 'Ali. *Muruj al-dhahab.*

Mengin, Félix. *Histoire de l'Égypte sous le Gouvernement de Mohammed-Aly, ou Récit des Évenemens politiques et militaires Qui Ont Eu Lieu depuis le Départ des Français jusqu'en 1823.* 2 vols. Paris: Chez Arthus Bertrand, 1823.

Michaelis, Joannes David. See Abu'l-Fida.

Minutoli, Baron Heinrich Freiherrn von. *Reise zum Tempel des Jupiter Ammon in der Libyschen Wüste und Nach Ober-Aegypten.* 1 vol. of text and an atlas. Berlin: Bei August Rücker, 1824.

Minutoli, Baroness Wolfradine-Auguste-Louise de. *Mes Souvenirs d'Égypte.* 2 vols. Paris: Napveu, 1826. (English translation: *Recollections of Egypt.* London: Treuttel et al., 1827.)

Montagu, Edward Wortley. "A Letter from Edward Wortley Montagu, Esquire, F.R.S. to William Watson, M.D.F.R.S. containing an Account of his Journey from Cairo, in Egypt, to the Written Mountains, in the Desert of Sinaï." *Philosophical Transactions* 56 (1766):40–57.

———. "A Letter from Edward Wortley Montagu, Esquire, F.R.S. to William Watson, M.D.F.R.S. containing some new Observations on What is Called Pompey's Pillar, in Egypt." *Philosophical Transactions* 57 (1767):438–442.

———. Also see Walpole.

Orosius. Cited in White in his *Ægyptiaca*, q.v.

Pausanias. *Description of Greece.*

Philostratus. *Life of Apollonius of Tyana.*

Pliny the Elder. *Natural History.*

Plutarch. *De Iside et Osiride.*

———. *Lives.*

Pococke, Richard. *A Description of the East, and Some Other Countries.* 3 vols. London: W. Bowyer (for the author), 1743–5.

———. *Inscriptionum Antiquarum Græc. et Latinum. Liber. Accedit, Numismatum, Ptolomæorum, Imperatorum, Augustarum, et Cæsarum, in Ægypto cusorum, e Scriniis Britannicis Catalogus.* London: Typis Mandati, 1752.

———. Also see White, *Abdollatiphi historiæ.*

Porphyry. *De Abstinentia.* (Also cited in Eusebius, q.v.)

Ptolemy. *Geography.*

Quatremère de Quincy, Étienne Marc. *De l'Architecture Égyptienne, Considérée dans son Origine, ses principes et son goût, et comparée sous les mêmes rapports à l'Architecture Grecque.* Paris: Barrois l'aîné et Fils, 1803.

———. *Mémoires Géographiques et Historiques sur l'Égypte, et sur quelques contrées voisines; recueillis et extraites des manuscrits Coptes, Arabes, etc. de la Bibliothèque Impériale.* 2 vols. Paris: F. Schœll, 1811.

Regnault, Michel. "Analyse du limon du Nil." In *Description de l'Égypte*, "Histoire Naturelle" vol. 2, pp. 405–406.

Rufinus. *Historia Ecclesiasticae.*

Salamé, Abraham. *A Narrative of the Expedition to Algiers in the Year 1816, under the Command of the Right Hon. Admiral Lord Viscount Exmouth.* London: John Murray, 1819.

———. "Translations from the Arabic, of various letters and documents, brought from Bornou and Soudan by Major Denham and Captain Clapperton." In Dixon Denham. *Narrative of Travels and Discoveries in Northern and Central Africa, in the Years 1822, 1823, and 1824.* London: John Murray, 1826.

Salt, Henry. *Egypt: A Descriptive Poem with Notes by a Traveller.* Alexandria: Printed for the Author by Alexander Draghi at the European Press, 1824.

———. Also see anonymous, "Observations relating to some of the Antiquities of Egypt . . ."

———. Also see anonymous, "Travels in Egypt, Nubia, . . ."

Savary, Claude Étienne. *Lettres sur l'Égypte, où l'on offre le parallèle des mœurs anciennes & modernes de ses habitans, où l'on décrit l'état, le commerce, l'agriculture, le gouvernement du pays, & la descente de S. Louis à Damiette, tirée de Joinville & des Auteurs Arabes, avec des Cartes Géographiques.* 3 vols. Paris: Onfroi, 1785–6.

Shaw, Thomas. *Travels, or Observations Relating to Several Parts of Barbary and the Levant.* 2 vols. Oxford: Printed at the Theatre, 1738.

Silvestre de Sacy, Antoine Isaac, Baron. *Observations sur l'Origine du Nom donné par les Grecs et les Arabes aux Pyramides d'Égypte, et sur quelques autres objets relatifs aux antiquités Égyptiennes.* Paris: C. Fuchs, 1801.

———. *Relation de l'Égypte, par Abd-Allatif, Médecin Arabe de Bagdad; Suivie de Divers Extraits d'Écrivains Orientaux, et d'un État des Provinces et des Villages de l'Égypte dans le XIVe Siècle.* Paris: Imprimerie Impériale, 1810.

Squire, John. (Journal extracts are in Clarke and Walpole, q.v.)

Strabo. *Geographica.*

Stroth, Friedrich Andreas. *Ægyptiaca, seu veterum scriptorum de rebus Ægypti commentrarii et fragmenta. Collegit F.A.S.* 2 parts. Gothæ: Sumtibus C. G. Ettingeri, 1782–1784.

al-Suyuti, Jalal al-Din. *Husn al-muhadara.*

Syncellus. (Surviving portions of his work were edited by Wilhelm Dindorf: *Georgius Syncellus et Nicephorus Cp. ex recensione Guilielmi Dindorfii.* 2 vols. Bonn: E. Weber, 1829. In *Corpus Scriptorum Historicorum Byzantinorum*, vols. 11–12.)

Tacitus. *Annals.*

———. *History.*

Thucydides. *The Peloponnesian War.*

Walpole, Robert. *Memoirs Relating to European and Asiatic Turkey, and*

Other Countries of the East; Edited from Manuscript Journals. 2 vols. London: Longman, 1817.

―――. Also see anonymous, "Observations relating to some of the Antiquities of Egypt."

Wesseling, Petrus. *Diodori Siculi Bibliothecae historicae libri qui supersunt e recensione Petri Wesselingii cum interpretatione latina Laur. Rhodomani atque annotationibus variorum integris indicibusque locupletissimis.* 11 vols. Biponti: Ex Typographia Societatis, 1793–1807.

White, Joseph. *Abdollatiphi historiæ Ægypti compendium, aribicè et latinè. Partum ipse vertit partim a Pocockio versum edendum curavit notisque illustravit.* Oxford: Clarendon Press, 1788.

―――. *Ægyptiaca; Or, Observations on Certain Antiquties in Egypt.* Oxford: Oxford University Press, 1801.

Wilkinson, (Sir) John Gardner. *Extracts from Several Hieroglyphical Subjects, Found at Thebes, and Other Parts of Egypt. With Remarks on the Same.* Malta: The Government Press, 1830.

―――. *Manners and Customs of the Ancient Egyptians.* 6 vols. London: John Murray, 1837.

―――. *Materia Hieroglyphica, Containing the Egyptian Pantheon and the Succession of the Pharaohs, from the Earliest Times, to the Conquest by Alexander, and Other Hieroglyphical Subjects, with Plates, and Notes Explanatory of the Same.* Malta: The Government Press, 1828.

―――. *Topographical Survey of Thebes, Tápé, Thaba, or Diospolis Magna.* London, 1830. (A map on six sheets.)

―――. *Topography of Thebes, and General View of Egypt: Being a short account of the principal objects worthy of notice in the Valley of the Nile, to the Second Cataract and Wadee Samneh, with the Fyoom, Oases, and Eastern Desert, from Sooez to Berenice; with remarks on the Manners and Customs of the ancient Egyptians and the productions of the country, &c. &c.* 2 vols. London: John Murray, 1835.

―――. (Wilkinson's early hieroglyphic publication is contained in Thomas Young, *Hieroglyphics, continued by the Royal Society of Literature,* q.v.)

Wilson, Sir Robert Thomas. *History of the British Expedition to Egypt; to Which is Subjoined, a Sketch of the Present State of That Country and Its Means of Defence.* London: Printed by C. Rowarth and sold by T. Egerton, 1802.

Xenophon. *Anabasis.*

Young, Thomas. *An Account of some recent discoveries in hieroglyphical literature and Egyptian antiquities, including the author's original alphabet as extended by M. Champollion, 1823.* London: John Murray, 1823.

―――. "Egypt," article in the *Supplement* to the *Encyclopaedia Britannica,* 1819.

―――. *Hieroglyphics, collected by the Egyptian Society.* London: Howlett and Bremmer, printers, 1823–1828.

————. *Hieroglyphics, continued by the Royal Society of Literature.* London: Howlett and Bremmer, printers, 1828.

————. *Rudiments of an Egyptian Dictionary in the ancient enchorial character; containing all the words of which the sense has been ascertained.* London: J. & A. Arch, 1831.

Anonymous.
Itinerarium provinciarum Antonini Augusti.
Mémoires sur l'Égypte, Publiés pendant les Campagnes du Géneral Bonaparte, dans les années vi et vii. 4 vols. Paris: Imprimerie de P. Didot l'Ainé, années VI–XI.
"Observations relating to some of the Antiquities of Egypt, from the Papers of the late Mr. Davison. Published in Walpole's Memoirs." *Quarterly Review* vol. 19, no. 38 (1818): 391–424. (Despite the title of this review article, it is mostly about Caviglia's labors at Giza and nearby sites, and it draws upon a manuscript memoir by Salt.)
"Travels in Egypt, Nubia, Holy Land, Mount Libanon, and Cyprus, in the Year 1814. By Henry Light." *Quarterly Review* vol. 19, no 37 (1818):178–204. (Here too the title is misleading, for over half the review is about the exploits of Belzoni. It also draws on Salt's unpublished memoir.)